CW00692955

TO THE ENDS OF THE EARTH

TO THE ENDS OF THE EARTH

HOW ANCIENT CONQUERORS, EXPLORERS, SCIENTISTS, AND TRADERS CONNECTED THE WORLD

RAIMUND J. SCHULZ

Translated by

ROBERT SAVAGE

OXFORD
UNIVERSITY PRESS

Oxford University Press is a department of the University of Oxford. It furthers the University's objective of excellence in research, scholarship, and education by publishing worldwide. Oxford is a registered trade mark of Oxford University Press in the UK and certain other countries.

Published in the United States of America by Oxford University Press
198 Madison Avenue, New York, NY 10016, United States of America.

Library of Congress Cataloging-in-Publication Data
Names: Schulz, Raimund, author.
Title: To the ends of the earth : How Ancient Conquerors, Explorers,
Scientists, and Traders Connected the World / Raimund J. Schulz.
Other titles: Abenteurer der Ferne. English
Description: New York, NY : Oxford University Press, [2024] |
"Robert Savage, translator" —Provided by publisher. |
Includes bibliographical references and index.
Identifiers: LCCN 2023053739 (print) | LCCN 2023053740 (ebook) |
ISBN 9780197668023 (hardback) | ISBN 9780197668047 (epub)
Subjects: LCSH: Travel, Ancient. | Voyages and travels—History. | Geography, Ancient.
Classification: LCC G84 .S3413 2024 (print) | LCC G84 (ebook) |
DDC 913—dc23/eng/20231205
LC record available at https://lccn.loc.gov/2023053739
LC ebook record available at https://lccn.loc.gov/2023053740

DOI: 10.1093/oso/9780197668023.001.0001

Printed by Sheridan Books, Inc., United States of America

The translation of this work was supported by a grant from the Goethe-Institut.

Contents

Introduction, or, An American in Carthage

> There was a time when countless tribes of mortals oppressed the lands with their weight, as they wandered over the broad surface of the earth.
>
> Cypria, Frag. 1

In Carthage there once lived a mysterious stranger with an interest in hidden parchments. He claimed to have come from a vast continent on the far side of the Atlantic. It was home to many people, he said, including Greeks who had settled around a gulf after being led across the water by Heracles. Four islands lay between the continent and Spain; one of them was Ogygia, home of the nymph Calypso. The voyage out could only be made by oar because the sea was so thick with sediment. Another island was holy, blessed with a mild climate and fragrant with ambrosia, for this was where Cronos slept in a 'cave of rock that shines like gold'. Every thirty years, the Greeks of the great land in the west would send envoys to serve the titan, only to be replaced by a relief party thirty years later. The stranger himself belonged to one such embassy, yet rather than returning to the mainland, he had journeyed on in search of wisdom and truth, traversing 'the countries of many men' before ending up in Carthage.

A bizarre tale, perhaps, yet one that would not have seemed so far-fetched to ancient audiences. Mysterious isles, faraway continents, sailors who brave the ocean in search of wisdom and adventure—these were popular themes even among serious scholars. One such scholar was Plutarch, who recorded the story in the first century CE.[1] But what are we to make of the Atlantic Isles and the land in the Far West? Is it America, as the great astronomer

Johannes Kepler and others believed? And if the ancient mariner came from a new world that had already been colonized by Greeks, are we to conclude that antiquity knew about America 1,500 years before Columbus? Or is this just another of the countless yarns that sailors have been spinning on the shores of the Mediterranean since time immemorial?

To this day, a satisfactory answer has been found. Yet one thing is certain: Plutarch transcribed the story at a time when ancient geographical knowledge had reached a peak that would not substantially be surpassed in Western Europe until the voyages of Columbus. Over the course of a millennium, Greeks and Romans had expanded their geographical horizons to take in Java and the South China Sea in the east, the Urals and the Siberian steppes in the north, the African interior as far as Niger and Lake Chad in the south, and Scandinavia and probably Iceland in the northwest.

Few doubted that the Earth was spherical, so the possibility of a trans-Atlantic voyage from Spain to India, and even the existence of unknown continents, was widely entertained by intellectuals and those with an interest in geography. This book seeks to explain how this came about, what drove the ancients to push the limits of the known world, how far they ventured, and the consequences this continuous expansion of the horizon had for developments in politics, society, and culture.

There are several reasons why no such comprehensive account is currently available. The last attempt, published in 1963, is conceptually outdated,[2] while more recent efforts focus on specific epochs, regions, or individual missions.[3] The history of ancient discovery was and is a delicate field owing to the paucity of sources—no single expedition report has been preserved intact—and their openness to interpretation. Audacious speculation sits alongside a hyper-critical attitude that would discredit any attempt at reconstruction. Then there are spectacular topics like Atlantis, Ultima Thule, or the Hyperboreans, which not only attract informed 'outsiders' but also offer endless scope for esoteric fantasy. In short, the history of ancient discovery is tainted by a whiff of frivolity. This may help explain why it was long ignored by the titans of the ancient historians' guild. They sought instead to grasp the essence of antiquity by analysing its cultural, political, legal, military, and economic developments, generally concentrating on classical actors at the centre of the Mediterranean world: Athens, Sparta, Rome. When their attention shifted to the periphery, it was usually to take in military events such as the Persian wars, Alexander's campaign, the Punic

Wars, or Rome's push into the European interior. While these episodes were acknowledged as milestones in the history of ancient discovery, very few scholars made it their central field of enquiry.

Scholars from countries with a long tradition of discovery—Spain and England, for example—have traditionally been more open to the topic, yet here too, specialist research on territorial and maritime macroregions (Indian Ocean, North Sea, etc.) prevails. The collapse of the Soviet Empire and the wave of globalization ushered in by the Internet age brought fresh impulses. The various 'turns' in academic history endeavoured to shake off old blinkers, but they have struggled to this day to establish the methodological profile of a modern world and global history. Ancient history was also yoked to this trend. Some referred to 'globalizing processes' that got underway around 3000 BCE.[4] In the course of the 'spatial turn', ancient geography was rediscovered by a number of scholars,[5] while ethnography, long an enclave of expert philologists, has regained international interest.[6] The disparate sources have likewise been made accessible. There is certainly no shortage of commentaries and collections of fragments.[7] Recently, Duane Roller wrote an instructive survey of the most important voyages of discovery and the ancient authors who used their findings to construct the geographical archive of antiquity. Unfortunately, he lacked the space to contextualize them in relation to the political, military, economic, and technical developments of their time.[8]

So historians have not yet succeeded in developing clear methodological and substantive criteria for combining all these initiatives into a panoptic overview of ancient discoveries or for establishing their world-historical significance, although analysis of the beginnings of historical globalization processes promises a wealth of insights. Ancient long-distance expeditions formed the basis for transregional cultural contacts, colonial settlement movements, military and political expansion, and economic integration. 'Hot' phases of opening alternated with periods of retrenchment, reflection, and stocktaking, when forces were regathered and recalibrated before once again being unleashed into the wide blue yonder.

All this regularly led to a re-evaluation of the world as the familiar was measured against the new and the unknown assimilated to the known. This process was documented in various fields in a vibrant literary production.[9] Exploration and expansion stimulated new ways of thinking and propelled a dynamic increase in geographical, ethnographic, and philosophical knowledge. To this day, however, we lack a modern synthesis that presents expeditionary travels over a longer time span in the broader context of ancient history rather than treating them in isolation. This book sets out to provide just such an integrated history of discovery: a holistic account that situates expansion and exploration in the context of political, economic, and cultural developments.

Viable analytical models are required if we are to do justice to the complexity of the processes involved. We need a template of factors that allows us to chart a course through the bewildering variety of forms of mobility and explains why some societies went beyond the limits of the familiar while others did not—and why they did so more frequently in particular times and from particular places. I call this template an 'explorative constellation'. It formed the basis of every consequential voyage of discovery and explains a good deal of what makes antiquity such an unique era.

There must, firstly, be people willing to leave their homeland, at least for a time, to endure the risk and hardship of expeditionary travel. Movement over long distances is an archetype of human existence, celebrated in song, transfigured in epic, and condensed in national and religious foundation myths. Yet societies like that of (Mediterranean) antiquity, where around 90 percent of the population subsisted on agriculture, require a particular *mental and social disposition* that motivates them to set out into the unknown even when compelled by no military emergency.

Many sources, not just the tale of the stranger from Carthage, suggest that transregional mobility was a relatively accessible alternative to sedentary life and that those who seized the initiative were admired much like heroes on the battlefield. Heracles, Odysseus, Jason, and Aeneas are the great wanderers who explore faraway seas and lands before returning to their homeland or founding a new one. Countless myths tell of young men who venture abroad to vanquish monsters, seek riches, and conquer the hearts of fair maidens before returning to prominence and power. This motif has a basis in reality, insofar as young men in antiquity were expected to prove their mettle in the eyes of the adult world by taking to the sea or the open road.[10] Might not this restive, questing mentality have given rise to a 'spirit of exploration' akin to that which animated the early-modern period? And if so, what sources inspired this mentality and how far would it carry these voyagers?

To answer this question, we need, secondly, to enquire more precisely into the discoverers' *aims* and to find out what *expectations* and *ideas* they brought with them to foreign shores and lands. At one point, Augustine notes the mosaics of anthropomorphic beings that could be admired on the Carthage esplanade: fantastic creatures with one eye in the middle of their brow or their face in their chest; others with enormous ears, canine heads, or back-to-front feet.[11] Light reading on these freaks of nature could be had cheaply.[12] They are the ancient equivalent of the aliens of classic science fiction: outwardly humanoid yet disturbingly different, sometimes offering friendship and assistance, sometimes wreaking death and destruction. Then as now, large or pointy ears were a sign of the unfamiliar, and these ancient aliens, like their futuristic counterparts, inhabited the threshold of previously unseen worlds.[13]

Lapping up stories of such worlds and enjoying images of distant marvels is one thing, but actually making one's way there is quite another: a far riskier undertaking that presupposes tangible *motives*. Every departure is bound up with the prospect of enrichment. This can be material in nature, taking the form of valuable primary products and metals that are unavailable domestically; it can involve cutting out the middleman and gaining direct access to lucrative trading goods. But it can also be political, as when the leader of a colonial expedition hungers for power and influence denied him at home, or when a military commander gains fame, recognition, and acceptance through his conquests; or intellectual, as when the traveller offers information and proclaims his expertise on routes, countries, and people that others know nothing about.

As a rule, these motives do not exist in isolation—conquest always promises material gains and involves a widening of geographical horizons. They generally form a mutually influencing ensemble of factors. In order to situate them against the background of their respective historical situations and grasp the dynamic of ancient discoveries as a whole, we must, thirdly, know their *political and economic parameters*.

Expeditionary travel was and is a communal achievement and, for that reason alone, already a political affair. Discoveries seldom occurred by chance, through natural events or the will of the gods; they depended on complex decisions, and these were made in a political order and socio-economic environment that could make or break an expedition. There was a reason why the stranger in Plutarch's story chose the metropolitan port of Carthage as his new home, just as there was a reason why the exoticism of the foreign was so present in this and other port cities. They were the point of arrival and departure for many a roving adventurer, and they were especially open to foreign expeditions and information from abroad. Passed down by word of mouth within seafaring communities, information was coded in mythic and epic form from prehistoric times. Deciphering these codes is one of the most exciting but also challenging tasks facing the historian of ancient discovery.

Were past experiences and future hopes of mercantile profit all that predisposed coastal towns and their inhabitants to discovery? How did these factors relate to the aims of conquerors who claimed to have found the end of the world or to have set foot in new worlds? After all, ancient discoveries did not just take place in an atmosphere of peaceful trade and friendly first contact; they also involved military violence that left deep scars in the places encountered by expeditionary armies and fleets. What was the relationship among military expansion, long-distance trade, and colonization? Did they travel on similar routes and steer a course for the same destinations, and what part did they play in expanding and then assimilating the horizon of their world?

All these questions can only be answered by examining, fourthly, the *geographical parameters of expeditionary travels and the actors' conceptions of space.* No captain, no pirate, no leader of a colonizing mission, and no general send their men and women into completely uncharted waters to chase phantoms. They must already have an accepted, internally coherent idea of the destination's location in relation to familiar places as well as an inkling of how to get there, even if the precise circumstances and duration of the voyage may (still) be unknown. These guidelines provided actors with assurance and authority, but how far did their ideas of space and their goals extend?

We have grown used to seeing the Mediterranean basin as classical antiquity's centre of gravity. Studies on the Mediterranean are both popular and indispensable for understanding the foundations and contexts of ancient history.[14] Yet they, too, fall short of the whole truth, and they sometimes betray a narrow perspective stemming from an interest in political phenomena at the Mediterranean 'centres'.

It is time to add a new perspective to the familiar optics by setting the Mediterranean within a larger framework (without ignoring its specificity) and understanding its supposed 'margins' as pulsating contact zones among several 'world regions' and 'world seas'.[15] It is time for people who were too often sidelined by the ancient literature of elites to be taken seriously as engines of historical change.

This requires a history that is no longer fixated on the traditional players Athens, Sparta, and Rome. It is a story of far-flung adventurers and the powers that launched them, of perspectives reaching far beyond the Mediterranean world, and of encounters with societies that had their antennae turned in the opposite direction, to the edges of Mediterranean space. This book cannot provide a history of ancient discovery through the eyes of Indians, Arabs, or central Asian nomads—a rewarding and appealing task that must be left to other experts. But it can connect those civilizations and their peoples with Mediterranean history in such a way that they no longer appear as passive objects of Graeco-Roman exploration but as equal, integral actors who sometimes arrived in eastern or northern Mediterranean contact zones, via maritime and caravan routes, long before their Greek and Roman counterparts.

Any reorientation always needs a standpoint—otherwise it would be arbitrary—and this will here remain the zone of Graeco-Roman civilization, the area in which I claim professional competence. Combining this standpoint with the perspective of other macroregions is one of the most essential and fascinating tasks facing a modern history of discovery. Only then can Graeco-Roman antiquity be released from its geographical and historiographical isolation and placed in the context of a world history of premodernity, which is more than a prehistory of globalization.

The scope of expeditionary travel always depended, fifthly and finally, on the *technical and material resources* that lay to hand. Is it true that maritime expeditions could only be launched from sites with access to timber and metals for shipbuilding? Are such missions driven by scarcity or plenty? And, more generally, what skills in orientation and navigation did ancient seafarers possess?

As a rule, scholars tend to underestimate the nautical prowess of ancient discoverers, with the result that they occasionally adopt an excessively critical approach to the sources. Ancient mariners, it is claimed, only sailed in coastal waters and shied away from the open seas; adverse winds and currents as well as stormy winters posed insurmountable barriers, as did inhospitable deserts. Mediterranean interlopers were incapable of using native caravan routes outside temperate zones. Such objections may safely be disregarded.

The idea that ancient seafarers always or mostly hugged the coast and never sailed in winter (*mare clausum*) has long been debunked as a myth.[16] It resurfaces from time to time, however, not least because the optics of ancient sources and modern observers have been shaped by the history of naval warfare, which for specific, non-generalizable reasons has largely played out near the coast. To this day, every wreck found in the Mediterranean has been coastal. But this is because finds can only be made in shallow waters. The Mediterranean's average depth of 1,450–1,500 m—the Baltic's, by comparison, is only 55 m—and the frequently navigated major basins with a depth of 3,000–5,000 m make it practically impossible to locate and salvage offshore ancient wrecks.[17] In all this, one can detect a certain scepticism regarding the technological knowhow and innovativeness of ancient navigators who were supposedly incapable of tacking against the wind,[18] and whose ignorance of the magnetic compass (probably invented in China in the eleventh century CE) was said to rule out open-sea sailing. These objections, too, have been convincingly refuted. Tacking manoeuvres were known to ancient sailors from the early first millennium BCE, even without a lateen sail (by adjusting the square-cut mainsail and turning the mast, providing the keel was deep enough). There are respectable theories that some carried a solar compass on board.[19]

In fact, from the middle Bronze Age, at the latest, seaworthy ships plied almost all the world's oceans, not just the Mediterranean. There is no need to cite the celebrated oceanic voyages of the (Lapita) Polynesians to show that people more or less regularly sailed beyond sight of land even without technical instruments like the mariner's compass and sextant to guide them.[20] From around 2000 BCE in the Mediterranean, ships travelled up to 200 km from Crete to Egypt and from Sicily to Sardinia—roughly the same length as the Pacific voyages of the early Polynesians.[21] Over the course of antiquity, distances increased and ships came to sail all year round. By the Roman Imperial age, they were traversing the Arabian Sea and Indian Ocean, while for the great grain transports, a direct trip from Alexandria to Sicily and the western Mediterranean was standard even in winter.[22]

This not only saved time, but also offered nautical advantages. Every sailor knows that heavy storms are more easily weathered on the open sea, whereas the greatest dangers lie close to land and the coast, where reefs and shallows, unpredictable currents, eddies and fall winds (especially on a lee shore), as well as pirates can quickly spell doom. There was good reason to fear that a ship might founder on a (possibly unknown) coast during a tempest or at night, a perennial refrain in ancient literature.[23]

If merchant and warships nonetheless preferred the coastal route and most exploratory voyages moved along foreign shores, this had less to do with fear of the open sea, let alone an inability to sail beyond sight of land, than with practical considerations. Then as now, sailors used the thermal winds of the Mediterranean littoral, particularly in summer, to pick up speed and sail against the wind 'at beam reach': the onshore sea breeze at dawn and the nightly land breeze. Among other arguments, this quashes the notion that ancient navigation was mainly confined to daylight hours. Indeed, sea journeys at night were often preferred because the unclouded night sky allowed more exact navigation by the stars.[24]

If freighters steered for harbour in the evening, then this was also because the nocturnal land breeze was weaker than the daytime sea breeze. Logistical, commercial, and political concerns played an additional role. When a captain ventured into unfamiliar or only half-familiar waters to pioneer long-distance trade routes or establish entrepôts and colonies, he sought suitable partners, settlement sites, and landing points on islands close to the coast or on the coast itself, preferably near riverine estuaries to secure potable water and easy access to the hinterland. Regular provisioning of food and fresh water from the coast also dispensed with the need to store copious supplies on board, freeing up space for merchandise, rowers, or marines. Travelling along the coast (in the form of cabotage) allowed more goods to be offered to far more customers in less time.[25]

On the other hand, warships propelled by numerous oarsmen were constructed primarily for rapid manoeuvring, ramming, and/or boarding near the coast rather than for deep-sea navigation (which is not to say that, lightly refitted, they could not equally manage sea routes). To reduce weight and cram the vessel with as many oarsmen or marines as possible, they also did without victuals and made landfall at night to search for food and places to sleep. Survivors of a naval engagement sought refuge onshore, while commanders aimed to stay within sight of the general stationed on land.

Yet there were also situations in which these considerations were irrelevant, such as when those looking for valuable metals or products set out to bypass intermediaries and staging posts. These cases called for an ability to cross the open sea without touching land and tackle seemingly endless routes skirting the most arid deserts. A key reason why the ancients had this ability was that they lived in much closer connection to nature and perceived flora, fauna, and the environment far more intensively than we moderns. Positions were determined by the 'path of the stars' and the 'signs of nature': at sea by the water's smell, colour, and temperature, by the winds and the atmosphere, the movements and incidence of birds, fish, and plant remains, and by the universally attested practice of sending out birds to gauge the distance to dry land; on land by the movement of dunes, marks, and surface structures.[26] So long as multiple units did not need to be coordinated in large-scale military operations, ancient mariners and overland travellers could therefore usually do without precise maps. Nose, eyes, ears, and a sixth sense refined over many generations were a reliable guide, especially when combined with the knowledge of caravan leaders and pilots as well as improved means of transport.[27] In the case of deep-sea navigation, there was the added factor that it unfolded in spaces that posed relatively few maritime difficulties. In this respect, the Mediterranean resembles the waters of Melanesia and differs from both the North Atlantic and the Red Sea.[28] As a maritime macroregion, it is comparatively predictable. The air currents are regular in summer, fog is rare, the tides are weak and dangerous only in a few areas (Lesser Syrtis, straits),[29] and there are no hurricanes. Storms are violent but short-lived. Sea voyages are avoided in winter mainly because the overcast sky makes it difficult to navigate by the stars.

In addition to its advantageous climatic conditions, the close connection between land and sea, particularly in the north, and its numerous islands made the Mediterranean an ideal training ground for sailors, who travelled from there via the Strait of Gibraltar, the Bosporus, and—indirectly, by river and canal—the Red Sea (or Persian Gulf) into the Atlantic, the Black Sea, and the Arabian Sea (or Indian Ocean), respectively, where they could draw on the nautical expertise of local sailors.[30]

Despite all this, long-distance expeditions were fraught with enormous risk: countless tales of anthropophagous giants and sea monsters, man-eating women and devious goddesses reflect common anxieties in epic and mythic form.[31] Fear of the sea and the desperate search for an island sanctuary are classical *topoi*, as are respect for the boundless steppe and the sad fate of those blown off course and killed by pirates or abducted and sold into slavery. Mobility over great distances was a business requiring a significant initial outlay and frequent write-offs, not to mention a degree of discomfort that is barely imaginable today.

Unfortunately, we know very little about life on board an ancient ship that emerged from the Red Sea to sail towards the Indian coast or on to the Sea of China. Nor has any record come down to us of the daily ordeals of an ancient caravan on the slopes of the Hindu Kush, in the Saharan Fezzan, or along the Taklamakan Desert. Yet one thing is certain: the privations endured were barely different from those of the Middle Ages and early-modern period.[32] Wealthy traders therefore avoided long routes and sent their subordinates in their place. On the other hand, the logistical means for transporting drinking water and animal and plant food did not lag behind the standards of the so-called Age of Discovery.

If there was thus little to distinguish antiquity from the early-modern period in terms of its technological and nautical preconditions (and perhaps also its explorative mentality), and if its geographical knowledge of the world was also comparable, why did antiquity fail to make the epochal breakthrough ushered in by the Portuguese circumnavigation of Africa and the Atlantic voyages of Columbus? Put differently, why did it take so long for people from the Mediterranean to overcome the barriers of the great oceans? In short, why did the 'early-modern period' begin so 'late' in this respect? This fundamental question can only be answered by providing a thick description of the political, economic, and cultural developmental background against which exploratory missions were launched. Such a description will be attempted in what follows.

Bearing in mind all these criteria for an 'explorative constellation', we can see why a history of ancient discoveries cannot begin with Homer or any other epoch from classical antiquity. It must start instead where the groundwork for organized exploratory voyages was laid: the Bronze Age of the third to second millennium BCE. This period brought about a fundamental shift. For the first time, written sources supplement the archaeological record. They attest to large-scale communities under monarchical government in the eastern Mediterranean (Mesopotamia, Egypt) that developed agricultural techniques, introduced a division of artisanal labour, and sent large armies into the field. Political stratification, social differentiation, and entrenched palatial rule created a regular demand for supplies from abroad: principally minerals and metals (tin, copper) but also timber (for building temples and ships), luxury goods, and exotic or medicinal natural products (incense, opium, amber, pearls, gemstones).[33] These products were often found only in remote regions of the Mediterranean, the east African coast, India, central Asia, or the North Atlantic.

In many of these regions, there is evidence from the same period of early forms of mining and metallurgy. Something like a supra-regional market was emerging, stimulating trade, networks, and human mobility over long distances and inciting corresponding cultural technologies such as storage and writing (initially for memorizing goods and in list form).[34] At the same time, or a little later, city-states in the territorial and maritime transfer zones (the Levant, Cyprus, Asia Minor) started specializing in buying and transporting goods.

Revolutionary transport technologies became available with the invention of the sail, which allowed ships to carry much greater cargos, to reach a speed of up to five knots (9 km/h)—three times faster than oar-powered vessels—and maintain a course of 90–100° off the wind.[35] The domestication of the donkey, which could shoulder a burden of up to 90 kg for up to 50 km a day, was supplemented by the domestication of the dromedary from Arabia and the introduction of the horse from the Russian steppes.[36]

All this culminated in a first 'hot' phase of organized exploration. The eastern Mediterranean world was dominated by cultures whose prosperity and identity depended in large part on their ability to control transit routes on land and at sea. From the mid-second millennium, we thus begin to see a difference in shipbuilding between trading boats and warships.[37] The archaeological evidence suggests that the great leap outward occurred in a competitive atmosphere that made mastery of long-distance travel, control of sea lanes and caravan routes, and access to exotic products and seaworthy ships a source of fame and riches.[38] With that, the foundations were laid for a new era that has lasted over two thousand years, beginning in the Mediterranean and extending step by step to the farthest reaches of the terraqueous globe . . . and beyond.

The chronological endpoint of this first 'hot' phase is the third century CE. From the mid-second century, and then especially in the third century CE, the historical prerequisites and frameworks conditioning ancient exploration changed fundamentally. Beset by foreign crises and mounting economic pressures, the Roman Empire lost the expansionary momentum that had previously fuelled the history of discovery. At the other end of Eurasia, the Chinese Han Empire collapsed more or less simultaneously. As a result, global connections that had been maintained in earlier centuries by the constancy of state power broke down or were weakened considerably. Emerging from within Germanic and Asian ethnic groups, new actors pushed into the Mediterranean region to give the history of exploration in the west a completely new character. Meanwhile, Byzantium revived routes to the Far East that had lain dormant for several centuries. These later Byzantine developments lie beyond the scope of this study. The west, however, preserved the essential conceptual knowledge and achievements of ancient expansion. Conveyed through the Middle Ages into the early-modern period, these became important preconditions for the great exploratory voyages of the Portuguese and Columbus, as will be discussed in the concluding chapter.

I

A World on the Move

Ancient Rulers, Traders, and Heroes

CAPTAINS AND WARRIORS OF THE BRONZE AGE

Shadows of the Past and Adventurers at Sea

Anyone fortunate enough to have seen the sun set at Kommos in southern Crete will have heard the calls and glimpsed the shadows: proud ships glide into the bay, escorted by songs and steered by men with salt-encrusted faces, confident, hardy, and satisfied—much like four thousand years ago, when Kommos was a way station for mariners who had made the sea their home and the horizon their destination.

They were no cause for alarm, these men from Syria, Egypt, Anatolia, and the Levant. Their ships, not much smaller than the *Santa Maria* of Columbus,[1] were built in Ugarit in northern Syria, one of the most important Bronze Age entrepôts. The captains who called at Crete probably hailed from there, too. Up to 8,000 people lived in the capital of the kingdom of Ugarit (modern Ras Shamra on the Syrian Coast, 3 km from the sea), a polyglot society with an excellent harbour (Minet el-Beida) and heavily timbered forests in the nearby hills. Like other city-kingdoms in the Levant, such as Tell Kazel in Amurru, Byblos, Beirut, and Tell Abu Hawam, it had dedicated itself to the sea and to maritime trade. We are unsure exactly how goods were bought and circulated. Clay tablets found in the palace archive in Ugarit can be weighed up against evidence from other kingdoms, but no clear picture emerges. What cannot be doubted, not just in Ugarit, is the dominant role played by the royal palace in initiating and organizing the transregional exchange of goods and merchandise. The king secured his power and prestige not just by protecting his land from attack but also by providing himself and his subjects with goods, raw materials, and foodstuffs in a world permanently threatened by natural catastrophe. The ability to source, administer, process, and distribute these goods formed the basis of the palace economy.[2]

The king operated at the centre of a network of dependents of varying degrees of proximity who traded in his name, exchanging the goods they brought back from overseas for domestic products and silver.[3] Whether there was a correlation between particular product types and intensity of royal oversight is disputed, but it is highly likely that the Ugarite king paid special attention to valuable metals and overseas grain as well as luxury goods, while responsibility for sourcing politically less important utilitarian wares such as pottery fell outside the narrow elite.[4] Those entrusted with official missions may also have traded on their own behalf, including in grain, exploiting the opportunities for autonomous commercial enterprise that sprung up on the margins of the palace network.[5] In the world of the eastern Mediterranean Bronze Age, however, no traders went about their private business interests completely outside the ruler's mandate and supervision. There were only varying degrees of dependence within the royal network, connected with other such networks by diplomatic channels and treaties. It is doubtful whether the word 'trade', as commonly understood, is even fitting. We should instead imagine a continuous, wide-ranging, diplomatically and contractually regulated exchange and purchase of goods between large- and medium-sized powers, dictated by the resources and needs of the various palace rulers.

What applies for goods and raw materials also holds true for those who worked as specialists (doctors, artists, master builders, or sculptors) at the courts. They moved in networks woven by the rulers. To be sure, there were limits to palace jurisdiction and control. Particularly in remote border regions, on the coasts, and along caravan routes, specialist communities plied their trade in small companies that operated on a familial basis. But there was nothing like an independent 'entrepreneurial class' that travelled by land and sea offering its services to the highest bidder, not least because specialists depended on the palaces for their livelihood and could not survive without them.[6]

For the historian of discoveries, all this raises some crucial questions. What impulses for an expanding horizon and an increasingly dynamic knowledge of the world could such a system generate? To what extent did it lay the foundation for future developments? And where did its capacity constraints and weaknesses lie? What cannot be disputed is that the impetus for importing goods from abroad developed in the palace centres and harbour towns, which were also the departure points for long-distance voyages. On the one hand, only palace lords had the resources and authority to commission large-scale purchasing missions; on the other, they needed exotic luxury goods (pearls, ivory, amber, precious metals) to display their power and prestige. Through such conspicuous consumption, they showed that they alone knew about the trade routes and enjoyed access to the remotest lands and their products; and in having these products adapted to their own needs by palace workers, they demonstrated their power to domesticate the foreign and exploit the magic associated with exotic goods (such as ivory) to their own ends.[7]

Not every kingdom regularly sent its own ships abroad. A kind of division of labour seems to have applied that was typical of later periods, too. Large territorial empires, such as the Hittites and later the Assyrians, relied on the specialist knowledge of maritime-oriented city-kingdoms. The king of Ugarit could thus invest in 'round ships' and mercenaries while dispensing with a land army, having established himself within the concert of powers as a distributor and purveyor of the commodities and primary resources on which more powerful empires depended. As a Hittite vassal, Ugarit enjoyed wide-ranging autonomy and even received a shipbuilding subsidy. These ships supplied the Hittites with grain from Egypt and Syria as well as olive oil, wine, and salt.[8] In return, the Ugarites dispatched metals and minerals to the land on the Nile. Tin was transported by caravan from central Asia (Afghanistan) to the Mediterranean coast, copper from Anatolia and Cyprus (Alashiya), one of the greatest copper deposits in the world. Both were needed to make bronze, the most widely available metal at the time.

Merchants from Ashdod, Cyprus, the Levant, Crete, and Mycenae were therefore a common sight on the Ugarit harbourside. With the help of interpreters, they purchased wares from faraway regions (tin) or those processed in Ugarit.[9] The Ugarites could add their own local products to the mix: the purple robes so highly prized at courts; wine marked for export to the Nile delta; furniture and building materials made with timber from nearby forests; materials wrought in copper and gold; and anything connected with shipbuilding.[10]

Seaworthy ships were the vehicles, established sea routes the indispensable arteries of purchasing and exchange networks. In a 15 m long, fourteenth-century shipwreck found roughly halfway between Ugarit and Kommos on the southwestern Turkish coast at today's Uluburun, 10 tonnes of copper in 500 ingots (probably from Cyprus), 1 tonne of pure tin and glass ingots, as well as 150 large storage containers (*pithoi*), most likely Canaanite in origin, were recovered. There were three jars containing Cypriot oil lamps and bowls, seven with pomegranates and olive oil, also resin for preserving wine, 135 smaller ceramic articles from Cyprus, and 24 stone anchors of the kind used in Ugarit, Byblos, and Cyprus; finally, a series of luxury items: a female figurine, Egyptian ivory, ostrich and turtle shells, faience drinking cups, hippopotamus teeth, gold, silver, and Canaanite jewels, and thousands of glass beads, 41 made of amber.[11]

What is striking is not just the enormous distances these raw and finished goods and perishable organic substances had travelled from their source countries—the amber must have been transported overland from the Baltic coast to the Adriatic or through the Balkans to the Mediterranean and processed further[12]—but also their variety and quantity. If the findings from the Uluburun wreck are combined with those from other wrecks as well as references in palace archives, a picture emerges of a commercial network extending far beyond the Mediterranean: south along the Nile to the land of Kush (Nubia), which in good years would pay Egypt up to 300 kg of gold in tribute (a quarter of Spain's annual gold imports from the Americas in the sixteenth and early seventeenth centuries);[13] in the southeast via the Wadi Hammamat to the Red Sea and from there to southern Arabia and Somalia/Eritrea, the legendary Land of Punt, where the pharaohs were already directing their ships in the early second millennium; and in the northwest to the Atlantic and, indirectly, the northern European interior and amber coasts. If we add to this the exchange in goods (lapis lazuli, copper, timber) between Mesopotamia and the Indus civilization, which broke off around 1800 but lingered in cultural memory, we find in the middle Bronze Age a Eurasian distribution network that in the Mediterranean, however, still excluded great swathes of the Far West as well as northern African waters west of Egypt.[14]

The Uluburun wares may have been the cargo of the Egyptian pharaoh or a minor king from northern Palestine; passengers probably included Levantine traders and two high-ranking Mycenaeans, judging from the customized swords and signet stones. They may have supervised the transport of goods in the name of their ruler. Both the cargo and the site where it sank suggest that the captain had connections with the northwestern Balkans and initially sailed for the Aegean and then Kommos. From there, Ugarite ships returned laden with grain, oil, and pottery.[15]

The men who sailed on such ships were ethnically mixed, multilingual, intrepid, and determined to seize every opportunity for acquiring resources overseas.[16] They were among the first discoverers of the ancient world. Even if they acted at the behest or with the permission of their rulers and competed with one another for their king's favour, they were motivated by a primordial human dream: to gain wealth, fame, and the privileges of power.[17] Sinaranu, one of the personal traders (*tamkars*) of the Ugarite king, was so successful in his voyages to Crete that, exempted from tax obligations, he became enormously wealthy and could use his own ship on official trips to buy goods such as beer, oil, and grain. He only needed to make occasional gifts to the king.[18]

It is hard to gauge the extent to which individual rulers authorized their agents to take the initiative, particularly at sea, but this must have made a vital contribution to the expansion of maritime networks and the geographical horizon. Some Ugarites did not return directly to Egypt or the Levant after taking on fresh water in Kommos, repairing their ships, and selling their wares to palace rulers in Phaistos and Knossos, but sailed on to the Far West. One of the swords in the Uluburun wreck originated in southern Italy. From here it was just a hop to Sicily and Sardinia. These islands boasted some of the most coveted treasures in the ancient world: rich ore deposits, iron, copper, tin, and silver. The Ugarites and other seafarers from the Levantine coast had established trade routes extending from one end of the Mediterranean almost to the other.[19]

Crete and Minoan Contacts

Crete occupied a central position. Like the Levant, it produced neither copper nor tin. As early as the so-called protopalatial period (1900–1750 BCE), the Minoans therefore sought to tap into the east Mediterranean trading network of the Ugarites and Cypriots, extending their contacts past the Cyclades to western Anatolia (Miletus). A list of shiploads with tin from the Syrian trade centre Mari names Cretan interpreters and gives Crete as the destination. One of the Mari texts refers to a Cretan tin buyer for Ugarit—evidently Ugarit was a distribution centre at the end of the eastern tin route.[20] Ties were even closer with the land of the pharaohs, which attracted Cretan artists, master builders, and textile makers as well as healers working with Cretan medicinal plants. In return, ivory, grain, and silphium were shipped from the region subsequently known as Cyrenaica.[21] The wind favoured a direct crossing from Crete to the Nile delta or farther west to Cyrenaica and from there to Egypt. A Bronze Age ship could cover up to 150 km in a day, meaning that a direct voyage from Crete to Egypt would take several days and require navigation by the stars. The Minoans had probably learned the details from the Egyptians, and their ships were very similar.[22]

It is hardly surprising that the Minoans were also active north of their island. The Aegean had been integrated into the eastern Mediterranean trading network since the third millennium thanks to the seamanship of its people and its valuable metal deposits.[23] Here the Minoans encountered Mycenaean palace culture, whose elites appreciated Minoan artists and their skill in metalwork. They may also have supplied the Mycenaeans with Egyptian products (ivory, Nubian gold). For their part, the Minoans were keen to acquire silver from the Aegean isles and copper (and silver?) from the mines of Laurion near Athens.[24] Conversely, the lords of Mycenae, Tiryns, and Pylos needed gold, amber, possibly even Indian pepper, and crude metal to secure their status and the loyalty of the aristocracy, but also to maintain their army; some of the tin and the 200 copper ingots salvaged from the Uluburun wreck may have been intended for making bronze swords at the courts in Pylos or Mycenae. In return, the lords offered pottery, olive oil, and textiles.[25]

At the end of the fifteenth century, the peaceful exchange between Crete and Greece came to an abrupt end. The Mycenaeans conquered Knossos and took over their trade connections. While most Mycenaean-Minoan products continued to be funnelled into the palatial exchange and supply system in the east, some travelled westward. The western domain of Mycenaean palace culture formed a natural launching pad for the sea crossing to southern Italy and into the Adriatic. It extended the maritime trade corridor along the south coast of Asia Minor and the Aegean, although the direct route by open sea from Cyprus via Crete and Sicily or Malta to Sardinia was sometimes also taken.[26]

The key reason for the western orientation was the search for tin and copper.[27] Mycenaean pottery as well as simple glass and faience beads in Italy and Sardinia point to contact with the amber processing hub in Fratta Polesine (Rovigo in Veneto). Tin from central and western Europe entered the Mediterranean basin through Italy. Perhaps the Mycenaeans sought to uncover the mysteries of the land route from the Po Valley to the amber regions in the Baltic; amber artefacts and pearls suggest connections as far afield as Britain.[28]

Italic Warriors in Mycenae?

All this should not be mistaken for a regular transaction in goods. We are dealing instead with tentative exploratory forays that did not condense into a 'metallurgical koiné', stretching from Sardinia to Cyprus, until the thirteenth century BCE. The term 'koiné' here designates a macro-region where ethnic groups came to be interlinked through the consumption, exchange, and processing of metals.[29] The contacts made by Mycenaean captains with local ethnic groups barely exceeded the radius of an offshore island or a coastal settlement where they could berth their ships. Aegean-Mycenaean artisans or merchants may have spent some time here, but it is unlikely that they moved inland. Mycenaean or Aegean products made it as far as Britain through local networks or intermediaries in the manner of a relay race, rarely through individual trade missions. Among the wares of Mycenaean and Cypriot origin (copper ingots) shipped to Italy, there are very few of the luxury goods typical of the east. This fits in with what we know about the demographics of the settlements: they lacked the production and organizational structures of the palace exchange system found farther east.[30]

Instead of the inter-palace networks, maritime transfer channels arose between the Aegean basin and both Italy and Sardinia. For people living in the west, these provided a gateway to the wealth of the eastern Mediterranean palaces. All the archaeological evidence suggests that from the fourteenth century, fighters from the western Mediterranean, perhaps Italy or Sardinia—called Šardana (Sherden) in the sources—moved in the opposite direction along the routes that their Mycenaean 'trading partners' had pioneered in their search for tin and amber.[31] The high-quality, Italian-made longswords they brought with them proved far more effective than eastern stabbing swords in slashing through their opponents' leather chest guards and smashing their bronze helmets, giving them an edge in close combat. The Mycenaean elites were probably the first to respond to this challenge by incorporating western fighters into their armies and arming their own soldiers with these 'modern' weapons.[32]

The new swords had their greatest impact in conjunction with a second innovation: while trading vessels relied on the wind for their long-range voyages, the Mycenaeans used oar-driven galleys that were designed for speed and could operate more independently of sea breezes. Each bank of oars required twenty-five men in vessels later termed 'fifty-oared' (penteconters). At some stage between 1300 and 1200 BCE, the same period in which Italic swords were introduced, this type of ship was fitted out with a mast attached at the hull and clewline rigging.[33] It was designed to attack other ships as well as coastal towns, and it could take on warriors whose new swords made them best suited for such operations, as contemporary vase paintings show.[34]

Thanks to this new type of vessel and the transfer of close combat technology from Italy, the Mycenaeans now had the means to launch surprise attacks on the coasts and islands of the eastern Mediterranean.[35] A Hittite king complained that a resident of Ahhiyawa (most commonly associated with Mycenae) had established a base in Anatolia and raided Cyprus. Mycenaean plundering expeditions also targeted the royal residence of Troy, a centre for silverwork that controlled access to the Sea of Marmara; from there they may have pushed through to the Black Sea area. In 1208 BCE they joined with the Šardana and other fighters to launch a seaborne assault on Egypt under its pharaoh, Merneptha (1213–1203).[36]

In itself, this development is hardly surprising. Based on contracts and diplomacy, the inter-palatial exchange of goods was anything but a peaceful transnational order that prevented wars or invasions. Every order produces people and communities that simultaneously uphold and disrupt it as they look for alternative pathways to success. Violence on and from the sea has plagued the Mediterranean for as long as ships have sailed its waters, but the Mycenaeans brought a newfound aggressiveness to the eastern Mediterranean that is also reflected in the importance placed on heroic military feats within Mycenaean culture.[37] This was a risky but potentially lucrative alternative to peaceful forms of purchase and exchange: pillaged luxury goods poured into the royal treasury, while prisoners could be set to work as slaves building palaces or making textiles, pottery, and oil.

The field of enrichment pioneered by the Mycenaeans acted like a magnet on other warrior groups, leading to a continuous increase in the number of combatants. In the first place, these included the warriors whose fighting technique had paved the way. Initially, only individuals or small groups of Šardana fighters may have fought alongside the Mycenaean lords and trained them in the use of the new weapons.[38] They are the first specialists who, unlike doctors or master builders, were not active *within* the exchange system of the eastern Mediterranean palace networks but entered or attached themselves to the palace system from *outside*. If we draw on historical migration models for comparison and correlate them with the archaeological and written evidence from the late Bronze Age, we may surmise that the first pioneers were followed by generation upon generation of ever-larger organized groups (along with their families), who spread out not just in Mycenae but all over the eastern Mediterranean and drew other foreigners in their wake.[39] Seeking their fortune in the wealthier east with its magnificent palaces, these newcomers acted partly on their own initiative as pirates, partly as close-combat auxiliaries in the chariot armies of the eastern kings and potentates, who probably rarely conscripted native infantry.[40] The Amarna letters, an archive of diplomatic correspondence from New Kingdom Egypt, mention Šardana warriors who fought as mercenaries (?) alongside Egyptian chariot divisions. They later fought for the pharaoh at the battle of Kadesh (Qadesh on the Orontes River, 1275 BCE) against the Hittites, who for their part drew on fighters from Lukka and Shekelesh in Asia Minor. The Šardana appear within a mixed Egyptian division stationed at the northern border. Their experience in close combat may help explain why Merneptha could repel the invasion of the Mycenaeans and other foreign groups (including other Šardana) towards the end of the thirteenth century.[41] In Mycenae, Šardana groups evidently patrolled and defended mountainous regions where chariots could not be deployed. A thirteenth-century fresco from Pylos presumably shows a unit, now armed with somewhat shorter Italic swords and spears, fending off invaders. The king of Ugarit likewise augmented his native warrior elite (*marayannu*) with Šardana troops.[42] The Italian-style swords and lances found in the Uluburun wreck suggest that Šardana fighters served as security guards on ships carrying valuable cargo.[43]

How and on what basis foreign fighters were integrated into palace armies remains unclear. The frequently used term 'mercenaries' implies a freelance militia that contracted its services to rulers for an agreed sum.[44] There is no evidence of this, although we do know that enemies taken captive were incorporated into the victorious army and rewarded for success in arms with land and promises of booty.[45] It is uncertain whether these groups were ever completely integrated into the palace economies, however. We also do not know how the resettled foreign troops related to their freely acting tribespeople. Military communities were still coming over from the west, operating between the palace networks and choosing the most opportune targets to attack. For that reason alone, they created an element of instability with the 'integrated' warriors that, by the end of the thirteenth century, had plunged many of the palace domains into a fatal crisis.

Collapse of the Palaces

We know very little about the details. They can only be inferred from an analysis of the catastrophic consequences based on the criteria of historical plausibility and the scant evidence that has come down to us. What is certain is that from around 1200, many Mycenaean citadel-palaces were destroyed or abandoned. The same fate befell Ugarit and other Hittite vassal kingdoms such as Amurru with its most important city, Tell Kazel (Sumur). The Hittite Empire entered a period of decline around 1900 before its capital, Hattusa, was destroyed and temporarily abandoned.

Today several, regionally distinct causes of this decline are typically identified; the factors that brought the Hittite Empire to its knees were surely different from those that claimed the Syrian coastal cities. The spectrum ranges from ecological changes (fluctuations in climate, drought, exhaustion of agricultural land) and natural catastrophes (earthquakes) through the collapse of the palace exchange system to rebellions and a general inability of the (hyper-)organized palace system to cope with the various crises that confronted it and made it vulnerable to attack. Evidence and plausible arguments can be found for many of these causes, yet the military factor is sometimes ignored.[46] The downfall of a whole series of territorial powers and principalities in a relatively short period without any hostile intervention from outside would, however, be unprecedented. In fact, there are clear signs of military threats and conflicts: before they were wiped out, for example, the lords of Mycenae and Tiryns ramped up their defence efforts, expanded their fortifications, and relocated their metallurgical workshops behind palace walls. New walls were built in Athens and elsewhere, while the lords of Pylos set about strengthening their coastal defences. Not all palaces were fortified, but this does not mean that there were no dangers, only that they were spread across various focal points. In Asia Minor and Ugarit, all available forces were mobilized against 'invaders from the sea', conventionally called 'Sea Peoples' because Egyptian texts describe them as coming 'from the sea', 'from the ocean', or 'from the islands in the middle of the sea'. They were commonly assumed to originate in the Aegean basin, western Anatolia, and Cilicia. However, archaeological evidence (weapons and pottery) indicates that many of the groups came from Italy, including the Šardana.[47]

Piracy and Šardana raids were an all-too-familiar phenomenon in the eastern Mediterranean.[48] Perhaps the protective measures taken in Pylos were routine, while the petty monarchs farther to the east were advised by friendly regents to build walls to the sea shortly before the ominous ships appeared on the horizon.[49] Besides an exponential increase in the number of western militias and pirate bands, longstanding weaknesses or a perfect storm of adverse conditions must have been a key ingredient in military defeat, at least in Mycenae.

One weakness lay in securing a permanent supply of plant-based and metal raw materials as well as the fact that import security rested more on the recipient's military and political prestige than on any services offered in return. If prestige suffered due to military failures or natural and organizational mishaps, provisioning of the palaces from abroad was also endangered. The Mycenaean rulers, for example, may have been far worse affected by the defeat of their forces in the Nile delta by Merneptha than the confederated Sea Peoples, who had no power centre of their own, were settled in enemy territory, or sought new territories to invade.

There was another problem: for the palaces, the regular purchase, storage, and distribution of goods and materials within the area they controlled played a far more important role than any consideration of what they could trade for the imports.[50] This 'redistribution system' would seem to have been especially pronounced in Mycenae owing to the resource-poor environment in which the palaces were located. The Mycenaean tablets nowhere speak of trade or trade goods, instead making only vague references to oil. The palaces evidently placed emphasis on storing grain, wine, and oil, and they oversaw pottery and textile production; yet their sale, along with the production of metalware, was left to local groups and merchants and regulated only through taxation.[51] The palace of Pylos evidently kept records on shipbuilding, shipbuilders, and crew, but instead of carrying out these works itself, it delegated them to coastal communities. These supplied shipbuilders, captains, and oarsmen and hence maintained an 'esoteric knowledge' of seafaring and of its conditions and resources.[52]

Knowledge of their *nautical* expertise secured the coastal communities a relatively autonomous existence, much as the foreign fighters settled in the border regions possessed an expertise in *military technology*; shipbuilding specialists, like the recruited soldiers, were probably rewarded with land for their services.[53] Archaeological finds suggest that in the last decades of the thirteenth century, groups of Italian warriors had assimilated to the social structure of the palaces in several northern Syrian coastal towns (Tell Kazel) while preserving their identity through the production of pottery and ornamental textiles. The palace nonetheless relied on their skills and had to hope that they respected the rules of the palace system. Whatever loyalty they may extend to their new masters, pioneer migrants tend to offer information and contacts to the compatriots who follow in their footsteps.[54] They opened gateways for intruders who could then undermine the palace defences, given the limited extent of central control. Applied to the situation towards the end of the thirteenth century, this meant that pirates like the *Lukka* or *Sikalaju*, 'those who live on ships',[55] were unable to conquer fortresses like those of Mycenae or Ugarit, and certainly not the Hittite capital Hattusa in the Anatolian Plateau. They could, however, emulate their predecessors by targeting the import trade that was the lifeline of the palace economy—particularly for the inland empires—at its Achilles' heel, its reliance on overseas supplies of grain and primary products (especially tin).[56] Like the Mycenaeans, the Hittite kings possessed only limited agricultural resources and were therefore extremely vulnerable when the Mycenaeans and other foreign peoples attacked their coastal outposts in Asia Minor. So long as the interior was rich and stable enough to repel the assaults with the help of their vassals and integrated warriors, this weakness could be concealed. But in the decades before the Sea Peoples overran the land, a period of drought seems to have shaken the agricultural foundations of the empire even as defeats at land (for example, against the Assyrians at Diyarbakir in southwestern Turkey) and royal intrigues weakened it to the point where it could no longer mount a concerted defence. The sources for the period leading up to the attack by the Sea Peoples mention that the Hittites tried to import grain from Egypt by Ugarit and that famine stalked the land. When the ships of their Cypriot allies turned against them and joined the Sea Peoples, the empire's very existence was imperilled.[57]

Similar scenarios may be assumed for large parts of the Mycenaean world. Many palaces relied on a steady stream of raw materials and foodstuffs (from Egypt?) and imposed payments in kind on their populace as a result. A system so dependent on imports will break down if rifts appear that are not mended quickly enough. Failed harvests, earthquakes, and palatial mismanagement may have opened these rifts. Towards the end of the thirteenth century, the Mycenaean palaces sought to raise taxes on the rural population as well as reassert control over the sea traders supposedly acting on their behalf, but actually operating ever more independently—to no avail.[58] Military setbacks in Egypt eroded the Mycenaean rulers' authority not just over the civilian populace, which groaned under a heavy tax burden, but also over those they relied on for their military expertise: the western fighters integrated into the local population and the coastal communities. According to a recent theory, the coastal communities that specialized in deploying warships exploited the weakness of their overlords and turned from indispensable allies into dangerous adversaries who cooperated with a disgruntled rural populace and the invaders.[59] Much the same may be supposed in the case of Šardana fighting under the Mycenaean banner. Perhaps the materially beleaguered palace organization proved incapable of supplying the foreign fighters and the populace, thereby driving them into enemy arms.[60] Deprived of its last resources, the Mycenaean military machine was no match for the invaders. The palaces were stormed, looted, and burned.

Some rulers may have given up earlier and planned a seaborne exodus (or evacuation) to new settlements on distant shores.[61] At any rate, the populace frequently took to their heels during the attack. Some regathered under local leaders (*basileis*), who filled the power vacuum created by the fall of the palaces and established themselves as 'big men'. Others joined forces with the fighters and pirates who delivered the palaces the *coup de grâce*.[62] Loaded with loot, the victors were followed by manual workers and others who hoped to better their lot by joining the Sea Peoples.[63] Their path took them to the coast of Asia Minor and to Cyprus, for generations the targets of raids by the Mycenaeans themselves. Troy would not have been spared on these plundering forays, but their greatest conquest was Ugarit around 1185–1180 BCE. Here, too, internal factors made the city more vulnerable: King Hammurabi (Ammurapi) had lost touch with traders and artisans while one-sidedly privileging the charioteer elite. Ugarit's hands were also tied through its obligations to the Hittites. At the time of the invasion, the Ugarite fleet was operating farther to the west, while the palace guard had been redeployed in the Hittite heartlands. Resistance thus crumbled when the *Shikila* (*Sikalaju*) made landfall with their penteconters. The townspeople ran for their lives as their houses were sacked and burned.[64] Street fighting broke out in Ugarit, but the people were unwilling to sacrifice themselves for an unloved king and fled. The palace was put to the torch.[65]

A similar fate would have befallen the nearby residence of Ras Ibn Hani and Tell Kazel, used by the Sea Peoples as a depot and operations base. Pottery remains indicate the presence of foreigners from Italy and the Aegean in most settlements, a further sign that the invaders oriented themselves on the routes of their predecessors and profited from their experience.[66] In the Levant, too, the Sea Peoples lit the fuse of a powder keg that the kingdoms had been sitting on for centuries. Their rule could only be maintained through tax pressure, levies, and grain imports and bore within it the seeds of opposition. Resistance simmered among marauding bands, desperate peasants, and parts of the functionary elite, before breaking out into the open when triggered by a land or sea assault.[67]

'Sea Peoples' in the Nile Delta

Egypt alone was better forearmed against these problems owing to the greater, religiously sanctioned legitimacy of its rulers and the abundant harvests bestowed by the Nile. The pharaohs also benefited from their experience in repelling mobile groups at sea. They were therefore much better positioned to ward off the invaders and their families, who were approaching the Nile delta along the Levantine coast following the destruction of Ugarit and Amurru. The men boarded their ships somewhere in Canaan. Clearly well organized, they then pressed on towards the Nile delta in several waves before being repulsed by Merneptha and Ramses III between 1190 and 1179. Egyptian artists condensed the decades-long fighting into a single battle scene on the temple wall of Medinet Habu.[68]

The invaders were in principle the same bands of *Ekwesh*, *Lukka*, *Šardana*, and *Shekelesh* who had raided Egypt in 1208 (see above, p. 21).[69] They included the Peleset, known to us from the Old Testament/Hebrew Bible as Philistines. Encompassing multiple ethnicities, their language was probably Indo-European in origin. Many came from Anatolia and/or the Aegean and had reached the Levant in several waves as pirates and mercenaries fighting under charismatic leaders; the type of galleys they deployed in the Nile delta points unmistakably to Mycenaean and central European tradition.[70] After or perhaps even before their defeat in the Nile delta, they settled, like the Šardana, in the southern Levantine coastal area that bears their name to this day (Palestine). Here, they developed a culture of their own that 'involved various foreign and local elements'. Largely autonomous and organized in city-states, they undertook garrison duties to defend their land from the 'kings' of Israel and Judea, among others.[71]

The Hebrew Bible teaches that the Philistines, again like the Šardana, were skilled close-combat fighters, while their seafaring activities go almost unmentioned following their resettlement.[72] The *Cherethites* and *Pelethites* (= *Chrethi* and *Plethi*) are said to have fought as personal guards and battalions under King David.[73] The most common theory regards the Pelethites as identical to the Philistines. They were obviously mercenaries from the Philistine borderland of the Hebrew kingdom.[74] The most famous duel in history, between David and Goliath, likewise points to the military tradition of the Sea Peoples. Goliath is a formidable adversary whose bronze helmet, spear, sword, scale armour, and greaves recall the heavily armed archaic heroes of Troy. We know of a comparable suit of bronze armour worn in duels from Mycenaean Greece (near Dendra).[75] The legend of Goliath's gigantic stature likewise originates in the Aegean-Mycenaean realm. It presumably reflects the plumed 'helmet'—elaborate by Near Eastern standards—also worn by the (Italic) Sea Peoples.[76] Invincible in close combat, Goliath is felled by a stone flung from afar, just as the Achaean hero Achilles can only be wounded in the heel by Paris' arrow. There is evidence that slingshots were part of the arsenal of Bronze Age armies.[77] While the Philistine warrior's external features may be anachronistic, the writers of Kings believed one aspect to be realistic. Goliath is the fulcrum between two eras: that of the Italic close-combat specialist seeking his fortune in the east, and that of the 'Greek' warriors serving the new powers that would establish themselves in the centuries following the Sea Peoples' migration.

PHOENICIANS AND EUBOEANS TAKE TO THE SEAS

The Rise of the Phoenician Ports

Even if the Sea Peoples were stopped at the Nile delta, pacified, or absorbed into the victors' armies, the upheavals they brought about were momentous. In Greece and on Crete, village communities and principalities led by influential men (*basileis*) replaced the palaces after a prolonged transition. In Asia Minor, minor kingdoms such as that of the Phrygians and Lydians emerged on Hittite terrain. The diplomatic exchange between the palace dominions as well as trade in luxury goods, large amphorae, and standardized volumes evident from the Uluburun ship came to a (temporary) halt in the eastern Mediterranean.[78]

Long-distance links to the west were less seriously affected. The *basileis* continued the Mycenaean art of shipbuilding[79] and conserved the maritime knowledge accumulated by Mycenaean coastal communities. Traders and artisans who moved with the Sea Peoples to the Levant offered wares that partly originated in Italy and the Balkans and were subsequently dispersed over Crete (Kommos), Euboea, and Cyprus. Their activities may also have been a reason why overseas trade in northern Syria declined yet remained intact. Ugarit's harbour was rebuilt, and from the ninth century, the Cypriots took over much of the overseas trade in pottery, copper, and textiles. The Levant delivered agricultural products in return for Cypriot copper and handcrafted goods; silver from Spain, Anatolia, Attica, and Sardinia arrived on the eastern Mediterranean coasts. Knowledge of routes and coastlines was passed on by word of mouth.[80]

The Levant also experienced an upturn. Byblos, Sidon, and Tyre had survived the depredations of the Sea Peoples almost unscathed and may even have cooperated with them. The elimination of the great northern empires gave them the opportunity to expand.[81] The city-dwellers called themselves Canaanites (*kinahhu*). The Greeks termed them Phoenicians, an allusion to the most famous product of their homeland, the purple dye (Greek: *phonikeos*, red) secreted by murex snails. The Phoenicians used a Semitic script and led an urban life among local princes ('kings'). The latter, supported by a council of elders, steered foreign policy, commanded the fleet, and oversaw their civic resources in a world that since time immemorial had been defined by power struggles among territorial empires.[82]

Whoever wanted to survive here with a good but limited agricultural hinterland had to possess skills attractive enough for them to avoid being gobbled up by their more powerful neighbours. Ugarit had paved the way: located at the intersection of eastern Mediterranean and Near Eastern trade routes, the northern coast of the Levant offered the best opportunities for satisfying Assyrian, Babylonian, and Egyptian demands for raw materials and artisanal products. An Egyptian 'travelogue' mentions twenty trading vessels in the harbour of Byblos as well as fifty units in Sidon.[83] Yet while Phoenician towns had previously exported cedarwood from their hinterland, by the tenth and ninth centuries the export base had shifted to textiles, fabrics, leather goods, ivory, metal containers, and wine transported in specially manufactured amphorae. This shift owed as much to the depletion of Levantine timber resources as it did to changes in demand. The diverse wares and products point to craft specialization, and they made possible a more extensive commerce by the open sea than the arduous timber trade, which had been confined to the coast. Conversely, the new production chains required raw-material imports that could only be secured by extending overseas links.[84]

Like the kings of Ugarit, the regents of the Phoenician cities appear to have rarely intervened in interregional trade. They maintained their monopoly on the sale of cedarwood, but that was all.

From the eighth century, an aristocracy probably assumed control of long-distance trade and settlements on faraway shores, competing with the cities for power and influence. Apart from Sidon, the most important such city was Tyre. The cities' power and wealth depended not least on their knowledge of the products and needs of foreign lands. The 'lamentation for Tyre' from the Book of Ezekiel in the Old Testament (sixth century BCE) names merchants from Sheba and Raamah (in southern Arabia) who traded spices, precious stones, and gold for Phoenician wares; contacts extended as far as Africa and Spain.[85]

Image 1 Excerpt from the relief in the palace of Sargon II in Khorsabad (late eighth century BCE, now in the Louvre). The relief shows Phoenician ships (evidently from Tyre) transporting cedarwood and unloading it on the coast. The rulers of Tyre also supplied the 'kings' of Israel with raw materials and skilled workers. They had to deliver timber as tribute when they came under Assyrian control. Credit: Wikimedia Commons.

The Tyrians were famous for their technical skills and their shipbuilding. They constructed full-bellied trading vessels and slender penterconters whose planks and ribs were held together with iron nails and stabilized by a prominent keel—clearly a legacy of the Sea Peoples.[86] The Phoenicians used their technological advantage by offering their services to land-based powers, not just as long-distance traders and intermediaries but also as master builders and craftspeople.[87] Hiram I of Tyre (971–939 BCE) supposedly sent King Solomon timber, raw materials, and master builders for the temple in Jerusalem and received foodstuffs (primarily grain) in return; Phoenician artisans created Solomon's ivory throne. Finally, Hiram was also said to have contributed sailors and ships to a fleet that Solomon built in Ezion-Geber (the Red Sea port of Aqaba) that sailed for Ophir—a mysterious land in the Indian Ocean, southern Arabia, or on the coast of east Africa (Sudan or Somalia)—and brought back vast quantities of gold, sandalwood, and precious stones.[88]

The archaeological finds cannot confirm biblical statements about a glorious tenth-century Solomonic kingdom, however. They speak instead for a modest rule of 'tribal kings' incapable of such mega-projects. Outside the Bible, moreover, there is not a skerrick of evidence for a powerful Tyrian king Hiram in the tenth century. It is far more likely that the composers of the Book of Kings superimposed ninth- or eight-century conditions (or those of Babylonian captivity) onto an earlier age. In the ninth century, the Omrides dynasty ruled the Northern Kingdom, while in the eighth century Judah flourished under Assyrian protection, evolving into an empire that matches many descriptions of the Solomonic era. The details about Hebrew-Phoenician joint trading ventures at sea probably date from this period.[89]

The Old Testament surely overstates the extent of Hebrew involvement in this lucrative enterprise. Yet it cannot be doubted that a thriving Hebrew dynasty relied on Phoenician know-how to supply its area of influence with metals, timber, and other resources. The Tyrians probably received grain and oil in return, perhaps also wine and honey, as well as permission to use the kingdom's area of influence in the Red Sea as the springboard for an expedition in search of precious stones, high-grade wood (sandalwood), and spices (cinnamon) against a healthy share in the profits.[90] Perhaps the Hebrews, who had a reputation as good fighters, served as marines. The expedition to the legendary Ophir would thus have been a pillaging trip for which the Hebrews needed the Tyrians' nautical knowledge and ships. This would also explain why the enterprise, in contrast to other Phoenician voyages, took place only once within three years (a second attempt failed a century later) and led to no lasting commercial contacts.[91]

The Greatest Adventure: The Circumnavigation of Africa?

If Ophir is identified with a coastal zone of the Red Sea or Somalia—as is generally the case today—then it might further be assumed that the Egyptians would have blocked any disruption to their gold monopoly in the 'Southern Sea' and the cinnamon and ivory sources of Somalia. They probably sought to harness the Phoenician interlopers for their own objectives and divert them elsewhere.[92] At the basis of these efforts was an expedition undertaken around 600 BCE, sponsored by Pharaoh Necho II (610–595), that again brought Phoenician mariners to the Southern Sea.

In the early years of his reign, Necho had been forced to withdraw from the Syrian-Palestinian region following a series of defeats at the hands of the kings of Judea and Babylon. He had concentrated his energies instead on controlling maritime trade in the Red Sea. To that end, fleets were built in the Mediterranean and a canal dug between the Nile and the Red Sea.[93] The climax of his efforts came when he commissioned Phoenician mariners (probably from Tyros), who had already made a name for themselves as Red Sea specialists during their Ophir expedition (and perhaps earlier on the journeys to the Land of Punt—a legendary country probably identified with modern Somalia—undertaken with 'Byblos' vessels), to sail south from the Persian Gulf, then follow the coast of Africa (Libya) ever westward until they reached the Pillars of Heracles. From there they were to make the return leg by the Mediterranean. The circumnavigation of Africa was successful, according to the Greek historian Herodotus—a sensational feat, if true.[94]

To arrive at a plausible evaluation, we should first analyse the reported details of the circumnavigation against the background of contemporary geographical ideas and the political context. At the start of the expedition, neither the Egyptians nor the Phoenicians were aware of just how far south the continent extended. They assumed that the ships would veer west after a relatively short voyage to the south, heading for Gibraltar along a more or less straight coastline curving gently to the northwest. Accordingly, the western leg on the southern African coast was expected to last no longer than the voyage back by the Mediterranean. The direction and dimensions of such a long journey were organically connected to the Punt and Ophir expeditions, and they stand in an authenticated, logical context: Levantine trade contacts as far as southern Arabia or even Somalia are indicated by the story the Queen of Sheba's visit to Solomon, for example. She brought balsam with her, which was then supposedly cultivated in the royal gardens in Jericho and Jerusalem and exported to Tyre.[95] The Phoenician fleet thus surely sailed past the same areas on the east African coast that the Punt and Ophir expeditions had made for in their search for gold, cinnamon, and incense. Some even speculate that earlier Egyptian expeditions had been led by Phoenician mariners.[96]

It all depends on whether we assume a journey farther south past the Somali coast (Azania) and a full circumnavigation of the continent to be realistic. Such a journey would have taken around five times longer than the projected itinerary, corresponding roughly to the length of the Mediterranean from east to west. The Phoenicians were technologically, nautically, and logistically equal to such a challenge: they could tack against the wind and row against the current. According to Herodotus, they hauled their ships ashore every autumn for three years (as was the custom in the Mediterranean), sowing and harvesting crops each time before travelling on early the next year. By the third year they had reached the Pillars of Heracles. This timeframe, including interruptions, is not unrealistic. However, the three-year journey time recorded by Herodotus could also be Phoenician-Levantine code for a 'very long voyage' (other Tyrian long-distance voyages purportedly lasted three years as well; see above, p. 32). In addition, *several* Phoenician voyages exploring the coasts of Africa in stages over a long period of time may well have been condensed in cultural memory into a *single* voyage, just as the pharaonic victory inscriptions condensed the protracted migration of the Sea Peoples into a single battlefield (see above, p. 27). Possibly the Phoenician captains became aware only gradually, rather than on a single expedition, of the phenomenon that Herodotus found so incredible: 'that in sailing around Libya they had the sun upon their right hand'.[97] In fact, after crossing the equator the midday sun stands to the west, at least when rounding the Cape of Good Hope, while the rising sun when sailing north from there along the west African coast to the equator stands to the right. Herodotus, however, assumed that the sun must stay in the same position as on a westward journey along the north African coast (in the Mediterranean). Theoretical considerations could also lead one to suppose that the sun would appear to the right south of the arid equatorial zone. Indeed, observations in the areas south of the Tropic of Cancer could already have led to that conclusion.

Another phenomenon needs explaining: the fact that the expedition was never repeated and—even more surprisingly—that it was not reflected at the time or later in antiquity in a transformed geographical view of Africa. If we disregard fourth- and fifth-century speculation about a counter-ecumene, an undiscovered counterpart to the inhabited world known to the Greeks, no ancient author offered even a remotely realistic account of the continent's dimensions to the south. The southern coast of Africa was believed to stretch more or less in a straight line from the south Somalian highland to the Atlantic west coast. So stubborn a refusal to pass on, or even acknowledge, the geographical lessons learned from the circumnavigation of Africa is strange. One possible explanation is that traditional, longstanding worldviews tend to resist 'singular' discoveries if they are not repeated and consolidated. In the case of the circumnavigation, the 'discovery' filtered into the Greek knowledge horizon from a Phoenician culture that was not always well regarded by the Greek-speaking world, which may not exactly have been conducive to its uptake among scholars.

The strongest objection to the circumnavigation is the enormous dangers involved, particularly at the Cape of Good Hope. If the earlier Ophir voyages had made for the littoral zones of the Red Sea or Somalia, from where a route led overland to the Nubian gold depots, it might be worth considering whether a similar combination of sea and land expeditions lay behind the later Phoenician claim to have discovered the continent's true dimensions through a purely maritime circumnavigation. There are signs, for example, that in the sixth century BCE the east African port of Rhapta maintained contacts with the inland.[98] In addition, transit routes from southern Sudan to the Lake Chad area, and from there farther west to the Niger and Senegal river systems, may be assumed. In some areas, archaeology for the period between 600 and 500 BCE could demonstrate proto-urban structures with copper- and ironwork (see below, p. 137).[99] A century after Necho's expedition, the Carthaginians showed a keen interest in the trans-Saharan routes. An earlier attempt to traverse them from the east African side cannot be ruled out.

Tartessos as El Dorado

Far less interest has been shown in the historicity of the enterprise than in its motivation: why would the pharaohs have mounted such an expedition? Scientific curiosity and a passion for exploration are not enough.[100] This would have been without precedent and reflects a modern perspective. The historical-political context is crucial. The circumnavigation of Africa was part of a series of maritime efforts launched by Necho in response to a loss of power in the Levant. The search for alternative spheres of influence was a consequence of the eastern Mediterranean coasts and their riches having slipped from Egypt's grasp.[101] While Ophir was a lucrative substitute, it was long familiar and insufficient in this difficult situation. The Egyptians knew from the Phoenicians themselves that greater riches were to be found in the Far West.

The Old Testament thus speaks of a 'Tarshish fleet' sent out by Solomon with Hiram's ships. It returned after three years—exactly the same time as the African voyage was supposed to have taken—laden with 'gold, silver, ivory, apes, and peacocks'.[102] If we apply the same authentication criteria to this tradition as to the texts on the Ophir expedition, we may conclude that such a joint venture could not have arisen until the eighth century BCE (if it occurred at all), especially since the destination was even more remote: Tarshish refers in all likelihood to Tartessos in Andalusia, a thriving civic culture renowned for mining and exporting silver. Of all the ancient lands, the Iberian Peninsula boasted the greatest mineral wealth. The other products mentioned in the Old Testament may have originated in west Africa before being sold onward in Tartessos.[103]

The Phoenicians were among the first foreign powers to show an interest in Tartessian goods. In return, they offered utilitarian wares and oriental luxury goods.[104] To facilitate this exchange, in the tenth century they set up trading posts on the Andalusian coast, the most important contact zone between the Atlantic and the Mediterranean world. The earliest (c. 900 BCE) recorded such post, Huelva, as well as the more southerly Gades (Cádiz), became the key arrival and departure points for all Atlantic voyages on the tin route north as well as to the Moroccan coast.[105] (Not coincidentally, both Columbus after his first trans-Atlantic voyage and Cortés after the conquest of Mexico made landfall in Palos de la Frontera, near Huelva.) In addition, both colonies offered good links to the silver and copper mines of Rio Tinto, the Sierra Morena, and the Spanish and Portuguese Estremadura. The colonies were therefore largely settled by artisans, potters, miners, and stonemasons. There were also Phoenician artists who introduced local princes to the art of mosaic design.[106]

That the eastern Mediterranean only learned of the treasures in Tartessos and the voyages of the Phoenicians around a century later is suggested by the prophet Jeremiah (625–585 BCE), who stated that the Tyrians imported silver from Tartessos.[107] Jeremiah lived in the time when Necho was commissioning Phoenician mariners to circumnavigate Africa. We therefore have reason to believe that the pharaoh, too, wanted to profit from Tartessian wealth to make up for his losses in the Levant. Following these losses, but also the rise of Carthage, charting an alternative route beyond the Mediterranean made sense in connection with what I am tempted to call his 'southern strategy'. The circumnavigation of Africa was thus an Egyptian project that the Levantine Phoenicians had no reason to pursue any further.

The Euboean-Phoenician 'Connection'

Phoenician interest remained fixed on the Mediterranean, in keeping with the tradition of Bronze Age seafarers. They used smaller ships that could navigate the open seas.[108] They sailed through the Aegean to Crete and Malta, and from there to southern Italy and Sardinia. In Kommos, Phoenician mariners erected a three-pillar, Canaanite-style altar inside a temple at the harbour in 800 BCE. A Phoenician master coppersmith may have settled at Knossos.[109]

In principle, the Phoenicians were motivated at this early stage by the same impulses as the Ugarites and other Bronze Age mariners: profit and the acquisition of valuable minerals. Later, military pressure from the Assyrians may also have played a role, forcing the Phoenicians to supply primary products—especially iron—to the kings of the Near East and their armies. But this was not yet a factor in the early journeys.[110] Access to valuable minerals and well-sited ports prompted the Phoenicians to intensify their contacts with Cyprus, colonizing Kition in the ninth century, at the same time as they were embarking for Ophir and Tartessos. Besides Cyprus and Crete, Greece's coasts and islands formed a natural stopping post en route to the west, with much better anchorage possibilities and wind conditions than the Greater Syrtis. In Attica and on several Aegean isles, olive oil could be taken on board before being traded in the west for precious metals. Merchants were equally enticed by the silver deposits of Athens (Laurion) and Thasos.[111]

Between Athens and Thasos lay the settlement of Lefkandi in Euboea, with which the Phoenicians likewise cultivated intensive trade relations. In the eleventh century, Mycenaean refugees and returnees had established here an aristocratic culture with a warrior king no less proud of his arms than of his far-reaching trade connections (in the east).[112] The Euboeans resembled the Phoenicians in many respects. Their agricultural resources were similarly limited, and they therefore turned to overseas trade from early on, exporting pottery, aromatic plants, olive oil, and wine. They further shipped grain, artworks, and minerals to customers in Greece and Asia Minor. Their relationship with the Phoenicians could veer between cooperation and competition, depending on the situation. Euboean and Phoenician traders encountered each other most often on Cyprus, in Tyrian Kition, and in the Levantine ports. Euboean amphorae for transporting oil and wine as well as finely decorated pottery were already found in Tyre between 950 and 900 BCE. In the first half of the eighth century, there was Euboean and Cycladic pottery in Samaria, the capital of Israel. A not inconsiderable number of Euboeans were integrated into 'oriental' settlements; Euboean nobles schemed to marry into families from Tyre.[113]

In this way, the Euboeans were able to plug into the communications channels that the Levantine merchants had established with the great Near Eastern empires. Bases located near the great trading zones served as way stations as well as offering access to the land's resources and markets. One such base was Al-Mina on the Orontes River in northern Syria. The Euboean colony may have been founded with the permission of local rulers.[114] From a relatively early stage, however, the warehouses and offices must have been shared with Phoenician merchants. Euboeans who settled semi-permanently in Al-Mina would have taken wives from the local area and from northern Syria. Al-Mina offered an agriculturally rich hinterland as well as access to Cypriot metals (gold, tin, and copper) and luxury goods from the Mesopotamian-Levantine-Egyptian realm. The site was also an ideal launching pad for men offering their services as mercenaries to the eastern powers (Assyrians) or embarking on raids—then as now, the boundaries between trade, piracy, and mercenary service were often blurred.[115] As in similar situations later on, the Assyrians may have been happy to see a counterweight to the dominant Phoenician influence in the region.

In the west, too, the Euboeans moved at least in part along the routes pioneered by the Phoenicians. Some believe that Euboeans took over the transhipment of Phoenician pottery to Spanish Huelva. Others, conversely, think that Greek pottery was loaded onto Phoenician boats.[116] Perhaps Euboeans and Phoenicians together moved up the Tiber to a settlement that may already have been called Rome at the time. Tyrian trade missions to the north African coast were also part of a trading zone crisscrossed by Cypriots, Syrians, and Euboeans. The literature of the fourth century BCE has preserved a whole series of Greek place names on the Tunisian coast such as Hippo Acra (Bizerte), Pithekoussai (Tabarka), or an island called Eubois. In all likelihood, these names refer back to the exploratory journeys of Euboean mariners.[117] Despite what later legends suggest, Carthage, too, was a trading post frequented by Phoenicians, Euboeans, and Cypriots as a stopover on the journey to the west; it may already have been known to the Mycenaeans.[118]

Pithekoussai, City of the Courageous

Pithekoussai, the most famous Euboean colony on Ischia in the Gulf of Naples, was similar. The name indicates the presence of monkeys (*pithekoi*) on the island. Since monkeys are confined to northern Africa, Italic Pithekoussai may have been a secondary foundation of its Tunisian mother colony.[119] Around 3,000 years ago, Ischia was home to around 10,000 residents—not just Corinthians living cheek by jowl with Euboeans and Rhodians, but also Phoenicians from north Africa, Spain, and the Levant: a melting pot of people who had everything to gain and very little to lose by trying their luck abroad.[120] Here ships were hauled ashore in the winter months and loaded with cargo before sailing on to Tartessos. On the Etruscan coast, tin, copper ore, and iron (from the Upper Austrian Hallstatt culture) and possibly gold could be traded for pottery as well as for oriental-style *objets d'art* made in Pithekoussai, ointment, and wine. The metals could then be processed for domestic consumption (as ploughshares or weapons) or sold on to the east. Grain also had to be imported from nearby Campania, since a community of this size, mostly made up of artisans, traders, pirates, and smiths rather than farmers, could not feed itself from the produce of the island alone.[121]

Excavations have revealed a culture that valued good living and good taste. Discoveries include perfume flasks and glassware used in sporting activities and all-male drinking parties (*symposia*). Phoenician and Etruscan gentlemen may have clinked glasses with their Euboean hosts. Just as the Euboeans in Al-Mina married into the local community, so too the Greeks and Phoenicians of Pithekoussai courted Etruscan women from the mainland. 'Orientals' took Italic wives and buried their children according to Greek custom.[122] Children grew up bilingual and played a vital role in oral and written communication within the island community and with the outside world.

Perhaps that is why it was precisely here, in a polyglot, ethnically diverse society so heavily reliant on east-west trade, that the Greeks adopted the Phoenician alphabetic script. Alphabetic writing had evolved in the late second millennium BCE as an easy-to-learn medium that allowed traders and other mobile individuals to record and transmit information beyond the cuneiform script used by professional scribes.[123] In Pithekoussai, the following inscription could be read on one of the large wine cups imported from the east Aegean: 'I am the drink-worthy cup of Nestor; whosoever should drink from this cup, desire for fair-crowned Aphrodite shall seize'.[124] Nestor was the oldest Achaean fighter in Troy, the owner of an enormous drinking vessel or *krater*; as the goddess of love, Aphrodite was fatally connected with the battle for Troy. No doubt everyone snickered at the irony of lines that promised to reacquaint the ageing warrior with the delights of Aphrodite by draining the cup. A shared aristocratic lifestyle and collective knowledge of old, continually retold stories were here taken for granted.

Outlines of a New Order in the Eighth Century BCE

After a millennium of sea travel, warfare, and political upheaval, a new order emerged that would set the path for centuries to come. In Greece, Cyprus, and the Levant, and later also in Sicily and Sardinia, the palace cultures made way for a new form of polity that we know as the city-state: independent communities (*poleis*) with an aristocratic elite, institutions of their own, and mostly planned, sea-facing urban precincts that offered good landing and defensive possibilities. There had already been something of the kind in the Bronze Age, but the new cities that came to dominate the coasts of Greece and the Levant were smaller. Above all, the civic rulers' claim to power seems to have been reduced or entirely replaced by aristocratic families. Here, too, the cities of the Sea Peoples and Phoenicians may have set a precedent, although no direct influence on Greek developments can be demonstrated.

The coastal cities of the Levant and the Aegean made the Mediterranean their field of action, although large stretches of the north African coast continued to be left out. The number of players crisscrossing the seas increased along with the overall population of the Mediterranean basin.[125] Their nautical knowledge was passed on by word of mouth, while their destinations and forms of mobility drew on the experiences of the Sea Peoples and their predecessors.

On the one hand, mercenary service in Assyria and Egypt was a magnet for footloose fighters. For the Greeks, in particular, it accelerated developments at home. From around 900 BCE, their hoplites entered the fray with their spears, iron swords, and round shields, proving so successful that close combat became the basis of the new political order. It rested on the readiness of every male adult citizen to take up arms under an aristocratic elite. These appropriated the title of *basileus* from the Mycenaean leaders who had established themselves as local strongmen at the time of the Sea Peoples movement or had led larger émigré communities to Cyprus and the Levant. For them and their followers, mercenary service provided an additional opportunity to gain riches and glory, and it allowed them to start afresh whenever they were defeated in an internal power struggle. They sailed for the same areas as the Sea Peoples before them. The Assyrian and Egyptian armies now demanded Greek professional fighters who had learned to fight man-to-man in a closed line formation or phalanx. The 'Dark Ages' are here not a break but a bridge that allowed Bronze Age structures to survive well into the archaic period.

Another legacy of the late Bronze Age, and closely linked with mercenary fighting, was piracy and pillaging.[126] The same target and conflict zones reappear: according to Assyrian sources, *Iavan(us)* overran the coast from Cilicia to the Levant, as had once the Mycenaeans and Sea Peoples.[127] *Iavanus* is equivalent to 'Ionians', a collective term for all Greeks, who from an Assyrian point of view came from the west; these were mostly Euboeans. Egypt, too, remained a preferred hunting ground. Strikes on foreign shores could generate quick profits in the form of slaves and luxury goods, which could then be sold on or kept for domestic use. The attackers used a modified form of the penteconter with an additional sail, a stable keel, and a ram for capsizing enemy ships.[128]

The boundaries between raids, piracy, and long-distance trade carried out by the *basileis* or their sons were fluid. It took a long time for the trade volumes of the Euboeans and Phoenicians to regain the heights of the late Bronze Age; nonetheless, their trade networks and sea routes remained intact. Phoenicians and Euboeans drew on Mycenaean and Ugarite connections, venturing to northern Italy and Sardinia and to southern Spain. Old hubs like Cyprus and Kommos were supplemented by new ones (Carthage, Pithekoussai). The search for minerals was now concentrated on iron—a regular iron industry arose—and shifted to the new elites.[129] The old 'palace trade' carried out with large ships was increasingly replaced by 'private' trade involving smaller vessels. A crew typically consisted of no more than half a dozen men of mixed origin: Canaanite, Syrian, Cypriot, Aegean, and Anatolian.[130] Freed from palace control, they were accompanied by artisans, artists, builders, miners, and metalworkers. They were sought-after specialists, always on the lookout for new opportunities, be it at the courts of the Assyrians, in the towns of Etruscan nobles, or among the chieftains of Spain. They experimented with new methods and swapped information, ideas, and experiences.[131] Individual initiative, combined with a taste for adventure and specialist skills, allowed Greeks, in particular, to survive abroad and propelled their expansion to the farthest shores.

They often established settlements or trading posts in the process, much as the Philistines had done in the Levant.[132] Not all were successful, but some of the Phoenician foundations in North Africa and Spain as well as Greek colonies in Sicily and southern Italy surpassed their 'mother cities' in wealth, agricultural resources, and population. The precondition was rapid demographic growth in the Levant and in the Aegean in the ninth and eighth centuries. Yet scarcity of land or famine rarely were the push factors for emigration. There was more than enough land in Greece, although human and animal labour sufficient to cultivate more than around 5 hectares was lacking.[133] More often, power struggles within the aristocracy forced the losers to try their luck abroad and seek to gain the influence denied them at home. No emigrant charted a random course; they made for areas already pioneered through voyages of trade and discovery. *Apoikiai* ('colonies') were not established in a 'New World' but within a Mediterranean world-wide web woven by traders, artisans, pirates, and artists, the 'nomads of the sea'.[134] They resulted not so much from unique founding acts as from the gradual agglomeration of smaller footholds or their merger with existing communities. In many cases, the native populace may have accelerated the growth of the city. Greek and Phoenician colonization, which within two centuries would cover the Mediterranean with a network of independent city-states, was only possible because voyages of trade and discovery had scouted the terrain and prepared the ground.

WONDROUS ISLES, BEASTS, AND BEAUTIFUL WOMEN

Secret Maritime Knowledge and Memories of Great Deeds

How did people in the transitional period from the Bronze Age to the early archaic period experience sailing into the wide blue yonder, struggling on the open sea, searching for gold and silver, and conquering cities? Such experiences must have been wrested from oblivion and committed to memory, just as the esoteric knowledge of sailors was passed down orally.

Observations of seafaring peoples show that experiences pioneering new routes, venturing into foreign lands, and encountering foreigners are integrated into the common store of knowledge and made available to the younger generation through coded narratives. The storyteller and the elders who confirm his words are of high standing in the community. They alone know how to get to the hidden treasures, they alone know the dangers and the means to overcome them.[135] Their medium is the verse narrative, accompanied by lyre and illustrated with vivid images. Their audience in the Bronze Age were the coastal communities and palaces that helped pay for long-distance voyages and whose fame was increased by the proceeds. The so-called naval expedition fresco (probably sixteenth century BCE) from the Minoan settlement on Thera shows several scenes, beginning with the departure of a seven-ship flotilla for a fortified town.[136]

For some, the decoration of the ships, the clothing of the crew, and the ceremonial order of the fleet suggest a parade or procession to mark the beginning of the seafaring season; but there are also soldiers on board who have fastened their boar's tusk helmets to the awnings. On the north frieze, we see a land-and-sea assault on a town with an imposing building and galleries facing out towards the beach, not unlike the halls of Kommos that scholars have interpreted as shipyards.[137] There are consultation scenes as well as a ship foundering in high seas or off a cape.

Such a sequence of images cannot be understood without the accompanying story. It deals with war and peace—a dual template later used by Homer to describe the world on Achilles' shield: a solemn procession and a raid by bold adventurers undismayed by the perils they face at sea and a city's defences. This was what the aristocratic society found worthy of

Image 2 Flotilla fresco from Thera (Santorini). This section of a 6-meter-long fresco from the island of Thera from the Minoan period (sixteenth century BCE) shows ships setting sail from the harbour of a well-ordered coastal town. The peaceful, ceremonious atmosphere is striking, which is why some scholars interpret the fresco as a kind of procession. Photo by DeAgostini/Getty Images.

commemoration. But paintings like Thera's had to be continually brought to life, and they whetted an appetite for more: professional bards spun out variations on the story's basic themes.[138] Audiences wanted to know more about the heroes and their plans, whether there was conflict and betrayal, who proved their mettle and which enemies they killed, whether the gods took sides and if they all came back alive. There arose a reservoir of stories that grew up around key events and were condensed in new scenarios, personae, and regions.

In the late Mycenaean period, Troy had already been singled out as one of the most popular targets of heroic pillaging voyages. Other cities subsequently joined it, including Thebes, famous for the heroic battles fought at its gates.[139] The cast of heroes increased. Some were especially popular. These included Heracles, the first to sail across the Aegean (with six ships, roughly equivalent to the Thera fresco) and conquer Troy. Heracles was the epitome of the heroic warrior; he undertook labours for foreign kings that surpassed the bounds of the humanly possible. And he moved at the same limits of the world glimpsed by Bronze Age seafarers in their quest for precious goods. In the Far West he steals the Golden Apples of the Hesperides—perhaps a mythical version of Baltic amber—from a guardian serpent and slays the Nemean lion, while beyond the Ocean River, on the island of Erytheia, he rustles the cattle herds of the three-headed monster Geryon. He even transgresses the limits ordained by the gods in abducting the hellhound Cerberus.[140] Heracles reflects the confidence of the 'master of animals' in his ability to subdue nature and free humankind from the monsters lurking at the margins and in the deep. The descent into the underworld is the ultimate test of courage for all heroes and proof of their uniqueness. The universal dream of gaining fame and riches through plunder and military combat is transfigured in his feats; vase paintings from the seventh century show the hero clad in heavy armour.[141] His field of action corresponds to the exploratory horizon that had been disclosed in the Bronze Age and then regained in the archaic period.[142]

Whole armies of heroes crossed the seas in Heracles' wake. The Thessalian Jason, for instance, pushed into the Black Sea with his hand-picked fellow fighters on the Argo—a classic penteconter—to steal the Golden Fleece. Or Achilles, venerated in Thessaly and hymned in Lefkandi, prided himself on having plundered twelves cities from the sea and eleven by land before taking part in the second campaign against Troy. Homer later fashioned an entire epic from the conflict between the most celebrated mercenary of archaic Greece and his overlord, King Agamemnon of Mycenae.[143]

Of Shipwrecks and Wondrous Isles

The hero did not always need to demonstrate his prowess in great battles. The elemental dangers of sea travel as well as uncertainty about what lay in wait on distant shores formed the background to many stories, such as the ancient Egyptian 'Tale of the Shipwrecked Sailor', probably set in the Red Sea, and the last chapter of the 'Report of Wenamun', composed around 900 BCE, which tells of an Egyptian temple priest who embarked on a journey up the Levantine coast and was blown off course to Alasiya (Cyprus).[144] The protagonists of both these stories deliver a first-person report—a trait typical of the 'travel narrative': tossed up by storm and wind on a paradisial island, the first encounters a friendly snake god while the second meets a queen who offers him a banquet and the delights of love; both look forward to a happy return to their homeland. The crossing of the boundary between the familiar centre (home of the first-person narrator) and the unknown yet alluring periphery (island) is explained by the influence of unpredictable natural forces (tempests) and divine will. It is bound up with the existential experience of fear of death: the traveller encounters the world of paradise and death at the same time.[145]

In another narrative type, the island (or insular coast) is not a destination arrived at by chance but a planned stopover on the way to even more distant fields. The most famous, known throughout the Near East, is the legend of Gilgamesh, king of Uruk, who sets out to find the secret of life after the death of his friend Enkidu. Following an adventurous march through mountains guarded by lions and scorpion men, he arrives at the bejewelled garden and tavern of the divine ale-wife Siduri, 'who lives by the sea'. From here he takes the ferryman Urshanabi's boat across the 'waters of death' to an island where Utnapishtim, granted immortality by the gods following the flood, lives with his wife. It is the land of the blissful and the dead 'where the sun rises'. Odysseus, the hero of the archaic Greeks, will later cross the Ocean River, guided by the sorceress Circe's instructions, to interrogate the souls of the dead at the entrance to the underworld.

The common background to such stories is a mythical geography accepted throughout the eastern Mediterranean and Near East. Its oldest surviving document is the Babylonian (or Assyrian) 'world map' from the late eighth or seventh century BCE. Although it represents the seventh-century worldview, it probably goes back to a template that circulated among many Near Eastern cultures and gave a geographical setting to legends about the heroes.[146] Accordingly, the known world and homeland (Babylon) lie at the centre of a circular disc of earth surrounded by a ring of water (*nar marratu* = salt lake or bitter river). The Greeks called this earth-encircling river Okeanos; the term is probably borrowed from the Semitic-Phoenician.[147] Five triangular, island-like 'regions' (*nagû*) are grouped on the far side of the *marratu*, their tips facing outwards.[148] The distance across the *marratu* to the *nagû* is given on the reverse in 'leagues'. It is written of the northernmost region that here 'the sun is not seen'. Fabulous beasts roam the islands, including the three-headed Geryon, whose cattle were stolen by Heracles. Here, too, lies the island of Utnapishtim, which Gilgamesh reached after crossing the 'waters of death'. And here, finally, is the land of the dead, reached by a string of islands inhabited by female deities who must first be compelled or persuaded to give onward passage.

Age-old experiences of mariners culminated in these islands. For them, islands were oases in the desert of the sea, providing orientation and salvation in mortal danger. That is why temples were erected there presided over by mostly female deities (with snakes or dragons to guard their treasures, according to legend): goddesses like Siduri or Circe who possessed esoteric knowledge about sea routes. Perhaps they also reflected knowledge of the high status enjoyed by priestesses and queens, who in later times (the Queen of Sheba and the 'Sutean woman' among the Babylonians) sought contact with rulers of the north.[149] The temples on islands or coasts served as a neutral rendezvous for long-distance traders, since the god's presence protected the exchange from fraud and guaranteed that promises would be honoured.[150] In this way, the legends of island goddesses encode what long-distance traders knew and had experienced about the origin of the most valuable commodities from abroad: from an Egyptian perspective, the Land of Punt (Nubia) and the tin island of Cyprus; from a Sumerian-Mesopotamian viewpoint, Failaka Island (in the Gulf of Kuwait), equivalent to the Siduri coast, and Dilmun (Bahrain), where Utnapishtim dwelled; for Phoenicians, Greeks, and Hebrews, the glittering port of Tartessos. Given the very real dangers of the voyage out, islands were important waystations for taking on fresh water (hence the constant reference to ever-flowing springs!) as well as gateways to unfathomable wealth: gold, copper (Cyprus and Bahrain), lapis lazuli, pearls (Dilmun), spices and perfumes, tin. For those travelling there from places where such treasures were lacking, such abundance must have seemed overwhelming, divine, in short: paradisical.[151]

Of Beasts and Princesses

A third variant is found in stories in which the hero has no need of islands but comes to his own rescue in his hour of need, not only plundering the faraway land but freeing it from dangerous monsters as well. Such was the case with Heracles. Bellerophon did something similar when he slew the fire-breathing Chimera, a hybrid of goat, dragon, and serpent, at the behest of King Iobantes.[152] Or Perseus, who is ordered by the king of Argos to cut off the head of Medusa, rids the Ethiopian coast of the sea monster and is rewarded with the hand of Andromeda.

Such episodes are unmistakeably rooted in old fairy-tale motifs of a hero who does battle with evil and wins the fair princess. In the Greek context, however, they stand for more: monstrous beasts represent the wildness of nature at the edges of the world, and when a Greek hero defeats them, he tames the uncivilized counter-world to the polis and thereby confirms its superiority—as great a sign of valour as the monster's grimace and his golden hoard. Marriage with the foreign princess symbolizes the transition to civilization and legitimates the takeover of power. Later, such motifs formed the basis for the origin myths used by Greek colonists to justify their usurpation of foreign territory. In the early days, however, it was far more common for heroes like Jason or Theseus to abduct native women than to marry them there and then. Kidnapping girls was a nightmare scenario for the society of the polis but also a kind of initiation rite for young aristocrats, a test of their manhood. The abduction of girls and women provoked violent reactions, spurring those affected to seek vengeance, launch search parties, and generate wars and conflicts spanning multiple generations, the most famous being the Trojan War. In the fifth century, Herodotus begins his *Histories* by discussing myths of female abduction and the vendettas that eventually gave rise to the Persian Wars.

As such complications make clear, those returning from abroad were not always welcomed back—indeed, failed colonists could be greeted with shots upon their homecoming. Their arrival represented a threat to the powers that be, which had often changed in their absence. In this context, it is striking that the myths devote more space to the heroes' return after their adventures than to the journey out. The 'tales of return' (*nostoi*) formed independent narrative complexes that appealed enormously to Greeks, in part because in the unstable world of the dark centuries, unlike in the monarchies of the east, they never knew what had happened at home while they were away: whether envious neighbours had taken over their wives and property, or even whether an attack awaited them from both, the fate that befell the Achaean leader against Troy. Moreover, lengthy absences as a mercenary, pirate, or trader offered ample material for sailor's yarns to fill in the gaps. Who knew if the man who had set out all those years ago had drowned at sea, or if he had abandoned any thought of return as he lay in the arms of a beautiful woman? And if he did eventually return, he would embellish his tales to exaggerate his own heroism.

Contacts with the East

Many stories about heroes doing battle with monstrous beasts take place in the east or reveal the influence of eastern models, as for instance myths of native gods fighting serpents and dragons, which often symbolize the primordial power of the sea or the hidden force of the life-giving earth.[153] Such stories survived the depredations of the Sea Peoples because the space from Cilicia through Syria to Palestine preserved its written culture along with its urban structures. Consonantal writing was used by Hebrews, Phoenicians, and Aramaeans and made reading and writing accessible to broad sections of the population.[154] At the latest, linguistic and communication barriers were overcome once the trader, mercenary, or pirate took a local wife, settled abroad, or entered the service of a foreign king. In such a constellation, the need to learn the foreign language was far greater than on a short-term trading mission. The children of mixed marriages grew up bilingual and became mediators in a multicultural world that teemed with stories of daring heroes, cruel gods, and frightening clashes with monsters. The Phoenicians, too, had myths and songs that could be threaded into the late Mycenaean and Euboean narrative context.[155] Phoenician silver cups show sieges and hunts, battles and royal courts, all of which point to matching recitations. Stories were told or sung not just at feasts but also on long sea voyages or on warm evenings in Pithekoussai or Al-Mina, where the ruling class's multilingualism guaranteed their survival. Drinking vessels from graves in

Pithekoussai suggest that Phoenicians and Euboeans ate together, enjoyed epic songs, and perhaps even swapped Greek and oriental legends.[156]

Stories of Philistines and Hebrews

There thus emerged a dense network of trans-Mediterranean stories that were commemorated in song, were narrated on voyages and at firesides, and entered the lifeworld of foreign linguistic cultures through mixed marriages, proving no less resistant to military upheavals than knowledge of maritime trade routes. Some stability was provided by the tradition of near eastern hero and god narratives, which encompassed the entire area from Asia Minor through the Mesopotamian cultural domains to the principalities of the Levant. Similar stories were told everywhere of the god who must wrestle with a sea monster to secure his rule, or of heroes like Gilgamesh, who defends himself against the envious goddesses he rejected as sexual partners, fights giants and beast, and journeys to the end of the world and visits the land of the dead in his search for immortality following the death of his friend.

Almost all these stories were recorded in the form of epic poems in the Hittite, Ugarite, and Assyrian palace archives and were written down, dictated, or learned by heart by a scribal elite. Experience suggests that epic material disseminates quickly over political and linguistic borders. Why should Greek emissaries not have been granted a glimpse into the epic literature stored in the palace archives? It was hardly a diplomatic secret. Time and again, the old legends were recited at the numerous feasts and drinking ceremonies attended by Greek guests.[157] Additional opportunities for swapping stories presented themselves on long sea voyages, which for all their occasional dangers could also be mind-numbingly dull.

In this way, not only were a number of Hittite and Ugarite stories preserved and introduced to the Greek world; conversely, the Mycenaeans and their descendants may have succeeded in injecting some of their own heroes' tales into the narrative reservoir of eastern myth.[158] If it is true that the Philistines came from the same Aegean environment as the Mycenaeans, then their close, by no means always antagonistic, contacts with Egyptians, Phoenicians, and Hebrews provided them with a conduit to pass on their myths. Philistine gods like Beelzebub were adopted by Hebrew writers, while the Philistines gave Greek names to Semitic gods and goddesses

(Aphrodite to Astarte, for example).[159] Seafarers take their patron deities with them and worship similar sea gods. Given mixed crews, it is hardly surprising that Phoenicians or Carthaginians and Greeks worshipped Poseidon in common, nor that they found in Heracles/Melqart a semi-divine hero whom they could venerate as a slayer of sea monsters. They therefore built temples and altars for him when establishing bases on coasts supplied with fresh water, just as Near Eastern mariners did for their mostly female deities on faraway islands (see above, p. 47).[160]

Differences were quickly reconciled on land, too: along with the motif of a divine battle against a sea monster, the Hebrews appropriated the metaphor of the winged ship from the Ugarites and Greeks. The story of Jonah, who flees Joppa on a Tarshish ship only to be swallowed by a giant fish and spat out on dry land, shows the influence of Mediterranean-Greek narratives, especially the myth of Jason (= Jonah?), who was likewise depicted falling into the maw of a snake-like monster (during the voyage of the Argo?) and being regurgitated at Athena's behest (similar to Yahweh's command).[161] Episodes linked to David and Samson show that Hebrews and Philistines were linked by trade and intermarriage and that Hebrew commanders fought for the Philistines. Hebrews and Greeks served as guards at Jewish or Egyptian fortresses. We thus have every reason to believe that in the ninth or eighth century, a Philistine and Hebrew soldier would share a drink at the end of a monotonous shift, tell each other stories, and keep Euboean cups as mementos.[162] Philistines and Canaanites evidently used Aegean symposium utensils (*kratēre*). We know of a widespread Ugarite drinking ceremony (*marzeah*) that resembled the Greek *symposion* and drew the ire of the Israelite prophets. This points to its popularity among Hebrews, too.[163]

As foot soldiers, they were all united in the conviction that victories over charioteers and the conquest of rich cities deserved to be commemorated and sung. The Greeks, like the Akkadians, cried 'alala' when they went into battle, while the Hebrews shrieked an almost homophonous 'hallelujah'. They all would have understood each other. As fighters, they were linked by a sense of fraternity: where Greeks bragged about the fall of Troy, Hebrews celebrated the fall of Jericho. Both cities were taken through unconventional tricks by a besieging army with flagging morale (the Trojan horse and the blowing of trumpets, respectively). Another theme was heroic duels: Menelaus against Paris or Achilles against Hector or David against Goliath.[164] And then there were the hardy warriors who succumb to the wiles of beautiful women yet remain true to their mission. Heracles was known in the east, and his labours recall Samson, who killed a lion with his bare hands and destroyed the house of his tormentors while chained between two pillars. Samson came from the tribe of Dan, which can perhaps be identified with the Aegean Sea Peoples, the Danaans (= *Danuna, Denyan*).[165]

In two respects, however, the stories of the Hebrews differ from those of their Euboean and Philistine friends. First, their heroic deeds predominantly occurred in their homeland or in nearby Canaan, whereas the heroes of the Mycenaeans, Philistines, and Euboeans celebrated their successes in foreign lands that could only be reached by sea. Second, and more importantly, the Greek heroes fought with the help of sympathetic gods yet ultimately owed their victories to their own skill, cunning, and valour. By contrast, the successes of the Hebrew heroes were not so much a sign of their own strength (or divine origin) as proof of the unrivalled power of their god. 'You come against me with sword and spear and javelin', David calls out to his opponent, 'but I come against you in the name of the Lord Almighty, the God of the armies of Israel'.[166] The Greek heroes bragged about their ancestors and feats of arms before delivering the fatal blow. The idea that great heroes or kings have divine ancestors or are themselves semi-divine was foreign to the Hebrews (and the Ugarites); it was imported from outside into the Canaanite domain.[167] This difference also has to do with the Hebrews' roots in the Levantine mythic tradition. Here the gods themselves did battle with monsters and dragons. Allowing mortal heroes to bask in the glory of victory might well have represented too radical a break with tradition. Here too, as so often, a unique political constellation welded a basic religious orientation and heroic tales into a new narrative complex.

Transcribing the Greek and Hebrew Epics

The Hebrews dwelling in the mountainous terrain of Jordan were latecomers to the world of small and medium-sized Canaanite states. In the ninth century under David and Solomon (if they really lived), later lionized as great rulers, they had only just attained the status of doughty freebooters and mercenaries with a still primitive centre in Jerusalem. It took a few more centuries for Judea and Israel to evolve into respectable kingdoms, although they soon came under pressure from the Egyptians and especially the Assyrians.

The rise of Assyria is one of the most important turning points in ancient history, comparable with the expansion of the Persians around two centuries later. For the first time, the Assyrians unified the entire near east under a single hegemonic power.[168] Judea could survive as an independent kingdom with reduced territory and annual tribute payments, with Jerusalem as its capital. The Northern Kingdom of Israel became an Assyrian province in the last third of the century but experienced an economic upswing, evident in a building boom and increased involvement in Assyrian trading and economic networks. At this time, at the earliest, although probably not until the period of exile, Yahweh rose to become the one God who tolerated no rivals.

Assyrian expansion was important for Israel and Judea in another key respect. It helped disseminate a scribal culture, previously unknown in this form, that elevated the written word into a source of religious and political authority.[169] With increasing urbanization, the Hebrews developed a culture of writing spearheaded by trained scribes who were vital to both the palace bureaucracy and the professional priesthood. They provided the kingdom with new opportunities for entrenching its power.[170] In this period, the Assyrian kings established numerous archives and libraries; Mesopotamian and Egyptian rulers collected books and stories; the final version of the Gilgamesh epic was transcribed in the eighth century and preserved in the archives of the Babylonian king, where around the same time the 'Babylonian' world map was created with an accompanying explanatory text—all signs that, with the expansion of the Assyrian and Neo-Babylonian Empires, a new interest in the order of the world, its margins, and its legends was stirring.[171]

In Greece, Hesiod pursued the same interest when he composed a genealogy of the gods (*Theogony*) and in his 'Catalogue of Women' described a mythic chase around the world.[172] Hebrew scholars and writers may likewise have been influenced by such attempts at synthesis and have owned world maps similar to the famous Babylonian one.[173] In order to give their heterogeneous population a new identity and keep alive the memory of Judea in Babylonian exile as well as counter the Assyrian chronicles with something of their own, the priesthood created an epic historical work that combined the marvellous adventures of the tenth and ninth centuries with old Canaanite myths to endow the current royal dynasty with a glorious dynastic past.[174] The centre of the kingdom was Jerusalem, and with Jerusalem there was to be only the one God, who had led the Hebrews out of Egypt through the Sinai Peninsula to the land of Canaan promised to their forefathers. The oldest texts in the Old Testament thus arose between the eighth and sixth centuries.[175]

Something similar occurred on the Aegean shore of Asia Minor. Between 820 and 800, Euboean merchants or colonists developed the Greek alphabet from the consonantal writing of the Phoenicians at one of their countless meeting points in Al-Mina or in Pithekoussai, or perhaps on one of their long shared sea voyages to the west. It was the first alphabetic script aimed at reproducing spoken language as closely as possible. Like the Hebrews, the Euboeans used their new script to record their heroes' tales. It became a universal marker for demonstrating knowledge of Greek myths. Unlike the Hebrews, however, the Euboeans did not use writing to assert themselves against culturally dominant territorial empires and to give a young kingdom an autonomous identity. Apart from Sparta, there were no territorial empires in archaic Greece, only independent city-states that fought over fertile plains but were never confronted by a military machine the size of Assyria's. Since there was no professional priesthood in Greece and priests had limited authority, literacy was also not tied to any religious agenda. Reciting heroes' tales was part of an aristocratic way of life: the *basileis* sought both to add lustre to their position by recalling the heroic age and to consolidate their knowledge about distant countries and sea routes, but they did not draw from the recitation any direct dynastic claims to sovereignty in the form of an institutionalized monarchy.

In the eighth century BCE, the Euboeans showed markedly less enthusiasm for maritime activity, probably owing to battles fought for control of the Lelantine Plain (on Euboea); the decline was not so dramatic as the plight of the Hebrew kingdoms as there were no external aggressors. Yet the initiative and interest in preserving old stories now shifted to Cyprus and the coast of Asia Minor. Here the Greeks, like the Hebrews, lived in close proximity to the Assyrian Empire, whose expansion favoured the dissemination of literate culture and the Near Eastern epics. The relationship between Assyrians and Greeks was by no means permanently hostile, despite reports of 'Ionian' pirates off the Cilician and northern Syrian coasts. Ionians sometimes served Assyria's enemies (Phrygia) and were involved in local rebellions. They nonetheless profited from the expansion of Assyrian power, plugging into their trading network and meeting the Assyrian armies' need for iron and warships in competition with Phoenician cities.[176]

The Greek myths nowhere betray a pronounced enmity, yet the Greeks were all the more aware of differences in how they organized their societies. 'A small city, well-organised and on a steep promontory', wrote the poet Phocylides, 'is better than foolish Nineveh'.[177] Nineveh was the residence of the Assyrian Empire, and although the saying dates from the sixth century BCE, when the Assyrian Empire had already been destroyed, it may be supposed that the *basileis* of Asia Minor had a similar sense of self-regard centuries earlier. Like the Hebrews, they sought to confront the Assyrians with an epic of their own that emphasized what made them stand apart.

Around 700, a poet called Homer responded to their wishes by composing two large-scale epics. Adopting a familiar frame narrative, he concentrated his tales on conflicts so typical of the Greek world that anyone could identify with them. Against the backdrop of the Achaean expedition against Troy, the *Iliad* invoked the quarrel between the best fighter, Achilles, and the supreme commander, Agamemnon, as well as its fatal consequences—a configuration that must have been only too common in the pillaging campaigns of the archaic period, especially among mercenaries. The *Odyssey* tells of a hero who is tossed from one foreign shore and island to the next following the decade-long siege of Troy until eventually, with the help of his son, he regains his home and wife. It distils the dreams and fears of archaic mariners, who always risked losing the old in their quest for the new. Although the *Iliad* is generally believed to have been written first, there is much to suggest that the two epics merely reflect different social roles and ways of life that made the Greek aristocrat, in his estimation, superior to the potentates of the east.

ODYSSEUS

Learning and Suffering

Homer knew all the stories about heroes doing battle in faraway lands, wondrous isles, and beautiful princesses; he understood the magic of

Mediterranean sailors' yarns and homecoming tales; and he was familiar with the basic features of eastern epic, the adventures of Gilgamesh, and his crossing of the world-encompassing river. Yet what he made of all this was something quite new. Like the *Iliad*, the *Odyssey* deals with the fate of a great hero, the death of many men, mourning, hope, and suffering, but this time the geographical setting is not limited to Troy but has expanded dramatically. Odysseus saw not one city but many on his voyage, we read in the epic's second verse, after the hero is introduced as the plunderer of Troy and the narrative thread of the *Iliad* is resumed. Then comes the surprise: instead of announcing how Odysseus destroyed these cities as well, freed them from monsters, and won the hand of fair princesses, Homer indicates how his hero's involuntary engagement with the wide world and its people has a completely different meaning: 'He saw and *learned* their minds'—a heroic characterization found in no other epic poem from the ancient world.[178]

Making learning the focal point of travel is a Greek innovation that expresses a restless curiosity about the new and the strange. It is the product of an ethnographic way of thinking that probably existed only here, in the Greek world of the Aegean and Asia Minor, where in Homer's day people embarked for new shores and interacted with eastern cultures as colonizers, traders, and pirates: openness to the foreign and a hunger for learning are ideals typical of seafaring and colonizing communities. They form the precondition not just for survival overseas but also for success at home: Odysseus' encounters over ten years with countless peoples and marvellous beings at the edges of the world equip him to reconquer his homeland, whereas Agamemnon, sailing directly back from Troy, naively falls into the trap set by his murderers. Later, the most important Greek legislators, philosophers, and historians legitimate their works by claiming to have seen half the world.

The travels of Odysseus are anything but a comfortable educational tour. Odysseus admits more than once to hating the sea and wanting nothing more than a speedy return.[179] Yet this is uncertain; learning rarely occurs voluntarily, and certainly not in a pleasant atmosphere of studious repose. Learning abroad comes at a steep cost. It cannot be had without suffering and pain. 'Many pains he suffered', Homer states in the third verse, 'heartsick on the open sea, fighting to save his life and bring his comrades home'. The sea and its shores are not the setting of glorious triumphs but of hardship and anguish. The battle for survival is accompanied by the gnawing loss of home and wife, just as present adversity is exacerbated by the certainty of future uncertainties that make the suffering interminable. In the end, Odysseus returns alone, all his companions having died en route.

Homer's audience understood all this intuitively. Menelaus, too, freely admits to having suffered much when he was blown off course following his departure from Troy with Helen; but alongside Odysseus (and Nestor), he is the only Achaean hero to be rewarded in the end with happiness and prosperity in his homeland.[180] Here we grasp an essential feature of Hellenic anthropology. All Greek literature conveys the pessimistic idea that human life is defined by inescapable hardship and deprivation.[181] Besides the battlefield, the sea is the most dangerous terrain for mortals, the primal source of evil and terror. Admiration for men like Odysseus who make a virtue of necessity is accordingly immense. Through his stubborn determination to survive, he demonstrates a resilience not even the gods possess. All his suffering at sea, his pain at the loss of his companions, and his cares for his home are a necessary test of endurance on the path to (self-)knowledge. 'Learning through suffering' will later be a core element of tragedy, so similar in spirit to the Homeric epics, while the historian Herodotus has his tragic hero Croesus say to the Persian king Cyrus: 'my sufferings, which have been bitter, have proved to be lessons of wisdom to me'.[182]

This was also an experience directed against the rulers of the east. Odysseus is given the epithet *polytlas*, which covers the full spectrum from curious learning to patient suffering: he is at once 'much-daring' and 'much-enduring', the intrepid discoverer and the man bitterly punished for his intrepid discoveries.[183] Yet since he persists despite and through his tribulations, he becomes the prototype for a new hero whose qualities are quite different from those of the oriental Gilgamesh or the wrathful Achilles: Homer presents Odysseus as *aner polytropos*, 'the man of twists and turns'. The core meaning of this epithet is the ability to prevail through adaptability, intelligence, cunning, and persistence, to cope with defeat and loss without losing sight of one's goal. These are the qualities in which the seafaring, trading, and colonizing Greeks rediscovered themselves, and which they self-confidently opposed to the wealth and power of oriental heroes.

Homer did not simply replace an old ideal with a new one. The Homeric Odysseus differs from the standard hero not just through his new qualities but also through the multidimensionality of his character. The brutal pirate who risks the lives of his crewmates for pure curiosity, and who languishes in the arms of exotic goddesses (a temptation Gilgamesh had spurned!), is ultimately impelled to return by longing for his wife and home. Odysseus suffers endlessly and thereby acquires endless glory, yet part of what makes a life glorious, according to the Greeks, is the ability to enjoy moments of happiness. Just as steadfastness was emphasized in times of need, so too romantic conquests and hard drinking were praised. This explains the captivating tension between the extremes that define the deeds and character of Odysseus: the 'tragic' fall from conqueror of Troy to destitute castaway, the suave guest and merciless butcher of the suitors, the compulsive search for adventure and yearning for domestic comfort, love affairs with exotic beauties and loyalty to his wife.[184]

Odysseys Old and New

Such a personality—this is the second innovation—cannot be captured in a simple linear narrative, as the Mesopotamian Gilgamesh epics or the stories involving Jason and Heracles tended to do. The multifaceted and dynamic character of Odysseus required an equally complex epic plot to do it justice. To this day, there is a widespread belief that the *Odyssey* recounts the hero's wanderings. In fact, they take up only a sixth of the entire epic and are narrated retrospectively by Odysseus shortly before his return (books 9–12). Parallel to this, his son Telemachus has set out in search of his father—his experiences are narrated in the first four books. The two plot strands come together after Odysseus makes landfall in Ithaca, culminating in the joint reconquest of the homeland and its aftermath. The motif of the hero's late return is intertwined with the initiatory voyage of the youth, who matures into a man in searching for his father. Both form the framework for the narrative of Odysseus' wanderings, which receives its meaning and specific function beyond an isolated series of adventure stories only within this context.

In several respects, those adventures nonetheless constitute the centrepiece of the epic composition, not just because they are placed in the middle and the prooemium expressly announces them, but because, like a classic travel narrative, they are told in the first person. The impression of immediate authenticity this gives them makes them seem so fresh and vital that even non-Greek audiences and twenty-first-century readers can understand them. While this contributes to their timeless appeal, it also conceals interpretive pitfalls: time and again, captains have set forth with the *Odyssey* in one hand and modern sea maps in the other in a bid to navigate the routes and find the destinations that the hero steered towards.[185] Considerable critical acumen has been devoted to detecting a match between modern coastal formations and ancient descriptions. The search is never-ending since the geography of the *Odyssey* cannot be confirmed by archaeological 'proof', such as that adduced by Heinrich Schliemann when he claimed to have found Homer's Troy after excavating the hill of Hissarlik. This has done nothing to curb the enthusiasm of 'discoverers' both old and new. On the contrary, Odysseus and his comrades sail the seven seas to this day, from the Black Sea to the Atlantic and Pacific, and they sometimes even succeed in circumnavigating the globe two thousand years before Magellan.

And then there are the spoilsports who dismiss even the most cautious attempts to retrace the hero's itinerary as fanciful speculation. Odysseus and his companions, they argue, moved in a fantasy realm much like Tolkien's Middle-earth; for reasons of genre alone, any localization is therefore spurious.[186] Their star witness is the Hellenistic scholar Eratosthenes (third century BCE), who ridiculed such attempts by asserting: 'you will find the scene of Odysseus' wanderings when you find the cobbler who sewed up the bag of winds'.[187] Although this viewpoint was already contested in antiquity, it has maintained its authority into the modern age. Yet the matter is not so easily put to rest.

Faction, Not Fantasy

In its bare outlines, the plot of the *Odyssey* can be traced back to archetypal fairy-tale motifs: the hero sets off on a great adventure (Trojan War) and is tested by man-eating giants, sorceresses, and monsters. He returns home in the nick of time to fend off the importunate suitors who want to marry his wife. Homer's achievement, however, was to disengage this template—so far as necessary and possible—from its fairy-tale, mythic context and bind it to a complex epic plot that met his audience's needs while amalgamating oral traditions and contemporary reality into an autonomous epic world. Through this epic makeover, his dramatis personae are endowed with individual characteristics and histories. Likewise, particular events are integrated into overarching structures, patterns of meaning, and leitmotifs that go far beyond 'fairy-tale morality': the tension between divine anger

(Poseidon) and autonomous human conduct (Odysseus), the importance of guest-friendship and its misuse abroad, and the question of the responsibility borne by a leader who risks the lives of his crew to satisfy his curiosity.

Accordingly, Odysseus' travels are narrated in first person rather than in an indefinite third person, leaving little room for fairy-tale elements. These only appear when inseparably connected with a mythic tradition in a specifically miraculous context, as in the case of the sorceress Circe, who transforms men into swine and is defeated through the counter-magic of the magic herb moly,[188] or the nymph Leucothea, who saves the hero from drowning with her veil.[189] All these are tied to mythic characters and epic formulae, yet they come across as strangely isolated in the context of the epic, having no bearing on the overall character of the journey and its hero. Odysseus himself is not a magician who deploys mysterious powers to vanquish nature and his enemies but a hero who overcomes dangers through his intelligence and versatility, in contrast to Moses in the Exodus epic, who is instructed by Yahweh to demonstrate his authority with magic tricks.[190] In a similar fashion, fairy-tale motifs from classic sailors' yarns—enormous fish, towering waves, ghost ships that appear from nowhere—are eliminated or rationalized by being assigned a clearly defined place in the mythic geography, unlike the Jonah story in the Old Testament. The sole exception is the 'floating island' of Aeolia.[191]

Odysseus' journeys do not unfold in the anywhere and anywhen ('once upon a time') of fairy tale; they occur after the fall of Troy in a historically identifiable ten-year period and parallel to other events, in a reality that may be mysterious at the margins but never drifts into the fictitious or make-believe. Leaving aside the fact that the Greeks could have neither imagined such a fantasy world nor represented it in literary form, the epic's generic laws demand that the faraway places visited by the hero be 'tangibly presented to the mind's eye'.[192] This is only possible if the unfamiliar space he traverses in his adventures lies adjacent to regions familiar from a shared geography. Herein lies the key difference between Homer's *Odyssey* and Tolkien's *Lord of the Rings*. Where the fantasy novel constructs a geographical universe entirely removed from the real world, even those episodes of the Homeric voyages most indebted to sailors' yarns could not have been narrated without sticking to the known geography of the mythic cosmos with its islands and world-girdling Ocean.[193] In this respect, too, Homer set a precedent: all later ancient maritime epics and utopian novels seek to situate their fantastic or fairy-tale narratives on real islands or seas and thereby transport contemporary ideas about the world to their exotic settings.[194]

That being the case, the epic has no need of portals connecting the magic world with the real one, the doors, mirrors, wardrobes, or fountains that abound in fairy tales and fantasy novels.[195] Storms or the plain-speaking guidance of a helpful goddess are enough to divert Odysseus and his comrades from their ordinary route to the edges of the world. Even when the Phaeacians dispatch the sleeping Odysseus to Ithaca on one of their automatic wonder vessels, this is so closely tied to the familiar reality of maritime and mythic experience (ships were ascribed divine attributes and powers) that here, too, the miraculous recedes against the effort to integrate the faraway into the near-at-hand and familiar. Alcinous had promised Odysseus that he would bring him home, even if 'landfall lies more distant than Euboea, off at the edge of the world [. . .] So say our crews, at least, who saw it once, that time they carried the golden-haired Rhadamanthus out to visit Tityus, son of Mother Earth'.[196]

The epic setting of the *Odyssey* is thus neither fantastic nor arbitrary. It is integrated into a mythic geography through fixed relations to the known world as well as through mythic guarantors like Rhadamanthus. Islands like Euboea and Ithaca are as much a part of it as Scheria or the island of Calypso, with the difference that the latter are located at the outer limits of the world and are generally only accessible to the mythic hero. For contemporaries, however, there was no difference between these realms so far as their authenticity was concerned. Both were accepted as true and real: there is 'no distinction between realities'.[197]

Experiences and Knowledge of a World on the Move

The question of *credibility* should be kept separate from the criterion of *reality*. In the epic, it too receives a meaning alien to the fairy tale. Much that is unbelievable can be narrated without taking leave of the real world. Upon returning to Ithaca, the disguised Odysseus himself spins a web of lies about his adventures as a Cretan in Egypt and among the Phoenicians, which come across as credible precisely because they are plotted against real-world coordinates. In addition, Homer's listeners were familiar with the countless merchants known for falsifying their travels to deceive competitors or talk up their wares. Later in antiquity, too, the criterion for exposing stories as untrue was almost never the content itself (which could rarely be verified) so much as the manner and quality of the report as well as the narrator's social standing.

This is exactly how Odysseus is judged by his audience at the court of the Phaeacians. Alcinous compliments the hero mid-report for his 'good sense within' and for telling his tale 'with all a singer's skill'.[198] The most prominent auditor of Odysseus' travels thus dissociates him from the seafaring traders who lie and deceive for profit and associates him instead with the epic singers. They were taken at their word because, like the storytellers of maritime coastal communities and the northern shamans, they were custodians of an esoteric specialist knowledge. Homer demonstrates such maritime knowledge when, for example, he has his hero build a seaworthy boat on the island of Calypso and steer his course by the Pleiades for seventeen days following his departure.[199] And he conveys lessons with a timeless significance for mariners and colonists. The didactic potential is evident precisely in enterprises that miscarry or threaten to miscarry, as when the Greeks, having arrived on foreign shores, eat unknown plants (of the Lotus-eaters) or animals (of Helios) in violation of local taboos and customs—an ongoing challenge for seafarers calling for the utmost vigilance. Or when the hero makes his crew responsible for losses incurred in attacking the Cicones, since they disregarded one of the basic rules of piracy: strike fast and disappear even faster. And that classic among seamen: forgetting their duties in the arms of beauties and hence jeopardizing the success of the entire mission.[200]

Learning from such mistakes and drawing the appropriate lessons is also the poet's concern. It accords with the narratives of sea-facing communities, which aim to teach the younger generation the behavioural routines needed to survive on foreign shores as well as impart knowledge about exotic plants, animals, and people.[201] The epic packaging is the best means for internalizing these lessons, bestowing on them an authority that sober rules cannot intrinsically command; for unlike the Hebrews, the Greeks could not dignify their injunctions with the religious legitimation of a single God. For that very reason, they formed a code understood by all the societies that lined the Mediterranean coasts.[202]

The sequence of people and places encountered by Odysseus during his travels also adheres to an age-old organizational principle by which mariners and coastal communities assimilate new discoveries into their existing stock of knowledge. Catalogue-like lists of foreign tribes are compiled and integrated into a mythic ethnography and geography that can easily be memorized, communicated, and expanded. Such lists reappear in the genealogical tables of Genesis, which in other respects, too—in the idea of the world river Gihon (= Ocean) and the Land of Kush (= Ethiopia)—displays parallels with the mythic geography of the Homeric epics.[203] They recur in the catalogue of ships from the *Iliad* and are epically reworked by Hesiod around the time the *Odyssey* was being transcribed, when he relates how the Harpies were chased by the winged sons of Boreas (= the Boreads). Later given the names *periodos* or *periplus*, they were further used by mariners hugging the coasts as well as by merchants and travellers operating farther inland.[204]

Additional classificatory and mnemonic stability was provided when tribes or place names—as in Ezekiel's prophetic warning about the downfall of Tyre[205]—were combined with their trade goods, or when the names of tribes and the heroes who visited them were brought into a genealogical sequence, as occurs to this day in illiterate societies. It is hardly surprising that this order drew on mythic names to create its own, ever-expanding mythical world. No other means was available to the archaic period for understanding the buzzing multiplicity of people and places far from home and converting it into communicable knowledge: myth and epic were the putty and scaffolding that allowed individual pieces of information to be assembled in memory. The composition of the Homeric voyages may also have relied on such lists, at least in part.

In this way, the poet recorded not just contemporary expertise but also exploratory knowledge that had been passed down in Mycenaean coastal communities for generations and was actualized in the aristocratic world of the *poleis* in Asia Minor.[206] Homer reflects the worldview and interests of men who ventured beyond the borders of their homeland in the eighth century to seek their fortune in the east, north (Black Sea), and Far West. Their thirst for knowledge is taken up by the poet when he has Odysseus listen to the Sirens, who know 'all that comes to pass on the fertile earth', while lashed to the mast, or when he prefaces individual episodes with detailed, not strictly necessary depictions of the islands and coastal landscapes that in some respects anticipate the later *periploi* of discoverers (see below, p. 149),[207] or when he relates that the Phaeacians were once driven from their homeland by the Cyclops and founded a new city in Scheria.[208] Odysseus himself depicts a classic colonial constellation when he steers for a fertile island near the Cyclops' coast, inhabited only by goats and blessed with a deep-sea harbour, before sending out a reconnaissance mission to 'probe the natives living over there. What *are* they—violent, savage, lawless? Or friendly to strangers, god-fearing men?'[209] Cyclops and Phaeacians lie at opposite ends of the spectrum when it comes to how strangers could be received abroad: a hospitable welcome and the princess's hand, on the one hand, hostile cannibals, on the other. They are epic symbols for liminal experiences on foreign shores represented through the criterion of civilizational achievement: here the highest stage of polis life, there the lowest level of barbarism.

Coded Knowledge, Not a Real Journey

All these links to maritime knowledge and proto-colonial teachings do not mean, however, that an actual itinerary could be pieced together by minutely comparing the geographical, nautical, and topographical information provided by Homer with their real-world equivalents. The epic formation of individual episodes and their amalgamation into a whole stand in the way of such a procedure. These always adhere to conventions and prior decisions that frustrate exact attempts at reconstruction and influence any possible real references and associations, not to mention that such an attempt runs counter to the expectations of Homer's audience. Homer thus has Odysseus set out with a large fleet and crew, only to whittle them down to the point where the hero undergoes his final adventures on his own. The 'unrealistic' reduction of participants conforms to a decision concerning the epic treatment of the material: some adventures (such as the Circe episode) require a large cast, whereas others (such as the Phaeacian episode) demand that the hero acts on his own behalf. In narrating his travels, moreover, Homer had to compete with other adventures such as the Argonauts' voyage to Colchis. He could no less ignore their plot structures (like the journey through the 'clashing rocks') than he could the fact that the course of their journey and their heroes were bound to fixed locales.[210] Finally, several of the episodes drawn on by Homer were structurally interlinked.[211] The adventure on the island of Calypso and the journey to the underworld form a unit corresponding to the link between the island of Calypso and the stay among the Phaeacians. Both groups involve making landfall on a foreign shore and crossing over into the realm of the dead. This was a classic narrative motif familiar to contemporaries from the Gilgamesh epic and other hero sagas; it could not simply be jettisoned, still less assimilated to the real itinerary of an individual captain. But it was flexible enough to be adapted to the experiences and expectations of Homer's audience. Mythical islands and kingdoms of the dead could not be imagined on familiar territory, in the Aegean or eastern Mediterranean, only in a zone beyond. But because this zone was not a fairy-tale realm, it had to be filled with stories brought back by sailors from the world's end.[212] What can be reconstructed, then, is not any specific journey but the distant exploratory horizon of seafaring contemporaries, which lay somewhere between proto-colonization and hearsay. This horizon needs to be determined when interpreting where the *Odyssey* stands in relation to the history of discovery.

Adventures at the Edge of Colonization—The South

All Homer's explicators agree that Odysseus first veered off course the moment north winds prevented his fleet from rounding Cape Malea (southern Peloponnese) and Cythera and sailing farther west. Instead, after a storm-tossed voyage lasting nine days they arrived at the coast of the Lotus-eaters, somewhere west of Egypt on the Lesser Syrtis ('Lake Triton') or Greater Syrtis; some identify the site at Djerba. At any rate, they landed in a region that was half familiar to the Greeks.[213]

The plot and its context are thus anything but extraordinary: the crew make landfall, drink from a spring or river, and satisfy their hunger. A scouting party is sent inland. There they meet the friendly Lotus-eaters, who greet the new arrivals by inviting them to taste 'the honey-sweet fruit'. The name 'lotus' is Semitic in origin; Homer was probably inspired by dates or by a plant eaten in Egypt or Libya; perhaps he had even heard of silphium, the subsequently famous plant from Cyrenaica.[214] According to Homer, the lotus has such an intoxicating effect on those consuming it for the first time that they refuse to travel any farther. This is no magic trick but an experience common to sailors who 'go native'. Odysseus responds like a responsible captain in the British Navy: he orders the derelict men below deck and puts the rest to the oars before any more succumb to the southern idyll.[215]

The onward journey likewise moves in a maritime world pioneered by both Greeks and Phoenicians. A brief journey leads to an island lying 'not close inshore to the Cyclops' coast, nor too far out'. It has a good harbour with a spring at its head; despite its fertility, 'the island just feeds droves of bleating goats'. This is no magical isle but an ideal colonization scenario; the description perhaps reprises experiences on the Sicilian or Libyan coast, which Menelaus depicts as similarly teeming with goats.[216]

Yet Odysseus wants to cross over to the territory opposite, and it could be said that here, a gradual, tentative, generations-long process of relocating from an island to the mainland (as could be observed on Pithekoussai, for example) is compressed into a few days as in a magnifying glass. In the ensuing tale of the encounter with the Cyclops, as elsewhere, Homer works through several traditions and experiences. The old fairy-tale motif of a hero doing battle with a man-eating monster, transposed from its former context to the epic constellation of the journey, is functionally connected with a motif already touched on in the Lotus-eaters episode: the question of the kinds of beings a mariner and colonist could expect to encounter on foreign shores. Lotus-eaters and cyclops stand for opposing extremes on the scale of possible first contacts: here friendly and guileless natives, there ruthless cannibals.

The storyteller again draws a moral from the encounter. It is at once hopeful and minatory, in keeping with the protagonist's ambivalent character: on the one hand, several companions must perish because Odysseus was lacking in foresight; on the other, Odysseus succeeds in vanquishing his opponent through his intelligence and the techniques unique to a seafaring civilization. Wisely foreboding that he would meet 'some giant clad in power like armour-plate', he had brought along a skin of especially sweet wine prepared for him by Maron, a priest of Apollo in Ismarus.[217] The giant will be powerless to resist its soporific effect. Odysseus thus turns the intoxication his men had experienced among the Lotus-eaters against an enemy who, in contrast to the Greeks, downs his wine undiluted in vast quantities (in the land of the Lotus-eaters, the unknowing Greeks had consumed too much of the sweet fruit). The lesson is timeless.[218] Greek 'firewater' becomes the secret weapon of all mariners, traders, and colonists, a prize export and ultimate ticket of entry even to the world of the most brutal barbarians. But the cyclops must not be killed, only blinded, since otherwise the Greeks could never have escaped his cave, blocked as it is by a massive boulder. With a seaman's expert eye, they choose the right stake to ram into the giant's eye: 'we judged it big enough to be the mast of a pitch-black ship with her twenty oars, a freighter broad in the beam that ploughs through miles of sea'. And it is Odysseus who then hoists the sharpened stake: 'I drove my weight on it from above and bored it home as a shipwright bores his beam with a shipwright's drill'.[219]

The contrast exemplified in the Cyclops story between primitive savagery (in the form of cannibalism) and superior civilization (in the form of intelligence, knowledge, and technology) has another, less martial dimension that may originate in the near east. Although Polyphemus may be a terrifying cannibal, he lives with his companions in an idyll that has conserved the paradisical state of the Golden Age. They know neither the advantages and secrets of civilization (like agriculture) nor urban settlements, laws, and religion. Yet they want for nothing, since Zeus has ensured that the bounteous earth, regularly watered by rainfall, provides them with everything they need.[220] They are sheltered in caves where, as Homer notes, they stall their flocks of sheep and goats at night. The cave of Polyphemus is surrounded by a yard walled up with boulders and tree trunks. The cave itself is stocked with cheeses, 'the folds crowded with young lambs and kids, split into three groups—here the spring-born, here mid-yearlings, here the fresh sucklings off to the side—each sort was penned apart. And all his vessels, pails, and hammered buckets he used for milking'.[221]

This is not the primitive land of nightmarish giants who feast on the raw flesh of their victims, but neither is it a world altogether 'divorced' from reality.[222] It is instead a liminal space that resonates with the experiences of colonizing seafarers. The country and livelihoods of the Cyclops offer an ethnographic and ecological typology that the attentive listener could rediscover in the western Mediterranean coastal areas, where even today it is customary to pen livestock in nearby caves to protect them from the elements and from wild animals. Homer describes a flourishing farmyard, including a dairy, that produces everything needed to sustain life besides grain. The Cyclops, according to an old tradition preserved by Hesiod, are peaceful artisans who helped the gods.[223] How should they react to intruders like Odysseus and his comrades? A gang of ruffians and vagabonds overrun their well-tended island, break into their storerooms, and help themselves to their carefully stockpiled provisions before making off at dawn. Anyone can understand why Polyphemus, returned from his day's work, might be angry to find such uninvited guests awaiting him, guests who have the effrontery to conceal their true names and—the height of their impudence—seek to justify their theft by asserting their right to hospitality. Odysseus and his crew are nothing but sea robbers who travel up and down the coast, raiding as they go, and who deprive these peaceful shepherds of the fruit of their labour. Homer is the first source known to us who uses the term *peirates*, 'pirates', to describe such people.

Zones of Proto-colonization in the Northeast

We can deduce that the land of the Cyclops lies west of the coast of the Lotus-eaters from the order of the stations that follow. After their escape from the Cyclops' island, Odysseus and his men reach the 'floating island' of Aeolus. This brings them within sight of Ithaca following a ten-day voyage on a westerly breeze (*zephyros*). After the bag of winds is released shortly before Ithaca and they are forced to return to Aeolia, the Achaeans are driven back to their starting point in the west.[224] Now the geography of the *Odyssey* becomes more complicated.

After another seven days' journey they arrive in Telepylus, the country of the Laestrygonians. They too are man-eating giants. Their story, likewise drawn from a fairy-tale context, has a compositional function: that of further reducing Odysseus' fleet and crew to allow the hero to face all the coming dangers on his own. Once the giants have consumed several Greeks and hurled rocks at the squadron, only Odysseus' ship is left standing.[225] At the same time, the episode varies the theme of dangerous first contacts, only this time not in a familiar western Mediterranean setting with a fertile island as point of departure and an opposing landscape of hills and caves. The Greeks sail instead into a harbour renowned for its natural defences, 'all walled around by a great unbroken sweep of sky-scraping cliff and two steep headlands, fronting each other, close around the mouth so the passage in is cramped'.[226] Like the Cyclops, the natives raise livestock, but rather than living scattered in caves and hillsides, they dwell in a town with a marketplace, ruled by a king whose palace takes pride of place.

The realistic, richly textured depiction is supplemented by an ethnographic detail that seems strange only at first sight. One Laestrygonian shepherd driving out his flocks calls to another bringing in his own that here, 'a man who never sleeps could rake in double wages, one for herding cattle, one for pasturing fleecy sheep'.[227] The epic phrasing invites us to imagine a country where the nights are so short that the days succeed each other almost without interruption. The description fits midsummer nights in the far north, where the sun disappears behind the horizon only briefly,[228] giving rise to speculation that Homer had been informed of the phenomenon by amber traders, who since Mycenaean times had ventured from Thrace to the Baltic, or by Scythian chieftains, who in the *Iliad* are said to 'drink the milk of mares'.[229]

In his account of the man-eating Laestrygonians, Homer may also have been influenced by the cult of human sacrifice practised by the Tauri on the Crimea, which later found its way into the Iphigenia myth.[230] In the eighth century BCE, the Pontus was surely already a magnet for traders and pirates from Asia Minor. The colonies that began to sprout there from the second half of the seventh century (Sinope, Berezan, Istros) would have been the culmination of a prolonged phase of reconnaissance or 'proto-colonization'. For all that, knowledge of the area was sketchy. In the so-called catalogue of rivers from the *Theogony*, Hesiod lists two rivers (Ister = Danube and Phasis) that empty into the Black Sea.[231] Starting in north Africa and continuing in the west, the guiding theme of first contact thus leads logically—almost predictably—to the north. The Black Sea was considered foggy and bereft of islands (like the Laestrygonian coast) but far from unpeopled: Homer knows the cities of the Paphlagonians,[232] and tales were told of the savage Tauri and 'mannish' Amazons who fought alongside the Trojans and took to the field against heroes like Bellerophon, Achilles, and Heracles. They are nothing other than a mythicized version of the Scythians.[233]

Over the Ocean

In the Amazon myth, the search for an identity-forming counter-image to the male-dominated polis is combined with knowledge of the female warriors typically found in the nomadic societies of the north.[234] Homer, however, links to yet another complex of myths that, like the Laestrygonian episode, refers to the Black Sea region. From the Laestrygonians, Odysseus makes his way to Aeaea, the island of the sorceress Circe. She turns Odysseus' shipmates into swine before being subdued and bedded with the help of the magic herb moly.[235] Behind the fairy-tale story stands an age-old motif, known throughout antiquity and even in the Bronze Age: the search for aromatic herbs as well as therapeutic plants and antidotes. Sorceresses and 'queens of animals' like Circe, who has a wealth of knowledge about remedies and drugs (*polypharmakos*),[236] are also found in the Jason myth. Here Medea, daughter of Aeetes, king of Colchis, helps the hero by drugging the dragon guarding the Golden Fleece using a magic salve. According to an old tradition, Circe was the daughter of the sun god Helios and the sister of Aeetes; an alternative tradition identifies her as Aeetes' daughter and Medea's sister.[237] Aea, the Argonauts' destination, would thus be identical with the Homeric Aeaea, or it might be the island that King Aeetes gave his sister.

For its part, the land of Aeetes has an ancient mythographic association. Eumelus of Corinth, probably writing in the early seventh century, labels Aeetes' dominion the 'land of Colchis'; a kingdom of 'Qulha' (Colchis) appears in inscriptions of the Urartian king Sarduri II (762–735 BCE).[238] According to the poet Mimnermos, who lived around 600 in Asia Minor, Aea, the kingdom of Aeetes, lay at the edge of the Ocean, where the sunbeams of Helios rest in a golden bed.[239] Homer similarly locates Aeaea, 'where the Dawn forever young has her home [. . .] and the Sun his risings'. He later states that Ocean River is only a day's journey from there.[240] Since the Laestrygonians dwell in the north and Aeaea is where the sun rises, Odysseus must be at the world's extreme northeast, beyond the sphere familiar to the Greeks, near the Ocean or verging on it.[241]

It has troubled many scholars 'that Odysseus, having already arrived in North Africa, is then driven back past the starting point of his voyage, Ilion, to the Black Sea'.[242] To resolve the dilemma, some argued that two epic traditions (Odysseus and the Argonauts) were conjoined in the transition to the Circe adventure, that the Odyssean voyage conflates different chronological layers and reworkings, and that the entire *Odyssey*, or at any rate parts of it, was initially set in the Black Sea region ('Black Sea hypothesis') before being transplanted to the west in the course of western colonization.[243] For Homer's audiences, such constructions were immaterial. In the context of a worldview formed by amalgamating mythic cosmography, real geographical knowledge, and legendary traditions, having a hero sail from the western island of Aeolus to the northern climes of the Laestrygonians and Circe's island in the Ocean was unproblematic, especially since Homer's listeners were still generally unaware of the northern coastline of the Adriatic or the fact that Greece was contiguous with the European continent in the north.

And since they were equally unaware that the Black Sea was bounded by land—it was instead taken to be part of the Ocean—a combination of the Black Sea voyage with a foray into Circe's oceanic realm contradicted neither the logic underlying the mythic geography nor real experience.[244]

The relocation of the voyage to the northeast edge of the world also accords with the directions that Circe—possessed of maritime knowledge—gives Odysseus, after a year's stay on Aeaea, for proceeding 'to the House of Death and the awesome one, Persephone',[245] there to consult the ghost of Tiresias.[246] 'Just step your mast', she tells him, 'and spread your white sail wide—sit back and Boreas' winds will speed you on your way. But once your vessel has cut across the Ocean River you will raise a desolate coast and Persephone's Grove'.

Boreas is the north wind. It drives Odysseus from the far northeast to the city of the Cimmerians 'hard by the Ocean's churning shore', at the entrance to the underworld, as old legends relate.[247] Here Odysseus digs a trench and summons the shades of the dead with libations of honey, mellow wine, water, and the blood of sacrificial animals. Mist shrouds the Cimmerians, and the sun's rays never reach them.[248] This strikingly recalls the old Babylonian world map, which marks an island north of the 'salt river' (*marratu* = Ocean), 'where the sun is not seen'.[249] Homer probably connects this template with vague information or Nordic legends—which may have reached him via the amber roads or the Phoenicians' northern voyages (as far as England?)—about a ghost-like people living on an island at the edge of Hades. Where the Laestrygonians' extended days had earlier evoked the Nordic summer, the unending darkness of the Cimmerians perhaps alludes to the polar nights of the Nordic winter.[250]

Islands in the Stream

After consulting the dead, Odysseus and his crew are borne on a fair wind back from Ocean's River to Circe's island, the land of dawn.[251] In twice crossing the Ocean, they thus follow the path taken by the sun from its rising in the east to its setting in the west and back again, with the difference that for the ancients, the sun either passes below the Ocean or is conveyed on a golden vessel on its return journey. With that, the *Odyssey* opposes a northwestern oceanic crossing, corresponding to the eighth- and seventh-century Greek colonization movement, to the epic of Gilgamesh, who in keeping with Mesopotamian interests had crossed the Persian Gulf 'to the rising of the sun' in his quest for immortality.[252]

Circe again gives further directions. First they must sail past the Sirens, 'lolling there in their meadow', who spellbind men with their song and tempt them to make landfall. As Homer's listeners knew, the Argonauts were only able to sail on because Orpheus drowned out the Sirens' song. Circe advises Odysseus to lash himself to the mast and stop his shipmates' ears with beeswax to immunize them against the effect.[253]

Circe then proposes an alternative. They could continue via the Planctae (or 'Symplegades'), looming cliffs lapped by driftwood from the shattered vessels that braved them; only the Argo sailed clear with Hera's help. Or they could hazard a passage through the 'two enormous crags' where the monster Scylla and the whirlpool Charybdis, respectively, lie in wait.[254] Through their epic association with the Planctae from the Argonauts narrative, the intrinsically placeless fairy tales of Scylla, Charybdis, and the Sirens are localized in the eastern sea.[255] Leaving aside their compositional function in reducing Odysseus' crew, Homer's aim was probably to indicate that the hero is now departing the Black Sea area. Behind the alternative 'Planctae' or 'Scylla and Charybdis' stand not just two different mythic traditions but also, perhaps, two broad exit routes from the Black Sea in the context of the mythic geography: one through the dangerous straits of the Bosporus, which Argonaut specialists tended to identify with the Planctae, the other by the bend in the world sea north of Greece, which Odysseus had already traversed when journeying from the island of Aeolus to the region of the Argonauts' adventures. This variant is favoured by scholars who connect the regular gulping down and vomiting up of the sea by Charybdis with the tides and think that Scylla, bristling with twelve claws and six necks, reflects stories about giant polyps and deep-sea squid—both phenomena found only in the Atlantic.[256]

Odysseus takes Circe's advice and opts for the northern route. As on the outward journey, Homer provides no details about wind, current, or location, instead using the relative temporal marker 'soon' to link the overcoming of Scylla and Charybdis with the landing on the island of Helios. Circe and Tiresias had warned Odysseus against setting foot on the island.[257] Yet the incessant north wind leaves the companions with little choice; perhaps—an attentive listener might think—they did not want to risk being blown again too far to the south at Cape Malea. But easterlies and westerlies roar there too, and Odysseus warns of a south wind whipped up from nowhere.[258] These references to winds coming from all directions establish a clear parallel to the island of Aeolus: both islands are the property of male deities. One is the homeland and origin of the winds, the other buffeted continuously by winds. And just as Odysseus was earlier seized by a powerful easterly just before reaching Ithaca, so too Zeus now summons a hurricane to sink the ship after the departure from Thrinacia.[259]

Odysseus clambers on to a raft, yet the north wind again drives him to the double cliffs of Scylla and Charybdis. After passing through the straits one more time, he again finds himself at the edge of Ocean River. He spends nine days adrift, clinging to the broken mast of his ship, before he arrives at Ogygia, the island of Calypso.[260] The name Ogygia probably has Phoenician roots. Calypso is the daughter of Atlas, who shoulders the pillars on which the sky rests. The island lies at 'the navel of the sea'. This refers not so much to the curvature that arises when gazing at the farthest horizon as to the island's imagined position at the centre of the Ocean, just as Delphi, the 'navel of the world', lies in the middle of Greece (and the ecumene).

This is supported by the fact that, according to Homer, a sea voyage of eighteen days separates it from the land of the Phaeacians, who say of themselves: 'We live too far apart, out in the surging sea, off at the world's end—no other mortals come to mingle with us'.[261] Homer's audience thus located Calypso's island in the western Ocean, just as Circe's island lies in its northeastern region. An ancient tradition places islands of sorceresses and goddesses in the world-encircling sea; in this respect, as in others, the islands of Calypso and Circe form a pair. In Homer's epic, they exert a magical hold on the hero, who is powerless to break free of them on his own. The only reason Odysseus can leave Ogygia after seven years is because Zeus decrees it.

The Phaeacians

Like Circe, the distraught Calypso dispenses secret maritime knowledge: she instructs Odysseus to keep the Pleiades to his left when sailing across the Ocean.[262] He thus came to the Phaeacians *at* the far end of the world (but not *in* the Ocean!). Their country lies on the homeward route, hence closer to Ithaca than Ogygia. Under Alcinous' predecessor, the Phaeacians came to Scheria as colonists, seeking refuge from the Cyclops, while the more distant isles of the goddesses in the Ocean are ruled out as candidates for human colonization. Thus, although the depiction of the Phaeacian world is shot through with fairy-tale elements—the king has a palace, a paradisial garden, and ships that fly 'quick as a bird, quick as a darting thought!'[263]—its account of the town and its inhabitants makes it seem far more realistic than the islands of Circe and Calypso.

Now that the hero has escaped the oceanic world, Homer reprises the general theme of colonial first contact. Where the besotted nymph Calypso had promised the shipwrecked Odysseus eternal life, the mortal Alcinous offers him a house, land, and his daughter's hand[264]—a dream come true for any young Greek colonist. On the one hand, the account of the Phaeacians echoes that of the city-dwelling, monarchically ruled Laestrygonians—here too the Greeks initially meet the king's daughter, like Odysseus in Scheria—and transfigures it into an image of the ideal polis. On the other, the Phaeacians are presented as a counter-society to the Cyclops: there the uncivilized barbarians ignorant of navigation, here the timid but helpful master mariners operating from a flourishing colonial city with a harbour, marketplace, and houses, as well as a clear political structure, an aristocratic elite of twelve *basileis* with an overlord at its head.

All this suggests at once familiarity (albeit epically exaggerated) *and* remoteness. It may therefore be supposed that here, too, in amalgamating fairy tales about a people living happily at the edge of the world with an idealized image of a thriving urban colony, Homer was inspired by information about real circumstances. As always, the epic coding of maritime-nautical phenomena provides us with important clues. When Odysseus is driven to the land of the Phaeacians, he sees a river flowing into the sea. In response to his cries for help, the river's god 'stemmed his current, held his surge at once and smooth[ed] out the swells'.[265] This detail, which is unnecessary to the narrative, can be taken as a vague reference to 'slack water', the temporary cessation of the river current during a tidal bore, just as Charybdis gulping down and vomiting up the sea epically transcribes the ebb and flow of the tides. Homer's listeners were familiar with the Strait of Gibraltar as a western gateway to the Ocean through the tales of Heracles, who ventured 'beyond the famous Ocean'. To mark his expedition, he had erected two pillars that we identify as the Strait of Gibraltar.[266]

It was difficult for Homer to set his hero's adventures closer to home; he could not defy his audience's expectations by transplanting them from near the 'famous Ocean' to his own watery backyard, as it were. This is also where all attempts to place Scheria near Greek waters must fail. Although the land was colonized, according to Homer, the colonists were the Phaeacians, who eschew the company of their fellow mortals and stand close to the gods. Before coming to Scheria, they lived in Hypereia, the land beyond.[267] In this context, they (and their ships) acquire a special mythic function initially obscured by their (realistic) role as inhabitants of an ideal colonial town. It has often been asked why they take such good care of their ships and are considered master mariners if they engage in neither trade nor war, shun other communities, and show no interest in nautical discovery.

The answer again points to the magical border zone at the Ocean's edge. Scheria is the last 'continental' stopover on the journey to the hereafter, and the Phaeacians are the 'grey men' whose miraculous ships ferry the dead over the Ocean to this final bourn; only in exceptional circumstances do they convey a mortal hero like Odysseus (or Rhadamanthus) in the opposite direction.[268] This idea of souls being escorted over the world sea to the beyond by mysterious ferrymen is one of the oldest elements in Indo-European myth; Gilgamesh, too, is conveyed to Utnapishtim by Urshanabi's magic vessel.[269] In these myths, the ferrymen live at the edge of the world sea, beyond the areas normally populated by mortals. That is why the country of the Phaeacians displays not only features of an ideal colonial settlement but also those of a Golden Age when mortals lived alongside the gods. The river's water is so pure that it washes clean the foulest filth, the grass so sweet that the mules savour it like honey. The ruling family emanate a divine radiance from their 'high-roofed halls', guarded by dogs of gold and silver. Untended by human hand, the palace orchard brings forth a year-round harvest of luscious fruit, 'for the West Wind always breathing through will bring some fruits to the bud and others warm to ripeness'.[270]

Like the older myth of the ferrymen of the dead, such a wonderland belongs in the oceanic world of the west—not by chance, the flora in Alcinous' garden resemble those found on both Calypso's island and the Isles of the Blessed in the Ocean River. When Homer set about adapting this mythic image to the maritime experiences of his contemporaries, combining it with an idealized portrait of a remote colonial town, he could hardly situate it in the Aegean, the Strait of Otranto, or the Strait of Messina, nor in the Tyrrhenian Sea and on its coast, known as Temesa, which according to Homer was visited by ore traders like Mentes, the guest-friend of Odysseus; at the time the *Odyssey* was first written down, Pithekoussai was at least a generation old.[271] The context referred instead to the outermost limit of the navigable zone on Ocean's shore, where knowledge of the world based on trade contacts and proto-colonization gave way to an unknown world swathed in rumour, a cosmos presented in myths as a place of fabulous riches (Apples of the Hesperides) rather than an area ripe for colonization.

To learn more about this zone, we need to consider the close contacts the Greeks of Asia Minor maintained with the Phoenicians, who in Homer's day were as renowned for their seamanship as the Phaeacians. It is perhaps no coincidence that Ino Leucothea, who directs the shipwrecked Odysseus to the land of the Phaeacians, is the daughter of the mythic Phoenician king Cadmus.[272] Phoenician ships, traders, and artisans were a common sight in Homer's time; vases based on Phoenician models depict episodes from Odysseus' adventures. Phoenician traders had already been in contact with Andalusian Tartessos for generations; colonies in Gades or on the Spanish Mediterranean coast may have been founded several decades before Homer.[273]

This gave rise to the conjecture that Phoenician half-truths about Gades or Tartessos may have inspired Scheria. Its oceanic setting, the peacefulness of the Phaeacians, their complete isolation at the edge of the Greek world, cutting them off from all mortals (besides the Phoenicians!)—all this may have been brought to the poet's attention by Phoenician sources. In describing Phaeacian ships that arrive at their destination even in darkness and fog, Homer may well have combined the myth of boats ferrying the dead with information about mariners who steered Phoenician vessels in foul weather and had mastered navigating by the stars at night.[274]

Menelaus in the Southern Sea

Finally, vague knowledge of the Andalusian Atlantic coast is suggested from the other side, Menelaus' homeward journey. Like Odysseus, Menelaus was blown off course at Cape Malea and came back—Nestor explains to the young Telemachus—'from people so removed you might abandon hope of ever returning home, [. . .] into a sea so vast not even cranes could wing their way in one year's flight—so vast it is, so awesome'.[275] He mentions visiting the Ethiopians, Sidonians, and Erembians, adding that he saw Libya too. The list evidently serves a different purpose than the catalogues from the proto-colonial neighbouring regions do. Directly or indirectly, all these people have something to do with Africa, which Homer designates for the first time in Greek literature as *Libya*. It is described as rich in sheep and lambs, abounding in milk, mutton, and cheese.[276]

The name Ethiopia already appears in Mycenaean-Pylian tablets; Hesiod knows them as the people who dwell farthest to the south, near a city of 'blacks' (*melanoi*).[277] In the *Odyssey* they are presented as a pious people who consort with the gods—Poseidon is their frequent guest—at both the extreme southeast and the extreme southwest of the world (Libya), a geographical doubling for which no satisfactory explanation has been found.[278] There is a similar double meaning for the Sidonians: on the one hand, they are inhabitants of Sidon in the Levant and thus function as a collective term for the Phoenicians; on the other, they can be identified with Phoenician colonies in the west (Spain), which occasionally call themselves as such in inscriptions.[279] The reference to the Erembians is the most difficult to interpret. The philosopher and grammarian Crates of Mallus (second century BCE) took them to be Indians, and some modern scholars speculate that Homer knew about the Indian Ocean 'on the basis of Phoenician reports'.[280] If, however, *Eremboi* derives from the Hebrew and Phoenician word *ereb*, meaning sunset or evening, then this people would be found in the west as well as the east; *Eremboi* would designate those living on the western edge of the ecumene.[281]

As varied as the mythic and historical contexts of the three ethnicities may be, they are united by the striking fact that they could be located and imagined on both the western and the eastern flanks of Libya. If this strange duplication is combined with Nestor's reference to Menelaus' unusually long journey in a sea 'so vast not even cranes could wing their way in one year's flight', we might conclude that Menelaus sailed from Cyprus along the Levantine coast initially to Egypt, before pressing on via the Red Sea (or the Persian Gulf, where the ancestral home of the Phoenicians was later presumed to lie) to the Ethiopians. He then rounded Libya to arrive at the western Ethiopians, the western colonies of the Phoenicians (Sidonians), and Tartessos, before finally encountering 'westerners' (*eremboi*) in the Mediterranean.

The list of the peoples visited by Menelaus would thus be an epic anticipation of the Phoenician circumnavigation of Africa (see above, p. 35), with the proviso that Homer's contemporaries had not the faintest idea how far the continent extended south and thus considered a circumnavigation feasible, just as Odysseus and the Argonauts could sail around the north of the world on the Ocean.[282] The attempted circumnavigation of Africa by the Phoenicians was undoubtedly preceded by lengthy preparations and tentative expeditions (against the backdrop of the resumption of trade with Arabia in the seventh century).[283] It is quite likely that Homer's listeners and the poet himself had met Phoenicians and received, along with exotic wares, fragmentary information about the routes and destinations of such expeditions—even in antiquity, Homer was said to have drawn his geographical knowledge from the Phoenicians.[284] Menelaus brought back a silver mixing-bowl from the Sidonians, and his palace hall is decorated with amber. Multiple references to the fragrance of the magical islands in the Atlantic suggest a vague knowledge of Phoenician imports from the Ocean. Perhaps some *basileis*—aristocratic commanders of the archaic period—joined in Phoenician voyages; as in earlier periods, crews were ethnically mixed. Odysseus has a valued crewmate called Eurybates, described as curly haired and swarthy; Homer and Hesiod knew of short, dark-skinned people (Pygmies) on the southern shores of the Ocean (Ethiopia).[285]

New Lessons, New Horizons

If we assume that Homer and his audience were familiar with the mythic geography of the world outlined in the Babylonian map, then his epic attests to a remarkable extension of this mythically coded knowledge to take in the farthest reaches of Ionian Greek expansion in the Black Sea area in the north and Phoenician voyaging to the Strait of Gibraltar, if not Guadalquivir (Tartessos), in the west. A vague awareness of the waters and lands beyond this zone, as well as speculation about the link between climate and mores (e.g., Laestrygonians), are epically encoded in the description of the more remote stations on the voyage. In many respects, the whole serves as a vehicle for transmitting the secret nautical and ethnographic knowledge that the Aegean coastal communities had been gathering since Mycenaean times. If it had once been the heads of those communities whose stories had documented the push into the unknown, now it is the goddesses of the magical isles and the old seers (Tiresias) who point the way to the farthest ends of the Ocean and back again. The mere fact that the hero is privy to this knowledge and gives a credible account of his travels

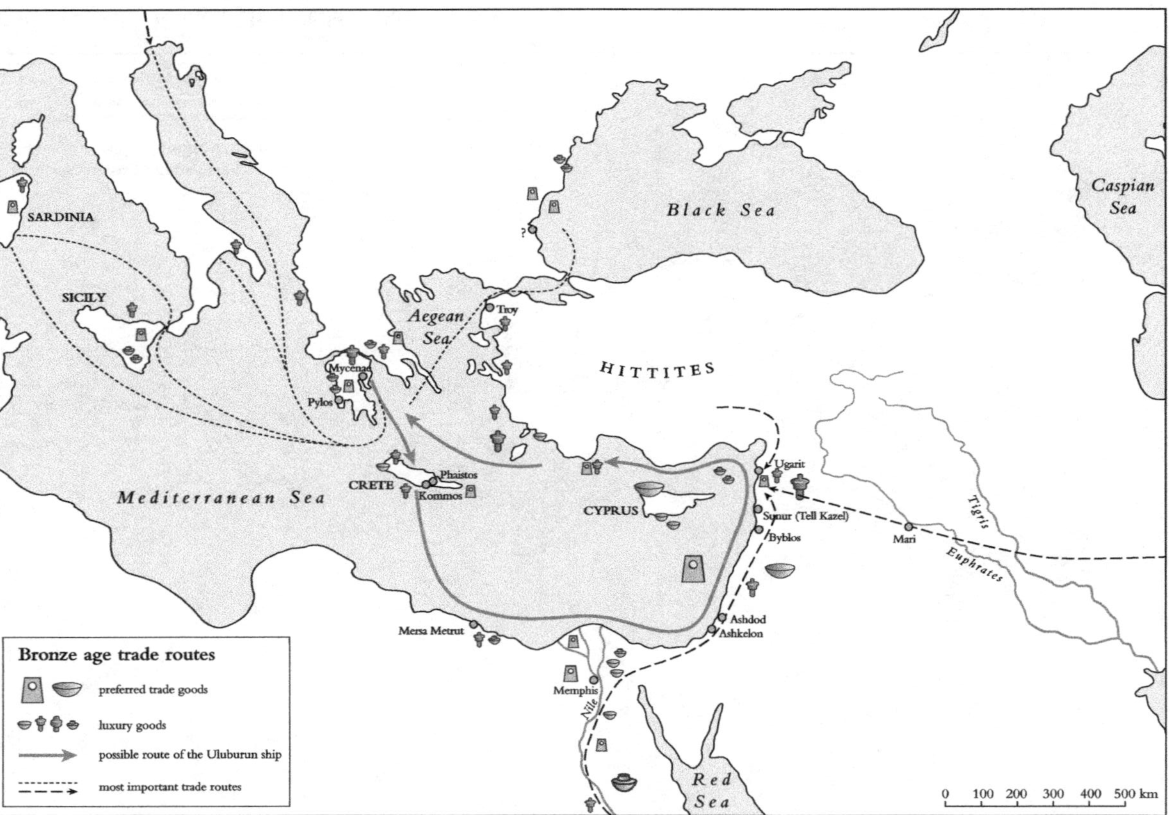

Map 1 Credit: Rudolf Hungreder/Klett-Cotta.

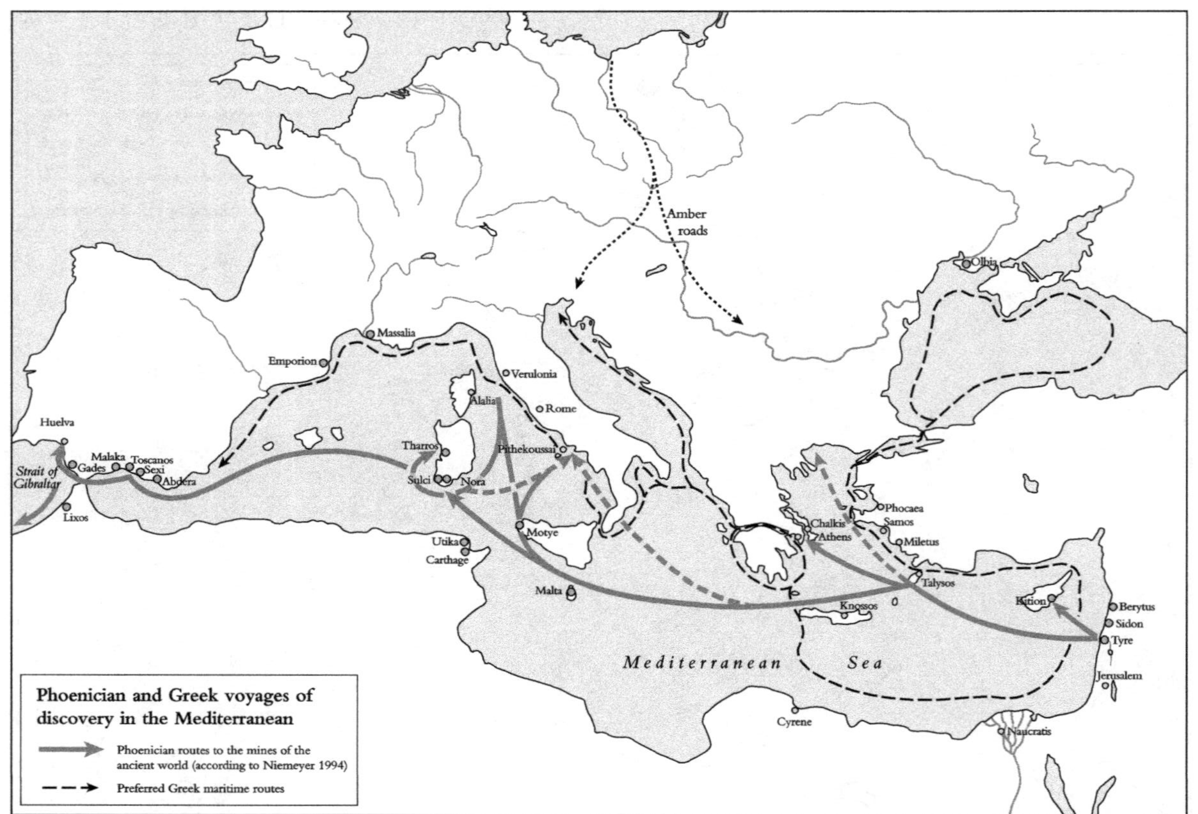

Map 2 Credit: Rudolf Hungreder/Klett-Cotta.

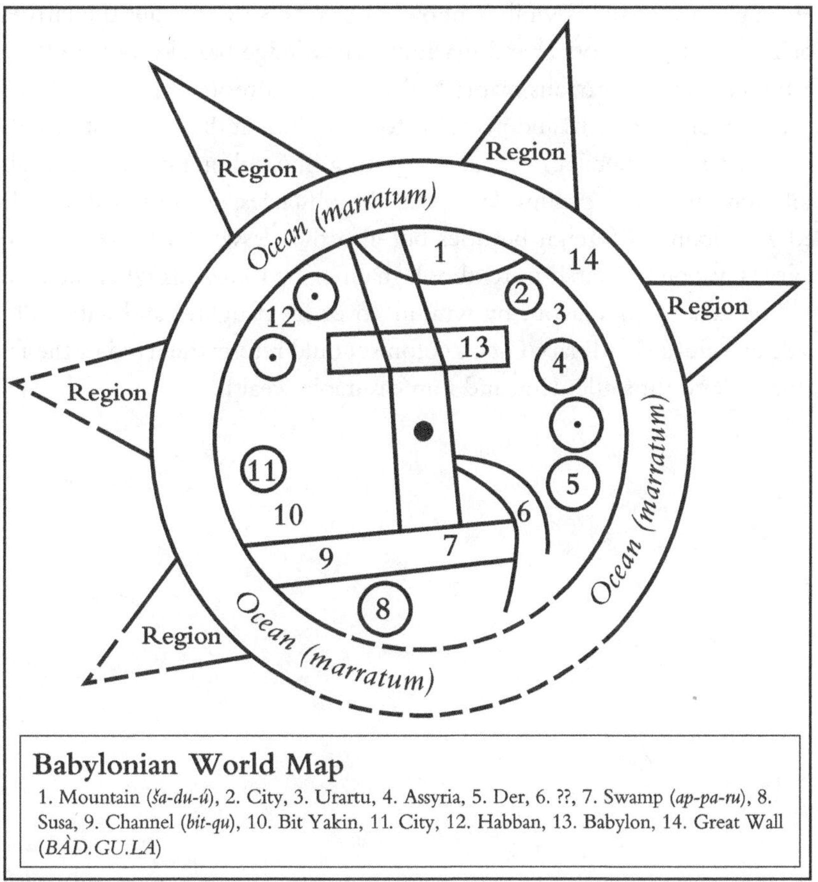

Map 3 Babylonian World Map. Credit: *New Directions in the Study of Ancient Geography*, edited by Duane W. Roller (Penn State University Press, 2020), p. 11.

lends him and the epic a sacrosanct authority, encouraging others to explore the limits of the world by following in his footsteps.

Pilots, prophets, and healers would have accompanied the early mariners and colonists on their long-distance voyages. And so the *Odyssey* contains in a nutshell all the lessons for dealing with foreign peoples that would make the Greeks—along with the Phoenicians—the greatest discoverers of the ancient world: a wary respect for diverse rituals and diets as well as for the tricks of native tribes, who would try to befriend mariners—in antiquity as later in the early-modern period—by claiming that their neighbours were cannibals; knowledge of the intoxicating effect of wine, which incapacitates the roughest barbarians while empowering traders to conquer the farthest horizons; not just nautical and maritime knowledge but also botanical expertise concerning various magic herbs and antidotes (*moly*), which would secure Greek physicians and mariners top positions at the courts of oriental kings—and, in general, the art of integrating into culturally and geographically remote ethnic groups despite all the obstacles: not just claiming the bed and brains of foreign beauties but also the classic *chercher la femme* of diplomacy, demonstrated in textbook manner by Odysseus when he gains the Phaeacian king's favour by winning over his daughter and wife and is made an offer no ordinary Greek colonist could refuse: the hand of the fair princess, land for settlement, and immeasurable wealth.

2

Apollo's Disciples

Exploration in the Seventh and Sixth Centuries BCE

SECRETS OF THE NORTH

GREEKS IN WEST SIBERIA

Odysseus' Final Voyage

The Greeks indulged in endless speculation about what happened to the hero after returning to Ithaca. Sometimes Odysseus dies in the Far West, sometimes he is transformed into a horse or killed by his (second) son, fathered by Circe. These bizarre sequels tend to ignore the crucial clue given by Homer himself about the hero's destiny: in his first night together with his wife after murdering the suitors, Odysseus reveals that the seer Tiresias instructed him to 'go forth once more [. . .] carry your well-planed oar until you come to a race of people who know nothing of the sea, whose food is never seasoned with salt, strangers all to ships with their crimson prows and long slim oars'. When another traveller calls the oar across his shoulders a fan to winnow grain, he should plant it in the earth and sacrifice to Poseidon. He will then live out the rest of his days on Ithaca.[1]

Of the many interpretations given these lines, still the most plausible is the one that sees Tiresias instructing Odysseus to undertake a kind of expiatory voyage to appease the still simmering ire of Poseidon. It takes him inland to people who know nothing of the sea and seafaring. When the native mistakes the oar on Odysseus' shoulder for a winnowing fan, he utters the redeeming word ('kenning') that frees the accursed one (Odysseus) from the spell (sea) placed on him by the demon (Poseidon).[2] Odysseus' 'final voyage' is far more than an epically reworked fairy-tale motif, however. It mirrors real attempts by seventh-century Greeks to investigate territories beyond coastal strips and islands. Which spaces did they have in mind? Or in epic code: where was the country and who were the people Odysseus was told to meet?

One clue is found in the *Arimaspeia*, an epic from the second half of the seventh century BCE. Its author, Aristeas, came from Proconnesos, an island city in the Sea of Marmara established by Milesians.[3] A fragment from the work reads: 'Here is another thing also that fills us with wonder, / Men that dwell in the water, away from the earth, on the ocean. / Sorrowful wretches they are, and theirs is a grievous employment: / Ever they rivet their eyes on the stars, their thoughts on the waters. / Often, I ween, to the gods they lift up their hands and they pray; / Ever their innermost parts are terribly tossed to and fro'.[4]

Aristeas clearly describes how those living in the interior of the country regarded island dwellers and seafarers with a kind of perplexed pity[5]—a revolutionary shift in perspective. Rather than expressing how seafaring Greeks viewed nautically illiterate landlubbers (Cyclops), the poet for the first time puts himself in the shoes of an inlander smugly contemplating the wretched existence of islanders, who devote all their lives, all their care and toil, to the sea and its dangers, never letting the stars out of their sight for fear of losing their way, racked by seasickness ('ever their innermost parts are terribly tossed to and fro') and praying to the gods for help. Whereas suffering at sea was for Odysseus a precondition for learning and heroism, for the landlubber it is senseless torture, a sign of uncivilized madness. Aristeas gives us the first 'noble savage' to hold up a mirror to the Greeks, showing them the futility of their own strivings.[6]

Later, the Greeks often used wise men from the Scythian north to voice criticism of civilizational values.[7] This northern orientation accords with the little we know about the epic's content and composition. Whereas Homer has his hero tell the story of his wanderings to the Phaeacian court, Aristeas describes his *own* journey to the steppes of the northern Pontus as far as the Hyperboreans.[8] The precondition may have been the sensational discovery made by colonizing Greeks that the Black Sea, contra Homer, is an inland sea. The *Arimaspeia* is the first document of a real explorer who no longer crosses seas by ship but, having been deposited on the northern shores of the Pontus, takes the overland route to the central Asian interior.

The Adventures of Aristeas

This exploit alone made the author a legend in his own lifetime. Aristeas was credited with bilocation, the ability to appear in two places at once; he vanishes only to reappear centuries later; his soul can leave his body to make further journeys on its own.[9] Aristeas himself encouraged these speculations by claiming at the beginning of his work to have been 'seized by Phoebus [= Apollo]' before embarking on his seven-year voyage.[10] For Greek ears, being seized by Apollo generally means 'veering off one's accustomed path'[11]—in today's parlance, temporarily taking leave of one's senses. The use of the phrase at the beginning of an epic and in connection with the start of a long journey is unique, however. It is not satisfactorily explained by stating that here, 'a second-rate poet sought to trump the usual appeal to the Muses through sensationalism'.[12]

Instead, Aristeas was already assumed in antiquity to have carried out his expedition as a journey of the soul, just as the legendary healer Abaris was said to have travelled around the world with (or on) an arrow, eating no food.[13] In the second century CE, Maximus of Tyre maintained that Aristeas' soul left his body and, taking flight like a bird on the wing, contemplated countries, lakes, rivers, and people in all their variety.[14] According to Pliny the Elder, 'Aristeas' soul issued from his mouth in the shape of a raven'.[15] Aristeas himself claimed to have travelled to Metapontum and told the people there to erect an altar to Apollo, placing beside it a statue bearing his own name.[16] A black-figure vase from sixth-century Athens shows a winged, fully armed warrior flying over the sea while watched by a raven perched on a rock. It most likely depicts an episode from the lost epic *Aethiopis*, the removal of Achilles from the funeral pyre to the 'White Island', identified by later poets with Elysium or the Isle of the Blessed. The inscription of a comparable vase points out that the winged warrior represents the dead man's *psyche*. The raven was one of the birds sent out by mariners to see if they were approaching land, and it was the sacred bird of Apollo. Later poets interpreted the scene as a journey of the soul initiated by Apollo.[17]

The poet Alcaeus locates the 'White Island' in the land of the Scythians, the same northern climes visited by Aristeas on his travels.[18] Homer had already identified the far north as the land of the dead and the hereafter (see above, p. 71). Just as Hermes, borne aloft on his winged sandals, escorts the souls of the dead over the Ocean past the 'gates of Helios' into the beyond, so one of the shaman's main tasks is to lead the spirit of the deceased to the underworld and deposit it there.[19] The shaman is a type frequently encountered in pastoral and hunter-gatherer cultures, an ecstatically gifted singer, priest, and healer who communes exclusively with the spirit world and is gifted with bilocation. In northern Siberia and America, the raven is revered as a shamanic ancestor and archetype, since it gains magical power and occult knowledge on its flight. Ravens—and birds more generally—tend to symbolize the soul, not just in ancient Greece; the shaman's soul could also assume avian form.[20] Finally, the seven-year duration of Aristeas' travels in the north and his disappearance for seven generations (= 240 years, as Herodotus calculated) upon his return do not just recall Odysseus' seven-year stay with Circe. The number seven has an equally important function in the cult of Apollo and in shamanism.[21] All in all, one suspects that even though Aristeas himself may not have been a 'Greek' shaman (accessories like musical instruments and ritual costume are missing) and did not embark on a shamanic voyage of the soul (this does not accord with the abrupt ending of the journey among the Issedones), he may have been inspired by a vague knowledge of it when composing his epic, much as Homer was guided by Hittite ritual ideas when he has Odysseus interrogate the souls of the dead in Hades.[22]

This interpretation also fits with his hometown's interest in the northern Pontus. Greek traders and adventurers had connections with this area even before they founded their first colonies (*apoikia*). As they colonized the Black Sea coasts and expanded trade links, a 'unique symbiosis and reciprocal assimilation of Greeks and Scythians' took place, including on religious terrain.[23] In a town called Gelonus in the land of the Budini—a tribe neighbouring the Scythians (probably Belsk, on an eastern tributary of the Dnieper)—Greeks and Scythians jointly celebrated a festival in honour of Dionysus at which they performed 'Bacchic dances', apparently entering a state of 'Dionysian' rapture through ritual dance and wine.[24] According to Herodotus, the Scythians throw hemp seed on red-hot stones, take vapour baths in the steam, and enjoy it so much that they 'shout for joy'.[25] There is archaeological evidence, confirmed by field experiments, that this was a purification ritual with narcotic effects. In itself, intoxication in the context of purification ceremonies does not yet entail shamanic ecstasy techniques or journeys of the soul. An almost catatonic trance-like state is more likely, such as the deep sleep the Phaeacians lulled Odysseus into before conveying him to Ithaca, or the soporific effect of Medea's magic salve (or potion) on the dragon guarding the

Golden Fleece—perhaps an epically coded reference to the cannabis found in Scythian graves or to the aromatic pastes used by Scythian women.[26] At any rate, ancient Iranian cultures like that of the Persians (and Indians) assumed that ritualized sweating during a state of intoxication enabled a journey to the beyond. In the Iranian realm, the raven was considered a messenger of the gods and represented the link to their world.[27] Metal frames have been found in Scythian kurgans (burial mounds) in the form of animal or bird figures, some with bells attached that recall shaman rattles.[28]

Open-minded observers like Aristeas could thus easily have drawn links between Scythian rituals and the practices of holy men who roamed Greece performing purification and expiation ceremonies (and also telling the future), entering a state of 'ecstatic madness' as they made contact with Apollo, the god of purity and derangement. Purification ceremonies and Apollo worship played a central role in founding a colony, a process in which Aristeas' family or the poet himself is known to have been involved. There is thus much to suggest that Aristeas, who like all ecstatically gifted charismatics was always on the look out for new 'occult knowledge', was informed by Scythians of shamanic magical practices from central Asia on his travels in the north. From a Greek perspective, the distance between a Greek sage—and seers and poets counted as such—and a shaman would not have been so very great. Both were in possession of geographical and ethnographic occult knowledge, both gave first-person accounts of their adventures at the margins of the world and in the underworld, and both told of their encounters with animals, hybrid beings, and the blessed, the key difference being that these stories were mostly set at sea for the Greek and on dry land for the shaman.[29] This may be why shamanic voyages of the soul struck Aristeas as a fitting vehicle to project himself into the world of people who had never even heard of the sea.

The Road to Western Siberia

Just as the shaman boosts his credibility by listing real locations as stages of his journey, so the poet consolidates his authority by realistically outlining the geographical and ethnographic context.[30] Herodotus' report indicates that Aristeas drew on a list of tribes in a way that recalls the account of Menelaus' wayward return journey in Homer, albeit with one key difference: for him, the Issedones (*Issedoi*) were the first *and last* stop in his itinerary after crossing the land of the Scythians. They informed him about all the other groups he mentions: Arimaspi, Hyperboreans, and griffins.[31] This self-limitation alone makes his account more plausible, as does the fact that Aristeas brings these tribes—reworked in epic format, to be sure—into a coherent historical context: 'The Issedones were pushed from their lands by the Arimaspi, while the Issedones dispossessed the Scythians'. Finally, the Scythians drove the Cimmerians from their lands by the South Sea (clearly the Black Sea).[32] This scenario of groups displacing one another reflects the demographic movement that repeatedly led to incursions of nomadic tribes into the sedentary cultures of Asia Minor and northern Mesopotamia. In the mid-seventh century BCE, a nomadic people that Greek colonists identified with the Cimmerians did in fact enter Asia Minor from Transcaucasia, attacking the Phrygians and Lydians and soon after laying waste to Greek cities on the Pontic and Aegean coasts.[33]

Aristeas had a keen eye for these realities. The scion of one of the first families of Proconnesos, he may have been a priest in the local cult of Dionysus. His fellow citizens knew he would enjoy great authority among the northern nomadic tribes as a charismatic 'holy man', endowed by Apollo with gifts in the ecstatic arts. He was probably sent by his hometown as part of an embassy to investigate political developments and to help local merchants, or one of the northern Pontic colonies, pioneer trade routes to the coveted goods of the north: alongside furs and medicinal plants (such as rhubarb) and above all gold, which according to the *Arimaspeia* was guarded by griffins.[34]

Two centuries later, Herodotus knew of a network of such routes, indicating the distances in days travelled. Their stations can be matched up with the groups mentioned by Aristeas and may therefore also have been used by him.[35] Retracing his itinerary from west to east, he would have wandered along the Hypanis (the southern Bug) through the land of the 'farming Scythians' to a forested region, home to the nomadic Scythians, that today is steppe land (Hylaia, east of the lower Dnieper). He would then have continued east, crossed the Don River (Tanais), and from there veered northeast to the land of the Sarmatians and Budini. Keeping again to the east, he would have spent seven days traversing a desert and finally arrived through 'stony and rough' country at the Argippeans, who inhabit the foothills of 'high and impassable mountains'.[36] Some scholars identify this rock-hard terrain with the salt steppes of the northern Caspian Sea; the

Argippeans would therefore be found at the Syr Darya (Jaxartes).[37] Another theory, taking its cue from the rivers that flow into the Black Sea, has the traders moving up the Don from the Sea of Azov to the region of Volgograd (at a bend in the Don), where the river was only around 80 km west of the north-flowing Volga. After crossing the overland section, they then continued upriver to the area of the Ural pass at Yekaterinburg (as Arabs would later do). The mysterious 'high and impassable mountains' would accordingly be the Urals, while the Argippeans could be a Kyrgyz tribe (e.g. the Bashkirs) or a Finnish people living at the western or southern foothills of the mountain range.[38] Their outward appearance—bald, snub-nosed, broad-chinned—reminds some readers of Mongols, while their peaceful ways and vegetarian diet, based on fruit and milk, recalls the Hippemolgi ('mare-milkers') and Abii mentioned by Homer (see above, pp. 68–69). As always, epic *topoi* are mixed with ethnographic data to characterize a people at the far limit of the horizon opened up by trade and exploration.[39]

To communicate with the Argippeans, the Scythians—Herodotus continues—had to bring along seven interpreters for seven languages, perhaps another allusion to the importance of the number seven in shamanic spiritual practices.[40] Herodotus reconnects with Aristeas when he states: 'But the country east of the bald-heads is known for certain to be inhabited by the Issedones'.[41] Greek and Scythian traders could evidently meet agents of the Issedones at Argippean markets in the Urals. They too were a real people with whom the Greeks traded in the seventh century; the poet Alcman refers to them as Essedones. Perhaps *they* were the model for the landlubbers in Aristeas (and Homer), who knew nothing of the sea.[42] In Herodotus' account, which draws in its essentials on Aristeas, they are depicted as peace-loving, law-abiding pastoralists. Women have the same power as men in their society. Whenever a man's father dies, a 'beast of the field' is brought by his relatives to be slaughtered and cut up. The father's corpse is then dismembered, mixed with the flesh of the sacrificed animal, and eaten at a feast; his skull is stripped bare, cleaned, and gilded.[43]

The emphasis on peacefulness and justice, like comparable *topoi* in Homer about the Abii, may refer to the Issedones' activities as traders and middlemen. The equality of the sexes, like the myth of the Amazonians, can be traced back to the observation that in nomadic tribes, women frequently carried out the same work as men. So far as the ritualized consumption of paternal flesh is concerned, a Greek observer may have misunderstood a burial postponed due to winter ice, or described a form of ritual (endogenous) cannibalism. Both point to a semi-nomadic people that roamed the Ekaterinburg area on the Iset River, in keeping with their placement in the *eastern* foothills of the *western* Urals. Others locate them farther south in the Jaxartes region (today's Syr Darya), west of the Aral Sea or southeast from Lake Balkhash.[44] Whichever the case may be, Argippeans and Issedones were an integral part in a system of northern trade routes whose existence from the archaic period onward is confirmed by findings of Graeco-Scythian artefacts along the Don, Volga, and Ural rivers.[45]

To the Altai Heights

By contrast, there are few archaeological remains of Graeco-Scythian trade goods north and east of the Urals. The descriptions provided in the ancient sources grow ever more outlandish in the absence of sustained contact: beyond the Issedones begins a land inhabited by one-eyed Arimaspi and gold-guarding griffins, and it may be supposed that large parts of the lost epic about the Arimaspi tell of their battles. One-eyed men had featured in the works of Homer and Hesiod. The griffin is a winged creature with the body of a lion and an eagle's head (with some variants). Widespread in Near Eastern cultures, it arrived in Greece via Crete and Mycenae, entering myth as a demonic predator but also as a companion of Apollo and Dionysus; today it resurfaces in fantasy novels and films.[46] In an epic context, Greeks did not take references to mythic hybrid beings or human populations with non-human characteristics to mean that they were moving in a 'completely make-believe' space, only that they had not (yet) seen this space with their own eyes. To tether it to the known world, they resorted to mythological set pieces that were flexible enough to be combined with both exotic folklore and vaguely grasped geographical data and functionally reinterpreted in the context of a 'new' epic world.

Behind the legend of the Arimaspi's battle with the gold-guarding griffins lies the old idea that the treasures of nature can only be wrested from it by doing battle with dangerous monsters, just as Heracles or Jason had to confront dragons, hydras, lions, or centaurs to win the gold of the Hesperides or the Golden Fleece.[47] Aristeas ascribes the role of heroic plunderer to the Arimaspi living 'in the northern interior', providing a positive variant to the Cyclops myth (see above, p. 67) and reviving the *topos* of the noble mare-milkers of the north:[48] 'numerous and very stout fighters, rich in horses and possessing many herds of cattle. They have a single eye in the middle of their fair forehead, they are shaggy with hair, and the toughest of all men'.[49]

The explicit reference to the human nature of these one-eyed warriors suggests that Aristeas sought to convey ethnographic facts with epic means: Herodotus later supposed that their name derived from the Scythian *armina* (= one) and *spu* (= eye), but it could just as easily be based on the Iranian word *aspa* (= horse); the Arimaspi would then be the 'people of wild horses'.[50] These were probably warlike nomads found between the Ural and Altai Mountains. Many had similar-sounding names: *almas*, *almasty*, or *albasty*, preserved in the Mongolian, Turkic, and Iranian languages of central Asia and the Caucasus as well as in southwest Mongolian place names. One-eyed beings were also present in Mongolian, Tibetan, and Turkic mythology—mostly as demons serving the underworld king.[51]

What about gold, the dream of all discoverers, whose magical allure drove Aristeas to the far north? Aeschylus, who drew on Aristeas, has the Arimaspi living on a 'golden river', which some take to mean the gold-rich Yenisei.[52] Numerous Scythian graves between Lake Balkhash and Lake Baikal and along the northwestern slopes of the Tian Shan and Altai Ranges contain spectacular gold artefacts. If we link these to the derivation of the name 'Arimaspi' from central Asia and the epic's spatial perspective—the Arimaspi live 'behind' the Issedones—then we can see here another allusion to a trade route into the Altai region, one of the 'richest ore regions in the ancient world'. 'Altai' denotes 'gold', the Mongols speak of the 'Golden Mountains'.[53]

The charm of this interpretation consists in the fact that it satisfactorily explains not just epic traditions, central Asian legends, and real knowledge, but also the role of the griffins. Its visual symbol frequently appears in Tschuden graves from the Volga to the Amur. Eagle-headed griffins decorate numerous objects found in graves of the Pazyryk people in the high Altais.[54] That the griffin is given the role of guarding the gold, otherwise assigned to dragons, serpents, or giant ants, perhaps stems from a misinterpretation of real objects: the great caravan route that skirts the Gobi, Turpan, and Gurbantünggüt Deserts between the Altais and the Tien Shan is one of the richest fossil repositories in the world. Many fossils show a raptor-like skull with a beak and a leonine body; perhaps their crouched stance made them appear to be brooding eggs. Scythians and Issedones may have combined these bizarre remains with old central Asian myths in the legend that these fossilized creatures died defending their gold—a monster story that had the additional effect of deterring gold-seekers from trying their luck in the Altais.[55] In the case of Aristeas, this tactic was successful in two respects: he dared go no further than the Issedones and had nonetheless found a material allowing him to link the Asiatic legends with both the Greek griffin tradition and the Apollonian 'rapture' he used to legitimate his epic. The griffin was not just considered a companion of Apollo (and Dionysus); griffins and Arimaspi are also interpreted as figures in central Asian folklore that tell of a mythic beyond as the destination of a shamanic journey. A shaman of the Altai region claimed in a poem to have crossed the Altai all the way to China.[56]

Apollo and the Hyperboreans

If the Altai region is home to griffins and Arimaspi, where are the Hyperboreans to be found, who according to Herodotus live 'beyond the griffins' and 'border a sea'?[57] An audacious yet popular hypothesis identifies them with the Chinese, as filtered through Issedone reports.[58] From a Greek perspective, the sea mentioned by Herodotus would be the eastern Ocean River, hence the East China Sea, and the trade route described in epic terms by Aristeas would be a northern arm of the so-called Silk Road. Such an explanation is not entirely far-fetched, given that the sedentary inhabitants of the Chinese settlement area played no role in the displacements of the central Asian nomadic tribes, as Aristeas says of the Hyperboreans. From prehistoric times, there was a lively commercial exchange between the Urals and the Far East (including China), with gold and silk playing an important role. As early as the second millennium BCE, Indo-European peoples functioned as intermediaries between European and Chinese settlement zones. In the sixth century, raw silk probably reached Celtic territory via Scythian middlemen. Silk was known in fifth-century Athens and probably exchanged for oil and wine.[59]

What speaks against an extreme eastward extension of the epic worldview to China, however, is the Greek myth of the Hyperboreans itself. They live—as the name says—'beyond (*hyper*) the north wind (*boreas*)'. Hesiod presents them in the 'Catalogue of Women' (see above, pp. 53–54) as horse-riding steppe nomads who live close to the mouth of the 'deep-swirling Eridanos', a river at the far northern limit of the world.[60] Where it does not contest their very reality, the tradition following Hesiod relocates the Hyperboreans to the edge of the Arctic, where the polar nights drive people into a six-month hibernation.[61] They are protected by the Riphean Mountains, not just from other people and their wars—according to Aristeas, they stayed out of the battles for territory fought between the other northern tribes—but also from the icy north wind sweeping down to the south. The geographical classification of tribes outlined in the Arimaspi epic permits a tentative identification of the Ripheans with the Altais.[62] The Hyperboreans live beyond this mountain range in a temperate climate without privation, sickness, and death (apart from one of their own choosing) as in the Golden Age, comparable to the Isles of the Blessed or Elysium in the Ocean, Olympus, or Aethiopia.

This ambivalent view of the north—on the one hand, as the origin of the aggressive, southward swarming nomadic tribes described by Aristeas, and on the other, as the homeland of a peaceful, semi-mythical people—is also found in the ancient Assyrian-Babylonian, Hebrew, and Indian (the divine beings beyond Mount Meru) traditions, which is why an oriental source of the Hyperborean legend has been surmised. Only heroes beloved by the gods, like Perseus, or exceptional mortals, like Abaris 'the Hyperborean' and Aristeas, can reach the Hyperboreans. To do so they need the support of a god, preferably Apollo, just as, according to Homer, archaic heroes were removed to Elysium.[63] Only Apollo visits them regularly, on a swan-driven chariot. He spends the winter pronouncing judgment and returns to Delphi at the start of spring, after the Delphians have summoned him with paeans and songs.[64]

The priests of Delphi associated the arrival of Apollo from the far north with the advent of the summer half of the year and his return on the swan chariot with the (in fact contrary) observation that in northern Italy and Greece, the whooper swan (*cygnus musicus*) flies north in the breeding season, when the fructifying zephyr blows, and only returns in autumn from the Arctic to the warmer climes of the south. The life cycle (*kyklos*) of the swan (*kyknos*) as Apollo's sacred animal in the north thus parallels the vegetative cycle in the south: it migrated to the Hyperboreans when spring brought new life in Delphi and returned in autumn when nature died.[65]

A similar cyclical idea of weaving together plant and animal life was associated with the Apollo legend on Delos. Here Leto gave birth to the twins Apollo and Artemis while leaning against a palm tree. Singing swans are said to have flown around her during the birth. The palm is called Phoenix; it fruits only in the hot south and grows a new frond each month. Better known is the bird of the same name, which dies each year and is born again from the ashes. The plant stands for the monthly lunar cycle, the bird (following an Egyptian model) for the annual solar cycle. Both myths are integrated in the Apollo story: Apollo represents the sun, his sister Artemis the moon, and the southern (Egyptian) phoenix is replaced by the northern swan.[66]

Perhaps the swan mythology, in conjunction with the solar cycle, further indicates a vague awareness of the northern European swan cult. Here the white swan gliding over the water symbolizes the sun chariot. It may therefore be the case that Scythian traders (who were occasionally identified with Hyperboreans[67]) or Greek merchants heading north via the Pontus or the Adriatic brought back word of it from their travels, which then merged with the cult legends of Apollo in Delphi and Greek mythology.[68] These likewise connect the sun in the form of Helios with the north. When his son Phaethon—according to Hesiod—was allowed to drive the chariot, he started a cosmic fire that almost destroyed the world. Zeus then struck Phaethon dead with a lightning bolt. His body fell to Eridanos, home to the Hyperboreans. His friend and sisters (Heliades) passed away from pain and grief. The gods took pity on them, transforming the friends into a swan and the Heliades into trees. Their tears turned into amber, mentioned by Hesiod in the 'Catalogue of Women' in connection with Eridanos and the Hyperboreans. Eridanos was the amber river, while amber was associated with divine lamentation and seen as a symbol of the sun.[69]

The Amber Road

The legends of Phaethon and the swans migrating north not only suggest contact with sun-worshipping northerners, but may also show a knowledge of the Amber Road, which since Mycenaean times could be reached from the Black Sea by way of the Bug, Dnieper, and Vistula Rivers and ran from the Oder and Elbe as well as the Rhine to the Rhône or Po.[70] The Eridanos—if given any credence at all—was identified with the Po or

Rhône. According to local Delian legend, each year Hyperborean envoys, guided by Scythians through the Black Sea and the Adriatic, brought straw-packed 'first offerings' (*aparchai*) to Delos. Here the first such envoys, two Hyperborean virgins, were venerated in Mycenaean graves.[71] The offering of first fruits in straw containers recalls northern European harvest festivals and processions. It also chimes with allusions to monthly and annual growth cycles in the Delian legend of Apollo. A link can even be made to Tiresias' prophecy that a race who knew nothing of the sea would mistake Odysseus' oar for a winnowing fan—this too is a reference to a fertility rite of Mycenaean-Minoan origin that the poet set in northern latitudes and combined with the bountiful grain of the northern Pontus.[72]

Their close connection with the Nordic swans and the amber of Eridanos has given rise to speculation that the Hyperborean gifts may not have been just first fruits but also swan eggs or amber (pearls), particularly as the envoys followed roughly the same route travelled by amber and other merchandise (cereals?) between the Adriatic and Black Sea by way of the Danube.[73] The Greeks were involved in the amber trade only as customers. It is not implausible to conclude that the Delians identified as Hyperboreans representatives of real people from the north who furnished them with amber gifts and other natural products, and thus integrated them into the local legends concerning Apollo; their gifts were subsequently regarded as Hyperborean.[74] But who were these people?

Greek antiquity already knew about the Celts, who from a seventh-century Greek perspective lived in the far northwest of the world, the same general direction as the Hyperborean envoys.[75] In the period between 650 and 600, the age of Aristeas, the Celtic late Hallstatt culture emerged in northern Europe. Monumental burial mounds near fortified hilltop settlements point to progressive social differentiation. Their elites smelted and refined iron and exported tin, copper, and other decorative objects to the Mediterranean, primarily in exchange for Greek wine and tableware. In a woman's grave from the Greek colony of Megara Hyblaea (c. 600 BCE), archaeologists found a necklace made of parts from all over the northern Mediterranean, from the Balkans to the Celtic Languedoc, symbolizing the various phases of the summer sun. In Gela, another Sicilian colony, gold rings were unearthed that originated in the Caucasus, the Colchis of Aeetes, son of Helios (see above, p. 70).[76] Taken together, these finds could also refer to the northern solar cult, which was transmitted to the Greeks, in however fragmentary a fashion, through decorative objects or sacrificial offerings (comparable to those made by the Hyperboreans) from Celtic emissaries, traders, or guest-friends. Like the Scythians, the Celts were among the northerners encountered ever more frequently by Greek adventurers during the centuries of archaic expansion.

GO WEST! LONG-DISTANCE JOURNEYS OF GREEKS FROM ASIA MINOR

One fine summer's day in the seventh century BCE, two ships were seen approaching the Mediterranean coast of Gaul. For the tribe of Segobrigii, this was no cause for alarm—these were hardly the first foreigners to visit their shores. Contact with Etruscans as well as Greek merchants and artisans had been maintained for generations. Yet this time, the Greeks arriving from Phocaea in Asia Minor came not with merchandise but with a request for a place to resettle. Their timing could not have been better. At that very moment, the Segobrigian king was preparing for the wedding of his daughter Gyptis (Petta, according to an older version). Local custom dictated that the bridegroom be chosen at the banquet. Suitors flocked to the court from near and far, so it was only natural that Protis, the leader of the Greeks, was invited along with his companions. Everyone was waiting with bated breath to find out which lucky man the princess would favour with the sign of water or wine. Without even casting an eye over the hopeful throng, she made straight for Protis and presented him with the drinking bowl. 'So it was that a foreign guest immediately became a son-in-law whose father-in-law gave him the land he needed to establish the town'.

A wonderful story still learned to this day, with minor variations,[77] by schoolchildren in the city founded by Protis: Massalia, today's Marseille. Much in it recalls fairy tales and epic motifs, like Odysseus' encounter with Nausicaa. We are dealing here with a foundation myth of the kind told in other cities of the west.[78] The best-known such myth circulated in the sixth century in Etruscan central Italy, where the hero Aeneas, following his escape from burning Troy and a long sea voyage, was said to have landed with several ships. Having won a series of battles, he married the local king's daughter (like Protis) and founded the town of Lavinium, named after his wife Lavinia. The story was probably brought to Italy by Phocaeans.[79]

For all their formulaic quality, legends give voice to real hopes and longings. Which young man leading an overseas colonizing expedition would not dream of winning the hand of a fair princess? At the same time, they have a legitimating function.[80] Later legends of other colonies compare the Greek's marriage with a local bride to tilling the land for its first crops. The new territory takes on attributes associated with female fertility and beauty, and colonization is justified as a founding act of civilizational order in a 'barbaric' environment. Sometimes the oekist—the individual chosen to lead the colonizing effort—is first purified by this success from a prior guilt that had compelled his emigration. As in the case of Odysseus' final voyage, ordained by Tiresias, the colonizing mission becomes a kind of expiatory mission only completed when new land is brought under the plough.

Whatever the political and ideological functions they may have exercised, these legends preserve historical truths. The oekists' guilt is a coded reference to political strife (*stasis*) in the hometown. Even more important is the fact that aspiring colonists would encounter communities and rulers who became their allies (through marriages and land grants) or occasionally antagonists. Modern maps of Greek colonization suggest that the Greeks steered clear of coastline occupied by rival powers. The Massalia and Aeneas legends as well as historical common sense teach us that this is a half-truth, at best. Of course, colonies could not be founded against the will of the great empires of Egypt and the Levant; for that reason, the eastern Mediterranean was generally avoided. But this does not mean, conversely, that the Greeks only set sail for unoccupied territory. Had they done so, not only would they have soon starved to death, but the colony's leaders would have found it impossible to crew so reckless a mission in the first place. No captain steers into completely uncharted waters, just as no leader of an emigrant community leads his people into uninhabited deserts. Overseas colonists therefore had to send out feelers to other cultures if they were to have any chance of surviving and thriving in their new home.

The Celts of the Hallstatt Culture

All such migrations were therefore preceded by numerous reconnaissance missions, trade contacts, and a lively exchange of information. The sum of these activities is called 'proto-colonization'. Medium-sized foreign communities, roughly equivalent in size to the prospective *poleis*, were ideal candidates for first or second contact. Unlike the great empires of the east, they exercised limited territorial rule and were willing to extend the hand of partnership to new arrivals. The Celtic tribes of the late seventh century BCE, which settled in today's France as far as the Mediterranean littoral, met these criteria. We usually assign them to the (late or early) Hallstatt culture, a term that goes back to a burial ground in the Salzkammergut in Austria and actually pertains more to the northern, central European zone, but can certainly also be applied to Celtic tribes in Provence.

The Celts, like the Greeks, were farmers. They were skilled in ironwork, which from around 800 BCE went hand in hand with occupational and social differentiation as well as the evolution of proto-urban structures. Alongside ditched and palisaded farmsteads ('Herrenhöfe') and settlements on low-lying ground, there were impressive castle buildings on ridges and plateaus with an integrated settlement area that could accommodate up to 2,000 people and corresponded to the dimensions of the Greek *poleis*. At the apex of the elevated settlements, as in Greece, stood an aristocratic elite ('princes') that ruled over 'relatively modest territories' and set the rest of the populace to work building monumental burial mounds adorned with Etruscan and Greek luxury goods. The leading men and women of the 'Herrenhöfe' were also buried with prestigious grave goods such as silk, which travelled long distances to reach Celtic territory.[81] All this suggests that the Celtic elites had been dealing with the Mediterranean world for some time and that Greek traders were well informed about the mores and customs of Celtic courts.[82]

The Massalia legend preserved this familiarity. The Segobrigii were a Ligurian tribe who, like the Celtiberians in Spain, had mixed early on with the Celts and were generally identified with them by Greeks. Although there is no evidence that the Segobrigian 'king' had a castle like that of some princes in the northern European Hallstatt culture, he too maintained contact with Greeks who had arrived at his residence in the wake of Etruscan traders and mariners. Justinus, the latest source for the Massalia legend, says that Protis and his fellows had previously forged an alliance with Rome, an Etruscan town at the time. While some believe this to be an unhistorical addition, the presence of Phoenicians in the Etruscan ports of Pyrgi and Gravisca has been verified.[83] His remark could thus indicate that Greeks did not blindly make for the French coast but had made enquiries and received consent from the Etruscans, who had set up a trading post (presumably for salt and Etruscan wine) not far from Massalia at today's St. Blaise, probably with native Ligurians, Celts, and Greeks.[84] This would also explain why the Phocaeans were self-evidently invited to attend the wedding festivities.

Furthermore, perhaps the legend has preserved real ethnographic details or at least fragments of Celtic legends. While it is un-Greek for a young bride to choose her groom by handing over a drinking vessel or other symbol (apple), the idea is familiar from Nordic legends.[85] The fact that the more recent version of the legend fills the vessel with water—in the older version, it brims with wine—appears at first glance to be a patriotic touch from the Massalians, who wished to express that they were the first to introduce the Celts to viticulture.[86] Yet perhaps the tradition also conserves a Celtic custom, such as a ritual act of purification upon the arrival of foreign guests, that the Greeks were fully conversant with: no one is surprised, and the husband-to-be plays his part to perfection.[87]

Besides, from the perspective of Greeks and Celts, the episode had a very practical basis. In all likelihood, the cultures of the European interior practised exogamy, that is, marriage partners were selected from out-groups rather than from the same tribe.[88] Greeks willing to resettle abroad belonged in this category, too. They fed a high demand for marriageable women. Because the emigrant ships were manned exclusively by (young) men, meeting the drastic shortfall of women was as much a requirement for survival as acquiring land. The episode of Gyptis and Protis is representative of the usual solution, which in reality took the more pragmatic path of prior negotiations but, as in the legend, mostly ended amicably. As a rule, the newcomers were far too weak and few in number to take women by force (as the Romans supposedly did to the Sabine women). The approach was one of cooperation rather than confrontation: according to the oldest version of the Massalia legend, found in Aristotle, the Greek leader was called 'Euxenos', meaning something like 'good guest' or 'good foreigner', and the princess adopted the name 'Aristoxene', 'best guest/foreigner', following her marriage; from their union issued the race of Protiads.[89] The names were meant to underscore the harmonious relationship between the ethnically distinct partners. Mixed marriages accompanied the founding of other colonies, and the site of the new settlement was often shared with natives. In the case of Massalia, indigenous settlers made up at least 20 percent of the population.[90] The high incidence of Etruscan pottery perhaps points to a Phocaean-Etruscan joint venture, comparable to Carthaginian-Euboean collaboration in Pithekoussai (see above, p. 39).

In one respect, however, the founding of Massalia differed from the earlier colonies in the west. The rocky settlement site around 43 km east of the mouth of the Rhône was suitable for growing wine and olives but lacked the agricultural resources needed to feed the population. How then could the new community survive? Massalia had an excellent port, so the town would have imported food from friendly tribes; Celtic settlements on the Rhône delta reveal storerooms for grain surpluses.[91] But what did the colonists offer in return and—the crucial question—why was their presence even tolerated?

Phocaea and the Rise of the Asia Minor Ports

Protis and most of his companions came from Phocaea on the Aegean coast of Asia Minor, today a small fishing village (Foca) yet in the sixth century one of the greatest cities in the eastern Mediterranean. Archaeological finds show that the settlement was an ironworking centre as early as the eleventh century BCE, which also explains its people's interest in the metals and minerals of the Far West.[92] By contrast, Phocaea (like Massalia) lacked particularly fertile farmland but had two excellent harbours in the vicinity of other *poleis*, which prospered despite their modest agricultural resources. They all imported grain from the agrarian colonies of Sicily and southern Italy, which was already generating export surpluses in the seventh century, as well as from Cyrenaica and Egypt; in the sixth century, these were joined by the northern Black Sea area. With that, the grain trade encompassed almost the entire Mediterranean.[93]

For their part, the coastal towns of Asia Minor supplied pottery, wine, and oil, making themselves indispensable as intermediaries between the Mediterranean 'peripheral and colonial regions' and the Aegean. They were reacting to the needs of their trading partners, not always peaceful in nature. The late seventh century was a time of political and military conflict that—as Aristeas already indicated—played out mainly on the margins of the Greek world or was imported into it. The *poleis* of the northern Aegean and the Sea of Marmara were forced to defend themselves against Cimmerians and Thracian tribes. Around the same time, the Lydian kings extended their empire to the Aegean coast. In Egypt, the dynasty sought to maintain its rule in Sais in the face of Libyan incursions, while the Sicilian and southern Italian colonies found themselves confronted with an expansionary Carthage and Etruscan competition.

All the powers involved in these struggles and threatened by them were desperately in need of military reinforcements, either because their own military capability was sorely lacking or because (like the elites of the western colonies) they had blocked the formation of a heavily armed citizen militia (hoplites) for domestic political reasons. The Mediterranean mercenary and privateering industries experienced another boom. Both led to important innovations in maritime technology. In Samos a transport ship was developed, based on the penteconter, that could bring mercenaries to Egypt, return with grain, and repulse enemy attacks with a below-water ram.[94] The penteconter remained the classic privateer and warship for longer voyages, but in the Phoenician-Carthaginian sphere of influence and/or in Egypt, engineers added a third row of oarsmen to build an even faster warship, the trireme of subsequent fame. In the seventh-century Levantine ports, hull parts began to be produced with pegs and grooves instead of simply overlapping wood, allowing larger units to be constructed (up to 40 m) and giving the ship greater stability; strengthening the keel with metal pins resulted in a more seaworthy vessel. Both these innovations made overseas trade more profitable and mercenary transport to all the Mediterranean crisis zones more cost-effective.[95]

The growing demand for maritime defence technology and mercenaries helped stimulate trade and integrate peripheral inland regions into the Mediterranean commercial economy. Greater quantities of precious metals (tin, bronze, iron) were needed to arm soldiers as well as fit out technologically advanced ships and their rams; mercenaries were paid in silver. Each mercenary was accompanied by at least one slave, and the rowing benches were probably also supplemented with slave labour. Because the age of large-scale enslavement in the Greek motherland was over by the early sixth century, the need for manpower had to be met from 'barbaric' regions.

The expanding slave trade may also have contributed to the spread of coinage to Greece and the western colonies, brought there by Greek mercenaries. Coins were a practical means for paying mercenaries, and regions like Egypt, which relied on them but had no silver deposits, needed vast quantities of precious metal from abroad. Moreover, Greeks employed in

Egyptian, Palestinian, and Syrian service expected to be provided with hetaerae (prostitutes), oil, wine, and tableware. Around the same time, markets for specialized pottery and marble sculpture from the Aegean emerged in Etruria, Spain, southern Italy, and the Pontus.[96]

The main beneficiaries of this development, besides several *poleis* on the Greek Peninsula (Corinth, Aegina[97]), were port cities on the coast of Asia Minor. Thanks to their trade connections and maritime experiences, they flourished as never before. Foreign rulers rewarded them handsomely for their services. In 550 BCE, for example, the Egyptian king Amasis gave Greek merchants an island in the Nile delta in exchange for a 10 percent tax on revenue. Under the name Naucratis ('city of Crates'), the settlement enjoyed a monopoly on the import-export trade between Egypt and the Aegean. One of the towns to establish a shrine in Naucratis was Phocaea.

Phocaean Fighters in Tartessos and Massalia?

The Phocaeans were also active in the northern Aegean and above all in the Far West. Herodotus emphasizes that they were 'the earliest of the Greeks to make long sea-voyages, [. . .] not sailing in round freight-ships but in fifty-oared vessels',[98] the classic warship of the archaic period, armed with a bronze ram. The statement is corroborated by the archaeological record. Phocaean success in the Far West evidently had less to do with their exports of pottery or oil and wine—these acted mainly as gifts and to open diplomatic doors—than with the services they offered as privateers and mercenaries, for which they received in return minerals and precious metals that were then sold in the Mediterranean, especially in silver-poor Egypt.[99]

Some time before the founding of Massalia, lucrative opportunities had emerged in Andalusian Tartessos. It had grown rich by exploiting local silver and copper mines (see above, p. 36). Like the Celtic tribes of the Hallstatt culture, it experienced a steep rise in population along with increased social differentiation, although it was a markedly more peaceful and less militarized society. As a result, Tartessian rulers were more reliant on foreign support against local rivals and the Carthaginians. Two Greek warrior helmets found in Andalusia may have belonged to professional soldiers in Tartessian service. Phocaeans may have been among them. The Tartessian king Arganthonios supposedly offered them land for settlement, as did the Egyptian king in Naucratis and later the Segobrigian king, according to the

Massalia legend. The offer was most likely part of a pay deal, such as we also find in Egypt.[100]

The Phocaeans turned down the offer, however, and refused to establish a permanent base on other, nearby stretches of the Spanish shore as well. While some may have been employed by local rulers as craftspeople, the overall evidence suggests that most belonged to military companies that, with the blessing of their home community, roved wherever they could to earn ready money and acquire valuable minerals. The remuneration offered by the king—his name derives from the Celtic word *arganto* (silver)—was so generous that the Phocaeans could use it to finance the construction of one of the era's largest city walls back home.[101] Yet in the end, both sides had miscalculated: in the mid-sixth century, Tartessos succumbed to Carthaginian dominance while the Phocaeans fled before the advancing Persians.[102]

The story was quite different in Massalia. Here a Phocaean 'company' (Justinus) took up the offer to resettle and had to engage far more intensively with local conditions and needs. Like most other Phocaean settlements, Massalia was probably set up as an *emporium*, a mixed-population enclave tolerated by the natives, and evolved only gradually into an independent *polis*.[103] However we imagine the process of colonization, one thing is certain: at least in its early stages, it too had nothing to do with any form of commerce. Archaeological references to exports originating in Massalia, or proceeding via Massalia up the Rhône into Celtic territory (wine, pottery), date only from around 540 BCE, some sixty years (or two generations) after the city's founding. Trade was initially sporadic, tentative, and unspecialized, more politically than commercially motivated.[104] Naturally, the Phocaeans did not arrive in Provence completely destitute, but the few objects and products they brought with them were gifts for the king; they do not reflect a plan to enrich themselves through trade. The dominance of Etruscan goods and amphorae was (still) too great for that. The few eastern Greek, Attic, and early Massiliote ceramics found in and around Massalia were for private consumption and were at best passed on as 'goods on consignment' or 'contact gifts' from the Etruscans.[105]

If not trade and trade goods, what made the Phocaeans so attractive to the native king that he offered them places to settle and marriage connections? The same as in Tartessos: assistance as mercenaries and privateers in addition to military and maritime know-how. Thucydides later related how the Phocaeans 'who founded Massalia' defeated the Carthaginians in a naval battle. Pausanias confirms that the colonists of Massalia proved superior to the Carthaginians at sea. Taken together, these sources point to early Massalian military activity at sea.[106] Justinus tells how the inhabitants of Massalia fought many battles against the Ligurians while mostly enjoying good relations with the Celts.[107] The Ligurians were notorious pirates, suggesting that the Massalians offered convoy protection against coastal raids and defended Celtic settlements against their competitors. According to legend, were not the vassals of Aeneas first active as warriors in Latium before they established their first settlement? At any rate, local rivals for the hand of the king's daughter had to be eliminated. In Justinus' account, soon after the Segobrigian king died, his successor plotted an attack on the young colony.[108] A version of the foundation myth preserved in Livy indicates that shortly after their arrival, the Phocaeans had to defend themselves against the Celtic Salyes. In doing so, they were supported by other Celts and fortified their town.[109]

All the available evidence points to a chain of events typical for the advent of Greeks in the Far West: after an initially cordial reception by a local prince, they became embroiled in conflict with competing regional powers—not just to secure their own existence but also in return for their welcome on foreign soil. Although there is no direct evidence of foreigners fighting in Celtic service until the first century BCE (see below, p. 272), the origin of the colonists as well as their military hardware speak for similar service already in the archaic period, a time when the mercenary trade and the transfer of innovations in military technology experienced an enormous upswing.

In fact, technical know-how moved with the Phocaeans as they made contact with native tribes and resettled. The construction of Celtic plank boats suggests a transfer of Mediterranean shipbuilding technology in the sixth century BCE that continued into the following period.[110] Justinus further claims that the Phocaeans taught locals to surround their towns with walls. The Phocaeans evidently gave the Celts advice on improving their military infrastructure, just as Greeks did in other parts of the world. Their assistance extended far to the north. Shortly after the founding of Massalia, but long before archaeologically verifiable trade activities, the Celtic hillfort of Heuneburg on the Upper Danube near Ulm was encircled with an impressive mudbrick wall and several outwardly protruding rectangular towers—a structure without parallel in central Europe. The most plausible explanation is that it was inspired by Massiliote engineers and built with their (on-site?) assistance.[111]

In these and other cases where Celtic princes accepted help from Greek architects and soldiers, a wish to consolidate their status and prestige within their own society and against Celtic rivals surely also played a part. The princes were the most important, if not the sole, consumers of luxury goods (wine, symposium ware) of Greek and Etruscan origin, which were used to enhance local drinking customs. They were also the ones to offer foreign colonists land and forge alliances with them through intermarriage.[112] By reaching out to the Greeks, they perhaps sought to create a counterweight to the dominant influence of the Etruscans, who in the first half of the seventh century exploited their extensive trade network to exchange wine and pottery for coveted minerals (gold, silver, iron, copper, tin), natural products (salt, amber, grain, timber), and slaves.[113]

Playing merchants, settler groups, and combat units off against one another was a popular strategy among local rulers. Fostering competition and diversity among those offering luxury goods and (military) services increased their prestige and made them more of a military threat, particularly if—like the Celts—they were vulnerable in a particular area such as maritime power or fortifications, or if they themselves invested more energy in 'peaceful' ways of securing their status (hunting, feasting, exchanging gifts) than in warfare, as some scholars suspect was the case for both the Tartessians and the Hallstatt Celts.[114] The king of Tartessos offered his friendship to the Phocaeans to push back against Carthaginian influence. Much the same can be suspected of the king of the Segobrigii, who aimed to mobilize the young warriors of Massalia against plundering Ligurians or all-too-intrusive Etruscan merchants and pirates.[115] This is always a high-stakes gamble, which is why a marital connection with his foreign allies would have struck the Celtic prince as the best guarantee that they would not turn their military power against him.

The Sea Route to Tartessos—and the Tin Islands?

Ultimately, the Phocaeans also profited from the arrangement. From the mid-sixth century, Etruscan exports by way of the Rhône system into the Celtic zone of central Europe declined significantly. Etruscan amphorae made way for those from Massalia. The Celtic princes had clearly developed a taste for the diplomatic gifts of the Massalians, who in turn had found time to perfect a wine-transport technique that could compete with the Etruscan amphorae: Massalia became the only Greek colony to develop its own type of amphora.[116] With its help, the Massalians succeeded in taking over the lucrative wine trade from the Etruscans (by peaceful means and perhaps with a profit-sharing agreement)—from then on, the Etruscans concentrated on northern Italy and the regions north of the Alps[117]—and towards the end of the sixth century, they used their trade network to flood the area all the way to the Upper Rhine and the Upper Danube with their wine. Their repertoire included pottery for everyday use as well as fine tableware for the drinking parties of the Celtic princes. Attic drinking bowls and giant vessels (such as the Vix krater) for mixing water, wine, and aromatic additives showed Greek war and combat scenes and thus in a certain sense preserved the Phocaeans' tradition as warriors, even if they had now turned to more profitable ventures.[118]

There is still debate over whether the Massalians themselves journeyed up the Rhône to the Celtic princely residences in central Europe, whether native middlemen transported goods on their behalf, or whether the Massalians placed their contacts (and military escorts?) at the disposal of foreign merchants in return for a share in the profits and customs duties. In any case, they succeeded in establishing their town as a central relay station for trade between the Mediterranean and central Europe.[119] One impulse for economic development was the influx of Phocaean settlers after their hometown was taken by the Persians in 545 BCE. It was only now—after two generations spent proving their mettle as fighters and privateers—that the colonists expanded their territory, established sub-colonies, and turned to long-distance trade. Only now did the town begin to issue its own coinage (from Tartessian and southern Celtic silver) and give itself a constitution in which the wealthy aristocracy called the shots and officials and councillors were chosen on timocratic (property-owning) and hereditary principles. A small settlement grew to become one of the leading trading and port metropolises of the western Mediterranean.[120]

It was not unusual for an initial spell of mercenary service to be followed by a switch to mercantile activity. A similar sequence can be observed in Saite dynasty Egypt, where Naucratis was only established several generations after Greeks from Asia Minor were hired as mercenaries. The trading post was used by Phocaeans, among others. Egypt received oil, wine, pottery, and especially silver in return for grain. But what were the Massalians seeking among the Celts in exchange for wine and pottery? On the one hand, the classic metals that had already enticed the Etruscans to the north: copper at the southern flanks of the Massif Central, iron, and gold; on the other, access via the Rhône, Saône, and lower Loire Valley to the overland routes to Galician and Atlantic tin deposits. Further incentives were salt, grain, and above all slaves, in great demand at the time in Italy (Rome) and the Mediterranean more generally (see above, p. 101).[121]

Maritime expeditions to the Atlantic tin deposits were launched in parallel to these overland missions. A sixth-century BCE coastal report outlines a sea route from Massalia to Tartessos and the tin trade routes overseen by its rulers. Its author was probably a captain or merchant from Massalia.[122] The preface describes the shores of Tartessos as well as the islands and peoples farther north in the Atlantic. Two days' journey separates the Oestriminic Isles (probably Brittany) from the islands of the Hirians and Albiones (England?). Here the Oestriminians acquired tin and freighted it to Tartessos. Either there or in southern Spanish Mainake, the cargo was transferred to the Phocaeans, who then presumably shipped it along the Mediterranean coast to Massalia and from there to the Mediterranean basin.[123]

There is much to suggest that the Massalians soon attempted to control this route—or at least the section of it that ran along the French Mediterranean coast—by setting up colonies and trading posts of their own (*emporia*). It is less likely that they made it as far as the famous Tin Islands. According to Pliny the Elder, a certain Midacritos was the first to import 'white lead' (= tin) from the *Cassiteridis insula*. Some assume he was a Phocaean or Massalian and date his voyage to before 500 BCE.[124] Yet this is no less certain than the popular identification of the Casseterides with Cornwall or the British Isles. It might just as well be an island off the Spanish or Breton coast where tin was sold. Quite apart from the fact that there are no parallel references to any direct contact between Massalia and Cornwall in the archaic period, the logic of the situation speaks against it. So long as relations with the Tartessians remained amicable, there was no reason to muscle in on their maritime trade links, especially as the Massalians had enough on their hands securing contact with the Celts and Tartessos.

Colaeus and the Samians in Tartessos

Before too long, exclusive links to wealthy funders and trading partners are guaranteed to whet the appetite of ambitious rivals. So it was that the Samian captain Colaeus was blown off course on a voyage to Egypt, stranded on an island called Platea, then driven by the east wind to the Pillars of Heracles 'and came providentially to Tartessos'.[125] In fact, no captain is ever involuntarily tossed up and down the entire Mediterranean by winds and divine intervention. The author wished to place the voyage and its stupendous result—Colaeus returned with the biggest profit any Greek trader had ever made (besides Sostratos of Aegina)—in an epic light.[126]

Reality needed neither gods nor freak winds. The Samians had good contacts with Egypt and Cyrene for importing grain. Four ivory combs of western Phoenician origin in the Heraion of Samos—whether votive offerings made by Phoenician mariners or dedications of Samian voyagers returned from Tartessos—demonstrate relations with the Phoenicians and Carthaginians. What could be more natural than to set out in their wake (from Cyrene) and attempt a journey to Tartessos, as familiar to the Samians by hearsay as to the less distant Phocaeans? After all, there is evidence that both called at the same Etruscan ports.[127]

Herodotus maintains that the Samians were the first to visit Tartessos, yet he states a few chapters earlier that Tartessos was discovered by the Phocaeans. According to a later source, the Rhodians arrived in Tartessos even before the Phocaeans.[128] These conflicting claims are typical for the history of exploration. Clearly, several *poleis* competed to chart a direct route to silver-rich Tartessos and each subsequently prided itself on having been the first. The Phocaeans probably pioneered the northern route via Sicily, Italy, Corsica, and the Ligurian and French coasts, securing it with trading stations and colonies (such as Alalia on Corsica), while Colaeus took the route along the southern coast of the Mediterranean preferred by Carthaginians and Phoenicians.[129] Like the Phocaeans, the Samians hired themselves out as mercenaries and had a reputation as privateers and pirates; the remains of a ship dedicated in the Samos shrine and sometimes associated with Colaeus belonged to a naval vessel. Some scholars link the military helmet found in southern Spain (see above, p. 102) to Colaeus. Like the Phocaeans, Samians established contacts with natives before venturing to the west. Based on the votive offerings found in the sanctuary to Hera, these extended from Africa and Egypt to Etruria and Spain.[130]

In both cities, such a far-flung network of contacts relied on support from the domestic aristocracy and the priests attached to civic deities. They were the guardians of knowledge about routes and contacts in the west and could draw on this knowledge if an emergency—such as that which befell Phocaea in the mid-sixth century—forced a community to emigrate.

They were the ones who used the proceeds from foreign trade to organize the construction of urban infrastructure (such as the city wall in Phocaea), allowed the entire community to enjoy the fruits of overseas success, and ensured that cities like Phocaea could regularly import grain and precious minerals.

The priests and their institutions exercised an additional function. There was a reason why Colaeus dedicated one-tenth of his profits to the Hera temple, while the Phocaeans probably made comparable donations to the temple of Artemis at Ephesus. If we consider the origin of votive gifts in various Mediterranean coastal regions, the Near East, and the Balkans, as well as the distribution of divine cults along trading routes and among colonies, we may conclude that temples such as those of Ephesus and Samos provided captains, mercenaries, traders, and colonists with a religious identity. They guided mariners over the waters and were thus an important motor for long-distance travel, mediating between captains and the community at large, much like the temple of Melqart for the Phoenician expeditions.[131]

What holds true for Phocaea and Samos surely also applies to other port cities of the eastern Aegean: for Chios, which transported slaves and hetaerae from Thracia and Phrygia to Lydia, Egypt, and the Levant, supplying the country with Thracian silver and the Mediterranean coastal regions with tableware; or for Miletus, which founded colonies on the Black Sea not just to satisfy the Mediterranean basin's appetite for metal but also to secure its citizens the arable land that seemed threatened by Lydian incursions.[132]

A NEW WORLD ORDER

LONG-DISTANCE TRAVEL AND COLONIZATION IN THE SIXTH CENTURY BCE

Natural Philosophers in Miletus

Residents of port cities in Asia Minor saw themselves as part of a dynamic world. Some learned from old stories how their families had once landed on these shores and founded the 'Ionian' *poleis* that were now flourishing as never before. Knowledge of the colonial past was linked to current expansion in the Black Sea and the Far West. Audiences listened spellbound to the stirring tales brought back by mariners, heard about bizarre landscapes and strange people with idiosyncratic customs, and marvelled at the variety and mutability of the world beyond the familiar borders of the Mediterranean littoral. At the same time, they admired the colonists who had successfully asserted themselves in this world, rubbed their eyes in amazement at the riches many a captain brought home, and celebrated their ships' ability to cross vast distances to reach their destination.

Whenever barriers are broken and personal experience takes the place of legend, people demand new explanations. From the first third of the sixth century BCE, at the height of the colonization movement from Asia Minor, men from Miletus enquired into the principle on which the world was constituted and the laws by which it changes. They were searching for a cosmic formula that brought about these changes and expressed an 'abstract divine omnipotence'. We call them 'natural philosophers'. Their reflections were speculative—exact measurements and chemical analyses still lay in the future—yet grounded in observation and logical argument. They are therefore considered to be the founders of philosophy. The ancient concept *philosophia* denotes a comprehensive love of wisdom that embraces natural-cosmological, religious, political, and in this sense also philosophical aspects of the universe. A lover of wisdom does not rest content with commonplace, traditional teachings but aims to find out more about the world and the laws that govern it. The Ionians called this search for 'extra knowledge' *historia*. Why did *historia* not rest content with explaining individual phenomena, instead expanding its perspective to take in the entire world, and why did it do so at this particular place and time?

According to Aristotle, the starting point of all philosophy is curious astonishment about the world and its changes. In Miletus, such astonishment was provoked by a range of different objects. Here trading routes from the eastern empires converged with shipping routes to the Aegean, the Black Sea, and the west. Here news of the latest discoveries made by seafarers and colonists mingled with ancient eastern wisdom literature and cosmologies. It was this mix of age-old wisdom and new experience that converted astonishment in the face of individual phenomena into a new kind of 'global' thinking and explaining. For astonishment alone yields no science, no *theoria*. Dogged curiosity is needed as well, along with a drive to ask new questions, come up with new answers, and accommodate these answers in an explanatory system. The Greeks believed that anyone spurred to enquiry by astonishment leaves behind the many small, confined worlds of everyday life; they broaden their mental horizons (from the Greek *horizein* = to bound, limit) to take in the world as a whole, the cosmos.

Besides influences from the east, the experience of maritime expansion seems to have been a decisive stimulus for this quest for expanded mental horizons. Admittedly, captains, shipowners, and colonists were not under the kind of permanent economic or nautical pressure that gave rise to a drive for innovation in the early-modern period. Yet their constant battle with the sea, the experience of colonization, and long-distance trade with diverse cultures contributed decisively to the emergence of a scientific and philosophical worldview. Unlike desert dwellers, who were also confronted each day with vast expanses of space, archaic mariners made the stupendous discovery that these expanses could be mastered with technical instruments, knowledge, and logic. Not by chance, almost all the natural philosophers embarked on long sea voyages in their youth and took a keen interest in geometry, astronomy, and navigation. Thales, an engineer from Miletus (and supposedly the son of Phoenician parents), considered the founder of Ionian natural philosophy, is presented in the sources as an astute politician and skilled navigator. He probably stood in close contact with mariners, merchantmen, and travellers.[133] After a journey to Egypt and the Middle East, he composed an astronomical manual for mariners, used geometrical proofs to calculate the distance of a ship from the shore, and explained the significance of the constellation Ursa Minor for navigation. According to Milesian tradition, his younger compatriot Anaximander founded the Black Sea colony of Apollonias, sought natural explanations for cosmic phenomena, and introduced the Greeks to the Babylonian shadow-casting rod (gnomon) for determining the time of day.[134]

Thales and his successors did not just adapt astronomical knowledge, however; they also pioneered global accounts of the world. The ocean's immensity opened their eyes to the nature of the universe and cried out for explanations. Anaximander offered them in his prose text 'On Nature'. The repeated process of founding a colony further fostered the capacity for creative abstraction and experimentation with pre-given templates and cognitive models. Given that mariners, long-distance traders, and colonists relied on practical experience and expertise and were keenly receptive to the new, it is hardly surprising that they would be the first to abandon the explanations offered by myth and its literary genres for models written in an alternative medium: prose, otherwise only practised at Delphi. Their writings formed the precondition for an additional stimulus: rivalry between thinkers and the resulting criticism of existing explanations. The superiority of a new approach needed to be justified—knowledge itself became the object of thought.

To be sure, the Milesians were not the only ones to ply the seas, carry out long-distance trade, and establish colonies. Specific socio-political conditions complemented the general intellectual, mental, and environmental climate. Unlike the inhabitants of many other Greek cities, the Milesians were not permanently preoccupied with securing life's necessities but had (according to Aristotle) the time and leisure to philosophize.[135] Miletus had grown rich from overseas trade. It enjoyed an unusual degree of domestic political stability that distinguished it from many other *poleis* of the Greek Peninsula and the Asia Minor coast. Since the failed siege by the Lydians in the mid-sixth century, it had also been protected from external threats and had built up an imposing naval presence. The city possessed one of the strongest fleets in the Aegean and enjoyed—like the Ugarites in relation to the Hittites but unlike other coastal *poleis*, especially Phocaea and Samos—special privileges recognized by the Lydian kings and also, until the end of the century, by the Persians.[136] The Milesians thus not only cultivated exclusive contacts with the royal courts of the east, but also combined prosperity and stability with an external security that released the philosopher from the confines of everyday political activity.

These factors formed the parameters for a thinking that veered away from earlier paths of wisdom. It was only natural for coast dwellers to believe that the disc-shaped Earth was like an island encircled by the Ocean. Thales then took from the Babylonians the idea that the Ocean flowed under as well as around the Earth. Homer and the myths had already venerated the Ocean as 'the origin of all things' and 'the father of all the gods'. Once these explanations were combined with the Milesians' existential confrontation with the sea, Thales' conclusion that water was the originating element of the world seemed almost inevitable.[137]

Anaximander also ascribed central importance to the sea when explaining nature. The basis of his account of the universe was the assumption that everything is in a state of constant flux. The first organisms arose in the sea, and humans, too, could trace their descent from fish. Anaximander's term for the primordial ground of all that exists was *apeiron*, 'that which is without limit', a condition characterized by disorder instead of hierarchy and formlessness instead of structure.[138] This resembled people's understanding of the Ocean. In the opinion of the epic poets and philosophers, it was the element from which all living organisms had emerged, but also the epitome of chaos and disorder in relation to the order founded by the Olympian hierarchy. By uncovering the opposition between order and disorder to explain the structure of the world, the philosopher replaced older mythical notions with a rational conception of the whole.

Divine Guidance: The Oracle of Delphi

The quest for a rational order based on empirical observation and plausible speculation did not mean, however, that the *polis* religion and its gods had fallen into abeyance. For all their technical ingenuity, mariners and colonists still needed divine support: the sea voyages and acts of settlement undertaken by men of diverse origin—some of Protis' companions came from neighbouring communities in Asia Minor[139]—required a stabilizing framework to imbue them with meaning. Much like in the early-modern period under the sign of the cross, 'colonization' was therefore always an act approved by the gods, who accompanied the process from beginning (departure from the homeland) to end (report of mission accomplished).

Apollo played a central role in many foundation myths. As *Apollon Delphinios*, he led emigrants safely over the waves like a dolphin, while as *Apollon Archegetes* he protected the colony at its foundation.[140] In other versions, Apollo flies ahead of the oekist in the form of a raven—a motif familiar from the Arimaspian epic (see above, p. 85).[141] Many stories tell of how the aspiring oekist travelled to Delphi, where the priests commissioned him to found an *apoikia* and gave him instructions on how to get there in the form of enigmatic sayings. The oekist had to decipher these sayings and so prove his fitness to lead the colony. Only upon passing this aptitude test could he be sure of Apollo's support. Now he possessed the authority needed to assemble a team and take command of the expedition.

It is unlikely that leaders of colonization missions regularly travelled from Asia Minor to the Delphic oracle in the seventh century BCE.[142] A visit to the oracle was an onerous undertaking due to the long journey and associated costs, and it could only be paid nine times a year; perhaps the nearby oracles of Didyma or Claros were visited instead.[143] It also presupposed that founding an *apoikia* was the sole goal of a journey previously agreed upon by the community, hence that the oracle merely gave divine sanction to a planned expedition rather than initiating it.[144]

Both may be assumed for the mid-sixth-century emigration of the Phocaeans necessitated by the Persian invasion but not, or not generally, before then. In the early archaic period, permanent resettlement was one alternative among several possibilities facing colonists abroad, depending on the situation.[145] Tellingly, the foundation myth of Massalia (and other colonies originating in Asia Minor) has nothing to say about a visit to the Delphic oracle. According to Strabo, the Phocaeans were given an oracle instructing them to take with them 'a guide received from the Ephesian Artemis' in the form of a sacred image, but this clearly refers not to the 'company' of Protis but to settlers from around fifty years later. They were the first to build a temple to Delphic Apollo (and Ephesian Artemis) on the headland by the harbour exit at today's *vieux port*, from where the god towered protectively over the city and gave orientation to sailors far out at sea. The inhabitants of Massalia's sub-colonies were said to have presented native tribes with objects sacred to Artemis, probably small cultic statues.[146] Aristeas, too, supposedly told the people of Metapontum to erect an altar to Apollo long *after* the colony was founded, prompting them to seek confirmation from the oracle.[147]

All this suggests that contact with the Delphic Apollo and the institution of the relevant cults in the new colony were generally put off until the second or third generation. Only once a young colony had become established was it customary to give thanks at the oracle sites and make donations. Now the visit also made political sense: as a neutral space not associated with any particular *polis*, Delphi offered a budding colony recognition as a new civic community unbeholden to the religious or political authorities of the mother-city.[148] From the early sixth century BCE, Delphi offered colonies a platform to trumpet their overseas success to the Greek world and burnish their attractiveness as trading partners.

The oracle stood to gain, too. With every successful colonizing mission, the Delphic priests increased not just their wealth but also their stock of knowledge about distant shores. While future colonists and sailors had access to this knowledge as well, Delphi gave them a sheltered space for sharing their experiences and receiving—in the form of an Apollonian pronouncement—an additional, universally recognized religious imprimatur for their missions. It would be stretching the point to attribute to the Delphic oracle an overall coordinating function comparable to that exercised by the papacy in the early-modern period—the influence of local temples and cults on the coast of Asia Minor was too great for that. Still, the priesthood constituted a supra-regional authority that combined its monopoly on information with religious authority and made Delphi an 'intellectual marketplace' for political solutions and, along with Miletus and Phocaean Elea, a centre of Greek thought. For that reason, the legend of the Seven Sages, four of whom were from Asia Minor (Thales of Miletus, Bias of Priene, Pittacus of Mytilene, and Cleobulus of Lindos), came to be associated with Delphi despite probably arising in Miletus. The supra-regional role of the sanctuary had its counterpart in the breach of local horizons by the philosophers. Anaximander placed Delphi at the centre of the world.[149]

New Religious Models: Transmigration of the Soul

Apollo watched over everything. For foreign ethnic groups as well as their rulers, he became so attractive that the potential for collaboration could sometimes arise. In the process, so-called middle grounds—contact zones between different ethnic groups in a still early phase of political organization like the young colonies near the mouth of the Rhône or in the northern Black Sea—may have been better suited to reciprocal influence than the Greek enclaves and settlements in Egypt, whose civilizational distance and venerable age were ever more clearly perceived and accepted by the Greeks. Lasting takeovers of Egyptian deities and their cults (Isis) first ensued four hundred years later, when a new 'Graeco-Macedonian rule' was established on the Nile with the Hellenistic kings.

When it came to the agrarian Celts and Scythians who lived in the Black Sea region to the edge of the steppes, the situation seems to have been more open. Here Greek traders and colonists, self-confidently aware of their independence, could more easily cooperate with the natives to their mutual benefit. All the archaeological evidence suggests that the archaic 'colonies' of the Pontus (just like the colony at Massalia) were inhabited by a mixed populace of Greek immigrants and native 'barbarians'. They combined local and Greek traditions, using dwellings adapted to the environment and climate ('pit houses').[150] For colonists from ports in Asia Minor, this must have seemed all the more natural because their forebears had made similar arrangements with the indigenous Carians when they first settled there.

Military conflict was never ruled out, and the intensity of contacts always depended on the political climate as well as on regional contexts.[151] Thus, the tales of Anacharsis and the Scythian king Scyles in Herodotus indicate that, without the backing of the indigenous nobility and enough time to build consensus, an all-too-abrupt imposition of Greek culture and traditions 'from above' could brutally backfire.[152] Yet precisely this tradition, which is confirmed by the archaeological record, shows how familiar Scythians and Greeks were with each other's myths and legends, to the point where they could adopt them while meeting on 'middle grounds'.[153]

All this presupposed long-standing contact and linguistic proficiency. Such communicative bridges can be assumed among locally active traders and—as always—in mixed marriages and their offspring in 'borderland' settlements. This was the basis on which common cults and places of worship could emerge under certain circumstances. For example, Greek merchants in the Scythian forest steppe of the northern Pontus erected an altar for Apollo that they probably shared with natives.[154] According to Herodotus, the Scythian *Geloni* worshipped Greek gods in the Greek fashion and spoke a Graeco-Scythian pidgin.[155] In a mixed-population colony called Olbia, as in other Milesian *apoikia*, there was a cult of Apollo Delphinios.[156] The legendary 'Hyperborean' sage Abaris is said to have introduced his people to a god the Greeks identified with Apollo. Herodotus equated the Scythian magic god (G)oitosyros with Apollo.[157] Conversely, Greek settlers on Samothrace, an important stopover for mariners, merchants, and colonists, appropriated elements of the Thracian mysteries for the cult of Dionysus.

Their proximity to foreign cultures and their 'hybrid' nature made the colonies unusually receptive to 'barbaric' practices, especially if these promised orientation and security. Ethnically mixed contact zones typically attracted miracle workers and itinerant preachers like Aristeas, who introduced the colonies of the northern Pontus to shamanic purification techniques and ecstatic practices (see above, p. 86). There was a reason why priests who interpreted oracles and performed purification rites did good business in the colonies: legends maintained that in establishing the colony, oekists had to flush out contagion (*miasma*) and keep all impurities at bay. Apollo's raven, which appears in connection with colonization legends and miracle stories, becomes the feathered *pharmakos*, the 'scapegoat' that takes all the guilt on itself so that the community might be washed clean.[158]

Besides their legitimating function in allowing a new community to distinguish itself from the old in an alien environment, such acts served a dual purpose. Every settlement on distant shores was fraught with risk. Many emigration projects failed in the critical early stages or had to be abandoned, not just because they came under attack but because the unaccustomed climate, unaccustomed flora, and ecological conditions caused the rate of illness to skyrocket—not coincidentally, writings from the corpus of Hippocrates devote particular attention to northern and southern colonization areas.[159]

From an archaic perspective, sickness in the literal sense was equated with impurity, but internal division and strife were also viewed as illnesses affecting the body politic. *Poleis* became patients and legislators the physicians who treated them. 'Political' and 'physical' illnesses were mortal dangers that threatened the existence of young colonies, in particular. It is therefore unsurprising that they worshipped Apollo as a god of healing, not just as a helper at the colony's foundation, and embraced cathartic cults and their priests.[160]

Elsewhere, too, there was a growing need for divine and human aid against illness. Increased sea travel brought with it increased susceptibility to disease. If we further consider the internecine feuding that often prevailed in the *poleis* of the 'motherland' before emigrations, as well as the risk of infection facing citizens crowded into small, growing communities and mercenaries stationed in Egypt and Sicily (see above, p. 101), we can understand why an army of charismatic healers, seers, and priests from the northern and eastern borderlands (like the mythical Abaris) swept over the Mediterranean colonies from the end of the seventh century. All were specialists in banishing present uncertainty and anxiety through atonement and prognostication.

The colonial zones functioned as vectors for various knowledge traditions. Their historical achievement lay in selectively combining the multitude of 'religious' offers with their own traditions and developing them into coherent systems of thought. We know that the Pontus colonies and their mother-cities in Asia Minor were remarkably familiar with the myths and legends of Scythian nomads in Eurasia and Caucasia, and that these stories were imported into the Mediterranean basin by traders and artisans.[161] The legends involving Aristeas demonstrate not just an encounter with shamanic ecstasy techniques (see above, p. 86); they also indicate a fundamental shift in spirituality in parts of the Greek world. In the sixth century, purification rituals and ecstatic practices fused with Egyptian, Indian, and Iranian (perhaps also Celtic) borrowings[162] into the idea of an immortal soul that must pass through various bodies before returning to its divine homeland. In the second half of the sixth century, itinerant Orphic priests combined this theory of a transmigration of souls (or metempsychosis) with an elaborate cosmogony that was taken up in the colonial zones of Sicily and southern Italy, on Crete, and in Thrace and the northern Pontus. In the fifth century, Orphic religious communities in southern Italy, Sicily, and the northern Aegean performed initiations and buried the dead with gold tablets providing instructions for their journey in the underworld.[163]

Pythagoras and His Teachings

Eschatological promises of salvation, initiation into occult knowledge, and purification rites address feelings of uncertainty that traditional religious and social authorities can no longer assuage. The colonies' proximity to foreign cultures facilitated the process of adaptation. The typical colonial need for a religiously underpinned identity in an alien climate may have provided an additional incentive for synthesizing old religious and philosophical models with new ones.

The success of the Samian charismatic religious leader Pythagoras in the southern Italian colony of Croton, where he turned up in 530 BCE, shows how such a process of amalgamation could provide political stability in a situation experienced as insecure. His teaching—so far as it can be reconstructed—takes up key Orphic ideas while adapting motifs such as reincarnation and metamorphosis from legends told in Aristeian circles and in the southern Italian colonial *poleis* (Metapontus, where Aristeas was worshipped, was a Pythagorean centre).[164]

Pythagoras, later dubbed 'the Hyperborean Apollo', found fertile ground in Croton. A plague had ravaged the city several years before, and after a devastating defeat at the hands of Locris and Rhegion, the aristocracy stood accused of luxury and decadence. By adopting Orphic doctrines and making the post-mortal existence of the divine soul dependent on its *moral* conduct in the here and now, he helped a battered aristocracy win back its self-confidence. Purity now became the *ethical* postulate of a strictly regulated life. In this respect, the Pythagorean *bios* reflected a rear-guard action by the elite—equally evident in contemporary poetry—to distance themselves from the rest of society through their moral qualities, moderation, and intellectual superiority.[165] Metempsychosis entailed vegetarianism, an old characteristic of the idealized peoples of the north that could perhaps only be realized at the time in cereal-rich southern Italy. Along with the idea that the body was nothing but an appendage of the divine soul, vegetarianism offended the norms of *polis* society. For that very reason, Pythagoreanism not only promised to give the aristocrats back their dignity, clearing them of the charge of excessive luxury and military failure, but also gave them the opportunity to redefine themselves against both the rebellious lower classes and the metropolitan aristocracy. This is what made the doctrine of metempsychosis so attractive, including for colonial tyrants. It drew attention away from the fact that they ruled by force and offered them religious validation for their politically precarious position. For the path from the divinity of the soul to the godlike human being was but a short one. The new doctrine of the soul was no longer just an emergency response; it expressed an optimistic self-awareness growing out of the successful assertion of power by monarchical governments in peripheral regions.

Together with princes, bards, and seers, physicians represented the highest social rank that the soul could attain in its cycle of rebirths. According to the Orphics and Pythagoreans, the soul's redemption from the cycle of reincarnation always involved purification or purgation (*katharsis*), which is why so many Orphics performed purification rites.[166] It is certainly not by chance that Pythagoras' arrival in southern Italy coincided with one of the greatest plague outbreaks ever to befall Croton. The Pythagorean ban on eating beans responded to favism, an occasionally fatal allergy to fava beans common in southern Italy and Sicily.[167] As a countermeasure, the Pythagoreans recommended moderation and austerity. 'For extravagance'—so the master—'ruins not only the fortunes of men but their bodies as well, since most diseases arise from indigestion, and that arises from extravagance'.[168] The warning against luxury as a political and ethical problem is combined with a dietetics that, along with gymnastics and music, became the foundation of the famed 'medical school' of Croton (and perhaps that of Cyrene). Its representatives—all Pythagoreans or sympathetic to the teachings of Pythagoras—believed that diseases could be cured or prevented solely with reference to their natural causes and required no religious explanations. Crotonian doctors like Democedes took their art eastward, tracing the opposite route to that which had brought Pythagoras to the west.

Revolutionary Cosmological Models: The Earth as Sphere?

This brings us, finally, to a phenomenon typical of contact zones in the north and west: colonists and sailors had to pay close attention to the nature of the world and its changes. Charismatic specialists also depended for their success on their observations of nature.[169] Empedocles of Akragas (c. 495–435 BCE), one of the most renowned Pythagorean seers, doctors, and preachers, was the author of a didactic poem 'On Nature' as well as one on 'Purifications'.[170] His cosmology was influenced by environmental conditions in Sicily. Pythagoras connected his ideas about the soul with a particular interest in the order of the world. His Samian background, the Phocaean foundation of Elea (Velia), the centre of Eleatic philosophy, and the voyages of the Crotonian physicians all point to a continuous exchange of knowledge and experience between east and west. This was also the precondition for a ground-breaking discovery made by Greek scholars at the end of the sixth century BCE.

Drawing on Babylonian-Hittite models, Anaximander of Miletus (c. 610–547 BCE) had used the expanded geographical horizon, travel reports, and descriptions of the coastline to construct a circular map of the entire surface of the earth (*ges periodos*).[171] It encompassed almost all the Mediterranean rim to the Strait of Gibraltar and was divided by the Mediterranean and Black Seas into two roughly equal halves: Europe occupied the northern semicircle, Asia the southern one; Libya was imagined as part of Asia. The entire ecumene was no longer surrounded by an oceanic river, as in Homer, but by an 'outer' sea. The raised edges of the earth's disc delimited it beyond the ecumene and prevented it from overflowing.[172]

Anaximander's construction was not designed to provide practical guidance, and unlike early Chinese maps of the world, his efforts served no administrative or political purpose. His goals were theoretical in nature: he wanted to grasp the earth as a harmonious structure (by the standards of oriental-Milesian geometry) and make it the object of calculations.

In his view, the discoid earth formed the surface of a cylinder. The pressure of the surrounding air caused it to float in the middle of a spherical universe, vaulted by the semicircular celestial sphere.[173] If the universe and planetary orbits were spherical—an idea Anaximander may have borrowed from the Near East (Babylon)—then it was only natural to assume by analogy that the earth was also a sphere.[174] The argument for the spherical form of the heavens, based on the visible movement of the stars, likewise applied to the spherical form of the earth.

What led Pythagoras, or perhaps one of his students (Archytas), to take this last step was not so much empirical observation—this would come later—as the endeavour to comprehend the earth as the most harmonious

Image 3 Arimaspe in battle with griffin (red-figure vase, fourth century BCE). The battle of the Arimaspi with the gold-guarding griffins was a popular subject in ancient art, especially in fourth-century Attic vase painting. The griffin is a hybrid creature with the body of a winged lion and the head of an eagle (see p. 90). The *Arimaspeia* of Aristeas, along with archaeological evidence such as the Kerch vases from Athens, named after the northern Black Sea site where they were mostly found, show battles with griffins and hark back to Asian-Siberian mythic traditions. Credit: Wikimedia Commons.

possible geometrical figure. The earth *had* to be spherical because the sphere was the most perfect geometrical body. This idea may have arisen from eastern models that represented the earth as a dice or square.[175] The Pythagoreans' interest in the earth's shape, and their thesis that this was spherical, may relate to the significance that the master's later students, at least, ascribed to number as the basis for cosmogony. Perhaps this thesis somehow arose with their efforts to calculate the earth's surface.

The imperial writer Diogenes Laertius (c. 200 CE) refers to a different context. According to him, Parmenides, a philosopher from the Phocaean colony of Elea who stood close to the Pythagoreans (mid-fifth century BCE), claimed to have been 'the first to declare that the earth is spherical (*sphairoiedes*) and is situated at the centre of the universe'.[176] If this assertion is true and Parmenides did not simply have in mind Anaximander's circular conic section, then his argument rested not on geometrical-philosophical speculations but on physical considerations: dense elements in the cosmos congregate in the middle, which explains why the earth floats at the centre.[177] Astonishingly, none of the sources cites the expected evidence that the earth is spherical, the empirical observations that would have been familiar to any mariner or coast dweller: how the water curves away when a

Image 4 Marriage of Protis and Gyptis. This painting by Joanny Rave (1827–1887) depicts the key scene in the foundation myth of Massalia, as recorded by the Romanized Gaul Pompeius Trogus in the first century BCE (see p. 96). In the style of nineteenth-century salon painting, the Greeks are shown entering the scene on a stage of white sand, set against the dark blue sea. The encounter with the gleaming white princess is presented with a certain romanticized pathos. The reality would have been far more prosaic. Credit: Bridgeman Images.

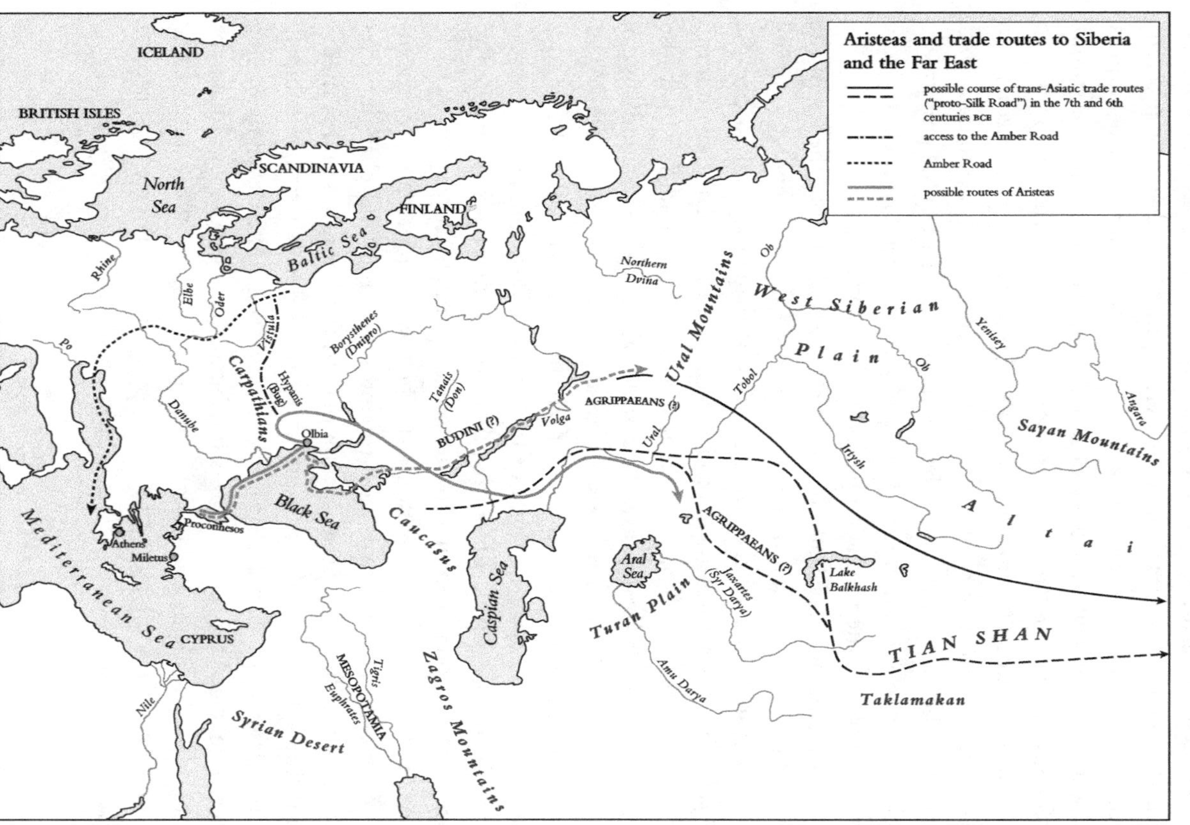

Map 4 Credit: Rudolf Hungreder/Klett-Cotta.

ship sails over the horizon, the shift in constellations when the observer's standpoint changes, or the circular shadow cast by the earth in a lunar eclipse. These explanations appear only a century later, in Aristotle—which, given the fragmentary state of the surviving material, does not preclude Parmenides having known about them. Without naming their sources, philosophers may well have drawn on such familiar observations as stimuli for further-reaching reflections that culminated, via interim solutions such as the idea of a trough-shaped basin, in the thesis of a spherical earth. From the end of the fifth century onward, it was a fixed, if not always uncontested, element in the Greek worldview. Found in no other part of the premodern world, it forms a continuum in a tradition of knowledge that stretches from antiquity through the mediaeval period to the modern age.

The scholars of Asia Minor, by contrast, long held to the theory of the earth's discoid shape, even if this gave them headaches when accounting for the constellations of the sun and stars. Perhaps they did so because the *poleis* in Asia Minor stood in closer contact to the great civilizations of the east, which never accepted that the earth was round. This may also explain why they tried to answer questions about the origin and laws of the material world with recourse to wisdom literature and cosmologies, but not to eschatological promises of salvation and a moral code. In addition, the strongly empirical bent of Ionian *historia* was eminently compatible with the disc form, which may have struck them as better suited to 'cartographic' representation. On one crucial point, however, they saw eye to eye with their western counterparts: they were all searching for meaningful order in a world that was growing ever larger and changing ever more quickly. This search gave rise not only to Pythagorean number theory and natural-philosophical arguments about the forces generating change in the universe; it also drove their attempts to organize their ever-increasing knowledge about the world and its inhabitants into geographical patterns. Without the broadening of horizons beyond the limits of the known, and without a constant willingness to make contact with foreign ethnic groups, these developments would not have been possible.

3

Beyond the Mediterranean

Carthage and Persia Explore Africa and India

THE CALL OF THE SOUTH

CARTHAGINIANS ON THE WEST AFRICAN COAST

The Rise of the Persians and Expanding Carthaginian Influence in the West

In the mid-sixth century BCE, two political changes—one originating in the eastern Mediterranean, the other in the southwest—gave renewed impetus to global exploration. In 553, Cyrus II (the Great) had usurped the Median throne in the Iranian highlands and united his kingdom of Anshan in ancient Persia (modern Fars in southwestern Iran) with that of the Medians. Thus, the Persian Empire was born. It would set the political coordinates in the Near East and the eastern Mediterranean for more than two centuries to come. Having barely taken the throne, Cyrus launched a military campaign directed first at the kingdom of Urartu and then at the Lydian kingdom of Croesus. Following his conquest of the kingdom, his generals stood at the gates of the Greek *poleis*. At an assembly of Greeks from Asia Minor convened in 546 BCE, Bias of Priene is said to have urged them to pack their valuables and flee for Sardinia. Only a few followed his advice, including the Phocaeans. When the Persians began invading their city, they sailed with their families first to Chios and then towards Italy. They eventually settled on Corsica (Kyrnos), joining the colony of Alalia founded twenty years before.[1]

Yet the times were changing in the west as well. Around 600, the Carthaginians seem to have used Gades' request for help as well as Tyros' loss of power to play an active role on the Spanish Atlantic coast and target Phocaean privateers. This objective converged with the interests of the Etruscans, who had been pushed out of Provence by the Massalians (see above, p. 106). Phocaean pirates were also disrupting maritime trade between Carthage and Etruria along the eastern Sardinian coast—reason enough for the affected powers to form an alliance. Between 540 and 535 BCE fighting broke out between the Carthaginian-Etruscan fleet and Phocaean forces off Alalia. The Phocaeans suffered such heavy losses that they were forced to abandon their colony on Corsica and retreat to Rhegion and southern Italian Elia (Velia). This allowed the Carthaginians to establish outposts on Corsica and Sardinia to protect their trade routes; within a few decades, Carthaginian commanders had carved out a sphere of influence in western Sicily.

The West African Coast and the Nile Question

By the end of the sixth century, the Carthaginians had emerged victorious from their rivalry with the Phocaeans. Only Massalia could hold its own.[2] At some point in the second half of the sixth century, a certain Euthymenes of Massalia navigated the Atlantic 'by way of the outer sea'. Perhaps he first sailed along Brittany in search of the Oestriminic Isles (probably the marshlands of Grand Brière near Saint Nazaire or the Scilly Isles off the English southwest coast) into the North Atlantic; he then returned to the Strait of Gibraltar before making for the west African coast. Here he arrived at the mouth of a great river, probably the Senegal.[3] Euthymenes thought he had discovered the Nile estuary.

This initially baffling claim makes sense once we bear in mind that many contemporary scholars puzzled over the Nile's upper reaches and internal connections. Some believed that it was linked to the Indus, while others looked for its origin in the western Ocean.[4] Euthymenes clearly shared this latter view and believed he had solved another, fiercely debated problem: the cause of the annual flooding of the Nile in Egypt.[5] His answer was as simple as it was startling: according to the few references to his travel report (*periplus*) that have come down to us, he observed that in the estuary of the river he identified as the Nile (in the Atlantic), fresh water flowed out into the sea so long as the wind was blowing from inland. When the land winds abated and the sea breezes picked up, the water retreated or was thrown back.[6] Because he posited a direct link between the mouths of the Nile in Egypt and on the Atlantic coast—Euthymenes pointed out that the wildlife on the Atlantic side resembled that in Egypt[7]—the Nile inundations had to be caused by the wind-influenced currents in the Atlantic. Some take this to be the first ever attempt to explain the tides.[8]

Such observations did not just have scientific merit. A possible river connection between the Nile delta in Egypt and the African Atlantic coast presented unimagined strategic opportunities. Suddenly it seemed possible to travel from Egypt through Libya to the coasts of west Africa, with their abundant deposits of gold, and from there access the riches of Tartessos and the Atlantic Tin Isles. This would have dramatically shortened the circumnavigation of Africa supposedly once undertaken by the Phoenicians. It is no coincidence that around thirty years later, the Persians (under Xerxes) also sought to chart a route to west Africa after conquering the land of the pharaohs. A certain Sataspes sailed from Egypt over the Mediterranean to the Strait of Gibraltar, navigated a considerable stretch of the west African coastline until at least southern Morocco, then returned after a months-long voyage; the 'dwarfish race' he encountered there, 'who made a dress from the palm tree', has been speculatively identified with a tribe from Senegal or Guinea.[9] The (official) objective was apparently to circumnavigate Libya, yet here too, a subsidiary aim of the expedition may have been to clarify the Nile question. This would explain why the voyage lasted several months. Perhaps Herodotus mixed the leader up with another Persian called Mago, said to have circumnavigated Africa around the same time.[10]

Carthaginian Expansion in the North Atlantic—Himilco's Expedition

It would be rash to take all this as evidence of a race to chart and control west African coastal waters. Yet as the tectonic plates of power shifted in the Mediterranean, this area clearly attracted increased attention from those states and cities that (like the Persian Empire) were driven by ideological or political imperatives to secure transregional links, or that (like Massalia) relied for their prosperity and independence on developing new maritime routes to valuable minerals. As one such actor, Carthage had a keen interest in keeping competitors out of the waters beyond the Strait of Gibraltar. By the 520s, it had consolidated so many bases in the western Mediterranean and on the Spanish Atlantic coast around Tartessos and Gibraltar that Punic hegemony over coastal zones and maritime trade routes appeared within grasp. At the beginning of the sixth century, the Carthaginians thus imposed maritime restrictions on Etruscan Rome encompassing Sardinia, north Africa, and probably Spain. The clauses of the treaty indicate that Carthage aimed to establish a kind of monopoly on trade with the north African coasts and Sardinia.[11]

In keeping with the logic of this development, the Carthaginians tried to stop pirates and merchants passing through the Strait of Gibraltar and to strengthen their own influence in Guadalquivir. In addition, they sought access to the source areas of Atlantic tin to make up for the metal's absence in northern Africa. Around the same time as the voyage of Euthymenes (c. 525 BCE) or in reaction to his Atlantic expedition, the Carthaginian Himilco set out from the Mediterranean via Tartessos to the northern Atlantic in search of the 'land of the Oestriminians'.[12] His destination may have been the tin mines of Galicia and Cornwall. Himilco seems to have gathered information about the northwestern Atlantic coastline and reached a large island near southern England given the name holy, *iera*: today's Ireland. The duration of four months suggests that he invested considerable time into building up a mercantile network.[13]

Hanno's *Periplus* on the West African Coast

Even as they were expanding in the western Mediterranean and on the Spanish Atlantic coast, the Carthaginians began extending their influence on the Moroccan coast. Still in the sixth century, they secured the permission of local Berber princes to establish the colonies of Tingis, Lixus, Rusibis, and Mogador. The *periplus* of the naval commander Hanno, known only from a single manuscript preserved in Heidelberg, details the course of one such expedition along the African Atlantic coast.

Around 500 BCE, the manuscript's author offered a Greek audience a selection of Punic original documents in a relatively free translation. The first part is based on a Punic inscription or written tablet from the sanctuary of Baal Hammon in Carthage. In the Greek version, it is headed *periplus*. *Periplus* means 'circumnavigation' and denotes a compendium of the kind of information that might come in handy for mariners sailing along the coast: safe places to drop anchor, topographical details, observations about the natives. Ordinarily, sailors conveyed such information by word of mouth. There is debate over whether the *periplus* in written form has Greek and/or ancient Near Eastern roots. By using the term, at any rate, the translator of the Punic original wanted to make clear to his Greek readers that this was an officially commissioned expeditionary report, just as the *periplus* of Euthymenes was most likely authorized by the council of Massalia. Accordingly, the text begins by naming the expeditionary leader and the official objective of establishing colonies beyond the Pillars of Heracles. This information would not have been included had the sole criterion been nautical relevance. The original inscription was probably composed and displayed by the leader or the relevant authorities after the expedition had come to an end.[14]

The second part reproduces a literary commentary or supplement in *periplus* form composed by Hanno himself. He describes the journey farther south along the African coast after the colonies had been planted. Here Greek motifs, poetic turns of phrase, and ornamental flourishes accumulate, prompting some to see it as 'nothing more than a conflation of ancient myths' with utopian elements.[15] The use of mythic elements is not necessarily a sign of inauthenticity, however; it can serve to connect the unknown with the known. Accordingly, the translator of the Hanno text may well have embellished the journey into uncharted waters and territories with literary elements that accorded with his readers' expectations and made it easier for them to follow along. This part should only be dismissed as a fabrication, then, if it is clearly incompatible with the historical, geographical, and nautical context.[16]

Doubts about the text's authenticity draw primarily on nautical objections. It was thus believed that a return journey from Senegal to Morocco was impossible against the prevailing north winds on the 850 km stretch from Cape Juby (southern Morocco opposite the Canaries) to Cap Blanc (Mauritania), an argument also advanced against the Necho expedition.[17] In fact, Phoenician ships fitted out with oars and sails could sail against the wind.[18] Moreover, coastal breezes could be used against the trade winds,[19] while even critics concede that when headwinds and counter-currents proved too strong, it was possible to continue overland on one of the west African caravan routes with the help of native guides until more favourable maritime conditions presented themselves.[20] It is unclear whether the ships were left behind, dismantled, and/or transported on ox-drawn carts. Perhaps the geographical distribution of petroglyphs in southern Morocco and Mauritania points to chariot routes connected with the coast. Depictions of ox-drawn chariots suggest that they could be used to transport moderately heavy loads.[21] Transporting prefabricated ship parts, even through the desert, was a practice known since earliest antiquity.[22] The tale of the Argonauts in Pindar's version, according to which Jason and his companions spent twelve days carrying their ship on their shoulders (the distance between the Red Sea and Lake Tritonis), may indicate that contemporaries would not have dismissed such overland transport on African shores as intrinsically impossible.[23]

The enterprise's dimensions likewise seem unique only at first glance. Hanno supposedly set sail from Carthage with a fleet of sixty pentecontters and 30,000 men and women.[24] The Phocaeans also took women and children with them on their penteconters when their city was besieged by the Persians, while a little later they confronted the Carthaginians and Etruscans with sixty units and planted colonies in familiar regions of the Tyrrhenian Sea.[25] Admittedly, in the sixth or fifth century the Carthaginians were not under attack by a foreign power like the Persians, yet in 480 BCE they suffered a painful defeat at the hands of the Syracusans at Himera when attempting to expand their influence in Sicily. Some believe that this 'emergency confronting the Carthaginian state' speaks against them mounting an African expedition so soon after Himera. Yet the same argument can be turned on its head: precisely because the Carthaginians risked losing access to the trade links and agricultural riches of Sicily, it was only natural for them to investigate alternative regions where no land-based military resistance could be anticipated, where they already had a foothold, and where new sources of wealth beckoned, especially gold. That is exactly what the Carthaginians did two centuries later after being defeated by Rome in the First Punic War for Sicily, and a comparable constellation of military setbacks on land had prompted Pharaoh Necho to concentrate his energies on exploring the South Sea and circumnavigating Africa (see above, p. 102). Why should similar circumstances not have led the Carthaginians to push farther into west African waters, especially as, after Himera, they demonstrably redirected their military efforts from the Mediterranean to the Libyan interior and conquered parts of Tunisia?[26]

Planting Colonies, Exploring the Senegal River

According to Hanno's report, the expedition's official goal was to plant colonies, which in reality also meant 'recolonizing' older Phoenician settlements.[27] As always in antiquity, these were located not far from existing settlements (in Morocco) in known coastal areas.[28] Two days after passing through the Strait of Gibraltar, Thymiaterion was founded at the mouth of the Sebou River. The ships then sailed farther west, offered sacrifices to Poseidon at Cape Soloeis, and continued for a day past a lagoon teeming with wildlife (including elephants). The colonies of Karikon Teichos, Gytte, Akra, Melitta, and Arambys were then planted. Their precise location cannot be determined with any certainty (Karikon Teichos is frequently identified with Mogador),[29] although as a rule they would have been found at river mouths in a zone stretching from Cape Cantin in the north to the ancient river Lixus, today's Oued Draa, in the south.[30] This area is contiguous to the Moroccan colonies.

With the planting of Arambys, the expedition's official mission had been accomplished in its essentials. Its next moves were aimed at securing the surrounding territory and forging trade links. To that end, Hanno sailed up the Lixus with a reduced flotilla, or perhaps just a flagship. 'On its banks', the *periplus* reports, 'a wandering people, the Lixites, were pasturing their flocks, with whom we remained some time, becoming friends'.[31] The Lixites may have been Berbers; Carthage had been in close contact with them for some time. They later served as interpreters and guides, another argument for assuming that Hanno was moving in accustomed latitudes.[32]

The Carthaginians would have learned from the Lixites that the 'Ethiopians' at the source of the Lixus were inhospitable, that their country was surrounded by high mountains, and that it was 'full of wild beasts'. They lived alongside strange cave-dwellers 'who are fleeter of foot than horses'.[33] The *troglodytes* are frequently identified with Pygmies, known to the Greeks since the days of Homer and Hesiod; some think the name refers to Libyan-Nubian tribes.[34] We should not imagine the Carthaginians passing through unoccupied territory as they made their way inland. Archaeological finds show that around the same time Hanno was making his voyage, iron-producing settlements were established on the middle reaches of the Senegal River that were most likely connected to the Atlantic coast and Morocco.[35] Although Hanno's report contains no direct references to this culture, it is clear that the expedition operated in an environment that made such contacts likely, and that the Carthaginians were interested in investigating foreign peoples and their products. Why else would they have brought along Lixite interpreters?

After sailing along the desert shore for two days to the south and another day to the east, the Carthaginians spotted a small island in a gulf. Here they established the settlement of Kerne, probably the islet of Herne in the Rio de Oro bay. Having entered unknown territory, Hanno was understandably concerned about the safety of a coastal base. As in the Mediterranean, he instead chose an island that offered some protection from assault while still lying close enough to the mainland to allow trading contacts to be made.[36] The reference to Kerne's location near the delta of a great river called Chretes suggests the hope of finding not just fresh water but also an inland route. Chretes is generally identified with the Senegal.[37] Hanno would thus have reached the point that Euthymenes had identified thirty years earlier as the mouth of the Nile. A reconnaissance journey upriver brought him to a lake with three islands. Hanno needed a full day to reach the end of the bay, 'which was overhung by great mountains'.[38] There, natives clad in animal skins threw stones at the ships and prevented them from landing. Because the outlook for trade looked so bleak, he changed course and returned to Kerne via a tributary of the Chretes (evidently the Senegal River).[39]

Gold and Other Products

Hanno's report is unmistakably embellished with epic motifs; the stone-throwing, pelt-wearing natives, for example, recall the Cyclops adventure from the *Odyssey*. Yet this does nothing to detract from the reality of the voyage of discovery and its objective. Like the Massalian Euthymenes, Hanno steered for the Senegal River and journeyed relatively far inland. Tellingly, he also mentions that the 'deeper and larger river' was 'teeming with crocodiles and hippopotamuses'.[40] This information, which is irrelevant for trading purposes, recalls Euthymenes' statement that the animals he came across in the river he discovered resembled those of the Nile. Clearly, the question of the Nile's western upper reaches and its connection to Oceanus was discussed not just in Greek circles (Massalia) but in Carthage as well. We will see later that even the Persians had an interest in this question (see below, p. 146), and perhaps Sataspes was instructed accordingly when he was sent to the west African coast.[41]

Carthage's main priority was probably finding pathways to the interior. The reference to elephants may suggest that they were looking for a new source of ivory to meet strong demand from the Mediterranean, not to mention other special items and animals (monkeys).[42] Even more importance was attached to minerals: the prime attractions in west Africa were copper from Akjoujt in Mauritania, tin from the Jos Plateau in Nigeria, and especially gold, assumed to be found by following the 'gold route' up the Senegal.[43] Precisely the absence of gold from Hanno's report points to its value; discoverers and traders tended to keep their lips sealed about their most precious booty. At any rate, Kerne soon became a centre for the gold trade; one Greek author writing in the fourth century BCE characterizes its inhabitants as rich in gold.[44] Herodotus confirms that the Carthaginians acquired gold on Africa's west coast, and he shows how it happened: 'To this [place on the west African coast] they come and unload their cargo; then having laid it in order by the waterline they go aboard their ships and light a smoking fire. The people of the country see the smoke, and coming to the sea they lay down gold to pay for the cargo and withdraw away from the wares. Then the Carchedonians [= Carthaginians] disembark and examine the gold; if it seems to them a fair price for their cargo, they take it and go their ways; but if not, they go aboard again and wait, and the people come back and add more till the shipmen are satisfied'.[45]

This is the earliest account of the 'silent barter' practised on the west African coast until the nineteenth century. Hanno may already have resorted to it, given that the Lixite interpreters he took on board could not communicate with all the natives they encountered. A fourth-century *periplus* confirms that the Phoenicians, having arrived in Kerne with their ships, transported perfume, glass, and Attic pottery on smaller boats to the mainland on the opposing shore, where the natives were waiting with deer, lion and leopard skins, as well as elephant tusks.[46] Although this trade may not yet have gotten underway in Hanno's day, his report still indicates the breadth of possible products that the Carthaginians hoped to acquire. It casually mentions that the Carthaginians found large quantities of sedge (or reeds) in a lagoon half a day's journey from Cape Soleis. Sedge was used in the ancient world for making incense, especially by the Phoenicians; the report goes on to note that Hanno sailed along a 'fragrant' coastline. The Phoenicians were famous for trading incense, which in the eighth century they imported primarily from Syria and Israel to Mediterranean coastal areas, shipping it on from there.[47] Under Persian rule, Phoenician cities like Tyre had lost their monopoly on the incense trade, so it is hardly surprising that the Carthaginians showed a keen interest in the plant as they explored the west African coast.

No less famous than the Phoenician incense trade was their trade in timber for shipbuilding, housing, and temple construction, as attested in

Old Testament references to the assistance the Tyrians gave Solomon. The Phoenicians themselves made high-quality furniture, using a kind of wood known for its pleasant aroma and marbled appearance. When Hanno set sail from Kerne and continued south along the coast, his ships anchored after twelve days on a shore from where a large, thickly wooded mountain range extended into the interior. 'The wood'—according to § 12 of the *periplus*—'was aromatic, and of various kinds'. This could refer to the citrus tree, which was widespread in ancient northern Africa.[48]

Besides the prospect of gold, the voyages thus clearly promised access to a range of valuable plants and animals in semi-familiar regions. But what drove the Carthaginians farther south on a twelve-day journey that offered no new commodities and no further trade connections? Why did they venture ever farther into uncharted waters if they had already accomplished their mission to plant colonies and search for precious products?

A Western Route around Africa?

Even in antiquity, there was speculation that the final stage of the expedition aimed to find out whether the circumnavigation of Africa that the Phoenicians had once supposedly undertaken from the east could be made from the opposite direction, despite the less favourable winds and currents.[49] Now, at the latest, the ancient mariners pushed into the unknown, and the references in the text to strange sights and natural phenomena proliferate accordingly. All this does not necessarily make the report fictitious. In line with ancient tradition, the captain of a long-distance expedition was expected to varnish his tale in this way, yet real places could still be made out beneath the mythical overlay. Having found the aromatic trees and taken on fresh water, the Carthaginians thus sail down the coast for five days to arrive at a bay their interpreters call 'the Horn of the West'. Here they again come across a large island with a saltwater lake, which in turn surrounds another island. At night they see many fires burning from the island and hear pipes, cymbals, drums, and 'confused shouts'. The sailors panic and take flight on the advice of their 'soothsayers'.[50]

Island adventures are part of the stock repertoire of epic narrative, yet what is striking here is that the Carthaginians do not seek adventure and intrepid exploits for their own sake. They wisely avoid taking risks and continue on their way. The reference to the saltwater lake is quite prosaic and reflects any captain's natural interest in possible sources of fresh water. What probably stands behind it is again the search for profitable natural products, in this case salt. In a different context, Herodotus refers to Carthaginian information about a lake on the Libyan coast where native girls extract gold dust from the mud with the help of pitch-covered bird feathers.[51] He was probably reinterpreting news from gold-rich regions in west Africa. As late as the nineteenth century, the renowned Africanist Mungo Park was still reporting that natives transported gold along the Niger in carriages made from feathers.[52] If these tall tales are compared with what Hanno writes about the sounds that reached the Carthaginian camp from the island, the epic embellishments are far less conspicuous: no monsters, only unknown songs, such as those heard by many explorers on African shores. We thus have little cause to doubt the veracity of his report on the island (in the Bight of Benin?).[53]

More important for understanding the mission is the fact that Hanno spent twenty days following the coast to the east rather than sailing farther south. From this he concluded that he was within reach of the Erythraean Sea. This confidence encouraged him to keep going. He sailed past 'a burning country full of fragrance, from which great torrents of fire flowed down to the sea. But the land could not be come at for the heat'.[54] The terrified Carthaginians supposedly hastened to quit these shores as well, although they may have been familiar with the phenomenon. In Sicily there was a fire- and ash-spewing mountain (Etna) that covered the land and sky with smoke whenever it erupted. But perhaps the Carthaginians were seeing fires lit by natives to drive out game on their hunts. Four days later, they saw a 'lofty fire [. . .] which seemed to touch the stars'; by day it proved to be a high mountain. According to their interpreters, the volcano was called 'Chariot of the Gods'.[55] To this day, natives call the 4075 m high Mount Cameroon 'Mountain of the Gods'.[56]

Ambition drove them on. After three days they arrived at a bay called 'the Horn of the South'. There they again spied a large island containing a lake in which there was a smaller island. What they had only heard on the first island they now saw with their own eyes: savage people, mostly women, covered from head to toe in hair. Because it was daytime and the creatures were known to the interpreters—they called them 'gorillas'—the Carthaginians set off in pursuit, caught three unfortunate women, and killed and flayed them, intending to exhibit their skins back home; the men escaped capture through their swiftness of foot. The later Roman author

Pliny writes that two ape skins were kept in Carthage, although not in the temple of Melqart but in that of Juno (Tanit).[57] Perhaps he was alluding to an economic interest in pelts. More clearly here than before, however, it is the discoverer's pride that drives the voyage to its climax and conclusion: 'We did not sail any further, our provisions failing us'.[58]

The truth was more complicated. If the Carthaginians had indeed reached Mount Cameroon at the Bight of Biafra,[59] they would have noticed that the coast now curved southward rather than continuing in a more or less straight line to the east, as they would have expected from their knowledge of the Phoenician circumnavigation and their preconceived ideas about Libyan geography. This convinced Hanno that a continuation of the journey to the Erythraean Sea was beyond his capacities. This, too, was a finding worth bringing home.

THE ROAD TO TIMBUKTU

CARTHAGE AND THE SAHARA

Trans-Saharan Caravan Routes

Around the same time that the Carthaginians were exploring the west African coast and river systems, they were intensifying their contacts with the African interior from the north. The widespread view that the Sahara is an impenetrable, deadly barrier of sand only partially applies in early antiquity, when wetter climatic conditions prevailed. In fact, 'only' a quarter of the world's greatest desert is covered in sand (9.4 million square kilometres), the rest consisting mostly of stone and scree. Anyone who has crossed the Sahara will know that the desert is (and was) full of plant and animal life. In the third millennium BCE, it could be crossed along the semi-arid zones of the Hoggar and Tibesti massif, especially in winter, when the air was cooler and summer rains still filled the waterholes. Mules, horses, and probably also oxen (for shorter distances) were used for transportation. Petroglyphs suggest that horse- and ox-drawn 'war chariots' were known in the Sahara (perhaps a legacy of the Libyan 'Sea Peoples'), with ox-drawn chariots predominating in petroglyphs from the eastern Sahara (see above, p. 129).[60] Oxen, at least, could pull heavy loads. Horses were prestige objects involved in slave hunts; better-off travellers would also have used them at certain stages on the desert crossing.[61] From the distribution of petroglyphs, some scholars have reconstructed a network of horse-drawn carts ('chariot tracks') that extended along two great axes from Morocco and Tripoli (along the Hoggar Massif), one running to the Niger Basin near Gao, the other farther eastward to Lake Chad from Leptis Magna. Camels, known in Egypt and Arabia in the first millennium BCE, probably only played a secondary role as transport animals.[62]

From the first millennium, at any rate, ecological conditions in the desert, knowledge of trans-Saharan routes, and transport adapted to the harsh environment made possible a sporadic exchange among semi-arid zones in the Mediterranean north (which were suited to farming and animal husbandry), the land of the Nile to the east, and the Lake Chad area and Niger river system to the south (equivalent to the Nile). From the seventh century on, migrants probably also trekked south from the Near East through the Sudan. Crucially, around the same time the Carthaginians were launching missions to explore the west African coast and the Libyan desert from north Africa, urban settlement structures with complex social stratification were emerging in the Lake Chad area at the onset of the sub-Saharan Ice Age in the form of the so-called Sao civilization (bordering the *firki* floodplains south of Lake Chad) and the fortified settlement of Zilum. The emergence of these civilizations was once attributed to trade relations with the north and changes in climate. Today, some scholars explain the breakthrough to urban culture with the impact of groups emigrating from the Near East following the collapse of the Assyrian Empire, and perhaps also with a retreat from Berber slave hunts in the northern Chad basin. Berber expansion may likewise have led to a transformation of the proto-urban Tichitt civilization in southeast Mauretania in the mid-first millennium BCE.[63] The iron-producing settlements of Walaldé on the middle Senegal, which were connected to the Atlantic coast and Morocco and sourced iron via networks of semi-nomadic cultures, date to roughly the same period.

Along with the southern spread of the Berbers, news of the emergence or further development of such iron-producing cultures may have been an important spur for trans-Saharan trade. In however sporadic a fashion, caravan routes now connected at least two urban points of contact in fertile regions of the south and north as well as centres of iron production on the Niger (Dia Shoma) and Senegal (Walaldé). While a trader would very rarely have traversed the *entire* route, transportable 'luxury goods' (amazonite and carnelian) and technologies (the chariot as prestige object, for example) circulated via integrated subnetworks, with the Fezzan, home to the Garamantes, acting as a hub.[64]

Evidence can be found in Herodotus that knowledge of this system had reached the Mediterranean.[65] He splits north Africa into three zones: the inhabited coast, the region of wild beasts farther inland, and the waterless desert farther south; a ridge of sand extends between the second and third zones, from Thebes in Egypt to the Pillars of Heracles.[66] There, salt hills containing freshwater springs punctuate the parched landscape at intervals of about ten days' journey. Native tribes live around these hills. Travellers journeying on a line from east to west would first encounter the Ammonians, ten days' journey from Egyptian Thebes; after another ten days, they would meet an unknown tribe at the oasis of Augila. The Garamantes, Atarantes, and Atlantes come next, all at ten-day intervals. More tribes live beyond the Atlantes, but Herodotus does not know what they are called.[67]

Such lists are familiar from archaic epics, with the difference that the epic combines mythic and real names and offers few topographic details. Herodotus supplements this principle—in him, too, tribes have marvellous traits (no weapons, no names, no dreams)—with more concrete information from other sources and itineraries,[68] just as he had done when describing the trade route to Siberia. The ten days' journey between tribes corresponds to the distance typically travelled by a trans-Saharan camel caravan between two oases, including in later periods. Assuming a daily march of 45–50 km, camping on open ground at night, a longer stay in an oasis was needed every tenth day to replenish supplies, take on fresh water, and rest the animals.[69]

Herodotus describes these oases—as he does north African flora and fauna in general[70]—with considerable accuracy, occasionally mentioning date palms as well as salt hills flowing with spring water. Some can be identified with a degree of certainty when the information provided by Herodotus is collated with later Arab sources. The easternmost, the first on the route from Thebes to the Ammonians, was the Siwa Oasis, located around 560 km west of the Nile. The next—explicitly named by Herodotus—was the oasis of Augila (the modern Awgila or Awjila in the Libyan desert[71]), while farther southwest came most likely the Oasis of Ghat. After that, the route clearly did not lead to the Atlas Mountains in Morocco but continued southwest to the Hoggar Massif (see map).[72] The seemingly incongruous reference to the salt hills documents one of the most important Saharan trade products: along with gold and slaves, salt was a staple of the trans-Saharan caravan trade.[73]

The Expedition of the Nasamones

What exactly were the destinations linked by this caravan route, and was there any connection to Carthaginian exploration policy? Here, too, Herodotus gives us a clue in a tale he heard in Cyrene. The larger context concerns the geography of the world and its seas. The author addresses the question of where the sources of the Nile might lie. Here, as on other occasions, Herodotus uses information acquired second-hand to defend his own worldview by confronting it with differing opinions; it may therefore be assumed that he tailored the story to suit his purposes. Yet this leaves its core message unaffected, and it is therefore generally assumed to be authentic.[74]

According to the story, a group of Cyrenians visiting the Ammon oracle in Siwa heard the following from the native king. Five men from the tribe of Nasamones (on the Libyan Mediterranean coast) were once selected 'to go and explore the Libyan desert, to find out if they could see more than had ever been seen before'. Amply supplied with food and water, they came south to 'the part which is infested by wild animals. Next, they started to travel in a westerly direction through the desert'. Because the Nasamones—as Herodotus reports elsewhere[75]—regularly visited the oasis of Augila to gather dates, the young men may initially have made for this destination so that, equipped with chariots and horses, they could join up with the main caravan route from Egypt.

They passed through the stations that Herodotus had enumerated in ten-day intervals: 'After they had crossed a great deal of sandy desert, they at last, after many days, saw trees growing on a plain. They approached the trees and tried to pick the fruit that was growing on them'.[76] According to Herodotus' list of oases and tribes, corroborated by later information about trans-Saharan caravan routes, the Nasamones must have turned southwest from Augila and arrived after ten days at the well-watered Fezzan Basin.[77] The Fezzan was (and is) one of the most fertile regions in the Sahara and one of the most important caravan junctions. The people Herodotus calls the Garamantes settled in Wadi al-Ajal (c. 1000 km south of Tripoli) near Zinkekra. From around 500 BCE, they grew wheat, barley, grapes, and dates with the help of an ingenious irrigation system that tapped the groundwater (foggara system).[78] The oasis described by Herodotus as 'a third hill of salt, with water and a great many fruit-bearing palm-trees', can be located east of modern Sebha (Sabha); based on the ten-day march of around 500 km, it is most likely Fuqaha.[79] When he goes on to note that the Garamantes would 'put a layer of soil on top of the salt and so have land to cultivate',[80] he describes a method for neutralizing saline soil that is practised to this day by oasis-dwellers, who take fresh alluvium from wadis and standing pools and scatter it on the ground. Herodotus clearly knew this region 'south of the Nasamones'[81] and its inhabitants so well because a second caravan route—still operating in modern times—ran from the Garamantes in the Fezzan all the way to the coastal land of the 'lotus-eaters', mostly identified with eastern Tripolitania. According to Herodotus, the journey lasted thirty days. The German explorer Gustav Nachtigal was the first European to take the route in 1869; he took exactly thirty days to reach Murzuk in the Fezzan.[82]

Timbuktu and the Niger

If the previous combinations hold water, then the Nasamones would be situated on the so-called Bornus Road, used from ancient times until the nineteenth century by traders making their way from Tripoli to central Africa. It terminated in Lake Chad, and there is much to suggest that the Nasamones did not, as Herodotus assumed on the basis of a faulty geography, continue farther west to Morocco and the Strait of Gibraltar—such a route did not exist in antiquity and would have led through trackless desert—but turned southwest to traverse the plateau between the Hoggar and Tibesti Mountains. The Oasis of Ghat on the Hoggar's western slopes, the land of the Atarantes, could have been their first stopover after ten days' travel (around 500 km); the next was perhaps the Oasis of Aïr (Asben).[83]

If we identify this last station with the land of the Atlantes at the Hoggar Massif, then this is where Herodotus' geographical information dried up. Entering this unnamed zone, the caravan kept threading its way through oases at the usual ten-day intervals.[84] 'They were set upon by small men of less than normal human stature, who captured them and took them away. The two groups—the Nasamones and their guides—could not understand each other's language at all'.[85] The 'small men' are generally identified with Pygmies, who lived farther north at the time than they do today.[86] But they could also have been black tribespeople who were less physically imposing than the Berbers.[87] 'They were taken through vast swamps and on the other side of these swamps they came to a town where everyone was the same size as their guides and had black skin. The town was on a large river, which was flowing from west to east, and in it they saw crocodiles'.[88]

The Nasamones were clearly dragged through subequatorial rainforests and swamps. But where were they taken? A common theory has them arrive at a native settlement near Lake Chad in the Bodélé Basin, surely infested by crocodiles in antiquity; the shore of Lake Chad could easily be taken for a river on account of its branching and size. This would have brought them close to the Zilum civilization (see above, p. 137).[89] A different interpretation, one that better fits the ten-day marches and the distances involved, identifies the city (*polis*) of stocky dark-skinned inhabitants with Tombouze (founded c. 500 BCE), predecessor to the celebrated Timbuktu.[90] The extensive swamps would then be the lakes and marshlands formed by the Niger near Timbuktu.[91]

The Great Goal? A Link between the Trans-Saharan Land Routes and the West African River System

Once all the clues are assembled and crosschecked against the stations named by Herodotus as well as the caravan routes known from later (Arab) times, there is much to suggest that the Niger was in fact the terminus of the Nasamones and that they did arrive at this goal.[92] In its entirety, the caravan route extended from the lower Nile Valley (near Thebes) to the Niger bend, roughly corresponding to the famous medieval route from Cairo to Timbuktu. Herodotus explicitly states that the river reached by the Nasamones was home to crocodiles and flowed from west to east. That fits the Niger, yet Herodotus clearly had something else in mind: the search for the trans-Saharan Nile, equally familiar from the *periploi* of Euthymenes and Hanno. As we have seen, Euthymenes speculated that its waters were driven inland by oceanic winds blasting from the Atlantic and thus flowed east at this time (see above, pp. 126–127). Indeed, following the return of the Nasamones, the king of the Ammonians claimed that the great river was the Nile. Herodotus appropriated this interpretation from him or the Nasamones because he was convinced of the parallel or mirror-image course of the Nile and the Danube.[93] He was not alone in making this mistake: a connection between the Niger and the Nile was still being discussed in the early nineteenth century.

There is a further connection with the Hanno expedition. Hanno had ventured far down the Senegal; its headwaters are located only a few kilometres from the upper reaches of the Niger. Early Arab geographers assumed that the Senegal and Niger formed a single river flowing from east to west; they called it the 'western Nile' or the 'Nile of the blacks'. A much-used caravan route ran from Lake Chad along the Niger to Timbuktu and then southwest to the Senegal. Northwest Africa's gold deposits were concentrated on the upper Niger. The gold trade was directed from the caravan towns of Timbuktu, Jenne, and Gao. Finding gold, or at least localizing the areas where it was mined, was surely one of the motives behind Hanno's voyage. The gold trade brought fame to the Carthaginian settlement of Kerne at the mouth of the Senegal; in the early middle ages, the Senegal was called 'river of gold'.[94]

Salt, the second important product traded on the caravan routes, also demonstrates a link with the Hanno expedition. References in the *periplus* to the lagoons on the west African coast and in the Senegal region could indicate an interest in saline water and salt harvesting.[95] That would fit the oases on the caravan route, which Herodotus describes as places with 'hillocks of salt and springs of cool, fresh water', as well as the salt mines on the route from the Fezzan.[96]

And there is a third link: according to Herodotus, the Garamantes who lived in the Fezzan and controlled trade with the African interior chased the 'troglodyte Ethiopians', the 'swiftest of foot' of all nations.[97] He was probably referring to the indigenous people of the Hoggar massif or the black tribe of the Tebu in the Tibesti Mountains. To this day, Tibesti oasis dwellers enjoy a reputation as excellent runners.[98] The Garamantes clearly carried out raids in the area and sold some of the captives as slaves while keeping others for themselves. Skeletal remains suggest that an enslaved black African population helped build the irrigation system, and perhaps also tilled the fields, while their masters devoted themselves to slave-hunting and commerce.[99] Hanno, too, had learned that 'people of various shapes' lived east of the Lixus, 'cave-dwellers, who, so the Lixites say, are fleeter of foot than horses'.[100] The authors were no doubt mixing up their topography; nonetheless, they ascertain here that the slave trade connected the west African coastal region (or the river system that drains into the Atlantic there) with the trans-Saharan caravan routes that ended in the Niger and Lake Chad.

It was this connection between west Africa and the Niger route that the Carthaginians were trying to tap from the west and north African coast.[101] Much of Herodotus' information about west Africa (and the Niger?) clearly had Carthaginian sources.[102] The Carthaginians possessed colonies not just on the west African coast but also in Tripolitania (Oea, Sabratha; Leptis Magna was planted in the seventh century),[103] a starting point for the caravan route to the Garamantes in the Fezzan and on to Lake Chad. It has often been surmised that one of the reasons for the importance of the Tripolitanian colonies lay in their role as termini for the trans-Saharan trade via the Fezzan.[104] Not by chance, the Carthaginians did their utmost to keep other powers away from this coastal region, just as they did from the Moroccan coast. Libyan inscriptions suggest a Phoenician presence in the Fezzan, while the Garamantes employed 'a method of recording their language, inspired by the Phoenician alphabet, which the Tuareg people still use today'.[105] Recent research points to the likelihood of Phoenician-Carthaginian influences on the societies of Lake Chad. Like the Phoenicians of the Levant, the Carthaginians were active (and notorious) as slave hunters and traders. It seems reasonable to assume that they used their widespread contacts, especially with the Garamantes, to supply their armies with black auxiliaries (they are mentioned in the fifth century) and their Mediterranean societies with slaves (see above, p. 101). It is not necessarily surprising that the sources are silent on this score. We encounter the same phenomenon in relation to the Portuguese in the far more copious fifteenth-century CE writings. All the same, black slaves started to appear in Mediterranean art from the sixth century BCE and were a common sight in urban cultures.[106]

The Carthaginians also traded with the Nasamones for gemstones (carbuncles), among other things.[107] A Carthaginian called Mago, who allegedly crossed the desert three times, probably took the caravan route previously used by the Nasamones from Tripolitania through the Fezzan to Timbuktu or Lake Chad. Perhaps he tried to cut into the gold trade on the Senegal and upper Niger.[108] A second route ran farther west from Algeria (Tlemcen) southwest to the Senegal and Niger Rivers.[109] Although the sources say nothing about a Carthaginian expedition from the Senegal encountering another coming from Tripolitania or Algeria, all the evidence suggests that they at least came close.

The Greeks were surely spurred on by their optimism. Mercenaries stationed in Egypt may have brought news of blacks back with them to Greece.[110] It is no coincidence that Pindar presented a new version of the Argonaut legend at precisely the same time as the Carthaginian expeditions in Cyrene, a version in which Jason and his companions made landfall at Libya on their return from Colchis via the Ocean and spent twelve days crossing the continent on foot before reaching the Mediterranean at Lake Tritonis.[111] As usual, the epic-mythical trappings express a new stage in knowledge about the world, in this case a confidence that southern climes no longer posed a serious obstacle to human endeavour.

THE PERSIAN ADVANCE INTO ASIA

THE EXPEDITION OF SCYLAX OF CARYANDA

Cambyses in the Libyan Desert

The importance of trans-Saharan trade is further evident in the fact that the Persian Empire occasionally took an active interest in the Sahara. In 539 BCE Cyrus had advanced to the borders of Egypt after capturing Babylon. In 522 his successor Cambyses conquered the land of the pharaohs. He split up his army upon entering Thebes. One group was dispatched to Ethiopia in present-day Sudan. A second army, supposedly 50,000 strong, was ordered to march on to the oasis of Siwa to enslave the inhabitants and burn down the oracle of Zeus Ammon.[112] This latter information is likely a fabrication of Egyptian priests or other eastern sources that sought to present the country's conquerors in a bad light. Herodotus developed it into a caricature of the Persian king that stood in contrast to Cyrus, the empire's founder.[113]

In reality, rational foreign and trade policy considerations were behind the plans. From Siwa, Egyptian traders brought African slaves to Naucratis.[114] Priests and residents of the sanctuary were very well informed about trans-Saharan trade, perhaps exercising a coordinating function similar to the Delphic oracle. Cambyses clearly had no intention of destroying the oasis and sanctuary—what could this have achieved? By showing his presence as new ruler, he wanted instead to secure the route to Siwa through garrisons as well as strengthen his hold on the strategically important trade hub at the Libyan border.[115]

According to Herodotus, the Persians reached an 'oasis' (probably el-Kharga) following a seven-day march. Nothing is known of their subsequent fate. The Ammonians claimed that a sandstorm buried the approaching army, a story that has given rise to the wildest speculations to this day. In the history of the Sahara, it was not uncommon for caravans to be swallowed by sandstorms; whether this could have happened to an entire army supposedly numbering 50,000 seems highly doubtful. The demise of Cambyses' army has recently been explained with their defeat at the hands of rebels, which was then reinterpreted as a desert storm. It is more likely that Cambyses was simply not up to the logistical challenges of leading a large army over caravan routes, and at some stage ordered them to retreat and/or they were led astray by local guides. The priests of the Siwa oracle turned this into a catastrophe that spared them the costly presence of garrisons.

India

Cambyses' Egyptian campaign was nonetheless a great success. Even the Phoenicians had made available their ships, so laying the basis for building the Persian fleet. There emerged a protected economic area, extending from the Aegean to the termini of the great caravan routes in the south, which gave Greeks opportunities for employment as artists, architects, doctors, or naval commanders.[116]

Cambyses died suddenly on his way north to suppress a rebellion. His successor, Darius I, came from a collateral line of the royal dynasty. After ending a lengthy civil war, he continued his predecessor's expansionist policy, targeting the maritime border zones and peninsulas of the lands conquered by Cambyses. By taking over marine coasts (in both east and west), he was perhaps making a claim to world domination in keeping with ancient eastern tradition.[117] In any event, strategic and material considerations played an important role: in the west, the coast of Asia Minor could only be secured by controlling the Aegean and gaining hegemony over Thrace and Macedonia. Covert expeditions had allegedly already explored the southern coastlines of the Balkan Peninsula.[118] In the east, by contrast, there beckoned a land that was connected to Mesopotamia by the Persian Gulf and had lost none of its lustre by the end of the sixth century: India.

According to Persian royal inscriptions, India (*Hindus*, in ancient Persian, *Sindh/Sindhu*, in Sanskrit) designated the middle and lower Indus Valley. The northwestern regions of today's Punjab, called *tagatus* and Gandhara by the Persians, had probably been conquered by Cyrus after 546 or 539 BCE. Twenty years later (519 or 518), Darius ordered his forces to sail down 'the great river' (Indus) from the Persian border zone in present-day Afghanistan to find out whether there was a maritime link to the Persian Gulf. The king's chief interest lay not so much in trade as in conquering the Indus region, which ensued a few years later. Darius' inscriptions mention *Hindus* (= Sindh) as a new province.[119]

Herodotus names Scylax from the Carian coastal town of Caryanda as a leading member of the Indus expedition.[120] Caria had been a part of the Persian Empire since the mid-sixth century. The Carians had a reputation as fearless pirates and mariners. Several documents attest to the presence of Carian and Greek mercenaries, ships' carpenters, and other specialists at royal courts in Asia Minor.[121] The Persians carried on this tradition: Carians transported Lebanese cedarwood from Babylon to Susa, while two Carians are recorded in Bannesu at Pihatu sa Dur-al-Arab; presumably there was a Carian marine station at Shatt al-Arab.[122] Scylax belonged in this circle. He may therefore not only have gathered a wealth of experience in Asia Minor and its southern waters—otherwise Darius would hardly have appointed him to captain the Indus expedition; he must also have been familiar with at least the basics of Persian geography before the journey began. The decision to explore and conquer the Indus region also goes back to global geographical reflections that recall Graeco-Carthaginian speculations on the course of the Nile (see above, p. 132). According to Herodotus, Darius wanted to know where the Indus—besides the Nile, the only river 'where crocodiles are found'—drained into the sea.[123] The strictly unnecessary reference to crocodiles living only in these two rivers recalls the conclusion by analogy drawn by Euthymenes, who had posited a link between the Atlantic and the Nile on the basis of the fauna and freshwater found at the mouth of the Senegal (Chretes).[124] If Darius now applied the same analogical reasoning to the wildlife on the Indus and investigated its mouth on the (eastern) Ocean, he clearly wanted to test the alternative theory of the eastward course of the Nile and find out if the Indus lay upstream of the river. This theory could find support in the similarity—also emphasized by Greek authors—between the Indians and Ethiopians, both peoples dwelling at the margins of the world.

To be sure, Greek sources like Herodotus were not privy to the discussions of Persian military planners, yet there were not just Phoenician but also Greek-Carian captains such as Scylax who must have been familiar with their paymasters' ideas about geography and could convey them to a Greek audience, at least in broad outline. Indeed, the matter-of-fact way in which Persian kings could be made to voice such geographical reflections speaks for a kind of common-sense geography that the Persians shared with Greeks and Carthaginians, and which they sought to exploit for their political ends.[125] Darius evidently wanted to find out whether the outer southeast limits of the Persian Empire (Egypt/Ethiopia) could be connected with India via the Nile/Indus. Just how closely such considerations were tied to hegemonic interests would be shown around a century later, when the Persian king Artaxerxes III (390–338 BCE) wanted to bring his rebellious Egyptian subjects to reason by redirecting the upper course of the Indus(!). Thirty years after that, Alexander made his way east in the conviction that the Indus and Nile were interlinked.[126]

The Indian Expedition of Scylax of Caryanda

Scylax's expedition began at a place called Caspatyros in the region of Paktia. The name Paktia probably derives from the modern Pashtun or Pakhtun, an Afghan people in the Indian borderlands.[127] Caspatyros may be equivalent to the 'town of Caspapyros in Gandhara' in the Gandhara Plateau near Peshawar at the confluence of the Indus and Kabul Rivers, perhaps Kabul, Casyapa-pur, or Casypa (Kashmir).[128]

The Kabul River was navigable from here, and it was at this point that the expeditionary fleet was built and launched. The next stages can only be reconstructed from the work of the slightly younger scholar Hecataeus of Miletus, who most likely had access to Scylax's travel report. He names a 'polis' called Argante in India (*Argantè polis Indias*), probably still in the Kabul Valley.[129] From the tributary of the Kabul River the fleet then sailed down the Indus.[130] At its lower reaches, it entered the realm of the *Opiai* and reached a 'royal fortress'.[131] Beyond the fortification lay a desert, probably the Thar Desert.[132] The *Kalatai*, a dark-skinned people who according to Herodotus were subject to Darius, probably settled east of the Indus delta, near present-day Palanpur. Along with the reference to the royal garrison, this could suggest that even before the expedition, Darius had already established a bridgehead in the Indus delta and had secured the cooperation of the local populace.[133]

From the delta, the fleet sailed along the old waterway to the Gulf of Oman.[134] It then probably did not turn into the Persian Gulf, since this was a familiar route. Hecataeus refers to 'Arabian isles' called *Kamarenoi*, probably an island off the southwest coast of Arabia, perhaps Kamaran near Ras Issa north of Hodeidah at the opening of the Red Sea.[135] Knowledge of this island could derive from Persian expansion in the Red Sea, which occurred independently of Scylax's voyage; yet because the other information provided by Hecataeus fits into Scylax's previous route, this information could also refer to his journey. Scylax would thus have been the first Mediterranean mariner to sail around the Arabian Peninsula.[136] Finally, Herodotus has Scylax sail back at the point 'from which [. . .] the Phoenicians had set out on the instructions of the Egyptian king to sail around Libya'.[137] Their journey's starting point had been the Gulf of Suez!

An Alternative Route?

If Scylax's journey west from the mouth of the Indus and his circumnavigation of Arabia already makes this one of the most momentous ancient voyages of discovery, the expedition was an even more sensational achievement if one recent theory is to be believed. According to this theory, the ships sailed down the Ganges, not the Indus. Herodotus writes that the river navigated by Scylax flows to the east, which only holds true of the Ganges.[138] Caspatyros could be Pataliputra, a city built on the Ganges. From here, an overland route extends to the west, and the Ganges flows around 250 km to the east.[139] The geographer Strabo (first century BCE) knows a land called *Gandaris* in the eastern Punjab. Other authors mention a race of *Gandaridai* or *Gangaridai* on the Ganges. To that extent, there is nothing to stop us identifying *Gandariké* with the region around the Ganges.[140] The population of the Ganges Valley rose sharply from 600 BCE, corroborating Herodotus' characterization of India as the twentieth satrapy.[141]

Yet all these and other combinations, such as the hypothesis of two expeditions (one down the Indus, the other down the Ganges),[142] run aground on a fact that makes the Phoenician circumnavigation of Africa appear questionable, too. It may well be the case that Scylax was informed by locals about a river flowing to the east. But if he used it and went on to sail around the subcontinent, and if later sources were aware of his travel report, it is hard to explain why they knew nothing about how far India extended to the south (until the first century BCE). If they had such knowledge, why did it not flow into contemporary depictions of the ecumene? All this aside, a voyage down the Ganges can only with difficulty be reconciled with the Persian king's planned conquests. He certainly had no interest in conquering the Ganges Valley. He aimed instead to expand his control of waters from the Persian Gulf to the mouth of the Indus and must have had his sights set on Arabia. The expedition's unusually long duration, sometimes used as an argument for a circumnavigation of India, can be explained by delays caused by the monsoon and the fleet's cautious reconnaissance of the Arabian coast.[143]

The *Periplus* on India

Scylax recorded his observations in a *periplus*. Yet, like the reports of Hanno and the leaders of the other expeditions, his report—so far as the seven fragments permit us to say—contained none of the nautical-meteorological facts (about wind, land breezes, or currents) that a mariner sailing in unknown waters might find vitally important.[144] This suggests that such information continued to be passed down orally, at least until the first century BCE. The real impulse for composing the expeditionary report was the intelligence the Persian king needed to conquer and rule the land. He accordingly expected a written report in prose—the writing style of Ionian scholars.[145] Leaving aside the scanty references to the *periplus* of Euthymenes, the Scylax *periplus* is the first prose work that goes beyond listing linear points to provide geographic information about nature, forms of political organization, and social phenomena. Along with his official report, he most likely composed a second version for his compatriots, incorporating elements from the Greek tradition, just as the translator of the Hanno *periplus* took greater liberties with the second part and enriched it with Greek motifs.[146]

Nonetheless, the original need for information of the Persian planners can still be detected behind the extant fragments. Thus, Scylax reports that the land around the Indus is wet due to the countless springs and canals. This statement is true for the rainy season, at least. It was of particular interest insofar as it could be used to calculate the food and water rations of the army as well as the land's potential tribute. According to another fragment, an abundance of timber lined the riverbanks, while on the mountain slopes grew a plant called *kunara*, probably the same as the Greek word *kinára* for 'artichoke'. Timber from India was always in high demand in Mesopotamia and would have interested the Persian king not just for building ships to sail down the Indus but also as a supplement for cedarwood from Lebanon. The artichoke was not the fleshy thistle familiar to the Greeks (which was unknown in India at the time) but probably a thorny bush, perhaps a rose bush.[147] Scylax's readers were unaware of this, although they probably knew of the artichoke's antirheumatic, choleretic, and diuretic effect. Around the same time, Greek physicians plied their trade at the Persian court, while Indian medicine stood in high regard. Indian and Greek medicine overlapped and influenced each other. Perhaps the botanical information supplied by Scylax has to do with the general patronage enjoyed by medicine at the Persian court.[148] In addition, Darius needed information about the country's political situation. Scylax's reference to the 'kings' standing far above their subjects might allude to the Vedic 'varna system'. It is realistic that he mentions nothing about cities, because although the Punjab was densely populated at the time, it was not until after the expedition that urbanization took off in the southern Indus Valley.[149]

In his later reworking of the report for a Greek public, Scylax must have itched to populate this faraway land with the marvellous beings that the epics had always reserved for places and islands at the edges of the world. Some peoples from the India book were thus familiar from the Greek tradition: the 'monopods' (*Skiapodes*), the 'one-eyed' (*Monophtalmoi*), the 'large-headed' (*Makrokephaloi*), and probably also the 'dog-headed' (*Kynokephaloi*) all clearly belong to the literary revision rather than the original report.[150] Perhaps Scylax transposed to India the 'dwarfs' (*Pygmaioi*, *Troglodytae*) that Homer, Hesiod, and the late sixth-century expedition leaders had placed in Libya.[151]

By contrast, there are no Greek antecedents for the 'winnowing-fan ears' (*Otoliknoi*) and the 'people that produce only one offspring' (*Henotiktontes*), although there are Indian counterparts for the *Otoliknoi*, at least.[152] With few exceptions, the other marvellous beings can also be found in Indian mythology. Scylax probably learned about them from his Indian informants. In reproducing their stories, he drew on Greek concepts and transferred elements from Greek epic and mythology onto a largely unknown country.[153] As in other cultures and at other times, here people with one eye served as a cipher for the strangeness of an unusual exterior.[154] The wondrous beings at the eastern limits of the world thus partly reflected Indian sources, but they also formed a code that made Indian stories and realities comprehensible to a non-Indian audience. Scylax thereby created a facet of the India that was to remain canonical—varied and augmented, but rarely called into question.

Integrating the Expedition Reports into a Panoptic View of the World: Hecataeus of Miletus

At the end of the sixth century, scholars were faced with the task of integrating into their worldviews the constant influx of knowledge about the far south and east generated by the expeditions of Scylax and other mariners. In doing so, they had to combine two contradictory principles for representing space: the linear descriptive itinerary of the *periplus* and the 'world maps' of the philosophers, which abstracted from empirical data and were built on geometrical harmony.

One of the first to succeed was Hecataeus (c. 560–480 BCE), an aristocrat from Miletus. He compiled the findings of expedition reports, the colonial knowledge of his hometown (especially in the Black Sea area), as well as the fruits of his own travels and investigations in the Persian Empire into a synoptic presentation of the earth in the form of a 'journey around the world' (*perihodos*, *perihegis ges*). While this form of representation drew on age-old models of geography, it was now thoroughly buttressed with empirical data. Hecataeus presumably appended it as an elucidation (or 'legend') to the Ionian 'world maps', as conceived by Anaximander, and probably drew an additional map of his own.[155]

Hecataeus divided the earth into a semi-circular northern and southern half, equated with Europe and Asia. He possibly imagined Libya as a third landmass, based on reports that had come in about the extension of the Sahara. Europe and Asia are separated by a waterline running from west (Gibraltar) to east (Phasis = Rion). Hecataeus further posited a north-south line running from the Danube to the Nile. The earth was thus split into four roughly equal quadrants. Within the quadrants were countries and landscapes in the form of geometrical figures (squares, circles, trapezoids); there was probably an additional categorization into climatic zones.[156]

The descriptive survey of the world (*Perihegese*) began in Spain and led via Europe, Asia, Egypt, and Libya back to the Pillars of Heracles. Persia, India, and Arabia are described as lying on the coasts of the Erythraean (= Indian) Sea. Hecataeus does not shy away from modifying the information provided by his sources. He organizes his material into chapters (*logoi*) on large geographic-ethnographic regions (Scythia, Egypt, Libya). The old genre of a 'catalogue of nations' was supplemented with information on cities, rivers, and ports as well as local manners, customs, economic life, diet, religious forms, and cults. Details about the country's topography, natural resources, ecology, flora, and fauna farther inland were also included. With that, Hecataeus continued a tendency, begun in Aristeas, of shifting the focus of attention away from the coast, something that made most sense where the coast and the interior formed a single political entity.[157]

As a few fragments indicate, the ethnographic data seem to have been far more vivid—at least in certain passages, and especially when Hecataeus could draw on his own travel experiences—than the scanty information about places and coastlines. For example, the lively account of a crocodile hunt in Egypt found in Herodotus probably goes back to Hecataeus. On the other hand, he left the Indian wondrous beings out of his description, evidently because other informants could not confirm their existence.[158] If he had too little information to make corrections or omissions, he left the faraway people wherever his predecessors and the epic tradition had placed them (Arimaspi, Pygmies, monopods).

One of Hecataeus' main objectives was to distil what was typical about a people and its environment from the available data—an approach that would continue to characterize Greek ethnography. In doing so, he may have been looking for connections among climate, physical appearance, and way of life. Historical contexts, by contrast, are mentioned only in the form of foundation myths and heroic legends; age-old myths are rationalized when he declares, for example, that the three-bodied giant Geryon, whose cattle were rustled by Heracles, was the real king of Ambracia. Hecataeus vouches with his own person for the correctness of his interpretations: 'Hecataeus of Miletus speaks as follows', his critique of myth begins: 'I write these things, as they seem to me to be true. For the tales of the Greeks are many and ridiculous, as they seem to me'.[159]

In this respect, as in others, Hecataeus was representative of Ionian scholarship, offering constructions based on observation and empiricism while feeling compelled to interpret individual aspects. With Hecataeus and the reworked expedition reports, Greek ethnography had found the two forms that would define its course in the following period: the presentation of a single land (e.g. *Indiká*) and the collation of individual reports into a description of the entire world. What would change were the interests, questions, and categories brought to bear by Greek authors, and these in turn were influenced not just by shifts in the intellectual and cultural climate but also on the political and military terrain. The Persian wars at the beginning of the fifth century BCE constituted the most serious break.

HUMAN EXISTENCE IN THE WORLD

DEVELOPMENTS IN ETHNOGRAPHY AFTER THE PERSIAN WARS

The Persian Wars and Their Interpretation

In 500–499 BCE, *poleis* on the coasts of Asia Minor rose in revolt against Persian rule. The rebellion was crushed within five years and ended with the destruction of Miletus. Athens and Eretria had briefly taken part in the rebellion, so King Darius ordered a punitive expedition. In 490 BCE his army was defeated by the Athenians on the plain near Marathon, on the eastern coast of Attica. Ten years later, a much larger army crossed the Hellespont under the command of Xerxes. From Thrace and Macedonia, they quickly overran central Greece. Only around thirty *poleis* under Spartan leadership dared to resist and formed a defensive alliance (the so-called Hellenic League). After initial defeats in Thermopylae, in September 480 they secured a victory at the naval battle of Salamis that was as devastating as it was unexpected. This was followed a year later by another victory on land at Plataea and the destruction of the remaining Persian warships at Mycale (on the coast of Asia Minor). In the years that followed, Hellenic League troops conquered the last Persian holdouts in the Aegean. The Ionian cities again shrugged off Persian rule and formed a naval alliance under Athenian leadership, pushing Persia further onto the defensive. At around the same time in the west, the tyrants of Syracuse had repelled invasions from Carthage and challenged Etruscan naval supremacy in the Tyrrhenian Sea.

Victory over the Carthaginians and Persians was an epochal event, above all for the Greeks of the motherland. For the first time, they had not only faced a well-armed aggressor on their home turf; even more momentously, they had unexpectedly held their own against the world power that had swept away all the empires of the east. This was a victory that needed explaining. The first attempt came from the Athenian Aeschylus. In his tragedy 'The Persians', first performed in 472 BCE, he reminded his compatriots of what had been at stake. 'O sons of the Greeks, go on! Free your fatherland, and free your children, your wives, and the shrines of your paternal gods, and the tombs of your ancestors! Now the struggle is for all!'[160] With that, he expressed what the Persian wars had first brought about: an awareness of having defended a form of freedom that had not fully been appreciated before. If this freedom had been so tenaciously contested, then the struggle must have unleashed forces superior to the Persians. Instead of fleeing in the face of overwhelming numbers, the Greeks had rushed to Salamis 'their courage high', the messenger reports to the Persian king's mother.[161]

The willingness of citizens to defend their freedom was a precondition of victory, not its guarantee. Other *poleis*, for example the Greeks in Asia Minor, had fought for their freedom in vain. As so often in such situations, the gods' succour and support proved decisive. They had decreed—according to Aeschylus—that Europe and Asia would never be ruled by a single power but would always belong to the Greeks and Persians, respectively. By crossing the Hellespont (and destroying Greek temples), Xerxes had violated the divinely ordained border between the continents and hence disturbed the equilibrium between Greeks and 'barbarians'. For this sacrilege he was punished: the gods invisibly fought on the Greeks' side in the great battles, stirred up favourable winds, and instilled courage in the Greek warriors. Only with their help could the Persians be pushed back.[162]

Two things are worth noting in this interpretation: first, the self-evident connection between a thirst for freedom and divine assistance; second, the fact that Aeschylus treats Greeks and Persians as equals against the backdrop of a divine world order by granting each dominion over their own continent. With the divinely sanctioned boundary separating Asia (Orient) and Europe (Occident), 'The Persians' stands at the beginning of an interpretation of the world that would leave a deep imprint on European intellectual history. In Aeschylus, however, it is not (yet) bound up with any degradation of the Persians.[163] They may at times be ascribed negative stereotypical qualities, such as luxurious wealth, emotional excess, and softness, that would soon be applied indiscriminately to all eastern peoples.[164] Yet these elements do not yet form an independent motivic context, and they are given nothing like the structural weight that the tragedy accords the theory of the sacrilege committed by the Persian king when he arrogantly crossed the Hellespont. Anyone can succumb to hubris, depending on the circumstances and character of the individual. With the ghost of Darius, Aeschylus thus brought on stage a purified ruler shaped by Greek cultural values, whereas Xerxes is presented as flawed because he flagrantly disregarded moral precepts and failed to grasp his fate.[165] The message is that the Athenians, too, could meet a similar end if they succumb to hubris and upset the divine world order. The search for means to restore that order is of a piece with the Ionian scholars' search for order in the natural world. Aeschylus expands this search to explaining a global military event and assures the Greeks that the gods had entrusted Europe to their hands. This was an astonishing message that catapulted the Greeks' self-confidence to unprecedented heights.

Man as Measure of All Things

Further successes confirmed the trend. In the eastern Mediterranean, Athenian warships attacked Persian positions in Cyprus and Egypt. Despite several setbacks, the city became the leading sea power and Piraeus the most important trade centre in the eastern Mediterranean. The Athenians grew rich, financing their extravagant democratic order with the tribute pouring into their coffers from their allies.

All these remarkable developments over such a short space of time prompted new questions. Were the gods really to thank for all this? Did not the successes of Athenian warships and their oarsmen prove that mortals were capable of achievements that knew no natural (or divine) boundaries? 'At many things we feel awe', writes Sophocles, 'But at nothing more / Than at man. This being / sails the grey-white sea running before / Winter storm-winds, he / Scuds beneath high / Waves surging over him / On both sides'.[166] Where Aeschylus still gazed reverently at the world ordained by the gods, and where the Greeks of his generation, animated by their love of freedom, repelled those who disturbed this order in the gods' name, humans could now impose their will on the world through their skill. The world was now to be mastered rather than husbanded. Divinely ordained nature had become the object of human *technai*.

This realization necessarily brought new impulses to reflections on what it meant to be human. What Sophocles so eloquently brought to the stage became, from the mid-fifth century on, a topic of discussion for scholars from a predominantly colonial background ('Sophists'). They spread throughout the Greek world, charging their students fees for tuition in all areas of knowledge, from cosmology and history to rhetoric and practical politics. Humans and their abilities stood at the centre of their interest, and they enquired into the applicability, implementation, and usefulness of the material they taught. Protagoras summed up the Sophistic position by declaring man to be the measure of all things. Traditions posed no obstacle to their brash self-assurance. Several Sophists countered the pessimistic ideas of a decline in human history, as represented by Hesiod, with the theory of a constant ascent in human culture to the giddy heights indicated by Sophocles. The gods played no role in all this, or at best a subordinate one. Some Sophists even claimed that they were a figment of the human imagination, created when worthy kings, benefactors, or inventors were posthumously deified.[167]

Discussions of Nature (*Physis*) and Human Conventions (*Nomoi*)

It was one thing to affirm human capacities and situate them against a cultural-historical evolutionary process. Understanding their causes and drawing the consequences was a far more difficult undertaking. The basis for discussions conducted throughout the Mediterranean was the contrast—first formulated by Hippias of Elis around 430 BCE—between human customs, institutions, and (legal) orders (*nomos*), on the one hand, and natural abilities and endowments (*physis*), on the other. There was heated debate about which should be given more weight. The Greeks had repeatedly come across new and (to them) bizarre customs during their voyages of exploration and colonization. Within the world of the polis, meanwhile, the sixth century saw a flurry of new constitutions. Both convinced many scholars that the significance of human-instituted law (*nomos*) would have to be relativized. Ultimately, according to Gorgias, it only mirrored real power relations and could be invalidated by the strength (*physis*) of those who took the law into their hands. From the diversity of human mores, others drew the conclusion that barbarians and Greeks were equal so far as their *physis* was concerned, that is, as biological beings, and differed solely through their customs (*nomoi*). Others, in turn, thought that different peoples imagined the gods according to their own *nomoi*.[168] All these reflections were based on knowing and classifying a plethora of folk traditions. Several Sophists seem to have created veritable ethnographic catalogues.

In a further step, such observations led to fundamental anthropological questions such as that concerning humankind's place in nature. At a time when there were still no clear disciplinary boundaries, numerous scholars from various fields of knowledge took part in these conversations. As Sophists called age-old norms into question, Greek physicians also began taking their distance from wandering healers and miracle workers (like Abaris or Aristeas), developing methodical principles and rationally grounded healing procedures that dispensed with religious or pseudo-religious support. This was bound up with a particular way of speaking about the objects of one's own endeavours based on critical reasoning. The progenitor of this 'medicine as science' was Hippocrates from Kos.

To arrive at a diagnosis, doctors needed to gain an overview of the physical condition (*physis*) and life circumstances (*nomoi*) of their patients. In their methods, they differed only in degree from philosophers who directed their attention to the nature of the world (*physiologoi*).[169] From the mid-fifth century, Hippocrates' students and followers sought to summarize their observations in rules that claimed validity for all human beings. These could then be elaborated into ethnographic-climatological models, already present in rudimentary fashion in Homer—according to him, the healthiest and longest-lived people dwell in a pleasant climate and fertile environment—and varied by Hecataeus. A text from the Hippocratic circle entitled 'On airs, waters, and places' (or: 'On the environment', 430–400 BCE) sets out to demonstrate that differences between peoples (and countries) derive from climatic and physical conditions. This could occur in two ways: either climate and nature directly influence the bodies and minds of the inhabitants, or environmental factors indirectly shape their way of life (*nomos*), which in turn shapes their physical and mental dispositions.[170] In developing this theory, Hippocratic authors drew on a wealth of written and orally transmitted data (autopsies, reports of discoveries, information from Greek colonies, observations of slaves).[171] Much of their evidence was taken from peripheral peoples, on the assumption that knowledge increases with distance and ethnic diversity. 'The nations that differ only a little from one another I will omit', notes the author of 'On airs, waters, and places', 'and describe the situation of those that differ greatly, either in nature (*physis*) or in their customs (*nomoi*)'.[172]

Along with the Libyan tribes, the peoples of the Black Sea offered an inexhaustible reservoir of information—not just because traders, travellers, and colonists had been in contact with them for centuries, but also because their nomadic way of life stood in such stark contrast to that of the polis Greeks. While the Scythians were discussed most intensively,[173] less populous and well-known tribes could also be cited if their way of life showed peculiarities that could not solely be explained by the influence of climate and soil. This category included the 'Macrocephali', first encountered in India by Scylax (see above, p. 150), but also said (presumably by Hecataeus) to inhabit a region west of southeast of Colchis on the Black Sea.[174] At first, the writer of 'On airs, waters, and places' asserts, 'it was their law [*nomos*] that had the greatest influence on the length of their heads, but now nature [*physis*] too contributes to what law started'.[175] Thus, the Macrocephali had adopted the habit of using 'bandages and suitable appliances' to artificially elongate the skulls of their infants. Nature had followed their lead: today, macrocephalous parents produce macrocephalous offspring without any need for intervention, just as children inherit baldness, blue eyes, or myopia. Here, *in nuce*, was a theory of hereditary or 'acquired' traits arising from the interaction between *nomos* and *physis*, although the author abstains from assessing the relative influence of the two areas.[176]

The Discovery of the Past—Herodotus' 'Histories'

Given the passion with which scholars throughout the Greek world sought to interpret, and use for their own ends, the influx of ethnographic data on human expressive forms and abilities, it must have dawned on them at some stage that similar methods could be applied to the past as well as the present. Sophistic teaching on ethnogenesis and the Hippocratic author's explanation for large heads both had a temporal depth dimension that clearly allowed for change. Homer, too, attests to an awareness of historical change that manifested in the different qualities of earlier and current generations.

The greatest achievement of the Greeks in living memory was indisputably their victory over the Persians. Aeschylus had turned this triumph into a tragedy that in fact drew on materials from a far more distant, mythic past. The Greeks themselves mythicized and heroized the Persian wars. This established a precedent for tying recent events to a mythic past and reworking them into a literary narrative. As optimism about the potential for human achievement soared, as Sophists taught techniques for success that could be learned by 'everyone' and denied the agency of the gods, and as natural philosophers and physicians sought to understand human nature through empirical means, old explanations such as that of the division of responsibility for the continents among the gods had to be revised or augmented with new arguments.

Intellectual impulses and literary models formed the essential preconditions for what might be termed the 'birth of historiography'. Real needs were also in play: from the mid-century, it was no longer so easy to find eyewitnesses to the Persian wars. The pressure to preserve and explain events and deeds grew as they became shrouded in myth. In contrast, many scholars saw the key to understanding humans and the world in empirical enquiry and observation. At the same time, with the emergence of direct democracy in Athens and other institutions that entrusted a larger number of citizens with political responsibility, and with the rise of Athens as a great maritime power, the post-war generation experienced change in the 'real historical' situation on a scale never seen before.

For all the pride they took in their achievements, such drastically accelerated changes generated a feeling of uncertainty that—as Sophocles expressed—could be deeply disorienting.[177] Guidance was most convincing when it came from outside in the form of an undistorted, sharp-eyed view of events. In the 440s, Herodotus gave readings in Athens from his work on the Persian wars. We have often cited it as a source on voyages of discovery and exploration, and not by chance. Herodotus was a widely travelled man from Halicarnassus, one of several *poleis* in Asia Minor that were not only home to scholars of the calibre of Thales and Hecataeus but from which many captains had set sail for distant shores.

Just how intensively Herodotus was involved in empirically informed discussions about human nature is shown by the preface to his work: 'Here are presented the results [*apodeixis*] of the enquiry [*historie*] carried out of Herodotus of Halicarnassus. The purpose is to prevent the traces of human events from being erased by time, and to preserve the fame of the important and remarkable achievements produced by both Greeks and non-Greeks; among the matters covered is, in particular, the cause of the hostilities between Greeks and non-Greeks'.[178]

The self-introduction is in keeping with the prose style of the time and recalls Hecataeus (and probably also *periplus* authors like Scylax). In presenting himself as a speaker on the stage, Herodotus announces something new, original, and contentious. Just as Sophists, physicians, and naturalists offered competing explanatory models, so too Herodotus raises a claim to discussing his topic in dialogue with differing opinions. Herodotus will typically use this first-person form of address when criticizing alternative views, sometimes to polemical effect. Ever since, critique, correction, and competition have lubricated not just scientific discourse but also history writing.

Accordingly, the form and method applied by Herodotus fit snugly into the mould of contemporary discussions. *Apodeixis* means something like the public presentation of an argument or proof. Sophists and Hippocratic doctors very frequently use the term in its verbal form at the start of their treatises. By using the substantive to caption his work, as it were, he makes unmistakably clear that he does not simply intend to tell a story but wants to argue convincingly and pleasingly while refuting or discrediting rival interpretations—the verb *apodeiknymi* appears some 137 times in his work.[179] And just as the Hippocratic authors claim to have developed their theories on the basis of observing and gathering empirical data from nature (*physis*) and human custom (*nomos*), so Herodotus uses the term *historie* to indicate that he approaches the object of his investigation with the same intention.

In setting out to wrest human deeds from oblivion, Herodotus shares with the scholars of his day an interest in the human world and connects with the universalizing ambition of Ionian scholars. But by applying empiricism and argumentation not to *present* conditions but to *past* human-caused events, he creates a new field of enquiry and—unbeknownst to him—a new genre that we now call 'history'. At the centre of his interest stand human achievements and deeds (*erga*), those performed not just by Greeks but by barbarians as well. The Persians are the barbarians par excellence, and it is to be expected that in presenting their deeds and the deeds of the Greeks (as in the epic), failures and defeats will be included. Like the Hippocratic physicians and Sophists, however, Herodotus makes no fundamental distinctions between Greeks and barbarians, treating them as equals. And just as physicians and Sophists do not simply collect observations and information but evaluate them for their theories, models, and guidelines, so Herodotus broaches at the end of his introduction the problem *he* wants to clarify in recording 'things done by man': the cause of the great war fought between the Greeks and Persians (tellingly, not the war instigated by the Persians against the Greeks). With that, the Persian war is established as the object of unprejudiced and (by contemporary standards) rational analysis, hence as a 'historical' topic.

Understanding the root cause of the conflict—and this is the next, no less revolutionary step—requires not just presenting its course but also analysing the events that led up to it,[180] just as the Hippocratic doctors sought to interpret unusual physiognomies (such as the large heads of the Macrocephali) by going back to their origins. The task Herodotus sets himself is more ambitious: where naturalists gather and interpret data about the nature of the world and human forms and customs, he must first search out the stories of the Greeks and Persians (*historie*) and develop his 'display' in critical confrontation with them (*apodeixis*). In doing so, he reaches far back into the mythic or epic past (prehistory of the Trojan war), which he does not completely disqualify as unreliable, but which he deems too vague and unproductive to shed light on the causes of the Persian war.[181]

The real starting point is a man 'who I myself know was the first to begin unjust acts against the Hellenes': the Lydian king Croesus. He loomed far larger in the collective memory of the audience, providing a convincing argumentative link to the still-raw memory of the Persian wars. The detailed presentation of the internal relations and foreign policy of the Lydian king culminates in his decision to wage war against the Persian (= Median) King Cyrus, a decision that backfires and brings Cyrus to the shores of the Aegean. The account of Persian expansion that follows takes up almost half the entire work; it ends with the Ionian rebellion, the sole encroachment from the Greek side, incited by two tyrants who had fallen prey to hubris. From there, Herodotus turns to the actual 'Persian war' of 480–479.

With his presentation of Lydian history and the conquests of the Persians (under their respective kings), Herodotus gave a cogent answer to the question of the causes or responsibility for the outbreak of the Persian wars. What resulted sooner or later in conflict with the Greeks was the expansionism of eastern monarchies, fuelled by the abundant human and natural resources at their disposal, as well as the tendency to hubris this amplified, as seen for the first time in Croesus and then becoming ever more pronounced in the Persian kings. Individual decisions (or mistakes) and 'deeds' as well as chance constellations of events are important catalysts; these are what make Herodotus' account so vivid and lively. The same holds true for the question of the causes of Persian failure. In Herodotus' view, these can only be deduced by interrogating the 'witnesses' and drawing on the events that can be reconstructed from their testimony. Here, too, chance and the unforeseen play a significant role. A fundamental lesson can be learned from all this: no single power can ever lastingly rule over all (a view that Aeschylus had justified solely with reference to the will of the gods); instead, human history is subject to continual shifts in power relations. Power and success often bear within them the seed of their own demise.[182]

The *Nomos* of Nations

In two passages of his work, Herodotus provides a more detailed answer to the question of how the Greeks could prevail against overwhelming Persian force. Thus, the Spartan exile Demaratus explains to Xerxes the night before the invasion that Greece is a poor country, yet poverty has strengthened the wisdom (*sophie*) and disciplined cohesion (*nomos*) of its inhabitants.[183] Both were the cause of that special virtue (*aretê*) that allowed them to overcome poverty and tyranny. This was especially true of the Spartans. They could hold their own against even the mightiest invader. Faced with Xerxes' riposte that even a Spartan could not cope with forces ten or twenty times the size of his own, Demaratus adds that their obedience to the *nomos* and their unique phalanx formation, not the *physis* of the individual, made the Spartans feel superior to every other people.

With that, Herodotus transfers arguments from the debate about the *nomos-physis* relationship onto a 'historical' event. He takes a clear stand by prioritizing *nomos* over natural endowments: this makes the crucial difference.[184] The same holds true for the Athenians, who according to Herodotus first became powerful following the expulsion of the tyrants and the introduction of the *nomos* of Cleisthenes' 'democracy'[185]—so powerful, in fact, that they could not only repel the depredations of their neighbours but even, thirty years later, turn the tide of the Persian invasion to become the saviours of the Hellenes. Here, too, *nomos* (in the form of democracy) determines success and failure (the Persians fought with equal persistence and bravery). It is thus entirely logical that Herodotus has the Athenians articulate a kind of Hellenic ethnic identity comprised of *nomoi*—a common language, religion, and way of life.[186]

In short, Herodotus presents *nomoi* as the key factors governing political and military success and failure as well as the historical vicissitudes to which all societies are subject. It is thus hardly surprising that the *nomoi* also form the central components of the ethnographic excurses (*logoi*) that punctuate the first five books whenever the Persians come across new peoples to subjugate. The Lydians appear at the beginning because they were the first to impose their rule on Greek cities. Then come the Persians themselves, the Egyptians and Scythians, Libyans and Thracians. Shorter sections on Ethiopia, Arabia, and India are included, as well as miscellaneous references showcasing the author's erudition.

The individual *logoi* essentially deal with four themes: (1) geography, ecology, and climate; (2) marvels (*thomata, thomasia*); (3) culture; and (4) history.[187] So far as the narrower realm of 'ethnography' is concerned, Herodotus is particularly interested in religious rites, customs, ways of life, and dietary habits—a list that recalls Hecataeus and Scylax. Yet Herodotus had access to far more information than his predecessors. Sophists and physicians sifted through this data to formulate theories about the relationship between *physis* and *nomos* and to deduce political or medical prescriptions. Herodotus used it to document the sheer diversity of *nomoi* and to define ethnic groups and their countries in their specificity as ethnographic-historical units. The astonishment at the world and its changes that had driven the Ionian natural philosophers mutated into astonishment at the variety of human cultural expressions.

Herodotus' ethnographic excurses attest to his familiarity with theories about the influence of climate and soil, as when he explains the excellent health of the Egyptians (and Libyans) by arguing that this is 'probably' (!) due to climate, particularly the absence of seasons: 'diseases almost always attack people when they are exposed to change, especially changes of seasons'.[188] To be sure, Herodotus adds, the Egyptians themselves attributed their health to a *nomos*, their habit of undergoing monthly purges. Similarly, the Libyans attribute their robust physical state to burning the veins at the top of their children's heads and about their temples (to prevent the 'flow of rheum from the head'). In fact, this reflects Hippocratic teaching, and Herodotus leaves undecided whether that is the real cause of their health. What is important is that the people themselves are convinced of their ability to influence *physis* with their *nomoi* rather than being helplessly exposed to iron laws governing climate and soil.[189]

Herodotus does not dispute that *nomoi* change with time and place. Through their exposure to luxury following their conquest of the Lydians, for example, the Persians had transformed from a simple, nomadic tribe adapted to their original harsh setting into a decadent people ruled by kings with a marked tendency to hubris.[190] And the Sophist habit of arguing in antitheses influenced his decision to establish a series of binary oppositions in his lengthy excurses on the ancient Egyptians in the south and the young, nomadic Scythians who roamed the north.[191] Yet all these conceptions have the status of secondary patterns and cannot be converted into a self-sufficient model. Thus, Herodotus cannot resist the temptation of integrating differences in *nomoi* into an evolutionary trajectory along the lines suggested by Sophist teachings about ethnogenesis. He remains equally sceptical about the potential for *nomoi* to undergo fundamental change in the future. Even though the aim of his lengthy excursus on the Scythians may have been to hold up a mirror to the Greeks, no moral appeal follows on from this that could conceal his true interest: the knowledge that from the perspective of the respective nations, *nomos* is all that counts. 'For if it were proposed to all nations to choose which seemed best of all customs, each, after examination, would place its own first; so well is each convinced that its own are by far the best'.[192] This is illustrated with an experiment supposedly carried out by Darius. He asked Greeks and Indians in turn for what price they would be prepared to treat their parents' corpses according to the rites of the other nation (burial or ritual consumption). Both adamantly refused to adopt the other's custom under any circumstances. With that, they proved that (as Pindar had already stated) *nomos* was king of all.

Comparative Ethnography and Persian Stimuli

On the one hand, then, Herodotus used the enormous amount of data gathered on travels and in interviews to relativize the customs of foreign nations (a similar phenomenon, albeit more complex and with amplified feedback effects, can be observed in the era of European colonial expansion). On the other hand, he developed the insight that *nomos*, whatever Protagoras may have said to the contrary, does not stand at human disposal but is ineluctably shaped by tradition, terrain, and climate. That is why *nomos* forms the crucial criterion for recognizing what is typical about a people. This insight raises the ethnographic tradition (Hecataeus) to a new level. With Herodotus, ethnographic thinking is converted into genuine ethnography, which in turn becomes a 'value- and ideology-free' end in itself.

One aspect of the new ethnography is explicit comparison. Even in the early-modern period, Herodotus was still considered a specialist in the 'comparative study of peoples' customs and mores'.[193] Comparisons inevitably arise when one is confronted with a multitude of ethnological data, and this was surely already the case for Hecataeus, who evaluated a plethora of *periploi* on foreign countries and ethnic groups. Similarly, in the text 'On the environment', several peoples of the north are explicitly compared under specific viewpoints. Yet Herodotus was the first to use comparisons of *nomoi* to work out the differences and similarities between Hellenes and Lydians, for example, or Hellenes and Egyptians.[194] Sometimes he draws parallels between greater (Egyptians) and lesser Greek ethnicities (Spartans). And he compares foreign nations with each other, as when he notes differences between Egyptian priests and Persian magi or commonalities among Babylonian, Egyptian, and Arabian burial rites.[195]

Certainly, Herodotus' historical topic encouraged *military* comparison of the combat strength, strategy, and size of the opposing forces. He was similarly used to comparing systems of government, as demonstrated in the famous constitutional debate supposedly held at the Persian court.[196] Yet all this does not explain the range of explicit comparisons referring to the ways of life of people living throughout the *entire* ecumene. Given that the original version of Scylax's *periplus* was a Persian commission, Persian models may have provided an additional stimulus. If there was something like a common-sense geography shared by Greeks and Persians, why should the same not have held true for the ethnographic domain? The courts of the Persian kings were cosmopolitan centres for exchanging ideas and experiences. The bas-reliefs adorning the monumental stairways in the audience hall at Persepolis formed a kind of 'ethnographic museum'. Among the visitors were Greek emissaries, exiles, and doctors who made a career at the Persian court and were dispatched by the kings on fact-finding missions (much like Marco Polo by the Mongol rulers 1,500 years later).[197] Herodotus refers on several occasions to the Persians' ethnographic interests in connection with their far-flung conquests. Before his Ethiopian campaign, for example, Cambyses sent out a fact-finding mission that, according to Herodotus, brought back information about the natives' way of life, longevity, and religious rites as well as their natural resources and idiosyncrasies.[198]

To be sure, such passages always conform to the logic of the narrative in which they are embedded. They meet the expectations of a *Greek* public and operate in a *Greek* discursive space. All the same, we know of questionnaires comparable in content designed to find out more about a country from non-Greek literary traditions as well, for example, the Hebrews.[199] Combining geographical information with ethnographic data was an old principle in the Near East. The Sargon Geography (see above, pp. 46–47) thus contains commentaries on conquered peoples such as the Amorites, 'who do not know grain'; the Lullubu, 'who do not know construction'; or the Karziner, 'who do not know burial, but cremate their dead'.[200] Ruling over so ethnically diverse an empire, the Persians relied on such empirical data, combined with geographical and ecological information, to maintain order in their multiethnic army, to govern their satrapies, to communicate with their subjects, and to assess and collect taxes.[201]

Herodotus surely lacked access to Persian or Near Eastern original sources, and he was also hardly in a position to consult participants in Persian expeditions or members of the Persian planning staff. Yet he could interview people who were familiar with Persian foreign policy and with Persian documentation conventions.[202] In any event, the evidence suggests that Herodotus drew *second-hand* on Persian narratives where they were available to him, as he himself emphasizes at the start when discussing the causes of the conflict between Greeks and barbarians. Even if this may have been untrue—Herodotus at least believed he could present his sources to his audience in this way.[203] The Persian Empire thus surely played a role in mediating knowledge of faraway nations in the east and southeast.

People at the Limits: India and Arabia

For Herodotus, peripheral nations formed the outer circle of an order encompassing the entire ecumene. At the Mediterranean centre, people lead an orderly agrarian life—albeit one burdened by the tribulations of the Iron Age—with elaborate burial rites. Then comes an intermediary zone, inhabited by nomads who feed on the milk and meat of their animals. Farther out live people who pay scant heed to their sustenance and occasionally cultivate a moderate form of ritual cannibalism (Massagetae, Issedones, Indian tribes). At the outermost limits (*eschatiai*) of the world, finally, can be found people (especially in the north) who consume nothing but raw food: grass, roots, fruit, fish, or meat.[204] These are tribes of cruel savages and even pure cannibals (*anthropophagi*), on the one hand; on the other, in the south and east, peace-loving communities like the Ethiopians, who, isolated from the hubbub of historical change, have preserved the happiness of the Golden Age and live to a ripe old age thanks to the fertile soil and healthy climate.[205]

While these categories recall Hippocratic models, they more strongly echo epic traditions. In Homer, the Cyclops and Laestrygonians represent the cruelly savage variant, Scheria and Ethiopia the bliss and closeness to the gods of nations on the southern and northern periphery. As the geographical horizon expanded in the following period, the same typologies came to be identified with new ethnic groups. With the help of the outlying extremes, one could rest secure in the advantages of one's own civilization, by contrasting it with primitive savagery, or criticize it, by opposing it to ideal conditions.

Herodotus does not slavishly adhere to this template but augments and modifies it as he goes. For him, *one* people does not possess solely positive or negative traits; instead, there are gradations and distinctions as well as ethnic groups that do not fit into the normative dichotomy governing people at the limits. Here too, there is a pronounced scepticism towards categorial global models that fail to do justice to a far more complex reality. He is thus unconvinced of the existence of the Hyperboreans and Arimaspi and ignores the large-eared, one-eyed, and 'people that produce only one offspring'. In the first case, they are mentioned by unreliable Greek sources. In the second, they form typical elements of *Indiká* (reports about India) that are incompatible with the scope of the *Histories*.

On the other hand, Herodotus is open to reports from peripheral regions if they come from non-Greek sources or have been verified. In India, for example, the natives risk their lives wresting treasure from gold-digging ants. In Arabia, winged serpents make it difficult to harvest incense.[206] Both motifs accord with contemporary climate theory, according to which lands in the far south are far more fertile and wealthier, but also produce unusual animals (Arabia is famous for its perfumes and spices, in India there are cotton-producing trees growing wild);[207] yet these motifs do not appear in the archaic epics, or for that matter (probably) in Scylax or Hecataeus. Indian epics, on the other hand, tell of 'ant-gold'.[208] The story is likely based on a local report about marmots that dug up gold-bearing sand when burrowing through the soil. The Ural-Altaic word for 'marmot' resembles the Sanskrit term for 'ant'. Accordingly, the gold actually found in northwestern India originally came from the Altai. Presumably, Herodotus' informants translated the Sanskrit word instead of the Altaic word, and thus the marmots turned into the Indian gold-digging ants.[209] Similarly, the flying snakes of Arabia can be traced back to Egyptian and Arabian folklore. They also feature in Hebrew and Assyrian

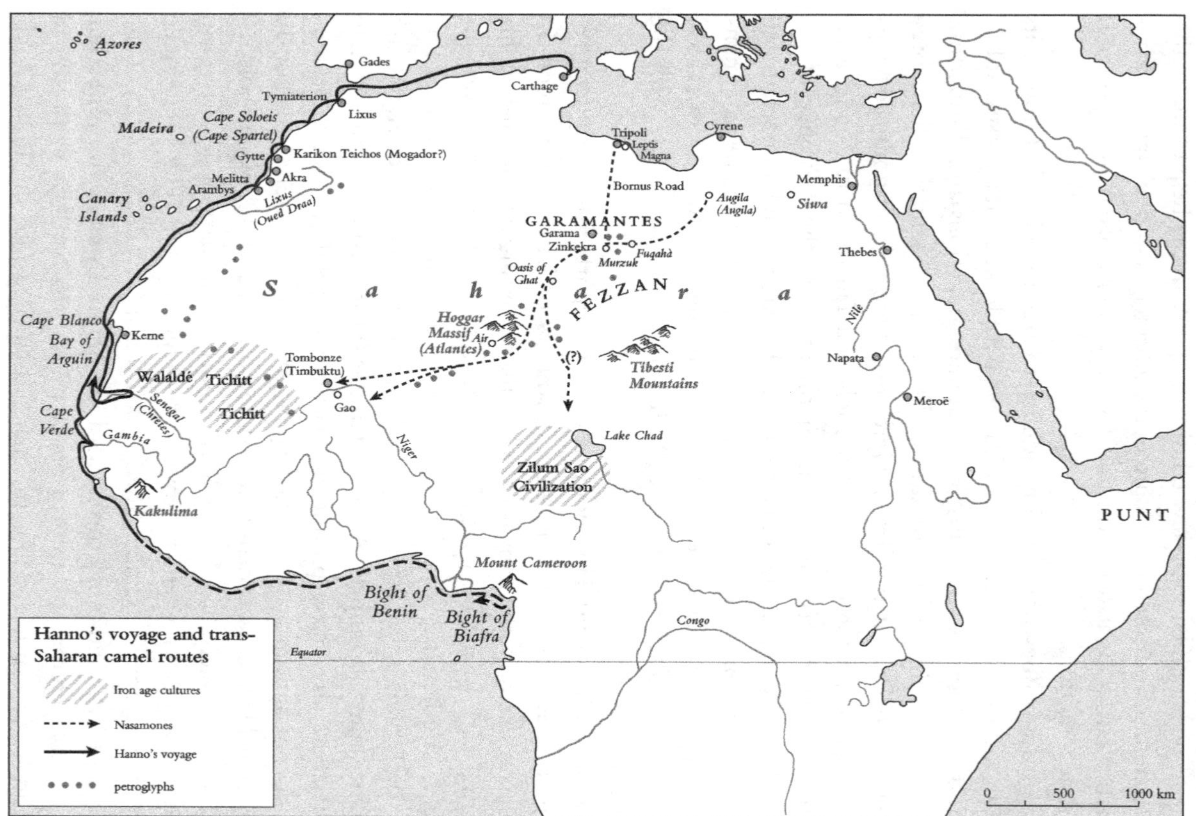

Map 5 Credit: Rudolf Hungreder/Klett-Cotta.

stories that combined the observation of migrating locusts with the topos of marvellous snakes.[210]

The crucial point is that Herodotus accepted these stories because they came from credible sources and because, in his view, they were a typical and essential characteristic of two major regions that, for all their diversity in ethnic *nomoi*, could also be presented as unified ethnographic spaces. And perhaps he recognized behind these two stories a pragmatic phenomenon: the Indians paid 360 talents of gold dust in tribute to their Persian overlords, the highest of any satrapy, while the Arabs sent 1,000 talents of incense each year.[211] It was hence in the Persian imperial interest to take seriously tales of gold- and incense-guarding animals.

4

New Horizons on Land and at Sea

GRAND DESIGNS

GEOGRAPHICAL AND COSMOLOGICAL FOUNDATIONS OF GLOBAL EXPLORATION

Herodotus' Critique of Ionian Geography

Given the sheer breadth of Herodotus' interests and his intense engagement in discussions about the nature of the world, it is unsurprising that he drew on the new information flowing into Asia Minor after the end of the Persian wars, not just in representing India and Arabia, but also in revising the *geographical* image of the world. He is the first author to use the term *ecumene* for the world, meaning 'inhabited world' or 'inhabited land'.[1]

He ridicules the Ionian scholars for depicting the world as a circle; likewise, those who claim that the earth was girdled by a ring-shaped oceanic river.[2] Both notions were incompatible with new reports about the Caspian Sea being an inland sea and the eastward extension of Asia. The basic division of the world into Asia and Europe was unaffected by all this, however, in keeping with the general theme of his work. Europe encompassed the northern half and was separated from the other landmasses by a line bisecting the Mediterranean from west to east; the straits of the Bosporus and Hellespont formed the border zone to Asia. The boundary continued through the Sea of Marmara to the Black Sea (Pontos Euxenos), then along the Phasis River, the Caucasus, and the Caspian Sea. Further orientation was provided by the Ister (Danube) and Nile Rivers, which originated in the west, flowed parallel to the east, and finally drained into southern and northern bodies of water, respectively. Their courses ran symmetrically to the west-east axis bisecting the Mediterranean. Three climatic zones were integrated into the continental order: the wet, cold north; the dry, hot south; and the Mediterranean temperate zone, the most favourable conditions being found in Greece.[3]

Herodotus himself devised this continental demarcation, paralleled in the course he charted for the Nile and Danube Rivers, as a way of ordering the immense mass of the ecumene. By contrast, geometrical classifications played no role when he conceived the shape of the outer seas. In place of the surrounding Ocean, he acknowledged only the Erythraean ('Red') Sea (roughly corresponding to the Indian Ocean), the Caspian (or Hyrcanian) Sea, and the great sea in the west, which he was the first to call the 'Atlantic'.[4] Whereas the Erythraean Sea was connected to the Atlantic, the Caspian was an inland sea. He ignored the Persian Gulf as a maritime space because Scylax had ignored it.[5]

Astronomical Interests

Herodotus' worldview could establish its authority not least because the Greeks' knowledge of faraway lands remained all but unchanged in the following generations. Exploratory energies dissipated during the wars between Athens and Sparta and their allies (the 'Peloponnesian Wars') or took a back seat to military objectives. Athens would have been the most likely candidate to launch expeditionary forays. Yet here again we see that the actors 'at the centre' of Greek history, unlike the *poleis* 'at the periphery', tended to play a subordinate role as discoverers or initiators of expeditions. Although the tragedies show an intimate familiarity with mythic geography and the stories of the northern Pontus, real information, especially about the Far West, was lacking. The comedians mention stockfish from Gades and eels from Tartessos, yet many also fell for the Carthaginian line that the sea was unnavigable beyond the Strait of Gibraltar.[6]

As almost always in antiquity, such pauses following centuries of expansion did not go unused. They offered an opportunity to think through the masses of information that had accumulated in the archaic period and integrate them into models that could function without any need for new empirical data. This process of refinement then gave rise to renewed impulses to venture into the unknown under changed political conditions. From the mid-fifth century, philosophers in Athens such as Anaxagoras and Hippias turned their gaze heavenwards despite (or perhaps because of) lagging progress in geographical knowledge, offered explanations of astronomical phenomena, and sought to measure the earth and skies with the help of a gnomon (a shadow-casting dial) and a scaphe (a hemispherical bowl representing the heavens). Many cultivated contacts with like-minded colleagues in Sicily and Asia Minor. After the Peloponnesian War, Plato—following the example of the Pythagoreans—called for astronomy to be placed on a mathematical footing; among his listeners was Eudoxus of Cnidus (c. 391–338 BCE), who would go on to become the founder of mathematical astronomy.[7]

In keeping with the tradition of meteorological farmers' calendars, the chief concern of Greek astronomy was to determine the appearance and disappearance of the fixed stars against the night sky; from this, Eudoxus developed his theory of planetary orbits in the fourth century. Beyond any practical application, the natural philosophers had shown a similar interest in the positions of the planets to embed their cosmic models in a harmonious order. Plato sought to integrate their efforts into his natural-philosophical writings and their myths of metempsychosis and cosmic visions. At the same time, he emphasized the use of mathematical astronomy for education as well as harmony and proportion as the basis for knowing about the world.[8]

Scholars have ranked these heterogeneous discourses, written in very different styles and for very different purposes, by their degree of scientific seriousness, just as ethnography tends to establish authorial credibility by drawing a sharp line between the 'hard facts' of empirical observation and the *topoi* of marvellous beings. Yet this perspective was largely foreign to the ancient mind. As in the Middle Ages (see below, pp. 373–374), there was a plurality of truths about the world that could embrace a wide variety of mentalities, methods, and discursive modes that sometimes complemented and sometimes contradicted one another. As *possible* pathways to knowledge, however, none was disqualified from the outset. That is also and especially true for the astronomical-cosmological discussions of the fourth century. These were conducted in a space of intense competition that not infrequently flared up in personal enmity (between Eudoxus and Plato, for example) and skirmishes between rival camps, but also allowed for mutually enriching exchange. They mirror the productive rivalry among the *poleis* engaged in active exploration, perpetuating it on a different level and with different actors.

All this did not yet entail any empirical expansion of the geographic horizon, nor did it confer any political or military advantage; this partly explained why ordinary people could scoff at astronomy as the folly of conceited aristocrats. Still, the will to get to the bottom of astronomical *and* terrestrial global phenomena created the foundation for a new way of seeing the world and for solving the problems bequeathed by the expeditions of the previous era.

Herodotus puzzled over why the mariners who allegedly circumnavigated Africa had the sun on their right. His theory that Libya extended south to ever more arid, barren climes was contradicted by the expedition of the Nasamones and by Hanno's voyage (see above, pp. 128–142). The division of the earth's disc into a cooler northern part and a warmer southern part no longer seemed plausible, yet what should take its place?[9] The phenomena of the far north were equally difficult to interpret. Herodotus had no explanation for the report that people who lived north of the Rhipaeans spent half the year in hibernation.[10] The long days could be deduced from the fact that on summer nights, the sun barely rose above the lowest points of northern latitudes. Yet it was hard to understand why the days and nights became ever longer the farther one travelled north, why the elevation of stars and constellations changed near the celestial pole when one moved north or south (they stand higher the farther one travels north and sink in the opposite direction), and why new stars appeared in the south that were unseen in the north.[11]

The only way to reconcile these changes with the expanded geographical knowledge base was to abandon the notion of an essentially flat earth—raised only at the edges like a trough, as Anaximander and the Ionians had maintained—with an unvarying horizon.[12] Rather, the changing horizons, light conditions, and stellar constellations were linked to *different standpoints* on earth. Once this step had been taken, the logical consequence was to relinquish the idea of a discoid earth. And here the theory of a spherical earth—far from commonplace at the beginning of the fifth century—offered itself as an alternative.[13] The proponents of this theory pointed out that for a pole-dweller, the sun sinks below the horizon for half a year at the autumnal equinox and is covered by the southern hemisphere; this would explain the six months' sleep recounted by Herodotus and already alluded to by Homer.[14] And now it could also be understood why the starry sky changed when the standpoint shifted from north to south, why the celestial pole rose to the north, why the pole retreated from the horizon or approached it when one moved towards or away from it, and why, finally, the sun's daily course changed with geographical latitude.[15] Xenophanes said that there were many suns and moons depending on the relation between the earth's climates, sections, and zones; even today we speak of a tropical sun and a polar sun.[16] The first measurement of the ecliptic (the angle between the sun's apparent course and the plane of the celestial equator) falls in the first half of the fifth century and is attributed to Oenopides of Chios; using the gnomon, he found this angle to be 24°.[17]

The theory of a spherical earth also made possible an orderly integration of climates. Parmenides of Elea (see above p. 122) categorized the sphere's surface, based on the movements and radiation of the sun, into five belts or zones (Greek: *zoné*). Following the Pythagorean model, he transposed the solar and stellar trajectories onto the earth's surface through central projection. Due to the sun's vertical position, the median zone between the tropics was a scorched, uninhabitable plain. Adjacent to the south and north lay a temperate and inhabitable zone that bordered the 'frigid zones' of the polar caps. For Parmenides, the scorched zone separating the temperate zones was almost twice as wide as the area between the tropics.[18]

Next, the known and newly discovered regions of the earth had to be integrated into this schema. The Carthaginian expeditions posed a problem. While the information they brought back from the west could be unproblematically transferred to the northern belt, their expeditions in the northern and southern Atlantic forced a correction of the borders of the frigid and torrid zones, since the habitable regions discovered south of the Tropic of Cancer intruded into the scorched zone.[19] A solution was offered by the widely travelled geographer, mathematician, and astronomer Eudoxus of Cnidus, not by chance the first to demonstrate the variability of the horizon by taking measurements with a gnomon and a celestial globe. He transposed Hecataeus' tripartite division of the ecumene into Asia, Europe, and Libya onto the northern temperate zone in the form of a rectangle twice as long as it was wide.[20] Probably influenced by the Carthaginian expeditions, he additionally assumed that Libya continued south of the torrid northern tropic to the temperate zone even farther south (beyond the southern tropic). This image accorded with the continent's actual dimensions, with the difference that the broad scorched zone stood opposed to the idea of a unified continent. Instead, Libya's extension south into the temperate zone formed a 'counter-ecumene', home to humans later referred to as 'antipodes'.[21]

A supplementary hypothesis posited that the Nile originated in the southern ecumene. Fed by winter rains in the south, it flowed north in a more or less straight line through the hot zone until it emptied into the Mediterranean. These rains swelled the river and caused the inundation of the Nile in summer.[22] Ecumene and counter-ecumene thus stood in an ongoing interrelationship that could be experienced physically. Nonetheless, Eudoxus probably assumed that no one could move from one ecumene to the other through the torrid, uninhabited zone between the tropics; that is also why the sources of the Nile remained undiscovered.[23]

If the sources of the Nile were to be found in a landmass extending south to the counter-ecumene, and if the Nile had no upriver connection to the Ocean (as Hecataeus and Euthymenes believed), was the counter-ecumene surrounded by the Ocean? Or did its arms embrace the outer sea in a gigantic arc that linked up with India in the east and made the Erythraean Sea an inland sea? And the most enticing question of all: if Libya continued far farther south than had previously been assumed, were there other ecumenes awaiting discovery in other parts of the earth, and if so, where were they in relation to the outer sea?[24]

All these questions were the subject of vigorous intellectual debate and spawned a number of different models, partly complementary, partly competing. The best-known answer was given by Plato. He was the first Greek author to have unambiguously asserted the Earth's spherical form (in the *Phaedo*, composed shortly after 378 BCE). In doing so, he put forward a theory that was clearly still revolutionary in fourth-century Athens.[25] The spherical Earth is envisaged as enormous. His famous saying that the people of the Mediterranean crouched around the sea like frogs around a pond targets a fixation on the familiar environs of a small ecumene. In fact, there were other continents on the globe. If the theory of the four terrestrial rivers developed in *Phaedo*'s concluding myth is understood to mirror the celestial realm, at least in part, what results is a spherical earth subdivided into four ecumenes by two 'oceanic belts' intersecting at right angles (the Ocean and the Acheron). This view of the Earth was to prove influential, probably providing the template for the bands on the medieval imperial orb.[26] In Plato's day, it accorded with popular ideas about the terraqueous world. The ocean extending from north to south would be equated with the Atlantic; that lying perpendicular to it can at least partly be identified with the Erythraean Sea. The upper-right triangular segment formed by the oceans would be the known ecumene, that beneath it the counter-ecumene (of the *Antioikoi*); the two fields opposite would be the ecumenes of the *Perioikoi* and the *Antipoden*, respectively. The east-west ocean roughly corresponds to the area occupied by the torrid zone in Parmenidean and Eudoxean teaching.[27] Water in the torrid zone should really evaporate; some scholars thus presumably removed the equatorial ocean from the model of oceanic belts and only accepted the Atlantic, which girdled the earth from north to south.[28] In the story of Atlantis from the *Timaeus*, written around 362, Plato speaks instead of an enormous ('true') continent that encompasses the Atlantic and the entire Ocean (the 'true sea') in the west.[29]

All these reflections reprise ancient myths, such as that of the realm of the dead beyond the Ocean (Homer) or the Isles of the Blessed, as well as contemporary speculations about a great southern land extending from India to Libya (later expressed by Aristotle, too),[30] and combine them with the need for a geometrically balanced distribution of water and land on the globe. As speculative as these constructions may be, they survived virtually unchallenged until the eve of the early-modern voyages of discovery: the antipodean continent furnishes the primary model for the *terra australis* with which Portuguese captains reckoned on their voyages down the west African coast, just as Columbus and his contemporaries never entirely dismissed the idea of a great western continent and Atlantic isles, even though the Genoese navigator promised a direct trade route to India. And the same discussions about the possibility of crossing and inhabiting the 'scorched equatorial zones' that would so preoccupy early-modern mariners have their origin here (see below, pp. 369–370).

Aristotle's Worldview

Even if connections and possible contacts *between* the ecumenes were rarely discussed, and even if a direct passage from Spain to India via the Atlantic was probably never seriously contemplated, these questions were embedded in the theory of how water and land were distributed on the spheroid Earth. In keeping with the Greek way of thinking, such questions were not approached with reference to nautical-technical criteria but on the plane of geodesical construction. Two options stood available to anyone wanting to find out the distance between the known and unknown ecumenes and whether they were linked by land bridges. Either they could combine calculations of the Earth's entire surface area with the east-west and north-south extension of the ecumenes, or they could draw on additional ethnographic, zoological, and botanical analogies, on the assumption that regions in the same climatic zone produced comparable flora and fauna.

Aristotle trod both paths. He broke new ground in seeking to prove the spherical hypothesis (although he rejected the Platonic idea that the Earth rotated on its axis).[31] The best-known proof rested on the observation that during lunar eclipses, the edge of the earth's disc displays a uniformly curved line on the moon's surface; his reference to changes in the horizon and the starry sky with even a slight northward or southward shift in standpoint was irrefutable. This fact convinced him that the Earth was relatively small, at any rate far smaller than Plato had suggested in the *Phaedo*. Drawing on the example set by the 'mathematicians' (probably including Eudoxus) and their calculations, he estimated the Earth's circumference at 400,000 stades (around 74,204 km).[32] The famous saying that the Earth is only a tiny speck in the universe rested on Aristotle's authority.[33] If the Earth was small, then the landmasses discovered on it had to occupy a relatively large space. This shrank the distances between them, and reaching the ends of the ecumenes, or discovering new ones, seemed simpler than on a gigantic globe.

At the same time, Aristotle modified the zonal theory by expanding the frigid zone and pushing the torrid zone farther to the north, past the Tropic of Cancer.[34] In the north, the land of the Scythians marked the border of the temperate zone, although whether this was inhabited in its entirety could, according to Aristotle, only be determined by experience, that is, by new expeditions. Like most of his contemporaries, he believed the southern counter-ecumene to be unreachable, with the result that Greek interest—in contrast to the Carthaginian tradition—again came to be focused on the west-east axis of the northern hemisphere.[35] Aristotle maintained that a single sea stretched from the ecumene's western to its eastern limit (Spain and India, respectively). While its breadth was open to interpretation, the sea could not be all that large.[36] On the other hand, similarities in fauna (elephants) made him think it 'not unlikely' that the region of Gibraltar and the eastern end of India were not only geographically close but are (or were) somehow territorially interlinked; whether this connection extended over the northern or southern hemisphere remained unexplained.[37]

With these reflections, as well as the idea of a relatively modest circumference of the Earth, Aristotle gave renewed impetus to would-be explorers. The more landmasses there were on a small earth, the greater the chances of encountering undiscovered countries in the temperate zone and placing academic constructions on an empirical footing. But in which direction should they set out? Should they go east, west, or both at once? As was so often the case, happenstance and political developments played a key role in deciding the outcome.

BRAVING THE NORTHWESTERN OCEAN

PYTHEAS OF MASSALIA'S VOYAGES OF DISCOVERY

The Celtic La Tène Culture

For the observer fixated on classical actors, it is easy to forget that, around the same time that the eastern Mediterranean was becoming embroiled in military conflict, no less momentous a revolution was taking place in the Celtic lands to the north. Together with a shift in power relations in Etruscan Italy, it would have a delayed impact on the Mediterranean world. From the mid-fifth century BCE, numerous fortified hilltop settlements of the Hallstatt culture were abandoned or destroyed. In their place appeared smaller settlements clustered around political centres, later classified by Caesar as *oppida*. We attribute them to the so-called La Tène culture to distinguish them from the Hallstatt Celts.

The reasons for the change are unclear. Perhaps the domestic agrarian economy was no longer capable of satisfying the expectations of elites and their hunger for luxury products, especially as the total population—if Roman authors are to be believed—was growing at the same time and needed to be fed. Perhaps the princes had overreached in their role as distributors of goods and services and deprived rival clan leaders of opportunities for power. The latter usurped their authority and cultivated—judging by their grave goods—a more martial bearing than their predecessors. Many carved out new fiefdoms. Others descended from the late fifth century on Italy, and later even on Greece, to seize in far larger quantities as booty what their predecessors had once received as diplomatic gifts. Rome was almost completely captured during one of these raids.[38]

Massalia was spared such massive invasions (the sources report only of a siege by a Ligurian tribe).[39] Yet the economic consequences of upheavals within Celtic territories were all the more severe. Archaeologists have found that trade with the Celtic north via the Rhône experienced a sharp downturn in the very period that saw the emergence of the La Tène culture.[40] Clearly, the old customers for Massiliote wares had been driven out, while the new ones took what they wanted by force or procured them through a closer-lying partner, the Etruscans.

The Etruscans had relocated to the Po Valley in the early fifth century, in reaction to Massalia's dominant role as a distribution centre for Mediterranean wares and after shattering defeats at the hands of the southern Italian Greeks. From here, they forged new trade links via the passes in the central Alps with centres of the La Tène culture on the Rhine, Mosel, and Saar.[41] The direct north-south axis proved more effective than the route up the Rhône monopolized by Massalia, especially as it could bypass the declining Hallstatt hillforts at Mont Lassois and the Heuneburg. At a time when Athens and Sparta were preparing to do battle for hegemony in Greece, the Etruscans had largely brought northern trade under their control and regained a monopoly on tin.

Massalia initially reacted by intensifying trade with the Mediterranean. Yet for a city that since the mid-sixth century had all but depended for its existence and prosperity on its contacts with the Celts, this development was a heavy blow in the medium term, particularly as the Carthaginians hindered maritime access to the Atlantic silver and tin mining regions of north-west Spain. First attempts at recovering lost positions may have been made at the start of the fourth century, when allied Rome waged war with Etruscan cities and central Italian tribes. The key to improving the situation was a revival of the Rhône links to the north, and perhaps necessity now gave rise to an unforeseen opportunity. If the Hallstatt rulers no longer came into consideration as tin and amber middlemen, what could be more natural than to go straight to the source? That way not only could costs be cut but the Etruscan competition could be shaken off as well.

Pytheas' Search for the Tin Isles

These thoughts may have spurred a Massiliote captain called Pytheas and his paymasters to seek a direct route to the Tin Isles in a bid to break the Etruscan stranglehold on the market. Here, as so often, a classic competitive situation unleashed an explorative dynamic that propelled those seeking a local commercial advantage to venture into ever more remote regions. On these last stages, at the latest, the clarification of scientific questions co-determined the voyage. Pytheas thus combined fourth-century geographic and astronomical scholarship with an ambition for discovery fuelled by mercantile interests. He anticipates the role of the scientifically productive writer-discoverer who would become the standard type in the early Hellenistic age, under the aegis of the Seleucid and Ptolemaic kings (see below, pp. 224–226).

The sources characterize Pytheas as *doctissimus* and *philosophos*; perhaps he was a student of Eudoxus who exploited his hometown's trade connections with Athens to learn about astronomic measuring methods and establish contact with Aristotle and his acolytes (while Aristotle, conversely, consulted Massiliote informants when drafting his constitution of Massalia).[42] Upon returning from the north, Pytheas composed a text 'On the Ocean'. It went beyond the confines of earlier *periploi* to encompass the sea in its entirety, in keeping with the expanded worldview of the fourth century. The few surviving fragments and testimonies show Pytheas to have been keenly interested in solving natural-scientific problems, such as the phenomenon of the tides, as well as in placing new astronomical and geographical data on a mathematical basis.

Some scholars therefore conclude that Pytheas, as Massalia's foremost astronomer, had his own observatory at a site near the temple to Artemis or Apollo and calculated the length of the shadows cast by the sun with the help of a 10-metre-high gnomon. At first, the gnomon had probably been used only for telling the time; Oenopides had then measured the angle of the ecliptic with it at a constant 24°, defining it as one side of a regular pentagon. Soon after, Eudoxus may have attempted to use the relations between the shadows furnished by the gnomon to ascertain the geographic latitudes of their respective locations (parallels north [+] or south [-] of the Equator).[43] Pytheas perfected this technique by calculating the ratio of the gnomon's height to the length of the shadow it cast at the summer solstice and converting this into degrees of latitude, thereby determining the geographical latitude (or parallel) of Massalia before setting sail. During his journey north, he repeated the procedure at least four times with a portable gnomon to gauge his relative distance from Massalia's latitude. This suggests the entire journey must have lasted several months, since the astronomical data for the far north required observing the sun's position during the winter solstice.[44] The calculations were so influential that the great mathematicians and astronomers Hipparchus (active around 160–130 BCE) and Eratosthenes (c. 276–194 BCE) adopted them along with other astronomic observations (e.g. on the polar constellations). They constitute one of the most important arguments for the authenticity of the expedition.[45]

Many scholars believe that Pytheas sailed with his own ship through the Pillars of Heracles past Tartessos and into the Bay of Biscay.[46] While this is possible, there is not a skerrick of evidence in the sources to support this assumption, which would be difficult to square with the fact that Massalia had known about the advantages of inland trade for centuries and, in view of the Etruscan competition, must have sought an alternative precisely here. Traders and expeditionary leaders were always eager to combine land and sea routes, preferring overland shortcuts to a longer seaborne voyage. Sailing around Spain to the Gironde estuary was a far longer and—given Carthaginian naval dominance—more perilous undertaking than travelling from Agde to the mouth of the Aude, then making the short trip to Tolosa before sailing down the Garonne and Gironde to the coast; or taking an alternative inland route via the Loire from the Rhône Valley or Narbo to Biscay.[47] Dispensing with a ship of his own would have offered Pytheas an additional advantage: native mariners familiar with the routes to the Tin Isles, and with ships far better adapted to the rough North Sea, could be used instead. This was also in keeping with the customs of fourth-century maritime trade.

Pytheas thus came without difficulty to the Spanish northwest coast (*Aremorica*), the *Ostimioi*, as well as an island called Ouexisame, probably today's Ushant. The *Ostimioi* are probably identical with the Oestrymnians, mentioned by Avienius and known to Massiliote sailors (see above, p. 126); Caesar later called them *Osismii*. Somewhere on the coast of *Aremorica* (perhaps at the ancient port of Le Vaudet), Pytheas carried out his second measurement of latitude. It came to 48°42′; the parallel ran through the coastline of *Celtica* (= Aremorica).[48] Navigating by the Pole Star, he then sailed on to the Tin Isles, surely aboard a vessel much like those later used by the Veneti.

The direct goal was the southwestern tip of England, today's Land's End in Cornwall. Here Pytheas could observe the sites where tin was mined and the methods for extracting it; cast into transportable form, the material was shipped from one of the peninsulas or offshore islands such as Ictis (St Michael's Mount or Mount Batten).[49] Cape Cantion, likewise used as a port of export, can be identified with Kent or the Isle of Thanet.[50] Natives called themselves Pretani or Pritani (probably Celtic for the 'painted' or 'tattooed' ones); if Diodorus is to be believed, it was from them that Pytheas borrowed the name *Pretannia* or *Prettantiké* for the island, and it was from them that he may have learned how far Britain extended to the north.[51] Pytheas had now moved beyond his earlier mission to scout tin-mining areas. As in earlier exploratory ventures (Hanno, Euthymenes), mercantile objectives could be furthered by pursuing the geographic, ethnographic, and astronomical interests that now came to occupy the centre of his attention.

Thule and the Push to the Arctic

Pytheas is the first Mediterranean explorer known to have traversed large parts of the island, starting out from Cornwall or Kent. His claim to have travelled all over Britain is exaggerated and has been taken to indicate the general untrustworthiness of his account. Yet his critics knew only the European mainland, which was harder to access by land and sea than the British Isles. There is no doubt that with the help of locals, Pytheas was able to gain a good impression of the islanders' way of life. While his report shows the same idealizing traits found in descriptions of other peripheral people (simplicity and frugality), it comes across as authentic with respect to diet and agriculture, in particular.[52]

Following his overland excursions, he continued by ship along the English west coast through St George's Channel to the north, passing countless islands en route (including the Isle of Man and the east coast of Ireland). Sailing up the channel, he may already have connected changes in the tides with the movements of the moon. He set anchor on several occasions to undertake further excursions into the hinterland: not just to learn more about the natives but also to measure the sun's height at noon at the summer solstice and to calculate how far north he had sailed from Massalia. Measurements were probably made at the latitude of today's Cambridge and Dundee as well as on the Isle of Man and Northern Ireland, subsequently fixed by Hipparchus at 54°14′. The northernmost measurement was most likely taken at the Outer Hebrides (Lewis); its latitude was calculated at 58°13′.[53]

As he sailed ever farther north, Pytheas noticed that the Sun still shone weakly in winter and moved from west to east, contrary to expectations.[54] Now began the most exciting leg of the voyage. From the northern tip of Britain, he probably sailed past Cape Wrath to the Orkneys, an archipelago that archaeological records show to have been densely populated at the time. Stone circles suggest that the natives made astronomical observations, which surely would have piqued the Massiliote's interest. His comment that there 'was no night' at the time of the summer solstice holds true of the Shetlands and Orkneys.[55]

Having now acquired the Celtic tongue, Pytheas would have listened spellbound to the stories of the Orkney islanders. They knew of an island farther north called Thule (Thoule) that could be reached in six days' sailing.[56] Pytheas immortalized Thule. We cannot know for sure whether he himself visited the island or merely passed on what his informants on the Orkneys or Shetlands told him (the latter case would resemble Aristeas' account of the land west of the Issedones).[57] The Romans later assumed that he had discovered the Shetlands; modern scholars point to the Norwegian coast or an island (or archipelago) off the coast of Scandinavia.[58] More recent scholarship tends to favour Iceland: the island is visible in fair weather from the Faroes, while there is a great deal to support (and nothing to disprove) a passage from the Orkneys or Shetlands, such as those later undertaken by the Vikings. The inhabitants of the northernmost islands of Britain were familiar with the currents and bird flight and would surely have charted a course for northern waters in their quest for fish, whales, or edible birds (on the Faroes), including during the winter months; it is not unlikely that they made it as far as Iceland.[59]

Pytheas recorded numerous observations about Thule's botany. His opponents (Strabo) later mixed these up with descriptions of other northern regions to expose him as a fraud. For example, a reference to natives making a drink from honey and grain applies to other regions and cannot be used as an argument against identifying Thule with Iceland.[60] By contrast, the claim that 'the people who live close to the frozen zone do almost or entirely without cultivated fruits and domestic animals, and they subsist on millet, wild herbs, fruits, and roots' holds true of Iceland. Idealizing *topoi* of a primitive diet may resonate here, yet Pytheas demonstrates his ethnographic expertise and anticipates later models when he makes links between nature (*physis*) or the cold climate and the people's way of life (*nomos*). At any rate, his descriptions were so impressive and cogent that, only a few decades after his work appeared, Hecataeus of Abdera relocated the homeland of the Hyperboreans to an island in the Ocean.[61]

The assertion that Thule lies in the Arctic Circle can likewise be applied to Iceland. Pytheas states that the distance of the summer tropic (Tropic of Cancer) from the Equator is equal to the distance of the Arctic Circle

('circle of the bear') (23.5°) from the North Pole, and that in Thule there is no night at the summer solstice and no day at the winter solstice.[62] The sole surviving exact quotation from his book on the ocean says just that: 'the barbarians showed us where the Sun goes to sleep; for around these places it happens that the night becomes very short, two hours for some, three for others, so that, a little while after setting, the Sun rises straightaway'.[63] What Pytheas here describes in figurative speech is a real phenomenon in the Arctic, as Irish monks in Iceland recounted a millennium later. For those dwelling in southern climes, the sun sets in the evening and where it hides at night remains a mystery. In the Arctic Circle, however, the midnight sun never completely disappears. Instead, observers can track how it comes to rest on the horizon or sinks temporarily behind a mountain range (its 'bed'?): it 'goes to rest' and 'rises again'.[64]

And Pytheas, finally, depicts other natural phenomena that sounded strange to his contemporaries only because they were hearing of them for the first time, in a language that strained against the limit of its expressive capacity.[65] North of Thule, probably a day's journey away, began the 'curdled' sea. This evidently refers to the Arctic Ocean with its glaciers and icebergs.[66] On the island there were places where the sea 'cooked' or 'lived'. If Thule is identified with Iceland, we might think here of volcanoes or geysers lying near the coastline. In keeping with this image, Pytheas observes a region 'where land properly speaking no longer exists, nor sea, nor air, but a mixture of these things, like a marine lung, in which earth and water and all things are in suspension'.[67] Perhaps he was describing the Northern Lights, or (in connection with the tides) shifts in ice using terminology that recalled a metaphysical concept, developed by Aristotle and Plato, according to which earth and sky merge at the edge of the world.[68]

Amber Roads

At some point, the Massiliote departed the far north and sailed back to the Channel, probably along the east coast of England. Now began the third stage of the expedition, which again combined geographic exploration with the search for raw goods and their regions of origin. The North Sea was famous for amber as well as tin; even in Herodotus' day, the precious material was said to come from the coasts of the northern Ocean. The Massiliotes knew that it was transported via rivers and bridle paths to the

Saône and Rhône or farther east via the Alps and the Danube basin to the Po region. Pytheas thus had a natural interest in exploring the river systems of the North Sea area and solving the mystery of amber's origin.

He probably proceeded on a local ship through the Wadden Sea of the Frisian Islands to the mouth of the Elbe, the point where amber entered the inland trade network. The Elbe would accordingly be the legendary amber river, Eridanus.[69] On the coast of the Wadden Sea, near the river's mouth, lived the Guions and Teutons, later classified as Germanic tribes by Pliny. Pytheas offers the earliest extant account of these tribes,[70] although their ethnic designation and difference to the Celts were unknown to him—these points were clarified around two centuries later by the Greek scholar Posidonius. In any event, the tribes chiefly interested the Massiliote for the insight they could give into the origin of amber. The Teutons purchased it from the inhabitants of an island called Abalus (the Celtic Avalon?), one day's sailing from the coast. The islanders supposedly used any amber they did not sell as fuel (perhaps for ritual purposes), an indication of the sheer quantity available. The name for the island found in other sources, *Basilia/ Basileia* ('royal'), suggests monarchical rule.[71] Many identify the island with Heligoland, which was larger at the time, and see it not as the source of the commodity—there are no indigenous amber remains there—but as a 'marketplace and warehouse' for trading amber from Jutland. This would accord not only with the comparable function of the islands off the southern English coast for the tin trade (see above, pp. 181–182), but also with the assertion that the Teutons bought amber there.[72]

Pytheas could have further pursued his objective by making for the west coast of Jutland as well. Some believe that he even sailed past the Danish islands to the Baltic (Samland) and the second major source region for amber, which first became accessible in the Ice Age. On this account, Bornholm, an island in the Baltic Sea (Gotland), or the Scandinavian Peninsula could have been Abalus. If this theory is correct, then Pytheas would have achieved what his compatriots had long hoped for: a direct route to the sources of amber that could compete with the Etruscans' inland connections.[73]

As is so often the case, the sources show no interest in the return journey. One possible itinerary would have taken him through the Heligoland Bight and the Channel to the Bay of Biscay and from there overland to the Mediterranean, or down the Elbe and then along the Rhine via one of the amber trade routes. Yet there are ancient voices suggesting a different route:

according to Polybius (quoted in Strabo), Pytheas 'traversed the whole of the coast of Europe from Gades to the Tanais (Don)'. Assuming Pytheas did not mistake the Elbe for the Don/Tanais, it may be supposed that he sailed from the Baltic via the Vistula (which he identified with the Don) and the Bug (Hypanis) or Dniester to the Black Sea and hence found the eastern arm of the amber road, returning from there to the Mediterranean and Massalia.[74] This theory is not as far-fetched as it may sound. If Pytheas did reach the Baltic, natives could have informed him about rivers that flowed south from there and had their source near rivers known to the Greeks that drained into the Black Sea (such as the Dnieper and Volga). Later authors had their reasons for comparing his travels with the voyage of the Argonauts![75]

Whatever the specifics of his itinerary may have been, the few reliable facts at our disposal suffice to qualify his expedition as one of the greatest exploratory feats of the ancient world. Yet comparing him with Columbus—as the modern-day Massiliotes are fond of doing—fails to do justice to his undertaking, and to ancient voyages of discovery in general. Pytheas was not sailing into uncharted waters. Like Aristeas before him on land, he was using established coastal routes and maritime connections, albeit more consequentially than ever before and aided by the latest astronomical navigation and measurement techniques. His achievement was to have traversed the partial routes used by various ethnic groups and combined them into a grand tour by land, river, and sea of regions only vaguely known to his compatriots.

Some contemporaries found this achievement so implausible, especially in regard to the far north, that they accused Pytheas of telling tall tales. The best-known such critic, Polybius, was a historian notorious for finding fault with his predecessors and mistrusting all mariners and traders. He also needed to disparage Pytheas' exploits to boost his own profile: in the second century BCE, Polybius himself carried out a journey along the African coast that, despite the patronage of Scipio Aemilianus, barely went beyond the Strait of Gibraltar (if it even made it that far). He therefore could not tolerate the fact that, two centuries earlier, a 'private man' had sailed much farther without such powerful backing. Polybius offered no serious geographic-ecological or nautical grounds against the authenticity of the voyage. Similarly, the geographer Strabo cast doubt on the voyage because no great ruler had commissioned Pytheas to undertake it, and because the northern regions of the Arctic Circle had to be uninhabitable, as stipulated by orthodox climate theory.[76]

Pytheas had demonstrated the exact opposite, and his assumptions have been confirmed by settlement archaeology. Furthermore, all the nautical, archaeological, and political data indicate that the conditions for such a voyage were in place. In view of the sources, there is thus no reason to doubt that it occurred (unlike in the case of the circumnavigation of Africa), especially considering that it fits with the scientific, political, and economic context of the time. Pytheas sought a direct route to the tin-mining areas and the amber lands, and he used mathematical astronomy to criticize older views and to calculate latitudes so convincingly that they were not only recognized by Strabo but adopted by later scholars like Eratosthenes and Hipparchus. They had no doubts about his voyage and acknowledged his scientific breakthroughs. He was the first to have penetrated the Arctic Circle (around 65°N); he extended the temperate zone farther north than his contemporaries (Aristotle located the border at 54°N) and described astronomical phenomena like the midnight sun on an empirical basis.[77]

Remarkably, neither ancient nor modern authors mention the sober self-assurance with which the Massiliote braved the unknown. No one—not even his critics—refers to the dangers and terrors that the North Sea and the unknown latitudes into which he was venturing must have posed for the Mediterranean mariner. It is the same self-assurance, known to the Greeks since Homer, with which Aristeas, Scylax, and others called on divine help as they set out to explore worlds that were somehow connected with their own. In the case of Pytheas, there is an additional confidence in drawing on native experience and scientific techniques to forge a path to the outer limits of the world in the quest for more knowledge. In this respect, too, Pytheas is a child of the fourth century. New knowledge on ethnographic, astronomic-geographical, or medicinal terrain was combined in complex models with diverse goals: to comprehend foreign lands, to develop theories of the Earth's surface, or to present remote regions of the world under the aspect of their medicinal utility.

For a long time, however, the voyage of Pytheas spurred no follow-up research trips to the north. During the expedition, or perhaps shortly before it, an entrepôt (emporium) called Korbilon/Corbilo was founded at the mouth of the Loire to facilitate access to the tin mines of Brittany.[78] That was enough for the lords of Massalia. Other powers, such as the Etruscans and Carthaginians, were mired in power-political conflicts in Italy and the Tyrrhenian Sea that made incursions into the North Atlantic an unaffordable luxury. Likewise, the Celtic world was increasingly seen in Italy and Carthage (and soon in Greece, too) as an enemy threat. It forfeited its role as a conduit to the world of the north, only to take it up again when Rome expanded to the Gallic Mediterranean coast.

THE NEAR AND FAR EAST

The Multifaceted Image of the Persians

The situation was different in the east. Even after Herodotus, this remained the major object of study and experimentation for the Greeks. Here, the Persian Empire formed a stable bridge to faraway places. Graeco-Persian relations were complex. On an individual level, the search for advancement in Persian service as physician, mercenary, expeditionary leader, or engineer predominated. On the level of the polis as a whole, the relationship was shaped by military and political considerations as well as by the attempt to square a sense of civic identity with the existence of this vast empire. Several interpretive models were developed within this multi-layered framework.

When Persia succeeded in extending its hegemony into the Aegean following the Peloponnesian War, the Greeks wavered between defiance and political resignation. Their sense of political failure could only be mitigated by an insistence on their cultural, intellectual, and technological superiority to the 'barbarians'. This compensatory strategy deepened oppositions that were already established in Aeschylus. The Persians were disdained as Asiatic barbarians who cowered before a despotic, cruel, and arrogant ruler and were therefore incapable of developing the best human qualities, in contrast to the freedom-loving Greeks living in Europe. This intercontinental opposition was politically instrumentalized in Athens, above all. Athenian politicians needed a powerful bogeyman, first to justify their dominion over the members of the Delian League and then, in the fourth century, to encourage their citizens to resume an imperial foreign policy.

For all that, a wide-ranging ethnographic interest continued to exist largely independently of political imperatives and prejudices. It was particularly cultivated by those Greeks who grew up under Persian rule and whose careers allowed or indeed forced them to arrive at a more nuanced image of the nature of the country and the *physis* of its inhabitants. Along with historians like Herodotus, these were mainly mercenaries and doctors active at the Persian court.

There were overlaps and influences between the two perspectives, and it is not always clear how they related to the way people actually behaved, just as it is generally very difficult to draw conclusions about broader social attitudes from literary evaluations and descriptions. Besides, attitudes and opinions were always overlaid by everyday conduct. Persia was and remained the archenemy, yet this did not prevent the elite of Athens from adopting elements of Persian grave design, fashion, and lifestyle (parasols), nor its politicians from orienting their building projects (Odeon), methods of rule, and representational forms on Persian models. In the fourth century, the people's assembly went so far as to issue decrees honouring Persian satraps and awarded them Athenian citizenship rights.[79] The weight accorded a given perspective additionally depended on political trends and moods. Thus Euripides, writing near the end of the Peloponnesian War, undermined the continentally and culturally determined Greek-barbarian binary by presenting the 'European' Achaeans as vicious barbarians and the 'Asiatic' Trojan women as noble victims.[80] This invited the conclusion that human behaviour is not always dictated by geography. *Nomos*, not nature, is the deciding factor, meaning that anyone can act with 'barbarian' cruelty or 'non-barbarian' nobility.[81]

Euripides, like the Sophists, was known for his critical diagnosis of Athenian society. Precisely because his plays so pointedly call into question the conventional Greek-barbarian dichotomy, this may be supposed to have been deeply rooted in the minds of his fellow citizens.[82] The same held true for the old idea that there was a correlation between geographic-climatological conditions and character traits.[83] Hippocratic physicians had posited links among climate, landscape, diet, and *physis*, transposing patterns they detected in regions (Scythia—Libya—Egypt) onto the continents of the ecumene.[84] According to the text 'On airs, waters, and places', Asia was favoured by nature; fertile and well-watered, it had been spared violent seasonal extremes in weather. Yet these were the very conditions that had made its denizens soft, indolent, and fit objects of monarchical rule. The Scythians were effeminate, too, due to their moist and flabby bodies, a byproduct of the northern climate. By contrast, the 'southern European' Greeks (in the

Golden Mean) had to cope with more pronounced seasonal variations in climate and an inhospitable environment. They needed to show courage and valour and could only live in freedom, which gave them the space they needed to develop their natural aptitudes.[85]

Although the text combines climatological and geographical determinisms with political institutions (monarchy), it does not draw any political conclusions.[86] In order to make political use of the physical determinants, these had to be tied to barbarian clichés in a setting that was open to such an approach. This occurred in Athens. In his *Republic*, Plato has the wise Socrates explain that the globe is divided into three cultural zones with differing ethical qualities. Aggressive courage was highly developed among Thracians and Scythians, the Greeks were formed by a love of wisdom and knowledge, while the Egyptians and Phoenicians farther south were characterized by their acquisitiveness. The Greeks are identified with the part of the soul that partakes of the divine and rules over the other parts.[87]

Aristotle drew political consequences from this model by linking it to the continental binary. The inhabitants of northern Europe were brave yet lacked the intelligence and skill that (civic) culture can foster. By contrast, those who lived in hot Asia, roughly corresponding to the Persian Empire, were intelligent and skilful but slothful. Only the Greeks, blessed with a moderate climate, maintain a balance between valour and intelligence. They are 'naturally' free, whereas the barbarians of the east are slavish. Accordingly, Greeks should rule over barbarians.[88]

This model, like the inertia attributed to the Scythians in the text 'On airs, waters, and places', was blatantly contradicted by real-life experiences with the northerners, who were considered exceptionally skilled warriors and were more than capable of creating a civilization. The fact that the Persians, the eastern barbarians par excellence, had acquired the greatest empire in history was equally incompatible with their supposedly lethargic nature. These were constructs based on a purely conceptual symmetry of simple binaries, whence they derived their intellectual appeal and political applicability. The Athenian rhetorician Isocrates radicalized the Aristotelian model. He posited an insurmountable ethnic-cultural opposition, setting a signal that was welcomed in the period after the Peloponnesian War: the Greeks felt themselves to be *culturally* superior to the whole world, yet they were paralysed by civil wars and no match for the Persians when it came to foreign policy. The solution was for *all* Greeks ('Panhellenism') to take up arms against the archenemy. Such a war would bring the Greeks freedom, release their brothers in Asia Minor from Persian bondage, and open new opportunities for fortune-seekers.[89]

The Mercenary's Clear-Eyed Gaze: Xenophon's Persian Friends

Isocrates drew his optimism not just from the philosophers' pseudo-scientific constructions but also from real experience. In 402 BCE Cyrus (the Younger), the Persian commander in western Asia Minor, marched east with around 10,000 Greek soldiers to oust his brother from the throne. The mercenaries proved their valour at the Battle of Cunaxa, yet Cyrus fell in the attack on the king. The Greeks were now stranded in enemy territory without their paymasters and had lost their officers to boot. They immediately elected new leaders, among them the Athenian Xenophon, before advancing through unfamiliar terrain to the Black Sea. Xenophon's report on the march, *Anabasis* (literally 'a going up, a march'), deliberately establishes a parallel with Odysseus' return to Ithaca.[90] A rich ethnographic source, it once again demonstrates the importance of mercenaries for exploration. The account of the feast hosted by the Thracian king Seuthes is one of the most valuable ethnographic descriptions in ancient literature.[91]

The *Anabasis* conveyed a message that could be understood without any need for philosophical models: the Greek professional fighter, battle-hardened in the Peloponnesian War, was so superior to the Persians even in their own land that they dared not risk open confrontation. The homeward march proved that a Greek army could traverse vast unknown spaces. The impression was confirmed by the successes of the heavily undermanned Spartan king Agesilaus against the satraps of Asia Minor in 396–394. In addition, the push for independence by Persian satraps and governors (like Mausolus) suggested that the once-mighty Persian Empire was crumbling from within. All this encouraged Isocrates to renew his calls for an offensive war against Persia.

Xenophon was not immune to this sense of self-confidence. He mocked the wealth of the Persian king and urged his compatriots not to bow and scrape over silver. However, he also stood in Persian service and showed greater nuance. Cyrus the Younger was a model general of whom 'nothing shameful was either seen or heard'.[92] Xenophon's *Cyropaedia* portrays Cyrus the Elder, the founder of the Persian Empire, as an ideal ruler who was a barbarian simply because he was not a Greek. According to Xenophon (and Plato), the Persians began their decline only *after* Cyrus, when they adopted Median customs and relinquished their traditional education system.[93] Even when he thematizes the deviousness of the Persian Tissaphernes in the *Anabasis*, he does so against a context of Greeks acting in similar ways. His account of the series of Persian defeats at the hands of Agesilaus is not intended to highlight the weakness and cowardice of the enemy; rather, it serves to increase the victor's glory and distract attention from his mistakes in Greece.[94] In the *Hellenica*, Xenophon depicts a conversation between Agesilaus and the satrap Pharnabazus in which each pays respect to the other's cultural 'code': the Persian appears in clothing fit for a king yet sits down on the ground beside Agesilaus and proves his intellectual superior when they argue.[95]

This positive image of the Persian ruling class from an *ethical-intellectual* standpoint was to prove influential. It established the basis for the union of the Graeco-Macedonian and Persian elites advocated by Alexander, even as a belief in the *military* weakness of the Persians gave hope that their empire was ripe for conquest. The two were not necessarily contradictory: the Persians' achievements could be respected even as they were targeted for invasion. Their overlordship over so many peoples impressed the Greeks, particularly at a time when their own alliance systems were proving incapable of concentrating and organizing power. Precisely because the polis had failed as an instrument of expansion, the monarchic principle, represented by a benevolent and rational regent, was embraced as a divinely sanctioned form of government. Plato represented Darius as a great monarch and legislator on the same level as Solon and Lycurgus, a view that accorded with the Persian kings' own self-appraisal. In his *Oeconomicus*, Xenophon draws on the template of the Persian monarchy when describing the household of large landowners in Greece.[96]

There were also personal reasons for using Persian examples to illustrate the positive side of barbarian elites. Unlike Isocrates, Plato and Xenophon were aristocrats who cared little for Athenian democracy and found Persian grandees more attractive interlocutors than the man on the street.[97] For them, the Persian Empire was far less servile, including in its interior, than it seemed to those who understood monarchy as inimical to freedom. Xenophon emphasizes that 'in Cyrus' province it became possible for either Greek or barbarian, provided he was guilty of no wrongdoing, to travel fearlessly wherever he wished, carrying with him whatever it was to his interest to have'.[98] This freedom was enjoyed, above all, by the growing numbers of hirelings engaged in Persian service. Thus, while Xenophon's depiction of Cyrus the Elder may have been oriented on Greek ideals, it incorporated a wealth of authentic details as well as oral and written traditions from the east. The last books of the *Cyropaedia* betray an intimate knowledge of the psychology and methodology of Persian rule. Knowledge of how a state was administered was also always knowledge of a land and its people. Like Herodotus before him, Xenophon therefore viewed all non-Greeks with an open mind—how could a mercenary officer survive otherwise?—and was familiar with climate theory. In contrast to the theorist Aristotle, however, he did not use it to interpret his ethnographic material in a degrading way.

Some maintain that Herodotus and Xenophon were exceptionally broad-minded, whereas the common man clung to negative stereotypes.[99] To be sure, we know very little about the 'common man' and his attitudes. Yet it might be asked how many Athenians were familiar with the theories of Aristotle—the 'common man' surely was not. What we do know is that the lectures Herodotus held in Athens were a great success and that Xenophon was widely read. All this suggests that Herodotus and Xenophon were not in the minority with their cautious perspective and their interest in authentic details.[100] At any rate, many of those who for professional or political reasons (as exiles) came into close contact with the Persians formed a different impression of them than the politicians back home.

The Physician's Hunger for Knowledge: Ctesias on India

One of them was Ctesias of Cnidus. To this day, his two books on Persia and India are a target for criticism that even calls into question the bare outlines of his life.[101] While much of the criticism is justified, it is taken too far at times, as when information about Ctesias or details from his writings are dismissed as 'fiction' just because they resemble set pieces from literary traditions or fail to appear in parallel sources, or because more had been expected of them than is contained in parallel or precursor sources. This involves a problematic reversal of the burden of proof. It pays insufficient heed to the fact that only a fraction of the ancient literature on the Persians, and hence also on the circumstances of Ctesias' life, has come down to us. Furthermore, modern scholars often implicitly judge the intention and literary quality of Ctesias' writings by modern criteria or against the standards set by the best ancient historians. Yet Ctesias did not see himself primarily as a historian in the manner of Herodotus or Thucydides, even if he supposedly later characterized his own work with the term *historie* (enquiry);[102] his professional interests led him down other paths.

If we disregard the hyperbolic criticism of his biography and rely solely on the ancient sources, Ctesias was said to have fought in the Battle of Cunaxa, albeit on the opposite side to Xenophon. From 405 he was engaged as a doctor at the court of Ataxerxes and used his position to write a 'Persian history'. It offered a kind of moral portrait of the court that contained invented and sensationalist material, yet he also took pains to record realistic details, although these rarely betrayed a specifically ethnographic interest. Such was not the author's intention, however. He set out to depict aspects of the Persian world left out by Herodotus in dramatic, novelistic fashion, focusing on the psychology, motives, and character traits of his *dramatis personae.* In this respect, he sometimes recalls the much later Plutarch, and many see the *Persica* as a forerunner of the novel and ('fictional') travel literature. Some suspect Persian models, while others interpret his imaginative stories and antithetical position to Herodotus as a deliberate provocation for the amusement of a Greek readership. That was not all, however. The Persian court and its elites offered a cautionary example of how, in a monarchy where luxury prevailed and powerful women exerted undue influence, good characteristics and dispositions (of kings) could turn bad; only under this aspect could they be presented as a mirror image of Greek virtues, although they provided no ammunition for sweeping and one-sided negative stereotypes about the Persians in general.

His second book, the *Indica*, took a thematically different approach. As Persia transformed over time from an existential threat to an imposing yet familiar neighbour, so the need grew among Greeks for more accurate information about the lands even farther south (Arabia) and east. The argument that the *Indica* served in part to hold up an idealizing contrast to the Persian monarchy is unconvincing not least because there was no comparable court in India.[103] Accordingly, so far as the surviving fragments permit us to tell, the subject of the book on India, unlike the *Persica*, is not people, their characteristics and intrigues, but ethnographic, zoological, and botanical particulars. Many scholars take it for a literary confection, a collection of tall tales and exotica with no grounding in reality. They cite ancient critics who denounced Ctesias as a fraud. Yet such wholesale denunciations of colleagues and predecessors were practically *de rigueur* in antiquity. In the case of Ctesias, they are especially trite. They were made by authors who took the works of later authors on India as their yardstick. Writing after Alexander, these authors could learn far more about the country, even beyond the Indus, owing to the completely transformed political situation. Any comparison between them and Ctesias would therefore necessarily be to the latter's detriment, without permitting any conclusions to be drawn about his credibility.[104]

Another aspect frequently overlooked by modern critics is that Ctesias saw himself not primarily as a historian embedding his ethnographic material in a comprehensive analytical framework, but as a storyteller and physician. As such, he needed to keep a watchful eye on everything foreign to assert himself in the contest for royal favour. His India book thus makes no claim to check all the facts and integrate them into a reliable historical context. It aims instead to collate extensive information from this faraway wonderland and present it to a Greek public in an appealing form. We must again avoid making all-too-sharp distinctions between hard ethnographic 'facts' and fanciful exotica. This division counted less for contemporaries; these were two manifestations of one and the same reality. Marvellous peoples and natural phenomena had been fixtures of the popular image of India since Scylax. Ctesias therefore had to reprise them if he wanted to conform to the genre and satisfy his readers' expectations.

The *Indica* depicts the 'monstrous' tribes only casually mentioned by Scylax in far greater detail, adding new ones from other parts of the world or from Indian traditions. The best known are the 'dog-headed' people, previously localized in Africa. They clearly derive from reports of apes.[105] There are apes in India, and they accordingly appear in Hindu mythology, the Puranas, and the great epics, along with the big-eared, the one-eyed, and the antipodes. Yet the Indians did not see them as exotic; they were a means for expressing social and political differences within their own country. The 'dog-headed' stood for communities outside the Brahman elite, for lower 'castes', or for the 'casteless'. There were further ancient Indian stories that identified non-Aryan mountain tribes in the Himalaya with dog-headed savages owing to their incomprehensible 'barking'.[106]

Today, it can hardly be doubted that Ctesias knew of such stories.[107] Like Scylax before him, he sought to combine them with Greek interpretive templates and information. While he expanded the world of Indian marvels and enriched it with multiple details, he invented or 'fabricated' nothing, as is sometimes alleged. Besides, it is not at all clear whether such stories were typical of the *Indica* as a whole. The extant sections are solely those selected and preserved by the following generations in the manner of a Reader's Digest. Even among the fragments, there are texts that make no mention of wonders (*thaumata*). Evidently the text contained much that was objective and sober. If it had been preserved in full, we could no doubt arrive at a more nuanced judgment.[108]

Yet even the marvellous tales do not in themselves demonstrate a lack of seriousness. The Sophists saw in them a vehicle for meaningful argument. Herodotus, in his very eagerness to grasp the world without prejudice, showed a pronounced weakness for unusual plants and animals from India and Egypt. Even Aristotle, one of the fiercest critics of Ctesias, composed a text 'On wondrous things' and drew on Ctesias' information about Indian flora, declining to name him as a source while at the same time denouncing him as a liar.[109] Finally, Hippocratic physicians were interested in the marvels of peripheral peoples because they hoped to find answers to human *physis* by comparing the extremes and because they relied on exotic therapies, medicinal plants, and aromatics; many products in Hippocratic prescriptions feature the phrase 'Egyptian, Ethiopian, and Indian'.[110]

Ctesias cannot be isolated from these trends. India was a preferred object of medicinal as well as geographic and ethnographic interest, while Indian medicine, along with Egyptian, was held in high repute in the fifth and fourth centuries—a matter of great importance for someone like Ctesias.[111] Like every doctor at the international melting pot that was the Persian court, he gathered information, quizzed merchants and travellers (above all from Bactria in central Asia), compared notes with his Indian colleagues, enquired about the origin and background of the gifts presented by Indian emissaries, and asked what was represented on the exotic artworks and pictures on display at the Persian court; perhaps he had access to royal documents. Xenophon took a similar approach when researching the *Cyropaedia*, and subsequent scholarship has often confirmed his findings.[112]

Even if Ctesias never set foot in India, the knowledge he could amass about this faraway land over a roughly fourteen-year period was unrivalled by any Greek before him. He combined this wealth of information not just with the unprejudiced curiosity of a Greek who felt at home in the Persian world, but also with an inquisitive physician's professional interest in ethnography.[113] Every doctor listens before passing judgment, gathers data, and compares what he has heard with what he already knows before jumping to conclusions. He scrutinizes what he has been told before rejecting it as nonsense, and he attempts to arrive at an overview that contains as many facets as possible and takes in multiple perspectives. It goes without saying that he must keep his patients (or his public) engaged. Yet this does not extend to presenting them with demonstrably false or fabricated material. Just as ancient doctors wanted to understand physical processes without being able to peer directly into the human body, so too Ctesias sought to bring across the nature of a country he had never visited himself by listening carefully.

In this context, he can draw on his empirical observations to correct received opinions, such as Herodotus' belief that all Indians, like the Ethiopians, are naturally black-skinned due to the extreme sunshine. In fact, he had seen two Indian women (probably at the Persian court) who were as fair as any in the world.[114] The criticism levelled at Herodotus in ethnographic literature has a rational kernel in such openness to experience. In other passages, Ctesias adopts older views of the health and longevity of people on the southern periphery, writing that the Indians live for 120, 130, 150, and sometimes even 200 years. Yet he adds, reverting to the discourse of a physician, that they are 'not afflicted with headaches, or toothache, or ophthalmia, nor have they ulcers in any part of their body'.[115]

Some scholars conclude that Ctesias followed his description of customs with a discussion of Indian medicine.[116] The fragments support this conjecture. A remarkable, at times marvellous, natural phenomenon is first depicted, followed by a reference to its medicinal use or the way the Persian king applied it. For example, a perfume much desired at court was extracted from the *karpion* tree, called 'fragrant rose' by the Greeks. Similarly, wonder-working Indian fountains are presented in terms of their specific function. One fountain yielded a truth serum valued by the king: 'If three obols' weight of this, mixed with water, be given to anyone to drink, he will reveal everything he has ever done, being in a state of frenzy and delirium the whole day'.[117] Such practices were confirmed by fifth-century travellers to India. A fountain called *Balladé*, an ancient Sanskrit word meaning something like 'useful', possesses curative properties. It casts up again anyone who enters it feet-first, as well as everything apart from iron, silver, and gold. The water is cold and sweet, makes a loud bubbling noise like water in a cauldron, and is used to heal leprous diseases of the skin—the Indians were evidently aware of the therapeutic effect of mineral springs.[118]

Even Indian fauna is investigated not just for its exoticism but with respect to its medicinal use. Ctesias mentions a kind of wild ass, at least as large as a horse, with a white body, red head, blue eyes, and a long horn on its forehead. Ctesias here describes the Indian rhinoceros (*Rhinoceros unicornios*); along with Iranian and Indian legends and images that could be seen at the Persian court, his account marks the debut of the unicorn. In claiming that 'those who drink out of cups made from it are proof against convulsions, epilepsy, and even poison', Ctesias draws on eastern traditions about the efficacy of rhinoceros horn as an antidote.[119]

It is not just his depictions of flora and fauna that provide an invaluable insight into Indian traditions and realities, however. Besides the Indian dogs that found favour at the Persian court, Ctesias describes Indian birds (budgerigars) and monkeys (langurs, among others). He is the first European to give a detailed account of the deployment of Indian battle elephants with mahouts. It was through Ctesias (and not Alexander) that the Greeks first learned that elephants were regularly used in India as a military weapon. His most vociferous critic, Aristotle, accepted all his information about Indian animals.[120] Wherever Ctesias relied on hearsay and visual material, he added marvellous elements, but these too are grounded in reality. The best-known example is the *martichora* (from the Persian *mard* = human being and *khora* = eater, hence 'man-eater'): a creature as large as a lion, with a human head, ears, and eyes as well as a tail like that of a scorpion; it is hunted with spears by natives mounted on elephants. It is the Indian tiger.[121]

Beyond this, the *Indica* are of inestimable ethnographic value. Its depictions of Indian customs and cults are based on native traditions that we would otherwise know nothing about, and which only later flowed into the Indian 'national epics'. Thus, Ctesias mentions a sacred spot, fifteen days' journey from mount Sardo, where the Indians worshipped Helios and Selene. As perhaps the first recorded allusion to an Indian cult of the sun and moon, this reflects the great importance that the epic *Ramayana* accords the sun as the personified god Surya.[122] And when Ctesias tells of 'a river of honey that flows from a rock', this recalls the paradise Uttarakuru described in the *Ramayana*, a land flowing with milk and honey.[123] Similarly, when referring to black pygmies in India, Ctesias by no means simply translates to India the Homeric tale of the African pygmies who battled against cranes, as is sometimes claimed (he says nothing about this story). Instead, he seeks to reproduce native stories about the short, dark-skinned indigenous populace with the means of Greek ethnography.[124]

Finally, the information Ctesias provides about eastern geography is not entirely free of set pieces found in other settings: abundant reeds, lakes producing oil that is skimmed off the surface by the natives, fountains brimming with gold.[125] But they also offer much that is new and original. Ctesias is the first Greek to report of the Dead Sea. The Hypobarus River (= Hyparchos, Spabarus), which flows from the northern mountains before draining into the eastern Ocean, may well be the Ganges.[126] Mount Sardo, fifteen days' journey from the sun and moon sanctuary, is today supposed to lie in the Himalayas or in the Aravalli Range near the Rajasthan Desert in northwest India.[127] Moreover, when Aristotle knows about the Paropamisus Mountains in the southeast, the river of Bactria, and the direction in which the Oxus (Jaxartes) flows, as well as the Indian Choaspes, he owes all this to Ctesias.[128] And Ctesia was ahead of his contemporaries in one other respect: he believed that India was habitable far beyond the Indus.[129] Here too he was to be proved right, as a young man from the ruling Macedonian dynasty was about to confirm.

ALEXANDER'S SEARCH FOR THE ENDS OF THE EARTH

The Macedonian Magnet

Spared the perennial warfare engulfing much of Greece, the kingdom of Macedonia in the peninsula's north had become a force to be reckoned with. From the mid-fourth century, the energetic regent Philipp II used the land's resources and its proximity to gold-rich Thrace to build up one of the most modern armies of the period. He alone seemed capable of harnessing not just ideological discussions about the Persian 'barbarians', but also the scientific energies of the fourth century for a new expansionary thrust.

Even earlier, the Macedonian kings had invited to their court poets and artists like Pindar, Bacchylides, Euripides, and Zeuxis, but also doctors like Hippocrates. Aristotle's father had been personal physician to Amyntas III. Aristotle himself was enticed to Pella by a fat fee.[130] Here he rose to become tutor to the young prince Alexander. In the 330s, when Alexander followed the call of Isocrates and began implementing his plan of a Panhellenic revenge campaign against Persia, he did not just dream of military glory; he was also spurred by Aristotle's hunger for knowledge. Both contributed to the dynamic behind Alexander's campaigns.

The young king was familiar with his teacher's geographical worldview, the *periploi*, as well as with discussions about the farthest reaches of the world and the Ocean. In addition, Alexander surely knew the work of Herodotus and let his fascination with the distant wonderland take flight on the *Indica* of Ctesias.[131] His officers also showed an interest in the botany and fauna of foreign lands. Children of the fourth century, they all shared its enthusiasm for integrating knowledge into complex theories and so moving a step closer to solving the riddle of the world. The army that crossed the Hellespont in early 334 was followed by a retinue of engineers, geographers, geologists, and naturalists, and a group of so-called bematists. Their task—perhaps proposed by Aristotle—was to measure the distance travelled by counting their steps and to record as much information as possible about the extent, fertility, and population of the lands they traversed as well as the availability of food and water. The leaders of larger expeditions were required to provide an account of the land and its people. Their reports were later turned into books by geographers and historians.

Alexander and his officers also knew their immediate opponents better than many a soapbox orator. The Macedonian royal family had long cultivated friendly relations with the Persians; a Macedonian princess had married into the Achaemenid dynasty.[132] Alexander would have come across Persian emissaries and exiles in Pella. Artabazos was one of them. He had taken a Greek wife and was related by marriage to the mercenary generals Memnon and Mentor of Rhodes, both of whom stood in Persian service.[133] Alexander also surely knew of Cyrus the Younger's campaign and the writings of Xenophon. They taught him that a well-organized army of professional soldiers could march practically without hindrance into the heart of the Persian Empire. On the other hand, his own encounters with Persian grandees, supported by what he read in Xenophon, must have convinced him that the Persian elite consisted of courageous men who took their duties seriously. They were well informed about the Macedonians and could afford to hire Greek mercenaries; indeed, they succeeded in repelling an advance Macedonian division dispatched to northern Asia Minor.[134] The great king appeared a respectable adversary at a time when the monarchical principle enjoyed widespread legitimacy in intellectual discussion and had demonstrated its superiority through the rise of Macedonia.

Alexander's Campaign against Persia

Under these auspices, the campaign of conquest that Alexander began in 334 BCE appears less the dawn of a new age than the climax of a development that had been underway since the end of the Persian wars. The certainty with which Alexander marched through Asia Minor and over the Taurus Mountains to Cilicia owed something to his knowledge of the path earlier taken by Xenophon. No less important was his awareness of the role played by the Persian king in warfare. Whereas the Macedonian king led from the front, his Persian counterpart was only symbolically the first warrior, standing behind the infantry without actively participating in battle. This had more to do with considerations of statecraft than with cowardice: the Persian king represented the order and continued existence of the empire. His death would have shaken it to its foundations. Like Cyrus at Cunaxa, Alexander therefore tried his utmost to decide the battle by taking out the king. He succeeded at Issus because his officers secured the flanks and, with the Companions, he commanded the best cavalry of the time. His successes were thus based on his calculated deployment of superior armed forces and exact information about the king's wartime role.

Defeating the Persian king on the battlefield was one thing, surpassing him as a conqueror was another. A march to Egypt was therefore imperative for more than just strategic reasons. Here, Alexander was greeted as a liberator by the majority and probably crowned pharaoh in Memphis. He then proceeded west to Paraitonion (Marsa Matruh) and from there 300 km through the desert to Siwa.[135] According to Herodotus, Cambyses had failed on his march through the desert, and Heracles and Perseus had reached the oasis—so the myth.[136] When Alexander attempted the same, he was motived above all by the need to prove his godlike powers of conquest against the harshest natural backdrop. The priests hailed him as the son of Zeus Ammon and probably prophesied that he would conquer the world.[137] What the gods had refused Xerxes—the union of Europe and Asia—they would grant Alexander.

A man appeared godlike not just by vanquishing his enemies on the battlefield but also by founding cities. Alexander's choice fell on the western estuary of the Nile delta, opposite an island mentioned by Homer called Pharos. The foundation bore the name of its founder: Alexandria. Perhaps it was meant to facilitate trade with Greece and make Egypt more independent of the Phoenician metropolises.

Bursting with confidence, Alexander set out in April 331 to conquer the Persian heartlands. He again defeated the reassembled imperial army on the plain of Gaugamela. The defeated king fled east as Alexander was proclaimed 'king of Asia'. The march into Persia resembled a triumphal procession. In Babylon, as in Egypt, Alexander was received as a liberator. The gates of Persepolis swung open in early 330. During the victory banquet, the palace went up in flames. Persian depredations in Greece had been avenged. The official mission had been accomplished.

Alexander at the Caspian Sea and Hindu Kush

Yet Alexander had to continue to Ecbatana, the summer residence of the Persian kings, to track down Darius and gauge the loyalty of the northern and eastern provinces of the empire. From now on, at the latest, his interest in geography combined with his ambition to gain undying fame into an unstoppable force that the sources and Alexander himself characterize as 'longing' (*pothos*). If the oracle at Siwa had prophesied him dominion over the world, then like Dionysus and Heracles he would have to venture to the farthest reaches of the ecumene. This goal burst the bounds of the Panhellenic revenge campaign. That is why the last Greeks were dismissed after the conquest of Ecbatana, although they were free to stay on as mercenaries.[138]

Darius had fled through the so-called Caspian Gates. In order to secure his homeward route, Alexander left behind his old companion-in-arms Parmenion with 6,000 Macedonians and part of his war chest. He himself continued up the Royal Road between the Persian salt desert in the south and the Elburz Mountains in the north. The Macedonians were now moving in regions where only deported Greeks, at best, had set foot before. The great voyage of discovery began in eastern Iran.[139]

In or near Rhagai, news arrived that Darius had been taken captive. Alexander immediately raced ahead with an elite unit, reaching Darius' final campsite at the edge of the Dasht-e Kavir Desert after two days of hard riding. Another 65 km on, he encountered a body at the edge of the road; it was Darius, stabbed by a courtier. Alexander had the corpse taken to Persepolis and buried with all the honours befitting a great king. His self-understanding as legitimate successor obliged him to apprehend the fugitive regicide, who himself laid claim to the throne under the name of Artaxerxes. He had retreated past the Hindu Kush to Bactria, a hub of caravan routes at the borders of the Indian, Chinese, and Iranian civilizations.[140] Darius' faithless courtiers, for their part, fled to the thickly wooded ravines south of the Caspian Sea. Alexander pursued them there, knowing full well that he could not assume the throne and secure his conquests without their cooperation. Late that summer he reached Zadracarta, the capital of Hyrcania, a luxuriantly fertile landscape that to the Macedonians, who had just crossed the desert-like tracts and gorges of Media, must have seemed like a New World.

Greek geographers were aware of the Caspian Sea, yet no one knew its exact dimensions. Many considered it a projection of the Ocean—the Caspian is a saltwater sea!—and precisely this fascinated the Macedonian king. For it gave rise to unforeseen strategic opportunities: Alexander, like Aristotle, assumed a relatively modest-sized ecumene (see above, pp. 177–178).

Accordingly, he believed that the world sea could be used to transport an army from one continent to another.[141] Even in Egypt, Alexander had supposedly dispatched an expedition to find the sources of the Nile, and probably also to ascertain whether the Nile could be sailed upriver to India, a question that had already preoccupied Darius and been discussed by Aristotle.[142] When he reached the southern shore of the Caspian Sea in 330, he voiced his impression that the sea was as large as the Euxine. His companion noted that its water tasted sweet, at any rate sweeter than seawater elsewhere. They also observed water snakes—their significance was familiar from Ctesias. And Alexander thus concluded in good Aristotelian fashion that the Caspian was an inland sea, 'no smaller than the Black Sea', which extended to the Sea of Azov (*Maiotis*).[143]

Circumstances allowed no time for a more thorough investigation; Alexander later tried to make up for it.[144] The pretender king Bessus was still lording it in Bactria, while to the south, in Aria, the satrap Satibarzanes was refusing to pay homage. Before autumn of 329, Alexander therefore turned again to the east. From today's Mashhad, two roads led to Bactria. One led northeast through mountains and desert via the oasis of Merv

(Alexandria in Margiana). The other, longer route snaked southeast to the desert regions of Sistan through the satrapy of Drangiana, from there following the Helmand River Valley northeast over the Hindu Kush.[145]

Alexander initially chose the shorter route before changing his mind, swayed by the thought of subduing the satrap of Sistan, west of Arachosia. On the march from Sistan through Arachosia, Alexander 'founded' both Alexandria Ariana (on the remains of a Persian citadel) and Alexandria Arachosia; they later became famous under the names of Herat and Kandahar. As his army approached the southern foothills of the Hindu Kush, a third 'foundation' followed, Alexandria in the Caucasus, on the site of the satrap's residence of Kapisa, northeast of Kabul. The name reflects the belief that the massive mountain range was a continuation of the Caucasus; the Persian name, Hindu Kush, means something like 'above the eagle's flight'. Greeks naturally thought of the eagle nibbling the liver of Prometheus as he lay chained to the Caucasus. Never mind that the eagle of the Persian name belonged to an altogether different legend—for Alexander, the mythic link was enough to integrate the mountains into the known world. Even the cave where Prometheus was said to have languished was 'discovered'.[146]

More than a mythic reconnaissance mission, what drew Alexander onward was the sheer audacity of crossing the mountains with his 30,000-strong army. Admittedly, geopolitical circumstances, the pursuit of Bessus, and the claim to Persian royal succession all drove him to Bactria—here, Cyrus the Great's historically authenticated campaign in the land beyond the Caucasus and Sogdiana was a model to be emulated.[147] At the same time, however, 'unpolitical' motives increasingly came to the fore: the ambition to prove the divine ancestry revealed in Siwa and outshine all the kings and heroes of old by subjugating nature itself. The march over the snow-capped, 3,500-metre-high Hindu Kush (probably at the Khawak Pass) was one of Alexander's greatest achievements, for all that it has been overshadowed to this day by his spectacular victories on the battlefield. Perhaps he was stiffened in his resolve by the *Anabasis* of Xenophon's 10,000 mercenaries over the snow-capped Carduchian mountains; the accounts of Alexander's later historians suggest as much. The risk paid off handsomely: Bessus, ensconced in apparent safety behind the massif, was taken by surprise and fled in panic over the Oxus River (Amu Darya). Alexander occupied Bactria and its important city Bactra without difficulty. From there, his army trudged through the 80-kilometre-wide stony desert of Turkestan towards the Oxus, crossed the river on self-made, straw-stuffed flippers (due to a shortage of timber), and pushed into the northeasternmost Persian province, Sogdiana, a barren, sandy steppe land. All this effort paid off: Bessus was surrendered and sent to the city of Bactra for further punishment.[148]

The campaign's political objective had been achieved. Alexander had consolidated his rule while exploring lands that intrigued the geographers of his day. Ctesias had learned about Bactria—the *ultima thule* of the east—at the Persian court and knew of Indian wine and cheese in this region. From reading Ctesias, Aristotle knew the Oxus by the name Araxes, assuming it was connected with the Tanais (today's Don). Besides a few merchants, most Greeks were familiar only with the Tanais' lower course and estuary.[149] When traversing Sogdiana, however, Alexander came across a second river, called Jaxartes by the natives, lined with fir trees on its far bank. He must have been convinced that this was the previously unknown upper course of the Tanais, which according to Aristotle communicated with the Oxus.[150]

Image 5 View of the ruins of Bactra. Bactra in northern Afghanistan, capital of the Bactrian Kingdom, was the crossroads of several trade routes connecting China with northern India, Iran, and Syria. In 329–328, Alexander stayed here on his march to India. Later, the town was integrated into the Greco-Bactrian Empire. The arid surroundings and ruins that greet visitors today offer little indication of its former significance. Credit: AKG1573553: Roland and Sabrina Michaud/akg-images.

In this he was mistaken: Alexander had in fact discovered a new river, the Syr Darya, and he was unaware that the Syr Darya and the Amu Darya drained into the Aral Sea. Still, the identification he and his officers made befitted a divine commander: the traditional view was that the lower course of the Tanais demarcated the border between Europe and Asia. This led him to conclude that the upper course of the Tanais in the Far East also marked Asia's outermost border.[151] Alexander may not have arrived at the northern Ocean, but he had reached a corner of the Asiatic continent that few—if any—Greeks had set foot on before him. He gave his final (and northernmost) foundation, located on the upper Jaxartes on the site of a Persian outpost, the programmatic name Alexandria Ultima (Alexandria Eschate, today's Khujand).[152]

The royal progress through the northern satrapies was crowned with a fairy-tale wedding. In early 327 Alexander married Roxana, daughter of a Sogdian prince. Amorous feelings coincided with the pragmatic goal of securing his succession and winning over the native elites. His father-in-law, Oxyartes, was appointed to the king's council and his sons integrated into the royal cavalry. These and other measures aimed at assimilating native dignitaries into the Macedonian military and political structure were buttressed by Alexander's efforts to adhere externally to Persian royal ceremonial by wearing the diadem and introducing proskynesis (prostration before the king). Alexander had been familiar with Persian customs since childhood and showed the same respect to the Achaemenid dynasty as Xenophon. For the natives of the northern satrapies, he was a new Persian king punishing a rebellious satrap.[153] To his officers and friends, however, his conspicuous appropriation of the Persian style of rule was a cause of bitterness—more because they felt slighted than due to any intellectual wish to preserve the Greek-barbarian divide.

Then there were the ordeals he imposed on his battle-weary army, especially in crossing the Hindu Kush and slogging through the desert wastes of Turkestan.[154] Reports of growing disquiet mounted, from open criticism to conspiracy. Alexander punished any sign of dissent from even his most loyal officers and friends (Philotas, Parmenion). The gulf widened as Alexander moved beyond his official mission to pursue his dreams of conquest without heed to Macedonian sensibilities. The sources explained his grim obduracy with reference to his hot temper, later chalked up as a character flaw. In reality, Alexander knew that even the slightest hint of insubordination from his intimates would jeopardize the entire undertaking. Given the dwindling numbers of experienced Macedonians in his ranks, there was no alternative to delegating rule to Iranian elites. He had to be unrelenting if stability was to be preserved. In the end, Alexander got his way. The army, which since Ecbatana had been swelled by mercenaries and Iranian units, stayed true to him even under the harshest conditions, on the snow-covered passes of the Hindu Kush and in the deserts of Sogdiana. We hear nothing of mutinies, which would have been the surest sign that the murmuring among his officers had a more dangerous basis. Yet the army was doubtless nearing the limits of its endurance. The next stage of the march would show how much farther it could be pushed.

The Indian Adventure

Even if Alexander no longer had regicides and rebels to pursue, his role as successor to the Persian king required him to secure the regions of the Punjab that had periodically been part of the Persian Empire. This explains the ruthless force, the destruction of entire localities, and the massacring of populations that marked and marred his Indian campaign. There could be no pardon for anyone who opposed his rule.

Yet Alexander wanted more that to assert his power and receive the homage of the rajas. Aristotle had significantly underestimated the extent of the eastern landmass and hence the size of India. Accordingly, he claimed that the eastern limit of the ecumene and the world sea could be glimpsed from the peaks of the Hindu Kush (= Parnassus).[155] Yet Alexander and his men had seen only unending mountain chains from the Khawak Pass. Was Aristotle wrong? And if so, where did the ecumene end in the east, and where did the Ocean begin? Alexander could not simply dismiss these questions; he was too much the child of his inquisitive age for that. Having reached the northern border of the ecumene at the Jaxartes, he now had to seek the end of the world in the east to realize his claim to world rule. India was considered the easternmost land, beyond which lay the Ocean; nothing was (yet) known of the vast tracts stretching all the way to China.[156]

To this was added a strategic calculation that had already motivated Darius to commission Scylax's Indian expedition and had also been shared by Artaxerxes III (see above, p. 147). Like the Persian kings, Alexander believed that the Indus was connected with the Nile and that the southern sea (Erythraean Sea) was enclosed by a land bridge extending from India to Egypt. He now saw an opportunity to conclude his foray to the eastern end of the world with a return journey via the Indus and Nile. His return to the land of the pharaohs would have closed the circle of world rule prophesied in Siwa and connected it with a triumphal 'ride around the world'.[157]

In the early summer of 327, the army set out from Bactra and again crossed the Hindu Kush in ten days, probably by the same pass as on their approach. That autumn they proceeded from Alexandria in the Caucasus to the Punjab. One part of the army marched over the Khyber Pass, the northeasternmost entry point for all India's invaders, to the Kabul Valley. Alexander himself chose a more difficult route farther north. Together, they traversed the ancient cultural landscape of Gandhara, reaching the Indus in early 326. The arrivals saw irrigated rice fields and soon encountered a plant eaten by Indian holy men. The Portuguese later termed it the 'Indian fig'. We call it the banana.[158]

All this is not to say that the area was *terra incognita*. There had been Greeks and Greek settlements in India since the days of Cyrus the Great.[159] Scylax had taken a similar route, and his work was consulted by both Hecataeus and Herodotus. Alexander and his officers knew the *periplus* of Scylax and the *Indica* of Ctesias. For the Macedonian warrior, tales of the Indians' extraordinary longevity must have been as fascinating as those of people with canine heads and enormous feet, bizarre animals—unicorns, Indus worms, and beasts with a human face and a scorpion's tail—not to mention the legend of the golden treasure dug out of the ground by industrious ants and guarded by griffins.[160] The scholars in Alexander's entourage were curious about the curative springs and plants mentioned by Ctesias.

Like all discoverers and conquerors, the Macedonians thus set out with preconceived ideas that awaited confirmation. Alexander's officers encouraged the king in his conviction that India had once been visited and conquered by Heracles and Dionysus.[161] As son of Zeus, Alexander was following in his father's footsteps. The precedent seemed to guarantee his success as well as set a lofty standard for him to compete against. It lent his Indian mission—for all its adventurous exoticism—a sense of the preordained.

Alexander's confidence was borne out by the ease with which his army crushed the Indian forces. Mobile siege engines were as little known in India as the combined deployment of heavy infantry and cavalry. And finally, the conqueror was haloed by an aura of invincibility. Unsurprisingly, many Indian princes signalled that they would recognize the new king's suzerainty even before he crossed the Indus. They familiarized Alexander with native war technology, especially the use of battle elephants. Their information about nature and fauna stimulated an intensive trade in exotic pelts and plants.[162] They, in turn, learned about the mythic ideas that Alexander had brought with him. Many were clever enough to pander to his expectations. They thus presented the Indian god Krishna as a manifestation of Heracles and hailed Alexander as Dionysus, not least to exploit the all-conquering Macedonians in their own power struggles against regional competitors.[163] Ambhi, the most important raja in the western Punjab (Gandhara), offered Alexander his support against Porus, the king of the Pauravas, whose kingdom extended from the Jhelum River to the Chenab. Alexander confirmed Ambhi in his rule on the condition that he comply with his wishes. Ambhi thereupon adopted the name of Taxiles.

In Taxila!

Alexander could now devote over a half year to fighting the Indian princes in the northern Swat Mountains. Taxiles protected his rear and supplied him with grain, tribute, cattle, and elephants. Alexander entered the caravan city of Taxila early in the year. The raja's residence was a flourishing settlement at the intersection of transregional transport routes from central Asia to northern India and farther west towards Kashmir. It was also a Buddhist pilgrimage site and centre of north Indian medicine, law, and Hindu learning.[164] Alexander's officers gathered data about the appearance of the native populace, marriage customs, and widow burning (sati).[165]

One day the Macedonians observed men who were provided with oil at a market and could take whatever they pleased. Alexander thought he could identify two 'schools' among these men: the long-haired and the close-shaved. Eager to speak with their masters, he instructed Onesicritus to seek them out. He and a fellow scholar were responsible for the reports on the Indian 'wise men' that belong to the classic repertoire of legends about Alexander.[166]

Near Taxila, Onesicritus found fifteen naked 'sages' standing, sitting, or lying motionless until nightfall.[167] With the help of interpreters, he managed to converse with two of them. Allegedly, they were familiar with Greek philosophers and knew Socrates, Pythagoras, and Diogenes. That is surely fabricated.

Onesicritus probably identified the Indian ascetics with the Greek school of philosophy that seemed to fit them best: the Cynics.[168] This act of cultural translation entailed distortions and misunderstandings: the Indian gymnosophists were not completely naked, as Greek bodily culture prescribed.[169] When asked his name, the older sage presumably replied with the classical Sanskrit greeting *kalyana*. The Macedonians consequently called him Kalanos, just as the Spanish in Mexico turned the native word *tectetan*, 'I do not understand you', into the name of the country, Yucatan.[170] Does not Odysseus' trick in identifying himself to the Cyclops as 'no one' reflect a similar linguistic confusion?

Yet there is no reason to doubt the authenticity of the meeting in Taxila.[171] Brahman tradition stipulates that a good king should study the Vedas and seek the counsel of sages. Further, the story of Onesicritus contains many un-Greek elements beyond the typical misunderstandings and transferences of Greek models.[172] After the conversation, the younger Indian sage followed Alexander for only a short time and kept his distance from the royal court. By contrast, Kalanos, the elder, remained one of the king's closest advisers until his death in Babylon. On his account, he was free to choose his own life after forty (or thirty-seven) years of 'discipline'. He was alluding to the first *asrama*, the thirty-six-year period of study (*brahmacharya*) and ascesis before he could change his clothes, wear gold rings, and start a family—although the sources indicate that he already had students and children prior to this decision. Perhaps he represented one of the less strict schools of Brahmanism found in the northwest India; or he may not have been a Brahman at all but a Jain or Buddhist.[173]

In any event, Kalanos was invaluable for Alexander. He provided his headquarters with information about political conditions, Indian beliefs, and the position of the Brahmans. He even carried out interrogations on Brahman captives. It may well have been at his suggestion that Alexander dealt as brutally with Brahmans who incited resistance as he did with any other 'rebels'.[174] He may also have alerted Alexander to the upcoming monsoonal rains. This made launching a lightning strike on Porus, Taxiles' competitor, all the more important. Reinforced with 5,000 Indian fighters, Alexander proceeded in summer 326 up the Hydaspes (Jhelum) to reach a site near today's Haranpur.[175] After several feints, he crossed the river and defeated Porus' army. He then confirmed his vanquished enemy as his vassal and founded the settlement of Nicaea ('victory city').

Towards the Ganges?

The path to the east was clear, yet now the monsoonal rains drenched the conquerors and brought the rivers back to full spate. The onward march turned into a hard slog. As Alexander pushed his men to attack the cities that still held out against him, around 100 transport ships had to be dismantled and dragged with ox carts from one river to the next, first from the Indus 60 km to Taxila, then a further 180 km to the Hydaspes and from there to Chenab and Beas, where they were reassembled.[176] All this was possible only with the help of native auxiliaries. Yet it once again shows what ancient discoverers could achieve when transporting ships.

The strain on the Macedonians must have been tremendous, particularly as they confronted many of the typical problems faced by discoverers. Somewhere near the Chenab River they apparently tasted 'pods like a bean' that were 'ten inches long and sweet as honey'. They were bananas; they gave the men such upset stomachs that Alexander—like Odysseus before him—forbade them from touching any of the exotic fruits.[177] Countless snakes sought refuge from the flooding in people's houses. Indian healers provided some relief, yet the psychological pressure remained immense. When the expeditionary army reached the Hyphasis (Beas), the easternmost upper tributary of the Indus, the officers for the first time refused to go farther. Alexander retreated to his tent for three days. Then he relented, ordering twelve enormous altars to be erected in thanksgiving to the Olympian gods. This marked the definitive end of his advance on Asia.

At first glance, the officers' refusal seems not just understandable but even rational, whereas Alexander comes across as an isolated monomaniac driven by his yearning (*pothos*) to find the far ends of the world—regardless of expense. Yet the matter is not so simple. The Macedonians had learned from native princes that a fertile land lay beyond the Beas with a wealthy nobility and a king (Xandrames or Agrammes) who allegedly commanded over 200,000 soldiers, 2,000 chariots, and 4,000 elephants. The situation resembled the arrival of the Spanish conquistadors at the threshold of the Inca Empire.[178] Xandrames' empire looked impressive, yet closer investigation revealed that it had passed its peak. Alexander had entered the once flourishing kingdom of Magadha. Its ruler resided in the palace of Palimbrotha, yet his rule was beset with internal conflicts and his army was a shadow of its former self—rich pickings for the seemingly invincible Macedonian forces.[179] Those forces had additionally been strengthened by around 35,000 fresh recruits from Greece, attracted by news of precious stones discovered on the Punjab rivers; they would have braved any battle under Alexander's command. With his 100,000-strong army, Alexander faced an infirm empire that could be reached with relative ease: a march of around twelve days on a well-maintained road led through desert to a large river that emptied into the Ocean. The centre of the Magadha Empire lay on its lower course.

The river was probably the Ganges.[180] Compared with the almost 20,000 km that Alexander's army had traversed over the previous eight and a half years on often difficult terrain, the roughly 250 km march to the Ganges and the 1,000 km from Beas to the river's mouth must have seemed a walk in the park, especially as news of the desert area lying between the two river systems turned out to be false.[181] In addition, a voyage down the Ganges would not only have eased transport problems, but also have made possible a return journey via the Ocean. From his Indian informants, Alexander had learned that the Indus and the Nile were unconnected, even though the Macedonians had discovered crocodiles and the 'sacred lotus' on the Chenab/Acesines, both of which were familiar from Egypt. Alexander could also correct the claim made by Hecataeus and Herodotus that the Indus flowed to the east.[182] And who knows: perhaps he made a link to Scylax, who according to one modern interpretation had sailed down the Ganges, not the Indus.[183]

All in all, Alexander's plan to cross the Beas and push farther east was by no means as irrational as is sometimes assumed. That his military objective was achievable was proven ten years later by the Indian hero Chandragupta, who conquered the Magadha Empire in a whirlwind campaign. If Alexander was forced to pass up the opportunity and turn back at the Beas despite favourable conditions, fresh reinforcements, and a realistic goal, this can only be explained by opposition from the officer elite, not the army as a whole.

Their resistance had three sources. First, fighting against Indian mountain strongholds in the Punjab had taken a heavy toll on the officer corps.[184] Discontent with Alexander's leadership was further fuelled by concerns that he was turning from an approachable warrior-king into an aloof eastern ruler. Alexander had ruthlessly suppressed an outbreak of dissension, and while the going was good and he could argue that he had no intention of straying beyond the borders of the Persian Empire, he could still count on his officers' support. The heavy casualties in the Punjab, the unpredictable climate, logistical problems following the monsoonal rains, and the fact that Alexander now seemed intent on making conquests beyond the Persian Empire now caused even previously loyal officers to throw in their lot with the serial grumblers.

Alexander could do nothing to quell the mutiny, yet he continued to act rationally by presenting the defeat in a way that left his authority intact. Here, at the latest, the image of a conqueror whose judgment had been impaired by his megalomania needs to be revised. Alexander knew exactly what he was doing and what it was possible for him to do. Had fortune dealt him a better hand, his life might well have ended in the palace of the Magadha rulers on the Ganges rather than in Babylon.

By Desert and Sea

What remained was the return via the Indus, which was also said to drain into a great sea. Alexander could make the case that he would reach the (southern) Ocean and the end of the world via the Indus rather than the Ganges. His fleet, supposedly consisting of 2,000 ships manned by experienced sailors from the eastern Mediterranean (Greeks, Carians, Phoenicians, Cypriots), was constructed and fitted out on the Hydaspes. In autumn, most of the army, commanded by the Cretan Nearchus, set out from Hyphasis and sailed first down the Hydaspes, then the Acesines, and finally the Indus. A baggage train accompanied the fleet by land. Even before reaching the Indus delta, Alexander detached Craterus with 10,000 veterans and infantry divisions as well as elephants; they were to take the familiar route back through Arachosia and Drangiana to Carmania and Susa. Alexander wanted to show his presence in these regions and induce their satraps to send supplies to the coast. He must already have settled on a plan to bring back part of the remaining army by sea.[185]

Following numerous battles at which Alexander sustained serious injuries, in July 326 the fleet arrived at Patala (Hyderabad) in the Indus delta. Here the Indus emptied into a body of water that had to be the Ocean, judging by the tides.[186] Alexander had reached *one* end of the world. He took to the open sea 'saying that he wanted to discover if there was any other land visible out there not too far away, but I [Arrian] would guess that his main purpose was simply the achievement of having sailed in the Great Sea beyond India'.[187] He made landfall on an island off the mouth of the

Indus and sacrificed to the gods, praying 'that no man after him might pass beyond the bounds of his expedition'.[188]

The Ocean was the object of a purely imaginary rivalry that Alexander conducted with himself (and the gods). Its watery wastes had their counterpart in the world's inhospitable deserts. Alexander had sought out this challenge when he crossed the desert that had once allegedly swallowed the army of the Persian king Cambyses on his way to the Siwa Oasis. Now he faced the Gedrosian Desert (today's Makran), which extended west of the Indus delta. An unforgiving, mostly waterless and sandy wasteland of eroded hills, it might have provided a fitting model for Tolkien's Mordor.[189] Cyrus the Great and the Babylonian queen Semiramis were said to have failed to cross it, or to have come out the other side with only a few men. Alexander wanted to outdo them and force even nature to do his bidding. The 750 km march (to Pura) with a 40,000-strong army would be the ultimate test of his divinity.[190]

That was one side of the enterprise. Once it was known that the Indus and Nile were unconnected, a journey by ship from the Indus to the Persian Gulf suggested itself. Scylax had avoided the Persian Gulf, instead sailing around Arabia into the Red Sea. Alexander knew of its existence through Persian, Egyptian, and Indian informants, yet neither Greek geographers of the time nor the expedition's leaders were sure of the exact coastline or where in the north it opened into the gulf.

To that extent, Nearchus' expedition was also a voyage of discovery. Alexander commissioned him to record all contact points, river mouths, the nature of the terrain, and the people who lived there; perhaps he hoped to establish a regular shipping route. Nearchus later wrote out his logbook for Alexander in the manner of a *periplus* before working it up for a broader public, just as Scylax had done before him. It has been preserved almost in its entirety in the book on India by the imperial writer Arrian, who added many literary embellishments, as well as in excerpts in Strabo.[191]

Yet the navarch's voyage was by no means exhausted in pioneering new seaways, charting the coastline, or transporting back part of the army. Alexander's plan foresaw the fleet maintaining close contact with the land army and meeting it at previously determined supply depots. To this day, there is debate about whether the army was meant to provision the fleet or vice versa; given the expected difficulties of the march through the desert, and given the precedent of comparable parallel operations at the time of the Persian invasion of Greece, there is much to speak for the second variant.[192]

What Alexander had not taken into account were the monsoonal conditions. Had the fleet set out in July, it could have used the prevailing south wind to sail west along the coast. Yet they let the opportunity slip, presumably to avoid exposure to the full force of the summer sun on the Makran coast. By the time the 150 ships with 3,000–5,000 men under the command of Nearchus and the navigator Onesicritus set sail, the wind was blowing from the southeast; the zigzag course they had to set considerably lengthened the voyage following the onset of the northeast monsoon in autumn. The journey to the Persian Gulf took about 130 days, ending in January 324. Yet the ships could only hold provisions for ten days and water for five.[193] They therefore had to make landfall almost every day, although maintaining contact with the land army and its supplies was hardly possible.

All this was of little concern to Alexander. The march to the Kolwa Valley led through regions watered by mountain streams and supplied with autumn harvests; some officers found time to describe the exotic flora.[194] Yet the situation deteriorated once they entered the desert southwest of the oasis of Turbat. It was not just that help from the fleet was unforthcoming. Alexander's land army increasingly lost their way, despite being led by native guides. Having previously crossed rock and gravel deserts, they now stumbled over sand dunes that made every step a torment. Soon they were forced to march only at night, yet then temperatures plummeted below 35°F. Many fell victim to hunger, thirst, or snakebite. They began to slaughter their transport animals. The triumph over nature had become a march through hell.

By the time Alexander finally crossed the Makran and entered the more inviting landscapes of Carmania, he had lost three-quarters of his forces, approximately 25,000 people. The non-Macedonian auxiliaries and their women and children were the hardest hit. The army itself remained largely intact, probably because it enjoyed privileged access to food and water.[195] Alexander could therefore claim to have passed this test of his unparalleled greatness—albeit at too high a price. The agriculturally productive regions of Gedrosia had been stripped bare, leaving hunger and despair to follow in the Macedonians' wake. This, too, did not overly trouble Alexander. He staged the rest of the march as a Dionysian procession, enthroned on a triumphal chariot and accompanied by women and musicians—a macabre spectacle given those left behind in the desert sands, but for Alexander a fitting means to celebrate his victory over nature.[196]

Nearchus, meanwhile, had fewer difficulties to contend with. He could only draw on the rations left behind by Alexander at the start of his journey, at the mouth of the Hub River. Yet the voyage along the coast offered him opportunities to exploit the—admittedly rather scanty—resources available on land and at sea (fish, mussels, seafood), just as Scylax had done two hundred years before him. Coast dwellers sometimes had their grain and meagre belongings confiscated.[197] These encounters posed little danger, allowing Nearchus to indulge his ethnographical interests. His description of the 'fish-eaters' (*Ichthyophagen*) is famous. Their dependence on fishing, which arose from their coastal living conditions, influenced all their other material and cultural expressions. According to Nearchus, the ichthyophages' consumption of raw fish put them on much the same level of human development as animals.[198]

Another reason for the voyage's success and minimal loss of life was that Nearchus, like the Carthaginian expeditions down the west African coast, had taken on board trustworthy pilots and interpreters. They did not hold back with tall tales: mysterious isles inhabited by spirits or sorceresses who turned all new arrivals into fish. Yet for a man like Nearchus, such tales were an incentive to visit the islands and stamp out the terror.[199] Whoever has time to spare for such investigations—the entire journey took a leisurely four months—is not threatened by more immediate perils. In fact, Nearchus showed himself swept up by the scientific ferment of the time. During the voyage, he made observations about the changing position of the sun and compared it with similar phenomena in Egyptian Syene and Meroë.[200] Around a century later, Eratosthenes would calculate the Earth's circumference using data collected in these locations. Moreover, the voyage of Nearchus yielded a trove of geographical and botanical information: shortly before departing, one of the captains had learned that Indian ships arrived after around twenty days at an island called Taprobane—the first reference to Sri Lanka in western literature. Nearchus was evidently the first to mention Chinese silk and acquaint the Greeks with the mangroves found in warm coastal waters. His botanical and geographical interests, already evident in the Punjab when he observed the moon-influenced flux of the Indus, probably dated back to his years spent studying under Aristotle.[201] And again, the contemporary interest in medicine played a role when he claims, for example, that Indian physicians, unlike their Greek colleagues, could heal snakebite.[202] When Nearchus depicts how his men cut out and consumed the hearts of leaves of wild palm trees, his account recalls similar passages in Xenophon's *Anabasis*.[203] The voyage west of the Indus is thus less an isolated feat of derring-do than a knowledge-gathering expedition resting on the shoulders of respected forerunners, hence a typical product of the fourth century. Even whale sightings disconcerted the mariners only briefly. Acting on the advice of natives, Nearchus steered directly for the monsters and repulsed them by having his men strike at them with their oars and chant war cries. The discoverers did not learn that whale meat was edible. Still, the existence of these animals confirmed that they were in the Ocean.[204]

The pilots knew the route to the Persian Gulf, and thus towards the end of 325 the fleet sailed almost without loss—only four ships went missing—through the Strait of Hormuz. Those familiar with the country advised laying anchor in a bay at the mouth of the Anamis River near the region of Harmozeia. The site in question was Hormuz (Ormuz), later a trade centre for Portuguese and English merchants. A reconnaissance team met a Greek-speaking, Greek-clothed man who explained—as if by a miracle—that he belonged to Alexander's army, encamped only five days' journey away. Soon after, the admiral and the general were reunited.[205] For all his losses, Alexander had proven himself a global strategist who could dispatch his armed forces through the world's deserts and bring them together anywhere, without the help of modern cartography and technological instruments. Not long after, Alexander came across Craterus' division.

Alexander's Maritime Thinking

Anyone who thought that Alexander would take a well-earned break after entering Susa in early 324 BCE was in for disappointment. Just as Odysseus after a twenty-year absence explained that, according to Tiresias' prophecy, he could not refrain from travel, so Alexander was driven on by the augury of the priests of Siwa. After all, his goal of ruling the world had only been half-realized. Alexander was in no doubt that it was achievable. Even if the world in the east was bigger than Aristotle had assumed, Alexander may still have shared his teacher's belief in a relatively small ecumene.

The voyage of Nearchus strengthened him in the conviction that the world could be explored via the Ocean and conquered by landing on every shore. Now, at the latest, his continental thinking was augmented—if not entirely replaced—by an oceanic paradigm: fleets and sea roads, not armies and land marches, would henceforth dictate his plans. In the north, Alexander now caught up with what circumstances had formerly denied him. He thus sent a certain Heraclides to the Caspian Sea to finally ascertain whether it was linked to the Ocean.[206] Parallel to this, the focus of his attention shifted to the south. With Nearchus' voyage, at the latest, Arabia had entered the king's field of vision. During his return march, he had already instructed his governors in Mesopotamia and Lebanon to fell timber for a new fleet. In Babylon he had a harbour built and hired sailors and colonists. Farther south, Alexandria on the Tigris was founded (later Charax Spasinu)—not just with the aim of repelling Arabian pirates and providing a centre for trade in southeastern luxury goods, but also as a launching pad for large-scale expeditions to Arabia itself.[207]

It was probably the expedition led by Nearchus that first identified Arabia as an independent subcontinent extending far to the south, even though it had already been circumnavigated by Scylax.[208] The land's interior was considered *terra incognita*, inhabited by nomads whose raids destabilized the Levant and Mesopotamia. Alexander needed to stamp them out. In the tradition of the Persians, moreover, a commander seeking to rule not just the ecumene but also its waves could not desist from integrating Arabia into his empire. At the same time, a classical fourth-century problem could be solved in the south of the ecumene, again parallel to the exploration of the Caspian Sea in the north. At the mouth of the Indus, Alexander had already refuted Aristotle's hypothesis that the southern sea was bounded by land. Yet it was still unclear whether Arabia, too, was completely surrounded by the Ocean. Material motives also played a role: Alexander knew from Herodotus that the Arabs delivered 1,000 talents of incense each year to the Persian court. A voyage around India was thus not just a precondition for military invasion; it also held out the prospect of fresh booty for an army demoralized by the long march back from India. And in the long term, it could perhaps prepare the way for a spice route from Babylon to Alexandria.[209]

First Archias of Pella, who had commanded a trireme in Nearchus' fleet, ventured as far as Tylos, the largest island in Bahrain.[210] Then Androsthenes

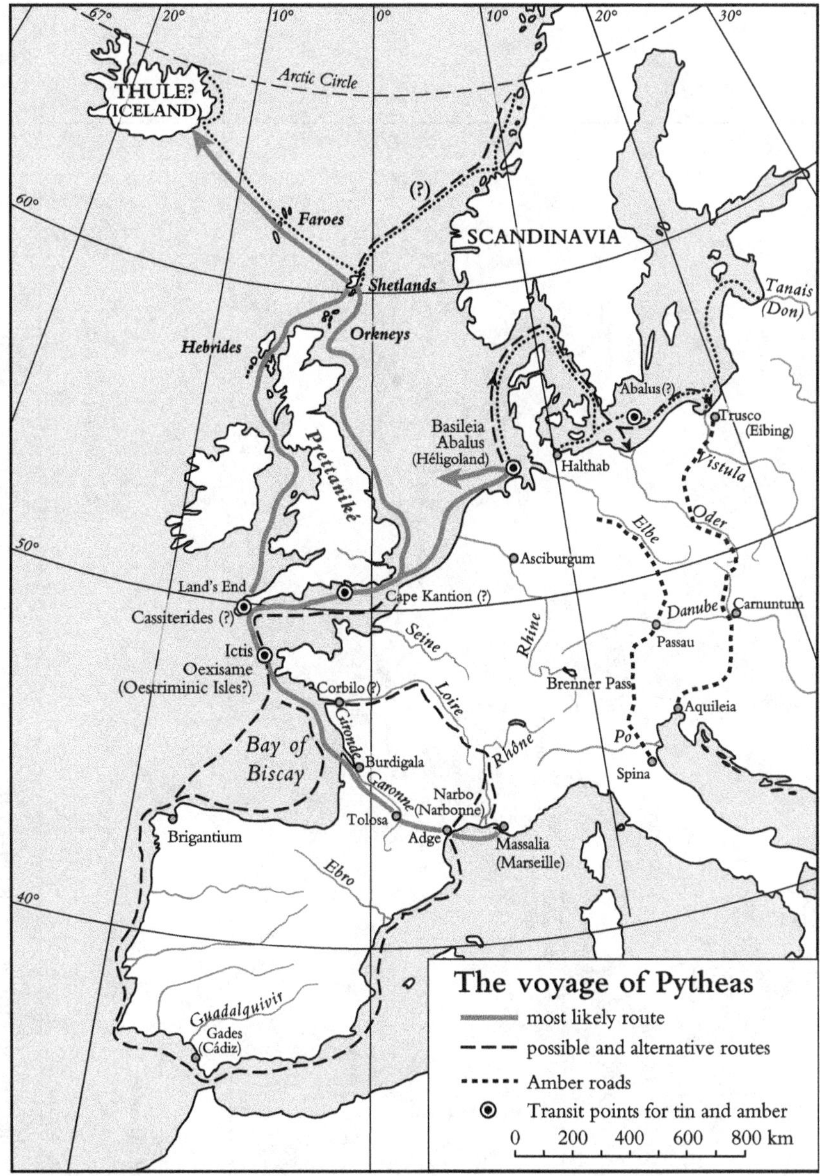

Map 6 Credit: Rudolf Hungreder/Klett-Cotta.

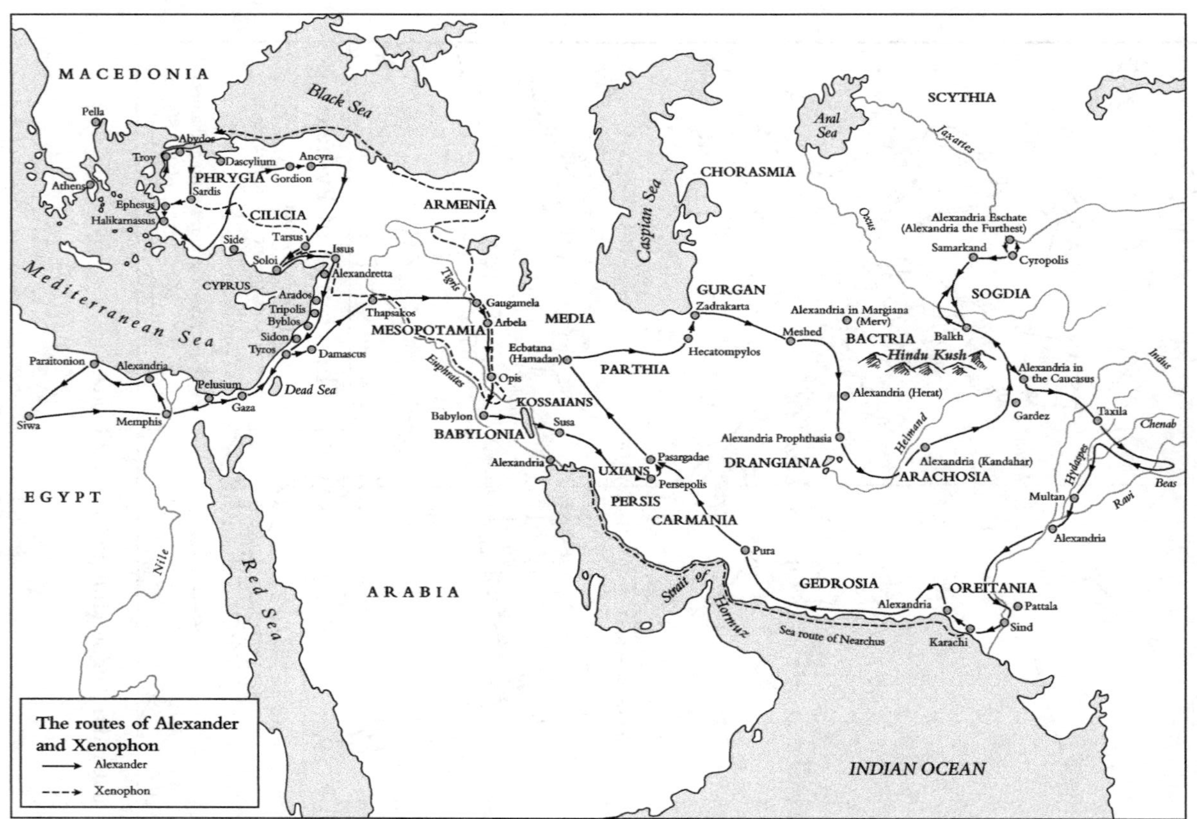

Map 6A Credit: Rudolf Hungreder/Klett-Cotta.

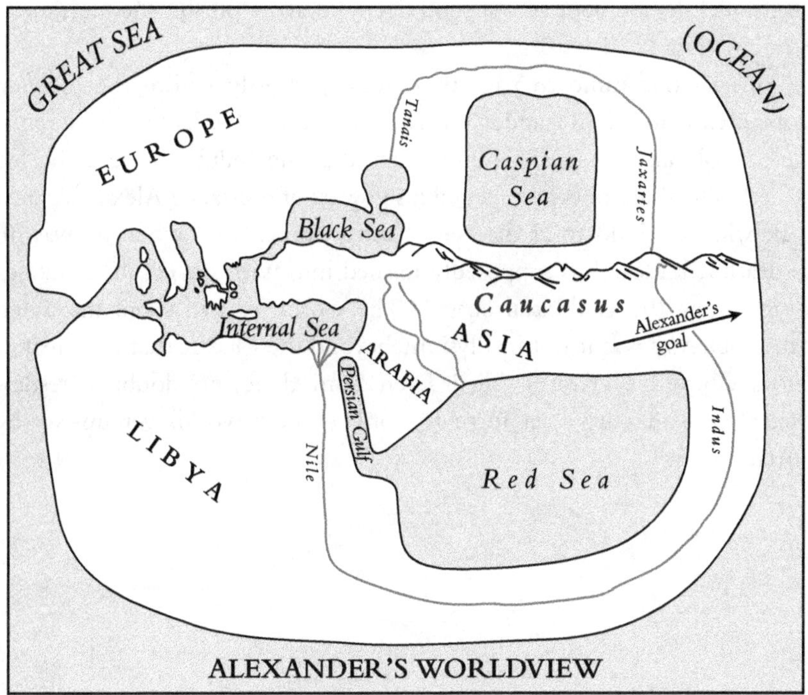

Map 7 Credit: Rudolf Hungreder/Klett-Cotta.

of Thasos was commissioned to skirt the west coast of the Persian Gulf and explore the shores of Arabia (324–323); his logbook became one of the most important documents on the Persian Gulf (see below, p. 224).[211] Other captains followed, although it is unlikely that any of them circumnavigated Arabia and reached Egypt. A journey in the opposite direction proved unsuccessful. Anaxicrates set out from the Gulf of Aqaba on the Sinai Peninsula, while a second voyage departed from the Heroonpolite Gulf (Gulf of Suez). Yet they made it only as far as Bab el-Mandeb and southern Arabia, respectively.[212]

Beyond their immediate military and commercial objectives, the Arabian voyages had a further dimension: they were the next step in the plan to conquer the world that Alexander had begun on the lower course of the Indus. Alexander still vastly underestimated the size of Africa (or rather 'Libya'). According to notes found in the royal secret archive, the voyages to Arabia were the opening move in a far more ambitious undertaking, the circumnavigation of Africa and conquest of the western ecumene through the parallel deployment of a second fleet and army on the Mediterranean coast of Africa.[213]

None of this came to pass. In June 323, shortly before the planned Arabian expedition, Alexander was racked by fever. He had probably contracted malaria, or a spear wound received at the Indus had never healed properly. Drinking bouts weakened his powers of resistance. Alexander died in Babylon on June 10 at the age of thirty-three. Even while he was on his deathbed, Nearchus supposedly regaled him with stories about his sea voyage along the Gedrosian coast.[214] The world sea had taken the dying man's soul. And was it not in Elysium, beyond the Ocean, that the greatest heroes enjoyed everlasting bliss? Even from there, no doubt, a restless Alexander would have set forth to conquer new worlds yet unseen by mortal eyes.

5

Investigating the East and South

Advances in the Hellenistic Era

SELEUCIDS AND MAURYANS

Alexander's Legacy

After Alexander's death, power fell into the hands of his officers. Three large territorial units emerged from the protracted power struggles and intrigues that ensued: in Egypt, Ptolemy founded the Ptolemaic Kingdom; the Seleucids reigned in the Near Eastern lands of the Persian Empire; while the Antigonids prevailed in the Macedonian heartland.

These kings had to demonstrate that they could make conquests, celebrate military victories, and present themselves as rulers over the ecumene. In doing so, they tapped into the legacy of exploration bequeathed them by the Persians and Alexander. Overall, though, they achieved less than might have been expected. The circumstances were propitious: with Egypt, Babylon, and parts of Syria, Ptolemy and Seleucus controlled access to the richest and most fertile regions of the Alexandrian Empire as well as prodigious financial resources (including the treasury amassed by Alexander). Yet while Alexander, secure in his victory over Persia, had been impelled ever onward by the elan of the great conqueror, his successors had to invest all their energies into maintaining their rule. At the same time, they were hemmed in by their perpetual rivalry. When they pushed at the outer limits of their spheres of influence, they did so with a view to securing, regaining, or consolidating their power. Mercantile and financial considerations could supplement their political strategy. By and large, however, the kings moved in spaces traversed or targeted by Alexander himself, or they appropriated the traditions of their antecedent monarchies without going much beyond them.

Exploratory thought was defined not by a breakthrough to something new but by integrating recent gains (through intensive colonization, for example) and working through the old. Expressed positively, one could say that the expansionary knowledge and dynamism of the fourth century reached a certain conclusion with the era of Hellenistic kings, a conclusion that was equally a climax: the speculative thought of the period following the Peloponnesian War as well as Alexander's no less untrammelled expansion now entered a consolidation phase. It created the space needed to intensify hastily forged links to faraway places and synthesize old knowledge with new.

In the ecumene's south, the maritime and mercantile activities of the Persians were continued. The ancient eastern empires had long sought to establish a presence in Arabia and lay hands on its legendary riches. The country remained largely closed off to the Greek world. This situation first changed with Alexander's expeditionary voyages. Probably during the lifetime of the great Macedonian (see above, p. 221), but perhaps commissioned by Seleucus I Nicator, Androsthenes sailed from the Euphrates to the Persian Gulf.[1] He left behind a much-read book entitled 'Voyage along the Indian coast'.[2] On the Bahraini island of Tylos, he continued the studies of mangroves begun by Nearchus. Since his voyage fell in the winter months, he and his crew could admire the blossoming date plantations in the island's north, near Manama. They further came across thickly wooded terrain containing valuable timber (teak) as well as cotton plants; these were familiar from India and had perhaps been imported from there.

From the outset, exploratory voyages in the Persian Gulf had a mercantile-political dimension extending from the Gulf to Arabia and India. It is quite likely that Seleucus I had already established a naval base in Ikaros on the island of Failaka, around 13 km off the coast of Kuwait. The naval expeditions of the kings in the Persian Gulf and the refoundation of old Alexandria on the Tigris under the name of Antiochia Charax (under Antiochus III, the later Spasinu Charax) may also have been intended to consolidate and promote maritime trade.

Knowledge of the fauna of the Gulf countries increased in this context. Androsthenes' observations, together with the reports compiled by other expeditions and information contributed by Alexander's bematists and historians, found their way into the 'Enquiry into plants' (*Historia Plantarum*) by Theophrastus of Eresos (Lesbos, c. 370–285 BCE), who led the Peripatetic School following the death of Aristotle. In his work, the botanical and climatological interests of the period before Alexander were combined with the empirical expansion of knowledge to the east and south in the first work of the discipline to prioritize systemic clarity and morphological terminology; in this respect, it remained unsurpassed until the sixteenth century.[3] Yet Theophrastus was also deeply indebted to fourth-century scholars. For example, he applied the theory of climatic and geographical influences on humans and animals to the appearance of plants, drawing conclusions for their cultivation and management.[4] And in the last book of the *Historia Plantarum*, he discussed the medicinal use of saps, gums, and plant parts. In a shorter work, *De odoribus*, his investigation of the fragrances produced from plant extracts was informed by the rich tradition of Near Eastern and Egyptian lore. His work thus spans the euphoria of discovery and the search for an overarching synthesis of empirical knowledge in the fifth and fourth centuries. In this respect, too, Alexander's campaign was not so much a clean break as a dynamizing continuation of pre-existing interests.[5]

In the north, too, Seleucus I attempted to finish what Alexander had planned but could no longer bring to fruition. Between 310 and 304 BCE, he set out with an army to northern India to secure lost or politically destabilized northeastern regions of the former Persian Empire as well as the trade routes from Babylon to Bactra (Balkh), capital of the populous province of Bactria.[6] One army division was led by Demodamas of Miletus, a city with which the first Seleucid kings cultivated close relations; he probably served as satrap in Bactria and Sogdia. He crossed the Jaxartes (modern Syr Darya), a river believed to empty into the Caspian or Black Sea. On the northernmost border of the ecumene and Seleucid territory to the nomadic steppe world, Demodamas erected altars, reorganized and revived 'Alexandria Eschate', and founded 'Antiochia in Scythia' in his king's name.[7]

Around the same time or somewhat later (285–282 BCE), Seleucus I and Antiochus I commissioned Patrocles, a high-ranking general from their inner circle, to explore the Caspian Sea and determine once and for all whether it was an inland sea or a projection of the Ocean. The search for the mouth of the Jaxartes was part of the same exploratory mission. It too reflected the agenda of Alexander, who shortly before his death had sent

Heraclides to the Caspian Sea to find out whether it was linked with the Black Sea or the Indian Ocean (see above, p. 218). Patrocles had access to the royal archives and knew the old expeditionary reports, and he was an emissary in India soon before or after his voyage. His real objective may therefore have been to search for an oceanic northeast passage from the Caspian Sea to India.[8]

His voyage was limited to the Caspian's west and east shores, however. He identified one of the rivers (perhaps the Uzboy) with the Oxus or connected native reports about the nearby Aral Sea and its tributaries with the Caspian Sea. A later report of Indian goods being shipped to the Caspian Sea and making their way from there to the Black Sea may belong in this context. Entering the saltwater Kara-Bugas Bay and observing seals may further have convinced him that a passage to India was possible from here.[9]

The expeditionary report convinced Selecus, too. On its basis, he planned to dig a canal north of the Caucasus from the Black to the Caspian Sea with the aim of extending trade routes from the Aegean to the Caspian and India and exacting transit duties. He may also have seen the potential to dispatch warships to the Mediterranean and India. Pliny later made the fanciful claim that Patrocles sailed with the Diadochi kings (Alexander's successors) from India to the Caspian Sea.[10] However outlandish such accounts may be, they show that the Seleucid kings shared Alexander's oceanic vision, as had the Persian kings before him. The idea of a northeast passage has its counterpart in Darius' exploration of the southern seas and Scylax's search for a link between the Red Sea and the Indian Ocean, just as the planned canal in the north corresponds to the restoration of Necho's canal from the Mediterranean to the Red Sea. Not least thanks to Patrocles' report, the notion that the Caspian was connected with the Ocean became immovably lodged in the ancient geographic imagination.

The Seleucids and the Mauryan Empire

At the same time as the northern borders of imperial territory were being explored, overland links to India intensified. The starting point was a political revolution originating in northwest India. Here, twenty-five-year-old Chandragupta from the Mauryan dynasty (called Sandrokottos by the Greeks) completed the project that the Macedonian king had been forced to abandon: he advanced to the heart of the Nanda Empire, killed its king, and founded the Mauryan Empire in Pataliputra. Rapidly extending his sphere of influence to the west, he drove out the last of the Macedonians and integrated the realm of Porus into his empire in 317 BCE.

It took over a decade for Alexander's successors to respond. In 305 Seleucus led an army across the Hindu Kush. It is uncertain whether a pitched battle was fought. What we do know is that the two sides signed a treaty preserving their mutual interests. Chandragupta was recognized and kept the regions in the Punjab he had annexed or claimed as well as Gandhara, parts of Arachosia, and Gedrosia; the western border of the Mauryan Empire was secured for generations. Conversely, Seleucus could largely dispense with the need to garrison military forces in the east. In return for making territorial concessions, he also received five hundred war elephants with Indian trainers and mahouts. Even if the figure is exaggerated, this still gave Seleucus more war elephants than his rivals in the west. The agreement was crowned with a 'marriage clause'. This may have granted kings from the two dynasties the right to marry their counterpart's daughters; the more likely scenario, however, is that it sought to regulate mixed marriages between Indians and Greeks by giving children civic rights, on the Greek side, and, on the Indian side, allowing Greeks and Macedonians to be admitted into the warrior caste.[11]

The contract formed the basis for a century of peaceful neighbourly relations. It paved the way for the most intensive relations to date between India and the Asiatic-Greek west. An important presupposition was that the Seleucid and Indian empires were structurally similar. Mauryans and Seleucids both ruled over multiethnic and multilingual areas that lacked a distinct 'national' identity. Just as the Seleucids planted colonies to bind the eastern periphery of their empire to its western centre, so the Mauryans developed an active settlement policy. Like almost all Hellenistic monarchies, they endeavoured to optimize the country's tax regime in order to finance their standing army and bureaucracy; as in the Ptolemaic Kingdom, there were state monopolies on trade goods and primary products (metallurgy, mining), and as in the Hellenistic empires, the Indian kings were great landowners.[12]

Besides comparable ruling conditions, perhaps these parallels also derived from an exchange of information and experiences. This is most apparent on military terrain. Hellenistic kings took on Indian elephants with their trainers, while the Mauryans showed an interest in siege warfare techniques. Deimachus of Plataea, who lived in Pataliputra, wrote a work on siege machinery (poliorcetics). The Mauryans partly owed their military success to what the Macedonians had taught them about storming fortified towns.[13]

Trade—especially overseas trade as far afield as China—formed a second basis for common interests. It was part of a migration wave that, with the establishment of Hellenistic empires from the third century BCE, encompassed Greeks of all stripes and led from the coast of Asia Minor along the great trade routes to the expanses of central Asia. Settlers and colonists, mercenaries, artists, philosophers, and physicians joined in the exodus, as did artisans and merchants drawn by the prospect of acquiring valuable minerals (gold, silver, including in Bactria) and plant products from Arabia and the Far East. Theophrastus had extensively discussed Indian rice, cotton, barley, and pepper as well as incense, myrrh, cinnamon, and cassia.[14] Seleucus ordered the aromatic plants amomum and spikenard to be shipped to his empire for domestic cultivation, sending costus, cinnamomum (Ceylon cinnamon), and cassia to the oracle of Apollo at Didyma. The period that ensued saw the increased importation of Indian (and Arabian) spices and cosmetics via the Persian Gulf and Indian intermediaries. Europe's infatuation with the magical fragrances wafting from the east, which would persist well into modernity, finds its origin here.[15]

In agreeing to the treaty with Chandragupta, the Seleucid king may have been thinking of the improved access to eastern products it would provide. His counterpart pursued comparable interests. Thus Bindusara (300–273 BCE), Chandragupta's son, supposedly asked Seleucus' successor to send him sweet wine or grape syrup (*glukos*), figs (*ischades*), and a 'sage' (Sophist).[16] Wine numbered among Greece's top exports, even reaching the Far East. The figs may have been those discovered by Androsthenes on the Bahraini island. Identifying the 'sage' is more difficult. Philosophers were swept up in the great wave of migration that carried Greeks all the way to Afghanistan and the threshold of Mauryan rule. One of them, a certain Clearchus (presumably from Soli and a student of Aristotle), brought the moral precepts of the 'Seven Sages' from Delphi over 5,000 km by land to the Bactrian city of Ai-Khanoum at the confluence of the Kokcha and Oxus Rivers (Amu Darya in northern Afghanistan at the border to Tajikistan). According to an epigram, the maxims were here inscribed in the temple enclosure (*temenos* of Kineas).[17]

Ai-Khanoum had been re-founded at the beginning of the second century BCE for Greek settlers from Macedonia and Asia Minor. Under Eucratides (171–145 BCE), it was built up into a large-scale royal capital overlooking the rivers at a strategically significant site already used by the Persians. The confluence of the Oxus and Kokcha shielded the city on two sides and fed a cleverly designed irrigation system. And there were multiple sources of wealth. Ai-Khanoum controlled the extraction and sale of lapis lazuli from nearby mines in the southern Badakhshan ranges. In the palace's treasury, 75 kg of unprocessed blocks were found alongside a smaller quantity of worked material.[18] Architecturally, the city reflects classical Greek (gymnasium, theatre for 6,000 visitors), Bactrian, Persian, and Mesopotamian influences. Here, Greeks lived cheek by jowl with non-Greeks, and there would have been many mixed marriages, as in other towns founded by the Seleucids. In this respect only, these towns resembled the archaic colonies, which were the initiative of aristocratic groups and polis communities rather than a monarch.[19]

Moral doctrines such as those Clearchus brought with him to Ai-Khanoum affirmed migrants in their identity and beliefs. Yet they also lent themselves to transcultural contact in spaces with similar written and intellectual traditions. They met with keen interest in India and adjacent territories, in particular. There were parallels between Indian and Greek philosophy that had already struck Onesicritus in Taxila. Since Alexander's campaign, contacts between philosophically educated westerners and their Indian counterparts, the Brahmins, had been not uncommon. They were always connected to political rule, just as the transfer of Delphic maxims to the royal capital occurred at the behest of the Seleucid king.

As Alexander already knew, the rajas took advice from Brahmins, while the Brahmin legal code Manu (Manusmriti) demanded that rulers study Vedic scriptures.[20] In the age of Chandragupta and his successors, however, many other (ascetic) schools and religious movements, including Jainism and Buddhism, gained ground at the royal courts alongside the Hindu religions. Here, a climate of openness to foreign ideas prevailed. Given the array of wisdom offers confronting the Mauryan kings, an exchange of ideas with Greek Sophists did not seem out of place.[21]

This context also explains an unprecedented initiative of the third Mauryan king, Ashoka. Ashoka was the first Indian ruler, and indeed the first Indian, to proclaim his will in the form of inscriptions. Besides several

Image 6 Statue of the gymnasium director of Ai-Khanoum. This herm (a half-statue surmounting a pillar) of a man from Ai-Khanoum, dating to the first half of the second century BCE, might depict the director of the gymnasium. In Hellenistic times, the gymnasium served as a centre of Greek education and identity, even and especially in so remote a location as present-day Afghanistan. The full beard and clothing identify the subject as a respected older citizen.

smaller inscriptions in Greek and Aramaic, seven pillar edicts, and two regional edicts, fourteen major rock edicts have come down to us.[22] According to the thirteenth edict, he sent emissaries (*duta*) to teach the ways of the *dhamma*—universal law or righteousness—to Antiochus II (261–246) in Syria, to Ptolemy II Philadelphus, to Antigonus Gonatas of Macedonia, to Magas of Cyrene, and even to Alexander of Epirus.[23]

Although the word *dhamma* has religious connotations in Buddhism, it also appears in non-religious documents such as early legal codes. In sending his envoys far and wide, Ashoka was not so much launching a proselytizing campaign as asserting his claim to rule the world (perhaps as *chakravarti*).[24] Presenting an ethical framework that drew attention to the ruler's social responsibility helped integrate heterogeneous parts of the empire and their religious tendencies. Ashoka further sought to reach out to cooperative Greeks and stimulate an exchange between Buddhist learning and the ethics of Stoic and Peripatetic philosophers, whose teachings on political virtue were much discussed at Hellenistic courts at the time.[25] Rulers clearly saw these philosophical models as compatible. In this context, Buddhism seemed more open and flexible than the ritual precepts of the Brahmin Hindus. Ashoka's Greek inscriptions at Kandahar translate *dhamma* as *eusebeia* (piety); Deimachus of Plataea, who spent time at the court of Bindusara as an ambassador of Antiochus I, wrote a work *peri eusebias* as well as a book on India.[26]

In addition, the sources point to regular correspondence between Antiochus and Bindusara. The *dhamma* envoys may have been preceded and accompanied by letters, as was customary among Hellenistic rulers.[27] The Greek texts of the Kandahar inscriptions can only have been written by a scribe (a resident Greek?) who was equally at home in Greek philosophy and the world of Buddhism. There must therefore have been a great many scribes who were familiar with the foreign language and diplomatic conventions.[28]

. . . and Again: Doctors as Mediators

Even if we do not know what became of the emissaries and how far they roamed, the edicts presuppose an exact knowledge of transregional trade routes and the geographical locations of western rulers and their residences. Not by chance, Indian overseas trade to the west (the Persian Gulf) and south (Sri Lanka) significantly increased under the Mauryans and with the rise of Buddhism. As always, such transfer routes no doubt also facilitated diplomatic and 'religious' contacts.[29] For their part, the Hellenistic monarchs would not have resented the Mauryan diplomatic offensive; on the contrary, they may even have welcomed it. From the thirteenth edict, we learn that the envoys were 'medical men'. We have already seen that doctors played a vital role in travelling abroad and gathering information. In the period after Alexander, the migration of Greek physicians was for the first time matched by a comparable mobility among Indian adepts, who were every bit as professional as their Greek colleagues.

The rise of Buddhism was responsible for this. Buddhist ascetics (*sramanas*, *samana*) and monks ignored Brahmin prohibitions on physical contact and eschewed magical-religious healing practices. Instead, much like their Greek colleagues in the west, they developed an empirical, rational medicine based on observations of the body, nature (winds, seasons etc.), and diet, prescribing their patients plant-based medicines (pepper extracts, for example) and foods (dietetics).[30] And just as Greek physicians ventured to peripheral zones, so too medically trained Buddhist ascetics broke through the narrow constraints that the Brahmins had imposed on the Indian populace. They trekked to faraway villages, treated non-Aryans, and made no distinction between Indians and Greeks. Their monasteries were healing centres open to everyone. Under Ashoka, they sprung up along the great trading routes, and they enjoyed financial support from wealthy merchants. The Buddhist monks were therefore predestined to spread the teachings of the *dhamma*. Ashoka proclaimed in the second rock edict (near Girnar) that medical care should be extended to both humans and animals, and that medicinal herbs, roots, and fruits should be planted everywhere. This concern with universal welfare, subverting the Brahmins' social hierarchies and ritual taboos, breathes the spirit of Buddhist asceticism. A Greek observer characterized the ascetic physicians as 'philosophers in relation to humankind', which accords well with the claim of *dhamma* teachings.[31]

It goes without saying that their growing influence caused tensions and provoked counter-reactions from the Brahmins. These are reflected in the different versions of the famous Indian work *Arthashastra*, with which Brahmin scholars sought to win over the Indian ruler for their interpretation of the *dhamma*.[32] While Buddhist physicians could therefore not fully suppress the Brahmins' magical-religious healing methods, they could still supplement them with a new kind of medicine. The increased array of medical practices was matched by a panoply of competing philosophical offers, confronting the Mauryan ruler with the delicate task of maintaining an attitude of impartial benevolence towards them all. In this way, and with the intensification of trade contacts and diplomatic and philosophical exchanges, the Indian kings promoted the development of medicine on both sides.[33] Together with artists, philosophers, and astrologers, Greek doctors probably resided at their courts and in the mercantile centres of their empire.[34] The result was a wave of globalization that swept all the way from India to the Mediterranean and western Asian ecumene and made possible a culture of knowledge transfer extending from the Bay of Bengal to Gibraltar.

GREEKS ON THE GANGES

MEGASTHENES AND THE GRAECO-INDIAN EMPIRE OF MENANDER

There is no other era in ancient history in which the Greeks could learn more about the wonderland of the east than in the two generations after Alexander. Classics were written in this period that would shape how the European west perceived India for over a millennium and are considered among the most important sources on Indian antiquity. The first were histories of Alexander, which in the tradition of the fourth century sought to establish connections between climatological and physical conditions and ways of life. The comparison between India and the Nile region remained central. The fertility of both countries was generally believed to derive from the warm climate and its influence on the air as well as the abundance of water, helped in India by the monsoonal rains.[35] India was further blessed with gold, precious stones, and pearls, hence the Indian kings' luxurious lifestyle. Cleitarchus of Alexandria (c. 300 BCE) offered many details he could only have known from the tales of Indian envoys. Accounts of royal splendour were matched by admiration for the ascetics who, 'living simply and rustically in the wilderness', strove for wisdom and immolated themselves in old age.[36]

Anyone wanting more precise information had to make their way to the Mauryan court. There were now ample opportunities to do just that. Just as Indian emissaries sojourned at the Seleucid courts, so too Greeks travelled to the royal residence on the Ganges. The most important was Megasthenes from Asia Minor. He arrived at Pataliputra (near today's Patna) around twenty years after Alexander's death, possibly sent by the satrap of Arachosia or by Seleucus Nicator; he may even have helped conclude the peace treaty with Chandragupta.[37] He stayed in the king's residence or field camp for more than a decade. He also spent time with the Prasioi, a tribe based in the Mauryan heartland on the lower Ganges. He could ask natives for information about southern India. They confirmed Onesicritus' report of a twenty-day sea voyage to Sri Lanka from a port on the Ganges estuary.[38]

During or after his stay, he wrote a work on India (*Indica*) from which later authors quoted at length.[39] It most likely originates in a report on his activities for Seleucus, which was then revised for a broader public (as was the case for other *periploi* and *Indica*). Its three or four sections covered geography, fauna, flora, and climate, then early ethnography followed by an account of the cities, administration, society, and philosophy of the Mauryan Empire. Megasthenes significantly added to or corrected the old image of India, initially in the realm of geography: India's centre shifted from the Indus to the Ganges, and the size of the subcontinent was reconceived in light of the discovery that it could be sailed around from the Ganges delta.[40]

Ethnography posed different challenges. Like his predecessors, Megasthenes wrote for a Greek public and could only represent foreign institutions by drawing on Greek categories. For all that he strove for authenticity, we should therefore assume that he did not fully grasp Indian conditions or simplified, generalized, or falsified them by accommodating them to Greek patterns of thought. Tradition also weighed heavily on him. Megasthenes was an ardent admirer of Alexander and sought to authenticate the legends constructed by him and his officers with reference to Indian traditions. Thus, Dionysus had not only conquered India but introduced its people to agriculture, urban life, law, and the art of war. Heracles followed in his footsteps fifteen generations later and completed his work by founding and fortifying more cities; his most important foundation was Pataliputra, the Mauryan residence. Here Heracles rose to become the last king of all India.[41]

It is not entirely clear what Megasthenes was aiming at with this developmental model. Some suppose that he wanted Alexander's achievements to appear in an even more glorious light. Whereas Dionysus and Heracles had strolled into a defenceless country of nomads (still no mean feat when compared with the Persian king's failed Scythian campaign), Alexander had overthrown a worthy adversary, a kingdom left by his ancestral heroes in a state of military preparedness.[42] Others posit a link with Seleucus' foreign policy. Accordingly, in bestowing the blessings of civilization on the east, Dionysus and Heracles mirror the role in which Seleucus cast himself when subjecting his Asiatic territories to his rule. On the other hand, the fact that he encountered in India a well-defended kingdom, thanks to the efforts of Greek heroes, explains why this kingdom could not be conquered, 'only' made a treaty partner.[43]

However speculative they may seem, all these factors may have influenced Megasthenes' account.[44] They reflect the way in which ethnographic descriptions never existed independently of personal circumstances and political relations. Megasthenes was further constrained by his topic: unlike his predecessors, he faced the dilemma of reconciling a tradition established after Alexander with the current state of an urbanized empire that communicated with the Seleucids at eye level. The solution he found was conceived not just as a political programme but as a new *ethnographic model*, one that took up Herodotean models (such as the Scythian nomad discourse) and combined Greek traditions with contemporary findings.

In this context, he also reprised familiar motifs concerning the wonders of India: the gold-digging ants and one-eyed men; the mouthless and fleet-footed marvels found in the tales of the Brahmins, the epics, and the tradition of *Indica* established by Scylax and continued by Ctesias; the fertile climate and fecund fauna as well as the justice and happiness of the inhabitants, which the historians of Alexander saw realized in the kingdom of Musikanos and in the ascetic life of the Indian sages.[45]

Megasthenes went a step further, however: he transferred onto *all* Indians what his forerunners and contemporaries claimed to have found in specific groups or areas. They prided themselves on their gold jewellery and clothing while living modest, moderate, and happy lives, and they treated strangers with fairness and honesty.[46] He even resorted to outright falsehoods in support of this utopian image, as when he claimed that slavery was unknown in India.[47] He probably did not regard the slaves he saw labouring in the fields and houses as an unfree class in the Greek sense, since these were drawn from all levels of society and were not required to dispose of excrement and corpses, tasks traditionally reserved for the casteless *chandala* (untouchables). He then linked these scattered observations with the Brahmins' abhorrence of Aryan enslavement and the ideals of a slaveless society and an equality of all human beings—ideals that the Brahmins themselves would have vehemently opposed.[48]

Megasthenes on the Society and Governance of the Mauryan Empire

Megasthenes sticks closer to reality when he approaches the centre of Indian royal power and tries to describe society from this perspective. To be sure, his account of the Mauryan state is informed throughout by the model of the Seleucid Empire.[49] Yet these transferences still allow Indian realities to shimmer through. On the one hand, Megasthenes is a useful source on the military and the king's relationship with the army. On the other, mythologically embellished references to the wise men and physicians at court conceal valid insights into the diversity of the schools of wisdom competing for royal patronage.

Megasthenes was thus probably the first to describe Jainist ascetics.[50] They followed a strict vegetarian diet for fear of harming any living creature. Some swept the ground they walked on and covered their mouth and nose with strips of cloth to avoid crushing or inhaling insects. Megasthenes derived from this the long-lived story of the *Astomoi*, people without mouths who sustained themselves on the smell of roasted meat and the fragrances of some flowers and plants. That they lived on the Ganges and sought contact with Chandragupta accords with what Indian sources report on the Jains.[51]

The most controversial text concerns the division of Indian society into seven professional groups or classes (*méros*):[52] (1) the 'wise men', who stood in the highest repute (the Brahmins?); (2) the farmers, who were exempt from military service but paid the king tax; (3) shepherds; (4) artisans and merchants; (5) soldiers; (6) overseers and spies; and (7) more senior and older officials, who were responsible for running the courts and the administrative system. Although there are no Indian texts that mention this classification *as a whole*, the groups appear *individually* so often in the sources that

Megasthenes presumably provided a precise depiction of Indian society as he observed it in and around Pataliputra, at least.

Some scholars even maintain that this categorization of people based on their work reflects a vague knowledge of the Indian 'caste system'.[53] The term 'caste' was unknown in the ancient world; it was first used by Portuguese traders of the sixteenth or seventeenth century, who transferred a word originally applied to plants and animals ('castas') to the Indian society of their time. It cannot adequately convey the complex conditions and concepts of Indian antiquity, which waver between theoretical constructs and real social stratification.[54] At any rate, the Brahmin sources refer to only four social 'classes' (varnas): the Brahmins (priests), Kshatriya (warriors), Vaishya (traders, craftspeople, and farmers), and Shudra (untouchables), and these do not neatly match the groups named by Megasthenes. In addition, they belong to a different hierarchy: overseers and spies take first place in Buddhist sources and administrative lists. Like his predecessors, Megasthenes seems to have been unaware of the untouchables (Shudra). On the other hand, several details he mentions are confirmed in Vedic and Brahmin texts, for example, the fact that the king owns all the land and the farmers are exempted from military service but instead have to contribute a quarter of their products to the king's treasury, from which he finances the state, its officials, and the army.[55] The veneration shown the 'wise men' who 'know all of philosophy', and advise the king,[56] had already been remarked on by Alexander's historians.

It would be premature to conclude from all this that Megasthenes lacked the cultural understanding and vocabulary to grasp the various social categories he encountered in India and their causes.[57] There is much to suggest that in Chandragupta's day, the late Vedic varna system, which originated in northwest India, was not yet established in Magadha. To that extent, we would be wrong to criticize the Greek observer for describing it imprecisely or not at all, whatever his Brahmin informants may have told him.[58] In any event, his aim was to present key professional or administrative activities and categorize them in a manner oriented on familiar models. He thus borrowed his terminology for describing India's social classes (*meros* means 'part' or 'segment') from Aristotle's critique of the planned city of Hippodamus, which was divided into three classes of artisans, farmers, and soldiers. The number seven is clearly taken from Herodotus' account of Egyptian society, and it recurs in Plato's ideal state.[59]

There is one difference, however, that shows that Megasthenes was not slavishly imposing a Greek template on his ethnographic material. Plato's 'Republic' is based on a community of women and children; a person's position in one of the seven 'classes' is determined by talent, not by birth. In India, by contrast, as Megasthenes rightly points out, marriage outside the clan (*genos*) is forbidden, while professional specialization is monopolized by families and inherited. The varna system was indeed carried by lineage groups (*gotras*)—an aspect that played no role in the Greek parallel models.[60]

The same holds true of certain aspects of the Indian system of government. The king's advisers, listed by Megasthenes as the seventh group, were renowned for their wisdom and justice, and the local princes were selected from their ranks.[61] These 'princes' were evidently the *mahamatras*, who as district-level officials mediated between the residence in Pataliputra and the provinces. An old maxim passed down in the Vedas stipulated that they should serve as royal counsellors. Moreover, Megasthenes knew both of the great advisory councils: the exclusive council of ministers (*parisad* = those who sit with the king) and the assembly of officials (*raja-sabha*), said to have numbered 500 under Bindusara.[62]

How much Megasthenes knew about other details of the system of government is disputed. It partly depends on how we interpret the *Arthashastra*, rediscovered in 1909.[63] Arising in Brahmin circles, the work was intended to show the king how he could increase his power and limit the influence of rival potentates. For this, the king needed a well-organized spy system that fed him information and crushed internal enemies of state while fomenting unrest in neighbouring kingdoms.[64] However, the dating of these (and other) parts of the book is unclear, and it is also unknown whether they were grounded in specific phenomena or only in a very general, ideal perspective shared by some Brahmins. It may be that Megasthenes learned of their ideas by observing and conversing with them and found confirmation here for his own view of the slaveless society of the Indians.[65] According to the *Arthashastra*, the state rested on seven pillars: the king's character, the ministers, the provinces, the capital, the state treasury, the army, and the state's allies. If we consider that the varna system of the Vedic period had become more fluid by the time of the Mauryans,[66] it is possible that a foreign observer mixed up several categories, reclassifying the seven areas that enabled the king to expand his power as seven professional groups that corresponded to the seven social classes of Greek tradition.

Greeks Conquer the Ganges Valley

Despite these insecurities, what emerges is the portrait of an efficiently organized regime and a king who assiduously pursued the goal of generating as much revenue as possible by keeping himself well informed about his country and its people. This allowed him to finance the standing army, bureaucracy, and court, but also to mount further expansionary campaigns, as when the third Mauryan ruler, Ashoka, annexed the land of Kalinga in 261 BCE. Yet he must soon have realized that additional conquests would only fuel tensions, and that the empire could not be maintained in perpetuity through military force and surveillance.[67] By propagating *dhamma* teaching, Ashoka therefore sought to provide his vast empire with a moral foundation and defuse inter-religious conflicts by orienting them towards a shared ethics. At the same time, the *dhamma* was intended to remind subjects of their duties towards a 'purified' ruler.

As so often in history, however, the success of this state-mandated 'moral renewal' proved elusive. Perhaps the arrogance with which officials asserted their claim to moral leadership met with resistance from both the rural populace and the Brahmins, who felt threatened in their position as royal advisers; at any rate, no comparable edicts were issued by Ashoka's successors. Yet they too failed to unite the empire. It splintered into several parts and became ripe for invasion.

Not for the last time in Indian history, the danger came from the northwest. Bactria had always been notorious as a hotbed of political unrest. From 256 BCE the Greek satrap there, Diodotus, began pushing for independence from Seleucid rule, roughly coinciding with the secession of Parthia. In 238 he had himself crowned king of a breakaway 'Graeco-Bactrian' empire.[68] His son, Diodotus II, was overthrown by a certain Euthydemus (from Magnesia). He expanded the empire to the east and north (to the Oxus Valley) and especially to the south, as far as the Hindu Kush, forcing Antiochus III (223–187) to recognize him as a king in his own right. Its advantageous situation on the Silk Road, combined with its fertility and advanced urbanization, made his kingdom one of the most successful states to emerge in the wake of Alexander's campaigns. Ai-Khanoum became the residence of a Graeco-Bactrian governor and boomed as a local trading, tax, and tribute hub, reflected in the numerous Indian coins that have been found in the palace precinct.[69]

Like the Seleucids, the Bactrian kings promoted a Hellenistic way of life without rejecting Indian and Iranian influences. As they expanded over the Himalayas, the magnificent coins on which they had themselves portrayed began featuring the native language (Prakrit) on the reverse side.[70] The kings relied on experienced local administrators and on the collaboration of Indian families who were willing to appropriate Greek language, education, and culture as status symbols. The most famous example is Sophytus, an Indian with a Hellenized name, presumably from Kandahar (Arachosia), who imitated verses from Homer in his Graecian grave stele.[71]

In 183 BCE Demetrius I, probably Euthydemus' son, ventured beyond the Hindu Kush to Arachosia, Gandhara, and Taxila, ultimately conquering the entire Indus Valley; the old harbour town of Patala was renamed Demetrias. The Greeks then chased Alexander's dream: Apollodorus (155–130 BCE), perhaps a son or brother of Demetrius, led an army along the coast to Bharukaccha (Broach, Bharuch), which as Barygaza would later become

Image 7 Coin of an Indo-Bacrtian king (Agathocles?) with (Buddhist?) spoked wheel, Bactria. The Greek kings who resided in Bactria and northern India minted silver coins that incorporated local and Indian symbols. The eight-spoked wheel on the coin found in Ai-Khanoum (on the Oxus in northern Afghanistan) could be equated with the Wheel of Dharma (Dharmachakra) set in motion by Buddha (see p. 242). Credit: AKG1823586: Roland and Sabrina Michaud/ akg-images.

important for Roman trade in the east.[72] A second army reached Pataliputra. A rebellion in their homeland (led by Eucratides) forced them to break off the siege, yet the campaign was still the most significant expeditionary enterprise of the Hellenistic age. It secured the Greeks a dominion that extended from the Ganges to the Indus and to today's Baluchistan. Demetrius I resided in Sagala as the first king of the Indo-Grecian Empire.[73] Eucratides I (171–145 BCE) launched another Indian campaign, but the Bactrian part of the empire, weakened by power struggles and conflicts with Parthia, soon fell to the central Asian Yuezhi people. In the course of these upheavals, the residential city of Al-Khanum went up in flames.[74]

King Menander and the Encounter with Buddhism

South of the Hindu Kush, by contrast, Menander I Soter ('the Saviour'; 166–150 or 155–130 BCE) succeeded in stabilizing the situation. He is the most important king of the Greek Empire on Indian soil and, along with Alexander, the only Greek ruler whose memory is preserved to this day in Indian folklore. Probably with the help of Indian 'vassals'—the Seleucids pursued a similar strategy in Iran and the eastern reaches of their empire[75]—he ruled a large area from Kabul and the Swat Valley to the Punjab. Like the Mauryans before him, he could only survive as ruler by engaging representatives of the various religious and philosophical groups as his advisers.

On the Indian side, Buddhist monks were especially likely to seek out Greeks. Many had come under pressure following the downfall of the Mauryan dynasty and now sought protection from the new king, seeing in him a defence against a resurgent Brahminism. Some Buddhists may have been Greeks, who since Ashoka had acted as intermediaries between rulers and the local elite. Indianized names for Greeks (*Yona*) are found in Pali texts and inscriptions. A Greek monk probably took part in the mission sent to Gujarat and the Himalayas after the Third Buddhist Council (c. 250 BCE).[76]

The alliance between Greeks and Buddhism begun under Ashoka perhaps led, under Menander's reign, to an intellectual exchange at the highest level, such as had probably also taken place at the Mauryan courts. The most celebrated record is the *Milinda Panha* ('The questions of Milinda = Menander'), a dialogue between Menander and the otherwise unknown monk Nagasena on the problems of *dhamma*.[77] The text was disseminated in different versions as far as Sri Lanka and China and today counts among the most popular Buddhist classics. Menander is characterized in the opening chapters as 'wise, experienced, eloquent, and highly talented'. He emerges as a fair questioner who never unnecessarily interrupts his interlocutor but patiently hears out his explanations. At the end he supposedly converted to Buddhism, like King Agathocles before him.[78]

The *Milinda Panha* is of limited value as a historical document. It is not even an authentic historical text: the Greek influences it was once thought to reflect have proven spurious. Much of it was interpolated from Indian traditions and legends about the Buddha.[79] Similar reservations apply to the archaeological testimony. Menander's coins feature an eight-spoked wheel sometimes identified with the wheel of dharma (*dharmachakra*) set in motion by the Buddha. Yet the wheel depicted on the Ashoka pillars has twenty-four spokes; it is more likely that Menander's coins represent the star emblem of the Macedonian dynasty. Furthermore, Plutarch remarks that the dead king's ashes were distributed among all the towns of the empire, a way of honouring the dead known to Buddhism. Yet the striking parallels to the Buddha's funerary rites, as reported in Indian sources, may also suggest that Plutarch retroactively incorporated elements of these stories into the Menander legend.[80]

However tentative the interpretation must remain in its particulars, it at least shows how Greek and Indian religious symbolism, iconography, and ideas could easily be compared and combined, just as the philosophical systems of the two cultures were viewed as compatible. To that extent, it is unsurprising that Greek migrants had few difficulties adapting to their new country's religious customs, especially if they exercised official functions. In a pillar inscription from Besnagar in today's state of Madhya Pradesh, Heliodorus, who visited Prince Bhagadhadra's court as ambassador of the Indo-Greek king Antialcidas (c. 115–95 BCE), declared himself a devotee of the Hindu god Vasudeva-Krishna and a follower of the Bhagavata sect (c. 110 BCE).[81] Just as the Indian Sophytus imitates Homeric verses and prides himself on his Greek education in the Greek political and administrative context of Arachosia, so Heliodorus presents himself as 'Indianized' by alluding in his inscription to the Sanskrit epic, the *Mahabharata*.[82]

Against this backdrop, and given the broad opening towards the culture of the 'other side' occurring at the time, the question of which religious movement the ruler favoured or whether Menander converted to Buddhism plays a secondary role. When Menander's successors minted coins on which Zeus and Athena or the kings themselves imitated the Buddhist gesture of an outstretched right arm with extended index and middle fingers, or when they had their coins embossed with the ancient Indian Kharosthi (Gandhari) script along with a Greek legend and Buddhist characters and symbols, this does not signify a *specific* confession of faith by the rulers—that is to adopt a modern or Christian perspective. It stands instead for an attempt by the rulers to present themselves as benevolently disposed towards the multiple religious and philosophical currents swirling through the Graeco-Indian Empire. The kings and their officials and emissaries could use religious and philosophical sign systems that would be understood and interpreted in their own way by both the Greek and the Indian populace. This is what constitutes the enduring fascination of Indo-Greek relations, which began with the treaty between Seleucus and Chandragupta and reached its climax with Menander. This was one reason why Buddhist monks brought knowledge of the Greeks to Sri Lanka, where to this day every Singhalese Buddhist remembers King Menander (Milinda) with admiration.[83]

EXPEDITIONS OF THE PTOLEMIES AND THE GEOGRAPHY OF ERATOSTHENES

The Ptolemies' Voyages of Discovery in the Red Sea

The Ptolemies were in contact with Indian kingdoms as well. Under Ptolemy II Philadelphus, an ambassador named Dionysius stayed at the court of Bindusara or Ashoka—and he was surely not the only one, as Pliny suggests.[84] Ashoka himself had sent *dhamma* envoys to the court of Ptolemy II (see above, pp. 231–232). The Ptolemies nonetheless placed less value on relations with India than did the Seleucids. They ruled over an ethnically far more compact empire and directed their interests—leaving aside the strategically important Levant—primarily to the Red Sea. The first Ptolemy had already dispatched his admiral Philon to the Ethiopian coast, where he discovered Topaz Island (Zabargad) and brought back to the queen a large gemstone.[85] Under the second Ptolemy, after 277 BCE, Pythagoras 'the Navarch' explored the Arabian side of the Red Sea, describing the precious stones he saw in Arabia as well as the animals and humans he encountered along the coasts.[86] A few years earlier, Timosthenes of Rhodes had commanded royal ships to Arabia, east Africa, and the Sudan. In the books they wrote upon their return, the expeditionary leaders set down richly informative accounts of ethnography, geography, botany, and zoology. Their voyages brought knowledge of the Red Sea coasts and their hinterland to a level of detail unmatched until the Portuguese reports of the seventeenth century.[87]

To the Southern Sudan and Meroë

It may seem surprising that none of these expeditions ventured beyond the southernmost exit from the Red Sea, the 'Gate of Tears'.[88] It becomes understandable, however, once we consider that the Red Sea has a north-south extension of around 2,190 km, roughly equivalent to the distance from the Levant to Sardinia. Patrolling and financially exploiting such a vast, nautically hazardous area was a challenge that initially forestalled any push farther south. Instead, the Ptolemies—much like the Seleucids from 220 BCE in the Persian Gulf—sought to profit from maritime trade by raising customs duties of up to 50 percent, especially on the Arabian perfumes (incense, myrrh, cassia) and spices (cinnamon, saffron) they monopolized. In order to secure sufficient quantities for domestic use (in temples) and for exporting on to the Mediterranean (perhaps also to India), Ptolemy II wrested control of the Marib-Petra incense route from the Nabataeans. From the mid-third century onward, the flow of goods was diverted via Gerrha to the Arabian east coast and from there to Syria and Egypt.[89] The expansion of transport routes between the Red Sea and the Nile as well as the reopening of Necho's canal shortly after 280 BCE created a direct link to the capital. Planting colonies such as Myos Hormos (Mussel) near Quseir on the Arabian coast and Leukos Limen or Arsinoe and Berenice on the African coast at the Gulf of Eilat made it easier to control the sea lanes and combat Nabataean piracy.[90]

Yet there was another reason for the Ptolemies' engagement, which far surpassed that of their predecessors: by the end, over 270 bases and ports had been established along the Egyptian coast to the Strait of Bab-el-Mandeb.[91] Ever since Alexander's campaigns, war elephants had formed an important part of Hellenistic armies. The Seleucids sourced theirs from India, blocking access to other powers. At the same time, they extended their influence in the Persian Gulf and on the east Arabian coasts at least as far as the islands of Failaka and Dilmun, the old way stations for Indo-Mesopotamian maritime trade.[92]

Because the Ptolemies were almost always fighting wars for control of fertile Syria, they needed to find alternative hunting grounds. The hinterland of the Red Sea south of the fifth Nile cataract was considered the African pachyderms' preferred habitat. What could have been more natural than to explore these regions from the coastal bases and by sailing upriver? The third Ptolemy seems to have assigned a military detachment to the Red Sea hunting grounds and hired Indian mahouts to catch and train elephants; perhaps they were recruited by his emissary Dionysius.[93] A certain Satyrus was commissioned to fortify the desert route from Edfu via the Wadi Abbad to the sea and reconnoitre the elephant hunting grounds in the land of the troglodytes. During his expedition, launched at some point after 270 BCE, Philoteris was founded south of Arsinoe. Ptolemy had previously established Berenice (Trogodytice) at the end of the caravan route from the Nile and ordered special ships to be built for transporting elephants. To finance this transport and pay the soldiers, the kings sold Ethiopian ivory and sought access to the gold and amethyst mines of the deserts east of the Red Sea approaching the northern Sudan.[94]

Greeks in Meroë and on the Blue Nile

Eumedes established a base south of Port Sudan with the telling name Ptolemais Theron ('Ptolemais of the Hunts', today's Marsa Aqiq). The site could only be reached with small boats, however.[95] For that reason, a trade route ran overland to the Nile and on to the Nubian realm of Meroë; the city lay on the right bank of the Nile, 90 km south of Atbara. From 230 BCE, the Meroite king Ergamenes controlled all Ethiopia. His successors employed Greek sculptors and musicians and received envoys and scientists from Alexandria.[96] For the Ptolemies, these contacts opened the way to the gold mines of Wadi Allaqi as well as the Cinnamon Coast of Somalia. From here they could source not only elephants but also exotic animals (pythons, camels, apes) for the parades and royal zoo in Alexandria. On one of Ptolemy II's parades, 'Ethiopians' bore ivory, ebony, gold, and silver.[97]

Men like Simonides, Bion, and Basilis (who also wrote an *Indica*) or Damocritus and Charon spent several years in Meroë, the 'Nubian

Alexandria', writing books on the kingdom as well as *Ethiopica*; under Ptolemy II, a certain Dalion was said to have been the first Greek to venture beyond Meroë into Ethiopia. They became experts on the south and supplied important astronomical and geographical data. Thus Philon, sent by Ptolemy to the Ethiopian coast, ascertained that the sun stood at its zenith for forty-five days in Meroë before the summer solstice. Like Pytheas in the north, they also corrected the zonal theory by demonstrating that the habitable zone extended much farther south than had previously been believed. In making contact with the 'island of Meroë', as they called the fertile region bounded by the Atbara, the Nile, and its tributaries, and in exploring the desert from the Red Sea to the Nile, the Greeks also first learned of Lake Koloë (Lake Tana) and the Blue Nile (Nil el Azrag) and White Nile (Nil el Abyadh) as far as the swamplands below its confluence with the Sobat River (Astasobas). Travellers may have brought news of Lake Albert and Lake Victoria; the Greeks came quite close to the sources of the Nile.[98]

The farther abroad they roamed, the more frequently they simply mentioned the names of tribes and supplemented them with classical topoi on peripheral people: beyond the desert lived tribes whose kings had only one eye on their foreheads, cannibals, cynocephali, and men who went around on all fours.[99] Such tall tales were still being peddled in works of natural science from the sixteenth century. Yet there were also ethnographically valuable reports, above all those composed at the behest of the king by captains sent on exploratory missions. In the third century BCE, Timosthenes of Rhodes wrote an eleven-volume *periplus*, entitled 'On harbours', drawing on his own experiences and literary sources. This gigantic work probably set out to provide a systematic account of the entire ecumene. Only around forty fragments and quotations survive; the information they provide on nautical, geographical, and ethnographic matters as well as on buildings near the coast goes beyond the usual *periploi* to offer a kind of scientifically ambitious 'descriptive geography'.[100] Estimated distances are coordinated with information about the relative position of harbours and other coastal features; the significance of Massalia as a reference point for describing the western Mediterranean is based on its astronomical latitude, recalling Pytheas. The central position accorded Rhodes and the sea route to Egypt likely reflects the Ptolemies' claim to maritime dominance in the eastern Mediterranean.[101]

No less interesting are the ethnographic details. In one fragment, Timosthenes states that the Caucasian peoples were so savage and distrustful that they never communicated with each other and all spoke different languages. This reference resembles the report of another Ptolemaic expeditionary leader, perhaps Simmias, who encountered native tribes while voyaging along the 'Ichthyophagi coast' of the Red Sea.[102]

> In general, they do not come into contact with other tribes, nor does the strangeness of the appearance of those who visit them influence the natives, but, gazing at them intently, they remain impassive with their senses unmoved as though no one was present. For not even if someone draws a sword and strikes on them, do they flee; nor if they suffer insult or blows, do they become angry. Further, the people as a whole do not share in the anger of the victims. Sometimes, even when their children or women are slaughtered before their eyes, they remain unmoved by what has happened, giving no indication of anger, or, again, of compassion. In general, even if they experience the most fearful horrors, they remain calm, looking intently at what is happening and nodding their heads to each other. For this reason, people also say that they speak no language, but that they signify everything necessary by imitative gestures of their hands.[103]

As always, familiar motifs recur in such descriptions: in this instance, Nearchus' tale of the 'fish-eaters' who, according to other late second-century reports, lived on the Red Sea coast.[104] Their passive endurance recalls the age-old topos of the peaceful Ethiopians, and perhaps also the Indian Brahmins. Yet all these elements cohere in a realistic context. This is a first contact scenario between two worlds that can communicate through gestures, yet one that involves natives who have learned to mistrust strangers, having been taken captive as slaves or forced to assist in elephant hunts. An unwillingness or incapacity to communicate was a favoured theme of the Hellenistic period (Timosthenes tells a similar tale); some even suspect an ethnographic-ethnological experiment.[105] No less important was the interest of the royal paymaster, who needed to know exactly which tribes populated remote coasts.

Alexandria and the New Cosmic Model of Eratosthenes

If ever there was a centrally organized 'scientific' institution in the ancient world that not only prepared, financed, and coordinated long-distance exploration but also continuously processed the findings, then it was to be found under the first three Ptolemies in Alexandria. All the reports arrived in the library of the Museion that Ptolemy I (Soter) had established near the royal palace. A Museion was a temple to the Muses. Ptolemy created one in new dimensions and with a new orientation. Framed by columns and covered walkways, the shrine was dwarfed by the royal library. Monarchical libraries were hardly a novelty; the tyrants Peisistratus and Polycrates had previously owned such collections. The state archives of Near Eastern kingdoms likewise preserved 'sacred' and literary writings. Yet this new library was encyclopaedic in scope: containing up to 500,000 scrolls, it purported to assemble and make available to scholars the *entire* knowledge of the age. Originally conceived as an educational facility for the princes, it became the centre of a university under royal patronage and the most important research institute in antiquity.

In 245 BCE Eratosthenes of Cyrene was appointed chief librarian by the third Ptolemaic king. Eratosthenes had studied with the great philosophers in Athens and acquired an excellent reputation as a poet, philosopher, and mathematician. In Alexandria he achieved renown as a polymath, attracting the malice of envious colleagues. He worked in the areas of philosophy, mathematics, astronomy, music theory, chronology, history, and grammar; but his most important writings, from the point of view of a history of discovery, were on geography.

His chief goal was to create a new model of the Earth on a mathematical footing. Eratosthenes was the first scholar to use empirical and mathematical methods to estimate the Earth's circumference, probably with technical and financial support from the king, who wanted precise information about the surface area of his kingdom in order to calculate his tax revenue.[106]

Simple geometrical ideas were at the basis of Eratosthenes' calculations. The sun, he reflected, was so far removed from the Earth that its rays could be seen as parallels. On June 21 each year at twelve noon, the sunlight shone directly down on the southern Egyptian town of Syene (Aswan), an estimated 4,900 stadia from Alexandria. There, Eratosthenes carried out his measurements with the help of a gnomon. In Alexandria, he calculated an angle of 83° for the sunlight falling at midday. The scholar transferred the complementary angle of 7° to the Earth's centre and thus produced the triangle: centre of the Earth–Syene–Alexandria. He reasoned that 7° related to the distance between

Syene and Alexandria as 360° to the Earth's circumference (C). It followed that C / 360 = 4,900 / 7 or C = 4,900 × 360 / 7 = 252,000 stadia. The result was imprecise because it proceeded from several false assumptions—for example, that Syene and Alexandria lay on the same meridian—but it came much closer to reality (40,077 km) than any previous estimate. Even more importantly, it resulted from a procedure that could be repeated and improved.

No less important was his *Geographica*. The title indicates his interest in measuring, categorizing, and drawing (*graphein*) the Earth (*geo*) rather than merely describing it. The same principles he had applied when measuring the Earth were now used for mapping the ecumene, based on calculations about where places were located and the distances between them. Eratosthenes took his data from the information provided by Alexander's bematists and the expeditionary reports collected in Alexandria: not just those of Androsthenes' and Timosthenes' voyages, but also the *periplus* of Patrocles, the ocean book of Pytheas, the *periploi* of Hanno and Euthymenes, as well as the writings of Megasthenes, Deimachus, and perhaps the ambassador Dionysius.[107]

Drawing on all these sources, Eratosthenes arrived at a rough outline of the ecumene, which he first bisected along a degree of latitude running parallel to the Equator (*Diaphragma*).[108] He then added five parallel circles and four meridians, each oriented on a large geographical or morphological entity (thus the first, easternmost meridian retraced the course of the Indus). This cartographic grid formed the basis for the map. Collating the data from the *periploi* and itineraries at his disposal, Eratosthenes ascertained that the inhabited Earth was 38,000 stadia wide and 77,800 stadia long. As a result of progressive discoveries, the ecumene had broadened to both east and west. Because Eratosthenes simultaneously assumed a lesser circumference for the Earth than Aristotle, the sea between the western (Spain) and eastern (India) ends of the ecumene had to shrink. The consequence was that it was now possible to sail from Spain over the Atlantic to India![109]

The information about coasts, rivers, mountains, cities, and countries compiled in the expeditionary reports was now plotted against the cartographic grid and linked to ethnographic, climatic, economic, and political data—a triumph of synthesis that for the first time combined the mathematical focus of geography with the cultural-ethnographic tradition.[110] Several countries were grouped in rhomboid 'seals' (*Sphragides*). While the map depicted the Mediterranean, northern Africa, and northern Arabia with considerable accuracy, the edges of the world were distorted due to insufficient data and a tendency to simplify coasts and landforms into abstract geometrical shapes. The southern reaches of the Indian subcontinent were thus replaced by a line running east at the latitude of Meroë. This pushed Taprobane (Sri Lanka) much too far to the east and not far enough to the south. The African continent was likewise foreshortened to the south. To the north, the Caspian Sea was shown as connected with the Ocean. Britannia was included as an obtuse triangle. Thule appeared beneath the Arctic Circle.[111]

Eudoxus of Cyzicus and the Sea Route to India

By the late second century BCE, two developments had forced the Ptolemies to lift their gaze beyond the Red Sea and the east African coast. On the one hand, from the end of the third century (following the fourth Syrian war), elephants had lost their lustre as a weapon that conferred a decisive military advantage; the search for east African hunting grounds no longer had top priority. Accordingly, from Ptolemy IV Philopator (221–202 BCE) onward, no more bases were established on the Red Sea coast, while the existing footholds were repurposed to protect maritime trade and caravan routes. On the other hand, the Ptolemies were increasingly hard pressed by the Seleucids, who had wrested control of all Syria following their victory at Panium and marched on the land of the Nile around thirty years later. The Ptolemies survived only thanks to Roman intervention, yet they relinquished their Mediterranean outposts and were cut off from Levantine-Syrian trading networks. Much like the pharaohs a thousand years before (see above, p. 33), they thus looked for alternatives elsewhere. Finding a direct sea route to India was an obvious solution.

The crossing had not previously been attempted because Arab mariners kept the monsoon system a closely guarded secret. Matters were further complicated by a geographical problem. Eratosthenes had concluded from the reports of Patrocles, Megasthenes, and Deimachus that the subcontinent was a rhomboid that barely extended to the south. The southernmost region was thought to lie on the same parallel as Meroë, with the isle of Taprobane occupying the same latitude as the Somali coast. Accordingly, any ship that headed east from the Red Sea threatened to sail past India unless it was quickly propelled north by southerlies; but this was a risk no responsible captain was willing to take.[112]

These conditions could only change once news of India's true dimensions filtered through to the west. This revelation roughly coincided with the Ptolemies' relative decline in the mid-second century BCE. Around 1,000 km to the east, the Bactrian Greeks under Demetrius attacked the Mauryan Empire and charted the Indian coastline east of the mouth of the Indus. In the ensuing period, Greek mariners explored the west coast farther to the south; the Bactrian Greeks learned that the subcontinent continued all the way down to the Malabar coast and the Tamil kingdoms. Over the following generations, this information must have reached the ears of the Ptolemies. The *periplus* 'On the Red Sea' by Agatharchides of Cnidus was written around this time; it recounts the tales of traders and Ptolemaic expeditionary leaders and describes the dangers involved in their ventures. His chapters on the Red Sea's coast dwellers, botany, and fauna exemplify Hellenistic ethnography at its finest. They attest to the wealth of knowledge that had now been accumulated at the Alexandrine court.[113]

Now, for the first time, the Ptolemaic kings ordered their captains to sail beyond the Strait of Bab-el-Mandeb into the Gulf of Aden. Diodorus of Samos reached Azania, while Charimortus (probably under Ptolemy IV) made it as far as Cape Guardafui and the island of Socotra, ideally located for the voyage to India. There, Indian and Arabian traders offered their wares to Egyptian merchants. A captain hazarding the journey to the west coast of India from one of these starting points need no longer fear sailing past his destination. The only thing still missing was exact knowledge of the monsoon.[114]

How this last obstacle was overcome is depicted in one of the most famous discovery narratives of antiquity. Written around 100 BCE in Gades by the scholar Posidonius, it was still inspiring historical novels in the twentieth century.[115] According to Posidonius, a certain Eudoxus of Cyzicus (on the Sea of Marmara) turned up at the Ptolemies' court in the late (or mid-?) second century as part of an embassy. Cyzicus was a well-known port with excellent connections to the eastern Mediterranean. Eudoxus was one of the wealthy dignitaries who probably wanted to profit from expanded trade to the Far East; one of the oldest Mediterranean coins found in India originated in Cyzicus.[116] Even if the sources focus in what follows on the person of Eudoxus, it may be supposed that he was acting in the interests of other dignitaries (or in competition with them). Because his hometown already had commercial links to India, Eudoxus was likely interested in establishing a direct sea route to the Indian west coast.

He thus learned during a journey down the Nile that the Arabian coast guard had found an Indian sailor 'in a ship, alone and half dead', and brought him to the court of Ptolemy VIII (Euergetes). The sailor then offered to reveal the sea route if he were provided with suitable men and ships to bring him home. This seems far-fetched. If the Ptolemies had wanted information about the monsoon voyage, there was no need for them to wait for an Indian mariner to turn up on their doorstep. They could simply have asked one of the mahouts or Indian merchants and captains in their service, who had been crisscrossing the Arabian Sea for generations. And information about the Scylax voyage could surely have been found in the royal archives. The political conditions of the late second century, not a chance storm, was what encouraged the Ptolemies to use their knowledge of the monsoon system to circumvent Arabian middlemen and attempt a direct voyage, steered by Indian pilots. In Eudoxus, they found a captain willing to helm the risky undertaking.[117]

The crossing, probably from Berenice to Barygaza (Bharuch), went off without a hitch. Eudoxus returned richly laden with spices and gemstones (onyx?). That he felt cheated when he set about off-loading his goods—Ptolemy had a monopoly on imported Indian and Arab wares—recalls the tales of other discoverers; yet this episode serves above all to propel the plot. For it was not Ptolemy but his successor, Cleopatra III, who appointed Eudoxus to lead a second voyage. During his return journey, the northeast monsoon drove him past Cape Guardafui onto the Ethiopian coast. He eventually found his way back to Egypt with the help of native guides.[118]

This part of the narrative contains novelistic features as well. Yet this in no way detracts from Eudoxus' achievement. Support from Indian mariners and the second crossing under his command suggest that he was the first Greek to exploit monsoonal winds to sail directly from the Red Sea to India and back. The wind that bore the ships from the Arabian coast to India was named *hippalus*, probably after the promontory from which it seemed to blow into the sea. The passage to India could now be shortened by three-quarters of a year. Like Eudoxus, a certain Diogenes was blown off-course by the northeast monsoon on his return from India and washed up on the Ethiopian coast. He evidently reached the sources of the Nile, further increasing the credibility of the Eudoxus report.[119]

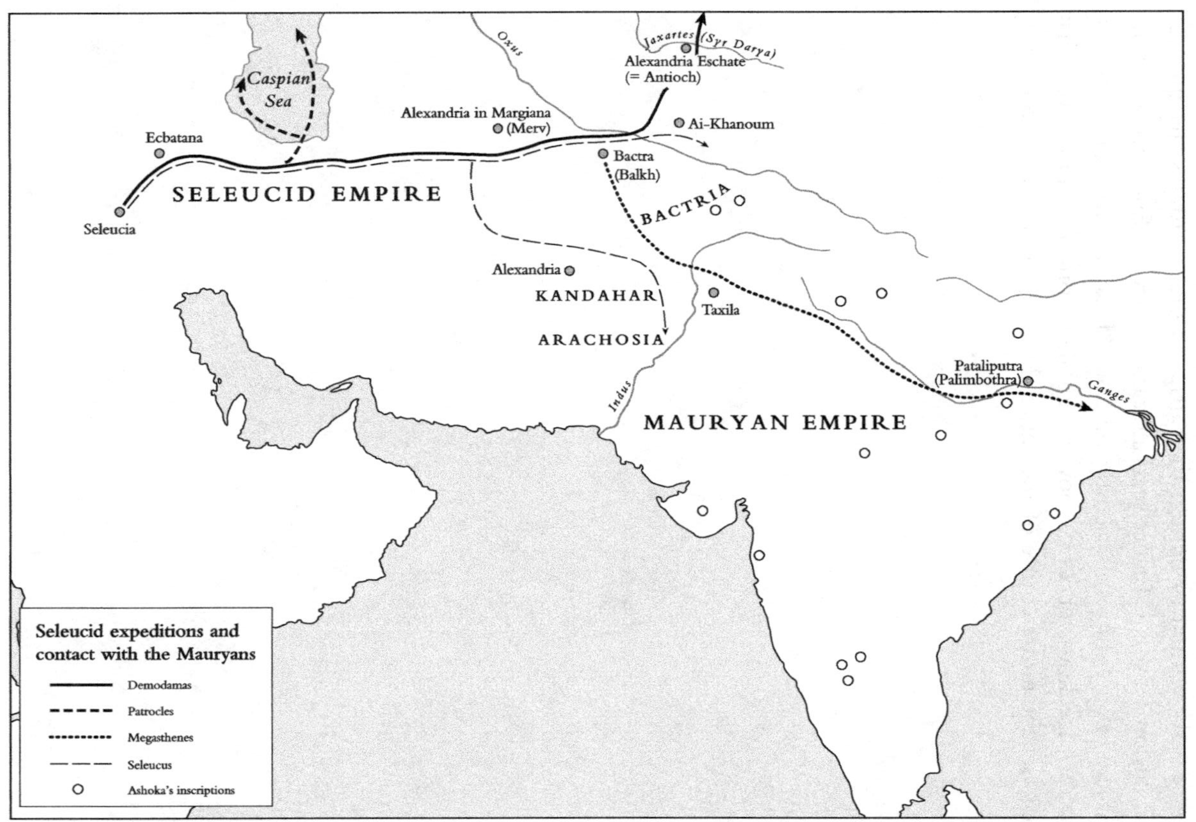

Map 8 Credit: Rudolf Hungreder/Klett-Cotta.

The Ptolemies recognized the advantages of the monsoon system, reorganized the administration of their coastal provinces, and entrusted responsibility for the Erythraean Sea and Indian Ocean to a senior official. They clearly wanted to tighten their grip on the sea routes and increase their customs revenue. Eighty years after the voyages of Eudoxus, one hundred and twenty ships were setting sail from Alexandria to India each year. By that stage, however, a new power had taken control in Egypt, one that would set the future course of ancient exploration in the west: Rome.[120]

6

The Romans Explore the North

WESTWARD HO!

THE ATLANTIC ISLES IN THE SECOND CENTURY BCE

The Fall of Carthage and the Expedition of Polybius

The second part of Eudoxus' story begins when he came back from India. Having washed up on the Ethiopian coast and won over the natives with gifts, the mariner came across the prow of a ship in equine form. It was brought by men from the west who had been shipwrecked offshore, he was told. Upon his return to Alexandria, he showed the galleon figure to shipowners and captains. They thought it came from Gades, some even claiming to know the ship. Apparently, it had sailed along the west African coast to Lixus; nothing more had been heard of it since.[1]

An electrifying report! If the missing sailboat's prow had been found in east Africa, then it must have sailed around the continent. Many dreamed of such a voyage, though few had dared it. The prospect of adding a southwest route to the newly discovered southeast sea road to India must have so enthralled Eudoxus that he did not consider the possibility that Gaditan ships had reached the Ethiopian coast via the Mediterranean and Necho's Canal. Some scholars dismiss the whole story as just another sailor's yarn.[2]

Yet such objections neglect key historical events. After Eudoxus had accomplished his mission at the Ptolemaic court, he needed new goals. The search for a western passage from Spain to India was a logical consequence of his previous voyages and suited the times. Rome had destroyed Carthage fifty years before, putting an end to the city's monopoly on west African sea routes. Roman generals may have gained access to Hanno's report around the same time. Shortly after Carthage's destruction, command of a fleet 'for exploring Africa' was entrusted to Polybius, who was detained in the house of the Scipios as a Greek hostage. It sailed 'along the coast', although it is unclear how far it went.[3] Polybius saw himself as a new Odysseus, knew Eratosthenes and the ocean book of Pytheas, and was said to have written a work entitled 'On the habitability of the equatorial zones'.[4] All this suggests that he followed in the wake of the Carthaginian and Massiliote explorers at least as far as the Draa River, and perhaps all the way to the mouth of the Senegal. Conversely, some scholars doubt that he even ventured beyond the Strait of Gibraltar.[5] This minimalist interpretation is supported by the absence of any other reports about the voyage or follow-up missions. Soon after the end of the Third Punic War, Rome was not prepared to take over Carthage's role, especially as politicians were redirecting their attention to domestic conflicts.

The Voyage of Eudoxus on the West African Coast

With *state* expeditions in the Atlantic drying up, new opportunities for long-distance trade beckoned. Since the fall of Corinth and Carthage and the annexation of Macedonia, Greece, and Asia Minor, enormous sums of money had flowed up the Tiber. Proceeds from raids, pillaging, and the sale of war captives filled the pockets of commanders to a previously unimaginable extent. Much of the bonanza was funnelled into property, while ever more slaves were bought to provide manpower for estates that now shifted to the more profitable production of olive oil and export wine. Cato the Elder recommended investing in long-distance trade and moneylending.

The funds that came pouring into Rome and Italy called for new investment opportunities as the general drive for self-enrichment spread to elite circles, the *nobiles*. That drive was driven partly by ever more extravagant campaign spending, partly by the desire of patricians to model their lifestyle on Hellenistic rulers. They adorned their villas and gardens with expensive paintings and statues, bought opulent silver cutlery and carpets, and enlivened their dishes with exotic spices. Indian pepper could easily be had in Rome, while Greek doctors drawn to the Tiber needed aromatics and spices to concoct their medicines. They advertised the therapeutic benefits of products sourced from the Far East.

The growing demand for luxury goods and specialists, on the one hand, and the unending stream of money and integration of far-flung economic zones through the mass transhipment of slaves, grain, wine, oil, and wares from the Far East, on the other, led to an unprecedented boom in maritime trade and economic production in the Mediterranean, as reflected in the number of wrecks and transport amphorae. Well-off Romans turned to specialized intermediaries to acquire exotic products. Seaborne trade had long since departed from the principle of the one-man enterprise, where a merchant (*emporos*) sailed alone or with a partner from port to port. This form of *cabotage* still existed, but the real money was now made by consortia (*synergoi*) of traders, financiers, and transporters with access to a Mediterranean-wide network of contacts across multiple ports. They could react more quickly to emerging needs, speculate profitably with certain products (grain), and spread the risks among themselves.[6]

The same conditions governed the trade in goods from the eastern Mediterranean (Alexandria) to Italy. Puteoli was the main destination port. There, big money combined with the know-how of the traders, transporters, and bankers who organized trans-Mediterranean trade by arranging, say, for the export of Italian wine to the east in return for pepper or cinnamon: manufacturing the necessary quantities of amphorae, assigning tasks to their contacts or family members in Alexandria, and drawing up contracts with financiers. At times they themselves came aboard: Plautus, the comic dramatist, mentions a *trapezita* (banker) and *naukleros* (captain or shipowner) returning home from India; a loan agreement from the time of Eudoxus refers to a 'spice-producing land', probably Somalia; shareholders in the enterprise included a Massiliote, a Carthaginian, and an Italian.[7]

A man like Eudoxus would have been familiar with such arrangements as he again sniffed out new commercial opportunities from Alexandria. Not by chance, he sailed for Puteoli following his brief return to his homeland. It is obvious what he was looking for: investors and partners for his plan to chart a course around Africa in the hope of importing the Indian and east African luxury products so coveted by the Roman elite, bypassing the costly intermediate trade through Egypt. In return, he offered them the latest in Aegean sailing technology, a square sail supported by a spar from the mast (or sprit) that was one of the most effective rigs in antiquity.[8]

It is unsurprising that his efforts to finance the venture proved unsuccessful. In the ancient world, innovative maritime technologies had to contend with the ballast of tradition. Logical considerations played only a minor role. The foremast had already marked a significant improvement in navigability when it was first introduced in the Mediterranean around 500 BCE; the sprit sail could not quickly supersede it.[9] Finance was also an obstacle: Puteoli's merchants derived most of their profits not from the spice trade but from the trade in grain and slaves. This was conducted via the Aegean (Delos) and Egypt. Their operations in Egypt were managed on the ground by relatives and freedmen. The proposed alternative route around Africa may have been attractive, yet it exclusively targeted goods from India and thus aimed to corner a market that, whatever its future potential, was still negligible for the traders of Puteoli. Under these circumstances, Eudoxus' plan seemed too risky, especially as the commercial networks they had spent so much time and energy cultivating in Egypt would have suffered in the event of its success.

Eudoxus could take solace (and pocket a hefty fee) in being entrusted with a commercial mission to the west.[10] He was bound for Massalia, a city whose maritime traditions raised expectations of a far greater interest in an Atlantic voyage along the African coast. Yet here, too, he met with no success. He was advised to try his luck in Gades, for centuries the starting point for all expeditions into the wide blue yonder. Here he staked everything on a single card. He invested the rest of his fortune in equipping three ships and hiring a crew, additionally recruiting physicians, artists, and musicians. These not would only prove useful on a long voyage (Francis Drake also took along musicians to entertain his crew on his circumnavigation of the globe), but could presumably help win over the natives, too; Greek 'courtesans' were as popular at the Indian royal court as Greek doctors.[11]

Yet all these preparations were again to no avail. Shortly after setting sail from Gades, part of his crew apparently mutinied and forced the leader to land on the west African coast. Undaunted, Eudoxus continued his voyage with a new penteconter until he came across tribespeople who allegedly spoke the same language as the Ethiopians on the east African coast—an assumption rooted in the Homeric idea that there were western and eastern Ethiopians. Like his contemporaries, Eudoxus drastically underestimated the length of the African coastline and had no idea how far south the continent extended.[12]

Eudoxus would have soon recognized that he had barely sailed beyond the Moroccan coast. Told that the Moroccan kingdom of Bocchus (c. 120–80 BCE) was nearby, he turned around and landed in Mauretania, sold his ships, and made his way to the court of Bocchus in Volubilis, hoping to persuade him to finance a new voyage. When this attempt likewise failed—Bocchus may well have feared for his lucrative role as middleman in the maritime trade with India[13]—he probably returned from Roman Numidia to Spain, where he again ordered a penteconter and a freighter to be built. Eudoxus must have realized that a voyage around Africa would take longer than originally anticipated. The transport ship would convey seeds and farming equipment to allow the crew to reap a winter harvest on the coast, just as the Phoenicians had done five hundred years before when they circumnavigated the continent from the east. Eudoxus set out again, yet at this point our source dries up. Perhaps—it concludes by surmising—more could be learned of the explorer's fate in Gades or Spain.[14]

Islands in the Atlantic: From Madeira to the Canaries

Like almost all travellers to Africa, Eudoxus came across a 'well-watered and thickly wooded yet uninhabited island' on his return leg, having been directed there by the Ethiopians of the southern Moroccan coast. A little later, King Bocchus allegedly planned to abandon the pesky Greek on a desert isle.[15] Island adventures were a staple of discovery narratives. Yet in this case, the Mauretanian king's familiarity with the island is great enough for reality to displace fiction. And Eudoxus, too, was sailing in waters that remained well within the bounds of human experience.

Indeed, it is hard to imagine that the Carthaginians and the seafarers from Gades who followed in Hanno's wake did not at some stage sight the archipelagos located just off the west African coast. Some speculate that Hanno himself already sailed past the Canaries.[16] They lie only around sixty miles off the African coast; Fuerteventura can be glimpsed from the mainland. Even if there are no explicit references to a discovery in the third or second century BCE, it was almost impossible for ships sailing along the west African coast to miss it. An expedition mounted a century later by the Nubian king, Juba II, shows that the kings of Mauretania were aware of the archipelago. He had evidently transferred parts of the Carthaginian state library to his palace, including the writings of Eudoxus, and had written a commentary on the Hanno *periplus*. According to Pliny, he visited the Canaries on several occasions and gave them names. The only surviving name is Canaria itself, clearly derived from the indigenous dogs, two of which were brought to the royal court. Juba apparently came across ruined buildings and temples yet found no trace of the natives.[17]

The Carthaginians may have gone farther still. The historian Diodorus (first century BCE) tells of a large island in the Atlantic discovered by the Phoenicians (Carthaginians) several days' sailing from the African coast when one of their ships was blown off course. The island was extremely fertile; it boasted navigable rivers, fresh water sources, and heavily timbered mountains. This island could not have belonged to the Canaries, which lie too close to Africa. It was more likely part of the archipelago described to the Roman rebel Sertorius by Spanish sailors several decades after the Eudoxus expedition. This island lay around 1,800 km from Africa; many later identified it with Madeira.[18]

Destination America?

There is another interpretation, however, which raises one of the thorniest problems in the history of ancient discovery. Some aspects of the description of the island in Diodorus are hard to reconcile with the actual geography of Madeira or the Canaries. Its remarkable fertility, health-giving springs, and carefree, well-fed inhabitants all point to the topos of the Isles of the Blessed, which Greek authors possibly conflated with Carthaginian reports. Yet essential idealizing features are missing, including the islanders' longevity and justice. On the other hand, several striking elements, such as the island's densely wooded ranges and navigable rivers, belong neither to the repertoire of Greek ideal landscapes nor to the real topography of Madeira. The claim that Carthaginians mistook lowland basins flooded with summer rain for rivers is as unconvincing as the argument that ancient forests first fell to the axe in modern times.[19] In fact, Madeira was never covered in dense, biodiverse forests. The idea of a flourishing landscape supporting a variety of flora is a product of modern revegetation schemes. These contradictions are hard to explain. Greek texts offer either internally coherent idylls along the lines of the Isles of the Blessed or (from the fourth century BCE onward) botanically precise descriptions of real landscapes. Neither applies here, whether the island is identified with Madeira or dismissed as fantasy.

One part of the world known to antiquity seems a better fit for the island described by Diodorus: India, with its two mighty rivers, wooded hills, and proverbial fertility. Ctesias mentioned countless therapeutic springs, while the rajas' passion for hunting was well known in the west—all key aspects of Diodorus' description. Yet how did India end up in the Atlantic? The same way as 1,500 years later, before Columbus' voyage of discovery. Given the Earth's spherical shape, Aristotle had already entertained the possibility of a journey west from Spain over the Atlantic to India, and Eratosthenes had confirmed him in this.[20] Distances seemed to be shrinking: the ecumene had expanded with the discovery of the Ganges and Britain, while the Earth's circumference had been reduced to just 180,000 stadia (33,400 km), the estimate given by Posidonius at the end of the second century. A smaller Earth and wider ecumene meant a narrower Atlantic. Posidonius concluded that, 'starting from the west, one might, aided by a continual east wind, reach India in so many thousand stadia' (70,000 = 12,950 km). A century later, Seneca suggested that with a fair wind, the journey could be made in a few days.[21]

Diodorus' island also lay only a few days off the African coast, just as the Carthaginian ship was said to have been propelled by favourable winds. Did the Carthaginians really make it as far as the coast of the American continent (or rather, from the perspective of the ancient sources, a new ecumene in the west), which they, like Columbus after them, described with Indian features because they believed they had reached the subcontinent? In the late Hellenistic period, geographers and philosophers were not the only ones who toyed with this idea and contemplated a trans-Atlantic crossing in both directions. Pliny relates how in the first century BCE, certain Indian merchants 'had been driven by tempests into Germania' while attempting an Atlantic crossing before being brought before the Roman governor of Gaul.[22] This recalls the shipwrecked Indian who was picked up at the entrance to the Red Sea, was escorted to the Ptolemaic court, and initiated Eudoxus' passage to India. While such tales warrant scepticism, what is crucial is that contemporaries saw them as evidence for the navigability of the Ocean between Spain and India; they established a tradition of similar incidents that continued into the modern age. Around the time that the Indians arrived in Germania, Statius Sebosus, a learned friend of the consul Catulus, wrote about India's marvels and collected all the reports he could find on the Blessed Isles in the Ocean. He probably sailed from Gades along the west African coast to the Canaries. Some believe that he, like Eudoxus, subsequently navigated the Indian Ocean.[23]

Whichever way we choose to read them, these accounts make one thing clear: the fear of the Atlantic once caused by Carthage's dominance in the late archaic period had given way to a confidence that no natural or divine impediments stood in the way of an Atlantic voyage to India. The plan for such a voyage lay in the air: the utility of a direct sea route was obvious from the mid-second century BCE, when the Ptolemies redoubled their efforts in this direction. From the perspective of Mediterranean countries, the overland routes may not have been blocked, yet they had become increasingly unsafe following the Parthian conquest of Bactria and the territorial isolation of the Graeco-Indian Empires.

And much as Columbus reckoned with the possibility of an unknown continent between the coast of west Africa and India—a suspicion that firmed into a certainty on his second American voyage—so too intellectual circles in the ancient west were abuzz with speculation that several worlds existed on the same latitude as the known ecumene. Crates of Mallus, head of the library of Pergamum, spent 169–68 BCE in Rome as the envoy of his hometown and may have used the typically long waiting period to introduce interested circles to his terrestrial globe, featuring two Atlantic ecumenes. Cicero reprised this worldview around a century later in his work 'On the state'.

Crates' globe may have been the model for representations of the world on Roman coins from 76 BCE.[24] Contemporaries were likewise aware that the Carthaginians were the earliest candidates for having mounted a trans-Atlantic voyage. In his dialogue 'On the face of the moon', Plutarch narrated how a Carthaginian reported having sailed in a rowboat from the western isles of the Atlantic (one of which was Ogygia) to the great continent around 5,000 stadia away, from which—as he expressly remarked—countless rivers drained into the sea. Was such an Atlantic crossing technically and nautically feasible?

In principle, a journey west from one of the islands off the west African coast required no great feats of seamanship. The shortest crossing between west Africa and the New World, from the Cape Verde islands to Brazil, is only a little longer than the direct sea route from the end of the Red Sea to the west Indian coast, and it could have been made in three to four weeks if travelling at the usual rate of knots maintained by Phoenician-Carthaginian ships. Ancient sailboats were not much slower than modern caravels.[25] Provisioning on longer sea voyages—taking on board edible animals such as turtles, salted fish, fruit, and fermented fish—did not necessarily fall behind the standards of early-modern expeditions; indeed, amphorae seem to have been better suited to storing fresh water than the later wooden kegs. It

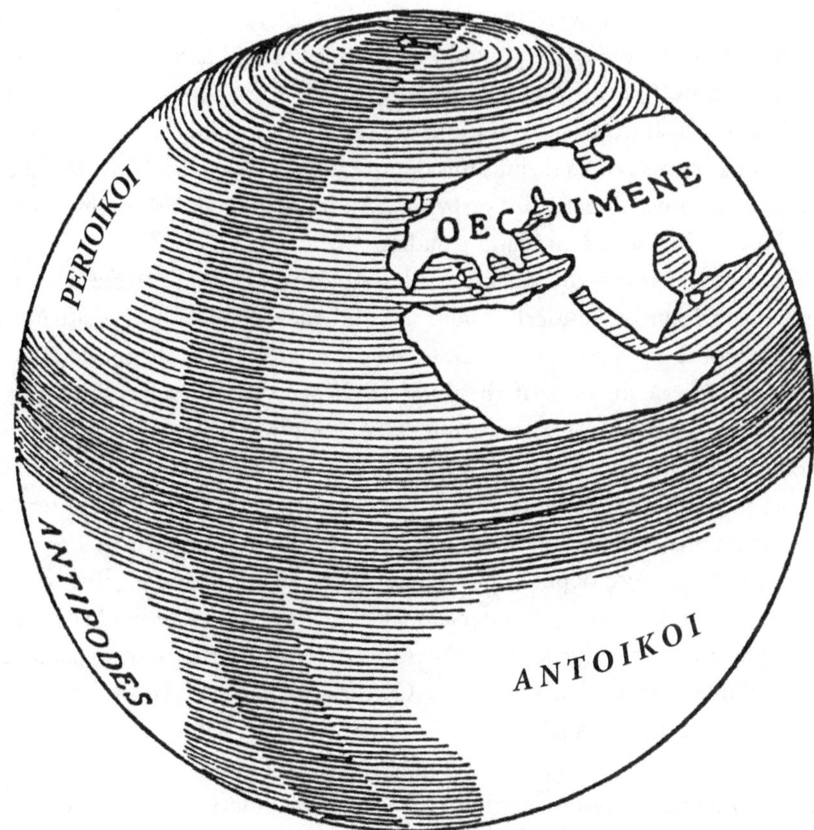

Image 8 Ancient globe. Reconstruction of the globe made by the scholar Crates of Mallus in the mid-second century BCE. In addition to the familiar ecumene in the northeast (in the upper right segment), it features three other 'terrestrial islands': those of the *antoikoi*, the *perioikoi*, and the *antipodes*. The cruciform Ocean flows between them towards the poles and along the equator. One of the most influential ancient models of the world, it was passed down through the Middle Ages to the age of Columbus and hypothetically anticipated the discovery of the two Americas (see p. 373). Credit: Author/Klett-Cotta.

is therefore entirely possible that a ship sailing at the latitude of the Canaries could have been driven to the Brazilian coast by the North Equatorial Current. This is exactly what happened to Pedro Cabral in 1500 CE, when, sailing along the west African coast towards southern Africa, he was blown out into the Atlantic by the northeast trade wind and the North Equatorial Current and became the European discoverer of Brazil. And who knows, perhaps Eudoxus, who steered the same course as Cabral from his starting point in Gades, met with the same fate. If ancient mariners had landed in the Brazilian tropics, they would have encountered natural phenomena that Diodorus/Ephorus deemed characteristic of the mysterious island in the Atlantic: lush tropical vegetation, dense mixed-species forests, navigable rivers. That new arrivals should misidentify the coasts of the New World as islands or peninsulas is hardly surprising: Pedro Cabral also thought at first that he had discovered an island paradise.[26]

All these factors—the matching descriptions of nature, references to trans-Atlantic links, nautical conditions, and the overall political situation in the second and first century BCE—help explain why early-modern explorers were convinced that they were following in the wake of the ancients and were only rediscovering what their predecessors had already known. And yet: unambiguous evidence that ancient mariners made the crossing to the New World has never been found. Ancient coins in America and the Azores, a likely stopover on a return journey, have turned out to be forgeries or were deposited at a much later date.[27] While an absence of archaeological evidence is understandable in the case of individual ships, it weighs more heavily against the recently revived thesis of a planned crossing of Carthaginian fleets. The Carthaginians usually only launched such expeditions, especially those occurring shortly before their city was captured in 146 BCE, when they intended to plant colonies abroad. There is no evidence that they did anything of the sort in America. A push factor of this kind, which was present in the Mediterranean (Phocaeans) and on the west African coast, would also be unique in the context of early-modern Atlantic crossings. Here other motives were in play than the need to save the populace of a Mediterranean metropolis from the depredations of aggressive powers. To be sure, commercial considerations were also involved in the second and first centuries BCE; the goal of reaching India by rounding Africa and crossing the Atlantic also exercised minds in Carthage and Gades. Yet the lack of support that Eudoxus received from state authorities is striking. Controlling the intermediary trade centred on the west African coast and the routes to the tin regions clearly seemed more rewarding than braving an Atlantic passage to the fabled riches of India, especially as such a voyage would have driven ships to the east coast of the subcontinent instead of the west.

When Carthage fell, and with it the sole power that could have undertaken that voyage (possibly excepting Gades), only Rome still had the financial and political clout needed to mount a large-scale expedition. Yet the Republic let the opportunity slip, even though it had taken over the Carthaginian state library in 146 BCE and could have learned about past Atlantic expeditions from the material amassed there. Polybius' voyage in 145 BCE would remain the sole expedition under Roman command for a century, and it barely went beyond Morocco, if it even got that far.[28] After the fall of Carthage, some Greek geographers maintained an interest in commercial voyages in the Atlantic; in his 'Periplus on the outer sea', Xenophon of Lampsacus, probably building on Pytheas, added more detail to the vague picture of the Baltic. But it would be a long time before any attention was paid to these texts in Rome.[29]

ROME'S ADVANCE INTO THE CENTRAL EUROPEAN INTERIOR

CAESAR CONQUERS GAUL AND 'DISCOVERS' THE GERMANIC PEOPLE

Posidonius among the Celts

A band of rough Viking warriors has set up camp on the banks of the Volga. To one side, the Arab scholar Ahmad ibn Fadlan pricks up his ears. At first, he understands nothing, but then he pieces together scraps of conversation and decodes short dialogues, until finally, to everyone's astonishment, he starts speaking in the language of the northerners. The despised foreigner becomes a respected member of the roving community and soon their 'thirteenth warrior'.

Scenes like this one from the eponymous film may well have played out in the 90s of the last century before Christ in the borderlands between Gallia Narbonensis and 'free Gaul' when Posidonius, born in Syrian Apamea, took part in a feast of a Celtic prince. He was not invited to join the band of brothers, however, nor was his aim to conduct trade or recruit mercenaries, as had so often been the case in previous centuries. Posidonius represented a new generation of scholars who used Roman provincial rule in the west to learn more about the land and its people, much as the Persian Empire had once given footloose Greeks the opportunity to gather more detailed information about the east.

The first destination was the Spanish Atlantic coast. Greeks had previously made their way there primarily on account of the tin trade and the inland silver deposits. Now men came with other interests: Asclepiades of Myrlea (Asia Minor), one of the leading rhetoricians and philologists of his day, moved to the Guadalquivir Valley, taught Greek to the natives, and wrote a treatise on the tribes he encountered there. After interviewing Gaditan merchants, Artemidorus of Ephesus drew up a map of the Spanish coast consisting of itineraries.[30]

Posidonius was also drawn to Gades. Efforts to demonstrate causal links between natural and cultural phenomena, underway since the fourth century and intensified by Alexander's campaigns, reached their climax in his writing. As a proponent of Middle Stoicism, he viewed the entire cosmos as a living organism animated by divine reason and a creative, vital force whose laws are valid everywhere. Even the Ocean lives. Its waves continuously lapping the shore resemble respiration, while the seaweed, flotsam, and jetsam it deposits on the beach flush it clean of foreign matter. The idea that everything is linked by vital forces led him to new solutions for old riddles. Scholars had grappled with the phenomenon of tides since the fourth century. Following Plato and Crates, several saw its cause in the interconnection of the four oceanic rivers. Pytheas detected the influence of the moon. His observations were augmented by a certain Seleucus in the Red Sea. Posidonius continued on this path, noting the tidal changes in Gades over a thirty-day period. The tides were strongest at full moon, when sun and moon stood in conjunction or opposition. With the influence of this constellation (the 'sympathy' conjoining heaven and earth), he had found the answer that would prevail until Newton's theory of gravity.[31]

His research findings flowed into his work 'On the Ocean and the surrounding areas'. Here Posidonius, having scrutinized numerous expeditionary reports (including those of Eudoxus and Pytheas), concluded that the entire ecumene was circumnavigable and posited—in line with Platonic tradition—the existence of other continents in the Ocean. The ecumene itself took the form of a slingshot, 'broad in the middle from south to north, but narrowing towards the east and west, although in the east the Indian region is broader'.[32] He estimated the Earth's circumference at 180,000 stadia (around 28,350 km), the length of an Atlantic voyage from Spain to India at only 70,000 stadia (little more than 11,000 km).[33]

Ethnography was integral to his account of the world. Posidonius followed Hellenistic convention in explaining even the most apparently primitive human customs with people's need to adapt to diverse climatic and environmental conditions. This is how Nearchus had described the 'fish-eaters' of the Gedrosian coast and Agatharchides the tribes of Ethiopia. Complex networks were also assumed to regulate the realms of botany and zoology, as when ingenious theories about the mutual influence of solar radiation and moisture were drawn on to explain India's greater fertility relative to Egypt and Ethiopia.[34] The search for causal links had previously been concentrated on the east (India) and south of the ecumene (Meroë, Red Sea coast). The west and north had served merely as complementary counterparts. All this changed with the rise of the Romans, as narrated in Polybius' history. Now an all-powerful western people stepped onto the world stage. The expansion of Roman rule offered the chance to apply anthropological-ethnographic theories to the Celts, generally held to inhabit the northwest of the ecumene as far as the Scythians. Interest in the central European north was further stimulated when the Cimbri invaded Italy towards the end of the second century BCE. They came from the same mysterious world on the Oceanic fringe from which barbarian hordes had periodically emerged to engulf the Mediterranean and threaten its civilization.

Posidonius sought to redefine all these phenomena in the context of a world geography and world history. Like most scholars, he was convinced that formations of human society derived from the interplay of climate, solar radiation, and physical nature as well as from the resulting adaptive capabilities. Unlike his predecessors, however, he assumed fluid transitions and sought out the vital quality that increased from north to south. After studying the Spanish coasts, their inhabitants and botany, he made his way via New Carthage to the battlefield of Aquae Sextiae, where Marius had defeated the Teutons and Ambrones ten years before. In contemporary opinion, these were Celtic tribes (Celto-Scythians). In arguing that the inundation of their homeland by the Ocean had forced their emigration, Posidonius reveals just how closely historical events were intertwined in his thinking with the laws governing the natural world.[35]

After this, Posidonius travelled—perhaps with support from a host—from Massalia to the land of the Celts. Even if he did not get very far, he still came away with a knowledge of the land and its people that was practically unequalled for his time. He summarized what he found out about the Celts in an excursus to his universal history. In his work on banquets, Athenaeus (second–third centuries CE) cites a fragment that has lastingly shaped our image of the Celts:

> The Celts serve their food with an underlay of hay and on wooden tables raised a little from the ground. Their food consists of a little bread and a great deal of meat boiled or roasted on charcoal or on spits. They are clean eaters, but with a lion's appetite. They select whole joints in both hands and gnaw bits off, or if a bit is hard to tear away, they slice along it with a dirk which lies to hand with its sheath in its own box. Those who live by rivers or by the inner or outer sea also eat fish, baked with salt, vinegar and cumin; the last they also sprinkle into their drinks.
>
> They don't use olive oil because of its scarcity, and they find its taste unpleasant because they are unused to it. In larger dinner parties, they sit in a ring with the mightiest in the middle, like a chorus leader, distinguished from the rest in his coolness in war, or in family or wealth. The host sits next to him, and the rest in order of honour of rank on either side. Their shield-bearers stand behind, and the men-at-arms share in the feast, sitting opposite in a ring like their masters.
>
> The servants carry the drink round in vessels like carafes, either of pottery or silver, and the platters on which they serve the food are of similar ware, but some also of bronze, others baskets of wood or wicker. The drink among the rich is wine transported from Italy or the Massiliote region. It is drunk undiluted, but sometimes with a little water added. Among the poorer classes a beer is made from wheat with honey added, and the majority drink it neat. It is called 'corma'. They sip from the same vessel a little at a time, but they do that rather often.[36]

These lines, too, stand in a long tradition of descriptions of northerners that veer between idealization and vilification yet also process real experiences. The time of the great Celtic invasions of the third century BCE was over. The description of the Celtic banquet is therefore free of 'barbarisms' and seeks to appreciate the foreign society as an (exotic) aristocratic culture. In doing so, it combines motifs from Homeric epic (such as the animalistic tearing of the meat) with authentic information about the significance of the seating arrangement and retinue, silverware, and wine as well as the Celts' trading relations (to Massalia and Italy/Etruria). What results is a vivid image of the banquet as a practice by which the Celtic elite maintained their status. Other passages describe their clothing and outward appearance, weaponry, and social structure.[37]

He goes on to generalize about these people from individual statements, drawing links between their climate, environment, and way of life.

According to the classical theory of climate, the reduced amount of sunshine in the north prevented moisture in the human body from evaporating. This explains why northerners had such large, 'bloated' bodies, pale skin, lank, reddish-blond hair, blue eyes, deep voices, and copious blood. This abundance of blood made them braver in battle but more susceptible to heat. The Celts charged at their enemies without forethought or understanding; they were impetuous, impulsive, and unrestrained—all qualities that, under the heading of *thymos* (passion), Aristotle had already ascribed the people of the north. They drank unmixed wine so immoderately that they became drunk to the point of delirium; they committed homosexual acts in full public view.[38]

These characteristics could change, however, if they broke free of the adaptive pressures of their climate and approached the Mediterranean lands and their civilization. Then they set aside their uncouth ways and developed a willingness to exercise their intellect, represented by bards, soothsayers, philosophers, and druids.[39] The immortality and transmigration of the soul taught by the druids allowed the Celts to go into battle undaunted and unprotected by armour ('naked')—a claim that preserves real knowledge of the ritual nakedness of elite Celtic warriors. Yet their disregard for death drove them to acts of wanton cruelty: the 'most savage' people of the north practised cannibalism, cut off the heads of their fallen enemies, and 'slaughtered' their captives 'like sacrificial animals'. When exchanging gifts at banquets, some chieftains even allowed their throats to be slit in a form of ritual suicide.[40]

Roman Interest in the World

Such reports satisfied Roman readers' appetite for sensationalism. The Republic's elite was familiar with the ethnographic-climatological models of Hellenistic origin. Their underlying idea that even the most uncivilized barbarians could be transformed would later become a cornerstone of Roman imperial ideology under Augustus. Yet all this lay ahead. At the time of Posidonius, Roman politicians and generals, guided by pragmatic considerations, drew only selectively on the ethnographic systems to describe nearby lands. In this they were following the example of Polybius, who had abandoned his earlier interest in charting the world's outer limits in favour of a practically oriented geography of familiar countries. The tradition that built on Posidonius thus frequently referred to the role of the druids, the Celtic system of allegiances, as well as the modalities by which elites secured their position and kept in touch with their retainers. This information gave governors or commanders insight into the military, political, and social structure of their potential adversaries. They were also interested because the Romans always sought to uphold their rule on the periphery through contact with indigenous elites.

A second focus was the precious metals produced by the nature (*physis*) of the land, which the Celts extracted from rivers—supposedly without effort—and worked into jewellery or offerings for their gods. 'There was gold all over Celtica', Posidonius asserted.[41] 'It was their lakes in particular which preserved the inviolability of their treasure, for they sank great masses of gold and silver in them'. He was also aware that the Romans were keen to get their hands on this prize. After establishing the province of Gallia Narbonensis, 'they sold off the lakes on the state's behalf, and many buyers found millstones of hammered silver in them'.[42] Everyone knew the story of the trove of Tolosa in the land of the Tectosages (northeast of the Pyrenees), which had once been seized by the proconsul and had then mysteriously disappeared. Traders told of the gold jewellery that adorned Gallic clothing and confirmed Posidonius' report that the lavish gold offerings made to Celtic sanctuaries and temple precincts were left untouched. Perhaps the sources' pronounced interest in the druids has to do with the fact that they tended these groves and sanctuaries.

Caesar on the Spanish Atlantic Coast

News of a second Dorado—alongside the Iberian one—in the land of the Celts piqued the interest of Rome's aristocratic elite. Many welcomed a lucrative military campaign to recoup their exorbitant spending on political campaigning and replenish their depleted coffers. Among them was a young man called Gaius Julius Caesar from a venerable yet impoverished family (*gens Julia*). In 69 BCE he was sent to Gades as quaestor of the province Hispania Ulterior to organize the manning of the provincial war fleet. He may have taken the opportunity to consult the writings of Posidonius. Following his return from Spain, Caesar climbed the next rung on the career ladder, albeit at enormous cost. As aedile, he indebted himself to the tune of 25 million denarii. Only a posting to the provinces could save him from ruin, yet his creditors demanded security. At this critical juncture one of the richest men of the time sprang to his aid: Marcus Licinius Crassus.

His father had been proconsul in Hispania Ulterior in the 90s and had bequeathed his son Spanish silver mines. But Crassus wanted more. One of his relatives had set out from Spain in search of the legendary Tin Islands, thought to lie opposite the Spanish Atlantic coast. In Rome, not much more was known about 'Britannia', as the mysterious island had come to be called by Caesar's day, than early-modern Europe knew about Mexico or Peru before the conquests of Cortés and Pizarro.

Previous attempts at prying the secret of the route from the Gaditans had been unsuccessful; now Crassus offered the young Caesar a loan of 830 talents (around five million denarii) to help him find the tin-mining areas. In 61 BCE, when Caesar was named proconsul for Spain following his praetorship, preparations began in earnest. Supreme command of the expeditionary fleet was entrusted to the young Decimus Junius Brutus, whose grandfather boasted of having subjugated Spain all the way to the Ocean. In summer the ships set out along the Atlantic coast, with Caesar following on land much like Alexander in the Gedrosian Desert. Those fleeing to offshore islands were taken captive. The ships then sailed on to Brigantium near modern-day La Coruña. There Caesar must have realized that the Tin Islands lay farther afield than he had thought. Still, northwest Galicia contained enough tin, gold, and silver deposits to compensate the cash-strapped commander and finance the next stage of his career.[43]

The Advance into 'Free Gaul'

Two years after his return, Caesar was named consul with the support of Crassus and Pompey. In the absence of any serious external threats to the Republic, the new consul sought a suitable stage to increase his fame and forge an imposing military machine. Yet the dream of the Tin Islands never faded. The People's Assembly and an intimidated Senate assigned him the proconsulship of Illyricum as well as Gallia Cisalpina and Gallia Narbonensis. From Illyricum, a foray into gold-rich Thracia beckoned, yet Caesar chose Gaul instead—probably because, while equally rich in treasure, it would let him revive his plan for an Atlantic expedition and combine it with territorial expansion.

Although the sources do not indicate whether Caesar pursued this grand strategy from the outset, it accords with both the striking sequence of his military activities since his praetorship and the political circumstances of the time. Rome had defeated all its Mediterranean neighbours, assimilated them as provinces, or turned them into client states. Nonetheless, the Roman ethos continued to demand victories on the battlefield, at least from ambitious patricians. These would now have to be won on the periphery and spread over the entire ecumene. In its own way, Roman expansion thus caught up with the global thinking of Hellenistic-era Greek geographers. Against this background, it was only a matter of time before Roman generals started modelling themselves on a figure who stood like none other for conquests extending to the farthest limits of the world. Men like Lucullus and Pompey, who led their troops east as far as Armenia and nearly reached the Caspian Sea over the Caucasus, saw themselves marching in the footsteps of Alexander, given the epithet 'the Great' in this very period. Two years before Caesar's Gallic campaign, Pompey had commissioned a statue of himself with a globe in one hand on the Campus Martius and claimed to have extended the boundaries of the Empire 'to the ends of the earth'.[44] Yet there were gaps on the balance sheet of Roman success: the northwest and the Atlantic, which Alexander had envisaged but not attained. Caesar had indicated the scale of his ambition in Gades by comparing himself to Alexander and sailing for Brigantium. The Gallic campaign was a logical continuation of his quest for the Ocean.

Yet troops first had to be brought into the country. The writings of Posidonius contained information on the Celts' fighting style and the role of the druids. Insights into the current political and geographical conditions were provided by former governors, Celtic envoys such as Diviciacus (resident in Rome in 61 BCE), and merchants who had advanced up the Rhône to Lake Geneva and up the Saône to Burgundy, selling as many as 100,000 hectolitres of Italian wine each year in exchange for slaves, metals, and pelts. They all depicted a fragmented world of rival tribes led by noble families engaged in a fierce struggle for supremacy. Lacking the power to launch an attack on the provinces, they relied instead on the goodwill of Roman commanders.[45]

This constellation provided a pretext for intervening: when the tribe of Helvetians, harried by the Sequani and their Suebian mercenaries, asked for permission to move through the Roman province to their new settlement near Tolosa (Toulouse), Caesar refused. The Helvetians then turned against the Aedui, allies of Rome. In response to their pleas for help, Caesar crossed the border to the Celtic lands in 58 BCE. The Helvetians were not only a suitable adversary—Caesar defeated them in a single campaigning season—but also famous for their treasure. Five years later, when Caesar returned from conquering almost all of Gaul, the price of gold in Italy had sunk by a quarter.[46]

The Expedition to Britannia

Caesar again crossed the provincial boundary in early 57. His new enemy was far from unknown: the Suebians had served the Celts years earlier as mercenaries, and their leader Ariovistus had subsequently built up such an imposing power base in Gaul that the Senate bestowed on him the honorary title of *rex* and included him in its list of allies.[47] For Caesar, the Suebian king was an upstart whose unwillingness to take orders from Rome made him an obvious target. Ariovistus, too, was defeated with lightning speed. The ensuing war would assume dimensions that far exceeded the political and material confines of Rome's early years, leading to one of the most momentous shifts in the geographical and ethnographic horizon of all antiquity.

Having notched up further successes against the Belgians and their neighbours, Caesar turned west to Aquitania to confront the tribes of the Atlantic coast. In summer he ordered his legate, Publius Licinius Crassus, whose family had an interest in the tin trade, to subdue the northwestern coast-dwellers. All areas of operation lay along the tin route to Britain; some contained rich tin, copper, and silver deposits. Crassus wintered on the lower Loire near the ancient maritime trade centre of Corbilo/Korbilon, whose inhabitants Scipio had already interrogated about the route to Britain in 150–51 BCE.[48] In early 56, Caesar had warships built on the Loire and ordered more Ligurian units to march past Gades to the Breton coast. There his lieutenant Decimus Brutus defeated the fleet of the Veneti, who 'excel the rest in the theory and practice of navigation' and 'hold as tributaries almost all those who are accustomed to traffic in that sea'. The Veneti evidently had a stranglehold on maritime trade with Britain. Subjecting them was a necessary step on the path to the Tin Islands, not least because Caesar could then commandeer their ships, purpose-built to withstand the rolling Atlantic tides.[49]

Caesar later offered military justification for his invasion of Britain: he wanted to deprive his Gallic enemies of the help regularly sent them from across the Channel. This was an exaggeration but not entirely untrue. From the mid-fifth century BCE, Celtic tribes had settled alongside the established island-dwellers, a particularly intensive exchange arising between the Belgians and coastal communities. To that extent, it could easily be argued that Gaul could only be pacified if southern Britain, at least, was brought under the yoke of Rome.[50]

Yet again, however, material and mercantile hopes were bound up with military considerations. Following his successes against the Suebians and Belgians, Caesar had released Roman merchants from the steep customs duties exacted by local princes at border crossings and fords.[51] Now, delegations of traders from Gallia Narbonensis made their way to Caesar's headquarters, hoping to break the monopoly on trade with the British Isles enjoyed by Gallic merchants and chieftains; besides tin, pelts and slaves were the most lucrative products. The aristocratic officer corps were impressed by rumours of silver, gold, and precious pearls, even though these resources did not occur naturally in Britain. Clearly, legends of Atlantic wonderlands had become mixed up with tales of Gallic treasure, perhaps augmented by reports of the gold and silver coined minted by Celtic tribal leaders north of the Thames. Where gold coins were in circulation, gold deposits could not be far off.[52]

Caesar thus took with him the expectations of a money-hungry generation of traders and aristocrats, the former providing the ships, the latter the military muscle. Gallic merchants were not prepared to share their information, and an initial reconnaissance mission to the Kentish coast failed to identify clear landing points. Caesar nonetheless assembled a fleet of around eighty ships in the autumn of 55 BCE, probably in Portus Itius (Boulogne-sur-Mer or Wissant). The fleet set sail at midnight and ploughed the dark waves of the Channel to arrive at the coast near Dover; yet the Celts made a landing impossible. Caesar then sailed northeast along the coast until he found an opening. With great difficulty, and flanked by a protective cordon, he succeeded in establishing a bridgehead.[53]

The Atlantic unleashed its full fury overnight. Eighteen horse transports were lost in a storm, while spring tides—unknown to Posidonius—flooded the warships. Almost the entire fleet was destroyed. The Celts renewed their attacks the next day. The whole invasion threatened to end in catastrophe, and it was probably only due to the sangfroid of the general and his officers that their enemies could be held in check and the damaged ships repaired or replaced. Now the victory over the Veneti paid off: Caesar could procure supplies from the continent without interference. Had the Gauls ruled the waves, the Romans would have been cut off from help. In the end, he made peace with the Celts on terms recognizing Rome's supremacy. Instead of gold and silver, he made off with twice the number of hostages.[54]

The first invasion of Britain gave Caesar the information about landing places and enemy tactics he needed to dare a second expedition on a far larger scale. For the winter, he ordered a massive fleet better suited to Atlantic conditions. 'He ordered those things which are necessary for equipping ships to be brought over from Spain',[55] again showing how closely his governorships in Spain and Gaul were connected and how much forward planning went into the invasion. In the summer of 54 he crossed the Channel with an armada of 800 units, five legions, and 2,000 cavalry. It was the first large-scale amphibious expedition in northern waters.

This time the coastal tribes put up no resistance. His troops could land unchallenged southeast of Kent. Then Caesar probably marched from the Stour River (near Canterbury) to the Thames. Here he conquered the residence of Cassivellaunus, the influential leader of the Trinovantes. After further successes against neighbouring tribes, Cassivellaunus surrendered and sued for peace. In return, he was given privileged access to Roman trade goods (especially wine), much to the satisfaction of the merchants in Caesar's camp. The treaty brought Rome annual tribute, hostages, and recognition of Roman hegemony, but—as Caesar acknowledged to Cicero—only modest booty.[56]

Still, the commander could shed further light on an island that had been shrouded in mystery since the days of Pytheas. An excursus in Caesar's *commentarii*, probably integrated later, reports on the ethnography of the Britons.[57] Especially impressive were the chieftains' chariots, an archaic combat device that had long been abandoned in Gaul and reminded some Romans of the heroes of the Homeric age. 'I see now', Cicero wrote to his brother serving as an officer in Britain, 'what splendid material you have to write about! How interesting are the regions, the character of events and places, the mores and customs, the tribes'.[58] Caesar himself asserted that, like a second Odysseus, he had seen 'into the character of the people, and got knowledge of their localities, harbours, and landing-places'.[59] Carrying on the tradition of Pytheas, he had also measured the daylight hours, finding that the nights were shorter than on the continent, and investigated the time of the winter solstice. And he named two islands off the west coast: Hibernia (Ireland) and Mona (Isle of Man).[60]

In short, Caesar saw his invasion of Britain as equally a voyage of discovery, or at least he wanted it to be seen in that way. Disregarding his technical and military achievement in ferrying a whole army across the Channel and forcing a well-armed enemy to acknowledge Roman supremacy, he could thereby divert attention from disappointed hopes of booty. And once again, competitive rivalry played an important role as an impetus for long-distance exploration. In his own words, Pompey had pushed the Empire's borders 'to the ends of the earth'.[61] Caesar extended 'Roman rule *beyond* the borders of the known world'; by invading Britain he had—according to a historian of the next generation—brought an 'other world' (*alter orbis*) into contact with the familiar one.[62] Reports trickled into Rome of the enormous rocky barriers blocking passage into this 'other world', an image that accorded well with the idea of the indomitable Ocean. Yet Caesar, like Alexander in the east, had imposed his will on nature. He proudly had a statue of the chained Ocean borne through Rome on his triumph and dedicated a shield decorated with British pearls to Venus Genetrix (as sea goddess), thereby trumping Pompey, who had paraded a pearl-bestrewn likeness of himself.[63]

All this shows the extent to which political rivalry at home and feats of arms abroad had expanded the Republic's perspective beyond the borders of the world. It was no coincidence that the Ocean figured so prominently in Roman literary discourse in the first century BCE: according to Sallust, Sertorius intended to retire to the far edges of the Ocean; Cicero claimed that in merging his troops with those of Sertorius, Mithridates aimed to connect his kingdom of Pontus on the southern coast of the Black Sea with the Ocean. Following Pompey's war against piracy, Roman sea power had spread over the entire Mediterranean. If Caesar's 'subjugation' of the Ocean in the west (emulating Alexander's in the east) was now celebrated as a deed of unsurpassed glory that paralleled Rome's dominion over the ecumene, then this apparently logical continuation of the quest for maritime expansion could be understood as an imperial counterpart to the research on the western Ocean undertaken by Posidonius. Caesar's expedition against the Britons—in the words of Plutarch[64]—'was celebrated for its daring. For he was the first to launch a fleet upon the western Ocean and to sail through the Atlantic sea carrying an army to wage war against an island of incredible magnitude'.[65]

Yet his exploits were not yet at an end. In the same year, he crossed the Rhine and entered territory no Roman conqueror had set foot on before. Now he could claim to have twice victoriously surpassed the borders of the known world, at sea and on land. With that, he had definitively relegated Pompey to second place. 'He had advanced far enough to serve both honour and interest', Caesar noted when he returned to Gaul that summer.[66]

Caesar as Ethnographer—The Invention of the Germans

'Over regions and nations which no book, no traveller, no report had made known to us, our general, our soldiers, and the arms of the Roman People have found a way', Cicero exulted in Rome.[67] The multitude of *new* tribes and landscapes was what counted in the last century of a Republic whose generals had reached the limits of the familiar. Some had illustrated itineraries made to allow the domestic public to share in their successes. Pompey had presented pirates and princes in local costume in his triumph, including female captives paraded as Scythian rulers (Amazons). Caesar drew on the crossing of the Danube and Darius' Scythian campaign, as described by Herodotus, when staging his advance beyond the Rhine.[68]

After five years of warfare, Caesar knew more about the land of the Celts and the territories on the right bank of the Rhine than any general before him. Yet instead of unfurling this knowledge against the background of Hellenistic erudition, the geographical and topographical information provided in his *commentarii* maintained a narrow military and strategic focus. They were intended to suggest to readers that the commander had registered, surveyed, and mentally mastered the geography of Gaul and its periphery (Britain, Germania) with a view to his military and political tasks. The lengthy description of the Hercynian Forest and its fauna is probably a later interpolation.[69] Besides the excurses on Gauls, Britons, and Suebians (whose authorship is likewise disputed), there are only a few Celtic concepts and barely any ethnographic details about eating customs, clothing, marriage rituals, and the like.[70] Caesar was a military man, not a scholar. Unlike Posidonius, he had no interest in compiling a comprehensive report on an *ethnos*; he wanted instead to demonstrate that he knew his enemy inside out and was therefore well positioned to optimize his chances of success on the battlefield.

He thus focuses exclusively on military affairs, social order, and the power hierarchy in the Gallic tribes: their factional groups and system of retainers, the influential druids, and the princes (*principes*) who deployed their private armies of debtors and clients in a ruthless struggle for power. This reduction of ethnography to the military and political domain had its counterpart in the literary genre of *commentarii* and is Caesar's own invention. It allowed him to dispense with the baggage of Hellenistic scholarship in surveying this *terra nova*.

Previously, Greek scholars had divided the northern parts of the ecumene into two large ethnic groups: the Scythians in the northeast and the Celts in the northwest. Where the two groups converged, they spoke of Celto-Scythians. Consequently, the Teutons advancing into the Alpine region and northern Italy were seen as Celts, the Cimbri as Celto-Scythians. In the period that followed, mercenaries and robber bands repeatedly descended on the land of the Celts from beyond the Rhine to profit from the ongoing feuds of local warlords. The Suebians under Ariovistus were the most successful. When Caesar recognized during his final round of negotiations that the Suebian king spoke Celtic as a foreign language, he drew the obvious conclusion that the Suebians were a non-Celtic people. Caesar called them Germans, a concept that Posidonius had probably applied to an east Celtic tribe and which the Romans transferred in the 60s from a group living in northern Gaul to Ariovistus' confederation. Once Caesar had defeated them and crossed the Rhine, he referred to everyone living on the right side of the Rhine as *Germani*. With that, he had introduced a broad new ethnic category in the north and given the entire space from the mouth of the Rhône to the Atlantic and Rhineland an independent historical-political profile that it had not previously had. The term *Germania* was probably intended as a counterpart to *Gallia*. The Germans were now domiciled between the Celts in the northwest and the Britons and Scythians in the northeast. They were cut off from the Celts by the Rhine; in turning this natural landmark into a boundary between distinct ethnicities, Caesar thus became the inventor of the Rhine border as a cultural construct.

There is speculation to this day about what lay behind this move: hardly ambition on Caesar's part to inscribe his name in the annals of ethnography; more likely the attempt to impose order on the vast heartlands of central Europe and legitimate his campaign. Caesar feared that the Suebians could field an army of up to 100,000 warriors based on their agricultural and military constitution, which alternated each year between farming and warfare. Private property was unknown to them, and permanent settlement was forbidden. They therefore lived freely but relied on pillage and conquest.[71] This made them the most dangerous enemy Caesar had ever encountered. And what was true of the Suebians, Caesar suggested, applied to all Germans. 'Their whole life is occupied in hunting and in pursuing the arts of war; from childhood they devote themselves to fatigue and hardships'. They glorified chastity because it increased their strength and hardened their muscles. To keep them primed for war, their princes assigned them land for a year at a time and then forced them to move on.[72] Idealized stereotypes of the peoples of the north, living modestly and in harmony with nature, combined here with sociological observation into the image of an unusually belligerent ethnic group that could threaten even Rome. That is why, for Caesar, the Cimbri and Teutons are also Germans, and he reminds his readers that the Romans had once trembled at the approach of these people.[73]

But if all Germans were so bellicose, and hence far more dangerous than the Celts, then Caesar deserved the highest praise for vanquishing them on their home turf.[74] To be sure, his campaigns had only been brief. Perhaps he wished to make clear that there was no point waging war against them again. For how could a people who, unlike the Gauls, wandered incessantly in a trackless wilderness, without fixed settlements and beyond the pale of civilization, be permanently integrated under Roman rule? The fact they had neither gold nor silver may have confirmed the futility of further campaigning. The territories that Rome now controlled left of the Rhine had to be protected. While this did not rule out future expansion, Caesar's political heir Augustus would come to appreciate the difficulty in defining the objective of such a mission.

Familiar ethnographic ideas lay behind this political-military message. Posidonius took the Celts living farthest from the Mediterranean to be the most ungovernably savage and cruel, putting this down to their adaptation to the northern climate. Caesar emphasized their distance from Roman civilization (in the form of the province) and its goods but reversed the normative perspective by ascribing the old category of justice—alongside superiority in armed combat—to the peoples of the northern periphery.[75] This gave him an additional self-justifying argument to explain developments in the field: the Gauls had once surpassed the Germans in military prowess but had forfeited their advantage as they opened their doors to merchants and dissipated their energies on feasting and infighting. Their nobles had become unjust, squabbling for material gains and making decisions without heed to the people's welfare. By contrast, their simplicity, lack of avarice, 'moral rectitude', and *iustitia* had allowed the more remote Germans to preserve and increase their *virtus*.[76]

The reference to the detrimental impact of provinces, merchants, and their wares on the 'good' qualities of the northern peoples recalls the dire picture that Caesar's contemporaries Sallust and Cicero were painting of the *nobiles*' moral decadence. Caesar shifts the perspective by expanding the negative impact of Roman civilization to the barbarians living beyond the provincial borders. At the same time, he assures his readers that Roman military power has not (yet) succumbed to the deleterious influence of their own civilization. Victory against the Cimbri and Teutons had already confirmed Posidonius in the belief that Mediterranean-Roman civic culture, for all its weaknesses, would prevail over Nordic military valour, not least because the Romans—like the Greeks before them—enjoyed an optimal, temperate climate at the centre of the habitable Earth that granted them both physical and intellectual vigour.[77] With his success over Ariovistus, Caesar proved that even the *virtus* of the Germans was no match for the *ratio* of the Roman general.

TO THE ELBE AND THE BALTIC

Ruler and Conqueror of the World: The New Order of Augustus

Caesar's decision not to press ahead with an invasion of the territories on the right bank of the Rhine also owed something to the situation in Gaul. In 53–52 BCE the Arverni chieftain Vercingetorix led a coalition of tribes in revolt against Roman rule. The brutal war that ensued concentrated on the enemy's supply lines and fortifications, culminating after numerous setbacks in the siege of Alesia. At the climax of hostilities, legionaries spent four days holding their position in a dual front made up of defenders and a relief army. The Romans emerged victorious despite suffering horrendous casualties. Vercingetorix capitulated. A million of his compatriots were said to have perished in the war, a million more sent off in chains.

Caesar could not rest on his laurels for long. Once again, the remorseless machinery of late Republican political rivalry cranked into gear; having once driven the dynamic of imperial expansion, it now turned inward. With his victories in Gaul, Caesar had done serious damage to Pompey's reputation as the greatest military commander of his age. For a time, the love match between Pompey and Caesar's daughter Julia staved off conflict. But when the third member of the triumvirate, Crassus, fell against the Parthians in 53 after Julia's death the previous year, the two great conquerors were no longer bound by personal ties. Caesar's enemies sensed an opportunity. Caesar had treated the *nobliles* with such open disdain during his consulship, and had built up such a formidable military power base in Gaul, that his removal from power now seemed necessary. Besides, Caesar was laying claim to a status that far exceeded the legitimate bounds of aristocratic striving for honour and influence (*dignitas*). Only another consulship could have sheltered him from a flood of prosecutions. But when the Senate insisted that he would have to stand for office as a private man in Rome, he saw this as more than just a political ploy. From his perspective, his compeers were denying him the honours he so richly deserved. He chose war. His opponents had since given Pompey supreme command over troops in Italy and the provinces.

Caesar prevailed in a power struggle lasting two years, yet he could not find a way to maintain his one-man rule indefinitely and reconcile it with the *nobiles*' claim to equality. His assassination on the Ides of March in 44 BCE was followed by more than a decade of bloody civil war, occasionally interrupted by peaceful interludes. Grand foreign campaigns in the style of Pompey and Caesar were off the table; Mark Antony, residing in Alexandria with Cleopatra, came closest when he launched the Parthian War. The military decision would fall in the Mediterranean heartlands. In 31 BCE Octavian defeated Antony at Actium. For the first time in antiquity, one man could unite the entire Mediterranean under his rule.

His first task was to consolidate the power he had usurped on the battlefield and win over the surviving aristocrats, without whose help the Empire could not be governed. In 27 BCE he was applauded for relinquishing his extraordinary powers and formally restoring the Republic. In return, he received the title *Augustus* (majestic, venerable), multiple honours, as well as official powers that gave him uncontested control of the state, governance of all unpacified provinces, and supreme command over the entire army. Augustus claimed that his rule rested on legal powers oriented on

Republican traditions. Everyone knew that it was the sum of individual powers combined in his person that was unprecedented and secured him unassailable power. Augustus bragged that he towered above his contemporaries in influence and prestige. Where leading senators in the Republic had once been called *principes*, now Octavian became the sole *princeps*. No one else could lay claim to this title.

Prestige derived primarily from military valour (*virtus*). When Augustus claimed to surpass all Romans in *virtus* and *dignitas*, the Senate and people of Rome expected him to demonstrate his pre-eminence by conquering new lands. Augustus was determined to fulfil what Jupiter had prophesied the Romans (in Virgil's *Aeneid*). 'To the Roman race I set limits neither in space nor time: / Unending sway have I bestowed on them'. Augustus had—according to the title of the report of his deeds—subjected 'the whole wide earth to the rule of the Roman people'. Poets dreamed of triumphs over India and China.[78]

Indeed, Augustus was ideally placed to organize a new kind of expansionism. Through the integration of provincial auxiliary troops, the (professional) army had become a pliant instrument of the imperial will, ready to march wherever it was ordered. The centralization of military high command afforded an opportunity to pursue a coherent military policy that no longer depended on chance or internecine power struggles but instead reflected long-term planning. The most advanced logistics in antiquity drew on the entire Mediterranean basin as a single distribution and transportation network, making it possible to launch far-flung operations guided by comprehensive strategic objectives. And now a concerted effort got underway to collect and evaluate geographical expertise, ethnographies, and itineraries.[79] The advantageous geostrategic situation, a pacified interior, centralized command of the most formidable army of the era, an unbroken legacy of imperial achievement—all these factors combined allowed antiquity to experience another enormous growth spurt and broaden its geographical horizon to dimensions that would not be regained until the early-modern period.

Old Enemies, New Goals

Just two years after the Principate was founded in 27 BCE, an army under Aelius Gallus set out on the incense trade route to southern Arabia. In 20 BCE the advance of six legions under Tiberius sufficed to install a

Rome-friendly king in Armenia and push back Parthian influence in the land. The Parthians agreed to return the lost standards of Crassus. Without having to fight a single battle, Augustus thus avenged the disgrace of Carrhae and stabilized Rome's foreign policy situation for decades to come. Gaius Caesar, Augustus' grandson and adoptive son from the marriage between his daughter Julia and his lieutenant Agrippa, led another expeditionary army to Mesopotamia and the Gulf of Aqaba. Yet Arabia proved an unsuitable base for provincial rule. Marching the army farther east would have removed it from the emperor's control and overextended the Empire's forces.

Augustus instead devoted his energies to a target already envisaged by Caesar: the northern European interior. Governors of the provinces in Gaul were constantly fending off German incursions. In 16 BCE the legate Lollius suffered heavy losses against the Sugambri and lost his eagles. Augustus could not accept such defeats if he wanted to live up to Caesar's legacy and the reputation of a world ruler.

Caesar had already tried to bring the nearby Alpine passes under his control. With the provincialization of all Gaul, the Alpine region had become even more important as a transit and communications space. Traders and merchants knew the pass routes, and no Roman had forgotten that Hannibal had invaded northern Italy via the Alps. Nonetheless, the conquest of Alpine territories that got underway in 25 BCE was an explorative achievement. The generals penetrated regions no Roman army had set foot on before. Over a series of campaigns, the Alpine Valleys between Lake Como and Lake Garda were subdued. Then Drusus, Augustus' son-in-law, marched from *Gallia Comata* into the Alps while his second son-in-law Tiberius led an army through the Val d'Adige and the Eisack Valley over the Brenner Pass to Lake Constance and from there to the Black Forest. Here he defeated the Raeti in a major battle.[80]

The Alpine campaigns yielded a wealth of new geographical information. The Hercynian Forest, hitherto perceived as an impenetrable mass, resolved into several mountain systems. Tiberius apparently glimpsed the source of the Danube a day's journey from Lake Constance. Its upper course had previously been known only in vague outline, yet now the river was definitively identified as Germania's southern boundary. Augustus' campaign in Illyricum provided further clarity about the river's course. By subjugating Pannonia, he also created a land bridge between Gaul and the provinces of Noricum and Raetia, established in 15 BCE, as well as the Illyrian provinces on the near side of the Rhine-Danube system.[81]

Roman Cartography as a Basis for Military Strategy?

In retrospect, it appears as if the Roman high command had set out to plug the territorial gaps in their rule and systematically extend their hegemony towards the north. Such a view is seductive when we look at modern maps. Yet did the Romans share our conception of space? Can we assume that they oriented their operations on geographical models, drawing on new information to broaden their geographical horizons in a way that went beyond their immediate administrative and military needs?

The meagre geographical details given by Caesar raise doubts. Many scholars therefore suggest that the Roman military relied on one-dimensional drawings (itineraries) of routes and fixed points, comparable to the *periploi*. On the other hand, it is difficult to imagine that carefully coordinated campaigns directed at a common target area were feasible without large-scale maps. There was a long tradition in Rome of depicting conquered lands in the form of publicly displayed, painted 'maps' and pictures; geographical data concerning the territories traversed or administered by commanders may not have been systematically evaluated, but at least they were preserved in archives from the first century BCE. The most important works of scientific geography were known to educated nobles and generals, who would have consulted the relevant specialist literature before venturing into *terra incognita*.[82] Still, Roman commanders had no need to face the challenges of transferring data onto a world map. The cartographic model aspired to by scientific geography—one derived from astronomical and mathematical calculations that made allowances for the curvature of the Earth's surface—was of little value to them. They were more interested in investigating a delimited region than in arriving at a mathematically exact representation of the world. For their purposes, it was enough to integrate information about rivers, lakes, mountains, and trading centres into a serviceable template in the form of a square or rectangle. Similarly, late Hellenistic historians had relied on military reports and regarded geographical knowledge as imperative for mastering the art of war and understanding historical connections.[83]

Nonetheless, the conditions for gathering and analysing data had changed. The Republic lacked an institution like the Museion in Alexandria where data collected on individual military expeditions could be collated into an all-encompassing cartographic project. Caesar's brief dictatorship left no time for this. All this began to change under Augustus, however. The emperor could now centrally plan and coordinate his campaigns. Client kings like Juba provided him and his advisers with memoranda on peripheral regions and composed geographical works about Libya and Arabia.

His closest friend and son-in-law M. Vispanius Agrippa probably played an important role in sifting through these works. As a leading general in the civil war and as governor of various provinces in the Empire's northwest, he was intimately familiar with remote landscapes and the geographical problems involved in preparing, organizing, and executing military operations. Charged with overseeing infrastructure projects in the Empire's interior, including building roads and aqueducts, he gained expertise in surveying and the mathematical modelling of space. Finally, he operated in an intellectual climate that drew numerous Hellenistic scholars, historians, and geographers to the imperial court. One of them was Strabo of Apameia, who wrote a *Geographica* of the ecumene ruled from Rome that dealt only summarily with those living outside the imperium.[84] There, he charted a middle course between the mathematical-scientific and the descriptive approach: when depicting macroregions and islands, he oriented himself on the principle of geometric shapes (rhombuses, triangles, rectangles), as prefigured in the 'seals' (*sphragides*) of Eratosthenes and in Polybius, yet he made no attempt to integrate the era's vastly expanded knowledge of the world's outer limits into a new picture of the Earth.[85] Agrippa may have studied these writings as well as Eratosthenes' work before he collated the knowledge gained on his campaigns and governorships with existing itineraries into a grand 'geographical commentary'.[86] It formed the basis for the plan to produce a world map that would provide visual support for Rome's claim to world domination.

Some twenty-five years after Agrippa's death, Augustus finally completed his friend's project and had a 6- to 10-metre-high map mounted on the walls of a portico on the Campus Martius (*porticus Vipsania*).[87] The main sources for the ecumene's north—data for the Far Eastern regions were taken from 'scientific' works—were presumably campaign notes in the form of itineraries and *commentarii*, as recorded not just by Caesar but probably by other generals and Augustus himself, as well as Roman provincial statistics and measurements, such as those Caesar had made in Britannia. On this basis, Agrippa depicted several macro-regions such as Britannia, Gaul, and Germania in rectangular form and indicated their north-south and east-west dimensions. For all their geometrical abstraction, the rectangles' congruent angles and proportional sides gave viewers a sense of the relative size of the Empire's dominions. Taken together, the individual rectangles offered a synoptic overview of the world known to the Romans. To the north, it probably extended to the Baltic coast and showed the Vistula as the border between Germania and Sarmatia, no doubt owing to the river's importance for the amber trade (see above, p. 185). Following Eratosthenes, the rectangle's central orienting line (*diaphragma*) was fixed at the 36th parallel north, stretching from Gibraltar to the Gulf of Alexandretta and on to India. Agrippa may have used other parallels as well.[88]

Campaigns to the Elbe and Warships in the North Sea

Agrippa's map is in many ways representative of how the Augustan age saw the world. In keeping with the calculations of Posidonius, the total extent of the ecumene may have been vastly underestimated.[89] Such a constellation had already strengthened Alexander in his conviction that he would soon reach the ends of the earth and could conquer the ecumene from the waves. Now politicians and writers felt confident that the gods had chosen the Romans to rule the world and to incorporate yet unconquered spaces, especially to the north, into their Empire in the foreseeable future. Indeed, the world map was not just a product of Roman imperial ideology; with its combination of linear and punctual location information and abstract yet proportionally congruent surfaces, it also accorded with Roman generals' ideas about space.

This is illustrated by the military operations launched in 12–9 BCE by Drusus against the Germans and by Tiberius against the Pannonians on Illyrian terrain. In 11 BCE the Romans under Drusus first reached the Weser, perhaps travelling along the Hellweg as far as Höxter and Corvey. Two years later they arrived at another large river, vaguely known to the Greek scholarly world as the 'amber river', Eridanos. The Romans called it Albis = Elbe. A Roman commander had once again set a new boundary marker at the end of the world; perhaps taking his cue from Alexander, Drusus had a monument erected to document his achievement. Upon his return, he was celebrated for pushing Roman power into new lands, much like Pompey at the Caucasus or Caesar on the Rhine and in Britain.

Thresholds to an unknown world are full of magic and mystery: a giant woman is said to have appeared out of nowhere on the riverbank, ordering Drusus to turn back and prophesying him an early death. Perhaps the Romans had encountered a Germanic embassy with a seeress. Yet the legend was probably invented to place the Roman high command's decision not to cross the Elbe in a mystical light. Some would have recalled Alexander's retreat at the Hyphasis; this had the effect of elevating Drusus' German campaign to the same mythic stature as his predecessor's march to India. In reality, as so often in the history of discovery, supply problems made turning back seem advisable. When Drusus died unexpectedly on the homeward march, this only gave credence to the legend of the Germanic clairvoyant. Tiberius then assumed command and could report after another year that all tribes 'between the Rhine and the Elbe' had capitulated. Five years later, coming from the Danube or upper Main, L. Domitius Ahenobarbus accomplished what had been denied Drusus: he crossed the Elbe, probably between Wittenberg and Schönebeck, and advanced farther east of the river than any previous Roman commander.[90]

From the outset, spectacular fleet operations accompanied the conquest of Germania. After Drusus had repulsed the Sugambri on the Lower Rhine in 12 BCE, he sailed down the Rhine to a point near Vechta and had a canal dug from a Rhine tributary to the Ijsselmeer (*fossa Drusiana*). He then continued by ship to the North Sea, subjected the Frisians, and sailed on to the island of Byrchanis, probably Borkum (*Burcana*), which was much larger in antiquity and was probably linked to Juist and Nordeney. From there he discovered the Ems estuary (*Amisia*) and fought the Bructeri at sea. His fleet was surprised by the tide on the return voyage. Clearly the Roman leadership had not yet sufficiently absorbed the nautical information about the Wadden Sea that the Greeks had already assembled. Frisians escorting the fleet from the coast came to the rescue. Before the onset of winter, the fleet returned via the Rhine. Drusus was celebrated as the first general to have navigated the northern Ocean, although the accolade rightly belongs to Caesar.[91]

Drusus' North Sea voyage suggests that army high command had drawn up a series of maps at the time that, like the works of Agrippa and Strabo, were based on the northwestern part of Eratosthenes' world model. Germania was bordered by the Rhine and the North Sea coast. The goal of the naval expedition was probably to determine the precise location of river mouths and their distance from the Rhine.[92] Further marine operations from the mouth of the Rhine explored the remaining East and West Frisian islands and reconnoitred the North Sea coastline as well as the Jutland Peninsula. Twelve years after Domitius Ahenobarbus had advanced from the Danube into the lands east of the Elbe, a fleet sailed along Jutland's west coast to the 'Promontory of the Cimbri' (Cape Skagen). It then entered the Skagerrak, where the Romans saw 'a vast sea in front of them or learn[ed] of it by report',[93] before proceeding to 'the region of Scythia and regions numb with excessive moisture', probably the west coast of Scandinavia, or perhaps a larger island on the German Baltic coast.

As a rule, North Sea voyages remained bound by their mission to provide offshore support for infantry while establishing connections between river systems and the Ocean. Learning more about the coasts, imperative for coordinating infantry and fleet movements, was also a key objective. Some therefore maintain that the fleet turned into the Elbe after rounding Jutland, sailing upriver to meet an army that Tiberius had led all the way through Germania. Such a rendezvous is unlikely, given that the spectacular foray into the Baltic would have been difficult to coordinate with a parallel land-based operation. Perhaps an impetus to strike out into the unknown had become untethered from political or military considerations, as with Alexander at the Hyphasis. A proximate goal could have been finding the land of amber as well as the 'northeast passage' from the North Sea to the Caspian, still assumed to be a projection of the Ocean. This would be a feat in keeping with the princeps' claim to have opened all seas and lands for the Empire. It was an astonishing achievement, given that there were no precedents for such operations in the north. They are hard to imagine in the absence of a geographical conception that could accurately gauge the relationship among routes, coasts, and territories.[94]

Assault on Maroboduus and the Campaign of Germanicus

This became even more apparent in 6 CE, when the Romans planned a large-scale expedition to the kingdom of Maroboduus in the Bohemian basin. According to Roman intelligence, Maroboduus had forged an army of some 70,000 footsoldiers and 4,000 cavalry that posed a lasting threat not just to Noricum and Pannonia, but to Italy itself. Two Roman columns were to enclose the enemy in a pincer movement: one, under the legate Sentius Saturninus, would march from the Rhine (Mainz) through Chatti territory and the Hercynian Forest while the other, under Tiberius, advanced northwest from Carnuntum (on the Danube). Coordinating large fighting units over such vast distances and combining them for a timed assault required precise knowledge of the terrain. The reference to the threat facing Italy and the provinces likewise indicates that Roman leadership had a clear idea of the size of the central European interior and sought to extend the area under its control to a line marked by the Elbe and Danube, lengthened by a connecting line between them.

A few days before the armies were due to converge, all hopes were dashed when a rebellion broke out in Dalmatia and Pannonia. After concluding a hasty peace with Maroboduus, Tiberius led his troops back over the Danube. Three years later, Roman legions under Quinctilius Varus suffered a crushing defeat against the Cherusci under Arminius, fighting in Germanic lands beyond the Rhine that had seemingly been pacified and were believed ripe for provincialization. Rome was determined to avenge the humiliation. Tiberius ordered a retaliatory strike. Under the command of the heir presumptive Germanicus, a son of Drusus, the largest army Rome had ever fielded pushed deep into the German forests to recover what had been lost. Once again, the Romans demonstrated their ability to coordinate long-range attacks involving several units. Four legions under Caecina marched from Xanten through the North German Plain to the middle Ems. Around Rheine, where the river was still navigable, they joined forces with Pedo's cavalry, which had come through Frisian territory, and the remaining four legions, led by Germanicus from the Lower Rhine through the Drusus canal to the Zuiderzee and then via the North Sea coast up the Ems.[95] The united armies proceeded along the Ems to the area of present-day Paderborn. After visiting the site of Varus' defeat and seeking unsuccessfully to do battle with the Cherusci under Arminius, the supreme commander led his troops back to the Ems. On the return march to winter quarters, Caecina unexpectedly intercepted and bested his German foes.

Germanicus had since returned with the fleet, having suffered heavy losses from the Wadden Sea tide like Tiberius before him. He did not achieve a military breakthrough until the following year, when he crossed the Weser—once again coming from the Ems—and crushed Arminius' troops at Idistaviso (between Porta Westfalica and the Steinhuder Meer), subjugating the Angrivarii a little later. Even if the return voyage along the Ems brought heavy losses due to summer thunderstorms and treacherous shallows, Germanicus could point to an impressive record: he had defeated Arminius and restored Roman military honour.[96]

Yet this very success caused Tiberius to break off the Germanic wars. In the (likely) event of a definitive victory, it was to be expected that Germanicus would be proclaimed emperor. Weighing up the costs and benefits of further expansion in light of the domestic consequences, Tiberius recalled his best general, abandoned bridgeheads in *Germania Libera*, and transferred his troops to the lands left of the Rhine. While the Romans would repeatedly cross the river borders into enemy territory, these incursions lacked the momentum of coordinated pincer manoeuvres. Now a different policy determined their planning. The wars of the Augustan age had yielded a wealth of information about Germania. Never before had a Mediterranean power had such intimate insights into the conditions of the Germanic tribes, the unstable basis of their economy, the permanent rivalries among their elites, and their reliance on glory and booty. From now on, the Romans used this information to play off chieftains against each other, supporting their allies with gifts and arranging to have their enemies assassinated.

The Baltic Sea

This policy met with lasting success, yet in retreating to the left bank of the Rhine, the Roman appetite for exploration waned. Tacitus complained that no one had ventured into the North Sea since Germanicus' storm-tossed voyage; indeed, no Roman wreck has yet been discovered in those waters.[97] While the conquest of the Ocean remained a fixture of imperial propaganda, it was enacted only symbolically and in places where success was guaranteed. Caligula contented himself with having his men gather shells on the North Sea coast and sending them to Rome as proof that he had tamed the Ocean.[98] When Emperor Claudius dispatched an army to conquer Britain, he could claim to have extended Roman rule to the farthest limits of the world; his presence for a few days near the end of the campaign was enough to celebrate a triumph.[99] Even the fleet that Gn. Julius Agricola, governor of Britain, sailed around the entire island was not engaged in discovery; it confirmed the far more detailed reports of Pytheas from 400 years earlier. Still, Agricola seems to have reached the Orkneys and perhaps even the Shetlands.

Yet when Tacitus claimed that the Orkneys had previously been unknown and wove in reminiscences of Pytheas' report, he did so to stylize his father-in-law as a new Alexander. In fact, the geographer Pomponius Mela, writing forty years earlier, had been well informed about the Orkneys and

Hebrides. Other writers had registered the expansion of the geographical horizon and could quiz German emissaries or Germans living in Rome once the imperial campaigns were discontinued.[100] Tacitus' complaint that the Elbe and the lands farther east had been forgotten is therefore to be taken with a pinch of salt; imperial diplomacy reached far beyond the borders of empire.[101]

In the mid-first century CE, Pomponius Mela and Pliny the Elder also painted a more accurate image of the Baltic (*Codanus sinus*) than that sketched by their predecessors: unaware of Jutland, Strabo had imagined the North Sea coast running in a straight line to the Black Sea and had depicted the known world ending at the Albis (Elbe).[102] Pliny was one of few writers to have spent much time in Germany. As a naval officer, he had easy access to coastal *periploi* and knew the rivers east of the Albis. He conveyed an accurate understanding of the land barrier of Jutland. His gaze then turned northward—he named *Scatinavia* as a large island as well as southern Norway (*mons Sevo*)—before sweeping east towards the Vistula and entering the North Sea via Skagerrak. He showed a good knowledge of southern Sweden (Uppland) and its inhabitants.[103]

Several decades later, Tacitus added more precise information about the Pomeranian, Prussian, and Baltic coasts and first mentioned Finland, which the Empire apparently knew more about than Norway. The Finnish Sitones supplied furs and hides, while the Suiones in Uppland and the inhabitants of the Baltic and Prussian coasts were familiar through the amber trade. The Baltic was now regarded as an inner sea separated from the outer Ocean by the Norwegian coast.[104] Yet unlike in the Hellenistic period, increased knowledge about northern climes did not lead to a revision of the worldview established by Eratosthenes, despite Pliny's familiarity with the principles of scientific geography. The *periplus* remained the sole medium on which he and Pomponius Mela oriented their description of the Baltic. Both men probably drew on the geographer Philemon, who had described the growth in knowledge since Augustus and had probably first used the term *Scandinavia*. Philemon proved that the new information could be categorized and interpreted by the standards of Hellenistic scholarship, yet he too made no effort to integrate the northern realm into a new worldview. Geographers parcelled their material into lengthy *periploi* that described the Mediterranean and the seas of the north and southeast without (yet) summoning the strength to attempt a synthesis on a mathematical basis.[105]

Mercantile Expeditions and the 'Amber Road'

With the abandonment of large-scale offensives in Germania, the impetus for exploration swung back to those earliest pioneers of discovery: merchants. These had always supplied geographers with essential knowledge, and without their help, neither Caesar nor the generals of the imperial period could have celebrated their triumphs. Horace writes that a Roman trader could sail the Atlantic 'thrice a year [. . .] undamaged'.[106] Trading also continued largely independently of military planning and power constellations; merchants from the provinces appeared at the court of Maroboduus, for example, before the planned pincer attack. Even once Roman maritime operations had come to a halt, traders continued to ply the routes from the mouth of the Rhine to Britain and the North Sea and Baltic, although far fewer voyages were undertaken by Romans than by locals.[107]

Nonetheless, maritime operations in the North Sea fuelled a demand for settlements that specialized in storing supplies and provisioning Roman units while also re-selling Roman pottery and amphorae to German chieftains. One such example was the settlement at Bentumersiel on the lower Ems, used by the Romans as a naval base and supply depot. Similar facilities sprung up at the Elbe estuary and other strategically advantageous coastal locations. There emerged a trade network of emporia, settlements, and princely seats near the coast.[108]

The discontinuation of the Teutonic wars after Tiberius did nothing to change this constellation. On the contrary: the *limes* formed an additional trade zone. The merchants living in this border zone knew the needs of Germanic princes and made long journeys into the interior. They brought with them luxury goods, bronzeware, and glass vessels for the upper class. Production centres shifted in the early imperial period to Gaul and the Rhineland and hence closer to central and northern European customers. From the Rhine, one route led to the Danish islands, while an overland route from the Danube brought traders to Bohemia and Slovakia, hence into lands ruled by Maroboduus and the successor realm of Vannius, and from there into territory east of the Elbe. Eventually, the sea and land routes converged at the Vistula.

Yet what drew traders to the Baltic coast? Besides pelts and slaves, one product was in hot demand among Roman elites: amber. The 'gold of the north' served as an incense substitute and was applied medicinally in the form of a powder or salve; above all, it was coveted as jewellery. Pliny

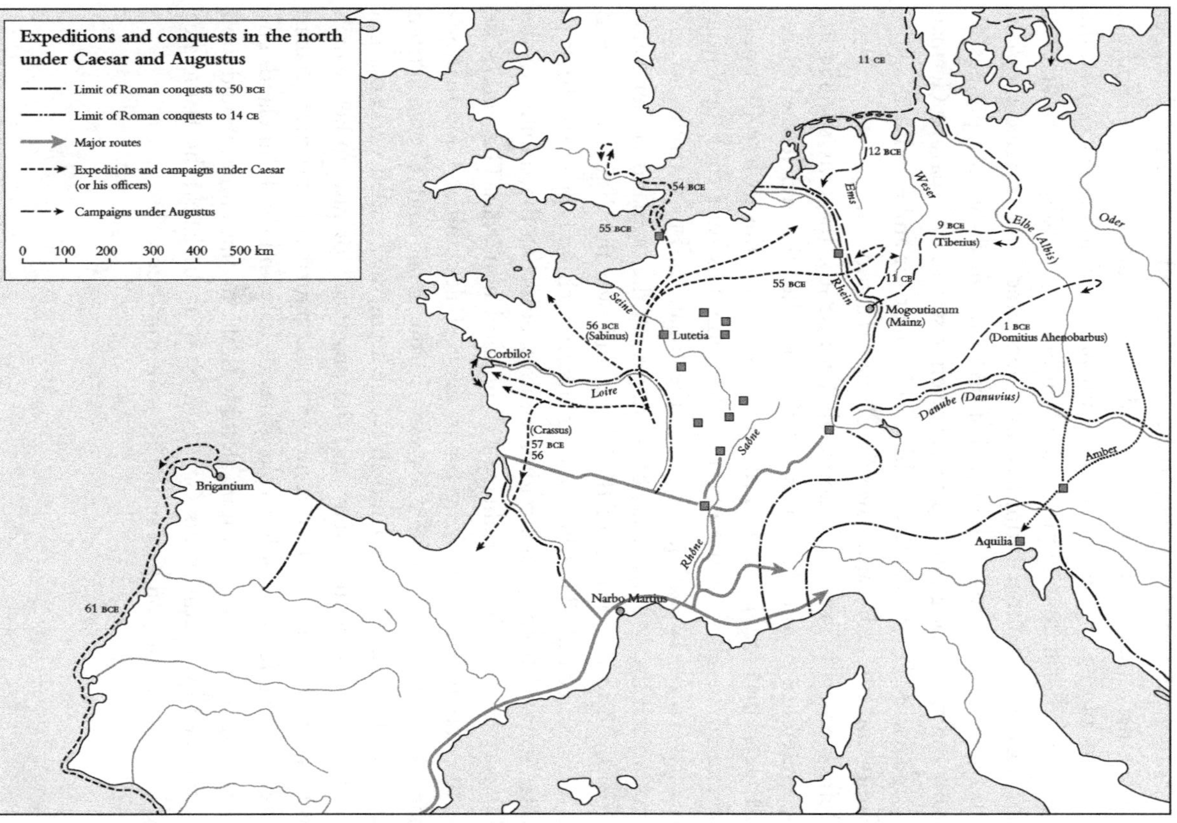

Map 9 Credit: Rudolf Hungreder/Klett-Cotta.

tells how in Nero's time, a Roman knight, clearly a trader with experience in Germany, was sent to Sambia (near present-day Kaliningrad) by the *procurator* of the gladiatorial games. 'Traversing the coasts of that country and visiting the various markets there', he returned with so much amber 'that the nets used for keeping the wild animals away from the podium [of the amphitheatre] were knotted with pieces of amber. Moreover, the arms, biers, and all the equipment used on one day, the display on each day being varied, had amber fittings. Amber-decorated litters carried the slain gladiators from the arena. The heaviest lump weighed thirteen pounds'.[109] Clearly the trader sought to tap a new revenue stream by bypassing German intermediaries. He probably combined his quest for amber with the purchase of aurochs, bears, and slaves for gladiatorial combat.[110]

Pliny's report is important, above all, because it is the only specific literary reference to the Amber Road that matches the archaeological record. Germans brought the prized commodity along this road to Pannonia. The knight travelled in the opposite direction. His path took him from the northern Adriatic (Aquileia) over the Julian Alps to Carnuntum and then through the Moravian Gate. Uniting with the overland amber route, it continued to the mouth of the Vistula and over the Vistula Lagoon to the Sambian coast.[111] That he could transport such vast quantities back to Rome, sourced from several trading centres, points to the stability of the trading system despite all military and political upheavals. The enterprise was the start of a century-long boom in the Baltic amber trade that enriched Roman merchant families such as the *Barbii* and *Caesarnii* from Aquileia. Harnessing their Danuban connections, they traded wine, oil, and manufactured goods from Italy and the provinces for raw amber, which was then worked into necklaces, intaglios, and figurines in northern Italian workshops before being sold to the elites of Italy and the Rhineland. The reports imported into the Empire along with the natural amber would soon be processed by Tacitus in his *Germania*. Now, at the latest, the Baltic area had become an integral part of the Roman worldview.[112]

7
The Globalization of Eurasia in the First and Second Centuries CE

PEPPER AND INCENSE
IN SEARCH OF THE TREASURES OF THE INDIAN OCEAN

The Imperial Economic Boom

By the late first century CE, the Empire had abandoned its plans to expand farther to the northwest. This was not a sign of weakness. Incursions into the *Barbaricum* demonstrated ongoing military strength and the capacity to launch strikes in any part of the world. The Parthian Empire was too riven by internal power struggles to pose a serious threat to Roman supremacy. For the time being, the Mediterranean and its peripheries enjoyed lasting peace under a single regime that seemed invulnerable to external attack.

These formed ideal preconditions for a continuation of the economic boom that had begun in the late Republic. The urbanization of the West, Rome's transformation into a megacity of around a million inhabitants, an increasingly wealthy landowning elite, and the standing army all created new 'centres of demand' that were serviced by a growing farming and manufacturing sector and spurred growth in long-distance trade. The Empire's financial and resource base increased to an extent not seen again in European history until the discovery of the New World.[1] The takeover of the Ptolemaic treasury, the integration of the rich provinces of the Levant, and the intensive exploitation of mines in Spain, Noricum, Pannonia, and Dacia provided the imperial household with a constant inflow of precious metals and coinage (totalling up to a billion *denarii*). These funds were injected into the economy through disbursements for the army, court, administration, and salaried officials, as well as for public works, festivals, and games. In its early years, the Empire was thus awash with cash.[2] Together with imperial investment in maritime infrastructure, ports, and canals, the creation of a unified legal and coinage system encompassing even remote provinces reduced transportation and transaction costs while facilitating access to credit for profitable trading ventures, with interest rates falling as low as 4 percent under Augustus.[3] At the same time, these developments eased the flow of information—vital for traders and merchants—and the dissemination of technical innovations (such as 'turbine-driven' watermills) along with new, more efficient agricultural practices (the targeted application of manure, chalk, and compost). As new farmland was brought under the plough in the provinces, the Empire's population shot up more quickly than ever before in Mediterranean history.[4] Manufacturing boomed, evident in increased production of pottery and metalwork, in the agricultural sector, in shipbuilding, and in the transport industry.[5]

The expansion of the moderate tax system to the provinces stimulated local production and created new markets that gave further impetus to pan-Mediterranean trade, leading to innovations in maritime infrastructure. The hydraulic mortar, probably invented in Campania in the second century, revolutionized the construction of harbours, allowing breakwaters to be built far out to sea even on unprotected coasts. These offered mooring points for larger transport ships in 2- to 3-metre-deep water. Specially constructed dredgers protected ports from silting as new crane designs expedited cargo handling, with transport amphorae of up to a hundred litres as well as 2-metre-high vessels capable of storing almost 1,000 litres. The invention of the chain pump (for discharging bilge water) according to the paternoster principle made possible the deployment of 1,000- to 1,200-tonne transporters (299–350 tonners were the rule), which exceeded even the largest Venetian ships of the early-modern period. If archaeological shipwreck finds are any indication, seaborne trade volumes reached heights between 200 BCE and 200 CE that would not be regained until the sixteenth century. Time-saving voyages over long distances on the open seas with two- and perhaps three-masters were commonplace even in winter.[6]

Taken together, all these factors—the favourable political situation abroad, legal and political stability at home, the steady influx and investment of ready money, a general increase in production, technical innovations in shipbuilding and harbour construction, and, last but not least, an unusually high level of basic education and literacy—made the Empire in its first centuries the most productive and economically advanced polity in antiquity, boasting a concentration of resources and mercantile activity in a global space that would not be seen again until the trans-Atlantic empires of the seventeenth and eighteenth centuries.[7]

Although the driving force behind the boom remained the mega-rich landowners of Rome and Italy, people outside the senatorial and equestrian class now also found access to previously unknown wealth. None more dramatically illustrated these opportunities than the manumitted slaves who, frequently sponsored or protected by their former masters and endowed by virtue of their background with the commercial advantages of multilingualism, mobility, and a willingness to take risks, rose 'from shoeshines to millionaires' (but also suffered enormous losses) in the most varied fields: as directors of large building projects, moneylenders, tax farmers, merchants, or shipowners. Beneath the wealthy elite, there emerged an affluent 'middling class' comprising around 10 percent of the population, while the masses enjoyed a higher standard of living than in the centuries before. Even small farmers could profit from new agricultural techniques, investing relatively modest sums for impressive returns. Meat consumption—an important index of prosperity in the Mediterranean—took off in Italy, at least.[8] Archaeological evidence from the western provinces suggests that large parts of the imperial populace were gripped by a 'consumption revolution'. It fed growing demand for products that had to be transported across vast distances from beyond the Empire's borders.[9]

Hunger for Products from the Far East

Ever since the campaigns of Lucullus and Pompey, at the latest, spices and perfumes from the Far East had found their way into wealthy households (see above, pp. 256–257); under Augustus, the flow of goods expanded to cover a broader customer base. Horace still described pepper as rare and expensive. A generation later, it was adding savour to the meals of 'ordinary' citizens. According to graffiti found in Pompeii, it was an everyday consumer good for a family of three, even though a pound of pepper still cost thirty-two times as much as a pound of bread.[10] For the wealthy, in particular, pepper was a must-have ingredient. The recipes of Apicius regularly call for liberal doses of the spice.[11] The *horrea piperataria* warehouse in Rome could store up to 5,800 tonnes of spices at a net worth of around 240 million sesterces, meaning that each person in the Empire consumed an average of one-fifth of a pound.[12] Along with incense, pepper was exempted from the 25 percent import tax in the Roman economic zone, in part because the emperor felt a sense of obligation towards his subjects, but mainly because he wanted to secure provisions for the army and relieve them of financial burdens: even legionaries at the remote northern borders had acquired a taste for pepper, as indicated by finds from the Augustan military camp in Oberaden and later at Vindolanda near Hadrian's Wall. A pepper shaker from northern France in the form of a black slave shows the spice's presence at the Atlantic.[13] Under the Roman Empire, the practice of seasoning dishes with pepper and other spices first spread throughout Europe and the Atlantic trade network.[14] Other Far Eastern spices and botanicals were regarded as luxuries for the elite. Myrrh, incense, cinnamon, and aromatic oils had been used since time immemorial for temple sacrifices and funerals (not least for hygienic reasons). At burials, we read in a first-century poem, the harvests of Arabia, Cilicia, Saba, and India filled the air. The imperial cult increased the demand even further.[15]

Far Eastern spices and aromatics were no less important as medicines and antidotes, an aspect already touched on in the oldest epics, as when Odysseus uses the magical herb moly to counteract Circe's sorcery. For Ctesias, Indian plant extracts were an effective remedy.[16] With the wars against Mithridates in the first century BCE, knowledge of the therapeutic benefits of Far Eastern plants travelled west; a prescription for mithridate, a theriac involving some thirty-six spices that supposedly provided immunity to every possible poison if taken daily, was known in Rome.[17] From the late Republic onward, the best doctors of the east brought the most advanced Hellenistic medicines as well as numerous therapeutic drugs and healing ointments to the Tiber. The encyclopaedia of Cornelius Celsus (first century CE) recommended treating coughing fits or liver disease with a mixture of pepper, frankincense, myrrh, and other essences.[18] In his book *De materia medica*, Dioscorides of Cilicia explained how myrrh, cinnamon, cassia, spikenard, and malabathrum could be used to clean wounds and prevent infection, and as an antidote to poison. Even spiced wines had curative properties: rosé wine against stomach ache and diarrhoea, myrtle wine against inflamed gums and tonsils, pepper wine against catarrh and coughing, wine infused with spikenard and malabathrum against kidney and liver complaints as well as jaundice.[19]

The frequency and matter-of-factness with which such sources refer to Far Eastern healing products suggest their widespread availability. The boundary between serious medicine and quackery was fluid. Writers recommended exotic essences as aphrodisiacs, while fragrant salves and oils were applied as deodorants: what for most was a rare outlay reserved for emergencies (illness) or ceremonial occasions (burials) became for the imperial elite an indispensable element of a new lifestyle. When Nero sprinkled a guest with a precious essence, the guest responded by inviting the emperor into a room fitted out with gold and silver pipes from which aromatic ointments 'gushed freely, much like water'.[20]

For all its extravagance, this example gives an inkling of how many Far Eastern aromatics and unguents were consumed and how quickly they could be procured. As their opportunities for political involvement shrank, Roman elites poured vast sums into documenting their social status through the display of luxury goods from abroad. Such goods flowed overwhelmingly (although not exclusively: even farmers wore amber jewellery, and even serving girls preened in silver mirrors) into the villas of the super-rich, just as parrots and ivory statuettes from India became a fixture in senatorial households, signs of an exotic luxury few could afford.[21]

Most of these goods came from the east, always notorious for its dissolute, profligate ways. Accordingly, Roman authors deplored the supposedly one-sided cash outflow and fretted about the moral decline of their fellow citizens.[22] One trend was especially illustrative: even in the late Republic, Chinese silk could be bought in the fashionable *vicus Tuscus* district. The new fabric revealed more than it concealed, although it was perfectly suited to the summer heat. By the early imperial age, silk textiles had become so common in high society that in 16 CE a Senate resolution banned men from wearing the 'dishonourable' material. Few took much notice, least of all the emperor: Caligula was *seriacus* (clad in silk), Vespasian and Titus wore silk togas at triumphal processions, and Heliogabalus was said to have appeared exclusively in silk.[23]

Imperial Military Policy

Some scholars maintain that the elite's enormous demand for Far Eastern goods even influenced imperial military policy. They cite the campaigns waged in 25 BCE by the Egyptian prefect Aelius Gallus and in 1 BCE by Gaius Caesar, the grandson and adoptive son of Augustus (see above, pp. 282–283). Both supposedly gave the emperor direct access to the incense-producing regions of Arabia and better control of the India trade.[24]

Gallus sailed with a newly built fleet from a port near Suez to Leuke Kome.[25] He then marched with 10,000 men, supported by an auxiliary contingent of Arab Nabataeans, along the west coast of the Arabian Peninsula to principalities in southern Yemen. His goal was likely the kingdom of the Himyarites, who had recently brought the ports of Aden and Mesala under their control. Having taken several towns, however, he advanced only as far as Mariba (Marib), capital of the Sabaeans (near Sama). Here he was forced to turn back after a failed siege. Yet procuring incense can hardly have been the reason for all this effort, given that it was not even cultivated on Sabaean territory, nor were the Sabaeans involved in the incense trade. They were, however, known for their military valour.[26]

Over twenty years later, the emperor sent his grandson Gaius east 'to manage Parthian and Arabian affairs' (*ad Parthicas Arabicasque res*). Gaius' eastern campaign was clearly intended to give him an opportunity to stage himself as Augustus' heir and win over the troops.[27] 'Parthian affairs' referred to the succession to the throne in Armenia, yet Gaius was prevented from deciding them in Rome's favour when he suffered a fatal injury. He had previously turned to Arabia 'to gain glory'. Collating this information with references in other sources, some conclude that he destroyed *Eudaimon Arabia* (Aden) and gathered information about the incense tree.[28]

Yet can we infer from all this that Augustus was pursuing 'commercial interests' along with the objective of grooming his adopted son to become emperor? Did he set out to destroy foreign ports and conquer or intimidate Arab kingdoms because they stood in the way of Roman trade interests and to provide Roman merchants with new revenue streams? Leaving aside the fact that the destruction of Aden rests on a shaky combination of sources[29]—what commercial advantage could it possibly have given him?—were Roman soldiers and merchants expected to occupy the port and take over the role of native traders and sailors?

This is unlikely, given their ignorance of the complex maritime and geographical conditions as well as their total inexperience in Arabian trade. This also distinguishes the situation in Arabia from conditions in Gaul and Germany, where Roman traders went far ahead of Roman arms in both time and space. No doubt generals of the late Republic considered the 'commercial' interests of their clients from the equestrian class when planning and executing campaigns. Caesar prided himself on having freed *mercatores* from Gallic customs stations.[30] Marcus Aurelius wanted to 'profit his knights' through his Parthian war.[31] Yet these objectives were always secondary to political and military motivations. Although some Romans may have hoped for cheaper access to Arabian wares from a war in Arabia, such considerations were surely not central to imperial war policy.

Strabo makes the key point: Augustus wanted to conquer *Arabia Felix* and seize its riches, known to the Romans since the days of Pompey and Gabinius.[32] Pliny connects Gallus' plans in Arabia with those in Armenia; power politics, not trade policy, was paramount. When he cites a thirst for glory as Gaius Caesar's only motive, on the one hand this points to Augustus' domestic strategy of bolstering his adopted son as his designated successor. On the other, the Arabian campaigns stood squarely in a Roman military tradition aimed at achieving success on the battlefield and conquering new territory. Augustus needed to do both to legitimate his power; not without reason, the *princeps* boasts in his *Res Gestae* ('deeds done') that two armies had marched to Ethiopia and Arabia under his auspices, won many battles, and conquered many cities.[33] No mention is made of trade; all that counts is imperial *gloria*.

Not coincidentally, the campaigns of Gallus and Gaius resembled Alexander's Arabian plans; perhaps they aimed not just to conquer the land but to circumnavigate it, too. Augustus commissioned Isidore of Charax and Juba of Mauretania to write 'memoranda' on Arabia and Parthia, much as Alexander had reconnoitred Arabia before setting out to conquer it. Just as scholars in Alexander's army studied the botany of the Far East, so too Gaius collected information on the incense tree and made it available to Juba.[34]

Such imitations of Alexander never operated in a power-political vacuum. By linking the Armenian question so closely with Gaius' expedition to Arabia, Pliny suggested that they shared a similar objective: that of weakening the Parthians. Both campaigns would strengthen the Roman position in Arabia by destroying principalities that were friendly to Parthia and supporting those friendly to Rome. Gallus' undertaking was probably part of a strategic initiative to isolate the Parthian Empire by conquering its Arabian client kingdoms, such as the Hadramites.[35] Augustus pursued a comparable policy towards Maroboduus in the west.

In this context, the Gallus campaign should be understood as a kind of test to gauge the possibility of turning southern Arabia into a Roman province; this is what Strabo has in mind when he writes that Augustus wanted to conquer *Arabia Felix*. The 'failed' campaign taught the emperor—like the Ptolemies before him—that the difficult march routes and complicated supply situation gave an expansion from Egypt little hope of success. Here, as later in Germania, Augustus clearly recognized that the financial benefits of direct rule would be more than outweighed by the enormous logistical and military costs. Accordingly, he made do with a policy that his successor Tiberius likewise pursued in free Germania (see above, p. 290). He relied on 'client kings', who indeed sent envoys to the imperial court after the Gallus campaign and strove to maintain *amicitia* (friendship), while still reserving the right to launch punitive expeditions against ill-disposed powers.[36]

Financial Interests, But No Trade Policy

Reconnaissance missions, punitive expeditions, and the establishment of friendly relations with Arabian rulers extended Rome's reach in southern waters. Naturally, these did not rule out pecuniary interests. When Strabo states that the emperor wished to secure the riches of Arabia, he means war booty, first and foremost. This is what motivated the legionaries, who had to be kept occupied and rewarded now that the civil wars at the imperial centre had come to an end. Many would have hoped for copious quantities of myrrh and incense, to be sold to the accompanying traders and later collected as tribute. The idea that Gallus and Gaius journeyed overland to Arabia to bring the Incense Route and India trade under Roman control and eliminate Arabian middlemen seems unlikely not least because incense was almost exclusively seaborne, while the India trade was also becoming increasingly detached from Arabian way stations like Aden.[37] Rome had no state merchant fleet, nor were there 'state enterprises' that could have influenced foreign policy in the manner of modern trading companies. In addition, there are no signs of a continuation of Ptolemaic trade monopoly, nor any attempt to direct trade flows or develop new markets. Even the Ptolemies' unconventional engagement in the Red Sea had military and financial causes (see above, p. 254).[38]

The emperor's interests were thus fiscal in nature: once Augustus had declared Egypt crown property (officially: property of the people of Rome), it was only logical that he would seek to cream off as much profit as possible from the land and its adjacent territories. This mainly involved maximizing customs duties at the external borders, which at 25 percent of the value of the traded goods promised lucrative returns. Proceeds from long-distance trade with southern Arabia, east Africa, and India at the start of the second century CE have recently been estimated at around 200 million sesterces per annum—almost enough to pay the entire imperial army for a year! This sum was augmented by interprovincial tariffs of 2.5 percent.[39]

Under these circumstances, emperors had an obvious interest in maintaining frictionless maritime trade, which they sought to shield from pirate raids and the depredations of enemy powers. That is one reason why Augustus took so many petty Arabian (and perhaps also Indian) kings into his *amicitia*; it is also why Roman warships patrolled the Red Sea as early as the first century CE. We find soldiers supervising local markets, collecting taxes, protecting Egyptian caravans (with luxury goods), and even as 'supercargos' on ships. In the second century, a Roman military support base (prefecture) was established on a main island of the Farasan archipelago in the southern Red Sea. One of its tasks may have been protecting commercial ships from piracy. Others speculate that the prefecture housed a customs station and that soldiers were posted there to combat smuggling at the entrance to the Red Sea.[40]

Yet all this has nothing directly to do with 'trade policy' or 'managing trade flows'. Filling state coffers was always the top priority. Setting aside the fact that protecting provincial production centres and transport routes from thieves and pirates was an obvious duty of the state, the security Rome extended to gold and gemstone mines in the desert west of the Red Sea, along with its control of trade and transport as well as markets and customs stations, served chiefly to increase state revenue, not least to finance the army. This security did not come free of charge: thus, Roman soldiers sold passes on the emperor's behalf for using the central caravan routes that passed through Koptos.[41] As the establishment of a Roman customs station at the Nabataean Red Sea port of Leuke Kome (on the Hejaz coast) shows, boosting customs receipts did not even require conquering foreign land. Tellingly, while emperors invested in building and expanding such stations, in forts and in roads, and in a coastal fleet to protect tax and mining revenue, they did not invest in the infrastructure of the Red Sea ports that were so vital for the India trade.[42] Even the 'Suez canal', reopened by Trajan, is mentioned in the sources only once in connection with the India trade; it therefore probably served strategic ends, as it had under the Persians.[43] In 116 CE, when Trajan conquered the most important port in the Persian Gulf, Charax Spasinu, during his Parthian War, economic or mercantile aspects were of little importance; he instead exulted in having taken a town founded by Alexander! The emperor had started the war to attain military glory, and when he saw ships sailing for India, he dreamed of Alexander's conquests, not the fat profits that motivated their captains.[44]

It could be argued that the sources deliberately suppress such 'profane' motives as profit-seeking since they clash with the emperor's military glory. And there are quite late and vague hints about the advantages of a 'world trade' dominated by Roman power.[45] The complaints of imperial-era writers about the drain of gold and silver from Rome (see above, p. 299) have been taken as evidence of a negative balance of trade that prompted the emperor to intervene. Yet such speculations do not stand up to scrutiny, given the literary context and lack of serious corroborating evidence. It is questionable whether a one-sided trade deficit even existed: Roman elites certainly paid good money for 'luxury products' from the east (as Pliny deplored), but in reality, only a fraction of that money left the Empire. Most ended up in the pockets of Roman middlemen and tax farmers and flowed back into the imperial treasury through tax and customs intakes (although the imperial administration could not trace all the details). If we multiply the average value of the goods freighted to India on each vessel, nine million sesterces, by the 120 ships that sailed annually from Myos Hormos, then export goods valued at around 108 million sesterces left the Empire each year. Goods imported in return, however, were worth at least 1,080 million sesterces, reaping the state over 300 million sesterces in annual customs revenue. This was an enormous sum, considering that state expenditure totalled around 800 million per annum.[46]

We can see now why the emperor publicly supported the complaints of Stoic moral apostles yet did nothing to suppress the trade with eastern luxury goods or staunch the supposed cash haemorrhage—he would have cut off one his most important sources of income. It may be the case that the imperial family paid freedmen silver money to procure them goods from abroad. Yet such transactions reflected a 'private' need for eastern products, not official state policy.[47]

Profits and Costs of the India Trade

Trade with Far Eastern products thus occurred largely independently of state directives.[48] Military conquests and shifts in power set the parameters, but private investors, consumers, and traders determined the quantity, economics, and spatial direction of commodity flows. *They* drove discoveries in the Baltic, just as in earlier times the search for exotic medicinal plants and aromatics had been an important motor for long-distance exploration, but now with increased profitability and intensity of trade over vast distances. We should be wary of overestimating the volumes involved in the India trade in the imperial age: it was always only a fraction of the total goods traded within the Empire.[49] Nonetheless, commercial transactions with India offered the prospect of extremely high profits (supposedly up to a factor of ten) owing to the hefty sums wealthy purchasers were willing to pay. At the same time, however, they demanded considerable capital outlay—several million sesterces, generally—due to the length of the transport routes, the risks of piracy and natural disasters, as well as harbour fees, customs duties, and commissions charged by middlemen.[50] Modern calculations assume that a cargo of pepper that could be sold in Rome for around 4 million *denarii* (16 million sesterces) would require several million sesterces in advance. These went towards the purchase price in India, the 25 percent import duty on the value of the goods levied in Red Sea ports or in Alexandria (*ad valorem*), as well as harbour fees (*ellimenion*), taxes in Mediterranean ports for the offloaded and reloaded cargo (*eisagoge*, *exagoge*), and camel transport—with pepper not even being the most expensive commodity.[51] According to a loan agreement drawn up in the Indian port of Muziris, a cargo assembled in India (4,700 tonnes of ivory and 790 pounds of textiles) had an initial value of around 9 million sesterces. After customs duties of 2 million (!) had been deducted, this had gone down to 7 million; by comparison, an entire legion cost 12 million sesterces per annum![52]

Individual traders and their families could not afford such sums because, unlike the trading companies of the early-modern age, they lacked access to fixed capital. Instead, they had to join forces to form *consortia* or *societates* and find four or five investors, on average, for every major undertaking. For a typical Indian freight of 1 million sesterces, each would have to pay 200,000 sesterces through a nautical loan (*pecunia traiecticia*), although there were probably also more modest contributions from 20,000 sesterces. The more partners and the larger the number of financed ships, the lower the risk.[53] But there were also cases of financiers from the equestrian or senatorial elite commissioning several merchants to carry out the enterprise or delegating it to freedmen. In parallel to this, a number of families with transregional contacts in Alexandria and the big Red Sea ports probably specialized in moneylending and credit transfer.[54]

So long as interest rates for loans and credit remained relatively low—capped by law at 1 percent per month—and capital was readily available, as in the reign of Augustus, finding creditors seems to have posed few problems, despite the protracted interval between investment and return (a voyage from Puteoli or Ostia to India and back lasted ten months, on average). Creditors could insure themselves against total loss through shipwreck or piracy, or wealthy investors could get their emancipated middlemen to shoulder the risk. In addition, the fact that the 25 percent tariff on imported luxury goods (apart from pepper) did not choke the India trade—the rate corresponds to today's punitive tariffs—shows that there must always have been enough consumers who were willing and able to foot the bill.[55]

Ships Bound for India

Yet once interest rates gradually began rising under Tiberius, eventually reaching a critical level for investors and traders, and signs of a cash shortage became apparent (first evident in 30 CE, then again under Nero), merchants had to find new ways to maintain their profit margins. A common solution in antiquity, as in the modern age, was to increase the tonnage of each journey. In this respect, changes in commercial shipbuilding in the early imperial age formed an important precondition for the boom in the India trade. According to archaeological finds from the Red Sea ports of Myos Hormos and Berenice, at least some of the ships plying the Indian Ocean were built to the same design as ships deployed in the Mediterranean.[56] Whereas 60- to 80-tonne vessels were the rule in the Mediterranean (apart from grain ships), including in the Indian Ocean, Roman two-masters and perhaps even three-masters with a tonnage of up to 500 tonnes were not unknown in the Red Sea ports and as far afield as the Bay of Bengal, as graffiti and literary references attest. Their robust hulls and stable design were clearly superior to Arabian boats (*madarate*) and better equipped against winds and storms, which during the (southwest) monsoon could reach 7 to 10 on the Beaufort wind force scale. This reduced the risk of loss and allowed additional mercenaries and archers to be taken on board to defend against piracy.[57]

A further cost-cutting measure was the transition from shell to skeleton construction in ancient shipbuilding, which saved both material and time: a commercial ship of 300 tonnes cost around 400,000 sesterces in the Mediterranean, the minimum amount of wealth needed to qualify for the equestrian class. New vessels were thus cheaper than comparable units from the fifteenth and sixteenth centuries, and in any case worth less than the wares they transported across the Indian Ocean. If the number of middlemen could be reduced while still using the routes they controlled—as a Roman knight did on the Amber Route during Nero's reign[58]—then astronomical profits lay in wait.

The Persian Gulf and Arabian Trade Networks

This was easier said than done. Mediterranean merchants intruded on established networks of foreign traders who had far more experience and a wider range of contacts in the Indian Ocean. Freight in the Persian Gulf—still a hub of long-distance commerce between east and west—was almost completely dominated by Arabian traders and trading towns; there is no evidence of Roman merchants in the narrower sense in the ports of the Persian Gulf, although there were many men from the oasis town of Palmyra, which became part of the Roman Empire under Tiberius, at the latest. Their nobles organized, protected, and directed caravan trade, which moved from the land of the two rivers via the Syrian desert to Antioch (where tariffs were probably charged on goods arriving by the Palmyra route). In addition, Palmyrene merchants sailed in the mid-second century CE from the Mesopotamian kingdom of Characene through the Persian Gulf to the northwest coast of India and were active in Red Sea ports and Egyptian caravan routes; a Palmyrene was even satrap of the Characene king on Tylos (Bahrain).[59] They surely owed some of their commercial success to the fact that they were simultaneously perceived as imperial subjects—some Palmyrenes were Roman citizens—*and* as natives who could draw on networks built over many generations, extending from western India across the Persian Gulf, southern Arabia, and the Red Sea to the Mediterranean.[60] Their role as middlemen in the Syrian transit trade allowed them to take advantage of the Gulf route that provided an alternative to the longer overland route through the desert. Goods shipped up the Euphrates through the Syrian desert from the kingdom of Characene and its main harbour, Charax Spasinu, probably reached the Mediterranean coast in time for the Mediterranean spring sailing season. By contrast, those delivered via the Red Sea arrived in autumn because the monsoon detained them in India until November. The two routes thus complemented rather than competed with each other, providing traders with relatively secure earnings and Mediterranean consumers with a biannual supply of goods from abroad: spices, silk, aromatics, exotic animals, and Indian slaves.[61]

A second important actor involved in commodity flows from the east were the Arabian Nabataeans, allied with Rome since the first century BCE. With Leuke Kome, they controlled a port on the Red Sea that Nabataean captains had been supplying with Arabian aromatics and Indian products since long before the Romans arrived on the scene.[62] Rome expected them to combat Red Sea piracy and actively support their expeditions in Arabia. Thus, the Nabataean commander Syllaios participated with 1,000 warriors in the campaign of Aelius Gallus (see above, pp. 299–300). If Syllaios had ambitions to rule southern Arabia, as Strabo alleges,[63] then perhaps he hoped, like the Palmyrene satrap in Bahrain for the king of Characene, to function as Rome's representative in this strategically important region.

Even if this never eventuated and Augustus instead cultivated *amicitia* relations with native princes and potentates, the Nabataeans still profited by exploiting Roman military might, much like the Palmyrenes did in the Persian Gulf. According to a bilingual inscription from Sirwah (Yemen), during the reign of their king Haritat (= Aretas IV) in the first decade of the first century BCE, Nabataeans could make an offering to their own god in the temple of the chief Sabaean deity.[64] Such privileges normally point to an ongoing presence of traders or seafarers in foreign lands. If this is the case here, then the Nabataeans would have extended their trading contacts in the slipstream of Rome's annexation of Egypt and the emperor's financially motivated interest in protecting Red Sea shipping from the Sinai Peninsula and northern Arabia to the Persian Gulf, where Nabataean traders were likewise active, and southwest across the Red Sea to southern Arabia. The caravan routes from Arabia, the Red Sea, or the Persian Gulf converged in their capital, Petra, whence commodity streams were redirected to Mediterranean ports; several Nabataean nobles owned warehouses and docks in Puteoli and Ostia, and some even ventured into the Atlantic.[65]

Alexandria, Gateway to the East

Given the dominance of Arabian and Palmyrene traders in the Persian Gulf and on transregional caravan routes, it seems only logical that Egypt and its Red Sea ports became the crucial base of operations for Mediterranean traders wanting to do business in the Indian Ocean.

If, after the Eudoxus expedition, no more than twenty ships had sailed east from the Red Sea ports each year, now entire fleets departed for India, as Strabo writes.[66] Egypt acted as a pivot between the three great maritime trading areas: the Mediterranean, the Arabian Sea, and the Indian Ocean. Despite the rise to power of southern Arabian and Ethiopian kingdoms, it was less beset by military and external political crises than the Syrian-Mesopotamian area. The land of the Nile rose to become the most important exporter of grain in the Mediterranean, and the route between Alexandria and Ostia was the busiest trade route in the ancient world. At the same time, Alexandria formed a transit point and depot for Arabian aromatics and Indian spices as well as for Mediterranean wares travelling in the opposite direction. According to Dio Chrysostom, 'Alexandria is situated, as it were, at the crossroads of the whole world, and it serves the world as a market serves a single city. It connects the most remote nations, and its market brings all kinds of people together in one place'.[67]

At the top of the wish list of Indian princes and social elites stood red corals, oil, textiles (linen), saffron, and high-quality glassware, whereas wine was evidently not intended for the Indians themselves but primarily for Mediterranean expatriate traders. Egypt exported its own handicrafts made from glass, copper, tin, gold and silverplate, coral, and textiles; it also supplied the arid regions of southern Arabia with wine, horses, mules, and grain. Eastern goods (incense, myrrh, and textiles, above all silk) were processed there before being re-exported to the west.[68] Having forfeited its status as royal seat of the Ptolemies, Alexandria could thus maintain and even expand its function as the most important commercial metropolis in the east. With around half a million inhabitants, Alexandria was one of the biggest cities in the world during the imperial era.

Even less well-off traders could still do good business in partnership with a motley crew of merchants: Greeks, Syrians, Jews, Arabians, and Indians as well as men from east and west Africa. Conversely, Alexandrians could be found in almost all the Mediterranean ports, including Ostia.[69] Merchant families from Puteoli like the Peticii or the Annii had relatives or freedmen in Alexandria or the mercantile centres on the Nile to see to their affairs on the ground.[70] In the case of the Peticii, the oldest traceable generation was involved in the grain trade, the next in wine, until the last also developed a sideline in eastern wares. This is presumably why, even in the Early Empire, the major Puteolian trading houses combined their activities in grain transport with the export of (Campanian) wine and the import of goods from the east. To finance their ventures and spread the risks, they collaborated with globally connected banking families and investors based in Puteoli or other trade centres.[71]

The Red Sea *Periplus*

The increased interest of Italian traders in trade with Far Eastern products does not mean that they themselves boarded their ships to set sail for the Indian Ocean. The mariners mentioned in the sources generally have Greek names; those who braved the passage to India were merchants residing in Syria or Alexandria. Italian traders rarely transported ships of their own to the Red Sea. Boatbuilding on the Red Sea was expensive and time-consuming owing to the timber shortage in Egypt. Materials and dismantled ships had to be transported to the Red Sea ports.[72] Only a politically well-connected general like Aelius Gallus had the wherewithal to build 80 warships and 130 transport vessels in Clymsa.[73] When Italian- or Egypt-based businessmen had ships in the Red Sea, numbers were far more modest; indeed, ownership of a ship was sometimes shared.[74] Larger units were frequently chartered at Red Sea ports, including from Indian shipowners who still dominated the trade with the pepper coast of Malabar at the start of the first century; or Greek and Alexandrian captains were hired who were familiar with the waters of the Red Sea and had already completed voyages to India with Egyptian, Indian, or Greek sailors.[75]

One of them left behind an account of all the routes, ports, and commodities shipped across the Indian Ocean. The author of this 'Periplus of the Erythraean Sea' (*Periplus Maris Erythraei*), written in the mid-first century CE, was probably a merchant or 'shipmaster' based in Egypt—he used Egyptian terms for months alongside the Roman calendar—with a wealth of experience in western India and east Africa. His notes may have served as a kind of navigation manual or guide for traders or their agents who, like those of the Peticii or Annii, were new to the India trade and principally dealt in luxury goods.[76] It is the only surviving work by an ancient trader, as befits a period when specialized sailing and navigation manuals (*grammata kybernetika, libri navales*) were being produced in the Mediterranean and elsewhere (clearly intended for Roman grain dealers and military commanders).[77] The *periplus* painstakingly lists products and describes what can be bought where and in which quantities, how to get to ports and markets, as well as the winds and currents—both nautical and political—that traders would have to navigate. Much as the *military* interest of Roman generals in the west led to a consequential reduction of ethnographic data to what was pragmatically indispensable, so too the growing interest of Roman-Mediterranean *traders* necessitated, in the case of the *periplus*, the ruthless excision of all ethnographic excurses, curiosities, and historical background. Everything boiled down to the type of information a shipmaster needed to know. Where the *periplus* of Agatharchides from the second century BCE still offered digressive and partly anecdotal stories about elephant hunts and native customs, the new *periplus* generally makes do with brief entries on tidal conditions in foreign ports and the political constitution of the power that controls the coast and hinterland. References to pirates and cannibals are included to alert sailors, not to pander to a taste for sensationalism.

Once a trader in Alexandria had concluded his preparations, he would usually sail up the Nile to Koptos (Qift), the ancient trading hub and customs station on the middle Nile.[78] Here wares were unloaded to be sent on camelback under military escort along the shortest route (six to seven days' journey) to the Red Sea port of Myos Hormos (Queseir al-Quadim?) or Berenice, located 300 km farther to the south. Goods would travel the same route in the opposite direction. The two ports emerged in the Early Empire as the most important on the African Red Sea coast, attracting most of the Indian transit trade. Here commercial links extending from Gaul to the South China Sea (China, Vietnam, Java) converged, and here agents of merchant families from Puteoli negotiated with tax collectors and officials for more favourable customs and harbour fees.[79] In both ports, a trader could directly purchase Indian wares or book passage and stowage to pursue commercial opportunities in the east.[80] Wealthier merchants chartered and crewed entire ships, including mercenaries for guarding against piracy. There were also fabulously rich entrepreneurs living in Alexandria—some of them women like Aelia Isidora and Aelia Olympias (late second century CE)—who operated their own commercial fleets in the Indian Ocean, perhaps in convoy, invested capital in import businesses, and engaged in moneylending. This network of millionaires, moderately well-off merchants, and small traders kept the India trade afloat and held out the prospect of considerable returns to anyone willing and able to shoulder the risk.[81]

Somalia and Arabia

The *periplus* recommended lifting anchor in September to avoid missing the autumn incense harvest. It took thirty days to travel to the incense groves of southern Arabia. The most important port was M(o)uza on the east coast of the Red Sea. Farther west followed the ports of Ocelis and Aden, controlled by King Charibael of Saba and Himyar, which probably first emerged as genuine trading posts in the second century CE. In Arabia, too, Mediterranean traders plugged into well-organized trade networks protected by native rulers. In the first century, Arabian Himyarites exercised limited sovereignty over nearby waters and had bases on the Somalian coast (Azania).[82] The island of Socotra, located beyond the mouth of the Red Sea, was ruled by a 'king of the incense land'.

The merchants and mariners of southern Arabia had learned early on to use the monsoon (a word of Arabic origin). In their ports, textiles, saffron, metalwork, wine, grain, rice, honey, and sesame oil could be traded for incense and myrrh as well as goods from other regions.[83] Many products, including aloes, incense, and high-grade ('Troglodyte') myrrh, were shipped to Arabian ports by Arabian or Somali boats. Merchants from the Roman Empire itself sailed only rarely to the southernmost trading station of Rhapta, situated north of Zanzibar, to procure ivory, tortoise shell, rhinoceros horn, cinnamon, and cassia. The latter was most likely sent from southeast Asia across the Indian Ocean at the latitude of the Maldive or Chagos Islands to Madagascar (which was settled from Indonesia) and thence to the coasts of Somalia and Tanzania.[84]

India!

According to Pliny, who knew several routes not described in the *periplus*, it was possible to depart for the south Indian coast from Ocelis in southern Arabia (at the entrance to the Red Sea) and sail back in December with the onset of the northeast monsoon.[85] Those wanting to steer a direct course from the Red Sea ports to the west coast of India, bypassing the coastal route, had to set sail in July. Having left the Red Sea, it took them around twenty days to reach their destination: Barbarikon and Barygaza (Bharuch/Broach at the mouth of the Narmada in Gujarat province) or Muziris and Nelcynda in the subcontinent's south.[86] 'Here lies the thriving town of Muziris'— in the words of a Tamil poet—'where the beautiful great ships of the *yavanas* [people from the west] make landfall and bring gold, spraying the white foam on the waters of the Periyar, before returning laden with pepper. Here the music of the pounding surf never ceases. And the great king shows his visitors the treasures of the lakes and the mountains'.[87] Slaves of both sexes could be sold in the northern ports, along with glass, gold, silver vessels, coral, patterned linen, incense loaded in one of the southern Arabian ports, and sometimes Red Sea topaz.[88] Bdellium and spikenard, lapis lazuli and turquoise from Afghanistan, ivory, cotton cloth, and silk were all purchased in return, yet by far the most important imports were black pepper 'beloved of foreigners'[89] (from the southwest) and long pepper (from southeast India).

In India, too, Mediterranean merchants had to adapt to an established system of maritime trade. Our customary fixation on the Graeco-Roman sources easily overlooks the fact that Indian traders had been making sea voyages as far as the Red Sea since at least the time of the Mauryans (332–184 BCE). Long-distance maritime trade is mentioned in India's oldest literary source, the Rig Veda (c. 1500–1200 BCE). Merchants who embarked on long journeys by land and sea in search of profit formed a respectable social class protected by the kings.[90] This tradition continued into the Hellenistic period. Indian traders lived on Socotra and in Alexandria long before the first Roman had set foot on their shores.[91] Centuries before western merchants appeared on the scene, Buddhist (and Jainist) monks and pilgrims had promoted urbanization on the subcontinent, expanded trade networks, and introduced the Mauryan coinage system to coastal areas. Like the Ptolemies and Mauryans, many Indian princes exercised monopoly control over certain goods; the prince of Chera sold ivory from royal elephant parks at Muziris. They also levied taxes for the security they could offer captains from piracy and fraud, building warehouses and supporting local guilds with the proceeds.[92]

While rulers in the north were interested in trading with the west but did not allow Roman and Greek merchants to settle permanently, preferring to deal with Arabian mariners from the Persian Gulf, Mediterranean traders met with more favourable conditions in the south. Here the commercial infrastructure was less developed, and many coastal rajas thought they could profit from western know-how. Quarters set aside for Graeco-Roman merchants (*yavanas* = Ionians) arose in Barygaza and Muziris.[93] They resembled the foreign enclaves conceded by nineteenth-century rajas. According to Tamil sources, *yavanas* worked as technicians and engineers, palace gardeners, and mercenaries at courts in Madurai, Pumuhat, or Kaveripoompattinam. In addition, they served as intermediaries between their compatriots and Indian potentates and organized the transport of goods back to Alexandria.[94] Some of the western products unearthed in Indian coastal cities—primarily glass, wine (amphorae), and Italian and southern Gallic pottery (*terra sigillata*)—may well have been used by the traders domiciled there, not just sold on to local rulers or re-exported to the Far East (China, the Pacific).[95] *Yavanas* maintained their accustomed lifestyle, which did not prevent them from worshipping Buddha and donating to the Buddhist monasteries whose infrastructure they profited from. Their presence promoted local manufactories for cotton goods and glass beads.[96] The 'foreigners' quarters' evolved into vibrant centres for cultural and technological exchange. And once again, the push into the unknown was driven not by soldiers and generals but by highly mobile, adaptable, and multilingual merchants.

THE ISLAND OF JEWELS

TAPROBANE AND THE EURASIAN TRADE NETWORK

New Challenges

Romans trading in the east benefited from tried-and-tested techniques for transporting goods and preserving foodstuffs. Wine amphorae of Campanian origin have been found in India and Red Sea ports in far greater quantities than those for oil and garum. Mediterranean staples fetched a lower price than Indian export goods, however, for the simple reason that demand for eastern wares in the Roman Empire far outstripped that for western wares in India.[97] When merchants sailing to the Indian west coast brought with them heavily tariffed Mediterranean wine, they therefore had to stump up enough coinage to fill their holds with pepper and other products for the return voyage.[98] Silver coins dominated until the end of Tiberius' reign, the high value of their metal contrasting with India's fluctuating, locally differentiated currency; not by chance, hoards of around 6,000 *denarii* bearing the stamp of Augustus and Tiberius have been found in west India.[99] Yet gold coins then grew in importance; they were worth more in India than in the Roman Empire. Following Nero's reduction of the silver content in the *denarius*, the import of coins shifted to pre-Neronian *aurei* (gold), which merchants collected and set aside for the India trade.[100] A Tamil poem about the *yavanas* confirms: 'They arrive with gold and leave with pepper'.[101] With 800,000 sesterces in gold, they could buy Indian goods that would sell for around eight million in the Mediterranean. In a trade system still mostly conducted by barter, coins were 'commodities' that could be exchanged for Indian products.[102]

Gold coins significantly increased investment costs at a time when, parallel to the relative debasement of the coinage, lending rates were rising in the Roman Empire. Two avenues for addressing these challenges were available to captains and their partners: either they sought out powerful patrons to help them negotiate special terms for paying customs duties and fees, or they entered state service and combined tax farming with their private mercantile initiatives. Such a combination was not unusual; even in the Republic, tax collectors had been involved in moneylending and the slave trade. Under Augustus, too, licences to charge Egyptian road tolls and port fees were auctioned off to private operators who entrusted their freedmen with the particulars. Unsurprisingly, they adopted a relatively flexible approach when setting customs duties (which were not fixed by the state, besides a few 'commodities' such as slaves), profitably juggling their own affairs with their tax-collecting and toll-levying activities. Over the course of the imperial period, this led to excesses that increasingly made them the subject of legal and bureaucratic oversight, until they were finally forced to relinquish this lucrative sideline. Until the mid-first century CE, however, this was not yet the case for the India trade, and the combination of duty collection and private business provided enterprising freedmen with an ideal basis for supplementing their income.

The Island of Jewels

Pliny tells the story of one of these freedmen. During the reign of Claudius (41–54 CE), he was commissioned by Annius Plocamus, apparently a Greek residing in Alexandria who had acquired Roman citizenship through the good offices of the Annii, to collect the 'Red Sea tax' (*vectigal*)—presumably the *portorium* and/or the 25 percent tariff on imported goods.[103] While sailing to the southern Arabian coast, he was blown off-course by fierce northern winds and washed up fifteen days later at the port of Hippuros on Taprobane (Sri Lanka). There he enjoyed the king's hospitality for six months, learned the local language, and answered questions about his homeland. His host was especially impressed by the freedman's *denarii*, evidently the proceeds of his tax collecting. Despite having been issued by different rulers, these were all equal in weight. The king thereupon sought friendship with the Romans and sent an embassy to the Tiber.[104]

Some parts of this story recall typical sailors' yarns: adverse winds have always intervened to turn a regular voyage into an adventure. In a similar way—albeit in the opposite direction—an Indian had drifted over to Egypt before the Eudoxus expedition (see above, p. 252); like the freedman, he learned a foreign language (Greek) and allowed the Ptolemies to establish direct contact with his homeland. The currents and winds east of Aden were indeed treacherous. However, western captains avoided sailing to Sri Lanka primarily because it was too time-consuming and the narrow straits between southern India and northern Sri Lanka were too difficult for their big ships to navigate. The colony of western traders in Arikamedu on the Indian east coast was evidently only frequented by smaller Indian boats (*sangara*) or reached via the overland route.[105] The freedman's customs ship was smaller than the large transport vessels, however. He may even have commandeered an Indian boat. Traditional Indian outriggers were not suited for the monsoon, but we know that in the Indian Ocean (and farther east) there was a brisk traffic between Indian and Mediterranean shipbuilding materials and techniques. In first-century India, ships with up to three masts and a 75-tonne load could be built and repaired according to the traditional Mediterranean pegged mortise-and-tenon technique, while

Indian teak could be used alongside cedarwood from Lebanon to ensure that they could be deployed even during the monsoon.[106]

The freedman's six-month stay in Taprobane suggests that he took advantage of the monsoon winds. This is precisely how long other traders tarried in India if they planned to return to the Red Sea in winter. Not by chance, he landed at Hippuros ('Horse Mountain'), a port in the island's northwest. The area is probably identical with the Tamil Kudiramalai (also meaning 'Horse Mountain': Sindu Kanda in Old Sinhalese) in the 'Iogana' area, a name that points to the regular presence of Greeks and 'westerners' (*yavana*).[107]

In fact, the names of Plocamus and his *libertus* (Lysias) are also found on a graffito near the well-travelled caravan route of Koptos.[108] The evidence dates from 6 CE and is thus around forty years older than the voyage mentioned by Pliny and placed in the reign of Claudius; yet we may be dealing here with two generations of the same family.[109] It was not unusual for successive members of a family to be involved in the Orient trade over half a century. Alternatively, Annius Plocamus may have initially engaged in long-distance trade and acquired his tax-farming contract decades later. At any rate, the freedmen of the Annii clearly combined tax collecting in the Red Sea, which probably extended to the coast of southern Arabia, with trade missions. Over time, they ventured ever farther in search of pearls, pepper, and ivory. Former Indian slaves who knew their way around their native waters may have been among them.[110]

What made Sri Lanka attractive enough for a freedman to brave the difficult sea route there, spend such a long time on the island, and even establish contact with native royalty? He had to learn the local language, which shows that the island had previously been excluded from Roman trade with the Orient. Indian merchants had deliberately supplied false information about Taprobane's size and location.[111] In Taprobane, not only could the same goods be bought as in India—pepper, pearls, cinnamon, honey, textiles, ivory, tortoiseshell, tigers, and elephants—but there was also said to be gold; the rumour alone acted like a magnet.[112] Taprobane was even better known for its pearls; Buddhist sources characterized it as the 'island of pearls'. Chinese pilgrims and Christian merchants referred to a fiery red gemstone. It was perhaps the same one that Marco Polo mentions as having belonged to the Sri Lankan king and been coveted by Kublai Khan. Sri Lanka's major port lay to the west of the famous pearl banks of the Gulf of

Mannar. To this day, the pearl banks extend over 80 km from Adam's Bridge to Puttalam.[113]

Previously, Indian middlemen had dominated the export of Sri Lankan goods; they may have favoured the southern port of Godavaya.[114] If they could be bypassed, western traders stood to boost their profits in a way that more than made up for the rising costs of loans and credit. And there was yet another advantage: the Sri Lankan king was so amazed at the quality of the freedman's *denarii* because he had never encountered them before. If we accept the basic authenticity of Pliny's tale, then this detail suggests that Roman coins were worth more on Taprobane than in India, where the southern Indian princes were used to the *denarius* and had already amassed currency reserves. The freedman could thus trade in greater quantities on the island than on the mainland.

The Secret of the *Rachias*

Roman coins were not the only product with which a Roman trader could profiteer on Sri Lanka. Red corals were at least as prized. Across the entire Indian Ocean region and beyond, they were valued as highly as eastern pearls in the Mediterranean.[115] We do not know whether the freedman had corals with him on board. Yet the very certainty that he came from the Mediterranean and traded with Mediterranean wares would have been enough for the Sri Lankan king. He sensed an opportunity to break free from Indian intermediaries and source coral directly from the west. According to a commentary to a fifth-century Sri Lankan chronicle (*Mahāvaṃsa*),[116] King Bhatikabhaya (35/8–63/6 CE) once sent an embassy to 'Romanukharattha' (the Rhomanukha Empire) to procure large amounts of red coral for his temple-building projects. 'Romanukha' is most likely an expanded form of 'Romanus'; 'Romanukharattha' would therefore designate the Roman Empire. The reign of this king overlaps with that of the emperor Claudius. All the evidence suggests that he was the king who extended his hospitality to the *libertus* and who so admired the Romans.[117]

Both sources mention an embassy that the king sent to Rome. Like other regional powers, he probably aimed to conclude an *amicitia*. Official contacts with the emperor and political stabilization of trade held out the prospect of more *denarii*, as well as corals, exquisite textiles for gift-giving, and gold and silver plate—all much desired in the Orient. Other embassies dispatched to the Roman court by Indian and Arabian princes pursued similar goals.[118] Perhaps the king of Taprobane even hoped to tap into the lucrative Arabian and Red Sea trade network at the expense of his Indian rivals, just as Sri Lankan rulers would do with the Venetians a millennium later. In the aftermath of the downfall of the Mauryan Empire, at any rate, the Sri Lankans probably succeeded in moving pearl production from the subcontinent to their island.[119]

The king's efforts should be seen against this background. The political acceptance of minor princes in the Indian Ocean, including Taprobane, derived from their trade and customs revenue as well as their display of foreign luxuries. To that extent, their support of domestic traders and artisan guilds had not just a fiscal but also a political objective. Given the ongoing rivalry among multiple small powers, friendship with the Roman emperor may also have conferred a competitive advantage. The title given the embassy leader, *rachias*, denotes a military rank that was ordinarily bestowed on ambassadors-in-chief, possibly equivalent to supreme commander of the armed forces.[120] In return, the king may have offered the Romans special concessions, such as access to domestic timber for boatbuilding (a rarity in the Indian Ocean) and protection from pirates.[121]

Yet the embassy leader revealed something else to his hosts, something far more remarkable: during a trip to the north (beyond the *Hemodi*, probably the Himalayas), his father had met with 'Seres'. They were of above-average height and had red or blond hair, blue eyes, and a harsh voice, and they spoke an unintelligible language.[122] The Greeks had been known as 'Seres' since the second century CE. Their name probably derives from the Chinese *sī*, meaning silk. The 'Seres' were accordingly 'silk people', yet clearly these were not Chinese *producers* of silk but rather people who *traded* it.[123] Reports of a blue-eyed, blond-haired people had been dismissed as ethnographic fantasy until they were confirmed by spectacular finds of Europoid mummies in the Tarim basin, the central corridor connecting China with northern Iran. A trade route led from the western end of the Tarim basin through Bactria to the Indian ports. India hence also serviced the Far East and acted as a way station for goods funnelled from one end of Eurasia to the other.[124]

The Silk People

Rachias' tale of the 'silk people' makes sense only against this background. Silk fabrics were already known to the Celts and Greeks, and the Romans had seen them among the Parthians. Silk garments were worn by the fashionable elite in the Early Empire (see above, p. 299).[125] Increased Roman trade with the east coincided with a boom in silk production in the Han Empire (206 BCE–220 CE). Silk travelled west along multiple pathways: via Bactria and northern Mesopotamia and the Syrian desert (Palmyra), via Patna on the northwest coast of India to Barbarikon, or via Sialkot, Mathua, and Ujjain to Barygaza and Muziris (southwest coast). Roman goods were transported by the same routes to central Asia.

A third route ran along the Ganges via Palimbothra (Pataliputra) to Tamralipta (Tamluk) on the Bengal coast. From here, products were conveyed by land or sea to the ports of the Malabar coast for sale to the Empire.[126] The Sri Lankans had contacts in Patna; the writer of the *periplus* knew the Bay of Bengal as an important market for Chinese silk and cinnamon leaves, which may have been brought there by the Seres and local middlemen.[127] The father of the Sri Lankan ambassador-in-chief, likewise a *rachias*, may thus have met the 'silk people' on an official mission in Patna or Bengal, with Buddhist monasteries possibly acting as intermediaries.[128]

The *rachias* knew that silk was an expensive luxury in the west owing to the long freight routes and complicated supply chain. The prospect of a direct maritime route to China must therefore have seemed as enticing as the route to the Indian and Arabian coasts. Taprobane played a key role here. The island formed a natural stopover for mariners on the long voyage to southeast Asia. The combination of the northeast monsoon with corresponding currents in the eastern Indian Ocean brought ships more reliably to the coasts of Malaysia than to the Bay of Bengal (although this was also easily reached from the island).[129] In short, the *rachias* sought to persuade the Romans that, with Taprobane as an ally, they stood the best chance of finding a direct sea route to the land of silk. Perhaps he could even point to his contacts at the Chinese imperial court, if the information provided in the Chinese chronicle Hanshu about a journey of the emperor's agents in the Indian Ocean pertains to the island. Red corals were as coveted at the Chinese court as they were at the court of Taprobane.[130]

Taprobane had links with other worlds. The main port of Manthai was a production centre for glass beads distributed as far as the Pacific. Perhaps the Sri Lankans reminded the Romans that in addition to silk, the east produced many medicinal plants and aromatics prized in Rome, not least due to the overexploitation of silphium on Cyrenaica.[131] Cinnamon was assumed by Greeks and Romans to originate in Somalia, yet its real homeland was southern China and southeast Asia. In all likelihood, it was brought west in part by 'Austronesian' boats sailing directly to Madagascar and Azania, in part via India and Sri Lanka, where it was called *kurundu*.[132] Malaysia supplied India, China, and the west with scented woods such as costus, used as an antidote and perfume (probably the Malay *putchuk*, Chinese *mù xiāng*, India/Buddhist *ku-so-t'o*), and tarum or aloeswood (Chinese *chén xiāng*, *kilam*, or *bac*), said by Pliny to come from the border of the cassia and cinnamon district; further, the ginger plant amomum, also found in Thailand, Cambodia, Laos, and Java, and still used in China today for medicinal purposes.[133] From China came the spices galangal, ginger (an ingredient of mithridate), and camphor; an aromatic substance made from cassia (*gùi zhī* in Chinese) had by the third century BCE become so prominent that the ruler of the north named entire provinces after it: Guizhou, Guangdong, Guangxi. Like benzoin and sandalwood from India and Indonesia, ginger was traded via Sri Lanka. Even pepper—one could learn in Sri Lanka—grew east of India on the Malay Peninsula.[134]

'CORALS AND SILK'

CHINA, ROME, AND THE EURASIAN WORLD

To Cattigara! Alexandros Sails for the China Sea

However great the temptation may have been, it took time for a seafarer to seize the opportunity to explore 'India beyond the Ganges' (our southeast Asia). The author of the *Periplus Maris Erythraei* was familiar with the eastern Indian Ocean as far as Malacca and knew of an overland trade route that led from the Bay of Bengal to China (Thin, derived from the first Qin dynasty).[135] Yet he had nothing to say about a direct link along the Malaysian coast (the peninsula of Chryse). The geographer Ptolemy (second century CE) was the first to break the secret. He was already better informed about India's east coast than about its west coast. His informant for the area beyond the Strait of Malacca was a captain named Alexandros.[136]

Alexandros was probably following a trail blazed by Indian mariners who had ventured into south Asian waters after the fall of the Mauryan Empire in search of the 'Golden Isles'.[137] In the late first century CE, his ship sailed from the Bay of Bengal along the Burmese coast before possibly threading the narrow Strait of Malacca—not without its dangers owing to the threat of piracy and wild weather. In this case, the 'Golden Chersonese' would be identical with the Malay Peninsula. Alternatively, he may have passed through the Sunda Strait south of Java, which Ptolemy seems to have known as Jabadiu.[138] From there, southern summer winds and favourable currents drove the ship in twenty days northeast to a harbour town called Zabae, perhaps Singapore or Kampot on the Gulf of Thailand. Alexandros sailed on for a few days southeast towards Cattigara, the easternmost point ever reached by a Mediterranean seafarer. Martianus, the author of a *periplus* on the outer sea, calls the town 'a place inhabited by the Sinae [Thinae = China?] and the starting point of the unknown earth'.[139]

Where exactly Cattigara was located has been the subject of much debate. Some identify it with Singapore, others favour Hanoi, while still others argue for Guangzhou or another Chinese port near modern Haiphong (Vietnam) in the Gulf of Tonkin or in Hangzhou Bay on the southern arm of the Yangtze River, from where the Grand Canal or an overland route wound its way through the cassia and cinnamon groves to the centre of the Han Empire and its twin imperial residences, Chang'an and Luoyang.[140] What cannot be disputed is that Alexandros had found a link to maritime trade in the China Sea and access to the products of east Asia—a feat of navigation no less remarkable than the sixteenth-century voyages of the Portuguese.

An 'Embassy' from the King An Dun

As so often in the history of ancient voyages, however, Alexandros' adventure seems to have borne no *immediate* fruit, even if we cannot rule out the possibility that other traders and captains sailed in his wake. Chinese sources are more direct: according to a credible chronicle from the early Han period (Hou Hanshu), an embassy from the king An Dun of Daqin sailed sixty years later 'from the Annamese border' (probably Tonkin) via the Chinese outpost in Vietnam to the Han emperor's court. Daqin most likely designates the Roman Empire, and An Dun may refer to the emperor Marcus Aurelius.[141] Yet there are justified doubts about whether this was an official embassy. Western sources are silent on this score, and what would have been its purpose? The Roman administration generally maintained diplomatic contacts only with powers neighbouring its provinces. In the absence of military or political motives, relations farther abroad were left to traders and merchants.

Tellingly, the 'envoys'—according to the chronicle—brought with them gifts of ivory, rhinoceros horn, and tortoise shell. These products were not classic Roman exports but came from the Indian Ocean. The chronicler suspects that the 'envoys' withheld more valuable gifts such as precious gemstones.[142] Gemstones and jewels from India and Sri Lanka were processed in the Mediterranean before being reexported east. These were evidently Syrian or Greek traders who passed themselves off as ambassadors in hopes of a better reception at court. They probably claimed that the Parthians had prevented them taking the overland routes; the Chinese were unaware that the Parthians only intercepted envoys, not traders from the Roman Empire. This ruse was intended to conceal the traders' true motive: to access Chinese silk and spices at the source, bypassing Indian and Indonesian intermediaries.[143]

We do not know how convincing they were or whether other mariners came after them. In the third century, Chinese sources report merchants from the Roman Empire travelling to Indochina (Fu-nan = Cambodia), Jih-nan (Annan), Chiao-chih (Tonkin), and eastern China. One chronicle mentions a certain Qin Lun (Leon?), who landed in Tonkin in 226 CE and was brought to the imperial court at Nanjing.[144] Yet Indian and Arabian seafarers continued to dominate long-distance trade in the Indian Ocean (including Sri Lanka), and most embassies that reached the Chinese capital arrived by sea from India and Sri Lanka.[145] The Chinese may also have been aware that Malaysian and Indonesian sailors (on boats with double outriggers) transported cinnamon and benzoin (*cancanum*) on a more southerly direct route to Madagascar and from there to Rhapta on the Somali coast (see above, p. 312).[146]

The 'Silk Roads'

Although Alexandros had thus pioneered the maritime route to the China Sea, he and other western merchants remained outsiders in commerce east of the Indies. The same holds true of the Chinese mariners. They barely ventured beyond Tonkin.[147] Chinese rulers turned their attention to the sea from early on, but mainly towards Japan and Korea. According to the first

Chinese chronicle, during the Qin period (late third century BCE), a man from Qi was sent to the eastern islands to gather magical herbs, probably a kind of immortality drug for the emperor—a motif recalling Gilgamesh's journey to the island of the immortal Utnapishtim (see above, pp. 46–47). Perhaps the 'eastern isles' should be identified with Japan, from which a genuine interest in Japanese natural products may be inferred. Yet the succeeding Han rulers—much like their counterparts in Rome—were more interested in extending their *political* influence south than in mercantile activity. To that end, entire war fleets were constructed in the second and first century BCE, shipbuilding was intensified, and nautical and astronomical information was collected and enhanced. In the context of these efforts, intelligence about India (Huangzhi?) and the Indian Ocean reached the imperial court, yet it barely registered against the power politics of the South China Sea. No impulses for Chinese trade missions in the Indian Ocean emerged, especially given the daunting natural obstacles: shoals and adverse currents made a voyage around the Malay Peninsula especially perilous, and if a Chinese merchant in the first centuries CE had sailed into the Gulf of Siam (Thailand), he would have switched to an Arabian or Indian sailboat before rounding the Malay Peninsula. From a Chinese perspective, land routes were less risky and cost-intensive; one such route probably led over the Malay Peninsula, linking the Gulf of Tonkin with the Andaman Sea.

The preference for overland routes was in keeping with the general political priorities of the Han emperors. For all that they may occasionally have deployed formidable war fleets in the South China Sea to expand their sphere of influence, coastal areas remained 'politically and economically secondary'. They were chiefly interested in the Asian mainland. For this was where the greatest danger to the Empire lay. Even before Alexandros' voyage, a network of overland routes connected China and the west. These are generally summed up under the heading 'the Silk Road', a misleading term known neither to the Chinese nor to the Romans. There was never a single 'road' but rather a cat's cradle of self-organizing routes that, in addition to connecting the east and west of the Eurasian continent, extended to southern Siberia as well as the great maritime routes of the Indian Ocean in the south. Although important, silk was far from the only product traded—others included cinnamon, medicinal plants, pottery, textiles, glass, gemstones, metals, and cattle—and the trade was certainly not unidirectional. At the major junctions such as Bactria and the edges of the Tarim basin, high-worth local products, above all textiles, were fed into the network; technologies, ideas, and beliefs circulated alongside goods.[148]

People used the major rivers where possible: the Yangtze in the east, the Oxus in the west, the Indus and Euphrates in the southeast. They skirted the central Asian deserts on mountainside paths to the north and south, where meltwater and oases allowed for the planting of crops. The oldest overland route ran from the Yellow River estuary past the Altai to the southern foothills of the Urals and from there north of the Caspian Sea along the Tanais (Don) to the Black Sea. Aristeas and Herodotus were dimly aware of it (see above, pp. 87-91). Gold, silk, and sable furs were irregularly conveyed along this route as early as the archaic period. Silk fabrics were worn at the Persian court and reached Athens in the fifth century. They arrived in Celtic territory a century earlier, possibly brought there by Scythian dealers or via Massalia and the Belfort Gap. Silk exports have been definitively established in the permafrost graves of the eastern Altai from the fourth or third century BCE and in Scythian kurgans in the Crimea and on the middle Volga.[149] The pathways survived and proliferated into the Late Republic; campaigning in the Caucasus during the final war against Mithridates VI, Pompey gathered information about a Caspian trade route to India, much as Alexander and the Hellenistic expeditionary leaders had done before him.[150]

The Tarim basin between the Tian Shan Mountains and the foothills of the Tibetan Plateau formed a second junction for Eurasian transit. It borders the Pamir in the west and thus extends almost to the Karakoram Mountains explored by Alexander. Moreover, there were passes over the Hindu Kush to northern India, while in the east, the route led through northern China. Extremely challenging to traverse, the Tarim basin connected diverse vegetation zones and ways of life at its edges: to the west and east, the urbanized agrarian spaces of Mesopotamia and Bactria, the north Indus region, and the Yellow River; to the north, the steppes from the Mongolian Plateau along the Altai to the Hungarian Plain, an almost uninterrupted ecological zone that permitted pasturage and horse breeding in its western reaches; and finally, the forested taiga to the north.

Each of these three zones yielded products and resources that were desired—and sometimes viewed as necessities—by inhabitants of the other two: thus, alongside pelts, the hunters of the taiga supplied nomads with amber and gold, which were worked by the nomads (with the help of itinerant artisans) and traded for natural products with the agricultural societies of the south.[151] It was this exchange of goods among the three biomes that caused regional contact zones to grow and solidify into transregional transfer spaces. As a rule, this gave agricultural societies the greatest opportunity to flourish and expand. Horse-riders responded to the resulting wealth imbalance with seasonal plundering, then with large-scale raiding. From the seventh century BCE, the people of Asia Minor and northern Mesopotamia were not the only ones to suffer the depredations of Asiatic nomadic bands ('Massagetae', see above, pp. 87–88). In the fifth century, the same threat hovered over the seven princedoms that battled for supremacy in the Yellow River and Yangtze regions during the 'Warring States period' (475–221 BCE).

The Expeditions of Zhang Qian

The most powerful of these nomadic tribes—labelled Xiongnu by the Chinese—descended from the Mongolian grass steppes onto the northern kingdoms of Qin, Zhao, and Yan. Hastily built ramparts could only prevent horsemen from invading farmlands without warning. To take the fight to the nomads, in the fourth century Chinese princes began replacing their chariot armies with infantry and cavalry divisions. From the end of the third century, the Xiongnu—probably in reaction to the expansion of the Qin and the establishment of the Han Empire—joined forces in a grand federation and redoubled their attacks on the territories they had lost, primarily in the Ordos region. When they inflicted a devastating defeat on the founder of the Han dynasty in 200 BCE, the Chinese reacted by expanding their defensive fortifications in the north, keeping a few openings for trade. They also sought to stave off the nomads through peace treaties; annual gifts in the form of gold, silk, rice, and grain; and arranged marriages with their leaders (policy of 'harmony and kinship').[152]

At the same time, they continued building up their cavalry—a process that the Romans would repeat three centuries later in response to Sarmatian and Hunnic mounted forces. This was of vital significance for the development of the silk roads. The Chinese had only limited horse-breeding experience and were unprepared to convert farmland into pasturage, meaning that the demand for horses could not be met domestically. The need to purchase or import warhorses was thus a constant in Chinese foreign policy from the Han dynasty, at the latest.[153] One solution lay in the Far West, where 'blood-sweating' steeds of the Ferghana (Uzbekistan on the Syr Darya) could help replenish their stock. From a Chinese perspective, the agriculturally advanced Ferghana was the most remote of the 'western lands' grouped around the Tarim basin. Yet these were largely controlled by the Xiongnu. The sedentary population provided the nomads with the resource base they had lost elsewhere through Han expansion. From the last third of the second century, at the latest, Emperor Wu (141–87 BCE) and his advisers recognized that the Xiongnu could only be fended off if they were denied access to these resources, thereby 'cutting off their right arm'.[154]

It was equally clear, however, that the Chinese needed foreign allies if they were to stand a chance of expanding west and defending their northern borders; the costs were otherwise simply too high. One obvious partner was an Indo-European nomadic tribe they called the Yuezhi, who lived in the grasslands north of the Tian Shan and supplied Chinese rulers with both jade and horses (in exchange for silk). When the imperial court learned that the Xiongnu had also defeated the Yuezhi, the time seemed ripe for a miliary alliance that went beyond the horse trade. In 140–138 BCE, Emperor Wu commissioned a senior officer named Zhang Qian to find the Yuezhi.

After a true odyssey, ten years' captivity among the Xiongnu, and a host of further tribulations, he finally reached his destination, albeit not where he had expected to find it. Following their defeat at the hands of the Xiongnu, the Yuezhi had fled over the northern foothills of the Tian Shan to the region south of the Aral Sea and then settled south of the Amur River, known to the Greeks as the Oxus. When Zhang reached the Yuezhi across the Ferghana (Da-yuan) in Bactria (Daxia), he had gone farther than any Chinese before him. Two centuries earlier, he might well have come across Alexander's troops.[155]

Zhang spent a year at the court of the Yuezhi ruler, yet he could not persuade him to enter a military alliance. The Yuezhi had now adopted an agricultural way of life and faced the west and south.[156] The Chinese envoy's sojourn was nonetheless not in vain. In the long run, it was of world-historical significance. When Zhang returned to the imperial court after an absence of eleven years, he told his compatriots about a world that had previously only been the stuff of fable and now made its way into Chinese chronicles (Hanshu and Shiji).[157] He told of northern India (Chengdu) and the Parthians (Anxi) who had conquered the land of the Seleucids (Likan/Tiao Zhi); he depicted their politics, people, and customs; displayed unknown plants and herbs; and reported that in Bactria, a special kind of Chinese bamboo (qiong chu) as well as clothing from southwest China were exported to India. Zhang not only showed that links to the west and India existed independent of state initiatives; he also laid the groundwork for connecting the emperor's strategic plans concerning western lands with a commercial interest in their products.[158]

The old myths of the 'kingdom of the Great Mother' in the west who possessed the elixir of immortality already spoke of exceptional trees and animals, jade and gemstones.[159] They reflected a longing for exotic rarities, yet this longing also always had a political dimension. For the 'son of heaven', owning such treasures was proof of his world-spanning rule. They documented that he could draw the most remote peoples and their goods to his court. Symbolizing the isle of the immortals, the imperial park was stocked with tropical plants and exotic animals: a black rhinoceros, white elephant, and parrots.[160]

The imperial cult of the exotic was reflected in a demand for western luxury goods that matched the lifestyle of the court and its elite. Besides exotic animals for the imperial park, these included precious glasses, crystals, textiles, silver, tin, and especially red corals, which had the same value in China as jewels in the Mediterranean. In his quest for immortality, Emperor Wu supposedly erected a shrine with coral grilles amid coral trees; the king of Sri Lanka practised a similar magic (see above, p. 318). In other respects, too, the lists in the Han chronicles display a striking resemblance to the information provided in the Red Sea *periplus*, although exact locations are missing.

Emperor Wu's ears may therefore have pricked up when Zhang told him about a trade route that linked Chinese Shu (today's Sichuan province) with India and delivered exotic goods to the north.[161] Around five years after his return, the emperor sent him southwest. This time, however, his efforts availed nothing, at least so far as the desired goods were concerned. At least contact was probably established with the Parthian king Mithridates II, who reciprocated with an embassy of his own in 101–100 BCE. Through the Parthians, word of the 'Seres' reached the Bactrian-Indian Greeks before making its way to the Levant and into the history of Apollodorus of Artemita. The fall of the Bactrian kingdom is the first event mentioned in both Chinese and Indian sources.[162] The Romans were introduced to Chinese silk around a century later through Cleopatra's mediation. In the 30s, soldiers led by Crassus saw silken Parthian standards.[163]

Chinese Expansion into the Tarim Basin

According to an old theory deduced from several references in the sources, legionaries from Crassus' army were deported by the Parthians to Antiocheia Margiana (Merv in Turkmenistan), conscripted by the Xiongnu, taken captive following a battle with the Chinese army, and eventually resettled in a town named Liqian (today's Gansu province).[164] Although this theory has never been verified, it attests to the fact that the 'western lands', especially the Ferghana (Dayuan), which had already been conquered by Alexander and incorporated into the Graeco-Bactrian kingdom, were gaining in military and political importance for the Han Chinese.[165] When the rulers of the Ferghana refused to supply them with horses, even in return for gold and silk, Wu sent in his troops. In 101 BCE the Ferghana was conquered following the longest and most expensive campaign waged to that point in Chinese history.[166] Much like the Romans in the Egyptian desert, the Chinese safeguarded the route along the northern edge of the Taklamakan with garrisons and soldier-settlers who tilled the barren land with the help of irrigation systems. At the same time, they expanded the Great Wall of Gansu, the western 'horn' of China, along the Hexi Corridor (an arid zone between the Mongolian deserts, the Qilian Mountains, and the Tarim basin in today's Gansu province) to the so-called Jade Gate (Yumen). Anxi ('Pacify the west') became the new military headquarters.[167] The military engagement played a key role in condensing central Asian caravan routes into the Silk Road. It gave the Han emperor an overland link between his capital of Luoyang and the horse-producing region of northern Iran while facilitating diplomatic oversight of the powers lying along the way. Western products such as grape wine and crops could now also be supplied to China and traded for Chinese goods.

Caravans travelling from east to west departed from Chang'an, the older imperial residence and Han capital. Here merchants supplemented raw silk with ginger, cinnamon leaves, cassia bark, and other spices, as well as Chinese ink and semi-finished products and iron from the mines of Shanxi, Hubei, Gansu, and Sichuan.[168] From Fengxiang, the southern route proceeded through Lhasa across the Himalayas to Patna (Palimbothra) and the Ganges delta, allowing the Seres to deliver raw silk to the Bay of Bengal. A second route led from Yunnan to modern Burma and the coast near Yangon.[169] The main route west veered northeast to the new military base at Anxi, then threaded the oases of Turfan and Kucha and followed the Issyk Valley to the Jaxartes and Samarkand. The southern route avoided the Taklamakan, bifurcating to the north (Beilu) and south (Nanlu) before reconverging at Kashgar (Issedon Scythia) at the foot of the eastern Pamir.[170] The northern road was used primarily in summer and was protected by walls and forts from 100 BCE. The southern route passed the jade mines of Khotan; Zhang probably took it on his first expedition. A pass led over the Pamir to Bactria and from there to the ports of the Indian west coast, where western traders purchased 'Chinese hides' and 'Chinese yarn'.[171] In Merv the southern route united with the northern branch, which ran through the Ferghana basin via Samarkand. It continued through northeast Iran to the southern Euphrates. Here the commodity stream was augmented by silk traded over the Persian Gulf and ended at the Syrian metropolises of Antioch and Seleucia, where many western silk merchants had their headquarters.[172]

The Silk Road thus had its origins in the east, with military objectives going hand in hand with mercantile considerations. Silk was no longer simply traded for horses and exotic goods, but it was also used to ensnare enemies—the Romans pursued a similar policy towards the barbarians beyond the Rhine and Danube.[173] 'Every border market we establish must be filled with shops', decreed a Han official, 'and the shops must be large enough to serve between one and two hundred people. The Xiongnu will then develop a craving for our products, and this will be their fatal weakness'. 'A piece of plain Chinese silk', another commentator wrote, 'can be exchanged with the Xiongnu for articles worth several pieces of gold. By these means we can reduce the resources of our enemy'.[174]

Combined with military improvements in crossbows and cavalry, this strategy proved successful. In the course of the first century BCE, the Xiongnu coalition disintegrated, riven by hunger, discord, and Chinese trade policy.[175] As the immediate threat receded, however, the silk roads declined in importance. Isolationists who viewed close trade contacts with the west as incompatible with Chinese tradition grew in influence at court. Local client princes now relieved Chinese troops in guarding the northwest borders. 'Control the barbarians with the help of barbarians' was the order of the day. Contact with the west broke off in the first seven or eight decades of the first century BCE.

The Kushan Empire as Trade Hub

As so often in history, however, political and military changes could do little to block established trade flows. These found other ways to overcome political borders. China's military retreat from the Tarim basin thus occurred roughly parallel to the trade boom over the Red Sea and India.[176] Once awakened, the appetite for commodities could not easily be suppressed by state directives. Grape wine, in particular, offered a welcome alternative to rice wine; vines even seem to have been cultivated in China. Conversely, Chinese silk had become a prize export that neither the Roman elites nor the principalities lying *en route* to Iran wished to do without.[177]

Trade in these and other products thus survived the ebbing of expansionist energies and contributed to the emergence of a new geopolitical order. In the mid-first century CE China's longstanding allies, the Yuezhi, had crossed the Hindu Kush and united their tribes on Indian soil to form the Kushan Empire. This empire was to become one of the richest and most important powers in the ancient world. At its height, it extended from China's borders through central Asia to the ports of the west Indian coast. It thus spanned several ecological zones amid the territorial and maritime network of silk roads; numerous products desired in the west such as bdellium, spikenard, costus, lapis lazuli, or turquoise could only be acquired in the Kushan heartlands. The Kushans themselves were interested in western glass, silverware, gemstones, and statues as well as gold (*aurei* coins) for coin production. Modest customs duties and taxes, combined with a liberal trade policy, allowed handicrafts to thrive, promoted urbanization, and brought unprecedented prosperity to the region.[178]

Buddhism was again a driving force behind long-distance trade. In the earliest days, most of Buddha's followers had been merchants who had found accommodation in monasteries and made donations in return; Buddhist literature praises the wealthy merchant who supports the community. The Kushan ruler Kanishka I (first to second century CE) was probably a Buddhist convert who, like Ashoka before him, used his influence to promote the religion. Under his reign, the Buddhist pantheon was expanded by several deities and the idea took hold that gift-giving could bring one closer to the goal of immortality in paradise. The 'seven jewels' (*sapta ratna*) encompassed gold, silver, pearls, gemstones, and coral; many believers donated pearls, glassware, coral, silk, and lapis lazuli.[179]

Because many of these luxuries could only be acquired in the Far West (Rome) or East (China), the reorientation of faith and the boom in Buddhist monasteries provided additional stimulus to long-distance trade. Many monasteries engaged in trading; like Hellenistic temples, they served as financial agents and as protected trade centres. One monastery built distilleries for high-proof alcohol, probably at the suggestion of western wine dealers.[180] In the first century CE, traders and Buddhist monks jointly crossed the Khyber Pass to Merv and traversed the Tarim basin to China, where communities of Buddhist merchants and monks from India are attested in larger towns and the new imperial residence of Luoyang.[181] Indian and Kushan traders brought silk to India and Iran, while jade and other wares coveted in China were relayed in the opposite direction from the Indian ports to China. The Red Sea *periplus* mentions that all goods destined for export to barbarian lands were first transported upriver to a royal capital; this was most likely Purushapura, the northern residence of the Kushans near today's Peshawar in the region of Gandhara. The Han emperors therefore gave permission for traders from the Kushan Empire to enter their territory, ensuring that contact with the west was maintained despite the repeal of Emperor Wu's expansionary policy.[182]

Pan Chao and the Search for a Connection to Rome

From the 80s of the first century CE, nomads from the north once again disrupted the flow of trade. The western branch of the Xiongnu or their former subjects—named Xianbei by the sources[183]—resumed their raids on Chinese territory and probably also threatened caravan routes (although horses were hard to use in the desert), reason enough for the Chinese rulers to mobilize against the 'pirates of the steppe' and bring the Tarim basin under their renewed control. From 73 CE, General Pan Chao led several successful campaigns against the principalities at the edge of the Taklamakan and the northern Xiongnu. In 91 he was rewarded with the title 'Protector-General of the Western Territories', a kind of suzerainty over the Tarim basin almost as far as the Caspian Sea.[184] While the reconquest of the Tarim basin and the repudiation of cavalry attacks did not amount to a 'reopening of the Silk Road', goods traffic now acquired a previously known stability. The oases thriving on the southern and northern route of the Taklamakan led traders safely from the Jade Gate in the east to the borders of Afghanistan and Uzbekistan and from there to the Iranian Plateau or the Indian subcontinent.[185]

Improved security on caravan routes skirting the Tarim basin appears to have attracted long-distance Chinese traders, although it is unclear how they related to imperial commercial and military policy. Unlike the Roman emperors, the Han probably had monopolies on silk, iron, and salt. And in keeping with Qin tradition, they had sought to control foreign trade and the activities of Chinese merchants by establishing clearly demarcated areas in town markets, forcing traders to reinvest their profits in land, and taxing them at twice the rate. This did not reflect any fundamental hostility to trade, even if orthodox Confucian scholars, like their Roman counterparts, praised farming over commerce.[186] On the contrary, by introducing an empire-wide copper currency, standardizing weights and measures, and building up a road network, the Han rulers did much to improve trade. There is no evidence that trade was subject to any direct taxes or tariffs.[187]

The reasons for the limitations placed on merchants were instead fiscal and political in nature. Whereas Roman long-distance traders and their freedmen never competed with the emperor, the double tax and ban on an administrative career in China reflected a concern that wealthy merchants, with their access to goods that were vital to the emperor's legitimacy, could pose a political threat to the establishment. Sources friendly to the emperor justified this concern with the suspicion that merchants would corrupt officials. The obligation to invest profits in land made it easier to tax profits on trade, which might otherwise have slipped from imperial oversight.

These measures were not particularly effective when applied to merchants active within the Empire and near the capital; when it came to long-distance traders dealing with luxury products, they were a total failure. On the one hand, the imperial court relied on their cooperation in sourcing western and southern exotica; for that reason, the later Han emperors abandoned their repressive policy towards traders. On the other, wealthy merchant families such as that of Liu Pao had excellent connections with higher circles and military active in the west; they resided in Luoyang or Chang'an and had branches in every provincial capital (albeit only from the Northern Dynasties period).[188] When Pan Chao, three years after being named protector-general of the western territories, led a campaign against the kingdom of Karasahr in the northern Tarim basin, several hundred Chinese merchants came in his train, much as Roman traders followed Caesar into Gaul. And just as Cicero hoped for rich pickings in Britannia, so too Pan Chao's brother, the historian Pan Ku, wanted to buy woollen blankets and carpets.[189]

We see here how neatly official military missions aligned with individual acquisitiveness. Pan Chao's brother would not have been alone in exploiting this opportunity. Pan Chao had previously assembled a motley crew of mercenary cavalry (recruited from nomad stock) and adventurers; he would have valued the knowledge of the merchants who accompanied him and sought to reconcile their interests with his own, just as later governors traded with western products (gold, silver, horses).[190] Yet a sophisticated surveillance and taxation system also kept the court informed about luxury goods from the west and the Roman Empire: gold, silver, jade, pearls, and glass. Many ended up in the palace, although maintaining an army in the western regions as well as appeasing the barbarians consumed vast quantities of silk and precious metals.[191]

In getting their hands on these products, the Chinese found themselves in a comparably advantageous position to the Indian princes: like pepper in India, silk had been a mass product in China since the Warring States period (475–221 BCE), albeit one that required long and intensive cultivation and had a high exchange value abroad. Chinese experts were unaware that most raw silk was processed and re-exported by Roman and Syrian textile workers.[192] Probably only the profits made in this way allowed western dealers to keep investing in raw silk purchases. The lists of the later Han chronicles show that from the Chinese perspective, as for the Indians, gold was not so much a means of payment as a commodity. The more gold was needed for buying horses or appeasing the barbarians, the greater was the desire to cut out the middlemen who pocketed so much of it.[193] This was the reason why the Han emperor or his general was interested in a direct connection to the Roman Empire.

The rise of the Kushan Empire played an important role in all this. From the mid-first century CE, Indians and Kushans settled to the south of the Tarim basin (the north was preferred by Sogdians from today's Uzbekistan), and they turned up in Chinese towns as well as in the capital, Luoyang. From them, the Chinese emperor and his generals may have learned of an overseas trade link from India to the realm of the Romans, which the Chinese probably called Daqin. According to the Hou Hanshu, this empire enjoyed a ten-to-one profit margin on maritime trade with Parthia and India![194]

In 97 CE Pan Chao took matters into his own hands and sent his envoy Gan Ying to Parthia in what was the first and apparently only attempt by a senior Chinese representative to reach the Roman Empire. Gan Ying came from the Oxus via Merv to Tiaozhi, which could be the Chinese name for the Tigris or refer to a port on its banks near the sea, evidently Charax Spasinu, gateway to the Persian Gulf.[195] Gan Ying accordingly stood at the exact spot where twenty years later a wistful Trajan saw ships set sail for India (see above, pp. 303–304). The Chinese envoy turned to face the opposite direction. When he asked whether there was a sea route to the Mediterranean from here, he was told that the sea was vast. A crossing would take three months in fair weather and two years in foul.[196] This gave a fairly accurate impression of the difficulties involved in rounding the Arabian Peninsula from the east, even if the envoy was probably in the dark about the exact geographical circumstances and knew nothing of Arabia.[197]

The shorter and more frequently used connection from the Euphrates over Palmyra and the Syrian desert was not revealed to the envoy. The Parthians presumably wished to prevent Chinese traders from coming into direct contact with the Romans. The same Chinese chronicle (Hou Hanshu) reports in another context that the Romans were interested in making contact with the Han Chinese but were frustrated by the Parthians, who were keen to monopolize the Chinese silk trade.[198] If this report refers to the embassy of Gan Ying and not to the much later one that came by sea to the imperial court in 160 (see above, pp. 322–323),[199] then the Chinese source was misinformed here. Pan Chao undoubtedly wanted to find out whether the Romans could be reached by sea. Yet it is hard to see how the Parthians would have been disadvantaged by such contact. The Palmyrenes were more likely candidates. They depended for their existence on their central role in the east-west transit trade.[200] Nothing of the sort could be said of the Parthians. Other than the previously cited source, there is no evidence that they monopolized the silk trade. Too many players were involved: besides the Palmyrenes, there were the Kushans and the Indian intermediaries. Had the Parthians succeeded in suppressing contact between Romans and Chinese, they would have been depriving themselves of one of their most important income streams. Conversely, even if their governments had reached an understanding, western or Chinese merchants would still have had to travel through Parthia and make payments accordingly. The 'travel guide' of Isidore of Charax—the territorial pendant to the Red Sea *periplus*, as it were—shows that the path through Parthia to central Asia (and China) was well trodden in the first century.[201]

Parthia's concern for the loss of a trade monopoly probably concealed a far more serious fear: that of a global power shift. The Parthians had been familiar with Chinese policy since the early first century BCE. They knew that the empire subordinated mercantile objectives to its strategic and geopolitical interests: not without reason, it was an official envoy who made enquiries in Parthia about maritime connections with the Roman Empire. With the rise of the Kushans, the Parthians saw themselves confronted with a rival in the east that had its own interest in contacting Rome and its eastern provinces. The Kushans evidently imitated Roman *aurei*, and the Kushan ruler Kanishka II used the title 'kaisar' while regularly plundering Parthian territories. War even broke out between the two empires in the second century CE. In the Chinese, with whom they first made contact under Mithridates II, the Parthians had hoped to find an ally against their common neighbour.[202] When Gan Ying enquired about a direct route to Rome, he threatened to foil this strategy. Worse still, there were fears that an alliance could be formed between the Romans and the Chinese, who had advanced to the northern borders of India, just as the Chinese had attempted with the Yuezhi against the Xiongnu.

The Agents of Maes Titianus in China

Whatever their motives may have been, while the Parthians dissuaded their Chinese guest from seeking maritime contact with Rome and successfully concealed the route through the Syrian desert, they could not prevent east-west connections intensifying in the north of their empire. When a Chinese envoy such as Gan Ying travelled from the Pamir to Parthia via Bactria, Merv, and Ecbatana, using the same route traversed by Alexander in the opposite direction, the news spread like wildfire among the merchant community. The message was clear: China was again interested in the Far West and had made the important Tarim basin transit zone safe enough for the anticipated profit to outweigh the risks, including for Western traders. The hope was to return laden with enormous quantities of Chinese products, especially silk, without having to deal with Kushan, Sogdian, and Palmyrene intermediaries.

A man named Maes, who also called himself Titianus, must have been electrified by the news. According to the geographer Marinus of Tyre (cited by Ptolemy), Maes sent 'certain people'—evidently his freedmen or 'agentes'—to the Seres.[203] While their goal is not stated, it is likely that they went to buy silk and other Chinese products. Some have therefore concluded that Maes and his family lived in Tyre and were personally acquainted with Marinus. This is nothing more than an ingenious speculation meant to explain his interest in trade. The Syrian coastal towns were renowned for their glass manufacture and textile workshops that processed Chinese raw silk and dyed silk purple; they therefore formed central production and processing centres for the most important export to and most valuable import from China.[204]

Against this background, Maes and his family may well have had business connections in Syria and been domiciled there for a time. However, Ptolemy's characterization of Maes as a Macedonian and the son of a Macedonian merchant suggests they were not native to the country, as does the fact that the Greek name Maes is largely confined to the Pontus region and Asia Minor. The name Titianus could have been freely chosen by the parents and the bearer. It was considered especially chic and commercially propitious in the east, but it does not authorize the conclusion that the man patronised by Titius was a Roman citizen. In such cases, a freedman typically adopted the family name of his former master (in this case, Titius).[205]

All we can say is that Maes and his agents probably set out on Bactrian camels from the Empire's east and took the same northern route ('the Great Khurasan Road')—from Ecbatana along the south coast of the Caspian Sea via Merv and Bactria—as that used by the Chinese envoy, which was also known to the Palmyrenes.[206] They may even have joined the Chinese party on their return journey. After passing the northern foothills of the Hindu Kush, the Macedonians came to the first large watchtower and customs station in the 'western territories', the 'Stone Tower', located somewhere east of Bactria between the Pamir and the Tian Shan Mountains, around 3,600 km from the Mediterranean coast.[207] Having dispensed with the formalities, Maes set his freedmen off on their great adventure. How far they came is the subject of dispute. Marinus of Tyre calculated seven months between their departure from the Stone Tower and their arrival in the *sera metropolis*. Some scholars contend that these details are borrowed from Chinese or Indian itineraries, but most connect them with the route taken by Maes' agents, probably escorting a caravan, along the northern or southern edge of the Taklamakan.

Their destination, *sera metropolis*, could refer to Chang'an (today's Xian), the early Han capital and marketplace for western and Chinese wares, Xianyang; the Qin capital; or the new Han residence of Luoyang.[208] The last interpretation is supported by Chinese sources that mention an embassy from around 100 CE bringing tribute from the lands of Mengqi and Doule. Read together, these names yield a compound noun that some take to be a translation of 'Macedonia', the homeland of Maes.[209] Western traders were known to pass themselves off as envoys. If Maes' agents made it as far as the Han residence, then they may have presented the 'son of heaven' with golden plates, coins, and silk garments.[210] Lavished with gifts in return, they set out on their return journey, arriving in Syria (or Macedonia) a year later.

Chinese scholars were not alone in finding such a scenario implausible.[211] There was no need to travel to the heart of China and the imperial residence to acquire silk, or even receive the emperor's 'Golden Seal and Purple Ribbon'. In addition, western sources contain no precise information about China's landscape and the appearance of the Han Chinese. The imperial court had a special bureau 'for dealing with foreign envoys' that sifted through reports of visitors from abroad; yet if Daqin does indeed designate the Roman Empire,[212] the Hou Hanshu has little to say about typical phenomena of the Empire, including walled cities, post stations, agriculture, the use of precious metals for coinage (the exchange rate given for coins is inaccurate), or botanical phenomena found only in the Mediterranean. The chronicle also contains elements that can be explained only as projections of Chinese ideas. The fanciful notion that Roman palaces were supported by crystal pillars, for example, reflects the Chinese appreciation for glass and crystal. There were apparently canopied chariots in Rome, although these were far more common in China. The idea that the ruler was legitimated by achievement stands much closer to Chinese tradition than the Principate ideology. In sum, the description remains beholden to indigenous social norms and (Daoist) utopias: Daqin is 'Great China', a wonderland full of gold, silver, and gemstones whose inhabitants are kind, honest, and noble.[213]

FROM CATTIGARA TO THULE . . . WITHOUT AMERICA?

THE IMAGE OF A GLOBALIZED WORLD IN THE SECOND CENTURY CE

The Transfer of Medical Knowledge and Religious Movements

Even if official contact was never made and the Chinese and Roman imperial courts knew next to nothing about each other, the journeys undertaken by Maes' agents and An Dun's 'envoys' are a high water mark in the history of ancient discovery. The entire Eurasian continent from the Sea of China to the Atlantic was now spanned by a web of maritime and territorial trade routes. These extended to the Pacific (by way of Malaysia), on the African continent at least as far as Lake Chad, and in the north via the Caspian Sea to the Siberian tundra.

Besides mercantile and strategic factors and a thirst for exotic products, such activity was furthered by another, frequently overlooked phenomenon: rulers, social elites, and many actors involved in trade in the Mediterranean, India, and China had compatible traditions for defining how otherness was perceived. These facilitated contact with strangers. All three areas were respectful of the enormous seas at their eastern, western, or southern coasts. All three understood the importance of the great inland rivers around which they organized their political rule and along which they ferried goods and people. All bordered to the north on the Eurasian steppeland and on nomadic people who were defined as barbarian in relation to their own civilization, but who could also be grasped in their difference and integrated into the order of things. Chinese writers developed ethnographic models that can be compared with those in the Greek cultural realm. The information about the Xiongnu related by the historian Sima Qian (c. 145–49 BCE) accords in large part with Herodotus' account of the Scythians, for all that it remains tied to a Sinocentric worldview.[214] Greeks, Indians, and Chinese (and also Persians) all told of legendary female steppe warriors. Such tales attest not only to knowledge of epic poetry from the Caucasus and central Asia but also to an archaeologically verified reality: among the nomads who roamed on horseback from the Black Sea to northern China, the two sexes led similar lives and women fought alongside men.[215]

Where more precise information was lacking, tenacious *topoi* filled in the picture. All three civilizational areas had cynocephali peopling the north together with warrior women; the legend probably originates in Mongol-Turkestani central Asia.[216] In Indian, Graeco-Roman, and Chinese texts, we also find paradisical counter-worlds in the far north (Hyperboreans, Ottorakorra = Uttarakuru in the Ramayana, located beyond the cynocephali) as well as in the western and eastern Ocean. According to legend, King Mu of Zhou discovered the paradise of the 'Queen Mother of the West'. At the beginning of the fifth century, Xu Fu set out to find the floating isles of the blessed in the eastern Ocean and fetch his lord the herb of immortality.[217] Gold and precious stones abounded in these paradisical realms; springs watered gardens teeming with wondrous plants that promised long life and immortality.

Such elements also reflect the age-old search for medicinal plants to vanquish the ailments and illnesses of the homeland. Even if medicine evolved on different timescales in Greece, Egypt, the Near East, and China; expressed itself in different forms; and was embedded in different social contexts[218]—plants, perfumes, and gemstones were everywhere attributed with magical and therapeutic powers. Chinese and Greek texts speak admiringly of the same Indian and south Asian medicinal plants. Some therapies, such as bloodletting, were administered by Greek, Indian, and Chinese physicians. From China, medical knowledge was conveyed via India to Rome and vice versa. In the west, physicians, envoys, and merchants acted as intermediaries. In the east, Buddhist monks were pioneers of a rational-empirical *materia medica* that seemed compatible with its Greek counterpart.[219]

The link between the spread of Buddhism and the intensification of Indian and Chinese trade routes has already been mentioned. It stands for a further historically significant phenomenon of Eurasian long-distance trade. Few professional groups rely on divine assistance so much as merchants and mariners, who brave seas and deserts, fear attack from robbers and pirates, and cannot know whether they will return alive. Buddhist monasteries therefore promised not just bliss in Nirvana but also a smooth journey in the here and now.[220] Greeks and Phoenicians founded temples to Heracles/Melqart after surviving storms and achieving commercial success. Others built in Muziris a temple to Apollo, while merchants in China gathered around the religion of their homeland. The Palmyrenes erected temples wherever their voyages took them for longer spells.[221]

The Indian Ocean was an especially fertile area for religious transfer and exchange, since here so many different ethnic groups were on the move and monsoonal conditions necessitated lengthy sojourns abroad and on the islands. On the island of Socotra, Indians, Arabs, and Palmyrenes used the same cave sanctuary for dedications connected with seafaring.[222] Merchants from Alexandria who spent up to five months in the ports of the Malabar coast knew of Buddha and his teaching; from them, Christians learned details about the master's birth. Conversely, Indian merchants and mariners in Alexandria and the Red Sea ports turned to the deities of their Graeco-Egyptian colleagues, as when a certain Sophron prayed for a safe voyage in a graffito in the Pan temple of El-Kanais and Edfu-Berenice. In Berenice, Nabataeans rubbed shoulders with men from Palmyra, Aksum, the south Sahara, India, and southern Arabia.[223] Indian travellers encountered the cult of Isis and Osiris in Koptos, where according to legend Isis learned of her husband's death, while traders from Koptos brought their cult with them to India. Syncretisms resulted between the Isis-Osiris cult and the Indian goddesses Svaha and Isis as well as parallels between Isis and the Indian goddess Pattini (in India and Sri Lanka). In a second-century Egyptian papyrus, Isis appears as Buddha's mother. Accordingly, it was only with the intensification of trade relations in the first century CE (and not earlier, at the apogee of Graeco-Bactrian culture) that Gandhara artists in northwest Pakistan and eastern Afghanistan produced Buddha statues modelled on representations of Greek gods, rhetors, and philosophers.[224]

The monotheistic religions and cosmologies had advantages over their polytheistic rivals: their devotees could practise their faith everywhere and congregate with coreligionists from different backgrounds, whereas the connection to polis and family played a greater role in the 'old' religions of the Greek world. Against this background, it becomes clear why commercial and missionary activity were so often intertwined: the merchant had his experiences and networks to offer, the holy man his blessing and divine assistance. Both were united by the imperative to journey far and wide and by the unconditional will to attain their goals. To succeed, both had to adapt to foreign customs and demonstrate an openness to local conditions in the target area. That is why Ashoka sent his '*dhamma* envoy' west along the great trade routes; according to the *Milinda Panha*, the Buddhist sage

Nagasena joined a caravan on the way to Pataliputra whose leaders wanted to be instructed in *dhamma* teaching. 'Great navigator' (*mahanavika*) was a term of respect in Buddhist literature and epigraphy.[225] Believers are saved by Buddha from sea monsters and maintain their composure in a tempest by meditating, just as Jesus succours his disciples and tames the elements during the storm on the Sea of Galilee.[226] Paul wrote: 'Three times I was shipwrecked, I spent a night and a day in the open sea, I have been constantly on the move. I have been in danger from rivers, in danger from bandits, in danger from my fellow Jews, in danger from Gentiles; in danger in the city, in danger in the country, in danger at sea; and in danger from false believers'. Leaving aside the references to Jews and false believers, this captures the anguish of maritime traders, who summed up their lives in almost identical turns of phrase and soon—in part to this day—worshipped Mary, the mother of God, alongside Isis as their protector and saviour at sea.[227]

All this has a real background. Christianity spread west predominantly over sea roads and ports and east—to Bactria and India—via trade centres like Alexandria and Syria, just as Mani did when disseminating his teaching. Manichaeans, Buddhists, and Nestorians used the same sanctuaries; Nestorian traders brought Christianity to China in the seventh century.[228] As a meeting place for traders and believers, Buddhist monasteries played a similar role to Christian monasteries on the caravan routes of western Arabia and to Christian churches on the coasts of the Indian Ocean from the second century.[229] Not by chance, Syria was home to the most intrepid merchants *and* the most zealous missionaries. Legends about Thomas and Bartholomew's missions to India built on a solid base of information concerning trade with the east. Later, bishops active on the Red Sea, in Ethiopia (Aksum), and in Arabia depended on the infrastructure of maritime trade.[230] Buddhism spread over southeast Asia parallel to the intensification of trade routes over the Khyber Pass to Merv and over the Taklamakan to China. Islam moved east and to north Africa along Arab trade routes. It tapped into communication networks laid down centuries before.

An Imperial Servant's Perspective—Pliny's Natural History

The intensification of trade networks and expansion of global horizons must have filled a Roman of the Early Empire with both pride and disquiet:

pride in the feats of arms that extended Roman hegemony to the outer limits of the ecumene and brought the most exotic delicacies within reach; disquiet at the chaotic multiplicity of a world that revealed ever-new peoples and wonders at its periphery. Did this all not risk exceeding the capacity of a regime that wished to rule a landmass even greater than that conquered by Alexander? And was there not a danger of losing one's internal compass, given the enormous increase in scale involved?

A tried and tested means for allaying such concerns is to gain oversight and precepts for action by collecting and sorting information. In antiquity, the term 'encyclopaedia' was coined for works that pursued this end. With the onset of the imperial age, the encyclopaedic gaze widened to take in the entire ecumene while preserving a strict Rome-centred hierarchy; similar developments occurred in China at the height of Han expansion. A generation after Strabo's *Geographica*, Pliny the Elder created the largest single surviving prose work of Latin antiquity, the 'natural history' dedicated to the emperor Vespasian. Like Strabo's cultural geography, the work focuses on the known, civilized ecumene, yet geography forms only one aspect, occupying books three to six after the section on cosmology. There follow books on anthropology, zoology, botany, and the medical aspects of animals and plants, as well as five books on mineralogy. The work was a compromise between Roman technical writing and the geographic-ethnographical literature of Hellenism. Although the author pressed traders and mariners for the most up-to-date information, he generally took his cue from the classical book traditions; he thus prides himself on having excerpted one hundred writers.[231]

The *naturalis historia* aims not to instruct but to present the *orbis terrarum* discovered by Rome, with all its wonders and astounding phenomena. These always remain tethered to the Roman world, either as a point of contrast or as confirmation of the Empire's power. The topical index placed at the start thus resembles a triumphal procession, and the following chapters are like a world map arranged in concentric circles around Rome.[232]

Pliny frequently remarks of animals, plants, medicines, and artworks that they were introduced as a result of imperial conquests and triumphs.[233] They thereby attest to the Empire's achievements. Expanding power and increased knowledge are two sides of the same coin. If the *mirabilia* at the periphery demonstrate the power of nature, then knowing about them demonstrates the even greater power of the emperor. Where the heads of the patrician aristocratic families had once administered knowledge in the Republic, now the emperor had sole authority to decree expeditions and determine how natural phenomena were to be explained and disseminated against the epistemic horizon of his subjects.[234] Pliny draws the conclusion: 'And yet who does not readily admit that now, when intercommunications have been opened between all parts of the world, thanks to the majestic sway of the Roman Empire, civilization and the arts of life have made a rapid progress, owing to the interchange of commodities and the common enjoyment by all of the blessings of peace, while at the same time a multitude of objects that formerly lay concealed, are now revealed for our indiscriminate use?'[235]

As guarantor of stability and universal peace, the emperor lorded over nature and its wonders. An understanding of the nature of the world went hand in hand with the capacity to govern it: to define the limits of nature was to strengthen the Romans in their conviction that they had found the best possible way of life under the emperor's sceptre. Bizarre natural phenomena and the extreme foreignness of barbarian peoples—the wretchedness of the Chauci, the unusual customs of the Essenes, the colourful physiognomy of Far Eastern tribes—all served to satisfy readers' appetite for sensationalism. At the same time, such reports conveyed the comforting assurance that life in the Empire was better, more rational, and more stable.[236]

Facets of Geography—Roman Writers and Ptolemy's World Map

An awareness of the Roman Empire's unparalleled dominance also influenced the geographical interests of Roman writers. Even though the spread of imperial rule inspired works that ranged widely across time and space, and even though numerous reports of the Indian Ocean, the European interior, and above all the Baltic had broadened the horizons of educated Romans since Augustus, this growth in information did not lead to any fundamental readjustment of the worldview oriented on Eratosthenes. What Roman writers offered their public was not a mathematical geography but an ethnography with literary pretensions, whether in the large-scale format of the encyclopaedia or in the smaller format of the handbook. Since ethnography was categorized as 'fine writing', scientific results were acknowledged but presented only sparingly; otherwise, the classics retained their authority.

Writing in the reign of Claudius, the geographer Pomponius Mela (c. 37–41 CE), like Pliny after him, thus integrates older sources, the latest empirical findings (on the Kattegat = Codanus, for example), and traditional myths about the north into the classical worldview. He holds fast to the idea that the ecumene is surrounded by the Ocean. Various distances are provided,[237] but the area around and beyond the Baltic is not significantly extended to the north, nor is any consideration given to the information about India's true dimensions to the south that Hellenistic explorers had been piecing together since the second century. Similarly, the picture Pliny paints of the country remains fundamentally indebted to Megasthenes, and he follows Eratosthenes in giving the subcontinent the shape of a rectangle. India, Taprobane, and the Indian Ocean appear to have moved closer to the Roman world,[238] yet empirical data about coastal and travel distances, the monsoon route, and regions recently opened to trade, such as the island of Chryse (Malacca, Sumatra, or Java), are omitted from the 'literary' sections on India, cited in the wrong place, or factually inaccurate. In this way, Pliny avoids subjecting Eratosthenes to fundamental revision. Old and new are juxtaposed higgledy-piggledy rather than being integrated into a comprehensive overview.

Pliny observes similar principles in the north, despite being better informed than many of his contemporaries. Like Mela, his knowledge of the Baltic leads him neither to reconceive the Ocean in light of that knowledge nor to posit a new *orbis*. The same holds true of Taprobane, which had earlier been taken for an *alter orbis* but is now an island seven days' sailing from India. The counter-ecumene in the geographical sense lies south of the Equator, without it being deemed worthy of further speculation.[239]

For Roman writers, the barbarian peoples of the periphery constitute the ethnographically and ideologically privileged 'counter-world' to the civilized centre of the Imperium Romanum. This is where the freaks and monsters familiar from Greek literature have their abode. Mela, Pliny, and later Solinus place them in the Indian Ocean; some—like the headless Blemmyes with faces on their chests—in the south; others in the far north. At the same time, the better-known zones are peopled with the ethnic groups with which Roman generals, soldiers, or merchants came into contact. Instead of giving rise to a new geographical model, the expanded empirical knowledge base expresses itself in the multitude of tribes that now fill the previously blank spaces of the Baltic countries and India, yet scant attention is paid to the geographical details.[240] This approach culminates in the *Germania* of Tacitus, for whom even the Elbe no longer plays a role as a boundary marker. Instead, the groups he names form a single settlement unit in distinction to the Sarmatians farther east.

Lack of interest in the further development of geography in Eratosthenes' sense, as well as a relatively uncritical acceptance of older reports, led Roman writers to adopt a position that would have important consequences for the later reception; it reflects in some respects the thriving maritime trade in the northern and southern Ocean, whose positive role in connecting the ends of the Earth is expressly approved by Pliny (and later even by Christian authors!). Buoyed by this confidence, Pomponius Mela and Pliny concluded from the expeditions of Hanno and Eudoxus that Africa could be circumnavigated from both east and west. Drawing on Cornelius Nepos, both know of Indians who had crossed the Atlantic on trade missions, although (as is typical in these tales) storms supposedly drove them off-course and cast them up on the Germanic coast—whereas Greek geographers such as the notoriously critical Strabo remained sceptical about such reports, particularly those concerning an African circumnavigation.[241]

Strabo did not think of himself as an expert geographer but as a worldly-wise scholar ('philosopher') who—much like Pliny in this respect—aimed to provide his audience with an encyclopaedic overview of the ecumene conquered and progressively civilized by the Romans. To that end, he composed a lost universal history and a 'cultural geography' of the world (*Geographiká*) that critically worked through expeditionary reports and ethnographic information. Strabo was convinced that the Parthian and Roman Empires had advanced markedly beyond Eratosthenes' time in their knowledge of the world and its remote regions.[242] He aims at a more accurate outline of the Indian subcontinent than Eratosthenes by imagining the two coastlines in the east and south as each 3,000 stadia (= 600 km) longer than the opposite side formed by the Indus and the Himalayas.[243] By contrast, he shows minimal interest in the Far East (China), south, and far north. He treats the areas beyond the Elbe as terra incognita, despite several Greek geographers having worked through the additional information that the imperial age had at its disposal. Yet even they were unable to give fresh impetus to research on the Baltic and far north. The Empire was sufficient unto itself, encompassing practically the entire inhabited Earth and its people. 'There is no need whatsoever now to write a book of travels and to enumerate the laws which each country uses', Aelius Aristides proclaimed to the emperor in Rome in the second century CE. 'Rather you yourselves [i.e. Romans] have become universal guides for all'.[244]

The situation was different in the east. Unswayed by Roman interests, geographers in Alexandria sought to assemble an improved cartographic view of the world from information sourced from as far afield as China. The most important representative of these endeavours was Claudius Ptolemy (second century CE). Alongside his masterpiece on astronomy, the 'Great Compendium' (named *Almagest* by the Arabs), he composed a *Geographia* or *Cosmographia*. The first book and opening of book 2 offer guidelines for drawing up maps of the ecumene. The following books, up to and including book 7, contain a compendium of around 8,100 locations, identified by longitude and latitude according to a uniform grid of coordinates that differs from the modern version only in its prime meridian. With the help of these data, Ptolemy produced a map of the world as well as twenty-six individual maps that took account of the Earth's curvature. Latitude and longitude are supplemented with information on ethnography and the natural resources of eastern lands, in particular, once again highlighting how ethnography could exert a bridging function.[245]

To calculate locations, Ptolemy drew on the notes of earlier geographers (Marinus of Tyre), itineraries, campaign reports, route descriptions, sailors' accounts, and distance specifications provided by merchants and captains: for the east African coast the reports of Greek traders and seafarers (Theophilus, Dioscorus, and Diogenes), for the seas beyond the Strait of Malacca that of Alexandros, for the north that of Philemon. For the south he consulted (through Marinus of Tyre) a certain Julius Maternus, presumably a Roman officer who set out from Leptis Magna on a Garamantes campaign and made it as far south as a country called Agisymba, 'where the rhinoceros congregate', probably the Sahara up to the wet region of Lake Chad.[246] For the overland and sea route to China, he used Alexandros' report and the details recorded by Maes' agents and summarized by their master (see above, pp. 336–338). They gave Ptolemy a realistic idea of the path to China; indeed, most of the information he sourced from the east and southeast struck him as accurate. He estimated the breadth of the ecumene from 15°W (the Canaries and Iceland) to 120°E (China) at around 16,740 km on the Parallel of Rhodes (36th parallel), the distance from north to south (Thule—southern Sahara) at around 7,440 km.[247] Since he calculated the circumference of the Earth at just 180,000 stadia (= 33,480 km), the maritime route between the ecumene's eastern and western extremities had to be further shortened. In the southeast, Ptolemy assumed a land bridge between Africa and China, probably based on the information he took from Alexandros' voyages to Cattigara; he may even have known of voyages undertaken by Indonesians along the cinnamon route to northwest Australia.[248]

The East between Ideal and Reality

Ptolemy belonged to a scientific community. His works were known only to a few Greek scholars. Pliny, on the other hand, represented the traditional interests of the Roman educated class, now focused on the Imperium Romanum as the political centre of the world. While one type of writing expressed a thirst for novelty and delight in critical argument, the other set out to convey a sense of security and intellectual mastery by arranging all the available information in accordance with established templates. Between these two forms, the geographic and ethnographic worldview had numerous gradations and literary variations. The diversity of expressive forms was practically a hallmark of how the imperial era dealt with the expanded global horizon. It offered an opportunity to interpret what had been experienced in different ways and fill gaps in knowledge with the help of the imagination.[249]

This is especially true of the lands at the outermost limits of the ecumene. Roman authors apply similar *topoi* when idealizing China as those applied by the Chinese to the land of Daqin. The Chinese are thus the most peace-loving people; they dwell in a fertile country with a salubrious climate that grants them a long, happy, and prosperous life; torture and legal compulsion are as foreign to them as theft and plunder. In this respect, the Seres take the place of the Hyperboreans. Christians locate the kingdom of the Seres in the vicinity of the earthly paradise.[250]

Being far older and better informed, the picture of India was more nuanced. On the one hand, Aelian (172–235 CE) and Pseudo-Aristotle offered colourful tales of the kinds of bizarre animals, plants, and people that Ctesias and Megasthenes had already reported on. On the other, Megasthenes could write sentences such as the following: 'The Indians eat simply, particularly while on campaign. They keep good order and abstain from theft. They do not drink wine, except at sacrifices. Their simplicity is also attested in their laws and contracts'.[251] Arrian saw things no differently four hundred years later when he claimed that the Indians had no money and disdained extravagance in their clothing and lifestyle. Pliny depicted them as a people on a primitive cultural level who subsisted on a diet of milk and meat (like the Scythians) and traded gemstones and pearls for imported copper and lead.[252] Many Romans were aware that this ideal image of frugal nomads stood in sharp contrast to the reality of the Indian principalities. Yet however much data was collected by traders and geographers, empirical knowledge was no match for the authority of the age of Alexander. Even when the Roman upper classes showed a renewed interest in India following Trajan's Parthian campaign, the image formed in the early Hellenistic period remained stubbornly immune to correction.[253]

Another key aspect of this image of India was its age-old wisdom, represented by the 'naked sages' (gymnosophists). They lived austerely in a land blessed with an abundance of natural resources, ennobling everyone they touched. If Egypt had been the ultimate study goal of Greek intellectuals before Alexander, now every scholar or miracle worker had to establish his credentials as a wise man with a fabricated voyage to India. Plotinus and Apollonius of Tyana supposedly made a pilgrimage to the subcontinent to be initiated into the mysteries of Indian wisdom, as had Plato and Pythagoras before them; even Alexander could mutate into a philosopher-king. Christians saw Buddha as the wisest eastern holy man; the ascetic Brahmans were kindred spirits who shunned the allures of nature.[254]

India and Germania as Counter-worlds and Mirrors

This multi-faceted image of India reflected not just literary conventions and expectations but also deep-seated longings for an ideal counter-world. Cicero had castigated the decadence and moral decline of his own society by drawing attention to the 'barbaric' Indians' imperviousness to cold and fire and the virtuousness of their women. Pliny may have been reminding his compatriots of their ancient virtues when he emphasized the Indians' simple ways.[255] In the imperial age, more than a few disgruntled senators registered that the *princeps* was increasingly trampling on their aristocratic liberties. Disappointment with internal developments redirected their gaze to the edges of the world, where they rediscovered much that had been lost under the Principate.

The world of the east was ambivalent, however. It was associated not just with self-sufficiency and wisdom but also with luxury, despotism, and licentiousness.[256] Pliny describes the kingdom of Taprobane as a model monarchy whose kings are chosen for their clemency and overseen by a people's council. In almost the same breath, however, he depicts the keen interest in Roman coins shown by the king; gold, silver, and gemstones are as treasured there as in Rome, even if there is less pomp and ceremony.[257]

The Oceanic northwest seemed to provide a safer, more fitting counter-image to Roman decline. Even though nature and life were anything but pleasant there, the classical phenomena associated with peripheral worlds were equally at home: Britannia was a country full of terrors and wonders, but for that very reason it was for Tacitus the only place where his father-in-law Agricola could shine as an ideal commander and Roman under Domitian's 'tyrannical' rule.[258] The wildness and primitiveness of barbarians could accordingly be positively reframed as freedom from political bondage and as primordial moral purity. The Germans were free men who (allegedly like the Indians) neither owned slaves nor lusted after gold and silver; their uncultured lifestyle resembled that of the Golden Age and could be used to mount a sustained critique of civilization.[259] In *Germania*, the only specialist ethnographic treatise from ancient Rome, Tacitus thus combines topical elements, ethnographic information, and the category of Germanic freedom into a counter-world that—precisely because it was enriched with verifiable details—could lay claim to objective reality in its critique of the Principate.

The regions even closer to the edge of the world, where earth and sky become one, were credited with the same wisdom and holiness as China and India. Hecataeus of Abdera equated the Celts with the Hyperboreans, who lived on a large island in the Ocean opposite Celtic country. According to a certain Demetrius (cited by Plutarch), the islands west of Britannia were inhabited only by holy men.[260] And did not the wise druids, with their doctrine of the immortality of the soul, resemble the Indian Brahmins? The two idealized images of the Far East and West could be mobilized more or less simultaneously: Seneca was said to have written a work on India just before the *Germania* of Tacitus.[261] Taprobane and the islands of the Indian Ocean with their utopian social order corresponded to tales of the Isles of the Blessed in the Atlantic. Sertorius had already contemplated retiring to the Iles of the Blessed, which Horace praised as a refuge for the disappointed.

There the Golden Age had been conserved that Augustus claimed for the ecumene, and there the ideal conditions could be rediscovered that were so wanting in the interior.

Utopian Travel Novels

The imperial public was thus confronted with an array of competing and corresponding models for assimilating new information. One such form was a genre that, like ethnography, could be used to critique civilization and outline a utopian alternative: the adventure story.

Shipwrecked heroes washing up on wondrous isles had long been a staple of Mediterranean and Near Eastern literature. Behind such tales stood the experience of traders who wanted to imbue their journeys to faraway coasts and islands with an air of mystery and danger. With Alexander, at the latest, India and the Indian Ocean became, alongside Egypt, the privileged setting for exotic adventures. In the imperial period, his feats were combined with the many legends and embellishments that had sprung up around them into the Alexander Romance of Pseudo-Callisthenes.

Other heroes soon followed in the Macedonian's footsteps. Their preferred pathway was the sea—unsurprisingly, given the boom in maritime trade. After several journeys sailing under the orders of the Macedonian king Cassander (305–297 BCE), Euhemerus of Messene claimed to have arrived at an island in the Indian Ocean called Panchaia. Here he found a temple to Zeus on a hilltop in a paradisical landscape. An inscribed stele inside revealed the origin of belief in the gods. Euhemerus evidently wanted to convey 'critical-enlightened' ideas about the Olympian pantheon and the Hellenistic ruler cult.[262] Diodorus thought that the journey was authentic, and to this day some scholars seek to identify Panchaia with a real island in the Indian Ocean (Socotra or Taprobane).[263]

Real information and literary *topoi* are even more clearly combined in another story. Seized by brigands in the incense-producing land of Arabia, the merchant Iambulus breaks free from his captors and sets sail for the Islands of the Sun, reaching them after four months. He spends seven years living on one of them among the strange natives: they are tall, unusually beautiful, and more powerful than ordinary mortals despite their floppy limbs. Women are held in common; children are forced to mount birds and take to the air as a test of courage; the natives have forked tongues and speak every language, including that of birds.[264] Driven off-course, the hero ends up at the royal court in Palimbothra after another four-month journey. There the ruler helps him return to Greece.

The king is a scion of the Mauryan dynasty, while the merchant's itinerary corresponds to the usual trade routes of the time. The novel clearly reflects Greek journeys to the Bay of Bengal, and the seven islands can be brought into connection with islands lying along these routes.[265] Once again, however, the realistic framework serves to convey an unrealistic message: that of a community of modest, peace-loving, and educated people living in a land of milk and honey. They rarely suffer from illness, live to the age of one hundred and fifty, and worship the universe, the Sun, and all the heavenly bodies. In short, they embody the ideal traits of people from the eastern periphery.

Adventure as Escapist Entertainment

Trials and tribulations at sea and on distant shores were also a source of sheer aesthetic pleasure when they artfully linked old motifs with new deeds.[266] society thus liberated from war, external threats, and severe hardship tends to develop a demand for exotic adventures, much as today's audiences immerse themselves in adventure or horror stories from the comfort of their armchairs or gaming consoles, secure in the knowledge that they can switch off their devices at any time. Many would have hungered for similar thrills in the imperial age: the Red Sea and Indian Ocean were popular settings precisely because there the dangers were still so acute. According to Pliny, 'companies of archers are carried on board the vessels, as those seas are greatly infested with pirates'.[267] In his treatise *On the Nature of Animals*, Aelian described sea monsters that, long vanished from the Mediterranean, lay in wait for travellers in those treacherous waters.[268]

The hustle and bustle of harbour towns provided an ideal microclimate for such horror stories. Here exotic animals were displayed at public games, here the most wonderful spices could be savoured, here images of the mysterious semi-mythical people who inhabited the far corners of the world could be viewed, and here a mixed society of mariners, slaves, traders, and prostitutes conveyed the whiff of foreign adventure. In this world, a story did not need a philosophical or political message for it to find a ready audience. Chariton, for example, was the hero of a play that became a fixture of the theatrical repertoire in Alexandria. Taken captive by pirates, he falls into the hands of Indian barbarians before being freed by his brother. According to Dio Chrysostom, the play was seen not just by natives but by Indians, Arabs, and Ethiopians as well.[269] While the Indian king spoke Greece, his retinue used Indian-sounding words that had a comic effect.[270] Another tale has two lovers being sold by pirates in Alexandria. The girl Anthia ends up in the hands of a rich Indian prince who is visiting the city on a business and sightseeing trip. His return journey takes him to Koptos, where he is killed by robbers who make off with his gold- and silver-laden caravan.[271]

Of course, these stories are not real in the sense that they actually happened. They also show no interest in conveying geographical information, although they do draw on solid data concerning the eastern maritime world. The thieves thus ambush the caravan on the very route frequented by merchants travelling to Ethiopia and Somalia.[272] In his 'Ethiopian Stories' Heliodorus describes how a captain, following the custom of the time, reserved part of his ship for merchants.[273] The non-fictional framework increased the story's credibility while offering opportunities for identification. In these stories, Greek traders, adventurers, and lovers prove their mettle in the world: nameless at the outset, happy, famous, and rich by the end. Perhaps their adventures also reflected the need of the mercantile elite to counter the disdain they encountered from the imperial ruling class and the Graeco-Roman literati with an ethos that valorized foreign travel and combined literary skill with expert knowledge.

This model was so successful that it could be appropriated by Christians. They too wanted to learn more about the acts and itineraries of *their* heroes. If India was for Greek philosophers the ultimate testing ground and fount of wisdom, for Christians it was the furthest goal of their evangelical mission. The Acts of Thomas were written in 240 CE, around the same time as the novel about Apollonius of Tyana. They recount how Jesus, adopting the guise of a businessman, arranged for Thomas to take passage with an Indian captain as a carpenter for King Gundafor (Gondophares). His passage to India follows the trade route from the Persian Gulf to the Indus Valley. Jewish women act as interpreters; feasting—as was customary in Greek ports—facilitates communication.[274] Just as *yavanas* served as craftsmen at the courts of rajas, so Thomas rises to become court architect. Yet the gold he is assigned for building a royal palace he instead redistributes to the poor. Before he is punished, Thomas performs miracles, preserves his bodily innocence (like the lovers in the romances), and spurns every temptation until he suffers martyrdom and returns to his heavenly abode, just as the Indian voyagers in the novels sail back to their terrestrial homeland once they have completed their adventures.[275]

The Northern Ocean and the Final Message of Antiquity

It was widely acknowledged that nautical conditions in the Red Sea and Indian Ocean were much more challenging, and posed far greater risks, than those in the Mediterranean. Even more threatening was the North Sea (*okeanos*), 'that breeds beneath its sluggish waves terrible monsters, ravening sharks, and sea-dogs everywhere'.[276] Its violent storms could wreck ships or mire them in mud. If it nonetheless figured less prominently as a setting for novels, then this was probably for want of Alexander's example. What remained were the legends centred around Aristeas, the Hyperboreans, and the voyage to the north of Pytheas. One of the most famous novels, the 'Wonders beyond Thule' (late first century CE), reassembles all the elements of northern peripheral worlds known to Greek culture: wondrous natural phenomena, magical practices, the living dead, enigmatic oracles, odysseys, and romantic adventures, all packed into the intricate plot of a story that has its heroes sail beyond the outer limits of the Ocean.[277] At the same time, Plutarch was discussing whether human life was possible on the moon and in the cosmos. He thought it likely, given that even the Earth's most inhospitable deserts and oceans support life. Other novels and pastiches depicted how Greek aeronauts flew by ship to the stars and set foot on the moon. The moon became the new ecumene. The stars were islands in the sea of the universe.[278]

The pleasure taken in devising new variants to old stories, and outdoing or parodying other writers through novel twists, probably also informs Plutarch's narrative about a mysterious stranger in Carthage who claimed to have come from a great continent beyond the Atlantic (see above, p. 1).[279] The story showcases a dazzling panoply of motifs that go back to real reports of Atlantic voyages, geographical constructions, and the oldest epics: Homer's land of the dead, Plato's Atlantis and 'true continent', as well as the legendary island of Meropis, which Theopompus of

Chios (378–323/300 BCE) described around the same time that Pytheas discovered Thule.[280]

Such speculations about islands and unknown landmasses proliferated in the imperial age as the optimism of discovery spread both east and northwest. The grammarian Demetrius of Tarsus was apparently ordered by Trajan to visit the isles north of England and reported back that some were named after demons.[281] Taking his cue from Crates, Tacitus wondered whether Odysseus had reached Germania and sailed on the Ocean.[282] Pausanias (c. 115–180 CE), probably alluding to the voyages of Eudoxus, told of a certain Euphemus of Caria, whose storm-tossed ship passed through the Strait of Gibraltar to arrive at an island inhabited by redskins (!) with horses' tails.[283] Strabo and Pseudo-Aristotle contemplated the existence of unknown worlds within the temperate zone, while Seneca was convinced that a time would come when 'the Ocean will unloose the bonds of things / and an immense land shall be revealed / and Thetis [protector of the Argonauts] will uncover new worlds'.[284] A thousand years later, Columbus applied the prophecy to himself on the Orinoco and merged the new worlds (*novos orbes*) into one: he thought he had rediscovered a New World already known to the ancients.[285] Was he right?

After Columbus, others pointed to references in Plutarch, Plato's narratives, and elsewhere to draw the same conclusion, maintaining that an ancient mariner (such as the mysterious Euphemus of Caria) had crossed the Atlantic and brought back news of the great land in the west as well as the islands offshore (the Antilles). For an empire at the height of its wealth and power, this would not have been beyond the realm of possibility. Yet such considerations frequently disregard both the literary genre and the intention of the sources, none of which originate in the geographical literature in the narrow sense nor in the meagre stock of 'real' navigational reports. All are based on speculative constructions and play with literary traditions. The various contexts in which they appear—the romance, the novel, the philosophical dialogue, the tragedy, the satyr play—were untouched by the latest geographical discoveries. Unlike in the novels set in the Indian Ocean, no contemporary nautical and mercantile information found its way into these tales. The impression of a condensation and intensification of old motifs of islands and ecumenes in the Atlantic thus cannot be put down to the influence of empirical accounts; it reflects instead the diversity of literary forms as well as the competitive urge to continually reinvent familiar themes. No doubt there was also a widespread sense in the imperial age that the Ocean and the world in its entirety could be understood and mastered as never before. Tellingly, however, the same writers who optimistically concluded that the Ocean could be fully circumnavigated in the south and the Atlantic crossed 'in a few days' from Spain to India—Pomponius Mela, Pliny, Seneca—knew nothing of a great continent in the west; Seneca looked vaguely to the future.

This is a sobering finding. The gateway for discovering America from Spain had opened more widely than ever before, yet in the absence of any compelling evidence to the contrary, there is nothing to support the conclusion that the ancients passed through it.

A Missed Opportunity?

Why did the ancients never venture beyond the Atlantic, or if they did, why has no firm evidence come down to us of their exploits, even though the prerequisites in the imperial age barely differed from those in the early-modern period (see above, pp. 262–264)? Like Columbus, the ancients knew the Canaries and a journey west from there posed no insuperable challenges—the return voyage was the far greater problem. Those who regularly braved the Red Sea and the Indian Ocean had no reason to shun it.[286] Pytheas had demonstrated that ancient ships could manage even the rough waves of the Atlantic. Pytheas also represents the undaunted curiosity of Graeco-Roman discoverers, who turned the perils of long-distance travel into an impetus for exploration, much as their Christian faith helped the leaders of modern expeditionary voyages overcome their fears and those of their crew. Their confidence was justified in view of the nautical technology at their disposal, which barely fell behind the standards of early-modern expeditions (see above, p. 264). Oceanic navigation by the stars or the Sun was not a problem for imperial-era captains. It was still the key navigational tool in Columbus' day, alongside observations of natural phenomena (wind, birds, currents, water). The compass merely supplemented it without replacing it—the Vikings did not need it to reach Greenland and Vinland/Labrador.[287] The nautical preconditions for an Atlantic crossing were thus given in antiquity, together with global conceptions of space and justified expectations of success. The plans were in the desk drawer, as it were, they were just never taken out. Why?

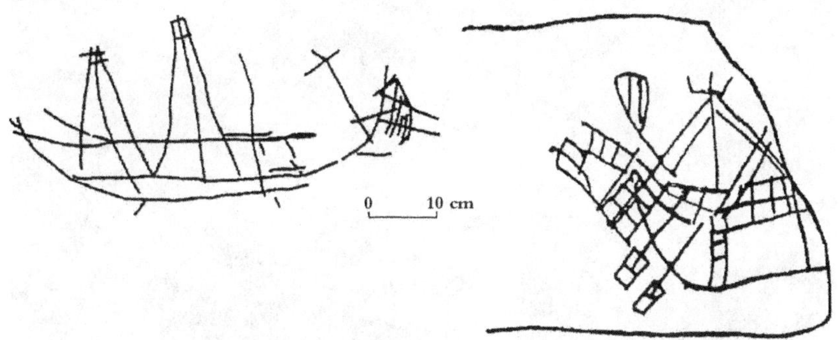

Image 9 Petroglyphs of the three-masted ships in the Red Sea (Myos Hormos) and Arikamedu (eastern coast of India), first century CE (?). The graffito from the Wadi Quseir al-Qadim near Myos Hormos, the famed port of departure for the India trade from the first century BCE, shows a large three-master. A similar model may be the basis for the fragment found in the port of Arikamedu, which was frequented by Western merchants. Some scholars, however, deny that this technology was known to antiquity. Credit: Author/Klett-Cotta

Roman grave relief showing the Peticii business-family who exported wine to India. *(Abruzzo Museum, Italy)*

Image 10 Funerary relief of the Peticii. This funerary relief attests to the far-flung connections of Italian merchant families in the early imperial age. The dromedary laden with amphorae alludes to the wine export business that the Apulian Peticii family conducted from Alexandria to the Far East (Arabia and India) via the Red Sea (see p. 310). Graffiti inscribed by a C. Peticius have been found on the desert route from Koptos to Berenice. Credit: Author/Klett-Cotta.

Image 11 Mural of Zhang Qian's expedition. The rock painting comes from a cave near the Mogao oasis on the Silk Road in present-day Gansu province. Buddhist monks covered the caves with paintings. This image from the early Tang Dynasty (seventh century CE) shows Zhang Qian taking his leave of Emperor Wu as he sets out on his expedition to the Western Lands (see p. 327). Credit: The Picture Art Collection/Alamy Stock Photo.

Image 12 Turfan/Xinjiang—central crossroads of the Silk Road. The oasis of Turfan (today in Xinjiang province in China) was one of the most important stations on the northernmost route of the so-called Silk Road in the eastern foothills of Tian Shan, probably used as early as the seventh century CE (see p. 325). The image gives a good impression of the extremely hot temperatures in summer (up to 50°C). Credit: AKG-images / Suzanne Held.

Image 13 Buddha statue with Greek drapery (Gandhara art). Found in present-day Pakistan, this third-century CE statue of Buddha combines Greek and Indian artistic elements in a manner typical of so-called Gandhara art. While the lavish hairstyle and lower garment likely reflect Indian fashion, the statue itself and the drapery of the upper garment point to Hellenistic models. Credit: Creative Commons Attribution 2.0 Generic license, Wikimedia Commons.

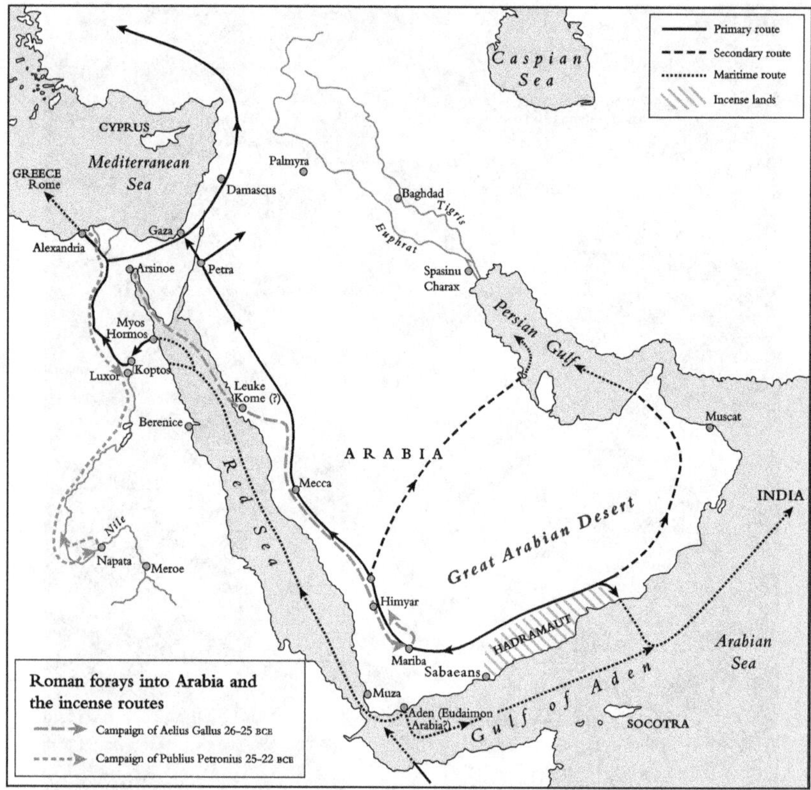

Map 10 Credit: Rudolf Hungreder/Klett-Cotta.

The key difference lay in the political and economic context. So long as the western Mediterranean benefited from a continuous flow of precious metals and products from the Far East, and so long as poorer provinces enjoyed food security, as in the Empire's golden age in the first century-and-a-half CE, there was simply no need to mount a journey west over the Atlantic. The associated expense and risks appeared to outweigh any advantages to be gained from bypassing middlemen and customs duties via an oceanic route. In the west, there were also no religious or social incentives to compensate for the lack of material imperatives, comparable to late medieval missionary zeal or the hope of acquiring social status through maritime discovery. Above all—and this is the decisive factor—the political situation was unpropitious. There was no state support and imperial patronage of the kind that had kickstarted other voyages of discovery in antiquity, including

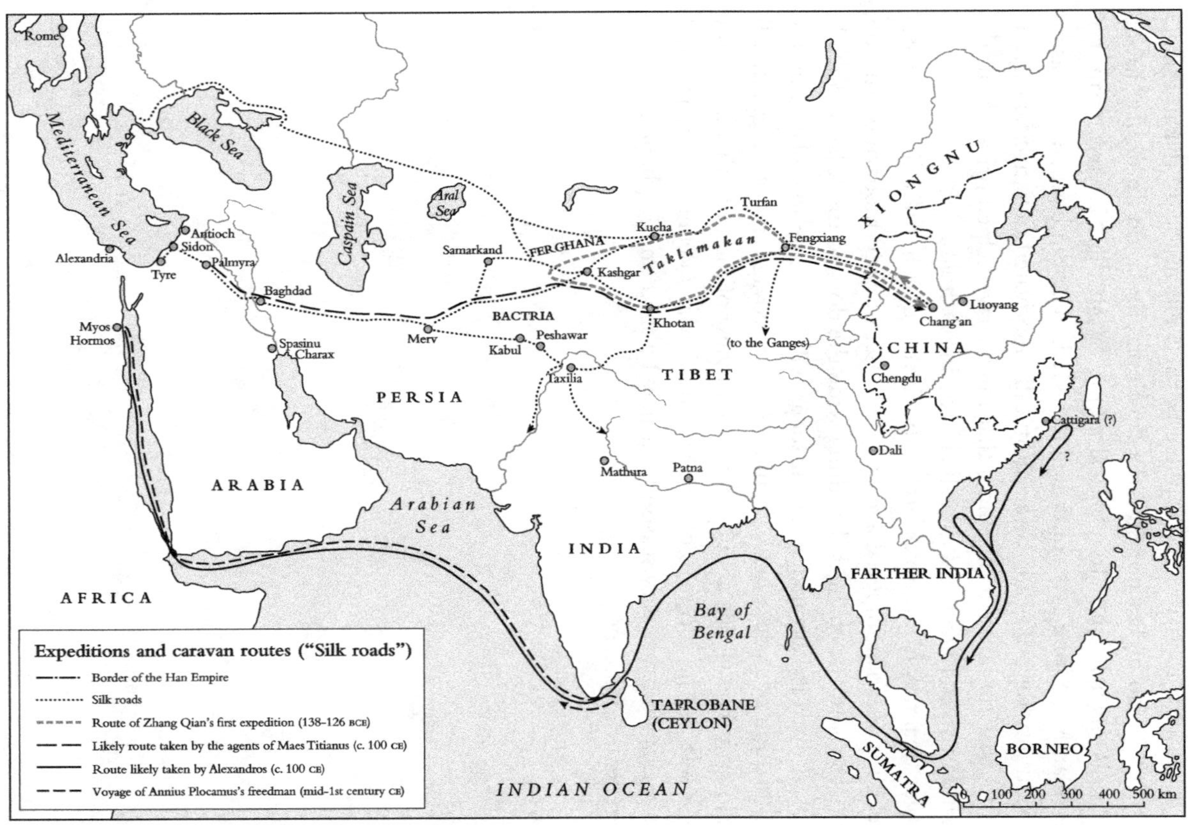

Map 11 Credit: Rudolf Hungreder/Klett-Cotta.

in the west. During the period leading up to the first voyage of Columbus, several kingdoms on the Iberian Peninsula competed in the waters off west Africa. They viewed the Atlantic as a 'second Mediterranean' where they could advance their own core interests, their expansionary dynamic held in check by no higher power. Such developments could never have arisen in the Roman Empire. Its political centre lay in the Mediterranean, not the Atlantic. So long as it controlled the Mediterranean basin, there was no opportunity for politically or economically motivated initiatives and rivalries to arise on its western fringes that might have helped bring about the Atlantic crossing imagined as realisable by intellectuals.

Our final task is thus to ascertain the factors that, in the millennium between the Roman imperial age and the onset of early-modern expansion, brought about the changes that flung wide the door to the Atlantic already cracked open by the ancients. Our focus will be on the role played by the transmission of ancient ideas about an Atlantic voyage and of geographical-explorative knowledge about the world. In view of the vast timeframe, only a few selected perspectives can be presented. Many details will be ignored, but perhaps for that very reason light may be shed on the phenomenon in its general significance.

8

How the Old World Came to the New

Ancient Knowledge and Early-Modern Expansion

Do not deny / yourself experience of what there is beyond, / behind the sun, in the world they call unpeopled . . . You were not born to live like mindless brutes / but to follow paths of excellence and knowledge.

Dante Alighieri, *Inferno* 26,116–117, 119–120

THE LOSS OF MEDITERRANEAN UNITY

From the mid-second century CE, and especially in the third century, attacks from German tribes threatened the political unity of the Empire. Relations with the Parthians deteriorated. With the rise of the neo-Persian Sassanid Empire, a new antagonist stepped onto the stage that was prepared to vigorously defend its interests in the Persian Gulf and Arabian Sea. At the eastern end of the silk roads, the Han Empire collapsed around the same time. Besides a brief period between 280 and 316 CE, China remained disunited for the next three centuries and lost its grip on Turkestan. In India, the Hephthatiles overthrew the Kushan Empire in the fourth century CE.

With that, the stable coexistence of the great Eurasian empires came to an end. Ties between China, India, and the eastern Mediterranean never fully broke off, but they became increasingly frayed from the beginning of the third century CE. In addition, an epidemic transmitted to China and Rome along the central Asian caravan routes (the 'Antonine Plague') resulted in a downturn in trade. Above all, the funds needed to keep regularly buying huge quantities of Eastern luxury products dried up in view of the worsening situation abroad. Changed consumer behaviour, combined with a shift in burial rites attendant on Christianization (interment), saw waning demand for African and Arabian aromatics.[1]

By the time the Roman Empire restabilized at the start of the fourth century, the world looked very different. The effects of fending off barbarian incursions and the internal wars fought over the imperial throne were most keenly felt in the west. Although Constantine managed to prevent the debasement of the imperial currency, he was unable to halt the decline in agricultural production and prosperity in Italy and in several provinces in the west. A thin upper class of superrich landholders still presided over vast latifundia, but they were less willing than in earlier centuries to enter state service and *voluntarily* sacrifice part of their fortune on public matters. The solidarity between state and private interests that had once fuelled overseas trade—between state revenue, financed by taxes and customs duties, and the elite's appetite for luxury goods—now fell apart.

All this significantly hampered the development of new maritime routes. While there had been insufficient economic and political pressure in the early imperial age, now the financial and political conditions that might have driven the search for alternative, trans-Atlantic pathways to the treasures of the east were lacking. From the early fifth century, as the western emperors ceded ever more land to Germanic intruders, the western empire was too preoccupied with its own survival to expend its dwindling energies on exploration. Now the all-conquering 'barbarians of the north' assumed the mantle of discoverers. They would not relinquish it for another 800 years.

The situation was quite different in the eastern part of the Empire. Here, several more centuries passed before the Arabs, rallying under the banner of Islam, became not just conquerors but great discoverers, especially in Africa but also on the southeast and perhaps even western oceans. In doing so, they were inheriting and perpetuating ancient traditions. In the meantime, a combination of skilful diplomacy and tribute payments helped the emperors in Constantinople contain the dangers that threatened from Germania (Goths) and Asia (Huns)—or they redirected these dangers to the west. In the east, large landowners could be more effectively yoked to state interests. Constantinople had the richest provinces in Syria and Egypt; Syria even experienced an unparalleled economic upswing in late antiquity. Trade with India, Arabia, Somalia, and the Far East could be resumed with new partners (Aksum in Ethiopia/Eritrea, the Himyarite kingdom in southern Arabia), even though these two regional powers fought each other in the Red Sea. Aromatics and spices once again entered the Empire via Alexandria. Trade, evangelism, and diplomacy sometimes complemented one another, as attested by the voyage of the Alexandrine merchant and missionary-convert Cosmas Indicopleustes to east Africa, Arabia, and Sri Lanka (perhaps also India), or the journey that Theophilus made to Arabia, India, and Aksum at the behest of Emperor Constantius II.[2]

Contact with China was also maintained. Byzantine historiographers and ethnographers knew it as the land of the *Sinai*, while Cosmas used the Persian name Tsinista for silk's country of origin.[3] Although the secret of silkworms came to Byzantium in 552, Chinese raw silk continued to be processed in Syria. Commodities sent in the opposite direction included wine and gold coins, around thirty of which (including imitations), dated between 450 and 641, have been found in China. Embassies were dispatched to secure overland silk imports along the Caucasus. Three or four Byzantine delegations ventured as far as China in 643–719 CE.[4]

No word of all this filtered through to the west. Jewish and Arabian traders supplied silk to the European interior, but this did not lead to the dissemination of remote geographical information. Most people no longer knew Greek, and access to Byzantine travel reports was lacking. Since the loss of the *Geographia*, the information provided by Ptolemy on Alexandros' voyage to the Sea of China and the extension of the ecumene to China, perhaps Java and Borneo, had disappeared from the west; knowledge of the Seres was limited to Pliny's vague hints.[5]

The west's ignorance of ancient Greek sources and contemporary Byzantine exploration went hand in hand with a changed relationship to knowledge of the world as a whole. The authority of Augustine was instrumental here. Like many of his coreligionists in the west, the church father was caught in a dilemma. On the one hand, the Christian obligation to proselytize required that the ecumene be explored to its farthest reaches (India); on the other, God had imposed limits on the human thirst for knowledge. While the world could be studied as God's creation, knowledge of its material structure depended on revelation. Because few were capable of partaking in this revelation through their intellect, God had provided holy scripture, whereas empirical data gained through the eyes and ears, by merchants and mariners, could safely be ignored[6]—an arrogance shared by not a few heathen writers.

So far as the writings to be consulted were concerned, the Bible naturally stood in first place. After that, however, things became more difficult. Augustine was comfortable drawing on Latin classics, and he accordingly had a 'profound geographical and astronomical knowledge'.[7] Others warned against poring over the 'pagan writings' of Greek philosophy and science.[8] As so often, the situation in the west was complex. Wrestling with themselves and the world, Christians were torn between the desire for knowledge and the fear of breaking God's commandments. Those prepared to countenance the study of pagan writings in view of their educational and propaedeutic function did so in the conviction that their authors had received a spark of the divine spirit. In this way, the encyclopaedias of Pliny and Solinus, Martianus Capella's didactic work 'On the Marriage of Philology and Mercury', and the Latin version of the Alexander Romance by Julius Valerius (early fourth century CE) could become authorities on the world's liminal zones, much as the post-Alexandrine writings on India came to be regarded as definitive in the imperial age.

Restricting the canon to a few authors gave rise to an enduring view of the Far East that reduced the more nuanced image of the imperial age to two poles: one that of a fertile, salubrious, and prosperous wonderland, the other that of a foreign counter-world populated by freaks and monsters—some harmless, others not. The former appeared mainly in India, the latter were fought by the Macedonian king in the Alexander Romance. Both poles could be linked to biblical motifs: on the positive side, Alexander's search for an earthly paradise or Land of the Blessed; on the negative side, the report that Alexander had enclosed the apocalyptic nations of Gog and Magog (including cannibals and cynocephali) behind the Caspian Gates. Since these would break free at the end of time, they could stand as substitutes for the real people (Huns, Mongols) who threatened to engulf Christian Europe from their heartlands in Asia.[9]

The innocuous marvels found a place in the Christian worldview, too. Augustine was not entirely convinced of their existence, but if they did exist, they were merely misshapen human beings and part of God's inscrutable design.[10] Others declared them to be the children of Cain who bore the mark of sin on their own bodies, while still others believed that Eve's descendants had disregarded God's warnings about eating dangerous plants and been punished with deformed offspring. No one considered that they might be figments of the imagination—Strabo's critique was unknown in the west. Even the most critical minds such as Roger Bacon (c. 1214–1292) or Albertus Magnus (c. 1200–1280) never doubted their existence.[11] Surely a fascination with exotic terrors, along with the need to secure one's own identity by defining it against the abnormal, played as significant a role here as in the Roman imperial age (see above, pp. 352–353). No less importantly, such creatures were reported on in the classics. What they said carried weight, especially as deformed human beings—as in the famous tympanum at Vézelay Abbey—could beautifully illustrate the evangelical mission to convert the heathen tribes awaiting discovery at the ends of the earth.[12]

Even as the west's view of the wider world was reduced to a few authorities and the *topoi* they conveyed, augmented by biblical motifs, one thing remained constant: the wish to ascertain humankind's place in time and space. Whereas the Greek east leaned more towards philosophy as an educational tool, history seems to have been the preferred medium in the west. Paulus Orosius was the first Christian writer to present geography as the setting of history. In the introduction to his 'History against the Pagans' (early fifth century), he confined himself to the inhabited ecumene.[13] Isidore, bishop of Seville, did the same in his *Etymologiae* (or *Origines*), written in the late sixth century. Based on word explanations, he set out there to provide an encyclopaedic overview of pagan and Christian learning. The writings of Pliny, Solinus, and Orosius formed the basis of geography and ethnography. The ecumene is subdivided into the three continents of Asia, Europe, and Africa (Libya) and connected with Noah's sons Shem, Cham, and Japheth. Asia is the most important, owing not just to its size but because it contains the chief sites of salvational history.[14] Isidore showed scant interest in new ethnic groups and border changes.[15] He knew nothing of China as a territorial or geographical macroregion; the Seres were 'a people lying toward the east, among whom wool taken from trees is woven'.[16] In India, mountains of gold are protected by 'dragons, griffins, and monsters of immense size'. The phoenix—important for Christian mythology—is born in Arabia, Amazons live in Scythia, and the 'griffins' cruelty' blocks access to gold and gemstones. Of the nations entering the Mediterranean zone, Sarmatians and Huns are mentioned alongside the Germanic tribes. They had 'burst forth from the crags of the Caucasus, where Alexander's gates had been keeping them back'. The description of Europe is cursory, while only the former Roman provinces in Libya elicit any interest. The Garamantes live farthest to the south. Clichés are recycled in relation to Ethiopia and the troglodytes.[17]

THE ANTIPODES AND THE EARTHLY PARADISE

However steadfastly his gaze may be turned towards the inhabited ecumene and away from the periphery, Isidore finds two other aspects worth mentioning besides the casually named monsters of Scythia and India. In the centuries to come, they would become shining lights on the far horizon, rekindling exploratory energies all but extinguished since the third century. On the one hand, he noted that there was a fourth landmass 'on the other side of the Ocean in the south, which is unknown to us because of the heat of the Sun'. This *terra australis* had been an object of speculation since the discovery of Taprobane in the fourth century BCE. Following Augustine, Isidore dismissed the idea that it was inhabited by Antipodeans as 'rationally' not credible,[18] yet doubts about its habitability did not imply doubts about its existence. Macrobius contemplated an Antipodean continent in the northern and southern hemispheres. Seneca, much admired by Christians, had prophesied the discovery of new landmasses in the Ocean (see above, p. 355), and the anonymous Ravenna Cosmographer wrote that enormous mountains (*maximi montes*) lay there by divine command. A space was reserved in the mediaeval imagination for the *terra australis* of the Antipodes. It provided a vital stimulus for looking beyond the limits set by more rigid contemporaries, and even for dreams of journeying on.[19]

A second object of speculative longing was the earthly paradise, located by Isidore at the eastern edge of Asia. According to Genesis, God had 'planted a garden in Eden, toward the east'. It was watered by a river that split into four arms after the expulsion from Paradise: the Pishon, 'that encompasses all the land of Havilah', where there was gold, bdellium, and gemstones; the Gihon, which flowed by the land of Kush; the Hiddekel (Tigris); and the Euphrates. In pre-Christian antiquity, the Gihon had already been identified with the Nile and the Pishon with the Ganges (or the Danube).[20] So far as the Garden of Eden was concerned, both Augustine and Jerome advocated a literal reading without completely rejecting a symbolic interpretation.[21] Because God had created humankind on Friday and driven Adam and Eve from the garden only a few hours later, Paradise not only was a real place in this world with characteristics that could be associated with the *topoi* of a rich and fertile east, it could also be precisely located at the dawn of historical time. The world maps oriented to the east accordingly reserve a prominent place for the Garden of Eden at the easternmost end of Asia, where the aromatic fragrance of the trees reveals their proximity to Paradise and its seed-bearing plants.[22]

If the Garden of Eden was here on Earth, could it still be reached today? After the expulsion of humankind—according to Genesis—God had stationed the cherubim and the flaming, whirling sword to guard the way to the tree of life.[23] Did this mean that humans could never re-enter it? References in the Old Testament echo what Greek writers said about the Isles of the Blessed or Elysium. Just as only a handful of heroes were admitted there by the gods, so God transported only Enoch and Elijah to Paradise.[24] To be sure, some sought to add to their company, much as Elysium was expanded in archaic Greece (Pindar). Thus Paul, at the final stage of his rapture, supposedly saw Moses, Peter, Luke, the great patriarchs and prophets, and even Adam in the earthly paradise alongside Enoch and Elijah.[25] But this version was destined to remain apocryphal. Most writers insisted that Elijah and Enoch were the only mortals to have been *physically* taken up to Paradise. There was no going back for the rest. They could only hope that their souls would reach Paradise *after* death in preparation for eternal happiness, just as Jesus had promised the thief on the cross.[26] In life, access was barred by a wall of fire stretching to the skies, by deserts and seas infested with beasts and snakes, or by the garden's location on a mountain towering to high heaven or on a harbourless island—the rivers of Paradise flowed underground to resurface in Asia or Africa.[27] The way there was never found, according to the Book of Enoch, so there was no point looking for it.[28]

As so often, however, the human imagination paid little heed to theological prohibitions. In the Middle Ages, a series of Christian writings recounted journeys to Paradise. They were modelled on the Alexander Romance and the legends associated with it. One story told of how the Macedonian king had gone in search of the end of the world and the Land of the Blessed (or source of life), arriving at the gates of Paradise before crossing the Ocean from there.[29] The Ravenna Cosmographer had to refute reports of people who had not only reached and beheld Paradise but even strolled through it.[30] There was no evidence for this, he asserted. On the contrary, 'most philosophers [= theologians] conclude that no one is permitted to seek the Ocean behind the ridge of India'.[31]

Impermissible, but not impossible. The hope of at least reaching the threshold to Paradise was barely suppressed by *theological* bans—not just because one could catch there a foretaste of eternal bliss, but also because the details given in Genesis about gold- and gemstone-bearing rivers suggested that nearby countries would enjoy immeasurable wealth, in turn confirming what pagan writers had written about the eastern edges of the world. For that reason, mediaeval maps located Paradise near India and Taprobane, the major gemstone-producing regions of antiquity, and had it encircled by a golden river (Chrysorrhoas).[32] That India (represented by the Brahmins) was viewed as a land of holy wisdom was a further indication that Paradise could not be far off.

The idealization of Far Eastern lands and blessed places at the ends of the earth thus fit snugly with the Christian notion of a terrestrial paradise to create a dream destination that would amply repay the labour needed to find it. It could even amalgamate with Graeco-Roman (Isle of the Blessed, Garden of the Hesperides), Celtic-Iberian (Avalon), and oriental motifs into the image of an island paradise in the Far West. According to the tenth-century version of the *navigatio* of Saint Brendan, the hero and his companions sailed for seven years until they penetrated a ring of thick fog (the Irish equivalent of the fiery wall) to arrive at an island paradise. Apart from the missing rivers, it had much in common with the Garden of Eden: it was extremely fertile, watered by abundant springs, and laden with eternally ripe fruit and gemstones. In later versions, an imposing gate and lance-wielding dragon guarded the entrance to the mountain paradise.[33]

GEOGRAPHIC-COSMOLOGICAL FOUNDATIONS OF LONG-DISTANCE EXPLORATION

Brendan's *navigatio* represents the successful attempt to combine classical and Irish-Celtic models of a wondrous island in the Far West with the

Paradise narrative in Genesis. Even if the west could never compete with the fascination of the east, the suspicion arose that the same place could be reached from different sides of the globe.

There is still a persistent view that the mediaeval mind, hamstrung by theological injunctions and further disadvantaged by the reduction of geographical knowledge to compact handbooks, abandoned key findings of ancient geography and cosmology. According to this view, the most prominent loss was the spherical Earth hypothesis, which was allegedly replaced by the archaic flat-Earth model only to be 'rediscovered' through the voyages of Columbus. It has been more than three decades since this popular idea was unmasked as a fabrication of seventeenth-century scholars wishing to present themselves and their age as enlightened and progressive through contrast with a benighted Middle Ages.[34] In fact, throughout the Middle Ages 'no cosmographer of note questioned that the Earth was a sphere'.[35] Pagan scholars were convinced of this anyway, and since Augustine had written that God had held the Earth's spherical mass (*moles globosa*) in His hands at creation,[36] the spherical model went uncontested among Christian intellectuals from the mid-sixth century onward (with a few largely unknown or neglected exceptions: Lactantius, Boniface, Cosmas).[37] In cosmological writings as well as in 'fictional' literature such as the Alexander Romance, it was preserved intact down to the modern age as one of the most stable intellectual legacies of antiquity. Christian interpreters had no theological reason to doubt it. They instead deployed the spherical model to shore up the account in Genesis, comparing the act of creation with the formation of the cosmic egg (in the Orphic tradition) and thus harmonizing the spherical-Earth hypothesis with scripture.[38]

Mediaeval maps of the world (*mappae mundi*), known as T-O maps on account of how they distribute the continents, are frequently cited but lack validity as a counterargument. They represent the world in a multidimensional sense that encompasses and even presupposes the idea of its spherical form. On a first level, they are intended to depict the providential meaning of God's creation in this world, which is why such maps—perhaps building on illustrations from Roman geography as well as the Book of Jubilees from the second century CE—confine themselves to providing a clear overview of the inhabited part of the Earth, that is, the three continents in the ecumene (corresponding to Noah's three sons and their descendants)[39] and their theologically significant topographical details. The biblical statement that God had brought redemption *in medio terrae* and set Jerusalem *in medio gentium* thus caused the holy city to be placed at the centre (after the Crusades and the loss of the 'Holy Land'); Paradise lay close to India.[40]

Their orientation to symbols and events germane to the history of salvation as well as their planispherical representation of the Eurasian and African continental plates did not mean, however, that theological imperatives overrode the representation of physical reality in these maps. On the contrary, spiritual places like Jerusalem and Paradise were 'real' parts of terrestrial geography that were to be located as precisely as possible, albeit not in accordance with present-day standards and with today's means. That is why the *mappae mundi* could so easily be adapted to breakthroughs in geographical and cartographic knowledge (Ptolemy, Byzantium, Arabs) and their political ramifications. Salvational geography required that the Earth, as God's creation, be represented as accurately as possible in its physical and scientific dimensions.[41] This allowed accompanying remarks on the wondrous peoples, animals, and products of the east (along with Paradise!) and the Atlantic isles; it also entailed the notion of a spherical Earth, which, given the oval or circular representation of the Earth on these maps, would have been taken for granted by viewers. For how else could a spherical section be displayed on a flat surface? In some mediaeval manuscripts the *mappae mundi* appear alongside zonal maps, which divide the Earth into two hemispheres and five climes: two cold, two temperate, one hot. Most surviving examples are from Macrobius' fifth-century *Commentary* on Cicero's *Dream of Scipio*. Isidore knew the zonal classification in the form of an easily memorized finger model. Zonal maps and classifications cannot be understood without positing a spherical Earth; it is hardly surprising, then, that the accompanying texts contain discussion on the globe.[42]

Harmonizing the climate theory and spherical model with the Christian worldview was uncontentious so long as it did not touch on the problem of whether other continents (such as the *terra australis* of the Antipodes) were habitable, and hence the theologically tricky question of how and whether people had arrived there through the torrid zone and if they had partaken of the good news.[43] By contrast, the classical view that climate determined ethnic differences, as expressed in appearance, character, and mores, was eminently compatible with biblical guidelines (the distribution of Noah's sons). It could also be used to differentiate oneself ethnographically, ideologically, and theologically from other groups—Muslims, for example.[44] Some even drew on the theory of climate zones to explain the nature and location of

Paradise. Christian authors described it in terms similar to those applied by heathen writers to the Golden Age: an everlasting springtime with a constantly pleasant, 'healthy' climate that brought forth an abundance of plant life and made possible a blissful existence without toil and strife.[45]

Early mediaeval cosmographers from Syria (Cosmas, Ephrem) fused the Platonic teaching of the 'True Continent' (see above, p. 176) with the idea of a land girdling the entire Ocean where Paradise beckoned.[46] This idea, which clearly presupposes a flat Earth, was unable to prevail in the west. Against this, Origen already advanced the classical thesis that there were four (inhabited!) ecumenes on the globe.[47] Discussion of the Antipodes south of the torrid zone and the tradition of the widely read Martianus Capella (fifth to sixth century CE) likewise indicate that Crates' theses on the distribution of the four landmasses on the quarters of the Earth's surface figured on the intellectual horizon of Christian encyclopaedists and cosmographers, particularly as the division into quadrants could be connected with the symbol of the cross. Perhaps mediaeval cosmographers such as the monks of St Gallen experimented around 1000 with the model of a globe (*spera*) that resembled Crates' version.[48]

Finally, the fact that the subjects of geography and natural history were taught in the arts faculty under the heading of geometry shows how receptive Christian thinkers were to the geographical constructions and calculations of antiquity. Geographical and astronomical textbooks accordingly described the classic computation of the Earth's circumference by Eratosthenes, which Senator Cassiodorus (c. 490–580), who served under Theodoric, had already cited in support of Christian knowledge of the world. Ambrose of Milan (c. 333–397) was familiar with the estimate made by Posidonius and accepted by Ptolemy (see above, pp. 260–261).[49] Isidore, too, engaged with Eratosthenes' calculations and their consequences. The Irish monk Dicuil (second half of the eighth to first half of the ninth century) composed a work *de mensura orbis terrae*; his compatriot, John Scotus Eriugena, took Eratosthenes as his model to calculate not just the Earth's circumference but the distance from the Earth to the moon.[50]

LATIN CHRISTENDOM AS BRIDGE

For all the political turmoil faced by Mediterranean-European civilizations from late antiquity, they never lost their curiosity and openness to different modes of understanding the world, provided these did not directly challenge the biblical tradition. Just as sailors' yarns, adventure stories, sober geographical reports, mathematical and descriptive geography, empirical observation, and philosophical-cosmological construction had co-existed productively in antiquity, so mediaeval thinking about the world resembled a broad current fed by numerous tributaries, canalized by Christian doctrine but only occasionally impeded in its onward flow. The influence of Graeco-Roman knowledge traditions on Christendom was too strong for intellectuals to turn a blind eye to classical natural philosophy, geography, and cosmology. On the contrary, Christian faith seems to have been a scaffold and motivation for human curiosity to overcome superstitious fear and gain further insight into the wonders of divine creation. Protected by powerful patrons and little influenced by Rome, several scholars from Ireland and Scotland justified their investigations into the visible world as a God-given task (as Origen and Tertullian had done before them).[51] All agreed that the prophets had revealed only a part of what could be known about the world. Yet whereas this led Augustine to eschew empirical research, it spurred John Scotus Eriugena (ninth century) to do the opposite: 'Yet divine authority not only does not prohibit the investigation of the reasons of things visible and invisible, but even encourages it'.[52]

The basis for such reflections was the endeavour to explain the information in Genesis, which God had revealed to Moses in mystical form, with the means of ancient science. Men like Eriugena, who could read Greek, turned to Bishop Basil of Caesarea (c. 330–379), who had consulted heathen writings (including Aristotle) during his studies in Athens and combined them with his own reflections to create a panorama of scientific knowledge.[53] The Christian message was subjected to a process of rationalization that, while not excluding myth, could place it at any time in the service of rational knowledge. Christendom thus retained an openness to the new while critically interrogating received ideas about the world.

It was thanks to this powerful critical impulse that the essential geographic and cosmological conceptions of antiquity, brought into conformity with Christian dogma, came to appear on the intellectual horizon of the Germanic world. In return, the latter added new empirical data and experiences on the habitability and navigability of the far north to the Romans' stockpile of knowledge, adapting them to ancient traditions such as that of Pytheas on the *zona habitabilis*, now extended farther to the north. In this way, Adam of Bremen recorded news of Viking voyages to North America (Vinland).[54] Latin Christendom was in this respect a conveyor rather than a destroyer of knowledge—not the gravedigger of classical geography and cosmology but a bridge linking them to the *ignorantes pagani* of the Nordic world. At the beginning of the thirteenth century, at the latest, the ancient spherical hypothesis superseded the flat-earth Nordic cosmology, just as Pythagoras and Parmenides had once been instrumental in replacing the Homeric disc-shaped Earth with a ball. The difference was that the Christian thinkers took up and developed this knowledge by confronting it with the seemingly deficient details provided in Genesis.[55]

In this context, the possibility of a sea link between the eastern (India) and western (Iberia) ends of the world remained present 'as a mental constant of spatial awareness'. It had only to be reconciled with the Antipodes thesis, Crates' continental model, and the problem of the Atlantic's true proportions. The decisive argument against surpassing the limits of the ecumene was initially theological in nature. In the east, Paradise blocked access to the world sea. In the west, religious fear of the enormous *Oceanus dissociabilis* acted as a deterrent;[56] only Noah's Ark had crossed it before landing on Ararat. Since then, the sea had been considered the site of the Last Judgment and barrier to the earthly paradise. Every Atlantic voyager had to reckon with God's punishment. Anyone who pushed on regardless should remember the story of Alexander, who before the gates of Paradise was prevented by the *ne plus ultra* from marching on and taking to the sea.[57]

Something was brewing beneath these self-imposed theological limits. One source of discomfort was empirical experience. Even in the west there was a sense that the Far East was attainable. Where else could the silken fabrics at Frankish courts have originated? And had not navigators from Britannia and intrepid adventurers from the north proved that the Atlantic could be navigated despite the cold, even if doubts were (still) raised about a *complete* crossing 'to the furthest ends of the Ocean'?[58] Still, such doubts were allayed by legends of wondrous isles in the Atlantic; these were tangible destinations and springboards to marvellous worlds that never ceased to haunt the mediaeval mind.

PREPARATIONS FOR DEPARTURE: MOBILITY, KNOWLEDGE TRANSFER, AND THE ARISTOTLE RENAISSANCE

As almost always in the history of discovery, these impulses were received and intensified thanks to a combination of political, economic, and social changes. From the mid-eleventh century, Christian Europe—driven by urbanization, demographic growth, economic prosperity, and transregional trade—was gripped by a mobility wave that made a virtue of individual and collaborative travel to faraway countries.[59] Missionaries, conquerors, and farmers infiltrated the last strongholds of Slavic groups in the Baltic. On the Iberian Peninsula, Christian kingdoms began wresting back territories lost to the Moors (Reconquista). During the Crusades, entire armies of knights set out with retinues of traders, priests, and colonists to 'free' the Holy Land from the infidel. Links with the north and south were intensified: Normans ('Northmen') left their homeland to cross the Mediterranean, founding in Sicily a kingdom legalized by the Pope. They ventured as far as Greece and fought in battles in Spain and the Levant.

Italian mercantile cities were the big winners. They offered logistical and financial support to the military campaigns in the east, eventually extending their connections to Alexandria, India, and China. Military mobilization was accompanied by a surge in the number of pilgrims trudging from northern (Scandinavia) to southern Europe (Santiago de Compostela) and via Constantinople to the Holy Land. Even scholars wandered from place to place in search of knowledge. Monks abandoned their vow of stability; 'those who travelled abroad were upheld as the model of society' (Hagen Keller)—a process that in many respects, not least in the transfer of culture and knowledge to royal courts, recalls the dawn of Hellenism. In Castile (Toledo), Norman Sicily, the Maghreb, and Constantinople, expansion fostered exchange between the Latin west and the Islamic-Arab south, previously connected by only a few channels. Through these contacts, the works of Arab astronomers and geographers who based their maps of the world on Ptolemy's *Geographia* were translated into Latin, as were the writings of Aristotle.[60] Beginning in the mid-twelfth century, the Aristotle renaissance encouraged those who had set aside their theological scruples to investigate the nature of the world with 'observation and experience instead of dogmatic tradition' (Jacques Le Goff).[61] The universities provided them with an inspiring forum for discussion, furnishing a new basis for reflections on the shape of the Earth, the relationship between land and water, and the position of the continents.

Aristotle's writings on geography and cosmology became part of the basic canon of the arts faculty and were diligently studied and commented upon. They adhered to the methodological principle that individual statements and observations should be derived from an overall system and set in relation to it. This was also true of the celebrated theory of elements. It served to underpin the idea of the Earth's spherical form in the divine act of creation.[62] Accordingly, the four elements earth, water, air, and fire had grouped together from unstructured matter (*hyle*) into four concentric spheres, based on the criterion of their weight and state of matter (solid, fluid, gaseous, fiery). Because earth was the heaviest element and the heaviest atoms clump together, a globular mass had formed at the centre of the universe (as Augustine had already written).

The model of concentrically tiered spheres with the Earth at the centre was compatible with the image of the cosmic egg, which Arab scholars had also used (see above, p. 371), and it was deployed as an argument for a fully circumnavigable globe. According to the French mathematician, Gossouin de Metz (1247), two people would meet on the opposite side of the Earth if they set out in different directions from the same place.[63] But this raised new questions: if the terrestrial sphere (*sphaera terrae*) was separated from the sphere of water, as Aristotle maintained, and if the former occupied the centre on account of its greater weight, how could a landmass like the ecumene, or other ecumenes like the Antipodes, emerge from the water to be elevated over the sphere of the lighter element?[64] In another text, Aristotle had dissolved the strict division between the two elements and posited a common sphere, without empirically applying it to the Earth's surface and its changes.[65] Late antique astronomers made similar arguments. Some assumed that God had intervened on the third day of Creation to establish the conditions for life by raising the earth from the waters.[66]

Finally, the question of the spheres was associated with a further core problem that had already preoccupied the ancients: the relationship between earth and water on the terraqueous globe. The Franciscan Roger Bacon (c. 1210–1292), who taught in Oxford and Paris, sided with Ptolemy, who in his lost text *De Dispositione Sphaeae* had claimed that only a sixth of the Earth's surface was habitable and the rest covered by water. In keeping with most Arab scholars, Bacon later revised this upwards to a quarter, the figure given in Ptolemy's *Almagest*. Others referred to the prophet Ezra, who inverted the ratio to assert that six-sevenths of the Earth's surface was dry.[67]

All these constructions bore directly on the old question of whether a full crossing of the Atlantic was possible. If most of the Earth was assumed to be covered by habitable land, and if, moreover, a relatively low estimate was given for the Earth's circumference, then the distance between the ends of the landmasses appeared relatively modest. Aristotle had estimated the Earth's circumference at 400,000 stadia. While this was a larger figure than Eratosthenes', he still pronounced it to be small 'in relation to other stars', a statement that had spurred Alexander in his mission to reach the limits of the world. Furthermore, Aristotle thought it not unlikely that 'the region around the Pillars of Heracles joins on to the regions of India, and that in this way the Ocean is one'. Since elephants were found 'in each of these extreme regions', it must be concluded that the sea was not very wide.[68]

The Arab-Iberian philosopher Ibn-Rushd (Averroes, c. 1126–1198) asserted in his commentary on *De caelo et terra* (as Aristotle's *On the Heavens* was called in the Middle Ages): 'India lies on the western horizon of Gades [Cádiz] and Spain on the eastern edge of India'.[69] Around 1260, Thomas Aquinas used almost exactly the same phrasing to argue that India was not so far away from Spain if one sailed west.[70] Roger Bacon connected the idea of a narrow Atlantic with the claim that well over a quarter of the Earth's surface was habitable. A century later, Petrus de Alliaco (Pierre d'Ailly, 1350–c. 1420), chancellor of the University of Paris, supported Bacon's interpretation of Aristotle's arguments by citing Seneca, who held that the sea could be crossed in a few days with favourable winds.[71]

THE 'OPENING OF EARTHLY PARADISE' AND THE SEARCH FOR PRESTER JOHN—FROM RUBRUCK TO MARCO POLO

These were academic discussions conducted among learned specialists with didactic intent. Two developments were needed to bring their scholarly models down to earth. First, the mental and religious barriers that still stood in the way of a circumnavigation of the Earth from east to west or north to south had to be overcome (as Pierre d'Ailly explicitly pointed out).[72] Second, the real-world situation had to change, and the impulses of the twelfth century steered to the sea, for a path to be cleared to the farthest destinations.

Until the mid-thirteenth century, the Latin west was largely cut off from reports on central Asia and the Far East (China) made by Byzantine diplomats and Arab and Jewish merchants.[73] A change came with the rise of the

Italian port cities that profited the most from the Crusades and Europe's growing demand for Far Eastern products (silk, spices) and sought to purchase these products from the source. When Mongol expansion reached the west in the thirteenth century, a trans-Asiatic land bridge emerged that later, following the collapse of Mongol hegemony, could be used to establish direct contact between Europe and Asia. This was an advance on antiquity, when there had been only isolated direct contact between the eastern Mediterranean lands (Syria, Macedonia, Egypt) and China. At the same time, Eurasia embarked on a century-long economic upswing, the likes of which the world had not seen since the golden age of the Han Empire and Imperium Romanum in the first century CE[74]—then as now an important prerequisite for intensified transcontinental links. Whereas Italian merchants hoped to pocket hefty profits by directly importing eastern luxury goods in exchange for easily transportable western commodities (amber, coral, jewellery), the Pope and some kings were enticed by the possibility of converting the Great Khan and forging a military alliance against the Saracens. In addition, many thought that the kingdom of the mysterious Prester John lay in the Far East near Paradise, from where he would lead an army of Amazons, exotic tribes, and Christians to support his coreligionists in their fight against the Muslims in the Holy Land.[75]

A mix of foreign policy objectives, financial hopes, and visions of power thus impelled thirteenth-century western missionaries, diplomats, and merchants to seek out the Great Khan's residence, first in Karakorum, then (after Kublai's accession) in Tabriz. They were followed at the start of the fourteenth century by missionaries who journeyed to China—sometimes via India—to build up their own ecclesiastical organization.[76] The intensity of contact began to wane with the end of Mongol rule in China and Persia and with the rise of the Ottomans, and the China mission came to an end with the establishment of the national Ming dynasty in 1368; yet the knowledge acquired en route remained. It was expressed, on the one hand, in an expanded global *geographical* horizon.[77] William of Rubruck, a Flemish monk who travelled to Karakorum, could settle the perennial conundrum of whether the Caspian was an inland sea. He also identified Cathay with the land of the Seres, while the Ganges delta marked the eastern end of the world from a western perspective.[78] With that, the west had in principle returned to the level of knowledge attained under the Roman Empire, despite the loss of Ptolemy.

On the other hand, the reports submitted by expeditionary voyages under papal and French instructions raised the bar of *ethnographic* analysis.[79] They gave new weight to eye witnessing as the criterion for providing credible information about places where readers would never set foot themselves. This development, a throwback to Herodotus, coincided with an increased openness to empirical experiment and first-hand observation. New writings could now be compared with old, and orthodoxies such as the Caspian Sea's debouchment into the Ocean could be convincingly criticized through on-the-ground experience, once again attesting to the importance of state patronage for the formation of ethnographic writing rooted in close observation.[80]

This phenomenon is familiar to us from antiquity, as is the fact that the missionaries entering Mongol territory still confirmed the existence of wondrous peoples in some form or another. They were as much a part of ethnographic reportage as details about the Mongols' way of life.[81] These two factors explain why the expeditionary reports ushered in a revival of travel literature drawn from *both* empirical observation and classical *topoi* concerning peripheral peoples. Sir John Mandeville's novel about his supposed journeys to the Holy Land, Africa, India, China, the Mongol Great Khan, and the kingdom of Prester John became a bestseller. Precisely because it offered so many marvels at the edges of the known world, contemporaries considered it to be authentic, or at any rate far more credible than the narrative Marco Polo wrote from Genoese captivity about his travels in the service of the Great Khan.[82] Today we know that the anonymous author who went under the name Sir John of Mandeville had never ventured beyond Jerusalem, at least, but had pieced together his information from a motley collection of sources. Besides the Alexander Romance, these included non-fictional works such as Rubruck's travel memoir. In contrast to Mandeville, they dampened hopes of finding the kingdom of Prester John—Rubruck never found him, and Marco Polo wrote that he died on the battlefield—while nonetheless idealizing the Far East as a far richer world. At the same time, they expanded the horizon of the west to a not inconsiderable extent. Through his news of Cipangu, the land of gold (Japan), Marco Polo pushed the eastern end of the world even further out into the Ocean.[83]

PARADISE SHIFTS SOUTH, PORTUGUESE ADVANCES IN AFRICA

What the reports on the Far East did *not* contain, or only very rarely, were references to an earthly paradise. Even Mandeville frankly confessed: 'Of

Paradise I cannot speak properly'.[84] This negative finding had far-reaching consequences. The farther east Europeans' *real* horizon of knowledge extended, the more easily the treasures of the east could be detached from the idea of a terrestrial paradise, the more frequently scholars began to doubt whether the localization of Paradise in the east was even correct. Some early fifteenth-century maps therefore dispensed with Paradise altogether. With that, one of the most important religious obstacles to an east-west oceanic crossing seemed to have been overcome. There was growing optimism about a possible circumnavigation of the Earth. Mandeville was sure that a ship with a good crew could sail around the world, provided mountains and lands proved no obstacle.[85]

No one yet doubted the existence of an earthly paradise. If it did not lie in the east, then perhaps it could be found in a different part of the world. And here the age-old (mis)identification of India with Ethiopia—shared by Byzantine writers—came to the help of scholars.[86] Identical ethnographic and natural characteristics had always been supposed in the two regions, and typical phenomena from one could be ascribed to the other. From the mid-twelfth century, some scholars moved Paradise south of the equatorial zone.[87] Was not the cherubim's flaming sword an allusion to the torrid zone? According to classical doctrine, the latter guarded entry to the temperate zone of the Antipodes, just as natural barriers (mountain, wall, water), combined with supernatural forces (cherubim), blocked access to Paradise. The peculiar charm of relocating Paradise to the south lay in undergirding this theologically motivated ban with a scientific argument drawn from ancient climate theory.[88] Even Roger Bacon weighed up the possibility that Paradise might await in the Southern Hemisphere, citing Aristotle's argument that the southern part of the globe was the best.[89] For the first time, the two great determinants of long-range projections in the Middle Ages—earthly paradise and Antipodean continent—had converged. They were joined by a third motif, the kingdom of Prester John, which from the fourteenth century (with news of a Christian Nestorian community) could be transplanted to Ethiopia, hence to the southern or southeast hemispheres.[90]

The relocation to the south of these mediaeval dream destinations went hand in hand with a longing to reach them. From the mid-thirteenth century onward, an awareness that the world had grown larger emboldened those who proclaimed that the equatorial zone was not just traversable but also habitable, as Arab cartographers and astronomers (following Ptolemy) had surmised, as Dante had hinted, and as Marco Polo had confirmed when he remarked that the North Star appeared to have dipped below the horizon in Java and Sumatra, suggesting that he had crossed the equator.[91] And it was now recalled that Pliny and Ambrose had written about people who dwelled beyond that line of latitude.[92] Pierre d'Ailly asserted that there were many settlements on its far side. Augustine's verdict on the existence of the Antipodes forfeited its binding authority. Nothing now stood in the way of a push into southern latitudes; indeed, it had come to seem imperative.[93]

Famously, the Portuguese took up the challenge around a century later, after conquering Muslim Ceuta at the start of the fifteenth century and rounding Cape Bojador in 1434. The search for the earthly paradise and kingdom of Prester John, now imagined as located on the upper Nile, were surely important motives.[94] As always, however, mental dispositions had to ally with hopes for concrete gains of a material and/or political nature for the investment to seem worthwhile. In this case, the chivalric-aristocratic ambition to perform glorious deeds at sea and the 'cursed lust for gold' (*auri sacra fames*) united the Portuguese in their fight against the Moor and drove captains south.[95] Henry the Navigator needed gold to keep his followers on side and secure his rule. At the turn of the fifteenth century, demand for gold in Europe had reached unprecedented heights as the one-sided east Asian trade led to a drastic shortfall of precious metals as means of payment.[96] For centuries, caravans had been supplying the metal from Ghana and the legendary Bambouk in exchange for glassware, textiles, copper, and coral. It was therefore only logical that Portuguese rulers seized the opportunity to make direct contact with the gold-producing territories.

They were supported by the know-how of Italian captains and merchant families from Genoa, who hoped for better prospects in the west than in the east. There, trade was still dominated by Venice and increasingly threatened by the rise in Ottoman power, and they themselves urgently needed gold to produce cloth of gold and buy goods from the Far East. Cooperation between political-aristocratic ambition and economic-mercantile self-interest had always been one of the most powerful driving forces behind voyages of discovery. It received an additional economic impulse in the mid-fifteenth century, when the Ottomans conquered Constantinople (on 29 May 1453) and threw into disarray the already disturbed trade relations between Italian cities and the Far East. Because demand for Far Eastern luxury products and spices as well as precious metals remained high and even grew (the European silk industry boomed in the thirteenth century, much like the Levant in the early imperial period), the search for alternative oceanic connections gained fresh momentum. The Portuguese stood to gain from this. The plan to reach India or China via the sea route around Africa now became a potentially lucrative endeavour, one that could additionally be justified with reference to ancient reports of successful circumnavigations (especially in Pliny). The Vivaldi brothers from Genoa had probably attempted to realise it in searching for gold at the end of the thirteenth century, when the Crusaders lost their last stronghold at Acre.[97]

COLUMBUS AND THE JOURNEY WEST OVER THE ATLANTIC

Seduced by hindsight, we can easily forget that the Portuguese crown, for all the pains it took to open up the west African coastal routes, never lost sight of the northwest Atlantic and its legendary islands. In the 70s and 80s, it even issued letters patent for discovering and occupying islands and lands in the west, and it never ruled out a voyage to India via the Atlantic.[98]

In all these undertakings, the Portuguese were supported by the Genoese, who had already participated in the economic development of Madeira and the Azores (through the introduction of sugarcane).[99] In making his way to the Portuguese court in Lisbon in the 1470s—like Cádiz of old, the gateway to the Ocean and centre of Atlantic shipping—Columbus was following in the footsteps of his fellow Genoese, just as his plan to reach India via the Atlantic was far from revolutionary. In some respects, Portuguese exploration of the African coast was a boon; they had reached the Guinea coast, thereby definitively disproving the idea that the equatorial zone could not be crossed and confirming Pierre d'Ailly's theory of its habitability. Climatological arguments against an Atlantic crossing on a southerly route from the Canaries (the Portuguese generally granted patents for the northern Atlantic) thereby fell away.

What remained undecided was the question of the Antipodes as well as other landmasses in the Atlantic. Given the centuries-long discussion about the Earth and its physical constitution, it is highly unlikely that Columbus had in mind an unobstructed passage with India (or the gold-rich Cipangu) as his sole objective.[100] Like all his semi-educated seafaring compatriots, Columbus was at least indirectly involved in this discussion. In Strabo's *Geographica*, translated in 1458, he found the electrifying sentence that two or more inhabited worlds could lie in the same temperate zone, 'and particularly in the proximity of the parallel through Athens that is drawn across the Atlantic Sea'.[101] Furthermore, he knew the famous Seneca prophecy (by reading the 1474–1484 Ferrara edition of the tragedies), replacing the plural form *novos orbes* with *nuebo mundo*. After observing large quantities of freshwater pouring from the delta of the Orinoco River into the Gulf of Paria during his third journey, he noted in his journal: 'I believe that this is a very great continent, until today unknown'.[102]

Since late antiquity, the Antipodes had been placed in both the Northern and Southern Hemispheres. Three years before Columbus presented his enterprise to the Portuguese king, Luigi Pulci had published a poem, 'Morgante' (1481/82), in which the 'demon' Astarotte explains that the world of the Antipodes lay beyond the Pillars of Heracles, with towns and kingdoms like our own but inhabited by heathen awaiting their conversion. Not long after, Columbus claimed this role of universal missionary for himself, the disciple who carries Christ over the Ocean (*Christopher* = *Christum ferrens* ['bearer of Christ'], as Columbus signed his name).[103] The fact that he did not rule out the Antipodes as his destination is shown by the response of a commission member to his project: 'Saint Augustine doubted it'.[104] Shortly after his first Atlantic voyage, the Humanist Peter Martyr (Pietro Martire d'Anghiera) wrote that Christopher had returned 'from the western Antipodes'.[105] Italian commentators described the newly discovered land in terms of the Antipodes.[106] And with the Antipodes, the dream of Paradise also stayed alive. Columbus believed he was close to it at the Orinoco.[107]

In contrast to what is frequently supposed in retrospect, Columbus reckoned with several partly complementary, partly conflicting possibilities: with a free trans-Atlantic passage to Cathay (or Asia); with the Antipodes (or some other new continent); or with the mythical Atlantic isles, Saint Brendan's Island, or Antilia, which Columbus hoped to find on his way to Cathay.[108] Even Ophir (thought to be in India) and Tarshish, the source of Solomon's gold, numbered among the possible destinations in an age that hungered for gold.[109] Columbus was ready for all eventualities prefigured in the ancient and mediaeval tradition and adapted what he said to the political circumstances and audience. The Spanish committee that considered his project after it had been passed up by the Portuguese named 'islands and continents' as the voyage's objectives, giving a good indication of the spectrum of possibilities.[110] Columbus sailed and argued on the bow wave of a thousand-year-old discussion that had developed a huge range of considered ideas about what lay between Spain and India.

What delayed the realization of his plan and prompted both the Portuguese and the first Spanish committee to turn it down was the incalculable length of the voyage. Debate about the Atlantic's dimensions was rekindled in the 1460s and 1470s, when the first Latin editions of Ptolemy's *Geography* were published in northern Italy. At 180,000 stadia (33,480 km), Ptolemy had not only estimated the Earth's circumference at almost a quarter less than the true figure (and half the figure provided by Eratosthenes); he had also extended the ecumene too far to the east, at 180 degrees longitude from the Canaries. Like most of Columbus' contemporaries, he assumed that it occupied half the Earth's surface, with the Atlantic taking up the other half, although the still undiscovered parts of the ecumene in the east might shorten a journey.[111]

Others cited Pierre d'Ailly, who joined Roger Bacon and Aristotle in claiming that most of the Earth was covered by land and even speculated that the Antipodes could be connected to the known ecumene. He drew on Marinus of Tyre, who argued against Ptolemy that the ecumene stretched some 225 degrees longitude to the east. Towards the end of his life, Columbus claimed to have proven Ptolemy wrong and Marinus right.[112] In 1474, the geographer and astronomer Paolo Toscanelli had already tried to interest the Portuguese court in the consequences of such a narrow Atlantic and a comparably short westward journey. He estimated the distance between Lisbon and Quinsay (Hangzhou) at 6,500 nautical miles, that between the Canaries and Cathay (China) at 5,000. The cosmographer Martin Behaim, who spent many years at the Lisbon court as a royal counsellor, applied Toscanelli's view to the globe he produced in Nuremberg in 1492; a year later, the Nuremberg-based physician and geographer Hieronymus Münzer (c. 1447–1508) called on the Portuguese king to investigate the Atlantic route.[113]

All this shows that the project of a trans-Atlantic crossing had been in vogue well beyond northern Italy since the 1470s. In this respect, too, Columbus was engaged in an ongoing discussion that had taken on a new lease of life with the translation of Ptolemy. Far from being an isolated visionary, he represented a well-established intellectual tradition that he modified to his suit his needs. He vehemently defended the Apocalypse of Ezra's statement about the preponderance of land over water on the globe.[114] He also owned a copy of Toscanelli's letter, probably even before his first voyage. To the information he picked up from Marinus, he added the Spice Islands (Indonesia) and Cipangu (Japan) mentioned by Marco Polo, both unknown to Ptolemy. After erroneously converting Arabic miles into Italian miles, he arrived at a distance from Cipangu to the west of 'only' 2,400 Italian nautical miles, roughly equivalent to 4,000 km.[115]

Even if Ptolemy contradicted Columbus' ideas about the dimensions of the Atlantic, in another respect he furnished him with an important argument for using the Atlantic crossing as an alternative to Portuguese attempts to sail around Africa. If Ptolemy was right in thinking that southern Africa was connected to India by a land bridge (the legendary Antipodean continent) and that the Indian Ocean was a vast inland sea, then maritime access to India was blocked and India could be reached only with great difficulty over land from its southeast flank. This possibility was taken seriously by the Portuguese, which is why they did not rule out a journey west over the Atlantic.

The reasons that kept them from taking up Toscanelli's initiative were primarily political in nature: Portugal was embroiled in an exorbitant war of succession with Castile. When Columbus presented the same project in 1484, the *Junta dos Matemáticos* rejected his proposal mainly because of its debt to Ptolemy and exposed flaws in Columbus' calculations. Moreover, journeys to Africa had just entered a crucial, highly promising phase: Diogo Cão had reached the Congo and brought back news of a flourishing kingdom ('the Congo Empire'), which many linked with the long-sought kingdom of Prester John. The discovery brought hopes that the coastline would soon curve into the Indian Ocean.[116] Three years later (1487–1488), Bartolomeu Dias rounded the southern tip of Africa and indeed discovered the sea route to India. In 1490 a mission was sent to the Indian Ocean to find out once and for all whether the Ptolemaic notion of a land bridge between India and Africa was fact or fiction.[117] The Portuguese were probably also convinced by Arab maps that Ptolemy was mistaken on this score. The 1459 map of Fra Mauro (a monk from San Michele in Venice), possibly commissioned by Henry the Navigator, was oriented south rather than east; it showed an African continent that stretched far to the east but was unconnected with Asia. Others added the critical caveat to the Ptolemaic land bridge in the south: 'Terra incognita secundum Ptolemaeum', unknown land according to Ptolemy.[118]

Depressed and beset by pressing financial difficulties, Columbus thus turned to Spain. Franciscan and aristocratic friends introduced him to new sources of funding and contacts with the royal house. The Spanish committee was also familiar with his calculation problems, albeit perhaps less so than the nautically experienced Portuguese.[119] Yet after the conquest of Granada, the last Muslim bastion in Spain, a new mood had set in. On April 17, 1492, following tough negotiations concerning money and privileges, official support for Columbus' voyage was finally granted under the Capitulations of Santa Fe.

THE OLD WORLD IN THE NEW

Like all great voyages of discovery, the decision to embark on the journey west was hence a product of political constellations and long-term trends. At its root was the cooperation between north Italian seamanship and a consortium of influential mercantile and financial interests, as well as the Spanish crown's determination to engage actively in the dynastic rivalry over maritime routes to India. In this respect, the journey may be compared to the expeditions to India the Carians once made under Persian command, or those the Phoenicians carried out in Africa under the Egyptian flag. The missionary idea may have played a subordinate role in the planning of its sponsors; like the Portuguese captains, Columbus did not even have a priest on board. Besides, the Great Khan was considered to be well disposed towards Christians.

Nevertheless, early-modern plans to circumnavigate Africa and cross the Atlantic operated in an intellectual climate that was directly and indirectly influenced by ancient sources, from whose authority they drew much of their confidence. Just as Greek mariners had once set out in the hopeful assurance that they were sailing in the wake of their great heroes Heracles, Jason, and Odysseus and moving in a world made explicable by myth, so the early-modern captains—for all their nautical experience—were certain that they were testing and realizing what the ancients had already demonstrated in theory. No one was too proud to refer to them when dangers lay ahead. 'The Infante'—according to the Portuguese chronicler on Henry—'well knew that Hanno, the Carthaginian captain, had sailed along the African coast until almost below the equator. The notes he made about his itinerary and what he saw clearly show that he must have advanced beyond today's Sierra Leone. He also held to be true what Herodotus, a highly serious author, [. . .] writes about the sea journey undertaken by experienced Phoenician mariners at the behest of Necho, an Egyptian king'.[120]

And so it was that Columbus, too, after sailing from a port near ancient Tartessos, calling in at the Canaries, and arriving at the Caribbean island of Guanahani (San Salvador) after a journey of thirty-six days, encountered a world he perceived (in part) through the lens of ancient writers and geographers. Among his favourite texts were the biblical tales of the Queen of Sheba and gold-rich Tarshish, which he linked with Cathay and Cipangu and later, following his trans-Atlantic crossing, identified with Hispaniola/Haiti and Jamaica; his patron Isabella owned tapestries showing the queen's visit to King Solomon and the riches of the kings of Tarshish. He later assured Pope Alexander VI that he had discovered Solomon's mines on Hispaniola, while on the Orinoco (in the temperate zone) he believed Paradise to be near.[121]

He was more restrained when it came to mythical motifs from classical antiquity. Columbus represents the view—widespread since the first Europeans had travelled to the land of the Mongols—that eyewitness reporting should be given greater weight than book learning, to which it could act as a corrective (see above, p. 380). In his letter from his first voyage, he reports that he failed to encounter the monsters (*monstra*) expected by many. Yet he could not wholly disappoint his readers. And so, he casually remarks that there were people born with a tail on one island (as Ptolemy had surmised there were in Indonesia).[122] He also glimpsed the Sirens (whom he had already encountered off the Guinea coast!) in Caribbean waters,[123] and was on the look-out for monsters and leather-clad warrior women on a desert isle, later taken by commentators to be Amazons. By contrast, the 'naked savages' on Hispaniola struck him as peaceful and innocent, although he did not draw the obvious conclusion that they had tarried in the Golden Age and, as the relics of a prelapsarian age, knew no shame; this would have entangled him in theological difficulties. He was sceptical about 'reports' of cannibals (anthropophagi), the Caribs on the Lesser Antilles.[124] Yet for all his sober observation and focus on material returns (gold, mastic), his continuing reliance on ancient *topoi* is revealed when he refers to natives telling him of 'men with one eye, and other with dogs' snouts'.[125] No Spaniard was in a position to infer the familiar *topoi* of cyncocephali and

Image 14 Marvellous peoples from the East in the world chronicle of Hartmann Schedel (1493). The 'monsters and fantastic creatures' of the New World from the *Liber Chronicarum* by the Nuremberg scholar Hartmann Schedel appear on an image bar in the margins of the text. Lifted from the catalogue of human marvels in Pliny and Solinus, they could be transplanted to the 'New World' following the voyages of Columbus. Credit: Author/Klett-Cotta.

cyclops from the words and gestures of their indigenous interlocutors; they were a projection of Columbus or his interpreter.[126]

And even when he and those who came after him realized that they had not arrived at Cipangu or the eastern end of Asia but a 'New World', they could not depict it otherwise than with the categories and images of the Old World. Amerigo Vespucci described the inhabitants of the Caribbean islands in similarly ambivalent terms to those used by Columbus or Mandeville in relation to the Far East: here peaceful, harmless, and naked savages who live to the age of 150 (like those living on the island visited by Iambulus, see above, pp. 351–352), there threatening cannibals. The humanist Peter Martyr compared the life of the islanders on Hispaniola with the

Image 15 Fantastic creatures in the New World. Levin(us) Hulsius, the Flanders-born, Nuremberg-based printer, published several accounts of voyages to faraway lands, including one to the imaginary Kingdom of Guinea in America. Here we see depicted those described by Pliny as having no heads (*akephaloi*) and having faces set upon their chests; in ancient times, they were thought to live in Africa (Libya). Credit: Author/Klett-Cotta.

Golden Age of Virgil and Hesiod, the Carib cannibals with the Thracians who once impregnated the Amazons on Lesbos.[127] Francisco de Orellana gave such a convincing account of female inhabitants of the great river in South America that the river was named not after him, its discoverer, but the Amazons. Cortés thought he had almost conquered their empire, while book illustrations showed America personified as a busty 'Amazon' with her subjects in the background taking gold from the mines of legendary Ophir and heaping it at her feet (Ophir was identified with Peru).[128] The arsenal of ancient dreams was thus dusted off to integrate the New World into the Old. Even the tribes of monsters reappeared in aggressive and irenic versions: book illustrations from the early sixteenth century show Indians as dog-headed cannibals or as relics of the idyllic Golden Age with faces on their chests. Hartmann Schedel's *Liber Chronicarum* from 1493 presents a complete catalogue of ancient wondrous nations in the New World as a colourful picture strip.[129]

And even as attempts were made to comprehend the 'Indians' in their ethnic originality and to debate their rights, those involved in such discussions continued to draw as if self-evidently on the ethnographic templates supplied by Herodotus, who enjoyed an unparalleled renaissance among missionaries, discoverers, and historians.[130] No less self-evident was the way they fell back on the tradition of the ancient botanists, Theophrastus and Dioscurides, when faced with the confusing variety of plant life.[131] Fernández de Oviedo y Valdez, author of the oldest history of American plants, animals, and people, confessed towards the end of his life that he found himself 'only just approaching the substance of those great and innumerable secrets, unknown to the ancients, [. . .] which await discovery in this second hemisphere and in these regions'.[132] Even as he acknowledged the ignorance of antiquity, the ancient world remained the yardstick for what could be known about the world.

Epilogue

All humans by nature desire to know.

Aristotle, *Metaphysics* 980A

In 1874 the director of the National Museum of Brazil published the transcription of a stone tablet that a slave had reportedly found near the Paraiba River. The content of the lost original was sensational. Writing in a Hebrew-Aramaic dialect, men from Phoenician Sidon described how they had landed on the coast after they had set out from the Red Sea 'in the nineteenth year of King Hiram' and been separated from the main fleet while rounding Ham (= Africa). Discussion of the document's authenticity has continued to this day.[1] Here, it seemed, was testimony confirming ancient stories about the continent in the Far West, not to mention the origin of the stranger from Carthage with which our passage through the history of ancient discovery began.

Even if scepticism predominates, enthusiasm flares up from time to time as sleuths both amateur and professional hunt for clues that ancient ships once landed on the shores of the New World. While they have been unable to furnish compelling evidence to date, they are spurred on by the conviction that ancient mariners must have been capable of such a feat. They recall the capacious view that the ancients had of the world, their faith in their ability to traverse seas and deserts to reach the farthest ends of the earth, at least in their own minds. Even if we will never know exactly how far ancient discoverers travelled, their real exploration of the world of Eurasia and North Africa, combined with their rational penetration of the entire globe, is the inspiring legacy they bequeathed the Modern Age. It is worth concluding by enquiring into the underlying causes, driving forces, and developments.

At the beginning stood the sailors from Ugarit and other coastal towns in the Levant. From the early second millennium BCE, they set out for distant shores to procure valuable goods for themselves and their powerful neighbours: metals needed to equip armies, build palaces, and manufacture temple implements—copper and iron from Cyprus, northern Italy, and the northern and southern coasts of Asia Minor, gold and silver from southern Spain and Nubia, tin from northern Europe. Others sought the exotic plants that were essential for temple service, medicine, and a luxurious life: incense and myrrh from southern Arabia and Somalia, soon also pepper from India and silk from China. Their places of origin became mythical wonderlands: Tartessos in Spain, rich in silver; Punt and Ophir in Arabia and Somalia; or Dilmun, the legendary stopover on the way to India.

No ruler could afford to do without products from abroad. The pride of showing them off at his own court was a source of his legitimacy. They revealed that the regent's arm stretched to the edges of the world and gave him access to the riches to be found there. Faced with the need to support large land armies to defend and expand their territory, pharaohs, Assyrians, Babylonians, and Persians sought to outsource technically demanding long-distance voyages to coastal communities that specialized in such tasks. For them, the sea was not a threatening liminal space but an escape route, an outlet for internal tensions, and the gateway to unimaginable wealth.

This constellation gave rise to the great maritime traditions of the Phoenicians and Greeks. In the ninth and eighth centuries, Tyre and Sidon sent their captains over the island and coasts of the western Mediterranean to the Atlantic to procure tin, silver, and gold for the Assyrians and Egyptians. Greek adventurers followed in their wake to Provence and Tartessos on the Spanish Atlantic coast. They explored the shores of the Black Sea, where according to legend Jason and his Argonauts had won the Golden Fleece.

The dynamic of their explorations could no longer be explained by political or material constraints, the unequal distribution of valuable goods in the Mediterranean, or the limited agricultural resources available in their homelands—after all, similar conditions prevailed in comparable regions around the world.[2] An urgent need for land or food rarely filled the rowing benches of their ships. They were driven instead by the prospect of profit and opportunities for success, along with an appetite for mobility and risk that was typical of port- and coast-dwellers. Routinized through constant experience, this is what led them to master uncertain routes and sail for destinations of which they were only dimly aware. The journeys embarked on by these archaic mariners manifested a *mentality of curiosity, audacity, and learning* that steered their thirst for knowledge towards distant horizons even when uninfluenced by state or religious authorities.

We find this mentality immortalized in the Homeric Odysseus, yet there is much to suggest that Bronze Age captains and Phoenician trading were already shaped by it. Odysseus—'much-daring' but also 'much-enduring'—is the prototype of the intrepid mariner. Through his adaptability, intelligence, and persistence, he endures one setback after another until he finally arrives at his destination, rich and famous. Odysseus became the model for all the great and not-so-great discoverers who set sail from Mediterranean coastal towns because their skills were wanted abroad: as physicians in search of medicinal plants and employment at the courts of the powerful; as captains of large-scale royal expeditions; as artisans and artists, mercenaries, pirates, and merchants, all of whom understood how to cater to the material needs of both their homeland and their new environs.

Such people are forced to adjust to alien cultures. They learn the language of their target area and wine and dine local grandees; if they settle down, they marry a native woman and have children who grow up speaking two languages. All this resulted in an intergenerational *experience of otherness* that probably did not exist in this form and over such a long period of time in other parts of the ancient world, yet shows remarkable parallels (and perhaps even continuities) to the mentality of early-modern Europeans.

Rulers of kingdoms facing inland used it for their own purposes. Tyre sent expeditions on King Solomon's behalf to the gold- and spice-producing land of Ophir. A Phoenician captain was allegedly commissioned by the Egyptian pharaoh to circumnavigate Africa from the Red Sea, probably to chart an alternative route to the treasures of Spanish Tartessos. Greeks not only fought as mercenaries for their foreign paymasters but cruised the Ocean for the Persian great king. One sailed down the Indus, continued to the entrance of the Persian Gulf, then rounded the Arabian Peninsula to land on Egyptian soil via the Red Sea.

This experience of mobility and otherness, combined with a mentality of inquisitive audacity recalling the early-modern age of discovery, helped people overcome their natural fears about putting out to sea for weeks or even months at a time. Greek seafarers and overland travellers were convinced that they journeyed on routes and steered for destinations pioneered by heroes and demigods like Odysseus or Heracles. Even as they neared the ends of the earth, they were sure that they would enter spaces that were inhabited and would therefore offer them some chance of survival. Otherwise, such expeditions could hardly have been countenanced and manned in view of the enormous risks involved.

From an ancient perspective, transregional mobility was therefore rarely a 'discovery' in the sense of a conscious, planned, and targeted breakthrough to something entirely new; indeed, novelty in general was of dubious value in antiquity. The Greeks lacked a concept for it. *Heuriskein* means 'to find' in the sense of *re*-finding something whose secrets could be fathomed through inquiry and research (*historie*).

The assurance that they were re-treading familiar paths and, like Odysseus, could find their bearings wherever the four winds carried them inspired the spirit of adventure rather than causing it to flag. Whereas an understandable fear of the unknown as well as the dangers of water and desert deterred people from other parts of the world from leaving their homeland, ancient travellers by sea and land saw here both an opportunity and a challenge: an opportunity to gain glory, wealth, and experiences that were valued back home; a challenge because these paths were lined by monsters and potentially fatal traps, and because, even when navigating supposedly known and familiar spaces, they could always cross a threshold to an unknown world that transcended their own experience.

Finally, an attitude of open-minded curiosity, mobility, and adaptability were important prerequisites for ensuring that voyages of exploration led to the planting of settlements on foreign shores, frequently in cooperation with natives. In this way, the archaic period (eighth to sixth century BCE) saw the points of departure for exploration on the eastern Mediterranean seaboard supplemented by new urban zones on the northern and western periphery. The *poleis* of the northern Pontos, Phocaean Massalia and its sub-colonies, as well as Carthage and its Atlantic foundations beyond the Strait of Gibraltar, were located outside the boundaries of territorial kingdoms. In their quest for gold, silver, tin, and other valuable products, and frequently in competition with each other, they could thus usher in a new phase of exploration directed at spaces beyond the Mediterranean: the world of the Atlantic tin isles and amber coasts, the vast expanses of southern Siberia, the deserts of the Sahara.

Where travellers penetrated farther inland, they took advantage of the great river systems along with caravan routes. Rivers such as the Rhône, the Guadalquivir, the Don and Dnieper, or the Senegal in west Africa were natural conduits to hinterlands that could never have been accessed on foot. Combined with territorial links, they formed mobility corridors that later showed many a conqueror the path ahead. By helping to develop these transit routes, city-states on the western and northern periphery became nodal points, distribution centres, and transmitters—not only of commodities but also of technologies, religious cults, and information. Through Carthage, news of the peoples, animals, and plants of northern Africa reached the Greek world. Amber traders acquainted the Greeks with Nordic myths and gods. Greek healers and merchants learned about shamanic wisdom from the Scythians. And it is surely no coincidence that a few decades after Aristeas set out for the southern Siberian steppes and Massiolite and Etruscan traders pushed ever deeper into Celtic territory, a new conception of the divine origin of the immortal soul spread throughout the Mediterranean, synthesizing with Greek myths into grand intellectual edifices such as Orphism.

While a dynamic of long-distance exploration and knowledge acquisition, largely divorced from any expansionist military agenda, thus unfolded on the northern and western periphery until well into the fourth century, the east remained the preserve of the great territorial empires until late antiquity. The Persian Empire formed the bridge on which products from, and information about, India and Arabia entered the Mediterranean basin. At the same time, it conserved ancient wisdom that had coalesced with the experiences of captains and colonists into a unique form of rational world-knowledge ('Ionian natural philosophy') even before Cyrus annexed the coastal towns of Asia Minor. When the Hellenistic monarchs who succeeded the Persians planned voyages of discovery to prepare for or accompany their conquests, they provided the material and logistics but still relied on the expertise of east Mediterranean coast-dwellers.

We should not allow the generals' prestige to deceive us: just as Darius drew on the experience of Carian-Greek captains when charting the sea route from the Indus to the Red Sea, so Alexander entrusted the Cretan Nearchus and Onesicritus from the island polis of Astypalaia with the voyage back from the Indus estuary to the Persian Gulf. A generation later, captains from Rhodes and Cyzicus navigated the Red Sea and the monsoon route to India for the Ptolemies. Greeks from Asia Minor settled in Ai-Khanoum in northern Afghanistan, while men from Miletus and the Aegean led armies across the Jaxartes (Syr Darya) for the Seleucid king and resided as envoys in Pataliputra on the Ganges. When Seleucus sent his general Patrocles to the Caspian Sea to search for a link between the Black Sea and India, he may have dreamed of the customs revenues the new trade route would generate. Of decisive importance were the strategic options of a northeast passage, which had already prompted the Persian kings and Alexander to initiate long-distance expeditions in the south (Nile).

The dynamic of exploration and colonization under the early Hellenistic rulers occurred against the background of a general wave of mobility that for the first time extended overland all the way to India and Afghanistan. It was supported by an economic upswing as well as the financial resources the kings inherited from Alexander and the Persian treasury. Yet the real secret behind the success of this third phase of ancient discoveries continued to be the symbiosis between exploratory missions launched from urban centres, the material backing of great empires, and their political ambitions. This is what distinguished the eastern Mediterranean from other regions, where these conditions were either non-existent or ephemeral. The extraordinary long-distance travels of Indian, Arabian, and southeast Asian captains on the Indian Ocean originated in small communities, but their regional princes were in no position to follow up these commercial exploratory missions with sustained military expansion; it can therefore be hard to reconstruct their movements. Cities in the Yellow River floodplains lacked maritime access to foreign shores and the opportunity to gain experience acquiring and transporting foreign goods. They fell under the sway of territorial rulers and then the Han emperor, who submerged autonomous city-states in a network of imperial distribution centres and subjected urban markets to ever-tighter controls.[3]

By contrast, Greek (and probably also Phoenician) port cities managed to keep their markets free from foreign interference. They allowed their traders enormous leeway (beyond imposing the usual tariffs and supervisory measures), as can be seen from the fact that they did not intervene in transactions involving foreign currencies below silver coins. They could even maintain their unity and a greater degree of independence than, say, the Chinese city-states when they were overshadowed by neighbouring powers or integrated into the territory of large empires. With that, they carried on a tradition that dated back to the Bronze Age and archaic period (Ugarit in relation to the Hittites, Miletus in relation to the Lydians). If they were nonetheless reconquered or destroyed, the new rulers sought out alternative partners or tried to compensate for the loss with new settlements.

Alexandria was the most successful, establishing itself as the gateway to the Indian Ocean, but many of Alexander's other foundations in Asia also became vectors of mobility and long-distance trade along or near the silk roads. Similarly, the exploration of the Red Sea and its hinterlands (Meroë) by the Ptolemies preceded an intensive wave of colonization along the coasts. Not by chance, Bactria, one of the most densely urbanized regions in Asia, became a hub for long-distance routes to China and India *and* the base from which conquering armies decamped for northern India.

Urban experience of the world coexisted with expansionary ambition not just because they profited from each other. They were also united by a factor that accelerated ancient discoveries and ensured they never came to a complete halt: competition between participant actors. Cities with maritime experience and far-flung trade links stood in permanent rivalry with other seafaring communities; leaders of colonizing missions had to hold their own against local and foreign competitors; merchants and traders fended off domestic and foreign colleagues. Captains and caravan drivers vied for 'secret knowledge' of routes and pathways (and therefore avoided fixing them in writing), physicians outdid each other showing off their expertise in exotic medicinal plants, and even the scholars who catalogued and processed their findings were driven by the urge to refute dissenting views, criticize their predecessors, and replace old information with new.

Ancient discoveries were thus sustained by a climate of productive rivalry—the 'agonal spirit', as it used to be called—that extended even to military enterprises. Kings insisted that their rule extended to the edges of the world, a claim they sought to substantiate in competition with others by displaying foreign-looking slaves and exotic plants and animals. Commanders competed with living rivals and dead role models (Alexander), not just over the number of their victories but over the range of their conquests, and when they had vanquished almost every opponent, they fought with gods and demi-gods or finally only with themselves, as Arrian said of Alexander.[4]

The achievement of the great conquerors lay less in discovering new lands than in bringing remote spaces, previously known only to traders, within the orbit of governmental and colonial authority. They thereby created new urban launching pads for expeditionary voyages and intensified contacts between faraway cultural realms that had previously been linked only by long-distance trade routes. Without Alexander's conquests, without the colonizing activity of the Seleucids, and without the rise of the Mauryan and Kushan Empire in India, Greek and Indian culture would never have become so closely intertwined, as manifested in Gandhara art, the exchange of physicians and scholars, or the adoption of Buddhism and Hindu religious ideas by Greek settlers, diplomats, and perhaps even Greek rulers on Indian soil. The fact that these adaptive processes took place precisely at a time when new coastal towns and residences were springing up in India yet again shows the importance of urbanity, not just as a springboard but also as a nodal point for long-distance exploration and transregional cultural exchange.

Around the same time the Bactrian Greeks were conquering northern India (second century BCE), Roman expansion ushered in the fourth and final phase in the history of ancient discovery. At first, the Romans emulated in the west what the Persians and Alexander had already modelled in the east. They conquered the Mediterranean littoral and assimilated Carthage and Massalia, those epicentres of exploratory activity, into their territory through military annexation or political integration, much as the Persians and Alexander had done with Phoenicia and the towns of Asia Minor.

When Caesar and the generals of Augustus ventured into the Atlantic and the central European interior, they used mobility corridors pioneered centuries earlier by traders from Massalia, Gades, and the Etruscan coast. Caesar drew on the maritime experience of Gaditans and Bretons when he made the crossing to Britannia. Augustus' generals may have pursued a similar strategy when guiding their fleets along the North Sea coasts and into the great inland rivers (Ems, Elbe) in parallel with land-based operations.

Even as they pushed into spaces no Roman had set foot on before (as Augustus boasted in the *Res Gestae*), their operations remained dependent on military goals and exigencies—*exploratio* meant something like reconnaissance of enemy territory.[5] They followed routes that captains and traders had plied for centuries, just as Nearchus had sailed on an established sea road from the Indus to the Persian Gulf (albeit one not yet known to the Macedonians). A commander cannot simply join a caravan or take a berth on a ship, as Pytheas had done; he must provision his army and rely on a supply line that can be stretched to breaking point in a strange land.

That is why Alexander turned back at the Hyphasis and Drusus at the Elbe; it is also why other Roman generals 'only' made it as far as southern Arabia, the Nubian border, and the Fezzan, and why the amber road was pioneered not by an army but by a Roman trader. The commercial traveller always ranged farther afield than the conquering soldier.

In the west, moreover, cultural exchange beyond the borders of empire comparable to what occurred in the Hellenistic east never arose as the Roman policy of urbanization broke down in the vast expanses of central Europe. In contrast to Bactrians and Indians, Germans and Sarmatians lacked a tradition of living in cities that might have meshed with Mediterranean civic culture. For the Romans, the land beyond the Rhine and Danube remained uncivilized 'Barbaricum', whereas they learned from the Greeks to respect Indian culture for its renowned fertility and wisdom.

To that extent, it is unsurprising that the last great exploratory push in antiquity was directed less to the west than to the Far East. The extension of Roman rule to Egypt allowed the seas from the North Sea and Baltic down through the Mediterranean to the Red Sea and Indian Ocean to coalesce into a single maritime trading zone. At the same time, the westward expansion of the later Han Empire led to a condensation of trans-Asiatic caravan routes. The Parthian and Kushan Empires closed the gap between Rome and China; small states and oasis towns at the junctions of trade routes could inject their own products and experiences into the pulsating network of global exchange. The nomads of the north took up artefacts from more southerly climes and distributed them over the Eurasian steppes.

An essential condition for expanding long-distance trade was the relatively stable relationship between the great empires. Rome waged war against the Parthians far less often than against the Germans—the emperor Caracalla reportedly even encouraged the Parthian king to join him in a common trading and economic bloc.[6] The Later Han Chinese sought to win the Parthians (and Romans?) as allies against the northern nomads; a conquest of the Indian Kushan Empire was never seriously contemplated.

Against the background of this geopolitical stability, the great powers experienced an economic boom. Agricultural production in both the Han and the Roman Empires increased in the first century CE. Both had urban centres of up to one million residents, promising certain profits for those catering to their needs.[7] The Mediterranean-wide *Pax Romana* led to a concentration of financial resources in a huge space, such as would not be seen again until the modern age. The imperial elites and significant sections of the army and urban classes had an enormous appetite for goods from the east, which they used to flavour their food and drink, for healing purposes, and to flaunt their own stylishness. This appetite coincided with a similar need among ruling classes of the eastern empires. This occurred in a region that was dotted throughout with urban or proto-urban connecting points ('oasis towns'), especially at the crossroads of the great caravan routes from the Syrian desert to the Tarim basin and the Malay Peninsula.[8]

The circulation of commodities thus assumed a scale that almost deserves to be called global.[9] Amber from the Baltic, Gallic coral, glassware, and pearls reached the courts of eastern rulers.[10] Indian cotton was no less coveted in China and east Africa than was Indian pepper in the Mediterranean and on the Yellow River.[11] Chinese raw silk was exported to India, Persia, central Asia, and the Levant, then refined into translucent textiles in Indian and Syrian ports and in Alexandria, and finally reexported to China and sold on in the Mediterranean. Arabia and the Somali coast sent incense and myrrh, obtaining in return precious metals (gold), glassware, Italic and Greek wines, and corals. Southeast Asia supplied China with cinnamon, which was traded west along with products from China (iron, pelts).[12] Attempts to cultivate pepper and millet in Italy, incense and pepper on the Nile, or wine in India did little to reduce demand for the original, since homegrown imitations could not compete with the quality and prestige of the genuine article.[13]

And as always, it was not just commodities and materials that were on the move but also knowledge and wisdom: concerning the art of shipbuilding, even more valuable in the hazardous waters of the Red Sea and the Indian Ocean than in the Mediterranean; concerning the art of healing, which continued to evolve in India, Greece, and China and developed similar techniques in particular areas; and finally, for proclaiming new messages of salvation. Christian missionaries used trade routes to journey to India in the same way that Buddhist monks used them on their travels to China and India.

The stability of this far-flung communication network was based on close cooperation among traders, shipowners, and bankers, who went about their business under state protection. Merchant families and investors of the Roman Empire had their counterparts in the trading families and merchant guilds of the Indian coasts, with their Buddhist financiers and monastic cash depots. They all chased profits with the backing of their rulers and patrons: Indian traders cultivated friendships with local princes, Roman traders took on treasury contracts, and Chinese merchants maintained close relations with commanders in the army.[14]

To be sure, the ruler's role and involvement in long-distance exploration varied according to political traditions and the military and geostrategic context. The ideology of conquering all the way to the limits of the world so beloved in the Graeco-Roman west was alien to the Han emperors. They used exotic products to ornament their court and demonstrate their universal power. Like their coevals in the west, they also sought to profit from the intensified goods flow. In the end, however, it was their search for warhorses and allies against the northern nomads, hence strategic and military calculations, that prompted them to expand south (to Vietnam), dispatch expeditions west (to the Ferghana and Bactria), and guard the silk roads skirting the Taklamakan with military bases.[15]

The Roman emperors eschewed a comparable policy of expansion and exploration in Asia, even if their poets sometimes urged them to pursue a different course. Spatially limited campaigns (primarily against the Parthians and the Nabataean kingdom) and treaties with local princes endeavoured to secure the buffer zones to the eastern provinces. Customs stations guarded by soldiers (such as those on the Farasan islands) and warships protected Red Sea trade routes from piracy and boosted state revenues; yet Roman generals never tried to make direct contact with Indian rajas or the Chinese emperor. Instead, captains and traders from Alexandria and the Syrian cities were the ones who, supplied with money and orders from Italic and Syrian merchant families, sailed through the Strait of Malacca to the China Sea and reached the Han capital along the silk road.

On balance, what was achieved is astonishing given the absence of modern navigation and communication technology, not to mention the lack of any non-state agency committed to promoting and funding geographical research. This partly explains why the history of ancient discovery was always subject to setbacks and reversals. Nonetheless, over the course of two thousand years, mariners, emissaries, traders, and generals traversed the entire Eurasian realm from west to east as well as large parts of north Africa as far as Lake Chad. They sailed from the North Sea and Baltic via the Mediterranean and Red Sea to the Indian Ocean and China Sea; explored the Caspian Sea in the north and large swathes of the African coasts to the Zanzibar Channel in the south, Cape Delgado in the east, and the Bay of Biafra (Cameroon) in the west; and perhaps even circumnavigated the entire continent—a massive expansion in horizon that needed to be assimilated and constantly spawned new reflections about the world.

Antiquity had a holistic view of the wider world. It was explored against the background of material and expansive objectives, systems of spatial orientation, and expectations of interpersonal contact. This last area exerted the most pressure to integrate the new, in keeping with the inquisitive mentality so typical of coast-dwellers. 'Many cities of men he saw and learned their minds', Homer sums up the wanderings of Odysseus,[16] and it is not the landscape or setting of Calypso's island that occasions the hero to land but his curiosity to find out 'what kind of people live there'.[17]

An interest in discovering natural spaces rarely provided the incentive for launching exploratory missions abroad. This came instead from encounters with unknown people and life-forms. The modern wish to reach natural fixed points like the North Pole or climb the Himalayas for their own sake was largely foreign to antiquity—there were no pure research trips into the unknown, even if some sources and modern scholars see things this way in retrospect. Men like Pytheas of Massalia who were supposedly motivated solely by a thirst for knowledge travelled against a backdrop of strategic or mercantile goals, which in turn depended on political and economic factors.

By contrast, scholars such as Hecataeus, Herodotus, or Posidonius, who by their own account left their homeland primarily for research purposes (*historie*), moved on well-trodden paths and in the narrow radius of long-familiar spaces, not at their unknown periphery. The search for the sources of the Nile or a northeast passage over the Caspian Sea may have whetted the curiosity of geographers, but for rulers and conquerors it was of eminent strategic-military, mercantile, and propagandistic value,[18] which is why they always prioritized investigating maritime, fluvial, or territorial connecting paths to inhabited spaces or communities.

The interest in people and life-forms is reflected in the huge importance assigned to *ethnographic thinking*, which accompanied voyages of discovery from the outset. All the great ancient cultures knew the fascination of magical places and beings at the edges of the world, expressed in legends of Isles of the Blessed, holy mountains, faraway continents, or paradisical lands with just, pious, and happy denizens, but also in the idea of human-animal hybrids. Yet while in China and India such ideas could only with difficulty be peeled away from their mythic and religious context, and in China depended for their empirical confirmation on the initiative of the celestial ruler,[19] the world of the Greek polis developed from the beginning an almost obsessive pleasure in painting the edges of the world in ever new colours and peopling it with weird and wonderful beings. These marvels were vividly present in everyday life: in the form of frescos at seaside piers, in cheaply available books, and above all in the tales of mariners, merchants, and adventurers like Odysseus, all lapped up by a ravenous public. They formed the mental ambience surrounding long-distance missions, and they were bridges to an undiscovered beyond. Mythic images, epic motifs, and ethnographic *topoi* were suited to integrating the new into the familiar and absorbing the shock of the unexpected even when they were supplemented or 'disenchanted' by findings on the ground.

Mythic thinking and epic storytelling are therefore not indicative of a primitive mentality gradually superseded by *logos*. Until the end of antiquity (and well beyond—consider the Portuguese national epic, *The Lusiads*), they instead formed flexible categories for preserving knowledge, working through long-distance expeditions in literary form, interpreting ethnographic data, and ordering all this against the world's buzzing diversity. They were so adaptable and absorbent that they could even be combined with foreign narratives (Celtic, Scythian, and Indian) to become—from a Greek perspective—a quasi-universal code for explaining the world.

Against this background, ethnographic thinking evolved into a versatile way of understanding and interpreting the world that could be applied to various fields of knowledge: medicine, whose representatives gleaned reports of faraway tribes for information concerning the human body and its treatment; history writing, which with Herodotus linked a sweeping war narrative with astonishment at the sheer range of human customs, recognizing it as an autonomous social factor; and geography, which combined striking folkloric details with fixed points in space to create a panoptic overview in the great regional descriptions (*Indica*, *Persica*, *Aethiopica*).

The Greeks in particular, and the ancients in general, have been accused of never having developed an undistorted view of foreign cultures, as evidenced by the fact that the Greeks never put much effort into mastering foreign languages. Yet this holds true only for those mercenaries and captains who lived abroad for a brief period, and particularly for the scribes who seldom bothered to go beyond what they already knew. It does not pertain to men like Ctesias or Megasthenes, who spent years at the courts of Persian or Indian kings, nor to the Greeks who entered the service of Indian rajas and became devotees of Buddhism or ancient Indian deities. It is especially untrue of all those who lived on the periphery and stayed in the closest contact with Scythians and Celts or with Bactrians and Indians. They were certainly in a position to develop an intimate familiarity with foreign cultures. Even if they did not understand everything and still drew on Greek analogies, they left behind a trove of information that is still used today to reconstruct the early history of the relevant regions.

Naturally, Greeks and Romans (and Carthaginians, no doubt) also used ethnographic data to degrade their enemies as barbarians and legitimate their conquests. Conversely, the utopian image of remote peoples harboured the potential to hold up a mirror to one's own civilization. However, only a small number of authors, politicians, and philosophers (such as Isocrates and Aristotle) made such constructs and only under certain circumstances, not least from the intellectual pleasure they took at drawing polarizing contrasts, whereas those on the ground offered more realistic assessments. Moreover, the political, self-critical, or fictional processing of foreign experiences never lost touch with empirical data.[20] A genuine interest in faraway peoples always shimmered through, proving flexible enough to allow widely contrasting interpretations of one and the same tribe to be developed and articulated in various literary genres: sometimes as an idealized counter-image in the form of the 'noble savage', the just monarch, or a pious and self-sufficient society; sometimes as the epitome of effete luxury or a caricature of man-eating barbarians; but always as the object of ethnographic research with an interest in the variety of human customs. Without this interpretive breadth, Greeks and later Romans would hardly have been capable of processing the steady expansion in their intellectual horizon brought about by their exposure to foreign people and mores. Indeed, this was so successful that it endured—refracted in multiple ways—into the early-modern age and was there applied to new worlds.

Closely connected with the ethnographic coverage of the world was the *natural categorization of the new*. Here, too, ancient voyagers achieved great things. Homer had already taken pains to create a coherent image of the people encountered by Odysseus in their natural surroundings, while literary travelogues (*periploi*) combined ethnographic data with information on the country's distinctive ecological and geographical features. Behind this endeavour stood the need of those who had commissioned the voyage to gain as detailed an impression as possible of the land, its assets, and its political and geographical circumstances.

It also reflected the interest in plants and natural products that had driven traders and healers abroad since the Bronze Age and had made physicians the secret heroes of ancient exploration. And finally, abundant nature, along with the associated hope of a long and healthy life, fascinated everyone who lived on Mediterranean coasts that offered neither. That is why ancient discoveries not only stimulated botanical and zoological works whose richly varied content and methodological premises remained unsurpassed until well into the modern age; an interest in nature also informed the great descriptions of lands in the east, whose exoticism continually stunned foreign visitors.

From the later fifth century BCE, this astonishment prompted enquiry into whether there were any links between the world of flora and fauna, on the one hand, and human culture, on the other. Philosophers, historians, and physicians, equipped with their specific research interests, went in search of an answer. They quickly ascertained correlations among natural regions that transcended political borders. These observations, and the analogical conclusions they licensed, gave rise to the famous theories of climate, which divided the globe into zones (or belts) parallel to the equator corresponding to their exposure to sunlight. Even if this schema only loosely fits with reality, it exerted a not unappreciable influence on the expectations of ancient (and modern) explorers by declaring the extreme regions of the Earth to be inaccessible on account of their intense heat or icy cold. It also made faraway destinations *within* the temperate zones seem attainable. Aristotle concludes a link between Spain and India from the occurrence of the same animals; according to Strabo, Eratosthenes reckons with 'two or several worlds [besides the ecumene] in the same temperate zone' and believes a voyage from Spain to India 'on the same parallel of latitude'—that is, within the same climatic zone—to be possible if the sea was not too wide to prevent it.[21]

Even if trans-Atlantic crossings were never attempted, and even if the mental barriers to the torrid and frigid zones were repeatedly overcome by intrepid travellers, climate theories made available rich interpretive and adaptive possibilities: they could be transposed, slightly modified, to different parts of the Earth and used to make sweeping generalizations about the inhabitants (southeast-hot = cowardly and slavish; northern-cold = rash and stupid), or to present one's own culture as a happy medium in comparison. This opened a huge field for political instrumentalization, especially when combined with negative *topoi*, but it also provided a mechanism for explaining links among climate, ecology, and human cultural expression through rational analogy and integrating them into an overarching interpretation of the world.

Such reflections reached a critical mass in the wake of Alexander's conquests. A wealth of ethnographic, botanical, and zoological data from India and Arabia as well as the coasts and lands of the Red Sea appeared on the intellectual horizon of Greek scholars and could be compared at the Hellenistic courts with the findings of the latest expeditionary reports. Agatharchides' treatise on the Red Sea, a typical product of this atmosphere, combined detailed observation with empathetic interpretation in a way that would not be equalled until the early-modern age. In the west, Posidonius carried on the tradition in describing the land of the Celts. However, later representations of the lands beyond the Rhine and Elbe failed to match the depth of the analysis directed southeast. People of the Mediterranean were clearly less enticed by the seemingly desolate expanses of the northwest interior, which were more the object of political and military strategy than the subject of detailed natural-historical and ethnographic research.

Finally, the fertile mix of data collecting, synthetic ordering, and rational-speculative modelling that was so typical of antiquity also defined how voyages of discovery were *processed geographically*. The geographical categorization of space did not serve primarily to guide long-distance voyages or campaigns; instead, its basic function was to demonstrate power. Of crucial importance here was the collation of individual pieces of information into a panoptic overview of knowledge oriented on rational criteria. This was set out in maps of the ecumene, which gradually came to relinquish the form of the circle; in a descriptive cultural geography; and (from the third century BCE onward) in a mathematical geography that captured landmasses in a latitude-longitude grid. All this relied on travellers and expeditions providing as much raw ethnographic and geographical data as possible. Ptolemy's *Geography* (*Geographike hyphegis*), the last great work of mathematical geography, thus documented the final boundaries of ancient knowledge as far as Java and the Sea of China.[22]

What lay beyond was of little interest, although the discovery that the Earth was spherical had created a new conceptual foundation for a truly global geography. Based on philosophical speculation and geometric analogical reasoning, and confirmed by empirical observation, it is for us today one of the most precious legacies of ancient geography.

The ancients themselves appear to have been less euphoric, perhaps because knowledge of the Earth's curvature was part of every seafarer's practical experience. In scholarly discussions, at any rate, the spherical Earth hypothesis figured less as a fundamental paradigm shift than as a welcome aid for better explaining astronomical phenomena, the sun's rays, and the movements of the constellations in the night sky than the flat-Earth model. From the third century BCE, at the latest, the 'globe' had become so much a staple of general experience that it figured as an indispensable element in the political self-representation of the powerful and successful.

At the same time, the spherical model acted in a direction that tied it to humankind's age-old fascination with remote worlds. Ever since the cultures of China, Mesopotamia, and the Mediterranean began reflecting on how their own civilizational space fitted into the Earth's surface, there had been speculation about faraway continents and the form and dimensions of the world's seas. Yet only with the idea of a *global* Earth could these ideas become the object of rational speculation and mathematical probability. Questions arose concerning how many continents were scattered across the globe, whether and how they could be linked up, and the proportion of the world's seas to its landmasses. The answers given no longer moved in the context of epic and mythic traditions but took the form of logically comprehensible discussions that could draw on the achievements of comparative ethnography and climate theory and—even more importantly—empirical and mathematical geography. The latter had developed imprecise but repeatable procedures for measuring the Earth's circumference and collected new measurements of distance between known places. Now it was possible, based on the ratio of the known ecumene to the entire Earth's surface, to estimate the size of the Atlantic and predict the existence and location of undiscovered continents.

This is the real birth-hour of globalization as a mental process. Steered by neither religious nor state authority, it unfolded in an exhilarating atmosphere of critical debate where the force of the better argument held sway, and where those who attempted a synoptic overview did so in the confidence that they had a vast array of empirical evidence at their fingertips.

This overview disclosed perspectives of world-historical significance. For if some dreamed of the possibility of a journey from Spain over the Atlantic to India, if others were convinced that the Far East could be reached by sailing south around Africa, and if still others imagined the land of the Antipodes and a *terra australis* in the south as well as an enormous continent in the west, then they were merely anticipating what the modern explorers would later realize. Columbus and his fellow navigators were certain that they were sailing in the wake of the ancients and encountering, in the New World, a world mapped out for them in advance. They would not have doubted the authenticity of the Paraiba tablet, which proclaimed the ancients' arrival on the coasts of Brazil. And who knows . . .

Acknowledgements

Over the many years I spent researching and writing this book, I was confronted by countless obstacles. A modern, integrated history of discovery must transcend conventional limitations of time and space and come to grips with cultures that lie outside the expertise of most classically trained ancient historians: the civilizations of the south Sahara, Arabia, India, China, and Central Asia. I needed to familiarize myself with the archaeology of these regions and the logistics involved in connecting them. I also had to navigate a body of literature that sometimes left me feeling out of my depth. Numerous colleagues, friends, and experts supported me with their advice and/or offered critical commentary on parts of the manuscript. I owe them all a debt of gratitude:

Franz Arlinghaus (Bielefeld), Ingrid Baumgärtner (Cassel), Frank Bernstein (Frankfurt), Reinhold Bichler (Innsbruck), Ronald Bockius (Mainz), Werner Dahlheim (Berlin), Christian Ellinghaus (Bielefeld), Beate Engelen (Bielefeld), Johannes Engels (Cologne), Antje Flüchter (Bielefeld), Klaus Geus (Berlin), Tommaso Gnoli (Bologna), Thomas Grammes (Berlin), Hermann Hiery (Bayreuth), Reinhard Krüger (Stuttgart), Matthäus Heil (Berlin), Jan Ottmar Hesse (Bielefeld/Bayreuth), Reinhard Jung (Vienna), Dierk Lange (Bayreuth), Arndt Latussek (Hildesheim), Eckhard Meyer-Zwiffelhoffer (Bielefeld/Tübingen), Jacqueline Passon (Freiburg), Robert Rollinger (Innsbruck), Felicitas Schmieder (Hagen), Peter Schuster (Bielefeld), Eivind Heldaas Seland (Bergen), Michael Sommer (Oldenburg), Tim Trampedach (Berlin), Thomas Welskopp(†) (Bielefeld), Josef Wiesehöfer (Kiel).

I extend particularly heartfelt thanks to my friend and colleague Uwe Walter, who took the trouble to read most chapters in a later version. He was never too busy to talk through key aspects and problems, and his historical sixth sense saved me from many an error of judgment. My former assistant Sven Günther (now Changchun University, China) worked on large sections of the manuscript, gave me invaluable suggestions, and put me in touch with Chinese scholars. I was further emboldened and inspired by Karl May, who sent his heroes to all four corners of the Earth; Jean-Luc Picard, who commanded his ship and its crew as they went in search of strange new worlds; and the eleven men who crossed the Ocean in 2014 and on July 8 conquered the green fields of Elysium in Belo Horizonte—'Beautiful Horizon'.

***

I am pleased and thankful that this book will now be published in the English-speaking world, which has traditionally been amenable to a global view of the world of antiquity. I hope it will help foster a more intensive exchange on processes of discovery that have shaped our historical heritage in many ways. Several colleagues and friends helped me on the English edition. In particular, I thank Stanley Burstein (Los Angeles) and Kai Brodersen (Erfurt) for their expert advice, tips, and wide-ranging discussions. I further thank my colleagues here at the University of Bielefeld. Elias Grebing showed a keen eye for detail in editing and proofreading the English version. Iris Kukla helped me clarify some tricky passages and oversaw the list of references. Julia Eyschen, Robin Dyck, Miguel Sanchez Sanchez, and Daniel Wache produced the index.[1]

Bielefeld, December 2023

Timeline

From c. 3500	Ugarit mounts long-distance voyages in the eastern and western (?) Mediterranean
c. 3000	Bronze Age begins
c. 2400–1100	Egyptian expeditions to Punt
End of the fourteenth century	Voyage of the Uluburun
c. 1400–1200	Mycenean palace culture, Mycenean maritime trade expands to the eastern Mediterranean
1300–1200	Introduction of the Italic longsword and evolution of the penteconter in the eastern Mediterranean. Mycenean seafarers reach southern Italy; Italic warriors (Šardana) infiltrate the eastern Mediterranean
1213	Merneptah's victory over Libyans and 'Sea Peoples'
1194 and 1186	Ugarit destroyed by the 'Sea Peoples'
1187–1156	Ramses III defeats Libyans and 'Sea Peoples'
c. 1000–609	Hegemony of the Assyrian Empire
c. 900	Phoenicians reach the Spanish Atlantic coast (Tartessos); Huelva and Gades founded
c. 800	Phoenician mariners and artists in Kommos (Crete)
c. 800	The Greeks adopt the Phoenician consonantal writing system
ninth century	Cypriots muscle in on Ugarit maritime trade
ninth century	Tyrians cooperate with Hebrews; expeditions to Ophir
c. 770	Euboeans (and Phoenicians?) found Pithekoussai
From c. 750	Greek colonies planted in the Mediterranean and, later, on the Black Sea

eighth century	Final version of the Gilgamesh epic transcribed
700–650	Homeric epics transcribed
eighth–sixth century Bible arise	Earliest sections of the Old Testament/Hebrew
From the end of the	Scholars in Miletus develop schematic representations of the world
c. 600	Phoenician captains sail into the Red Sea and allegedly circumnavigate Africa at the behest of Pharaoh Necho
c. 600	Phocaeans establish a first settlement at the site of later Massalia and serve the rulers of Tartessos as mercenaries
second half of the seventh century (?)	Aristeas journeys to the Urals and hears of trans-Asiatic trade routes; the *Arimaspeia* composed
Mid-sixth century onwards	Massalia extends its contacts to the Celtic Hallstatt culture (Heuneburg) and sends mariners to the Atlantic in search of the Tin Isles; Samians (Colaeus) and Rhodians establish trade contacts with Tartessos
	Miletus plants several colonies in the northern Black Sea area
	Delphi establishes itself as a meeting place and trade hub for colony leaders and seafarers
End of the sixth century (?)	Euthymenes of Massalia sails to the North Sea (the Tin Isles?) and along the Moroccan coast (to Senegal?)
	The Carthaginian Himilco seeks the route to the Tin Isles
	In the Italic colonies (Elea?), the theory of a spherical earth is developed
525–523	The Persian king Cambyses conquers Egypt and tries to reach the Siwa Oasis
518–516	Scylax of Caryanda is commissioned by Darius to navigate the maritime route from the Indus to the mouth of the Persian Gulf and probably rounds the Arabian Peninsula; at the same time, the Persians begin exploring the Red Sea

514 (?)	Darius wages his Scythian campaign
From c. 500	Proto-urban, iron-producing cultures arise near Lake Chad, on the Senegal River, and at the Niger bend
First third of the fifth century (?)	Voyage of the Carthaginian general Hanno along the west African coast (probably to Mount Cameroon), colonies planted in Morocco; exploration of the Chretes (Senegal?)
	Trans-Saharan caravan routes investigated by the Carthaginians (Mago?) and contacts made in the Fezzan (Garamantes and Nasamones)
End of the sixth/ beginning of the fifth century	Hecataeus (c. 560–480 BCE) collates expeditionary reports into a holistic representation of the Earth (*periegesis geo*)
c. 470	Sataspes is commissioned by Xerxes to explore the west African coast (to Senegal?)
Mid- to late fifth century	Heyday of the Sophists (in Athens). Herodotus gives public readings from his 'Histories' and works through new ethnographic findings in his excurses. Hippocratic writings.
Fourth century	Philosophical speculation on the size and shape of the Earth and its ecumenes (Plato, Aristotle), and on a possible sea link between Spain and India; Eudoxus of Cnidus (c. 391–338 BCE) pioneers mathematical astronomy and calculates the Earth's circumference.
Early fourth century	Ctesias of Cnidus serves as a physician at the court of the Persian king and writes *Persica* and *Indica*
401	'Retreat of the Ten Thousand' through the land of the Carduchians to the Black Sea; Xenophon's writings
Mid-fourth century onwards	Hallstatt culture makes way for the La Tène culture in central Europe
340–330 (?)	Pytheas sails to Britain, the Shetlands, and Thule (Iceland?); he possibly ventures as far as the North Sea (Heligoland?), the Baltic, and the starting points of the Amber Roads
334–323	Alexander campaigns against Persia and advances into Asia; 329–328: Alexander in Bactria; 327–325: in India

325–323	Nearchus sails from the Indus to the Euphrates; Alexander marches back to Babylon through the Gedrosian Desert
	Heraclides is commissioned to build a fleet in Hyrcania and explore the Caspian
324 (?)	Androsthenes of Thasos sails to Tylos and Arados and attempts to circumnavigate the Arabian Peninsula
	Anaxicrates ventures forth in the opposite direction from Hieropolis (Egypt); Hiero of Soloi explores the coasts of Arabia
311–304	Indian campaign of Seleucus; Antioch in Scythia founded; contract with the Mauryan king Chandragupta (Sandrakottos). A lively diplomatic and commercial exchange ensues.
310–300	Acting on the orders of Seleucus, Demodamas of Miletus leads an army across the Syr Darya (Jaxartes)
285–282 (?)	Seleucus commissions Patrocles to explore the Caspian Sea
c. 300	Ai-Khanoum founded (possibly Alexandria on the Oxus)
Mid-third century	The Mauryan king Ashoka (270–235) installs pillars inscribed with edicts in his empire and sends *dhamma* 'envoys' to the Hellenistic courts
Second half of the third century	Eratosthenes of Alexandria measures the Earth and writes his *Geographica*
From 280	Ptolemy II sends expeditions to Arabia, east Africa, and the Sudan under Ariston, Timosthenes, and Pythagoras 'the Navarch'
After 270	Satyrus establishes Philotera at the starting point of the pharaonic voyages to Punt; a little later, he founds Berenice (Trogodytice); Eumedes establishes Ptolemais Theron (Marsa Aqiq)
c. 238	Eucratides founds the Greco-Bactrian Empire
c. 180–160	Conquest of the Indus Valley and parts of the Ganges basin by Demetrius I and his successors

166–150 or 155–130	Menander I (Soter) king of the Indo-Grecian Empire; close connections to Buddhism
	Ptolemaic emissaries (Simonides, Bion, Basilis, Damocritus, and Charon) stay at the royal court in Meroë and write *Ethopica*
	Ptolemy II sends Dionysius to Pataliputra
	Under Ptolemy IV, expeditions pass through the Red Sea as far as Azania and discover the island of Socotra
First half of the second century	Agatharchides of Cnidus writes a *Periplus Maris Erythraei*
c. 145	Polybius is commissioned by Scipio to sail along the north African and (perhaps) west African coast (to Morocco?)
End of the second century	Under Ptolemy IX, Eudoxus of Cyzicus uses the monsoon system to chart a direct route to the west coast of India; thereafter he mounts several expeditions from Gades along the west African coast, hoping to circumnavigate the continent
138–114	Commissioned by the Han emperor Wu to find the Yuezhi, Zhang Qian travels from Longxi to Bactria via the Ferghana
	Another expedition takes him to the Wusun (on Lake Balkhash)
Beginning of the first century	Posidonius of Apameia conducts research in Gades and visits the land of the Celts near the Roman provincial borders
	Artemidorus of Ephesus maps the Spanish coasts
	Licinius Crassus sails along the Spanish Atlantic coast in search of the Tin Isles
61	Caesar advances by land and water to Brigantium (La Coruña)
58–54	Caesar pushes into 'free Gaul', defeats the Veneti, twice invades Britain, and crosses the Rhine. *Germans* and *Germania* are introduced as new ethnographic-geographical umbrella terms for the northern European interior.

c. 40	The Nubian king Juba II visits the Canaries (previously discovered by the Carthaginians)
27	Aelius Gallus campaigns in southern Arabia (Mariba)
25–15	Roman generals conquer the Alpine region, reaching Lake Constance and the Black Forest under Tiberius
25–22	C. Petronius marches with an army to the upper Nile in pursuit of Queen Kandake of Ethiopia
20–19	L. Cornelius Balbus leads Roman units against the Garamantes in the Fezzan
16 BCE–9 CE	Conquest and provincialization of the Alpine lands Raetia and Noricum
12–2 BCE	Agrippa's world map is displayed in the Porticus Vipsania
12 BCE	Drusus (Nero Claudius D.) navigates the Ijsselmeer to enter the North Sea and discovers the Ems estuary
11–9 BCE	Drusus travels from the Weser to the Elbe
7 BCE	Domitius Ahenobarbus marches from the Danube through the Thuringian Forest into territories east of the Elbe
1 BCE	Gaius Caesar journeys to Mesopotamia and the Gulf of Aqaba
5–3 CE (?)	A Roman fleet sails from the mouth of the Rhine through the North Sea and Cape Skagen to the Baltic and probably on to the west coast of Scandinavia; it may have sailed up the Elbe on its return voyage
16	Further North Sea expeditions as far as Heligoland (?)
65–66	Roman knights follow the Amber Road from Aquileia up through the Moravian Gate to the Sambian coast and the Baltic
84	C. Julius Agrippa circumnavigates Britain and reaches the Orkneys
First to second century	Italian investors and merchants become involved in the India trade via Alexandria

Mid-first century	The *Periplus Maris Erythraei* is composed
	Indian princes set up quarters for *yavanas* (westerners) in Barygaza and Muziris
	Roman tax farmers (Annius Plocamus) establish contact with the king of Taprobane (Sri Lanka). In the following period, envoys travel to Rome to conclude a pact of *amicitia*; Roman merchants receive information about links to China.
91	The Han general Pan Chao is appointed 'Protector-General of the Western Territories'
97	Pan Chao travels the Silk Road from the Tarim basin to the Caspian Sea.
	Pan Chao dispatches Gan Ying to the Parthian Empire as far as Mesopotamia (Charax Spasinu?) in a bid to link up with the Roman Empire
c. 100	Alexandros sails over the Indian Ocean through the Strait of Malacca into the South China Sea and on to Cattigara (Guangzhou?)
	Agents of the merchant Maes Titianus reach the Han Empire (Luoyang) via the (southern) Silk Road
	Coming from India, Diogenes calls at Azania (Rhapta)
	Julius Maternus ventures with the Garamantes to Agisymba (on Lake Chad?)
c. 160	Greek merchants (from Alexandria?) take the sea and land route to the Han court, presenting themselves as an official embassy from Marcus Aurelius

Notes

INTRODUCTION

1. Plut. De specie lunae 26 (= 941A–942D), Gárriga (2021), 97–101.
2. Cary-Warmington (1963).
3. Roller (2006) for the Atlantic, Timpe (1989a) for northern Europe, Stoneman (2019) for India. Fernandéz-Armesto 2006, 20–68 gives a global overwiew.
4. Moore/Lewis (1990).
5. Roller (2015) and the collection of more recent specialist contributions in Roller (2019), Dueck/Brodersen (2012), Raaflaub/Talbert (2010), Geus (2013), Romm (2010), Gómez-Espelósin (2010).
6. Dougherty (2001), Skinner (2012), Almagor/Skinner (2013), Dench (2007), Schulz (2005).
7. See Bibliography I.
8. Roller (2015, pb 2017).
9. Clarke (1999), 69–70; Elliot (1970).
10. Broodbank (2013), 326, 514.
11. Aug. civ. 16,8.
12. Gell. 9,4.
13. White (1991), 208–209.
14. See the introduction in Harris (2005), Abulafia (2003), Broodbank (2013).
15. See Abulafia (2019). On antiquity see de Souza/Arnaud (2017).
16. Morton (2001), Arnaud (2005), Beresford (2013), Harris/Iara (2011), Medas (2004), Whitewright (2011a).
17. Warnecke (2002), (2006).
18. For these stereotypes see Fabre (2004), xxi, 4–7 with literature.
19. Fabre (2004), 117; Medas (2004), 172–173, 191–199 (tacking).
20. Meijer (1986), 1–3; Medas (2004), 155–156.
21. Broodbank (2013), 330, 374.
22. Suet. Claud. 18, Warnecke (2002).
23. Jos. Bell. Jud. 3,9,3; App. civ. 5,10 (88–100); Plut. Dio 25,7–8; Sen. Epist. 53,2–3; Hld. 5,17,5; Arist. Or. 48,66; Lucian ver. hist. 1,6; Synes. Epist. 4, 160c–161c/164d–165a; Apg. 27,17–29.
24. Warnecke (2002), 98–99; Fabre (2004), 20–21; Medas (2004), 19–20, 54–57; McGrail (2001), 95, 156–157 with Plin. Nat. 7,209 and Strab. 16,2,24 (c 757).

25. Medas (2004), 12–13.
26. See the description of the Indian 'pilot' Suparaga in McGrail (2001), 258: '[he] knows the course of the stars and can always orientate himself; he knows the value of the signs, both regular, accidental and abnormal, of good and bad weather; he distinguishes the regions of the ocean by the fish, the colour of the water, the nature of the bottom, the birds, the mountains, and other indications'.
27. McGrail (2001), 101, 253 on Suparaga; Medas (2004), 13–14.
28. Fernández Armesto (2001), 13–14; McGrail (2001), 12.
29. McGrail (2001), 92.
30. Horden-Purcell (2000), 51–172; Cary (1949), v.
31. Dougherty (2001), 135–136; Fernández-Armesto (2001), 8.
32. Rougé (1981), 40; Fabre (2004), 110.
33. Fabre (2004), xvi; Hughes-Brock (2005), 310 with further literature.
34. Broodbank (2013), 277–283.
35. Broodbank (2013), 373; Bowen (1960); Roberts (1987).
36. Cunliffe (2011), 188–189; Broodbank (2013), 288–292, 327–329. Camels/dromedaries from Asia: Bulliet (1975), 28–56; Broodbank (2013), 453
37. Fabre (2004), 98; Broodbank (2013), 330.
38. Cunliffe (2011), 219; Broodbank (2013), 324–329: 'a new age of connectivity'.

CHAPTER 1

1. Sasson (1966), 132. Sherratt/Sherratt (1991), 364. On smaller ships, see Vichos (1999) on the Point Iria wreck.
2. Sherratt/Sherratt (1991), 361, 365; Bennet (2013), 206–207; Broodbank (2013), 393–394. On the ecological environment and palace of the capital, see Caubet (2000).
3. Liverani (1987), 67–72; Routledge/McGough (2009), 28.
4. Linder (1981); Pulak (1997), 356.
5. Burns (2010a), 118–119. Grain: Routledge/McGeough (2009), 24. Sherratt/Sherratt (1991), 365 and Broodbank (2013), 356–357, 394–396 assume that traders acted freely within diplomatic networks and paid customs. The palace rulers needed them to acquire goods from abroad. For a critical view, see Routledge/McGeough (2009).
6. Moorey (2001), 4. Broodbank (2013), 394–396, is more optimistic. Small companies: Broodbank (2013), 367. Limited range: Broodbank (2013), 356–359. Movement in networks: Zaccagnini (1983), 250–251; Moorey (2001), 9; Burns (2010a), 297.
7. Jung (2005), 51; Tartaron (2013), 16–20, 26–27; Bennet (2013), 177, 200–201 (Mycenae and Crete); Voutsaki (2001). Exoticism, marvels, and domestication: Burns (2010a), 32, 78, 133–135 (ivory), 174–178, 192–193.

8. Linder (1981), 33, 36–40; Sasson (1966), 132–133; Knapp (1991), 37 on grain. Emanuel (2021), 121 argues against 'a standing navy or a fleet of ships specially designed for combat operations'.
9. Linder (1981), 34; Sasson (1966), 132–135; Knapp (1991), 48. Naval programs: Sasson (1966), 132; financing: Knapp (1991), 21–68; foreign traders and mariners: Linder (1981), 35; Kuhrt (2000), 302; Demand (2013), 168. Interpreters and Cretans buying tin: Knapp (1991), 38.
10. Broodbank (2013), 393 (metallurgy); Kuhrt (2000), 302. Wood bound for Egypt: Knapp (1991), 34. In the second millennium, the Nile delta underwent a boom reflected in the quality and quantity of products and artefacts; see Broodbank (2013), 345.
11. Details in Pulak (1997); for an excellent, more recent survey see Broodbank (2013), 401–402.
12. Mee (2008), 364; Jung (2005), 54. Character and extent of bronze age trade: Tartaron (2013), 24ff.
13. Broodbank (2013), 389.
14. Burns (2010b), 290. On the 'disadvantaged maritime status of much of the African shore': Broodbank (2013), 79. Gold from Nubia: Sherratt/Sherratt (1991), 361; Punt: Fabre (2004), 38–42, 80–81; Broodbank (2013), 285; Ray (2003), 83. Harappa (probably the Meluha of the texts) to Mesopotamia, even after 1800: Ray (1994), 12; Ray (2003), 99; Broodbank (2013), 284; McGrail (2001), 58. Glass production also got underway around 1500. On Mesopotamia's early links via Dilmun, see the myth of Enki and Ninkhasarg, in which Enki proclaims to his daughter, patron goddess of Dilmun, that the land of Meluhha (= Indus Valley) will bring back marvellous carnelians, timber from Magan, and excellent mangroves on larges ships; Potts (1995), 1453. There was gold on the Indus, too; Ray (2003), 96.
15. Pulak (1997), 251; Burns (2010a), 300; Tartaron (2013), 26. Trade with Crete and Minoan exports: Knapp (1991), 29.
16. Broodbank (2013), 393ff. Smaller ships also sailed with mixed crews: Vichos (1999), 84.
17. Rivalries within Mycenaean palace society, fuelled by acquisitions of exotic products, are emphasized by Burns (2010), 115, 128, 161, 191–196.
18. Jung (2005), 46; Broodbank (2013), 394; Routledge/McGeough (2009), 24–27: 'Certainly, cases such as that of Sinaranu point to the existence of non-royal merchants with ships conducting overseas trade'. Their importance also depended on the character of the state in which they operated. Egypt offered merchants fewer opportunities than Ugarit, for example: Broodbank (2013), 396.
19. Demand (2013), 178–181. Sword: Pulak (1997), 254. Kommos supersedes Mochlos: Demand (2013), 137; Shaw (2004).
20. Dossin (1970), 97–106; Demand (2013), 143.

21. Knapp (1991), 33; Burns (2010a), 299; (2010), 94–97; Tartaron (2013), 82–83, 111–112 (navigation by the stars), 192; Sherratt/Sherratt (1991), 370 on Cretans in Egypt. On Cretan contacts in Avaris in the Nile delta, see Broodbank (2013), 383–389.
22. Meijer (1986), 3–4. Direct sea voyages navigating by the stars: Broodbank (2013), 465.
23. Broodbank (2013), 325–339.
24. Sherratt/Sherratt (1991), 369; Stos-Gale (2001), 199–204; Broodbank (2013), 353, 370 (silver, copper); Egypt: Burns (2010), 87, 94–95.
25. Cunliffe (2001), 259f., Knapp (1991), 43ff.; Knapp (1993). Pepper: Miller (1969), 81; Bennet (2013), 190–192. Exotic wares in Mycenae: Broodbank (2013), 410.
26. Emanuel (2021), 134; Broodbank (2013), 465 on the theory that Cypriots or others organized trade for the Mycenaeans; Yasur-Landau (2010), 42. Mycenaeans take over Minoan trade connections: Georganas (2010), 313.
27. Sherratt/Sherratt (1991), 358–359, 370–372.
28. Vanschoonwinkel (2006), 97; Harding (1984), 58–60, 68–87; Demand (2011), 145. Wessex/Britannia: Harding (1990), 139–154. Atlantic: Cunliffe (1999), on the major contact zones. Implications of the Minos legends for Sicily: Vanschoonwinkel (2006), 83. Amber: Vanschoonwinkel (2006), 97. On Mycenaean exports in Italy: Jung (2005), 61. Baltic amber via the Carpathians, then the Adriatic: Broodbank (2013), 432; contacts with Sardinia: 444.
29. Jones/Vagnetti (1991), 139.
30. Jung (2005), 62. No Mycenaeans in the north: Thrane (1990), 176. On the continental 'small chiefdoms' see Broodbank (2013), 431.
31. See Emanuel (2021), 184–192 and 340–342 for discussion of western Mediterranean origins.
32. Jung/Mehofer (2005/2006), 118–123, 131–134; Jung/Mehofer (2013), 177, 185–186.
33. Broodbank (2013), 464; Emanuel (2013), 6–8 with specialist literature in the notes; Tartaron (2013), 59–68; Georganas (2010), 306–307; Jung/Mehofer (2005/2006), 133.
34. Tartaron (2013), 59–68; Georganas (2010), 306–307; Jung/Mehofer (2006/2006), 133.
35. Emanuel (2021), 134–148.
36. Jung (2009), 145; Jung/Mehofer (2013), 185; Veenhof (2001), 197, 200. Šardana in Egypt: Jung/Mehofer (2005/2006), 134; Emanuel (2021), 193–194. Troy: Vanschoonwinkel (2006), 77–78. Silver in Troy: Broodbank (2013), 337; Black Sea area: Vanschoonwinkel (2006), 57ff.; Tartaron (2013), 36; Hiller (1991); Ivantchik (2005), 106 is sceptical. Petropoulos (2005), 17 interprets double axes and spearheads as guest gifts. Stone anchors resembling late bronze age Aegean anchors were also found on the Bulgarian coast. Mycenaeans on the coast of Asia Minor: Niemeier (1998); Margalith (1994), 73–75 on a Mycenaean colony in Ugarit and the Levant.

37. Cunliffe (2011), 196–197, 226–227, 234; Georganas (2010), 305. See Yasur-Landau (2010), 42–43. No Mycenaean (trade) goods were found in Ugarit, while Aegean traders are mentioned neither in Near Eastern sources nor in Linear B texts or Hittite documents; Yasur-Landau (2010), 55. Clearly, Mycenaeans were regarded exclusively as warriors and pirates!
38. Jung/Mehofer (2005–2006), 124–131; Jung (2009), 138; Jung/Mehofer (2013), 185–186 argue against a regular arms trade. See Deger Jalkotzy (2008), 389.
39. Jung (2009), 147; Sherratt/Sherratt (1991), 372; Broodbank (2013), 456–457.
40. See Drews (1993), 108–111, 140–149 on mercenary recruitment. Further Sherratt/Sherratt (1991) 373–374 on mercenaries and pirates. That the Assyrians maintained their own infantry from early on explains their survival during the 'Sea Peoples period' and their subsequent success.
41. Armana correspondence: EA 81, 122, 123; Ehrlich (1995), 78–79; and Broodbank (2013), 456 with a visual representation of Šardana warriors.
42. Jung/Mehofer (2005/2006), 134 with literature in note 175. Singer (2000), 24; Artzy (1997), 4. *Maryannu* as chariot fighters: Drews (1993), 112; hirelings as the basis of the bronze age economy: Artzy (1998), 445. Pylos: Dothan (1992), 219; Drews (1993), 141–147, 155; Jung/Mehofer (2005/2006), 120–121. Mercenaries in guerrilla war: Italy: Jung/Mehofer (2013); Libya: Driessen/MacDonald (1984).
43. Veenhof (2001), 201; Drews (1993), 153–154 on the Abydos relief, and 161. Close-combat fighters: Drews (1993), 137–139, 148–152; Barako (2003). Weapons: Drews (1993), 180, 201 on the sources in Medinet Habu.
44. For the older literature, see (among many others) Yasur-Landau (2010), 39 and passim.
45. Mercenaries: Broodbank (2013), 468. Emanuel (2013), 21–22 sees these conditions reflected in Odysseus' mendacious tale. Ugarites and Hittites may have sought to 'refit' the Lukka people for coastal defence: Artzy (1997), 5; Demand (2011), 196. The Lukka as pirates and mercenaries: Cline/O'Connor (2007), 111; Broodbank (2013), 469.
46. Overviews in Cline (2014), 139–170 and Dickinson (2010).
47. Discussion in Niemeyer (1998). Italy and pirates: Jung (2009), 41–44. Drews (1993), 218–219. Wachsmann (1998), 339–356. Lukka piracy: Broodbank (2013), 412, 461. Egyptian sources: Schipper (2005), 134; Helck (1995), 110; Noort (1994), 54–55. Fortifications, coastal defence in Pylos: Tartaron (2013), 18, 64–65.
48. Emanuel 2021.
49. See Jung/Mehofer (2013), 184; Dickinson (2010), 485 on the possibility of intra-Mycenaean conflict.
50. Snodgrass (1991), 16. See Broodbank (2013), 414–415 on traders' independence.
51. Whitelaw (2001); Burns (2010a), 189; Tartaron (2013), 16, 29; Yasur-Landau (2010), 36–37: 'It [the palace] did not monopolize crafts or industries such as metallurgy. The palaces exercised direct supervision over only the most

important industries that provided goods for trade, and they had a symbiotic relationship with a large private sector that practised much of its economic activity outside palace control'. For a critical view, see Routledge/McGeough (2009), 26. Mycenaean export goods: Mee (2008), 363. Ivory could also be processed outside the palace: Burns (2010a), 122–124.

52. Wedde (2005), 33–36; Tartaron (2013), 69, 75, 124–132, see Emanuel (2021), 162–163, footnote 13 with sources.
53. Yasur-Landau (2010), 48; Tartaron (2013), 124–138. Similar reflections in Broodbank (2013), 468.
54. Similarly, Yasur-Landau (2010), 189, 207, 215 on Šardana mercenaries (including in Egypt) as informants.
55. Jung (2009), 41.
56. On the dependence of bronze age trade on security and peace as well as the disruption caused by mercenaries: Artzy (1998), 445. Disruption to tin supplies: Drews (1993), 87.
57. Sasson (1966), 133 and Bryce (1998), 365 on supply problems; Yasur-Landau (2010), 98. Singer (2000) on other problems faced by the Hittite Empire, e.g., internal struggles for the throne, Ugarit's waning loyalty, loss of control in southwestern Anatolia.
58. This is the (not uncontested) view advanced by Sherratt/Sherratt (1991), 366–367, 371 with other literature. Failed harvests, etc.: Demand (2011), 196.
59. See Tartaron (2013), 69.
60. For the theory of a 'large-scale mutiny by mercenaries' as the true cause of the Sea Peoples phenomenon, see Goedicke, *The Report of Wenamon* (1975), 180–183. This is surely exaggerated (Emanuel 2021, 212), but it seems plausible that mercenaries like the Šardana were a destabilizing force.
61. Yasur-Lindau (2010) and Emanuel (2021), 162, 268–270 with Wachsmann (1998, 160) on the 'Rower Tablets' of Pylos, 'which may support an organised seaborne evacuation'.
62. Demand (2011), 204; Yasur-Landau (2010), 59, 69, 82.
63. Drews (1993), 14; Schipper (2005), 115.
64. Hoftijzer and Van Soldt (1998), 343–344. See Jung (2009), 39 on penteconters; Emanuel (2021), 111–113 on warnings of 'enemy ships'.
65. Jung (2009), 37–38; Yasur-Landau (2010), 164; Yon (1992). Date of the final destruction: Caubet (2000), 36.
66. On the connection among pioneers, bridgeheads, and invasion pathways, see Jung (2009), 44.
67. Sommer (2001), 174–175.
68. Demand (2011), 201–202; Cline/O'Connor (2003), 129–132; Emanuel (2021), 201–216. Sea Peoples fleet: Barako (2003). Attacks on the Nile delta: Jung (2009), 32. More migration than regular battle: Yasur-Landau (2010), 175. Families: inferred from the Medinet Habu relief by Yasur-Landau (2010), 177–179.

69. Dothan (1992), 145, 182–183; Drews (1993), 216–217.
70. Maeir and Hitchcock (2017), 250; Koch (2017), 192: 'well trained warriors'; Machinist (2000), 63–64 for their language. Wachsmann (2000) for the Mycenaean and central European galley type.
71. Veenhof (2001), 202–203. For the old, now superseded theory of Mycenaean origin and contacts, see Dothan (1992), 180–181, 191, 218; see also Margalith (1994), 42; Cline/O'Connor, 120; Yasur-Landau (2010), 180–196, Emanuel (2021), 249 and especially Maeir and Hitchcock (2017). The Philistines nonetheless copied Mycenaean pottery: Vanschoonwinkel (2006), 75; Cunliffe (2011), 240.
72. Emanuel (2021), 255.
73. 2 Sam 8:18; 15:18; 20:7; 20:23; 23:23; 1 Chr. 18:17. Not long-distance traders: Yasur-Landau (2010), 331.
74. Ehrlich (1996), 37–41; Machinist (2000), 66. The Cherethites (= Cretans?) were palace guards or bodyguards who had arrived as refugees; Hess (1992).
75. Peatfield (2008), 93; Georganas (2010), 310. Weaponry and comparison: Dothan (1992), 19; Goliath's armour and spear throw: 185.
76. See Yasur-Landau (2010), 208–209, 338; Yasur-Landau (2012).
77. Georganas (2010), 308; Tov (1986), 34–41; Margalith (1994), 49.
78. Tartaron (2013), 22. Knowledge of coastal communities: 126, 133.
79. Wedde (1998); Yasur-Landau (2010), 104.
80. Broodbank (2013), 494 (Phoenicians); Schipper (2005), 146; Tartaron (2013), 22–23.
81. Demand (2011), 207; cooperation with the Sea Peoples: Bikai (1992), 135–136, Yasur-Landau (2010). No changes: Röllig (1982), 16. On Phoenician links to Bronze Age traditions, see Broodbank (2013), 484–487.
82. Lane-Fox (2008), 21–22; Pappa (2013), 13–14.
83. Röllig (1982), 19.
84. Röllig (1982), 19–21, 25; Lane-Fox (2008), 21–22; Phoenician wine: Temin (2006), 143–144.
85. Ezekiel 27; Niemeyer (2006), 158–159.
86. Pritchard (1968), 100.
87. Barako (2003), 22–23; Niemeyer (2006), 146–148.
88. 1 Kings 5:15–32, 7:13–14 (Hiram and the building of the Temple); 9:26–28 (ships from Ezion-Geber to Ophir); 10:11–12 (gold, sandalwood, and gemstones from Ophir, see 2 Chron. 9:10); 22.48–49 (King Josephat's ships). Niemeyer (2006), 149 refers to parallels in the Iliad 6,288–295, where Paris brought experienced weavers and dyers from Sidon to his father's court. On Ophir's location, see Aubet (2001), 45. Older theories in Miller (1969), 265–267.
89. Finkelstein/Silberman (2006), 123–177; Liverani (2005), 108–116.

90. Acquiring sandalwood from Java ('algum' or 'almung') is mentioned in the Old Testament as an aim of Solomon's and Hiram's voyage to Tarshish; 1 Kings 10:11; 2 Chron. 9:10; Miller (1969), 62. Contractual basis: 1 Kings 5:25.
91. On Josephat's second attempt: 1 Kings 22:49; Margalith (1994), 60. Military reputation of the Hebrews: 1 Sam. 30:1–3; Joshua 11:11.
92. Miller (1969), 164–165. The Egyptians advanced from Mersa Gawasis to Punt during the Middle Kingdom; Cooper (2011), 206.
93. Hdt. 2,159.
94. Hdt. 4,42. The historicity is disputed, although recently the crowd of sceptics has thinned; Huss (1989), 2–3; Cunliffe (2001), 107; J. F. Quack, ZDMG 155 (2005), 609. The opposing positions are discussed in Cary-Warmington (1963), 114–117. Asheri (2006) is undecided; he takes the details found in Herodotus to be realistic but has doubts about a voyage that would be 'absolutely exceptional for the time'. Red Sea specialists: Fabre (2004), 156. Reference to previous journeys to Punt: McGrail (2001), 42.
95. Ez. 27.17; Miller (1969), 101.
96. See Miller (1969), 165, who see the quest for gold as the deciding factor. Queen of Sheba: Willeitner (2013), 30–31; Aegean and Phoenician mariners on early Punt expeditions: Dayton (1984), 364–366.
97. Hdt. 4,42,3 (transl. Rawlinson); realistic: Asheri (2007), 611.
98. Chami (1999).
99. Deme/McIntosh (2006), 317–347; Broodbank (2013), 572, 507 on Zinkekra in Wadi al-Ajat.
100. Cary-Warmington (1963), 118 points—albeit vaguely—to the opening of a new maritime route and corresponding trade opportunities.
101. See Asheri (2007), 611.
102. 1 Kings 10:22; 2 Chron. 9:21. Some explain the three-year rhythm of Tarshish ships with the monsoon cycle of the Indian Ocean: they set sail from the Red Sea in summer, carried out their business in Ophir (= Indian west coast) in winter, before returning early in the third year. The problem with this interpretation is that it requires identifying Tarshish with Ophir.
103. Cunliffe (2001), 44.
104. Aubet (1982), 324.
105. Pappa (2013), 32–33; Neville (2007), 83–112 for Gades and its hinterland, 146–147 for Huelva. Broodbank (2013), 491–492 on links between the Tyrrhenian Sea and the Atlantic.
106. Cunliffe (2001), 46–48, 256ff. Perhaps they had access to the Atlantic gold system.
107. Jeremiah 10.9; Lane Fox (2008), 26; Niemeyer (2006), 152.
108. Bikai (1987), 126; Demand (2013), 22ff.; Bronze Age traditions: Broodbank (2013), 494.
109. This is how the Tekke tomb has been interpreted; Coldstream (1982), 267f. An answer to the question of whether the grave finds are of local or

Phoenician-Canaanite provenance will depend on the technical prowess ascribed to domestic production; according to Shaw (2004), the altar served both locals and sea crew. Discussion in Lane Fox (2008), 166–167; Niemeyer (2006), 150.

110. Discussion of the Assyrian thesis in Pappa (2013), 177–178; Lane Fox (2008), 23–25, Niemeyer (2006); 159f.; Boardman (2006), 198.
111. Shefton (1982), 341 with Ps.-Arist. De mirabilibus auscultationibus, 135.
112. Broodbank (2013), 500–501; Lane Fox (2008), 55–57. A minority opinion holds that the king was a Phoenician aristocrat.
113. North Syrian women in Al-Mina: Lane Fox (2008), 108–109. Encounters of Phoenician and Euboean traders on Cyprus: Lane Fox (2008), 59–60. Euboean wares in Tyros: Waldbaum (1994), 54–57. Cooperation with mixed crews: Demand (2013), 228f. Euboea-Philistines: Lane Fox (2008), 89–90. Euboeans in the northern Aegean: Coldstream (1982), 266. On Thasos Hdt. 6,47 and Braun (1982), 11.
114. See Braun (1982), 9; Pappa (2013), 37.
115. Lane Fox (2008), 105. Al-Mina as launching pad for bandits and mercenaries: Lane Fox (2008), 111–113.
116. Demand (2013), 223. Shefton (1982), 343 speaks of a 'happy symbiosis of Greek material and Phoenician carriers'.
117. Boardman (2006), 196; Lane Fox (2008), 145–147.
118. Boardman (2006), 199; Lane Fox (2008), 147–148; Carthage: Niemeyer (2006), 162. Mycenaean pottery in Carthage: Fabre (2004), 64.
119. See Boardman (2006), 197–198; Niemeyer (2006), 150–151; Ridgway (1992), 108–110.
120. Broodbank (2013), 512.
121. Lane Fox (2008), 143–144; Buchner (1982), 295.
122. Buchner (1982), 294; Lane Fox (2008), 156–161 on Nestor's cup.
123. Broodbank (2013), 518; Pithekoussai: Buchner (1982), 296.
124. Wilson (2013), 552.
125. Estimates for 800 BCE run to 20 million; Broodbank (2013), 506–507.
126. Sherratt/Sherratt (1991), 373; Tartaron (2013), 71–72.
127. See Lane Fox (2008), 30–32, 85–88; post-bronze-age piracy: Tartaron (2013), 67.
128. Slaves: Lane Fox (2008), 131 on Sicily; penteconters: Tartaron (2013), 68.
129. Sherratt/Sherratt (1991), 374–377; iron production: Broodbank (2013), 451.
130. Lane Fox (2008), 93. Smaller ships: Sherratt/Sherratt (1991), 373. Phoenician ships had a carrying capacity of around thirty tonnes. Crew: Artzy (1998), 439–448.
131. Demand (2013), 235, 244; Niemeyer (2006), 150; Broodbank (2013), 375.
132. Structural parallels (fortification, mixed marriages) between Philistine and Greek foundations in the west are detected by Yasur-Landau (2010), 294, 314.
133. Foxhall (2005). Population increase in Phoenicia: Röllig (1982), 29–30.
134. Lane Fox (2008), 124–125.

135. Tartaron (2013), 26, 128–129.
136. Morgan (1988), Morris (1989), Emanuel (2021), 130–137 with additional representations from the Aegean.
137. Tartaron (2013), 40. Interpretation of ship engineering etc. in McGrail (2001), 113–122.
138. Morris (1989); Hoekstra (1981), 34; Lyra: Hurwit (1987), 48–49.
139. West (1988), 161–162; Hurwit (1987), 49; Broodbank (2013), 460.
140. Vanschoonwinkel (2006), 84–85. Geryon: Hes. Theog. 287–294. Amber from the Hesperides: Broodbank (2013), 432.
141. Brommer (1986), 65; 'master of animals', etc.: Burkert (1979), 94–96.
142. See Georges (1994), 4 on Heracles in Egypt against the pharaoh Busiris.
143. Hom. Il. 9,328–29; Lane Fox (2008), 57. Ajax is another pre-Homeric heroic figure.
144. Wenamun: Papyrus Moscow 120; transl. Breasted (1905); Text: Lichtheim (1976), 224–230 and Goedicke (1975) with commentary; Fabre (2004), 184–187; Emanuel (2021), 244. Shipwrecked Sailor: López-Ruiz (2014), 131–135.
145. See Demand (2013), 220–223. The queen's offer to spend the night with Wenamun recalls Odyssean adventures; Schipper (2005), 286–291, see Goedicke (1975), 128–129.
146. Horowitz (1998), 20–42; Rollinger (2013), 112.
147. The ring of water can already be demonstrated for Egypt of the nineteenth century BCE; here it is called the 'Great Green' and later the 'Great Encircler'. W. Helck, Lex. Äg. 3 (1980), 1276–1279 s.v. Sea ('Meer').
148. On whether the *nagû* was an island: Horowitz (1998), 32–33.
149. Sutean woman: Rice (1994), 116.
150. Rice (1985), 87–88, 103. In relation to the holiness of the island, parallels can be drawn with Delos and the Isles of the Blessed; Alster (1983), 59–60.
151. Dilmun = Bahrain: Rice (1985), 15–16, 99–102; on Failaka: 212–213; copper and pearls in Bahrain: Alster (1983), 39–45 identifies Dilmun with Arabia. Perilous voyage: Alster (1983), 49. From Dilmun, a god brought the Sumerians the art of writing: Rice (1985), 50–51; Dilmun = paradise: 52. Expeditions to Punt as the basis for the tale of the Shipwrecked Sailor: McGrail (2001), 36.
152. Lane Fox (2008), 218–221.
153. Consider the god Enki, who can be equated with the amphibious Oannes (Ea) of the Greeks; Rice (1985), 54, 111–113.
154. Burkert (1992), 9–11.
155. Lane Fox (2008), 29; Pritchett (1993), 68–69 on Helen in Egypt. Scenes on Phoenician ivory work and metalwork point to musicians: Lane Fox (2008), 125–127 on the Nora stela, which honours a god thanks for safe arrival after a storm.
156. Culican (1986), 581–614; Emanuel (2021), 154–155 on connections reaching into the bronze age.

157. Lane Fox (2008), 280–282; Burkert (1992), 11. Greek visitors may have heard the Hittite 'Song of Emergence' (c. 1200) in honour of Hazzi.
158. Ugarite myths in the Bible: Margalith (1994), 12–13.
159. Margalith (1994), 11–12, 28–40 on Apollo Smintheus, who brings a plague in the *Iliad*. Around half of the words in the Bible with Greek origin refer to dealings with the Philistines; Philistine names have Greek roots: Margalith (1994), 41.
160. Brody (1998), 23–37, 58–59.
161. Radermacher (1903), 66–68; Hamel (1995); Follis (1978); Brody (1998); 16; Isaiah 18:1; Hom. Od. 11,125.
162. Lane Fox (2008), 91; Yasur-Landau (2010) on mixed marriages between Canaanites and Philistines.
163. Broodbank (2013), 390. Philistines: Yasur-Landau (2010), 251, 264.
164. For a Hittite analogue see Hoffner (1968).
165. Margalith (1994), 32, 91, 123; Machinist (2000), 67. Battlecries: Burkert (1992), 19–20, 39–40.
166. 1 Sam 17.45.
167. Margalith (1994), 47–48, 95 (Ugarit) and 81, 84 on parallels with Hebrew and Greek myths. Heracles and Samson legends: 100–101.
168. See Lanfranchi (2000), 7.
169. See Schniedewind (2005), 66 and 17. Assyria as accelerating factor: Tadmor (1975), 36–48.
170. Finkelstein/Silberman (2006), 285–286; Schniedewind (2005), 66–67.
171. Schniedewind (2005), 74; Rice (1985), 254; Horowitz (1998), 25–26.
172. West (1986), 85–86. Alkman PMG 148 also offers a catalogue of mythical nations; see 156.
173. Hölscher (1949), 33.
174. See Finkelstein/Silberman (2006), 134–144; Demand (2013), 230.
175. Schniedewind (2005), 18–19, 89–90; Broodbank (2013), 534.
176. See Lanfranchi (2000), 12–21, 32–33.
177. Phocylides Frg. 4 (Gentili-Prato).
178. See Stanford (1963), 75.
179. Stanford (1963), 86–87 with Hom. Od. 10,464; 15,343–5. But see Hom. Il. 15,80–83. Cf. Hartog (2001).
180. Hom. Od. 4,81–90;.
181. The idea of a 'Greek pessimism' was influentially articulated by Jacob Burckhardt in the second volume of his 'History of Greek Culture'; GW 6, Basel 1956, 349–350.
182. Hdt. 1,207.
183. See Hölscher (1990), 43; Odysseus as 'wanderer' and 'explorer': Silk (2004), 39.
184. See Stanford (1963), 66–67, who sees in this a prototype of the worldly wise, noble pirate.
185. For the Argonauts, e.g., Severin (1985).

186. Lesky (1948).
187. Strab. 1,2,15.
188. See Marinatos (1995), 134–135; Segal (1968).
189. Petersmann (1981), 43–44.
190. Meuli (1921), 58; Hölscher (1990), 168–196.
191. Ballabriga (1998), 94–95; Page (1973), 73–78. Elimination: Petersmann (1981), 61ff.
192. Bowra (1964), 143.
193. Page (1973), 4; Roller (2015), 16–17.
194. Ballabriga (1998), 8.
195. Marinatos (1995), 134 perceives in Circe's island a 'bridge' or 'kind of gate' between two worlds. I find his arguments unconvincing.
196. Hom. Od. 7,321–2.
197. See Hölscher (1990), 140–141.
198. Hom. Od. 11,367–368; Tartaron (2013), 111.
199. Homer knows the circumpolar stars (Il. 5,5–6; 18,485–489; Od. 5,275) and the Great Bear. The Sun rises from Okeanos and falls back into it before disappearing under the Earth (that is, below the horizon). He also knew the (summer) solstices: Od. 10,470; see Hes. erg. 5,564–567.
200. Scodel (2004), 53; Stanford (1963), 73 (Cicones); Skinner (2012), 55–56 on the Lotus-eaters.
201. Scodel (2005), 156 emphasizes that the ethnographic descriptions in the *Odyssey* are pitched at an audience that was interested 'to learn about the world'.
202. See Skinner (2012), 49 on the universality of the ethnographic element.
203. Gen. 10 with Neiman (1980), esp. 39–41.
204. Hes. Frg. 98. Skinner (2012), 63. The chase of the Boreads in Hes. Frg. 150–157; Hirschberger (2004), 318–328. The air-borne pursuit proceeded from the Scythians over Asia and Africa.
205. Corral (2002), 151–153.
206. See Od. 5,270–277; Dougherty (2001), 31–33.
207. Scodel (2004), 48; Sirens and their 'global news-service': Stanford (1963), 77; Od. 12,191.
208. Hom. Od. 6,4–10.
209. Hom. Od. 9,174–175; Stanford (1963), 76 believes that Odysseus 'wanted to do some anthropological research'. It is more likely that he wished to investigate whether a crossing to the land of the Cyclops was feasible and advantageous.
210. Hölscher (1990), 159; Ivantchik (2005), 60–61.
211. See Hölscher (1990), 117.
212. See Lane Fox (2008), 124–125, who argues that news of Tartessos was integrated into the description of the region where the entrance to the underworld is found in Homer.

213. Hom. Od. 4,85–87ff. (Menelaus in Libya); 19,246–7 (the 'black' Eurybates); Vanschoonwinkel (2006), 88–87, Lane Fox (2008), 122–123, 147–148.
214. Hölscher (1990), 143; literature for identifying the plant in Pritchett (1993), 52.
215. Hom. Od. 9,97–104.
216. Hom. Od. 9,116–124; Dickie (1995), 35–36. Goat(skins) in Libya: Hdt. 4,189; Hippocr. de sacr.morb. 2; Herrmann (1926), 9.
217. Hom. Od. 9,214. Newton (2005), 138–139; Dickie (1995), 49–50.
218. See Meuli (1921), 80; Mondi (1983), 37; O'Sullivan (1990), 12–13.
219. Hom. Od. 9,321–324; 383–384; Dougherty (2001), 124: 'The narrative thus presents maritime expertise as the appropriate and successful response to the threats posed by the Cyclops'.
220. Hom. Od. 9,107–112; Mondi (1983), 19, 37; Scodel (2005), 148, 152.
221. Hom. Od. 9,219–224.
222. Hölscher (1990), 143.
223. Hes. theog. 146; Meuli (1921), 75; Mondi (1983), 18.
224. Hom. Od. 10,1–55; western voyage: Meuli (1921), 53; Maaß (1915), 15.
225. Hom. Od. 10,116–124.
226. Hom. Od. 10,88–90.
227. Hom. Od. 10,84–85.
228. Dicks (1970), 33.
229. Hom. Od. 10,82–86. The Scythians are first mentioned in the context of the Boreads' pursuit: Hes. Frg. 150; Ivantchik (2005), 26–27. Horse milkers: Hom. Il. 13,5–6; interpreted as nomads north of the Black Sea by West (2003), 154–155; horse milkers—Scythians: Ivantchik (2005), 66.
230. See Ivantchik (2005), 85–89.
231. Hes. theog. 337–345; Vanschoonwinkel (2006), 85–86; Petropoulos (2005), 16–19 and 21: 'For the time being, we can speak with certainty of the fact that during the 8th century B.C. the Greeks had not simply heard of the expanse of sea beyond the Hellespont though literary and oral tradition, but that they had also seen it first hand'.
232. Hom. Il. 2,851–855.
233. Amazons as Scythians: Mayor (2014). Hes. theog. 337–345; Petropoulos (2005), 17–19; the Black Sea: West (2003), 156–159.
234. West (2003), 159.
235. Hom. Od. 10,213–218, 392–397. The crew's transformation back into humans makes them younger and better looking, just as the plant given Gilgamesh by Utnapishtim restores his youth; Michaux (2003), 14.
236. Hom. Od. 10,210–218, 276 (expertise with poison). Circe as queen of animals: Marinatos (1995), 136–138. Homer indicates the export of remedies to Greece when he says that Helen gave Telemachus a drug 'to quiet all pain and strife, and bring forgetfulness of every ill'. This drug had been sent her by Polydamna, a woman of Egypt; Od. 4,219–232. The Lotus-eaters also know of

such drugs. An interest in exotic plants and animals is further evident in late geometric vase design.

237. Hom. Od. 10,136–137. Circe's island, originally conceived in the west, is moved by Homer to the east as Circe's niece Medea was 'abducted by the Argonauts a generation earlier'. He gives her the island Aeaea.

238. Eumelus F 3 Kinkel; Vanschoonwinkel (2006), 90. Lordkipanidzè/Léveque (1990), 167–187. The dating of the 'Korinthiaka' is contested; West (2002) holds that it was first committed to writing in the sixth century BCE, but older elements surely go back further; Ivantchik (2005), 63.

239. Mimnermos F 11, 11a; West, Vanschoonwinkel (2006), 90; West (2003), 159.

240. Hom. Od. 11,11; 12,3–4.

241. Hölscher (1990), 148; Gisinger (1924), 534; Käppel (2001), 17.

242. Hennig (1926), 273.

243. Black Sea theory: Maaß (1915), 15–16; layers: Herrmann (1926); a mixture: Kranz (1915), 99–102. Since Meuli, we have known that Homer worked through material from the Argonauts saga in books 10–12: overview in Ivantchik (2005), 60–61.

244. Black Sea—part of Okeanos: Ivantchik (2005), 67–106 with Strab. 1,2,10. The Argonauts saga is also set in Okeanos and in the Black Sea. The island of Leuke, where Achilles was transported after his death, can accordingly be interpreted as the equivalent of the Isles of the Blessed in the Ocean. Aea lies in the far north, and since Odysseus—like the Argonauts from Colchis—must return from the realm of the dead through the Planctae ('Wandering Rocks'), it seems likely that this second phase of Odysseus' adventures transpires in the Black Sea area.

245. Hom. Od. 10,491.

246. Hom. Od. 10,507–509.

247. Hom. Od. 10,507; 11,13–22. In another passage, the souls of the suitors drift past Ocean River and the rocks at Leuke to the underworld; the rocks are mentioned by Arctinus of Miletus (c. 750 BCE) as Achilles' burial site in the northern Pontus. There were clearly different traditions regarding the location of Hades that took in the northern sphere of the Black Sea.

248. Hom. Od. 11,14–16.

249. Ivantchik (2005), 58.

250. Bury (1906), 87–88; Hölscher (1990), 153–155. Perhaps Homer had heard of the historical Cimmerians who set out from southern Russia for Asia Minor around 700 BCE. It is also possible, conversely, that the historical people were given this name from the *Odyssey*. See Ivantchik (2005), 56–58, who argues against the interpretation of darkness as polar night. Bury (1906), 81–86 interprets the ghost-like people on the island of Brittia mentioned by Procopius (Persian Wars IV, 15,16) as a legend told on the Elbe that reached Homer via the Phoenicians; it became mixed up with the Cimmerians when Odysseus' travels were relocated to the Black Sea.

251. Hom. Od. 11,638–640; 12,1–4.
252. See Hölscher (1990), 155. Gilgamesh: Tablet 1, 40: '. . . who crossed the Ocean, the vast seas, to the rising sun'.
253. Hom. Od. 12,39–54.
254. Hom. Od. 12,60–110.
255. Meuli (1921), 86–89; Hölscher (1990), 156. Scylla and Charybdis were first placed in the Strait of Messina in the late fifth century; Eur. Med. 1342; Thucyd. 4,24,5.
256. Maaß (1915), 31–33. In the fifth century, Herodotus (4,85–56) identified not Scylla and Charybdis but the Planctae with the 'Kaneai' at the Bosporus and understood them as the 'gateway to the Pontus'. Homerische Untersuchungen, 165; Maaß (1915), 31. According to Strabo these are two islands at the mouth of the Pontus: 6,12,13. Atlantic: Maaß (1915), 33; Hennig (1934), 22–23, 32–33.
257. Hom. Od. 12,267–269.
258. Hom. Od. 12,287–288, 325–326; storms: 313–314.
259. Hom. Od. 12,403–424.
260. Hom. Od. 12,447–448; cf. 1,50–54; 7,244–245.
261. Hom. Od. 6,204–205; eighteen days: 5,278.
262. Hom. Od. 5,271–277.
263. Hom. Od. 13,81–88; 8,557–563.
264. Hom. Od. 7,313–314; see Thornton (1970), 19.
265. Hom. Od. 5,451–452.
266. Apollod. 2, 107; Hes. theog. 274; 294.
267. Hölscher (1990), 109.
268. Hölscher (1990), 109–110.
269. Cook 1992, 252; Michaux (2003), 20. On the fairy tale motif of the magic ship used by the hero, see Meuli (1921), 17.
270. Hom. Od. 7,85–128; quote: 118–119. Wealth of the Phaeacians: 5,38–39; 6,308–309; 7,86–92, 98–102; see Cook (1992), 242.
271. Hölscher (1990), 136–137, 172; Temese and Mentes: 1,184; Sicily: 20,383; 24,211.
272. Dougherty (2001), 112; directions to Scheria: Hom. Od. 5,344–345.
273. Hennig (1934), 41–42; vases: Gehrig (1990), 27–31.
274. Timpe (1985), 198; Meuli (1921), 65. The claim that Homer was thinking of a magnetic compass, or that self-steering ships recall an eye painted or carved at the bows, strikes me as too vague.
275. Hom. Od. 3,318–322.
276. Hom. Od. 4,85–89.
277. Snowden (1970), 102–103; Ivantchik (2005), 22–23; Strab. 7,3,7.
278. Hom. Od. 1,22–24; 5,283; Il. 1,423; 23,206; Romm (1992), 49. I accept the argument that the Ethiopians transformed from a mythical to a 'real' tribe with the discovery of black-skinned people south of Egypt in Homeric times.
279. Von Soden (1959), 27.
280. Berger (1903), 446; Hennig (1926), 272.

281. Von Soden (1959), 2629.
282. Around the same time, Hesiod (Frg. 252 Most) also thought it possible that the Argonauts carried their ship from the Ocean through Libya to the Mediterranean on their return journey.
283. Snowden (1970), 144; Rice (1985), 20–21; Crone (1987), 17. Herodotus maintains that the Phoenicians migrated from the Persian Gulf region to the Levant. Bowersock (1986), 399–401.
284. See Strab. 3,2,14 (c. 150); Roller (2018), 144–145.
285. Hom. Od. 19,245–247 (Eurybates); Hes. Frg. 98,15 (Most) in the context of the Boreads' pursuit; Romm (1992), 29; Ivantchik (2005), 23. Whether real ethnographic knowledge informed the account of the Pygmies is disputed; Snowden (1970), 102–122; Skinner (2012), 96. Silver mixing-bowl: Hom. Od. 4,615–619.

CHAPTER 2

1. Hom. Od. 23,267–273. The prophecy in Hom. Od. 11,134–135.
2. Dornseiff (1937); Romm (1992), 74.
3. Asheri (2007), 582. Dating: Sauter (2000), 108–109.
4. Ps. Longinus, de sublimitate 10, 4 (fr. 7). Text: Bolton (1962), 208; translation (and interpretation): Longinus, *On the Sublime*, transl. W. H. Fyfe (1927).
5. Romm (1992), 73 and Skinner (2012), 67.
6. Romm (1992), 72; Bolton (1962), 8–19 thinks that so unusual a shift in perspective cannot be attributed to Aristeas and the seventh century, a weak argument undermined by the reference to the Tiresias prophecy.
7. Pritchett (1993), 198.
8. Hdt. 4,13–16.
9. Hdt. 4,14–15; Philipps (1955), 162; Pritchett (1993), 25–26.
10. Hdt. 4,13,1. Prooemium: Asheri (2007), 582.
11. Burkert (1987), 109; Bolton (1962), 135–141.
12. It was widely believed in antiquity that Homer had been influenced by Aristeas. Quote: W. Burkert, Gnomon 35 (1963), 239.
13. Hdt. 4,36,1. Cleomenes and Abaris: Dodds (1951), 141; Eliade (1992), 42.
14. Maximus of Tyre, Philosophumena 10, 2–3, 38,3c. Dodds (1951), 141 and Philipps (1955), 162, 176 contend that Maximus preserved older explanations of a shamanic journey; see Dowden (1980), 491.
15. Plin. nat. 7, 174.
16. Hdt. 4,15; Philipps (1955), 176.
17. West (2003), 162–163. Raven and mariners: Medas (2004), 88–89. On the vase inscription: Ivantchik (2005), 74, ibid. also the interpretation of the Achilles vase. Removal of a person is frequently imagined in terms of flight: W. Burkert, Gnomon 35 (1963), 238–239. Achilles' post-mortem transport was probably suppressed by Homer because it did not fit conceptually with Odysseus'

nekyia; Edwards (1985), 223. Ikykos (PMG 291) and Simonides (PMG 558) relocate Achilles to the Elysian Fields, where he marries Medea.

18. Achilles becomes lord of the Scythians; West (2003), 164: Alcaeus frg. 354. Vogt = Z 31; from the sixth century, the White Island is identified with Leuke at the mouth of the Danube.
19. Thornton (1970), 26; Hermes as escort in the 'second *nekyia*': Hom. Od. 24,9–14.
20. Asheri (2007), 583; Philipps (1955), 176. Shamanism and bilocation: Dodds (1956), 140; Bolton (1962), 126.
21. Thornton (1970), 30. Raven as shamanic symbol: Phillips (1955), 176.
22. Bolton (1962), 123; Kingsley (1995), 226.
23. Timpe (1985), 191. Early trade contact: Bridgman (2005), 32.
24. Hdt. 4,108. There are functional overlaps between Dionysus and Apollo. An Etruscan mirror from the fifth century BCE shows an old man with wings on his back and a wine jug behind him. This is probably Calchas, the priest of Apollo, who embarked on a spiritual journey after being transported into an ecstatic state by wine; Thornton (1970), 25. On the location of the Budini, see Hudson (1924).
25. Hdt. 4,75.
26. Hdt. 4,75; Cannabis in Scythian graves: Taylor (2001), 393. On 'sweat baths', see the literature in Pritchett (1993), 208–209.
27. Turcan (1996), 221ff. on the Mithras cult.
28. Hdt. 4,73–75; Meuli (1935), 121–125.
29. Dodds (1951), 141; Kingsley (1994).
30. See Thornton (1970), 25.
31. Hdt. 4,16.
32. Hdt. 4,13.
33. Philipps (1955), 163; Bolton (1962), 76; Kristensen (1988).
34. Parzinger (2004), 14. Leading family: Hdt. 4,14 with Bolton (1962), 2, 131–132. Priest of Apollo: Bolton (1962), 141.
35. Asheri (2007), 586; trade goods: Hennig (1944), 72–77.
36. Hdt. 4,22–23.
37. E.g. How/Wells (1928), I, 310.
38. Hennig (1944), 72–76.
39. Hdt. 4,23–24. See Philipps (1955), 168–169; Thomson (1948), 62; Asheri et al. (2007), 598 and older literature.
40. Hdt. 4,24.
41. Hdt. 4,25.
42. See Bolton (1962), 9.
43. Hdt. 4,26; Herodotus draws on Aristeas: Bolton (1962), 76.
44. Asheri et al. (2007), 600–601. The description accords with the account of the Massagetae in Hdt. 1, 215–216. Cannibalism: Murphy/Mallory (2000). That

the tribe in question is the one mentioned in Chinese sources as the Wusun is by no means as widely accepted as Reichert (1992), 18 assumes.

45. Asheri et al. (2007), 599.
46. K. Ziegler, DKP 2 (1979), s.v. Griffon, 876.
47. Phillips (1955), 161; Romm (1992), 69.
48. Dodds (1951), 14.
49. Tzetzes, Chiliades VII, 687–692. See Romm (1992), 72.
50. Hes. frg. 98, 15; Romm (1992), 69–70; Phillips (1955), 173. Hesiod had characterized the Scythians as 'mare-milkers'.
51. Mayor/Heaney (1993), 54–59; Phillips (1955), 174. The Mongol *almas* was evidently reproduced with the Scythian *arimasp-*.
52. Hennig (1944), 76 on Aeschyl. Prom. 805–808.
53. Phillips (1955), 170; Asheri (2007), 595. Between 1860 and 1950, around a hundred ancient gold mines were discovered. They were active from 1500 BCE: Mayor/Heaney (1993), 52.
54. Mayor (2014), 113–115. The dragon standing guard over the mountain of gold belongs in the religious orbit of the mythical king who rules as a celestial father and figures as the ancestor of great dynasties among the Mongols, Chinese, and Turkic peoples: Phillips (1955), 174; Bolton (1962), 84. Tschuden: Hennig (1944), 75–76.
55. Phillips (1955), 171; Mayor/Heaney (1993), 49–52. In 1828, Adolf Erman (Berlin 1933, 711–712) reported that Russian inhabitants and traders in the Siberian tundra had given the name 'talons' to the frequently unearthed bones of the 'Rhinocerus teichorinus'. The indigenous people went further. They interpreted the skull as a bird's head and claimed that their forefathers had fought 'tremendous battles' against these birds. Erman immediately recognized parallels with the tales of Aristeas.
56. Phillips (1955), 176; Bolton (1962), 89.
57. Hdt. 4,13.
58. Bolton (1962), 100 with older literature (p. 31); Asheri (2007).
59. Athens: Stewart (1990), 166. Indo-European peoples: Mallory/Mair (2000), 39–42 (on Aristeas), 252–269; Mair (1995); Shankman/Durrant (2000), 2; Asheri (2007), 599; Hundt (1969).
60. Hes. fr. 98, 20–24; see Hom. Hymn. Dionys. 28–29; Skinner (2012), 63.
61. Hdt. 4,25,36; Bolton (1966), 102; Brown (1992), 98.
62. Bolton (1966), 92–97.
63. Brown (1992), 100–101; Thornton (1970), 24; Skinner (2012), 63; Bacchylides 3, 58–62 has Croesus transported to the Hyperboreans by Apollo.
64. Alcman frg. 307c V.; Aeschyl. frg. 68, 197; Pind. Olymp. 10, 29–47; Romm (1992), 64–65.
65. Käppel (2001), 22–23.

66. See Pritchett (1993), 102–103 on the Phoenix; the name is perhaps Mycenaean in origin (po-ni-ke) and was equated with the griffin. Van den Broek (1972); Käppel (2001), 23; swans circling Delos: Callim. Del. 249.
67. H. Daebritz, RE 9 (1914), s.v. Hyperborei, 278 with the sources. The mountain range that separated their land from other people was accordingly identified with the Haemus in northern Thracia; Bridgman (2005), 28–37; Timpe (1985), 185 on the Hippomolgoi (Hom. Il. 13,5).
68. Ahl (1982), 390–391; Käppel (2001), 25.
69. Hes. frg. 261a, b, 262 a, b, 98 v 24 (Most); Käppel (2001), 24.
70. Burkert (1987), 146; Ahl (1982), 395. Sceptical: Asheri (2007), 604.
71. Hdt. 4,33–34; Paus. 1,31,2; Plin. nat. 4,91.
72. Harrison (1904) with image (248).
73. Timpe (1985), 194, 201; Gisinger (1924), 538 considers knowledge of an old amber road proceeding upriver from the mouth of the Rhône, then along the Rhine to its delta; there were perhaps even reports of the Elbe. Harvest festival: Daebritz, RE 9 (1914), s.v. Hyperborei, 278.
74. Hdt. 4,32 ff.; Burkert (1987), 146–147; Bridgman (2005), 49; map in Bridgman (2005), 54.
75. They used the Adriatic route; see Hdt. 4,13.
76. Verger (2006), 48–53.
77. Athen. 13,576a–b; Iust. 43,3; Pralon (1992), 51–56. Greek artisans and traders among the Celts: Shefton (1994), 62–68.
78. Pralon (1992), 55; see Mahabharata 1, 185, 4–37, 3, 54–55.
79. Virg. Aen. 7,50–58; 358–362.
80. See Dougherty (1993).
81. Silk: Cunliffe (2011), 43; Kuckenberg (2010), 224.
82. Wells (1980), 21, 60–61 on contacts before Massalia was founded.
83. Bouffier (2013), 129.
84. Shefton (1994), 61–63; Bouffier (2013), 129; Hodge (1998), 143 on St. Blaise as 'a kind of joint Etruscan-Greek-Ligurian trading centre'; Hodge (1998), 65–66. Rhodians were at the mouth of the Rhône before the Phocaeans: Hodge (1998), 163.
85. Evidence in Radermacher (1916), including on Nanus, the 'dwarf'.
86. Aristotle in Ath. 13,576 a.
87. Pralon (1992), 54; Etruscan trade network in central Europe: Pape (2000), 74–75 with map.
88. Cunliffe (2011), 76–81.
89. Aristotle in Ath. 13,576b; Pralon (1992), 53.
90. See Morel (2006), 366; mixed marriages as integration factor: Morel (2006), 135. Shortage of women: Morel (2006), 365. Other Graeco-Celtic mixed settlements have been shown at Arles and Glanum: Hodge (1998), 160.
91. Strab. 4,1,5; Shefton (1994), 65–67; Morel (2006), 365. Grain in the Languedoc, import and Celtic granaries: Morel (2006), 381–383; Hodge (1998), 44–45, 59.

92. Yalcin/Özyigit (2013).
93. Just. 43,3,5. Morel (2006), 360; Broodbank (2013), 548 for the beginnings. Salmon (1984), 129; De Angelis (2003), 51; Osborne (2007), 283. Silos in Megara Hyblaea already indicate export surpluses by 700 BCE; in Metapontus, agricultural production outstripped domestic demand in the sixth century.
94. Wallinga (1993), 93–96; Möller (2000), 50, 78–80; 210; Rihll (1996), 90–91.
95. Pomey (2011). Invention in Phoenicia: Pomey (2011), 44, 53; image: 44. Triremes: Dunbabin (1968), 419.
96. Rihll (1996), 103–107, Osborne (2007), 293–294, Broodbank (2013), 556 on the Levant.
97. See Hdt. 4,152 on Sostratus of Aegina. Perhaps the city imported silver from Tartessos for its coins; slave trade: Broodbank (2013), 549.
98. Hdt. 1,163.
99. Shefton (1994), 72–73; Wallinga (1993), 70. Marginal importance of Phocaean export pottery in the west: Morel (2006), 371; Shefton (1982), 350–351 ('diplomatic gifts'). Silver shortage in Egypt and import by Greeks: Osborne (2007), 290. Penteconters: Hdt. 1,163; Braun (2004), 339–340; Morrison/Williams (1968), 109–112, 162, 194.
100. Hdt. 1,163; Shefton (1982), 345–346. Mercenaries: Wallinga (1993); mercenary contract and settlement: Domínguez (2000), 509. Shefton (1982), 345 speculates that the Greeks performed mercenary service for the Phoenicians.
101. Hdt. 1,163; Braun (2004), 337; Domínguez (2006), 434–440: interest in metals from Tartessos.
102. Domínguez (2006), 436, 453.
103. Malkin (2011), 156–157; Bouffier (2013), 129–130.
104. Shefton (2000), 33ff.; Bernard (2000), 150.
105. Wells (1980), 74 ('gifts presented to chiefs or kings for the purpose of making an alliance, securing a friendship, or establishing trade relations'). Shefton (2000), 39: 'diplomatic, "introductory" gifts'; Shefton (1994), 214–215 with A. 33–36.
106. Thuc. 1,13,6; Paus. 10,18,7; 8,6; Malkin (2011), 152–153. It is unlikely that the information here refers to the mid-sixth century BCE and the Battle of Alalia; the sources explicitly state that the Phocaeans who founded Massalia contested these naval battles.
107. Just. 43,3–5; see Strab. 4,1,5; H. G. Wackernagel, RE 28 (1930), s.v. Massalia, 2131; Timpe (1985), 208; Wells (1980), 73.
108. Bernard (2000), 150.
109. Liv. 5,34,8.
110. Bockius (2007), 267.
111. Kuckenberg (2010), 35–40 (but Kuckenberg [2010], 245 against southern influences); Shefton (2000), 38. See Wells (1980), 3, 25, 59, 74, on the origin of the 'architect'. The 'Palace of the Lady of Vix' on Mont Lassois, an apsidal

building without precedent in central Europe, may likewise reflect the designs of Greek (or Etruscan) architects. Kuckenberg (2010), 236–239.

112. See Wells (1980), 7–8, 51 on the 'chief' as 'centre of the economic system'. Kuckenberg (2010), 201 on marital connections, which may even have made Mediterranean women the wives of Celtic princes at a later stage.
113. Pape (2000), 75–81; Wells (1980), 38–46, 68–69 (grain and timber).
114. See Kuckenberg (2010), 97–98, 142–145.
115. See Braun (2004), 341; Wallinga (1993), 341; on the role of Greek products as prestige objects for Celtic princes, see Wells (1980), 96–97.
116. Van den Boom/Pape (2000), 44.
117. Pape (2000), 136–137; Wells (1980), 130–131; Kuckenberg (2010), 170–171 with maps.
118. Pare (1991), 191; Pape (2000), 86, 96–102, 120–123 (routes); 109 (symposia-like banquets). Wine for Celtic 'princes': Hodge (1998), 122; Wells (1980), 64–71 (Attic pottery).
119. Wells (1980), 62–63 and 74–75.
120. Shefton (1994), 64–65; Hodge (1998), 113; Bernard (2000), 152, 154. Constitution: Bouffier (2013), 131; wealth as qualification: Cunliffe (2002), 11. Influx of Phocaeans: Pape (2000), 124, and as 'crucial factor quickly leading to Massalia's dominance and far-reaching influence': Pare (1991), 191.
121. Morel (2006), 361, 384–385, 401; Malkin (2011), 154; Hodge (1998), 53–58, 116–117: slaves to Rome and the episode in Diod. 5, 26; Cunliffe (2001), 306; Pape (2000), 123 on tin. Massiliote wine amphorae along the Rhône and Saône to Heuneburg (map in Shefton [1994], 712): Hermary (2004), 67.
122. Timpe (1985), 203–205; Strab. 4,1,5 on the maritime orientation of the Massalian economy.
123. Hennig (1944); 96–107; Murphy (1977); Spain: Gisinger (1924), 559.
124. Plin. nat. 7,197; Morel (2006), 367–373. Scott, *Pytheas of Massilia* (2022), 13 and 126, who also discusses the value of the Avienus periplus, is sceptical. Dating: Domínguez (2006), 442, Malkin (2011) on Phocaean and Massiliote colonies and emporia.
125. Hdt. 4,152; Hennig (1944), 51–53; Asheri (2007), 678 with Hom. Il. 6,171; Od. 5,32.
126. Cunliffe (2001), 270; Shefton (1982).
127. Bouffier (2013), 129.
128. Timaios (Pseudo-Skymnos, Periegesis 202).
129. Shefton (1994), 61–62; Braun (2004), 337–338. Domínguez (2006), 442 argues for routes over the southern Mediterranean coasts. First contacts: Hdt. 1,163.
130. See Domínguez (2000), 507.
131. Domínguez (2000), 507; Malkin (2011), 196–201. Artemis sanctuary: Malkin (2011), 172–174. Strab. 4,1,4. Eighty-five percent of the votive offerings in Samos from non-Greek areas: Osborne (2007), 284.
132. See Tsetskhladze (1994), 125–126.

133. O'Grady (2002), 13, 96.
134. O'Grady (2002), 210–212; Dicks (1970), 45. On Thales' 'nautical astronomy': Van der Waerden (1988), 13–22.
135. Aristot. meteor. 981 b 20.
136. Hdt. 1,17, 141–143, 169.
137. Kahn (1985), 135.
138. Röd (1988), 40–42.
139. The leaders' names vary in the sources (Protis–Euxenos).
140. Strab. 4,1,4; Malkin (2000), 76.
141. Call. H Ap. 66–68 on Cyrene with Schmidt (2002), 23 as well as other parallels (two ravens show Alexander the way to Siwah); Apollo Archegetes instituted as a pan-Hellenic cult on Naxos: Thuc. 6,6,1; see App. civ. 5,109,454–5.
142. Malkin (2011), 151 holds otherwise; but see Londey (1990), 121–122; Scott (2014), 62–63.
143. That is why nearby, wealthy, and commercially active *poleis* such as Corinth and Chalcis (along with Crete) maintained close connections with the Delphic oracle in the early archaic period. According to legend, their colonists in Italy and Sicily received sayings from the oracle; Parke/Wormell (1956), I, 78; Morgan (1990), 116–117, 137, 161–168. On Crete Morgan (1990), 142–144. A Milesian exile consulted Delphic Apollo only a single time; Parke (1985), 10–11, 120. Sceptical: Londey (1990), 121–122. See Scott (2014), 62–63.
144. Londey (1990), 123–124.
145. This is also why Apollo plays no role when Nausithous, the prototype of early archaic colonization, founds Scheria; Hom. Od. 6,3–10.
146. Strab. 4,1,4 with interpretation by Malkin (2011), 199–200.
147. Hdt. 4,15.
148. Morgan (1990), 17.
149. Meier (1990), 42–45; Malkin (2011).
150. Tsetskhladze (2004), 226–278, esp. 247–256, 264–270; Tsetskhladze (2002), 81–96.
151. Marshall (2000) describes this using the example of the Cyrenians against the Libyans. On the northern Black Sea area, see Heinen (2001) and Okhotnikov (2001).
152. Hdt. 4,76–80 with Asheri (2007), 635–637.
153. For the Scythian side: Heinen (2001), on the Scythes legend and the question of linguistic proficiency. On the Greek side and the Colaxes of Scythian mythology in Alcman: Zaikov (2004), 69–84, and in more detail Mayor (2014), 104–106, 114–117, 358–361.
154. Petropoulos (2005), 53.
155. Hdt. 4,108,2.
156. R. Sherk, ZPE 93 (1992), 235–236; Pritchett (1993), 194.
157. Hdt. 4,59; Asheri (2007), 625.

158. Schmidt (2002), 27–28, 159. *Pharmakos* ritual and colonization: Burkert (1987), 84. Hdt. 4,178; Malkin (1987), 78, 90. Purification priests such as Abaris or Epimedes: Hoessly (2001), 58–63, 72–73, 83, 173–197.
159. Chang (2005); Kosak (2000), 37–38.
160. See Marshall (2000). Apollo as healer and founder god: Pind. Pyth. 4, 270–374, Apollo as 'physician': Call. Hymn. Apoll. 2,45–6. *Stasis* as civic illness: Brok (2000).
161. See Pritchett (1993), 195; Ivantchik (2005), 166–167, 245; Mayor (2014).
162. Dousa (2011). According to Diod. 5,28,6 the theory of the soul's rebirth was widespread among the Celts.
163. Parker (1995), 484–495, 502. Orphic doctrine and transmigration of the soul: Kalogerakos (1996), 343–344.
164. See Burkert (1987), 299–301; Pritchett (1993), 25–26.
165. Donlan (1980), 77–99. On Pythagoras in Croton see Morrison (1956), 143–144.
166. Kalogerakos (1996), 351–353.
167. Zhmud (1997), 127–128.
168. Diod. 10,7.
169. Parker (1995), 488, 492–493.
170. Kalogerakos (1996), 268–342.
171. Healing: Romm (1992), 26–27; Kahn (1960), 83; coastal descriptions as basis of Ionian geography: Timpe (1985), 183.
172. Aristot. Cael. 2,13; Ps.-Plut. plac. Phil. 3,10. Europe-Asia and surrounded by the Ocean: inferred from Hdt. 4,36 with Couprie (2011), 83 and the literature cited there.
173. Heilen (2000).
174. Gisinger (1924), 533, 542, 573; Heilen (2000), 57; eastern models: Berger (1903), 176.
175. Gisinger (1924), 541; Dicks (1970), 72–73.
176. Diog. Laert. 9,21.
177. Gisinger (1924), 573–574; Abel (1974), 996–998 with discussion.

CHAPTER 3

1. Hdt. 1,164–166. For Cyrus, the Medes, and Lydia see Waters (2014), 38–42.
2. See Huss (1985), 67. Fabre (1992), 12–13 proposes amicable relations with Carthage in the sixth century, when they faced a common enemy in Syracuse.
3. Fabre (1992), 14–15; Roller (2006), 16–18 (with arguments for the early dating). North Atlantic: Avien. Ora maritima 88–134, 363–298.
4. FGrHist 1F 18a (depiction of the voyage of the Argonauts).
5. The discussion's connection to the question of the Nile is the most important evidence for dating Euthymenes' voyage. With Fabre (1992), 13, I am satisfied by the arguments for dating it back to the first half of the sixth century, "probably before the Carthaginian Hanno".

6. Sen. quaest. nat. 4,2.22. See Carpenter (1966), 101. Euthymenes confused the etesians with the Trade Winds.
7. Sen. nat. 4,2,22.
8. Gisinger (1924), 566. According to Desanges (1978), 21, the etesians could only correspond to the monsoon winds that blow from July to October from the southwest. In that period, the river floods like the Nile. Two problems arise from this. Firstly, the fact that both rivers swell at the same time contradicts the assumption of communicating vessels. Secondly, the inundations of the Nile would have to exhibit blue seawater and not turbid freshwater, while conversely the Ocean just before the Senegal would have to be blue. These objections are not compelling. Euthymenes could have argued that the oceanic water from the Atlantic loses its transparency and colour on the long journey to the mouth of the Nile. It is further unclear whether he was aware of the coincidence in time. After all, this presupposes a stay of several months on the Senegal.
9. Hdt. 4,43; Ferguson (1969), 8–9. Cameroon: Asheri (2007), 613; Roller (2006), 21. To southern Morocco: Mauny (1978), 296. Identification: Snowden (1970), 105.
10. Heraclides Ponticus in Strab. 2,3,4 (c. 98).
11. Cf. Bosch-Gimpera (1944), 55–56, according to whom the Spartans were kept out of north Africa (Sirte).
12. Huss (1985), 84 identifies the Oestriminians with the Cassiterides mentioned by Herodotus, probably the Scilly Isles; Tartessos, mentioned in Avienus, likely derives from a translation of Himilco's report.
13. Cary-Warmington (1963), 46–47; coastline: Gisinger (1924), 531; Ireland and the Tin Isles: Roller (2006).
14. Omitted is the dedication to the gods normally found in Phoenician documents; Segert (1969), 509–510.
15. Fage (2002), 47.
16. Segert (1969), 518; Picard (1982), 179 on the division of the texts into two parts: Plin. nat. 5,8.
17. E.g. Mauny (1970), 22, 91–93; (1978), 296–297; Fage (2002), 47.
18. Lonis (1978); Picard (1992), 186–187 (tacking). Authenticity: Medas (2004), 143. Austen (2012), 30 regards the *periplus* as a "literary invention". However, the objections—nautical technology and a lack of archaeological evidence—are invalid or irrelevant for a voyage of discovery.
19. Medas (2004), 142 specifically on Hanno's voyage.
20. Mauny (1970), 93–99.
21. Cf. Lhote (1982), 48–49, 78–79, 86. Connection between chariot routes and the coast surmised by Mauny (1947), 341–357; discussed in Lhote (1982), 48–49.
22. Fabre (2004), 83–85 on Coptos and the good shipbuilding timber in the region; Theophr. H. plant. 2,4, 2,8. Prefabricated ship parts were clearly transported from Coptos to the Red Sea and reassembled there to bypass the unfavourable nautical conditions further north.

23. Vian (1982).
24. Hanno, Peripl. 1; Cary-Warmington (1963), 63; Oikonomides/Miller (1995), 3. The fact that the Carthaginians used penteconters does not rule out a dating to the time of Himera. Triremes were unsuited to large-scale expeditions and colonization. This against Rebuffat (1995), 24.
25. Hdt. 1,164–166. Sixty penteconters seems to have been the standard size of the Phocaean fleet; cf. Asheri (2007), 186 and Vivenza (1980), 104 on the parallels.
26. Cf. Hands (1969), 85. For a dating "rather later in the fifth century": Ferguson (1969), 5.
27. Pappa (2013), 47, 84.
28. Text and translation: Oikonomodes/Miller (1995).
29. Cary-Warmington (1963), 64.
30. Huss (1985), 79–80.
31. Periplus § 6; Cary-Warmington (1963), 64.
32. Interpreters: Geus (1994), 101. Lixus was already a Phoenician trading post in the eighth century. Important information passed through it from central Africa to Tyre, and later Carthage; Pappa (2013), 83–86.
33. Periplus § 7.
34. Cary-Warmington (1963), 64; Mauny (1970), 94.
35. Killick (2004).
36. Periplus § 8. Cf. Blomquist (1984), 56. Rio Oro: Huss (1985), 80.
37. Huss (1985), 81; Cary-Warmington (1963), 66. Location of Kerne: Vivenza (1980), 108–109.
38. Periplus § 9.
39. Periplus § 9–10; cf. Huss (1985), 81.
40. Periplus § 10.
41. Bichler (2011), 332.
42. Blomquist (1985), 58–61. They also acquired pelts and slaves; see Cunliffe (2001), 302.
43. Vivenza (1980), 108; Huss (1989), 4. Gold trade in the Senegal area: Ferguson (1969), 7.
44. Palaiphatos § 31; Law (1967), 188; Snowden (1970), 106.
45. Hdt. 4,196.
46. Ps.-Skylax Periplus 112,7.
47. Periplus § 15; Blomquist (1984), 57.
48. Blomquist (1984), 58.
49. Plin. nat. 5,8. That Hanno was commissioned to attempt a circumnavigation of Africa from the west is also assumed by Oikonomides/Miller 1995, 3. The Carthaginians were aware of the Tyrian circumnavigation and had access to information about the nautical conditions. See Vivenza (1980), 106–107; Oikonomides/Miller (1995), 3–4.
50. Periplus § 14. Cary-Warmington (1963), 67 translates "interpreters".
51. Hdt. 4,195.
52. Cf. Asheri (2007), 717.

53. Cf. Cary-Warmington (1963), 66; Snowden (1970), 106.
54. Periplus § 15.
55. Periplus § 16.
56. Huss (1985), 81 with A. 50 and 51.
57. Plin. nat. 6, 200.
58. Periplus § 18. Perhaps the rest of the text is missing.
59. Other attempts at reconstruction with maps in Beaujeu (1955), 162–162.
60. See Lhote (1982), 49–52, 81–87, 208, and 162 on the Libyan sea peoples.
61. Mauny (1978), 280–283; MacDonald (2011) is sceptical: he sees them as "sports cars for the local Saharan aristocracy" and dates the introduction of mules and horses much later.
62. Mauny (1970), 60–61; chariot routes and petroglyphs: 129–130 (camels); Mauny (1978), 278–292.
63. On the Tichitt und Berbers: MacDonald (2011), 72–75; MacDonald (1998), 91–92: "Chiefdoms" on the middle Niger. On the urban cultures of Lake Chad: Lange (2010); Breuning (2006). Connections of Assyrian traders or refugees via Nubia to the Chad region: Lange (2011).
64. Mattingly (2011), 50–58; Mattingly (2015), 779 on trans-Saharan trade. MacDonald (1998) and (2011), 74–75, 80; Killig (2004) on ironwork.
65. Sceptics (e.g., Austen [2010], 17) conclude from the non-existent or meagre evidence in the sources and archaeological remains that there was no trans-Saharan trade. The fact that Herodotus merely hints at slaves and gold as elements of this trade is entirely fitting. It is naïve to object that there are no physical remains of pelts in the context of the Sahara trade (Swanson 1975, 597); on this problem, see Mauny (1970), 81.
66. Hdt. 2,32,4. Asheri (2007), 261 speaks of four zones (desert and sandhills). Hdt. 2,32 and 4,181 suggests an unproblematic classification in three zones.
67. Hdt. 4,181–185.
68. Hdt. 4,174, 184; Liverani (2000), 498; Sommer (2011), 62.
69. Liverani (2000), 497–500. Now accepted by many: Mattingly (2015); cf. Lipinski (2004), 217–219 and Pappa (2013), 174–175.
70. Kádár (1972).
71. Law (1967), 183.
72. See Law (1967), 182–185.
73. Liverani (2000), 508. Oases: 499–502.
74. Hdt. 2,32. Carpenter (1966), 111–113; Pritchett (1993), 97–99; Asheri (2007), 261–262.
75. Hdt. 4,182.
76. Hdt. 2,32,5. Liverani (2000), 505, 511; Asheri (2007), 261; Mauny (1970), 63; (1978), 284.
77. Cf. Huss (1989), 7–8.
78. Cf. Mattingly (2011), 52–55.
79. Hdt.4,183,1; Liverani (2000), 501.

80. Hdt.4,183,1.
81. Hdt. 4,174.
82. Hdt. 4,183; Law (1967), 187; Liverani (2000), 512; Carpenter (1966), 117–118.
83. See Carpenter (1966), 128–129; Desanges (1978), 182; oasis of Ghat: Liverani (2000), 502.
84. Hdt. 4,185; Liverani (2000), 503.
85. Hdt. 2,32,6.
86. Mauny (1970), 120; Asheri (2007), 262. Sataspes also came across them: Roller (2006), 21.
87. See Law (1967), 186.
88. Hdt. 2,32,7.
89. Carpenter (1966), 128–131; Cary-Warmington (1963), 218–219. Bodélé-Basin: Asheri (2007), 262; Nachtigall (1881). Zilum: Magnavita et al. (2006).
90. On the predecessor settlements to Timbuktu: Park (2011), esp. 30–3339: "it is now clear that Timbuktu's prehistoric urbanism was far greater than it ever was during the historic period".
91. See Law (1967), 185; Mauny (1970), 120; Liverani (2000), 503; Mattingly (2011), 50.
92. Liverani (2000), 504; Thomson (1948), 70; Ferguson (1969), 3, 10.
93. Hdt. 2,33,2–34,2; Desanges (1978), 181–182. Other rivers in the Sahara that have dried up today contained crocodiles.
94. Search for gold: Liverani (2000), 513; Law (1980), 188–189; Senegal: Ferguson (1969), 7.
95. See Blomquist (1984), 57–58.
96. Hdt. 4,181–185; Law (1967), 182–184.
97. Hdt. 4,183.
98. See Asheri (2007), 706.
99. Law (1967), 183; Liverani (2000), 508. Skeletal remains and irrigation: Austen (2012), 35; slaves used in farming and irrigation: Wilson (2006) and Fentress (2011), 69.
100. Hanno Periplus § 7.
101. Huss (1989), 7. Still, the Carthaginians must have believed in the story: Cary-Warmington (1963), 219.
102. Hdt. 4,43; 195–196.
103. See Law (1989), 187.
104. E.g. Fage (2002), 44.
105. Austen (2010), 18. Inscriptions: Rouillard et al., in: Krings (1995), 776–844.
106. Snowden (1970), 24ff. with illustrations; Fentress (2011), 66–67. Black auxiliaries fighting for the Carthaginians: Frontin Strat. 1,11,18; Fentress (2011), 68.
107. Huss (1989), 6–7. Trade relations: Diod. 13,81,5.
108. Ath. II 44e; Mauny (1970), 120; Ferguson (1969), 8. Law (1967), 188 has Mago only make it as far as the Fezzan.

109. Mauney (1947), 341–357; Fage (2002), 45. Strab. 17,3,3–7 writes of the "charioteer-bandits" of the Nigretes (probably near the Tuat oasis in Algeria) and the Pharusians near the Atlantic coast, indicating a link to the west between Lixus and Tripoli.
110. Snowden (1970), 103–104, 122. Xenophanes F 16 describes the Ethiopians as having black faces with snub noses; a fellow mercenary in the army of Psammetichus II was also from Colophon.
111. Pind. Pyth. 4,20–21.
112. Hdt. 3,25.
113. Brown (1962); securing borders as a ruler's duty: Asheri (2007), 417, 423 with Hdt. 97,2. Apis: Hdt. 3,27 with Asheri (2007), 424–427.
114. Fentress (2011), 68.
115. Cf. Asheri (2007), 425.
116. Cf. Hdt. 4,87–88 on the engineer Mandrocles.
117. Rollinger (2013).
118. Hdt. 3,136.
119. On the historicity of Scylax's voyage see Allain, *The Periplous of Skylax of Karyanda* (1977), 54–57 and Salles (1988), 83.
120. Karttunen (1989), 40. Cary-Warmington (1963), 78 surmise that other Greeks participated.
121. See Pedersén (2005), 267–272.
122. Karttunen (1989), 41 with Herzfeld (1968), 8–9, 42–43 and 275–287.
123. Hdt. 4,44.
124. Hdt. 4,43.
125. Dan (2013), 89.
126. Sources and interpretation in Geus (2003), 239–241.
127. Hdt. 3,102; 4,44. Karttunen (1989), 41–42. Pactians are mentioned as Indian units in the army of Xerxes, Hdt. 7,67. Herodotus (3,93) distinguishes Paktuiké from the land of the Gandarioi and names a region called Paktyika near Armenia in the thirteenth satrapy. Paktuiky (cf. the Vedic Paktah) could be related to *pashtọ*, a language spoken in modern Afghanistan; Asheri (2007), 613 and Karttunen (1989), 44.
128. See Allain, *The Periplous of Skylax of Karyanda* (1977), 56. The land of the Gandaraioi is mentioned in Hdt. 3,91 and 7,66 as belonging to the seventh satrapy of Darius. Like the Bactrians, contingents of Gandharans served in Xerxes' army. Later references in Plin. nat. 6,48; Mela 1,2. Hindu legends refer to a Gandharan people who live in this region near modern Kandahar. Caspapyros: Hecat. F 295 (Pownall).
129. Hecat. F 297 (Pownall); V. Tomaschek, Argante, RE 2,1 (1901), 686.
130. Herodotus probably derived his claim that the Indus flows east towards the rising sun from the Indians' position at the easternmost edge of the world: Karttunen (1989), 42; Panchenko (1998), 213–214. Perhaps he identified the east-flowing Kabul with the Indus; Gisinger (1924), 622.

131. Hecat. F 299 (Pownall).
132. Panchenko (1998), 236; Karttunen (1989), 36.
133. Hecat. F 298 (Pownall); Hdt. 3,38.
134. This was where the tribe of Mukoi settled. This accords with the land of Maka on the coast of Carmania, named in Achaemenid inscriptions, and the Arab coast of the Gulf of Oman; Hecat. F 289 (Pownell); J. Wiesehöfer, "Myci", BNP 9 (Leiden, 2006), 402.
135. Hecat. F 271 (Pownell); Gisinger (1924), 630–631; Salles (1988), who refers to Scylax's knowledge of the troglodytes on the African cost of the Red Sea.
136. Breton (1999), 71. Persian expansion in the Red Sea: Salles (1988), 86.
137. Hdt. 4,44.
138. In early Greek literature there was no clarity concerning the existence of two great rivers. The south-flowing Indus shown in representations of the ecumene could be the course of the Ganges correctly given by Scylax, which was then transferred to the Indus by Herodotus; Panchenko (1998), 214–221. A further argument results from Onesicritus' statement that Taprobane lies twenty days' journey from the subcontinent; Plin. nat. 6,82. Hecataeus measured distances in days travelled, so the information might have come from Scylax, who sailed from the Ganges delta to Taprobane.
139. Sarao (2007); Strab. 15,1,11; Arr. Ind. 2, 4.
140. Strab. 15,1,30; Panchenko (1998), 213, 233.
141. Hdt. 3,94. Cf. Panchenko (1998), 237–238; Karttunen (1989), 37.
142. See Solomou (1992), 27–28, 34–35.
143. See Kaplan, *Skylax of Karyanda* (2009), Biographical Essay. The suspicion that we are dealing here with a set piece from Herodotus' story about the Phoenician circumnavigation of Africa (Asheri 2007, 613 and Karttunen 1989, 47 A. 313) speaks for a circumnavigation, not against it.
144. Medas (2004), 114–117.
145. Meyer (1998), 202–203; see Karttunen (1989), 65 on the prose report. The form of the *periplus* was used by the Persians on other expeditions as a suitable record: Hdt. 3,136.
146. Allain, *The Periplous of Skylax of Karyanda* (1977), 59–63; Karttunen (1989), 16–19.
147. F 296 (Pownell); Karttunen (1989), 66–67.
148. De Jong (1973), 136; Karttunen (1989), 21, 25; Filliozat (1964), 244, 257. Democedes: Hdt. 3,129–138; Indian timber in Babylon: Ray (1994), 56; Karttunen (1989), 25.
149. Kenoyer (2006), Karttunen (1989), 30–31; Ray (1994), 17. Varna/Caste system: Sharma 2005, 167–169.
150. Zambrini (1982), 106–107.
151. Karttunen (1989), 67. One-eyed: Aesch. Prom. 804; monopods: Alcman (steganopodes); Strab. 1,2,35; 7,3,6; macrocephali: Strab. 1,2,35; dog-headed: Dihle (1994), 25.

152. Karttunen (1989), 132.
153. Karttunen (1989), 126–134.
154. See Schmieder (1994), 210 on reports of Tartars. Niccolò de Conti recounted that Indians felt superior to "westerners" because the latter had only one eye.
155. Jacoby (1912), 2687–2688, 2700. Scylax and Hecataeus: Karttunen (1989), 69. The extent of his journeying is unclear, but Hecataeus could hardly have ventured beyond the Persian Empire and Egypt (Hdt. 2,143). I find it likely that Hecataeus made a map in view of the doxographic tradition, but above all because he is characterized by Eratosthenes as one of the first geographers.
156. Jacoby (1912), 2703; Gisinger (1924), 553; Heilen (2000), 47–48.
157. Heilen (2000), 46.
158. Heilen (2000), 51. Crocodile hunt: Hdt. 2,70–73; Dihle (1994), 31–32.
159. Hecat. F 1 a (Pownell).
160. Aeschyl. Pers. 401–404.
161. Aeschyl. Pers. 394.
162. Hdt. 8,109; Aeschyl. Pers. 744–751. Cf. 345, 362, 454–455, 472–473, 495, 513–516.
163. Scholars are divided on this point. Whereas Hall (1989) sees in the "Persians" the beginning of the negative barbarian stereotype, Gruen (2012), esp. 10–21, emphasizes the commonalities between Greeks and Persians. In my view, both are valid readings; indeed, it is a mark of the play's literary quality that it can be interpreted both ways by the audience.
164. Georges (1994), 119–120 on the *Persiká*.
165. Aeschyl. Pers. 321, 326–268, 441–444. Georges (1994), 82–89.
166. Soph. Ant. 332–337.
167. Xenophanes B 14, B 15, B 16; Prodicus of Ceos B 5; Democritus of Abdera A 75; Meister (2010), 120–127.
168. Xenophanes 21 B 16.
169. Thomas (2000), 14, 22.
170. Heinimann (1965), 14–19.
171. Thomas (2000), 43–46.
172. Hippocrates, Airs, Waters, Places, 14 (transl. Potter 2022).
173. Thomas (2000), 61–70.
174. Karttunen (1989), 133.
175. Hippocrates, Airs, Waters, Places, 14 (transl. Potter 2022).
176. Heinimann (1965), 27–28; Meister (2010), 84–85.
177. Meier (1990), 430–433.
178. Hdt. 1,1.
179. Thomas (2000), 222 and 221–228 on the significance of *apodeixis*.
180. See Meier (1990), 212.
181. Hdt. 1,1–5.
182. Hdt. 1,5,4; cf. Immerwahr (1966), 306–309.
183. Hdt. 7,101–104.
184. See Thomas (2000), 109–112.

185. Hdt. 5,66,1, 78. Democracy as *nomos*: Thomas (2000), 114–117.
186. Hdt. 8,144,2; Thomas (2000), 112 A. 19; Munson 2001.
187. See Müller (1997), 104; succinct overview: 113–114.
188. Hdt. 2,77,3; cf. 3,22,4; 3,22,106. Rood (2006), 297.
189. Hdt. 2,77,2; 4,187.
190. Thomas (2000), 108–109; Rood (2006), 303; Georges (1994), 181, 186.
191. Rood (2006), 302; Nippel (1990), 18–19, 22–26.
192. Hdt. 3,38.
193. Cited in Nippel (1990), 13.
194. Hdt. 1,35,1–2; 74,4; 94,1; 2,64; 92,1.
195. Hdt. 1,140,3; 1,198; 2,80.
196. Hdt. 3,80–83.
197. Lewis (1984), 101–111; Kim (2009), 24–27; Kim (2013).
198. Hdt. 3,23. Commissioned by Darius, Phoenician ships sailed along the Greek coast, "observ[ing] and record[ing]" them; Hdt. 3,136. Xerxes supposedly enquired into local customs and landscapes in Asia Minor and Greece; Hdt. 7,43, 128.
199. See e.g. 4 Mos. 13,17–20.
200. Northerners are "consumers of meat, milk, and roasted grain; their heart knows no oven, their stomach no beer"; Liverani (1999–2000), 83; Rochberg (2012), 35; Horowitz (1998), 92: "Like Herodotus, the author of *The Sargon Geography* seems to be interested in the customs and life-styles of foreign nations".
201. Kim (2009), 24–25 on the Persian perspective.
202. Murray (2001), 36–40; Wells (1923) on Persian contacts and their stories.
203. Hdt. 1,1,5.
204. Nippel (1990), 20 with evidence. Climate in Herodotus: e.g. 1,143; 3,106.
205. Fertile Tartessos was also ruled by a king who lived to 120, according to Herodotus (1,163,2).
206. Hdt. 3,107–109; 4,13, 25, 27, 191.
207. Hdt. 3,97.
208. Karttunen (1989), 53; (2002), 75–76.
209. Asheri (2007), 499, Cotton: Karttunen (1989), 52.
210. Romm (1987); Karttunen (1989), 171–176; Pritchett (1993), 93–94.
211. Hdt. 3,97.

CHAPTER 4

1. Dueck/Brodersen (2012), 37.
2. Hdt. 2,21,23; 3,113; 4,8, 36, 45.
3. Karttunen (2002), 457; Romm (1992), 20–22, 32–34 on the dichotomy proposed by Hecataeus.
4. Hdt. 1,202–203, Aristot. de mundo 392b 22–23.

5. Hdt. 1,180; 2,21–23, 4,8; 6,20; 7,80; Karttunen (2002), 457.
6. Gisinger (1924), 561–572. Plut. Alcibiades 17. Northern Pontus: Bacon (1961), 46–47.
7. Dicks (1970), 56–59, 151–153, 189, 357–358; Roller (2015), 75–76. Measurements: Szabó (1992), 129–143.
8. Plat. leg. 809c–d, 817e–818a; Rep. 820e–821b on Athenian complaints about the poor quality of astronomic studies; Dicks (1970), 108–110, 148–150.
9. Cf. Berger (1903), 121–123.
10. Hdt. 4,24–25; Berger (1903), 195.
11. Berger (1903), 126, 173, 190; Krüger (2012), 185–186 for the Middle Ages.
12. Aristot. meteor. 1,13 (350b); 2,1 (354a).
13. Heilen (2000), 56; Abel (1974), 1003–1005, 1013.
14. Od. 10,81–83; 11,41–43; Abel (1974), 993; Gisinger (1924), 578–579.
15. Abel (1974), 996; Gisinger (1924), 568.
16. Plac. Phil. 2,24 (Dox. 355); Hippolyt. Adv. Haer. 1,14. Cf. Berger (1903), 190–191.
17. Abel (1974), 1008–1010; Heilen (2000), 62; Dicks (1970), 157.
18. Heilen (2000), 58; Abel (1974), 999–1000; Roller (2015), 73–75.
19. Cf. Abel (1974), 1002–1003.
20. Cf. Eudoxos F 276a (Lasserre); Abel (1974), 1019; Dicks (1970), 189, Roller (2015), 75. Gnomon and celestial globe: Van der Waerden (1988), 93–100; Dicks (1970), 9–10.
21. Heilen (2000), 59; Couprie (2011); Plat. Tim. 63A. The southern ecumene corresponded to the southern temperate zone.
22. Eudoxos F 288 Lasserre. Heilen (2000), 59; Gisinger (1924), 582.
23. Abel (1974), 1018; F 289 Lasserre.
24. Gisinger (1924), 582 believes that Eudoxus assumed a similar landmass extending far to the north.
25. Phaedo 108e5 and 110b6–7.
26. Phaedo 109 b, 112e. Abel (1974), 1015. Perhaps Eudoxus already assumed periecumenes and antipodes; cf. Gisinger (1924), 582; Gemin. el.astr. 16, 1–2, 162–163.
27. Cf. Abel (1974), 1015; Gisinger (1924), 582 on models in Eudoxus.
28. Berger (1903), 311 with Strab. 2,5,3. Eudoxus argued that the Nile lost salt content as it flowed through the torrid zone from south to north due to the excessive heat and was therefore sweet by the time it reached Egypt.
29. Plat. Tim. 2424e–25a; Geus (2000), 58 with A. 14. This thesis likewise presupposes an enormous globe.
30. The basis is the Latin book *de inundatione Nili*; its dating and identification as a translated work by Aristotle are uncertain.
31. Aristot. cael. 2,13; 293b 30–32.
32. Cael. 2,14; 297b 30ff.; 2,298 a 15–16; Dicks (1970), 76, 196–197.
33. Abel (1974), 1022; Gisinger (1924), 576. Geminos el.astr. XVI 29 p. 176.

34. Arist. meteor. II, 5. 362b. Cf. Gisinger (1924), 580; Abel (1974), 1024–1025.
35. Aristot. meteor. 2,5,16, p. 326, 30–31. Berger (1903), 322–323.
36. Aristot. cael. 2,14. 298a 9–11; Gisinger (1924), 585; Abel (1974), 1026.
37. Cael. 2,14 298a; meteor. 2,5.362 b 27–29; Geus (2003), 233; Dicks (1970), 198; Roller (2015), 77. Perhaps Aristotle saw Atlantis as a former part of this land bridge, given the presence there of elephants, according to Plato; Crit. 114 E ff.
38. On the new La Tène elite and their migrations: Kuckenberg (2010), 259–262: Cunliffe (1997), 63–67, 73–89; Cunliffe (2002), 20; Pape (2000), 134–135.
39. Cunliffe (2002), 20.
40. Pape (2000), 134–135.
41. Cunliffe (1997), 75; Pape (2000), 134–139; Kuckenburg (2010), 171–172.
42. Cleomed. Met. 1,208–210; Mart. Cap. 6,609; Roller (2006), 63. Student of Eudoxus: Gisinger (1963), 316; Heilen (2000), 61–63. Dating: Roller (2006), 64–66. Tin and amber as goal: Scott, *Pytheas of Massalia* (2022), 6–7.
43. Heilen (2000), 61–63. Dicks (1970), 165–166 thinks that the *polos* is not a scaphe but a different name for the gnomon.
44. Roseman (1984), 4, 32, 34; Gnomon: Dicks (1970), 21–23.
45. Hipparch. Geogr. Frg. 53–55 = Strab. 1,4,4; 2,1,12; 2,5,8; Roller (2006), 68. Observatory and gnomon in Massalia: Journès/Georgelin (2000), 21–39. Measurements of latitude: Cunliffe (2002), 60–61.
46. Most recently Scott, *Pytheas of Massalia* (2022), 14–16. The old idea that the Carthaginians blockaded the Strait of Gibraltar is no doubt 'outdated' but this does not necessarily mean, conversely, that Pytheas used his own ship.
47. Roseman (1984), 148–150 and Cunliffe (2002), 54–6; Cunliffe (2001), 307–308, Roller (2015), 87.
48. Strab. 1,4,3; Roseman (1984), 24–29, 38 on Ouexisame and Ushant; Cunliffe (2002), 61–62, 68.
49. Diod. 5,22; Cunliffe (2002), 76–77. Tin bars: Ellmers (2010), 367–368.
50. Strab. 1,4,3; Roller (2006), 70–71. Cornwall: Diod. 5,22 with Roller (2006), 72. Cunliffe (2001), 92 f. Celtic ships: Cunliffe (2002), 103–106.
51. Cunliffe (2002), 94–95.
52. Pol. 34,5 = Strab. 2,4,1 (journey through all Britannia); Diod. 4,5,5 (sustenance, way of life etc.), cf. 5,21–22; Cunliffe (2002), 95–97, 107–109. Critics: Roseman (1984), 126; cf. Strab. 1,4,1–3.
53. Cunliffe (2002), 98–100, Hipparchus knew that summer nights were very short in the far north and that the sun remained visible through twilight; Roseman (1984), 43. Tides: Roller (2006), 75–78; Cunliffe (2002), 101–103. Galway: Ps-Arist. de Mundo 3 probably draws on Pytheas. St. George's Channel: Cunliffe (2002), 98.
54. Roller (2006), 71–72; Dicks (1960), 186–187. Pale sunlight at night: Pytheas F 28 (Scott) = Hipp. Geogr. Frg. 58 = Strab. 2,1,18; Roseman (1984), 57.
55. Pytheas F 19 (Scott) = Plin. nat 4,104; cf. Cunliffe (2002), 101; Roseman (1984), 92–93. Caesar Gall. 6,16 says later that the Gauls 'hold many discussions touching upon the stars and their movements'.

56. Plin. nat. 2,187; Roseman (1984), 75.
57. Discussion in Cunliffe (2002), 132–135.
58. See Kleineberg et al. (2011), 105–113.
59. Roseman (1984), 157; Cunliffe (2002), 119–135; Roller (2006), 81–87. Southern Iceland lies at 63–64° N.
60. Pytheas F 38 (Scott) = Strab. 4,5,5; cf. Roseman (1994), 138; Hawkes (1975), 37. For Iceland see now also Scott (2022), 75 and 154–155, who argues more for Norway.
61. Hawkes (1975), 38.
62. Pytheas F 31 (Scott) = Strab. 2,5,8; Cleomed. Cael. 1,5.
63. Pytheas F 7 (Scott) = Geminus, El. astron. 6,9; transl. Evans (2006), 162.
64. So Heilen (2000), 68; see Kleineberg (2011), 112.
65. Cf. Scott, *Pytheas of Massalia* 2022, 159.
66. See Cunliffe (2002), 126–7; Roseman (1984), 121.
67. Pytheas F 30 (Scott) = Strab. 2,4,1.
68. Roseman (1984), 127–128. Other interpretations 130–131.
69. Cunliffe (2002), 139, 143 on the amber region in Jutland.
70. Pytheas F 21 (Scott) = Plin. nat. 37,35; cf. Roseman (1984), 95–98.
71. Pytheas F 17 (Scott) = Plin. nat. 4,94–95; 37,35–36; cf. Cunliffe (2002), 146–149; Scott, *Pytheas of Massalia* (2022), 139 with further literature on *Basilia*. Alternatives: Funen, Zeeland, Sylt, or Amrum.
72. Cunliffe (2002), 152; Roseman (1984), 92.
73. Roller (2006), 87–89.
74. Strab. 2,4,1; cf. 1,4,3; Mela 3,33. So Hawkes (1975), 5–6; Roller (2006), 90–91, Roller (2015), 89.
75. Roller (2006), 91.
76. Pytheas F 33 (Scott) = Strab. 2,5,43; Cunliffe (2002), 162–170; Scott, *Pytheas of Massalia* (2022), 98.
77. Abel (1974), 1029–1030, 1045; Heilen (2000), 64–65; Van der Waerden (1988), 172–173. Correction of zones: Timpe (1989), 331. Aristotle's miscalculations: Dicks (1970), 210. For the Greeks, the 'Arctic Circle' was a circle passing across the sky with the celestial pole at its centre. We take the polar circle to mean a circle revolving around the Earth on the latitude where the celestial Arctic circle (in the Greek sense) coincides with the Sun's daily course at the time of the summer solstice.
78. Pol. 34,10 (= Strab. 4,2,1); Roller (2015), 37–38, 138–139.
79. Miller (1997), 218–220 on the Odeon with Paus. 1,20,4; Plut. Per. 13,5–6.
80. Evidence and discussion in Mitchell (2007), 27–28.
81. Mitchell (2007), 28–29. Archaic roots: Xenophanes DK 21 B 16, cf. 14–15; Pind. Frg. 215a 2–3. Along with negative cliches (Eurymedon vase), vase art shows from 460 Persians in scenes previously reserved for Greeks. On the positive view of Persians see Isaac (2004), 264, 269 with Hdt. 7,238 and 136.

82. He thus has Iphigenia (1400–1401) say that Hellenes should rule over barbarians, but not barbarians over Hellenes; Isaac (2004), 278.
83. Thomas (2000); Isaac (2004), 58–59; Kahn (1994).
84. Cartledge (2002), 40; Isaac (2004), 67.
85. Hippocr. aere 16; 20 (Scythians).
86. Isaac (2004), 62; Thomas (2000), 70–78, 91–94.
87. Plat. rep. 4,435e; Romm (2010), 224; Isaac (2004), 71.
88. Aristot. pol. 1327b29–32; cf. Romm (2010), 225; Thomas (2000), 71.
89. Isocr. pan. 179.
90. Xen. an. 3,2,25; 5,1,2; Mitchell (2007), 23.
91. Xen. an. 7,3; Hirsch (1985), 61–97.
92. Xen. an. 1,9,3; Georges (1994), 211–212; Isaac (2004), 288.
93. Xen. Cyr. 8,8,15; Mitchell (2007), 22, 132.
94. Cf. Hisch (1985), 42–43; Anabasis: Hirsch (1985), 14–38.
95. Xen. Hell. 4,1,29–39; Georges (1994), 218–219; Mitchell (2007), 21–22. Panhellenism and the folly of wealth: Georges (1994), 118.
96. Plat. epist. 7,332A–B; leg. 3,695C–D; Phaidr. 258 B; Hirsch (1985), 7.
97. Plat. Phaidr. 258b. Cf. Georges (1994), 109–221.
98. Xen. an. 1,9,13; Georges (1994), 50–53, 212–213; Isaac (2004), 290, 297.
99. Cartledge (2002), 51–57.
100. Hirsch (1985).
101. Attempts to expose Ctesias' position as physician as a literary fiction (Dorati 1995) seem overdrawn to me and have been refuted by Tuplin (2004); cf. Brown (1978), esp. 9–10.
102. Ctes. FGrHist 688 T 8.
103. Cf. Madreiter (2012), 131 and the literature cited there in A. 601, also 165.
104. I follow the argument of Karttunen (1991), 74–77.
105. Arist. Historia Animalium 2,8; Aeschylus in Strab. 7,3,6; Hdt. 4,191.
106. Ctes. Frg. 45, 40–44; Karttunen (1989), 180ff., Nichols, *Ctesias* (2011), 123–124; White (1991), 72–75. *Topoi*: Pritchett (1993), 272–273.
107. Cf. Stoneman (2019), 19, 32, 102–103.
108. Karttunen (1991), 77–78; Nichols, *Ctesias* (2011), 19–20. Stoneman (2019), 28–32, 101–102, 121–125.
109. Thomas (2000), 138; Karttunen (1989), 81.
110. Thomas (2000), 72; Hippocratic prescriptions: 138–139. Indian medicine: De Give (2005), 169–173.
111. De Give (2005), 169–173; Arr. Ind. 15,11–12; Strab. 15,1,45; 60.
112. Xen. Cyr. 1,2,1; 13; 1,4,25; 27; 8,5,28. Cf. Hirsch (1985), 62–67. Access to royal documents: Nichols, *Ctesias* (2011), 22–23. Bactrians as informants: Frg. 45 h (Nichols, 65). See Romm (1992), 86.
113. Cf. Brown (1978) on the Galen quote FGrHist 67: '[it] shows that he was not a traditionalist but a believer in improving medical practices by experimentation'.

Information on the faraway land: Nichols, *Ctesias* (2011), 20–24; Karttunen (1989), 83.

114. F 45, 19 Nichols, *Ctesias* (2011), 49–50. Hdt. 2,22; 3,101; Lenfant, *Ctésias* (2004), 175; Karttunen (1991), 79.
115. F. 45, 32; Lenfant, *Ctésias* (2004), 310. The Uttarakuru legend also refers to extreme longevity.
116. See Parker (2008), 29.
117. F 45, 31; cf. F 45, 33–35 on the use of poisons obtained from an Indian snake and the excrement of a bird called *dikairon*.
118. F 45, 49; Nichols, *Ctesias* (2011), 58, 138. Travellers to India: Lenfant, *Ctésias* (2004), 310.
119. F 45, 45; Pritchett (1993), 273–274. Lenfant, *Ctésias* (2004), 315–316; Nichols, *Ctesias* (2011), 130–132 on the identification with the rhinoceros and on Iranian-Indian parallels or models.
120. F 45 7; cf. Nichols, *Ctesias* (2011), 47, 96–97; budgerigars: 98; dogs: 100–101.
121. F 45, 15; Nichols, *Ctesias* (2011) 48–49; Karttunen (1991), 79; Lenfant, *Ctésias* (2004), 302; Pritchett (1993), 273.
122. Frg. 45, 16; Nichols, *Ctesias* (2011), 49, 106; Karttunen (1989), 80–81; Vassilaides (2004), 137.
123. Frg. 45, 29; Nichols, *Ctesias* (2011), 49 with commentary 115 as well as Lenfant, *Ctésias* (2004), 309–310.
124. Frg. 45,21; Nichols, *Ctesias* (2011), 50, 109–110.
125. Frg. 46 b 18–22; Frg. 45 a 41–45 (= 45 9, Nichols).
126. F 45, 36; Nichols, *Ctesias* (2011), 53, 121. Choaspes: Karttunen (1989), 83–84. More sceptical on the Ganges: Lenfant, *Ctésias* (2004), 312.
127. Cf. Karttunen (1989), 84; Nichols, *Ctesias* (2011), 101–102.
128. Bolchert (1908), 26–27, 39, 41.
129. Ctes. Frg. 59; Stoicheia 6,17,3; Phot. bibl. p. 47 b; Plin. nat. 37,39; Parker (2008), 33.
130. Lane Fox (2004), 48–55; Romm (1989).
131. Herodotus: Nichols, *Ctesias* (2011), 28; Parker (2008), 33. Familiarity with geography: Bolchert (1908), 67. Against any cooperation between Alexander and Aristotle: Romm (1989).
132. Hdt. 5,21,2; 8,136,1; Georges (1994), 78.
133. Cf. Georges (1994), 246.
134. Arr. anab. 1,17,11; Diod. 17,7,2–3, 8–10; Polyain. Strat. 5,44. Critical: Briant (2002), 817–818.
135. Arr. anab. 3,3,1–4,5; Curt. 4,7,5–32; Plut. Alexander 26,11–27,9.
136. Hdt. 3, 25; Arr. anab. 3,3,1.
137. Bosworth (1998a), 130.
138. Geus (2003), 237.
139. Wilcken (1967), 152. Deported Greeks: Holt (1988), 73–77.

140. Holt (1988), 11–13, 27–31 on urbanization, irrigation systems, and trade relations.
141. Geus (2003), 237.
142. Geus (2003), 237. That there was such an expedition to Ethiopia, evidently led by Callisthenes, is rightly disputed by Malinowski (2014), esp. 278–279 against Burstein (1976).
143. Wilcken (1967), 142; Lane Fox (2004), 275–276; Geus (2003), 237.
144. Arr. anab. 7,16,1–2; Geus (2003), 237.
145. Lane Fox (2004), 279–280.
146. Arr. anab. 5,3,2; Ind. 5,11; Geus (2003), 238.
147. Holt (1988), 38, 42, 46.
148. Lane Fox (2004), 299–300 on the Oxus, described in Arr.anab. 3,29,2–3 as Asia's greatest river. Desert of Turkestan: Holt (1988), 49 Curt. 7,5,1–18; cf. Arr. anab. 3,28,8.
149. Aristotle—Ctesias—Araxes: Burr (1947). Bactria: Ctes. F 45, 48; Holt (1988), 34–37.
150. Geus (2003), 238.
151. Burr (1947), 94. Greeks and Macedonians clearly knew nothing about the existence of the Aral Sea; Roller (2015), 96, 104.
152. Lane Fox (2004), 301; Holt (1988), 23, 54–55. Arr. anab. 4,4,1; Curt. 7,6,25–26.
153. Holt (1988), 53.
154. Holt (1988), 72–76.
155. Aristot. meteor. 1,13; 350a; Burr (1947), 95; Geus (2003), 235.
156. Cf. Lane Fox (2004), 331; Burr (1947); Bolchert (1907), 7.
157. Burr (1947), 96. Land bridge posited in Aeschyl. Prom. 807ff. Nile: Lucan. 10,272–275; Phot.Bibl.cod. 2489:441b; Geus (2003), 237. Erythraean Sea: Geus (2003), 240.
158. Cf. Bretzl (1903), 191–203.
159. Arr. Ind. 1,4–5; Thapar (1998), 129; Lascarides Zannas (1991), 63. Ashtadhyayi (of Panini) 4,1,49.
160. Bosworth (1998a), 83; Gold, silver, and gemstones: Thapar (1998), 75–76. Scylax and Alexander: Stoneman 2019, 39.
161. These interpretations drew on a Dionysus tradition that predated Alexander's campaign. This tradition had transferred the god's deeds to Arabia, Syria, and Ethiopia. Given the identification of India with Ethiopia, it was not difficult to relocate them to India; Bosworth (1998a), 121–124; De Give (2005), 43. That Alexander and his people knew the Scylax *periplus* is suggested by the fact that Nearchus relates that the Sun's shadow fell to the south during the voyage over the Ocean while casting no shadow at midday; he could only have learned this from Herodotus (4,42,4).
162. Bosworth (1998a), 83
163. Bosworth (1998a), 123–125. Krishna—Heracles: Bosworth (1998a), 183.
164. Lane Fox (2004), 347; Stoneman (2019), 53.

165. Diod. 17,91,3–4; Strab. 15,1,30; cf. Stoneman (2019), 65.
166. Strab. 15,1,63–65; Plut. Alex. 65.
167. Cf. Lane Fox (2004), 348–349.
168. Lane Fox (2004), 348–349.
169. Bosworth (1998b), 188.
170. Bosworth (1998b), 192–193.
171. Even Sedlar (1980), 69 argues for its authenticity.
172. Bosworth (1998b), 185–187.
173. Strab. 15,1,66 = FGrH 133 F 23. But see Bosworth (1998b), 186 A. 63 and 200, 202. The name 'Brahman' appears for the first time in Nearchus. First *asrama*: Agrawala 81–82, 2380–1; Manu 3,1. Bosworth (1998a), 93; (1998b), 192.
174. Bosworth (1998a), 94–97; information: Bosworth (1998b), 176, prisoner interrogation: 197–199.
175. Cf. Green (1991), 389; Lane Fox (2004), 351–353.
176. Arr. Ind. 5,8,5; Heckel (1992), 58–64.
177. Lane Fox (2004), 364–365; bananas (probably not mangos).
178. Lane Fox (2004), 371; Bosworth (1998a), 74–75. Cf. Green (1991), 407. On the historicity of the information about Xandrames' kingdom: Bosworth (1998a), 76–79; Jha (2004), 87–90 on the army of the Nanda empire.
179. Lane Fox (2004), 371–372; Bosworth (1998a), 199–200.
180. I follow Lane Fox (2004), 367–369, Bosworth (1998a), 186–200 and Stoneman (2019), 69. Green (1991), 407 favours the Sutlej; Geus (2003), 240 remains cautious.
181. Cf. Bosworth (1998a), 77–78.
182. Arr. anab. 6,1,2–3; Geus (2003), 239 on Indus crocodiles, with sources.
183. The Macedonians clearly knew from Ctesias that the Indus flowed south; Bolchert (1908), 7. Lotus and crocodiles: Bosworth (1998a), 70–71. Arr. anab. 6,1,5 with contrasting statements from Indian informants. Alexander and Scylax: Green (1991), 405 and Stoneman (2019), 39, 100–101.
184. Lane Fox (2004), 366.
185. Combined naval and land operations: Wilcken (1967), 194: Krateros with veterans and infantry: Lane Fox (2004), 382, 390; Bosworth (1998a), 181; Arr. anab. 6,17,3; Strab. 15,2,4–5;11, Just. 12,10,1.
186. Cf. Geus (2003), 240; Arr. Ind. 30,1.
187. Arr. Ind. 20,1.
188. Plut. Alex. 66,2.
189. Comparison in Bosworth (1998a), here: 171.
190. Surpassing Semiramis and Cyrus: Arr. Anab. 6,24,2–3; Strab. 15,1,5 (686), 2,5 (722) = FGrH 133 F 3; Bosworth (1998a), 126, 182–183.
191. Medas (2004), 144–145.
192. E.g. Green (1991), 430, who sees in the coordination of fleet and army a parallel to the 'highly successful amphibious strategy adopted by Xerxes' in Greece.

193. Arr. Ind. 23, 40,11.
194. Arr. Ind. 23,4 on grain at Turbat. Favourable conditions: Bosworth (1998a), 173–178.
195. Bosworth (1998a), 180. Plut. Alex. 66,5 is exaggerated; Lane Fox (2004), 398–399.
196. Arr. anab. 6,28,1–2; Curt. 9,10,24–28; Plut. Alex. 67,1–6. Lane Fox (2004), 399–400.
197. The far more advantageous supply conditions for sea voyages are a key argument against the few who still doubt the historicity of Scylax's enterprise.
198. Arr. Ind. 29.
199. Lane Fox (2004), 396–397; interpreters and the problems of acquiring information: Bosworth (1998a), 72. Arr. Ind. 30,3; Strab. 15,2,12 (725).
200. Arr. Ind. 25. He also knew the theory of climate zones.
201. Bosworth (1998a), 69. Taprobane: after Onesicritus: Diod. 17,93,2; 15,1,14–15; Plin. nat. 6,81; Pédech (1980), 143. Pioneering role of Megasthenes: K. Ziegler, Taprobane, DKP (1979), 516.
202. Arr. Ind. 15,11–12; Parker (2008), 89, 94. Strab. 15,1,28; 45.
203. Arr. Ind. 29,1 (= BNJ F 1 III), M. Whitby, Nearchus (133); Xen. an. 2,3,16.
204. Lane Fox (2004), 396–397; Geus (2003), 240.
205. Arr. Ind. 3, 35.
206. Arr. anab. 7,16,1–2; Geus (2003), 241.
207. Potts (1990), 8 with the sources.
208. G. Bowersock, Gnomon 59 (1987), 509.
209. Arr. anab. 7,20,2; Hdt. 3,89,95; 108–109; Plin. nat. 12,40,80. More sceptical: Potts (2011), 93; Bosworth (1998a), 153.
210. Arr. anab. 7,20,7; 8,18,3.
211. Geus (2003), 241. On Anaxicrates and Theophrastus (hist. plant. 4,7,7–8): Tarn (1929), 13; Amigiues (2005); Roller (2015), 101. Perhaps Androsthenes brought back incense, which Alexander then reportedly gave to his teacher Leonidas; Potts (1990), 9.
212. Arr. anab. 8,43,7; Theophr. hist. plant. 9,4,2–4; Strab. 16,4,4; Potts (1990), 6. Hieron: Arr. anab. 7,20,8.
213. Geus (2003), 241: 'There is no valid reason to reject them outright'.
214. Arr. anab. 6,28,6.

CHAPTER 5

1. The first Seleucid kings probably already maintained warships in the Arabian Gulf; Potts (1990), 10–11 with Plin. nat. 2,167.
2. Androsthenes FGrH 711; Potts (1990), 126; Roller (2006), 92. Arr. anab. 7,20,7; Strab. 16,3,2; Athen. 3,93; Roller (2006), 92.
3. Bretzl (1903), 29–30, 115–123, 132–145 with the additions of Potts (1990), 128–134.

4. Fraser (1994).
5. Cf. Parker (2008), 65 against an overvaluation of Alexander.
6. Plischke (2014), 173–179; resources and population: Mairs (2014), 28.
7. Kosmin (2014), 63; Plischke (2014), 46, 117; Roller (2015), 115.
8. FGrH 711–712; Strab. 11,6,1, 7,3; 11,7; Plischke (2014), 46, 198; Grainger (1990), 83, 153–154; Kosmin (2014), 68–69. Arr. anab. 7,16,1–3; Demodamas: Plin. nat. 6,49.
9. Cary-Warmington (1963), 185–186; Roller (2015), 116. Indian wares via the Oxus: Plin. nat. 6,52; Strab. 11,7,3. Great Indian road: Plischke (2014), 94.
10. Plin. nat. 6,58.
11. App. Syr. 55, 282; Strab. 15,2,9. Kosmin (2014), 33; Mairs (2014), 111–112, 132; Thapar (1997), 17.
12. Thapar (1997), 63–64. On contacts: Mairs (2014), 10.
13. Poliorcetics of Deimachus: Schwarz (1969), 297. Potts (2011), 96–97 suspects the influence of early Hellenistic poliorcetics in northeast Arabia. State monopolies, establishment of cities, and taxes in the Mauryan Empire: Jha (2004), 100–105.
14. Hist. Plant. 8,4,2; 9,20,1
15. Plin. nat. 16,135; Faure (1993), 198–200; Thapar (1997), 17. Seleucid trade with the Mauryans: Plischke (2014), 193.
16. Ath. XIV 67, 652–653; Plischke (2014), 194.
17. CVRAI 1968; Shipley (2000), 269–270; Mairs (2014), 73–74.
18. Mairs (2014), 28–29, 51–52, 59 as well as 38 on the irrigation system, 57–101 on the city as a whole.
19. Shipley (2000), 323; Mairs (2014), 68–70.
20. Manu 7,43. Alexander was reportedly praised by a Brahmin for wanting to deepen his knowledge.
21. Cf. Thapar (1998), 138–139; Halkias (2014), 84.
22. There are also the Laghman inscriptions; overview in Norman (2012). New inscriptions in Kumar Thaplyal (2009) and Gail (2009). Cf. Thapar (1998), 125–126. The Indians had previously been regarded by Greeks as an immobile, sedentary people; see Strab. 15,1,6–8.
23. Thapar (1997), 41–42; Norman (2007).
24. Rock Edict XIII. Nikam/McKeon, *The Edicts of Asoka* (1959), 27–30; Schneider (1978), 118–119. Against politically motivated 'conversion' to Buddhism: Jha (2004), 98–99; Hiltebeitel (2011), 43–44.
25. Cf. Thapar (1997), 3: 'The policy of Dhamma was a policy rather of social responsibility than merely of demanding that the entire population should favour Buddhism'; further 5, 37 as well as Thapar (1998), 137–181.
26. Thapar (1997), 17–18. On other parallels (the Delphic *eukrateia*) see Halkias (2014), 90.
27. Kosmin (2014), 58. In the edicts of Ashoka, only the Seleucid king is named 'Greek king', underscoring his stature and special relationship with Ashoka.

28. Ath. 14,652f–653a. Inscriptions and scribes: Halkias (2014), 88.
29. Halkias (2014), 87; Scott (1985), 133–135; Oceanic connections: Ray (1994), 21–28.
30. Cf. Zysk (2000), 5–6, 19, 24–25. Brahmins considered physicians unclean.
31. Megasthenes in Strab. 15,1,60; Zysk (2000), 28–29. Second edict: Zysk (2000), 44; Thapar (1998), 99. Monasteries and trade routes under Ashoka: Zysk (2000), 44, 118.
32. McClish (2009).
33. Thapar (1998), 99; Halkias (2014), 82.
34. Vassilaides (2004), 142.
35. Arr. Ind. 6,9; Strab. 15,690 and 694.
36. Curt. 8,9,23–31.
37. Arr. Ind. 5,6,2. Early dating in Bosworth (1996), 80; for an opposing view, see Stoneman (2019), 129–134 with strong arguments. Kosmin (2014), 38 on Megasthenes' role in the treaty.
38. Plin. nat. 6,82.
39. Kosmin (2014), 38; Zambrini (1982), 147–150. Strab. 15,1,53 (C 709) = FGrHist 715 F 32. That Megasthenes 'travelled extensively in the country', as Jha (2004), 97 claims, or 'probably travelled in areas outside the empire, as indeed did later travellers like Fa-hsien and Hsüan Tsang' (Thapar, 1997, 18), is speculative.
40. Kosmin (2014), 47.
41. Sources in Kosmin (2014), 41. Arr. Ind. 7,2–9 = FGrH 715 F 12; Diod. 2,38,2–6 = FGrH 715 F 4; Bosworth (1998), 125; (1996), 123. Dionysus and Heracles: Diod. 2,34 = F 4.
42. Bosworth (1998), 126.
43. Kosmin (2014), 38–46.
44. An excellent overview of these theories is found in Stoneman (2019), 135–138.
45. Scylax-Ctesias tradition: Zambrini (1982), 126–138. Ants: Arr. Ind. 15,5; Strab. 15,1,44; 53; wondrous people: Wittkower (1977), 89–90 and Stoneman (2019), 254–285.
46. FGrH 715 F 32 ap. Strab. 15, 1,53.
47. Arr. Ind. 10,8–9; Bosworth (1996), 88; Thapar (1998), 89–92.
48. Bosworth (1996), 88–89; Jha (2004), 107; Stoneman (2019), 217–220. No Aryan slaves: Diod. 2,39,5.
49. Kosmin (2014), 49–53.
50. Strab. 15,1,60; cf. Jansari/Ricot (2016) with Hosten (1912), 291–292. By contrast, Stoneman (2019), 280 argues for Brahmans who abstained from eating during their sacrifices at Chandragupta's court.
51. Janshari/Ricot (2016), 6–8. Reception: Strab. 15,1,57; Plin. nat. 7,25.
52. Thapar (1997), 57–61; Stoneman (2019), 212–217 with discussion of the scholarship.
53. Cf. Jha (2004), 106.
54. Singh (2008), 291–294.

55. Arr. Ind. 11,10; cf. Strab. 15,1,40 (704); Diod. 2,40,4.
56. Bosworth (1998), 93.
57. Bosworth (1998), 89; Arr. Ind. 11,1–12; Strab. 15,1,39–40 (703–704); FGrH 715 F 19; Diod. 2,40; 1–41,5 (FGrH 715 F 4). Caste system: Thapar (1987), 33–60.
58. Stoneman (2019), 216.
59. Aristot. Pol. 2,1267b 22–69a, 28.
60. Cf. Bosworth (1996), 124; Thapar (1997), 58; Stoneman (2019), 217. Diod. 2,40.
61. Bosworth (1998), 198–199; Arr. Ind. 12,6–7; Strab. 15,1,49 (707) = Megasthenes FGrH 715 F 19.
62. Bosworth (1998), 91; Thapar (1997), 62ff.; Arr. Ind. 12,5; Strab. 15,1,48 (707); Diod. 2,41,3.
63. Olivelle (2013) with McClish (2009).
64. Kulke/Rothermund (2016), 37–40.
65. Thapar (1998), 91.
66. Thapar (1997), 56.
67. See Jha (2004), 109.
68. Plischke (2014), 230–234; expansion under the Graeco-Bactrian kings: 63.
69. Mairs (2014), 49–50, 82: Graeco-Bactrian governor. Graeco-Bactrian kingdoms: Sidky 2000.
70. Alram (2002), 38.
71. Plischke (2014), 270–279 and Mairs (2014), 112–117 on Sophytus. Against Mairs (2014), 137, Dio Chrysostomos' report of the Indians who read Homer in translation may not just refer to the Indo-Greeks, but perhaps to later centuries of the Roman Imperial era.
72. The literary sources are meagre: Pomp.Trog. 41 Prol. PME 47; Kulke/Rothermund (2016), 47.
73. Kulke/Rothermund (2016), 47; Narain (1957), 76–81.
74. Mairs (2014), 90–91, 173–176.
75. Plischke (2014), 51. On Menander: Paranavitana (1971), 12; Narain (1957), 74–78.
76. Halkias (2014), 95; Vassiliades (2004), 145.
77. Text: Horner (1963/1964); classification: von Hinüber (2000), 82–86.
78. Horner (1963), 5; Halkias (2014), 91–93; Scott (1985), 141.
79. Von Hinüber (2000), 83; Vassiliades (2004), 147–149. Halkias (2014), 90–94 is more optimistic.
80. Plut. Mor. 821; Thapar 2002, 215; Vassiliades (2004), 148–149 with copious literature.
81. Mairs (2014), 117–128, 142–143; Greek monk: Halkias (2014), 95. In the second century BCE there was a largely mixed populace in Bactria and Arachosia; Mairs (2014), 140.
82. Mairs (2014), 123, 137–138.
83. Cf. Allchin (1997), 23–24; Halkias (2014), 103–106.
84. Plin. nat. 6,58; FGrHist 717 T Ia.
85. Plin. nat. 37,32.

86. Ath. 183–184, 633–634; Ail. Nat. 17,8; Juba FGrHist 275 F 73–76 (78?).
87. Hubbell (1935), 56, 69–71.
88. Tarn (1929), 9–10.
89. Huss (2001), 289; Diod. 3,18,4; Ios. ant. Iud. 8,163–164; Gerrha, Marib and Petra route: Potts (1990), 91–98. Lorton (1971) argues otherwise. Monopoly: Desanges (1978), 298–300. Products and subsequent processing: Sidebotham (1986), 10–14. The levying of customs duties was leased out: Sidebotham (2011), 34. Cultivation of incense and myrrh in Egypt failed. Seleucid maritime policy and customs duties in the Persian Gulf: Potts (1990), 11–20.
90. Reopening of the canal: Strab. 17,1,25; Plin. nat. 6,165; Desanges (1978), 263; Wilcken (1925), 87; Nabataeans: Tarn (1929), 15; Nabataeans as competitors in transit trade: Sidebotham (2011), 35. Streets: Manning (2005), 166.
91. Strab. 16,4,5; Plin. nat. 6, 167–168; Hölbl (1994), 56. Colonization policy: Desanges (1978), 267–270.
92. Cf. Salles (1987).
93. Burstein 1996. Hunting techniques and domestication of elephants, as described in Strab. 15,2,9; 16,1,42–43 and Arr. Ind. 13,1–14,9, resemble the methods used by the Ptolemies and residents of Meroë: Sidebotham (2011), 45–46.
94. Sidebotham (1986), 4. Agath. Photh. 23–29 (Diod. 3,12–14) on gold extraction in Wadi Alaki; Kortenbeutel (1931), 17. Ptolemy II may have sent Philon to Ethiopia for this reason. Gold, amethyst, and ivory: Sidebotham (2011), 43–44; Burstein, in: Boussac/Salles (2005), 152ff.
95. Strab. 16,76–17,78; PME 3,1. Elephant hunts: Huss (2001), 288. African elephants were not smaller than Indian elephants, as some ancient sources claim (Polyb. 5,84 on the Battle of Raphia), but larger: Hubbell (1935), 72. Strategic command: Wilcken (1925), 87.
96. Desanges (1978), 298–299; Burstein (1993); McLaughlin (2014), 62.
97. Huss (2001), 291–292; Zoo: Desanges (1978), 262–267; Hubbell (1935), 68–77; Strab. 1,4,2 calls the country south of Meroë 'cinnamon-producing'.
98. Strab. 17,1,2; Philon: Strab. 2,133; Ath. 9,390b; 13,566c; Agath. 64; Diog. Laert. 4,58. Simonides, Dalion et al.: Plin. nat. 6,183; Roller (2015), 110–112; Philon: Strab. 2,77; Plin. nat. 2,183; 6,171; Préaux (1957), 310; Snowden (1970), 127.
99. Plin. nat. 6,195.
100. Plin. nat. 6,183; Desanges (1978), 258–259; Prontera (2013), 208 (emphasis on the new as well as marine archive as sources); Meyer (1998), esp. 204–206. Three hundred tribes on the Black Sea: Timosthenes Frg. 25.
101. Cf. Prontera (2013), 209–212, 217. The details on 'nautical geography' later find their counterpart in the work of Eratosthenes, which Timosthenes drew on heavily.
102. Agath. Frg. 41; Meyer (1998), 209.
103. Diod. 3,18 = Agatharchides Frg. 41b Burstein (1989).
104. Arr. Ind. 26–31; BNJ 133 F 1b = Strab. 15,2,11–12; BNJ 133 F 1c = Strab. 15,2,13.

105. Cf. Desanges (1978), 292.
106. Aristot. cael. 2,14 298a15; Geus (2000), 78–79; (2002), 225–226; Roller (2010), (2015), 121–131.
107. Geus (2002), 282–284; Potts (1990) II, 6.
108. Geus (2002), 270–271.
109. Strab. 14,6, C64; Geus (2002), 270.
110. Geus (2002), 285; Roller (2010).
111. Geus (2000), 89–92.
112. Dihle (1978), 548–550; (1984d), 85 with sources.
113. Seland (2009a), 180–181.
114. Cf. Dihle (1978), 552–566; Dihle (1984a), 112–115.
115. Strab. 2,98–99; Poseid. FGrH 87 F 28. L. Sprague de Camp, 'The Golden Wind', New York (2014).
116. Ray (1994), 79. Early dating: Cary-Warmington (1963), 123–124, late dating: Dihle (1978), 548; Huss (2001), 617.
117. Cf. Thiel (1967), 16. Cyzicus and Eudoxus: Habicht (2013), 199.
118. Voyage back and northeast monsoon: Cary-Warmington (1966), 124; Thiel (1967), 16–17. On the Ptolemaic kings see Desanges (1978), 151–153. Ptolemaic monopoly: Habicht (2013), 199.
119. Ptol. geogr. 1,9,1 (after Marinus) with Geus (2013), 227–229. *Hippalus*: Desanges (1978), 158–159. Habicht (2013), 205–206.
120. Strab. 2,5,12; Desanges (1978), 303. The number is frequently regarded as exaggerated: Ray (1994), 66. Strategy, reorganization, and customs intakes: Desanges (1978), 304; Gabrielsen (2013), 73–77.

CHAPTER 6

1. Strab. 2,99; Cary-Warmington (1963), 124.
2. Thiel (1967), 23; Cary-Warmington (1963), 127.
3. Roller (2006), 100–104.
4. Polyb. 34,1,7; 5,9 (on Pytheas); Clarke (1999), 78, 91, 100–101, 112; Paus. 8,30,8.
5. Cf. Discussion in Roller (2006), 100–102 and (2015), 137–138.
6. Horden/Purcell (2000), 140–145; Gabrielsen (2013), 78–81.
7. Plaut. Cn. 426; P.Berl. 5883 and 5835; SB III 7169; Hauben (1985), 135–136; Whittaker (2004a), 163.
8. Whitewright (2011b), 92–93.
9. Whitewright (2011b), 93, 99–102.
10. Cary-Warmingon (1963), 124; Desanges (1978), 165.
11. Roller (2006), 108 with sources; Desanges (1978), 166.
12. Thiel (1967), 24–25.
13. Roller (2006), 109; Bocchus in Volubilis: Desanges (1978), 170.
14. Strab. 2,99.
15. Cf. Cary-Warmington (1963), 125.

16. Schmitt (1968).
17. Plin. nat. 6,201–205 = Juba frg. 43, 44; Cary-Warmington (1963), 69, 125; Schmitt (1968), 366–371. Roller (2005), 4–5, 159–160 on Asarubas, who composed a work on Mauretania's geography at Juba's court, 183–243 on Juba's geographical writings.
18. Diod. 5,19–20; cf. Plut. Sert. 8–9; Sall. hist. 1, F 100–102; Roller (2005), 46–54.
19. Cunliffe (2001), 10.
20. Strab. 1,4,6.
21. Sen. nat. 1 praef. 13. Posidonius: Strab. 2,2,2 (p. 95); 2,3,6 (p. 102).
22. Plin. nat. 2,170; on a similar story: Thomson (1948), 199.
23. Plin. nat. 6,201–202; Solin. 52; Schulz (2005), 183.
24. Ps.-Aristotle, de cosmo 392 b 24–30; Strab. 1,2,24; 2,5,10. Roller (2006), 51.
25. Cf. Medas (2004), 40–43. Speeds between one and five knots were possible.
26. Various sources therefore speak of an *Ilha de Santa Cruz;* Schmitt 1984, 172 fn. 2; Greenlee, *The Voyage of Pedro Álvares Cabral to Brazil and India* (1938/2020), 17.
27. Cf. Roller (2006), 54–57. Clarke (1967) doubts whether we can conclude knowledge of the Gulf Stream from Min. Fel. Oct. 32,4–5; inscription: Delekat (1969).
28. Plin. nat. 5,9.
29. Cf. Thomson (1948), 147.
30. Strab. 3,4,3 = FGrHist 697 F 7 (Asclepiades); Woolf (2011), 24; map: Brodersen/Elsner (2009); Whittaker (2004a), 64.
31. F 217–19 (EK), Reinhardt (1921), 123–124; Roller (2015), 148.
32. Eustathius, Commentarii ad Homeri Iliadem, 7, 446 = F200b (EK).
33. Strab. 2,3,5–6 = F49 EK = FGrHist 87 F 28 = Theiler F 49. Cf. Berger (1903), 574–582.
34. Dihle (1984c), 52–60.
35. Cf. Reinhardt (1921), 95. On Posidonius' journeys see Testimonia T 14–26 on Kidd (1999) III with commentary II, 16–21. Botany: Clarke (1999), 153, 173–183.
36. Ath. 4,151E-152D = F 67 (EK).
37. Diod. 5, 28, 1–3 = FGrHist 87 F 116 = Theiler F169 (appearance); Diod. 5, 30, 1 = FGrHist 87 F 116 = Theiler F169 (clothing); Diod. 5, 30, 1–4 = FGrHist 87 F 116 = Theiler F169 (weapons); Diod. 5, 28, 4 and Diod. 5, 31, 3–5 = FGrHist 87 F 116 = Theiler F 169 (social order).
38. Vitr. 6,1,3–10, not included in Edelstein/Kidd (wrongly, in my view); Diod. 5,32,7 = FGrHist 87 F 116 = Theiler F 169 (unrestrained sexual behaviour): Reinhardt (1921), 84–86, with Aristot. pol. 7,7 1327b, 23–25. Celts and climate theory: Tierney (1960).
39. Diod. 5,31,2–5 = FGrHist 87 F 116 = Theiler F 169 (not included in Edelstein/Kidd); cf. Kidd (1988), 308–310. Posidonius combines climate theory with

civilizational determinism by leaning on Parmenides' doctrine of zones and adding ethnic criteria; Strab. 2,2,2–3.

40. Ath. 4, 154 A-C = F 68 EK = FGrHist 87 F 116 = Theiler F 171a; Diod. 5, 28,5 (duels at banquets) = FGrHist 87 F 116 = Theiler F 169.
41. Strab. 4,1,13 = Theiler F 190; Woolf (2011), 75. Posidonious may have written his own work 'On gold and silver': Clarke (1999), 177.
42. Strab. 4,1.13.
43. Schulz (2005), 184–185.
44. Diod. 40,4 with Sen. suas. 1,9.
45. Woolf (2011), 85 assumes that later officials could draw on memoirs of Roman generals as well as administrative lists. Merchants: Caes. Gall. 3,1,2. Trade: Cunliffe (2001), 386–389. Cf. App. Celt. frg. 12,1 on a visit paid by the Averni king Bituitus to C. Domitius Ahenobarbus in southern Gaul in 120 BCE.
46. Posidonius in Strab. 4.3,3 (193; cf. 293).
47. Caes. Gall. 1,31,10; 35,1–2; 43,4–5; App. Celt. 16; Plut. Caes. 19; Cass. Dio 38,34,3.
48. Corbilo (Korbilon) was mentioned by Pytheas; Strab. 4,2,1; Cunliffe (2001), 335.
49. Caes. Gall. 3,12–16; Cass. Dio 39,40–43. Veneti as middlemen 'in the coastal trading networks': Cunliffe (2001), 395, 402.
50. Caes. Gall. 4,20,1. Relations with Celts in Britannia and Gaul and Caesar's motives: Webster (1999), 34–36; Peddie (1998), 6.
51. Caes. Gall. 3,1,2; Gallic trade: Cunliffe (2001), 386–389. Wine trade: Tchernia (2009).
52. Webster (1999), 41–51; Cunliffe (2001), 369; Cic. fam. 7,7,1–2; Caes. Gall. 5,4. Suet. Caes. 47 on pearls.
53. Caes. Gall. 4,23–27; Peddie (1998), 7; Roller (2015), 149.
54. Caes. Gall. 4,36,1. Spring tides: Webster (1999), 37.
55. Caes. Gall. 5,1,4.
56. March from Kent to Canterbury etc.: Webster (1999), 38–39; 'Trade agreement' and wine: Peddie (1998), 14–15; Cassivellaunus: Caes. Gall. 5,22,4.
57. Caes. Gall. 5,12–14.
58. Caes. Gall. 5,12–14.
59. Caes. Gall. 4,20,2.
60. Caes. Gall. 5,12,6–8; 13,7.
61. Diod. 40,4 (inscription in the temple of Venus Victrix).
62. Vell. 2,46,1. Rule beyond the borders: Plut. Caes. 23,3.
63. Plin. nat. 9,34,116; 27,1,11–12; Flor. 2,13; Cic. Quint. 2,16,4.
64. Plut. Caes. 23,2.
65. Plut. Caes. 23,2; Krebs (2006), 118.
66. Caes. Gall. 4,19,4; Krebs (2006), 127–130.
67. Cic. prov. 33; see also 22.
68. Cf. Krebs (2006), 130–132.
69. Caes. Gall. 6,24,2.

70. Woolf (2011), 87–88; Krebs (2006), 111–136; Bell (1995), 754–756.
71. Caes. Gall. 4,1,3 Krebs (2006), 122.
72. Caes. Gall. 6,21–23.
73. Caes. Gall. 1,40,5–7.
74. Explicitly stated in Caes. Gall. 4,16,1.
75. Caes. Gall. 1,1,3; 6,24,3–4. Cf. Hom. Il. 2,13,6.
76. Caes. Gall. 1,1; 6,24; cf. 2,15.
77. Vitr. 7,1,10–11.
78. Hor. carm. 1,12,53–60; carm. saec. 56 with Sidebotham (1986), 138–139. *Imperium sine fine*: Virg. Aen. 6,851–853. Report of deeds (Mon. Anc. tit.).
79. Cf. Whittaker (2004a), 71.
80. Hor. Carm. 4,4,17–18; Strabo 4,206; 7,292; Vell. 2,95; Suet. Tib. 9,1: Cass. Dio 54,22,3–4; cf. Plin. Nat. 4,79.
81. Aug. Res Gestae 30; Timpe (1989), 355.
82. Cic. Att. 2,4,1; 2,6.
83. Cf. Clarke (1999), 91, 105, 108.
84. Clarke (1999), 318; Roller (2015), 167–170.
85. Strab. 1,1,16–19; 2,1,22–23. Clarke (1999), 203–207, 236.
86. Cf. Roller (2003), 4: 'Juba was constantly sending information to Marcus Agrippa for his map of the Roman World'. Roller (2003), 71 on Juba II's relationship with Agrippa, 183–243 on Juba II.
87. Plin. nat. 3,17; cf. Whittaker (2004a), 66.
88. Hänger (2001), 138–139, 153. Timosthenes: Timpe (1989), 356–357.
89. Cf. Moynihan (1985).
90. Cf. Cass. Dio 55,10; Tac. Ann. 4,44. Quote: Vell. 2,97,4.
91. Cass. Dio 54,32–55,1. Strab. 7,290; Plin. nat. 4,96; pomp. Mela 3,31; Timpe (1989), 358 for Borkum.
92. See Hänger (2001), 181–182. On Caesar and Eratosthenes: Caes. Gall. 6,24,2.
93. Plin. nat. 2,167; Mon. Ancyr. 26.
94. Cf. Roller (2006), 121, who considers reminiscences of Pytheas.
95. Tac. Ann. 2,6,3; 8,1.
96. Tac. Ann. 2,23–34; Germ. 34; M. Annaeus Seneca, Suas. I, 15.
97. Tac. Germ. 34.
98. Suet. Gaius Caligula 44, 46; Cass. Dio 59, 25,1–3.
99. Cass. Dio 60,21,5.
100. Cf. Cass. Dio 67,5,3; Mela 54; Roller (2006), 123.
101. Tac. Germ. 41,2.
102. Cf. Hänger (2001), 140.
103. Plin. nat. 4,96–97.
104. Tac. Germ. 17,2.
105. The first to do so was Ptolemy, who introduced Saxony as a new Germanic ethnic group and named three Saxon islands, evidently Sylt, Föhr, and Amrum

(Ptol. geogr. 2,11,5 and 11). He also mentions the Silingi as an offshoot of the Vandals, whence Silesia takes its name (Ptol. geogr. 2,11,9–10).

106. Hor. carm. 1,31,13–15.
107. Cf. Cunliffe (2001), 407, 418–421. Merchants at the court of Maroboduus: Tac. ann. 2,62,2–3.
108. Cf. Schmid (1985), 451–459.
109. Plin. nat. 37,43; Erdrich (2014), 72ff.
110. Woolf (2011), 98–99. Cf. Cass. Dio 77,1.
111. Cf. Wielowiejski (1984), 75–76.
112. Wielowiejski (1984), 80–82; Koster (2014), 65–71.

CHAPTER 7

1. Hitchener (2005), 213; McLaughlin (2010), 28; Morley (2007), 574–580; Scheidel (2011), 33.
2. Whittaker (2004b), 170; Lo Cascio (2007), 628–629. Mines: Plin. nat. 33,96; Lo Cascio (2007), 643–644. Silver was also taken from Sardinia; Plin. nat. 33,66.
3. Hitchener (2005), 210–211; Lo Cascio (2007), 625; Jongman (2007), 609; credit and interest rates: Whittaker (2004b), 170; more sceptical with respect to trade: Bang (2008), 188.
4. Cf. Hitchener (2005); Bang (2008), 124.
5. Hitchener (2005), 213–217.
6. McGrail (2001), 158–159; Morley (2007), 572–573; Hitchener (2005), 212. Hydraulic mortars and ports: Wilson (2011), 225–226; dredgers etc. 226–228; amphorae and containers: 228–229. Voyages on the open sea, construction of 1,000–1,200-tonne transporters, chain pumps, and Venice: Ray (1994), 166; Wilson (2011), 222–224. Sailing in winter: Marzano (2011), 179, 184–186; Arnaud (2011a), 70–71. Sailing with mizzenmast: Arnaud (2011b), 147–160; Ray (1994), 166.
7. Hitchener (2005); Bang (2008), 126.
8. Jongman (2007), 594–618, 614–616. Hitchener (2005), 214. 'Middling class': Kehoe (2012), 115.
9. Hitchener (2005), 218; Bang (2008), 298; Morley (2007), 574.
10. CIL IV 5380; Cass. Dio 72, 24,1–2; Hor. epist. 2,1,270; Whittaker (2004b), 172; Tomber (2008), 16, 55; Young (2001), 23–24.
11. Whittaker (2004b), 172; Miller (1969), 10. Young (2001), 14.
12. Cf. McLaughlin (2010), 144.
13. Cf. Heimberg (1981), 8.
14. Whittaker (2004b), 172; Tomber (2008), 174; Miller (1969), 110.
15. Stat. silv. 5,1,210–213; Sidebotham (2011), 230; Tomber (2008), 16; Miller (1969), 25: black pepper and incense 'were considered to be necessities rather than luxuries'. Sidebotham (1986), 15.

16. The corals traded as far as China also had medicinal functions; Plin. nat. 32,11,24, pepper as remedy: Sidebotham (2011), 258.
17. Cels. 5,23,3; Whittaker (2004b), 164; Watson (1966), 35.
18. Cf. Sidebotham (2011), 14. Physicians on the Tiber: Miller (1969), 1.
19. Sidebotham (1986), 21; (2011), 14; Young (2001), 17. Indigo as remedy: Plin. nat. 35,27,46. Spicing the wine and dishes in the daily diet of both rich and poor is an imperial-era development that has its roots in the Republic; Miller (1969), 8–9.
20. Plut. Galba 19. Aphrodisiacs: Miller (1969), 4–7.
21. Parker (2008), 161 with Ov. am. 2,6,1–2; HA Heliogab. 20,4; 21,1 (parrots), 162–165 with image. Sulla's stepson Scaurus was the first to have a gemstone collection. Farmers and serving girls: Plin. nat. 34.
22. Plin. nat. 12,84; Young (2001), 25; Tomber (2008), 3. 50,000,000 sesterces is not an extraordinarily high figure—some senators were six times richer.
23. Senate decree: Tac. ann. 2,33,1; Cass. Dio 57,15; the emperor's silk garments: W. Richter, Seide, DKP 5 (1979), col. 78; Vicus Tuscus: Heimberg (1981), 28–29.
24. Sidebotham (2011); Groom 1981. According to Miller (1969), 13–17, Augustus was aware of the wealth of the southern Arabian Peninsula around Hadhramaut.
25. Mayerson (1995).
26. Beeston (2005), 57–60. In the first century BCE the situation was probably still different: Sidebotham thinks that the Sabaeans produced incense and myrrh and raised tariffs on the caravan trade. From their capital of Marib (Marsiaba), they held large swathes of southwest Arabia under their control until the first century.
27. Plin. nat. 6,141; 12,55–56.
28. PME 26; Tomber (2008), 102.
29. Seland (2009b) argues that *Eudaimon Arabia* refers not to Aden but to Arabia as a whole, in keeping with the Res Gestae of Augustus. Young (2001), 102–103 and McLaughlin (2010), 71 relate the destruction of Aden to the Gallus campaign, although the port had long since lost its trade-political importance. Perhaps we are dealing here with a gradual decline.
30. On the invasion of Britannia, see Crone (1987), 77: 'There is no doubt that the desire for wealth played a role in Caesar's decision, but it was made for booty, not trade opportunities'.
31. App. civ. 5,9.
32. Strab. 16,4,22; Young (2001), 101. Cf. Sidebotham (1986), 2 on Theophrastus' notes on Arabian and Indian products.
33. RgdA 5,26; Seland (2008).
34. Plin. nat. 12,55–56. Circumnavigation and Alexander: Miller (1969), 15; McLaughlin (2010), 72.
35. Sidebotham (1986), 170–171 believes that Roman engagement in the Red Sea in support of the India trade was partly motivated by hopes of better using the more cost-intensive, Parthian-controlled overland route to the east.

36. Young (2001), 101–102 on Plin. nat. 2,168 and 6,160. Client kings: Casson, *The Periplus Maris Erythraei* (1989), on Charibael (PME 23, 29–30).
37. Crone (1987), 18–26; Seland (2007).
38. Young (2001), 89; Whittaker (2004b), 167, 176. There is no evidence that Augustus ordered the construction of a 'commercial fleet [. . .] based on the Red Sea ports', as Miller (1969), 194 contends.
39. Bang (2008), 233, 236; Robinson/Wilson (2011), 7.
40. Speidel (2016); Villeneuve (2005–2006). Evidence for the previously mentioned surveillance and stationing functions in Alston (1995), 79–81. Warships and *amicitia*: Speidel (2007).
41. OGIS 674 = IGRR 1,1183. Tariffs: Sidebotham (2011), 219. Organization: Miller (1969), 225. Farasan a base against piracy: Wilson (2011), 233.
42. Cf. Ray (1994), 65; Tomber (2008), 154; McLaughlin (2010), 80; Robinson/Wilson (2011), 7. Leuke Kome: PME 19; McLaughlin (2010), 64; Young (1997), 266–268. Similar customs duties were levied in Palmyra.
43. Cf. Young (2001), 76–77. The fleet perhaps had its origin in the ships that Aelius Gallus had ordered built for his African expedition in Cleopatris (Egypt). Reduced transport costs: Sidebotham (2011), 180.
44. Cass. Dio 67,7; 68,17. Cf. McLaughlin (2010), 230–231.
45. Herod. 4,10.
46. Cf. McLaughlin (2010), 161–167. Sidebotham (1986), 38–39; (1991), 23; Young (2001), 202–204. The Empire's total annual revenue from provincial taxes and tariffs ran to over 680 million sesterces. Somewhat different figures in Parker (2008), 186 following Duncan-Jones (1994), according to which one-eighth of the Empire's entire budget of around 800 million sesterces was allocated each year to the Red Sea region. This would suggest that the figures named by Pliny (nat. 12,84: 100 million sesterces to India, Arabia, China; nat. 6,101: 50 million sesterces to India per annum) are not exaggerated.
47. Casson, *The Periplus Maris Erythraei* (1989), 33 A. 50; Sidebotham (1986), 89–91; Tomber (2008), 82. If the outflow of silver *denarii* was reduced from Nero onward, the reason probably lay in the reduced weight standards; others speculated that the emperor needed more silver coins to pay his troops; Whittaker (2004b), 175. Parker (2008), 178 suggests that local traders (in India) had earlier already lost their faith in the silver currency.
48. Cf. Whittaker (2004b), 176 and Young (2001), 62–63, 74; 135, 214–215. 'An absolute minimum of government interference and regulation'. The fact that entire bands of robbers lived off the India trade shows just how lucrative it was; Young (2001), 72.
49. Cf. Whittaker (2004b), 171. The number of transport ships that brought Indian pepper and other luxury goods over the Mediterranean to Italy came nowhere near the grain fleets of up to 1,000 ships that sailed each year for Rome.
50. Miller (1969), 222; McLaughlin (2010), 157. Plin. nat. 12,65 says that it costs 688 denarii to freight a caravan from southern Arabia to Gaza before the

tax collectors impose their levy; this equates to the annual income of three legionaries.

51. Plin. nat. 12,29 with Whittaker (2004b). Charges in Alexandria: Seland (2011), 402. According to the Muziris papyrus, a ship that transported 700 to 1,700 pounds of spikenard, c. 4,700 pounds of ivory, and 790 pounds of textiles, hence 7,190 pounds in total, cost 131 talents on a 500-tonner. By contrast, Arabian intermediaries (such as those in Palmyra) seem to have only charged customs if the goods remained in the country. Harbour charges and taxes: Arnaud (2011a), 66–67.
52. P.Vindob. G 40822, verso 29; McLaughlin (2010), 40, 158; De Romanis 2020.
53. Cf. Whittaker (2004b), 173–175; McLaughlin (2010), 157–158; Rathbone (2003), 211.
54. Cf. Whittaker (2004b), 173; Sidebotham (2011), 217–218; Rathbone (2003), 31; 208–210 on internationally active 'banks'.
55. Whittaker (2004b).
56. Ray (1994), 85; Blue/Whitewright/Thomas (2011); Seland (2014).
57. Cf. Casson (1991), 8–11; Casson, *The Periplus Maris Erythraei* (1989), 17, 35, 291–292; McLaughlin (2010), 29, 36. Two-masters etc.: Blue/Whitewright/Thomas (2011), 188, 195; Ray (2003), 60–63. Graffiti with three-masters: Tchernia (1998). On this: Plin. nat. 19,5; Pollux 1,91; Ath. 5–208e; Lucian. nav. 14, Pseudol. 27, Lexiphanes 15; Philostr. Apoll. 4,9 with Arnaud (2011b), 155. Larger ships against storms: Ray (1994), 85; Wilson (2011), 217, 232; 60- to 80-tonners in the Mediterranean and Indian Ocean: Rathbone (2003), 201; Whitewright (2007), 83–84. Arabian ships, built from Indian teak and coconut wood: PME 36; Ray (1994), 173.
58. Cf. Whittaker (2004b), 175 with Plin. nat. 6,101 and Petron. sat. 76.
59. Healy (1996), 33–37; Gawlikowski (1994), 27–33; Seland (2014), 375; Young (2001), 155–158. Exotic animal for Roman games: tigers, one-horned rhinoceroses, parrots, peacocks and other birds, hunting dogs, panthers, leopards, large snakes. Silk in Palmyra: Sidebotham (2011), 212.
60. McLaughlin (2010), 102ff. Palmyrene network: Seland (2013), 381–384,
61. Seland (2011), 401–406.
62. Nabataeans in the Persian Gulf: Plin. nat. 6,145 with Seland (2014), 374. According to Strab. 16,4,23 a caravan route Leuke Kome and Petra; likewise, PME 19; Sidebotham (2011), 177, 209; Young (2001), 19–23, 90–99; Tomber (2008), 68.
63. Strab. 16,1,22; 24.
64. Nebes (2009); Speidel (2007).
65. McLaughlin (2010), 150; Young (2001), 148. Characene and Charax Spasinu: Salles (1995), 116–117, 136–140. Nabataeans in Puteoli, Ostia, and Britannia: McLaughlin (2010), 155–156.
66. Strab. 17,1,13.
67. Dion Chr. 32,36; McLaughlin (2010), 141.

68. Young (2001), 53; Sidebotham (2011), 250–251.
69. Strab. 16,4,21; Dion. Chr. 32,40 on Indian traders in Alexandria; Sidebotham (1986), 101; Sidebotham (2011), 224;Young (2001), 55–60. On a raja who travelled to Alexandria for both mercantile and touristic reasons: Xen. Eph. 3; Young (2001), 62.
70. Casson, *The Periplus Maris Erythraei* (1989), 32; McLaughlin (2010), 34 on Gaius Numidius Eros, who following his return from India carved his name into a stone on the caravan route from Berenice to Koptos. Another example, attested in inscriptions on the Koptos-Berenice route, is Titus Vestorius, scion of a Puteoli trading and banking dynasty that brought the technology for producing 'Egyptian blue' (*caeruli temperationes*) to Puteoli; De Romanis (2005).
71. Cf. Whittaker (2004b), 169–170; Tchernia (1997); McLaughlin (2010), 156, on the Peticii. Bang (2008), 272–274 on the Sulpicii. Wine and wine amphorae: McLaughlin (2010), 19–20.
72. Ray (1994), 167; McLaughlin (2010), 37.
73. Ray (1994), 169; Tomber (2008), 65–66; McLaughlin (2010), 28.
74. McLaughlin (2010), 35; Rathbone (2003), 203–209. Trimalchio had five ships built for him on two occasions (Petron. 76,3–8).
75. Miller (1969), 190; Young (2001), 54; McLaughlin (2010), 33–39. Tomber (2008), 108; other Alexandrians in the southeast trade: Strab. 2,5,12. Indians are attested in Egypt through pottery and graffiti: Tomber (2008), 74–76. Indian shipowners: Ray (2003), 75.
76. Tomber (2008), 20; navigation manual: Miller (1969), 18; Ray (1994), 67. Luxury goods: Casson, *The Periplus Maris Erythraei* (1989), 16.
77. Strab. 1,1,21.
78. Cf. Tchernia (1997), 239; Casson, *The Periplus Maris Erythraei* (1989), 13 A. 10.
79. Merchants' agents: Casson, *The Periplus Maris Erythraei* (1989), 32. PME 1,19; in Koptos there was an 'association of Palmyrene Red Sea shipowners'. Their ships lay in Myos Hormos and Berenice. Sidebotham (2011), 196, 206, 223. Pearls were found in Berenice that were probably produced in Vietnam or Thailand. PME (56, 60, 63) and Ptolemy (geogr. 1,17,5) call the faraway lands Sinae (China) and Chryse Chersonnes (Malay Peninsula). Mediterranean lamps, cameos, and coins have been found in Thailand and Vietnam, among other places; Sidebotham (2011), 223.
80. Cf. McLaughlin (2010), 157; Bang (2008), 195.
81. McLaughlin (2010), 158; Young (2001), 42–51; Sidebotham (2011), 69, 185, 219. McLaughlin (2010), 40, 55 estimates that thousands of Roman soldiers arrived in India each year to protect merchants and as palace guards. Tomber (2008), 72 on eastern goods; black pepper from southern India as well as rice attested in Berenice and Myos Hormos; spikenard, costum, bdellium, and long pepper from north India, shipped in Barygaza: Miller (1969), 24. The price of eastern ointments from Indian spikenard fell from up to 300 denarii per litre to 100 denarii, according to Plin. nat. 12,85–98; cf. 13,18.

82. PME 23; cf. Tomber (2008), 100.
83. Miller (1969), 103–105; Ray (1994), 117; Tomber (2008), 54, 95; Plin. nat. 12,69; PME 7. Routes to Arabia: Robert (1993), 200–201; Azania: Young (2001), 36–37. Voyage length: Plin. nat. 6,26,104; Sidebotham (2011), 193. Monsoon: Liu/Shaffer (2007), 47.
84. Plin. 12,85, see Chami/Msemwa (1997), 673–677; Chami (1999), 205–214 and Gupta (2005), 148–149. Roman traders rarely on the Somali coast: PME 16 with Stern (1991), 114. The sources classify the voyages of a certain Diogenes and Theophilus as an exception; Ptol. geogr. 1,9; PME 6, 18; McLaughlin (2010), 69. Berggren/Jones (2000), 68. Produce shipped to Arabian ports on Somali boats: Young (2001), 20 and 35.
85. Young (2001), 34–35; Selvakumar/Shajan/Tomber (2009). PME 25, 56, 63; Plin. nat. 6,100–106.
86. Ray (1994), 11–47, 122; Young (2001), 29; on Barygaza; Stern (1991), 115; Tomber (2008), 125–130.
87. Text in Parker (2008), 173.
88. PME 49. Eudoxus already had slave musicians on board; Casson, *The Periplus Maris Erythraei* (1989), 21; Sidebotham (1986), 24. Some slaves were sold to China: Yü (1967), 180. Wine: McLaughlin (2010), 51.
89. Cf. Tomber (2008), 16. On Buddhist influence on trade see Ray (1994), 8, 121–143 and Chakravarti (2002), 24–31.
90. Prasad (1977), 11–25 with the sources and their interpretation; Cobb (2018).
91. Cf. Whittaker (2004b), 168; Tomber (2008), 108; Ray (1994), 79 on Socotra. On early oceanic voyages: Ray (1994), 2–3, 13 with references to the Rig Veda. On the organization of maritime trade and early Buddhist sources: Ray (2003), 75.
92. Tomber (2008), 147–148; Sidebotham (2011), 252ff. Taxes: Salles (1995), 132; prince of Chera: F. De Romanis, Ivory from Muziris, ISAW Papers 8 (2014). Buddhist monks: Ray (1994), 11–47, 122.
93. Cf. Dihle (1984d), 82–83.
94. Whittaker (2004b), 168; Sidebotham (1886), 27, 93, 100–101; Casson, *The Periplus Maris Erythraei* (1989), 14, 24. Young (2001), 30–31; Nappudanar, *Mullaippattu*, lines 59–66; Ray (1994), 84; Thorley (1969), 188; McLaughlin (2010), 18–19.
95. Stern (1991), 117–118; Raman (1991), 125–127, Comfort (1991), 135–148; Will (1991), 151–154.
96. Raman (1991), 131–132. Buddhism: McLaughlin (2010), 18.
97. Casson, *The Periplus Maris Erythraei* (1989), 17; Tomber (2008), 42–43 and 55, 148–150.
98. Young (2001), 28; Sidebotham (1986), 26. Return in winter: Plin. nat. 6,101–106; Monsoon in summer: PME 39,49,56. Arabian wine: Tomber (2008), 79. Customs passes in Berenice mention Italic wine amphorae for loading in ships: Tomber (2008), 81; McLaughlin (2010), 31.

99. According to PME 49 ships from the Empire brought gold to Barygaza. Most Roman coins, 70 percent silver, 90 percent gold, appear in hoards in the southwest, mostly from the Julio-Claudian era.
100. Cf. Wolters (1999), 390–393.
101. Sidebotham (1986), 21. PME names ports on the Malabar coast (53–55); Plinius recommends landing in Bakare (Becare), despite praising Muziris as *primum emporium Indiae* (nat. 6,104–105); the differing preferences perhaps reflect tribal rivalries.
102. Sidebotham (2011), 225. Cargo of 800,000 sesterces etc.: McLaughlin (2010), 161; Tomber (2008), 25; De Romanis (1997), 183–185. According to Strab. 16,4,22 traders from Arabia Felix also sold their wares for gold and silver.
103. Plin. nat. 6, 84–85; Abeydeera (2009), 148. According to Weerakkody (1997), 51 A. 5, the cognomen Plocamus indicates Campanian origins.
104. Plin. nat. 6,85: 'legatos quattuor misit'.
105. Weerakkody (1997), 10; Casson, *The Periplus Maris Erythraei* (1989), 24.
106. Seland (2014), 284, 382; Ray (1994), 179. 75-tonner: Plin. nat. 6,24.
107. Schwarz (1974), 168; Carswell (1991), 200; Weerakkody (1997), 14, 56. Hippuros is the rendering of Sindu Kanda in Ptol. geogr. 7,1,12.
108. Young (2001), 60. Other families of the same type: De Romanis (1996), 241–259; freedmen: Sidebotham (2011), 72.
109. Cf. De Romanis (1997), 188.
110. Cf. Young (2001), 60; Sidebotham (2011), 192 on the difference in time between the inscription and Pliny's dating. Tax-farming contract: Weerakkody (1997), 55.
111. De Romanis (1997), 181; McLaughlin (2010), 54.
112. Cf. Weerakkody (1997), 35; Young (2001), 32; goods from Sri Lanka: Sidebotham (2011), 193.
113. Plin. nat. 9,106; Carswell (1991), 200. Gemstones were processed in India under Graeco-Roman influence. Red gemstone: Cosmas Top. Chr. 11,14. Weerakkody (1997), 35. Western traders came to Poduca (near Pondichery), where pearls could also be acquired; Liu/Shaffer (2007), 51.
114. A wreck discovered in 2008 in the harbour of Godavaya probably contained glass- and metalware of Indian origin; Lawler (2012); Seeland (2014), 373.
115. Plin. nat. 32,21–24; cf. De Romanis (1997), 190.
116. Abeydeera (2009), 159; Mahâvamsa 34.50.
117. Schwarz (1974), 172–175; De Romanis (1997), 188–194, 200–203.
118. De Romanis (1997), 185–190; 201; Speidel (2016).
119. Cf. Gunawardana (1990), 38.
120. Weerakkody (1997), 57–58 and Abeydeera (2009), 151–153.
121. PME. 40; Gunawardana (1990), 31.
122. Plin. nat. 6,88; further details on the Seres in Plin. nat. 6,54; 7,27; 12,17; 12,38.
123. Weerakkody (1997), 72–74, Sidebotham (2011), 157. Archers and charioteers: Hor. carm. 1,29,7ff.; Prop. 4,8,23. The first author on Seres is Apollodoros

of Artemita (end of the second century VCE; FGrHist 779 F 7a); Seres = Chinese: Gunawardana (1990), 27.

124. Miller (1969), 195.
125. Suet. Cal. 52; Flor. 1,46,8 (*serica vexilla* in the Battle of Carrhae); Cass. Dio 43.24,2, 59,17, 3; HA Heliog. 26,1.
126. McLaughlin (2010), 44; silk in Barbarikon: PME 39, 49 (on Baryzaga), 56 (on Muziris) with Casson, *The Periplus Maris Erythraei* (1989), 30. PMA 56, 64 on the route to the Ganges delta; Ptol. geogr. 1,17,4. Routes to India: Chandra (1977).
127. Miller (1969), 75–76. Route connecting Sinai and the Seres via Patna: Ptol. geogr. 1,17,5. Perhaps some silk was transported by sea from the Strait of Malacca to the Ganges delta, Casson, *The Periplus Maris Erythraei* (1989), 27.
128. Inscriptions in Buddhist caves attest to a 'chief Raki'; Abeydeera (2009), 154–155.
129. Gunawardana (1990), 34; Seland (2014), direct contacts between Ceylon and China began in late antiquity; Prickett-Fernando (1990), 61, 71.
130. Ray (1995), 77–78 with PME 28,39, 49; Plin. nat. 32,11. Chinese chronicle: Werake (1978); Werake (1990), 220.
131. Miller (1969), 100; McLaughlin (2010), 170. Manthai: Carswell (1991), 200.
132. Miller (1969), 47, 74; De Romanis (2005).
133. Miller (1969), 30–38, 84–85: lakawood, the *serichatum* mentioned by Pliny; nutmeg and Mace from Indonesia (*Myristica fragrans*); sandalwood from Indonesia, Java, and eastern Australia is mentioned as *algum* or *almung* in the Old Testament as the objective of the Tarshish voyage: 1 Kings 10,11,2; Chron 9:10; also turmeric from China, Malaysia, and Indonesia.
134. Miller (1969), 38–57, 80–87; Ptol. geogr. 7,4,1; PME 36. Cassia and cinnamon: Miller (1969), 44; ginger: Parker (2008), 152. Cinnamon and cassia were already known to the Hebrews: Ex 30.23, Ez 27.19; Ps 45.8; also cloves, mentioned in Chinese and Indian texts (Ramayana, Charaka, Sushruta) and by classical authors as a perfume, medicinal ingredient, and dietary supplement. Route from Java to east Africa or Madagascar: Miller (1969), 66. Pliny's *siliquastrum* (nat. 19,87; 20,174) is probably cardamom, the 'pepper of Calcutta' known to the Portuguese in India as *silkiquastro*.
135. PME 64, cf. 55; Leslie/Gardiner (1996), 124.
136. I refer to the mariner by his Greek name to avoid any confusion with Alexander the Great. Ptol. geogr. 1,14,1; Leslie/Gardiner (1996), 124–125.
137. Hall (2010), 4–5.
138. Thomson (1948), 316–317. See also Martiani Heracleensis Periplus maris exteri (Schoff 1927), 43–45; Indian mariners and ships: Dihle (1984c), 215; Robert (1993), 259.
139. Marciani Heracleensis Periplus maris exteri (Schoff 1927), 46.
140. Ferguson (1978), 584; Leslie/Gardiner (1996), 14. Overland route via cassia-growing areas: Miller (1969), 141, 182; Ptol. geogr. 1,17,5.

141. Raschke (1978), 645; Leslie/Gardiner (1996), 153–158.
142. Miller (1969), 120; Bang (2009), 120; Leslie/Gardiner (1996), 156. Rhinoceros horns are listed as valuable import goods in a different chronicle (Sung-Shu 97 or Lieh-Chuan 57, in: Leslie/Gardiner [1996], 104).
143. Leslie/Gardiner (1996), 154–157; Casson, *The Periplus Maris Erythraei* (1989), 27; but see McLaughlin (2010), 134. Gemstones and jewels from India etc.: Miller (1969), 199. Fan Yeh comments: 'The document listing their tribute had nothing at all precious or rare. Thus one suspects that those who have written about it [Ta-Ch'in] have erred'. Leslie/Gardiner (1996), 51.
144. Leslie/Gardiner (1996), 100; 159–160; Ferguson (1978), 594; McLaughlin (2010), 136–146, 176. Roman artefacts in Indochina: Young (2001), 34; Kordosis (1992), 169.
145. Siriweera (1990), 125–126; Perera (1951), 301.
146. Miller (1969), 36; 147, 154–171; boats with outriggers: 157. PME 60 with McPherson (1990), 262–264.
147. Leslie/Gardiner (1996), 137–138, 159; Miller (1969), 180. There is a dubious report about a trade mission to Huang-chi (Kanchipuram) and Sri Lanka in the first century BCE; see Miller (1969), 184; Leslie/Gardiner (1996), 161–162 on Han shu 28B, 1671 about ships that sailed from Xuwen and Hepu (Guangxi and Guangdong) perhaps to Madras, also 'Chinese ships' to Arabia. These were ships 'from China' or those that transported Chinese products. Cf. Schottenhammer (2006).
148. Stauffer (2007). Also Pontic medicinal rhubarb, Liu/Shaffer (2007), 4.
149. Boulnois (2004), 40; Miller (1969), 140–141, 182.
150. McLaughlin (2010), 90–91.
151. Cf. Liu/Shaffer (2007), 5–15.
152. Cf. Lewis (2007), 31–32, 128–132; Liu/Shaffer (2007), 24–25; Di Cosmo (2002).
153. Cf. Boulnois (2004), 75–85; Lewis (2007), 129; Vogelsang (2013), 152.
154. Vogelsang (2013), 180; Yü (1990), 127–128, 131.
155. Liu/Shaffer (2007), 27, 31–32; Boulnois (2004), 16, 58–60; Lewis (2007), 141. Bactria as contact zone between China and the west: Lerner 2015.
156. Cf. Boulnois (2004), 65; Beckwith (2009), 72, 77; Harrison (2012), 308–310.
157. Leslie/Gardiner (1996), 24, 33–39.
158. SC 123,3166. Lewis (2007), 141–142.
159. Ying (2004), 338.
160. Lewis (2007), 94 (park = island of immortals), 152ff.; Ying (2004), 338.
161. Cf. Graf (1996), 200.
162. Leslie/Gardiner (1996), 23; Dihle (1984d), 85 (Indian philosophers in Clemens Alexandrinus); Dihle (1984c), 201 (Seres and Chinese).
163. Liu/Shaffer (2007), 28–29; Boulnois (2004), 66–68, 93. Alliance with Parthians and embassy: Thorley (1971), 71; Boulnois (2004), 71–72. Cleopatra's silk garments: Dihle (1984c), 202 and silk banners: Flor. 1,46,8 (3,11).
164. Cf. Manthe (2014).

165. Robert (1993), 35; Boulnois (2004), 58.
166. Liu/Shaffer (2007), 36; Lewis (2007), 143.
167. Cf. Liu/Shaffer (2007), 77–78, 82; Boulnois (2004), 88; McLaughlin (2010), 86.
168. Miller (1969), 121–123; 197; PME 6 and 39.
169. Miller (1969), 124–126; Yü (1967), 112.
170. Miller (1969), 123–124; Boulnois (2004), 90–91; Robert (1993), 214.
171. PME 39; these were unfinished and semifinished goods from which were produced the cashmere shawls worn in Greece (*kaunakai/gaunakai*). Miller (1969), 198; Plin. nat. 27,77.
172. Miller (1969), 120.
173. Liu/Shaffer (2007), 36–37.
174. Chi I, Hsin Shu 4,41; Huan Kuan, Yan Tie Lun 2,14; McLaughlin (2010), 4, cf. 84.
175. Thorley (1971), 72; Lewis (2007), 136–137.
176. Boulnois (2004), 97.
177. Liu/Shaffer (2007), 37.
178. Liu/Shaffer (2007), 44–58; Liu (1990), 3–8, 36 on trading cities and the goods valued by the Kushans. In contrast to China, the great mercantile families also exercised political leadership in the cities (40). Cf. also 80. Thorley (1979), 182–189 on Roman traders.
179. Liu (1990), 93–96, 175–176; Dihle (1984d), 80.
180. Liu/Shaffer (2007), 62; Liu (1990), 100–123.
181. Liu/Shaffer (2007), 63–70.
182. Liu/Shaffer (2007), 34–39.
183. Lewis (2007), 26.
184. Graf (1996), 200; Leslie/Gardiner (1996), 135, 141.
185. Cf. Liu/Shaffer (2007), 77. 'Reopening of the Silk Road': Miller (1969), 124.
186. Lewis (2007), 22, 63–70; Boulnois (2004), 70–71; monopolies: Yü (1967), 167 (iron); Liu (1990), 14–15, 48.
187. Lewis (2007), 63–65; Liu (1990), 49.
188. Cf. Liu (1990), 50, 80, 167; Lewis (2007), 76. According to Liu (1990), 48–49, trade employed more people than agriculture despite the laws in Luoyang and trade suffered no impediment.
189. HHS 77,4; Yü (1967), 138; Liu (1990), 16; McLaughlin (2010), 86.
190. Liu (1990), 44 on Hsü Miao and Yüan Hsien; Liu (1990), 18 supposes that the merchants were 'closely attached to the Chinese authority'. Mercenary cavalry and adventurers were a consequence of the professionalization of the army; Lewis (2007), 138–139.
191. Yü (1967), 123–124; Liu/Shaffer (2007), 80–83. Even the soldiers stationed in the Tarim basin paid for their living expenses with silk. Passport system: Liu/Shaffer (2007), 80; Boulnois (2004), 90; Liu (1990), 18; HHS 58, 2931.
192. Wei-Lüeh (in San-Kuo-Chih 30); McLaughlin (2010), 107; Leslie/Gardiner (1996), 72. Chinese sources assume that the Romans produced the silk; only

after 400 CE did it become known that only Chinese material could be processed into valuable commodities. Ferguson (1978), 590–591; Leslie/Gardiner (1996), 225–229.

193. Cf. Boulnois (2004), 75–85. Lists: HHS 88d, Leslie/Gardiner (1996), 49–50, 72–74.
194. HHS 88; Leslie/Gardiner (1996), 50, 61, 87–92; Liu (1990), 28; Liu/Shaffer (2007), 52.
195. Yü (1986), 461; Leslie/Gardiner (1996), 44–46, 140–147; Graf (1996), 200–202ff.
196. Leslie/Gardiner (1996), 46; Liu/Shaffer (2007), 53.
197. Cf. Graf (1996), 204; Leslie/Gardiner (1996), 147.
198. HHS 88; Leslie/Gardiner (1996), 51 A. 51; Hill, *Through the Jade Gate to Rome* (2009), 27; McLaughlin (2010), 107.
199. Dihle (1984c), 211–212; Leslie/Gardiner (1996), 26, 51, 146 (HHS 88).
200. Young (2001), 100, 111, 125; Graf (1996), 204.
201. Young (2001), 197–198; Schulz 2021, 149. Intermediate trade with silk as an income source: Yü (1967), 157–158.
202. Boulnois (2004), 72; Thorley (1979), 189. Chinese chronicles report of early hostilities breaking out between the Parthians and Kushan units when the latter conquered the Kabul region; McLaughlin (2010), 107, 129.
203. Ptol. geogr. 1,11,6; Young (2001), 196. Andrade (2015/2016), 61 considers them to be Asian merchants.
204. Cary (1956), 30–134; Paul (2005), 930.
205. McLaughlin (2010), 126–127; Heil/Schulz (2015). In Greek inscriptions from Syria the name Μάης is extremely rare, and it is an open question how the name would have been written in an Aramaic text: מה *mh*? Or perhaps מא *m'*? Neither yields a real name.
206. Young (2001), 190–194; Paul (2005), 944–960. Recently, Andrade (2015/2016) has argued that Maes took the more southerly route described by Isidore of Charax only 'into the Parthian lowlands', where he established contact with local traders or silk merchants ('Seres'). Yet would such a routine and unspectacular journey have been worth mentioning, and where would the clearly well-known 'Stone Tower' have been? Moreover, Andrade's argument is based on the highly unlikely assumption that Maes was a Roman-Syrian trader.
207. Boulnois (2004), 149–151; Paul (2005), 955–957.
208. Paul (2005), 958; Robert (1993), 216ff. Luoyang: McLaughlin (2010), 132; Xianyang: Reichert (1992), 55.
209. Leslie/Gardiner (1996), 14, 25, 164; Pulleyblank (1999).
210. HHS 4; Leslie/Gardiner (1996), 148; McLaughlin (2010), 127.
211. Zhang Xushan (2004); Andrade (2015/2016), 42–50.
212. For Leslie/Gardiner (1996), Daqin is the Roman Empire, and Haixi refers to Italy or Rome. Lewis (2007), 143 sees Daqin as 'a mythic realm of fantastic plants and animals'.
213. Ying (2004), 339; Kordosis (1992), 161–169.

214. Kim (2009), 115–124; cf. 61–62, 68–69 on Confucian foundations.
215. Mayor (2014), 31, archaeology: 63–83, India/China: 406–429.
216. White (1991) and Mayor (2014).
217. Kordosis (1992), 171–172; Leslie/Gardiner (1996), 238–239, 273–275. Daoist utopias: Bang (2009), 120; Raschke (1978), A. 840–850.
218. Lloyd/Sivin (2002), 61–66, 147–149, 247–249; Shankman/Durrant (2000), 48–50.
219. Zysk (2000), 47–48, 65–96; Ray (1995), 124–130; Nielsen (1987).
220. Ray (1995), 124, 133–150.
221. Sidebotham (2011), 255; Bang (2008), 131–132 on votive gifts for the goddess Nehalennia on the Dutch coast; 261 with Macr. Sat.3,6,11 on Palmyra. Greek and Indian astronomy: Van der Waerden (1988), 238–251.
222. Ruffing (2014), 148–149.
223. Ruffing (2014), 149.
224. Isis-Pattini: Sidebotham (2011), 255; Fynes (1993); Parker (2008), 300; Isis as Buddha's mother: P. Oxy. 1380. Christ—Buddha: Dihle (1984e), 101; Karttunen (1986), 193–194 on Buddhist monks in Alexandria. Sophron graffito: Ray (1995), 66.
225. Ray (1995), 36, 132, 153–154.
226. Mk 4:35–41; Lk 8:22–25, Mt 8:23–27; cf. Iambl. V.P. (28), 135.
227. Paul: 2 Cor. 11:25–26; long-distance traders: CIL IX 60, Z. 2–9.
228. Loewe (2005), 87; Parker (2008), 295.
229. Ray (199), 126–129; Seland (2013), 387–388; Seland (2012), 78.
230. Tomber (2007); Seland (2012), 78–83; Karttunen (1986).
231. Whittaker (2004c), 155; Naas (2011), 60.
232. Murphy (2004), 20, 23, 156–157, 211–214. Map and triumph: Nicolet (1991), 23.
233. Naas (2011), 62; Murphy (2004), 29, 45–47, 160–164. Both Pliny and Seneca (nat. 6,8,3–4) explicitly point out that emperors are responsible for investigating foreign parts of the world: Murphy (2004), 141, 155.
234. Naas (2011), 57–59; Murphy (2004), 213–214.
235. Plin. nat. 14,1,2.
236. Murphy (2004), 15, 213–214; Naas (2011), 57–67; Woolf (2011), 83–86; Pliny (nat. 2,189–290) was familiar with Eratosthenes' geography, climates, and their influence on people's ways of life; Murphy (2004), 134–135.
237. Mela 1,67; 2,4; 2,6; Dueck/Brodersen (2012), 47–48.
238. O'Doherty (2013), 16–18.
239. Plin. nat. 6,81–82, 89; O'Doherty (2013), 26; Timpe (1989), 376–377.
240. Cf. O'Doherty (2013), 15; Timpe (1989), 272.
241. Mela 3,90 and Plin. nat. 2,169.
242. Strab. 2,1,9.
243. Dihle (1984f), 178.
244. Aristeid. or. 102.
245. Cf. Clarke (1999), 142.

246. Ptol. geogr. 1.8,4; Roller (2015), 181–182. The ἐπερχόμενος points to a military context, as in the case of Septimius Flaccus in the Sudan (Ptol. geogr. 1,8,4).
247. Because Ptolemy posits 180 degrees of longitude for the ecumene, there is some cause for proceeding to the coast of China at 120°E, since here the known lands came to an end. Ptolemy additionally cleared up the confusing equivalence of the Seres and the Sinae. He located the latter northeast of the Indians, the former northwest of the Sinae; Dihle (1984c), 207–212; Clarke (1999), 142.
248. According to Plin. nat. 6,81, Taprobane was long taken to be the northernmost tip of an unknown southern continent (Antichthones).
249. Cf. Strab. 8,1,1 with O'Doherty (2013), 19 on the 'double image that is critical to the formation of geographical and imaginative conceptions of the Indies'.
250. Dihle (1984c), 203–215; Ferguson (1979), 592–593; Hor. carm. 1,12; 3,3,42ff.; Prop. Eleg. 3,12,1–14; 4,3; Stat. silv. 4,1.
251. Parker (2008), 62–63, 93, 107–108 on Strab. 15,1,53 (C 798 = Megasthenes).
252. Arr. Ind. 5,4,4; Plin. nat. 34,163; Parker (2008), 6; 43, 65, 161, 232–233.
253. Cass. Dio 68,29,1; Whittaker (2004c), 152–154; Parker (2008), 3–4, 126–128.
254. Parker (2008), 251–253, 270–276. Clemens Alex., Against Jovinianus 1,42. Brahmins as ascetes and holy people: Parker (2008), 285–286, Whittaker (2004), 149; cf. Socrates on the Indians (Eus. Pr. Ev. 11,3); Egypt and intellectuals: Kim (2009), 47. Wisdom of the land: Diod. 2,36,1 (Megasthenes); travels: Dihle (2000), 185.
255. Cic. Tusc. 5,77–78; Prop. 3,13; Parker (2008), 106–109; Woolf (2011), 100.
256. Herod. 3,101; Strab. 15,1,54/56; Arr. Ind. 15,4. Whittaker (2004c), 151.
257. Plin. nat 6,89; Murphy (2004), 108; Starr (1956); Murphy (2004), 106.
258. Woolf (2011), 91–94.
259. Strab. 15,1,34; 54; 66; Diod. 2,39; Arr. Ind. 10,1; Whittaker (2004c), 149.
260. Plut., On the failure of oracles 18; Woolf (2011), 93; Smith 2022.
261. Parker (2008), 70.
262. Diod. 5,41–46; 6,1; Holzberg (1996).
263. Winiarczyk (2011), 130–133.
264. Diod. 2,55–56; cf. Winston (1976), Holzberg (1996) and for the itinerary: Schwarz (1982).
265. Dihle (1984f), 178.
266. Arr. Epictet 3,13,9; Montiglio (2005), 221–222.
267. Plin. nat. 6,101.
268. Ail. nat. 16,18. The stories go back to Agatharchides; Seland (2009a), 182–183.
269. Dion Chrys. 32,40.
270. P Oxy. III. 413; Whittaker (2004c), 156; Tsitsiridis (2011).
271. Xenophon of Ephesus: Whittaker (2004c), 156.
272. Cf. X. Eph. 12–14; Parker (2008), 195.
273. Hel. Aethiopica 5,13–15; Bang (2008), 195.

274. Reger (2009); Karttunen (1986), 196–197.
275. *New Testament Apocrypha II.* Schneemelcher (1992); *The Acts of Thomas.* Klijn (2003). In the fourth century, Christian authors connected motives from the novel with the piety of Indian ascetes. A text attributed to Palladius depicts how a *scholasticus* searching for Taprobane trespassed on the land of the big-headed Bedsades. He is forced to work in the royal bakery, learns the language, and is released from service at the end because the king fears conflict with the Romans; Parker (2008), 278–279.
276. Albinovanus Pedo in Sen. suas. 1,15; cf. Hor. carm. 4,14,47–48.
277. Morgan (2009).
278. Coones (1983), 365.
279. Plut. de specie lunae 26, *On the Face Which Appears in the Orb of the Moon.* Gárriga (2021).
280. Theopompos of Cnidus in FGrHist 115 F 75; Aalders (1978).
281. Smith (2022); Trajan: Ebner (1906), 70.
282. Tac. Germ. 3,2; Woolf (2011).
283. Paus. 1,23,4–6.
284. Sen. Med. 374–379; Strab. 1,4,6 (65); Ps-Arist. de mundo 3,20.
285. Cf. Fernández-Armesto (1991), 32, 43, 128.
286. Dom João de Castro wrote following the return of the Portuguese Red Sea expedition in 1541: 'This sea [. . .] poses more difficulties than the Great Ocean itself, everything contributes to these difficulties: the winds, the lack of drinking water [. . .]'. Fabre (2004), 36; A. Kammerer, Le routier de Dom Joam de Castro, l'exploration de la Mer Rouge par les Portugais en 1541 (1936).
287. Krüger (2000), 46–47, 228. The early-modern cartographer Fra Mauro explains how sailors navigated the Baltic not with a map or compass but with a plumb line: 'per questo mar non se navega cum carta ni bussola, ma cum scandaio'. Falchetta (2006), 669; Hinkkanen/Kirby (2000), 283, A. 6.

CHAPTER 8

1. Crone (1987), 24–28; Nappo (2007); De Maigret (1991), 61.
2. Dihle (1984b), 102–108; Seland (2012), 83–84.
3. Kosmas 2,45–46; Wright (1965), 70; Kordosis (1999); Xu-Shan (2004).
4. Mango (1996), 145–159; Thierry/Morrisson (1994); Wright (1965), 271.
5. Wright (1965), 41–42.
6. Aug. civ. 11,2–3 with Lozovsky (2000), 141–142.
7. Schleicher (2014), 331.
8. Wright (1965), 47; Schleicher (2014), 39.
9. Stoneman (1994), 93–94, 97ff.; Wright (1965), 72–73; Karttunen (1987) for India. Search for Paradise: Pfister (1976); in the Middle Ages: Iter Alexandri ad Paradisum ed. A. Hilka (1935).
10. Aug. civ. 16,8; Scafi (2006), 111.

11. Simek (1996), 93; Steinicke (2005), 17–18.
12. Von den Brincken (1992), 95–96; Steinicke (2005), 43–45.
13. Von den Brincken (1992), 31–33; Lozovsky (2000), 14.
14. See Simek (1996), 40. On the tripartite classification of continents: Lozovsky (2000), 95.
15. The latest report about Gothia is that it is named after Magog and lies near Dacia; Isid. orig. 14,3,31; Lozovsky (2000), 107; Philipp (1911).
16. Isid. orig. 9,2,40. Isidore here uses 'older geographers'. Schleicher (2014), 367 concludes from this that the silk trade survived.
17. Isid. orig. 9,2,64; 125; 14,3,7; Sarmatians and Huns: Isid. orig. 9,2,66. Goths: 9,2,89.
18. Isid. orig. 9,2,133; 14,5,17; Augustinus: civ. 16,9; Randles (1994), 16, 19. Continents: 14, 3,1–15. Isidore seems to labour under a few misapprehensions: Schleicher (2014), 368–370.
19. Anon. Rav. 24; Krüger (2000), 93–95, 140–141; Flint (1984); von den Brincken (1992), 76 on Lambert of Saint-Omer. Augustine's authority could make recognising the Antipodes seem heretical. Boniface asked the Pope to condemn Virgil of Salzburg for heresy on account of his teaching on the Antipodes; Wright (1965), 56–57.
20. Kominko (2008), 146–147.
21. Aug. de Gen. ad lit. 8,1;7; Lozovsky (2000), 51; Grimm (1977), 58ff.; Kominko (2008), 146.
22. Anon. Rav. 14; Scafi (2006), 59, 89; Krüger (2000), 123–124. According to some interpreters, the plants of Paradise were ascribed special healing powers, cf. Grimm (1977), 143 on Ernaldus. Of the western exegetes, only John Scotus seems to have denied the existence of an earthly paradise.
23. Gen. 3:24.
24. Gen. 5:24 (Enoch); 4 Kings 2:1, 11.
25. Apocalypse of Paul, 46–51 (Schneemelcher [1992], 737–740).
26. Grimm (1977), 17–18, 36, 53; Krüger (2000), 125 on the Ravenna Cosmographer.
27. Von den Brincken (1992), 70, 94; Scafi (2008), 163; Isid. orig. 20,14,3, 2–4. Ephrem the Syrian describes the earthly paradise as a mountain that extends into the divine sphere. At its summit is God, beneath it the Tree of Life, in the middle the Tree of Knowledge. The region inhabited by Adam and Eve—reserved for the righteous—lies between it and the borders of Paradise. At the foot of the mountain are the cherubim with the flaming sword: Ephrem the Syrian, Hymns on Paradise, ed. Brock (1990).
28. Anon. Rav. 12,1; Grimm (1977), 80–90.
29. Phillips (2009), 36; Grimm (1977), 103ff. on Aethicus Ister (eighth century). Trips made to Paradise by Christian monks: Wright (1965), 263.
30. Anon. Rav. 1,7; Lozovsky (2000), 146.
31. Anon. Rav. 14, 19; Lozovsky (2000), 146.
32. Scafi (2006), 102.

33. Grimm (1977), 104–110; Sanchez (1994), 200; Moretti (1994), 269. Text and commentary: Burgess/Strijbosch (2006); Strijbosch (2000). Taking their cue from the legend of the Hyperboreans, some church fathers speculated on Paradise lying in the far north; Wright (1965), 71.
34. Simek (1996), 37–38; von den Brincken (1992), 3–4; Wolf (2004).
35. Krüger (2000), 152; (2012), 23–51, 66–69; Lozowski (2000), 120; Simek (1996), 6–24.
36. Aug. De Genesi ad litteram 1,21, col. 255. Krüger (2012), 43, 70–71, 207.
37. Exceptions: Krüger (2012), 92–95; von den Brincken (1992), 204–208; Schleicher (2014), 317 on Jerome's criticism of Cosmas and 169–264 on the Syrian-Antiochene school's opposition to the globular Earth. Its influence was relatively limited, however, and flickered out in Constantinople in the ninth century.
38. Wright (1965), 151; Krüger (2012), 73–75. Ephrem the Syrian had introduced the 'cosmic egg' to Genesis exegesis (306–373). Basil, Jerome: Parker (2008), 225; Marks (1985).
39. Gen. 9:18–19.
40. Psalm 73:12; Scafi (2006), 96–97, 153. Example: Vatican map (Pseudo-Isidore; late eighth century).
41. Cf. Schmieder (2013), 244–245; Scafi (2006), 87. Continental plates: Krüger (2012), 82.
42. Simek (1996), 26, 41–42; Krüger (2012), 79; von den Brincken (1992), 37–38. Isidore's finger model: Krüger (2000), 53–61, 85–86.
43. To get around these difficulties, many writers did not mention the Antipodes. Early church teachers—Clement, Origen, and perhaps Tertullian—had not objected to the Antipodes (Moretti 1994, 262–266). On the counterarguments and doubting authors (Beda Venerabilis, De temporum ratione 34, Eriugena [attributed], Glosses on Boethius, Liber contra Eutychon et Nestorium, ch. 5): Randles (1994). Theological problems raised by Crates' theory: Randles (1994), 20. Antipodes: Krüger (2012), 79–80, 84. Arguments against an inhabitable land of the Antipodes in Isid. De natura rerum 40,3.
44. Wright (1965), 180; Metzler (2009), 381–389; Phillips (2007), 45–46. Bartlett (2009), esp. 254–258.
45. Scafi (2006), 164; Plat. rep. 272a–b; Ov. met. 1,107–108; Hes. erg. 170–175; Hom. Od. 4,563–568; John of Damascus, de fide orthodoxa II, 11, PG XCVIV, col. 464; Isid. orig. II, XIV 3,2–3. On the one hand, the climate of Paradise was explained by the mountain on which it is located towering into the upper celestial regions (Scafi, 175, 187 A. 54; Alexander of Hales, Summa Theologica II. Inqu. IV., tract. 2, sect. 2, q 1). On the other, attempts were made to reconcile its location with the theory of climate zones. In some zonal maps, Paradise is attached to the globe in the form of a rectangle; Scafi (2006), 166–168.
46. Kominko (2008), 142–145; Schleicher (2014), 211–216, 245–246 on Indian influences.

47. Orig. sel. in Gen. 25.
48. Cod. Sang. 8125; von den Brincken (1992), 205; Wright (1965), 157–160. Crates' considerable influence in the Middle Ages: Stahl (1962), 41.
49. Ambr. hex. 6,7; Schleicher (2014), 307.
50. Lozovsky (2000), 27; 123–130; Krüger (2000), 20–25, 30–32, 83–84, 157–159, 224–236, 328–330.
51. Schneider (1970), 248–249.
52. Er. de divis. 3,35, Col. 723; Krüger (2000), 242–251. Similarly: John Scotus 3,35.7234 B–C, p. 263; Lozovsky (2000), 131: 'Ut enim per sensus pervenitur ad intellectum it per creaturam venitur ad deum'. Basil translation: Eustathius. Ancienne version latine des neuf Homélies sur l'Hexaéméron de Basile de Césarée, ed. E. Amand de Mendieta and S.Y. Rudberg, Berlin 1958.
53. Krüger (2000), 201–212; Grimm (1977), 71; Lindgren (1997), 514–516 on Eruigena. Quote: Er. de divis. 3,31, Sp. 708.
54. Von den Brincken (1992), 132–133; Wright (1965), 256; Krüger (2000), 88 on the *zona habitabilis* in Isidore; 166ff. on Dicuil and Pytheas, also 262 on Herman the Cripple and 396 on Adam of Bremen. The Crates map was known in Nordic lands: von den Brincken (1992), 130.
55. Krüger (2000), 97–100 on the interest of the Visigoth king Sisebut. High-level reflection: 135–140. Overcoming of Augustine: 205, 217. Transformation of the disc model: 380–394. Climate zones: 389–390.
56. Already in Sen. suas. 1,15,19–23.
57. Scafi (2006), 1(1994), 248 on Dante. Von den Brincken (1992), 167 on Hugh of St. Victor, De archa Noe mystica c. 14, PL 176, Col. 700D. According to Jerome, only the 'soul of man' can roam in regions and possible ecumenes beyond the Ocean, Schleicher (2014), 314–315.
58. Anon. Rav. 25; he knows (9) that land had been sought in the western Ocean; Krüger (2000), 20–24. On the other hand, he says that 'by divine command, the furthest limits of the Ocean cannot be found'. Early Christian writers believed that the Ocean was impassable: 1 Clem. 20,1.
59. Le Goff (1998), 34–36, 45–47.
60. Krüger (2012), 235; Arabs and globular Earth: Anawati/Hödl/Greiwe (1980); Goldstein (1991).
61. Von den Brincken (1992), 203–204.
62. Aristot. cael. 2,4; 14. Büttner (1979); Krüger (2012), 49–71. The late antique commentary of Alexander of Aphrodisias (second to third century CE) was important for handing down the theory of elements and spheres. It was translated into Latin in the thirteenth century; Sharples (1990).
63. Von den Brincken (1992), 203; Krüger (2012), 62, 92, 113–114, 270. Arab scholars came to the same conclusion around the same time: Vogel (2001), 228–230 on 'Earth voyages'.
64. Krüger (2012), 247; Randles (1994), 23–25; Vogel (2001), 119–125.
65. Aristot. de gen. 2, 4; cf. meteor. 1, 3.

66. Vogel (2001), 60–64, 135–136, 162–164.
67. Wright (1965), 188; Apocalypse of Ezra IV 6,42 (= Ezra II, 6 v.42). Text in Klijn (1983), 41; cf. Randles (1994), 23–28; von den Brincken (1992), 104, 187–189.
68. Aristot. cael. 2,14.
69. Krüger (2012), 63; De caelo et mundo = de caelo: Wright (1965), 9.
70. Krüger (2012), 20, 71; Thomas Aquinas, in Aristotelis libros de caelo et mundo (c. 1260).
71. Pierre d'Ailly, Imago mundi 8.
72. Von den Brincken (1992), 144–145.
73. Hyde (2009), 71–77.
74. Edson (2007), 112.
75. Knefelkamp (1986), 40–42, 55–57; Schmieder (1994), 24, 27.
76. Schmitt (1986), 95–124; Reichert (1992), 69–97, esp. 83 and Schmieder (1994), 167 on the *pax mongolica*. John: Hamilton (2009), 125–132. Rubruck, Seres, Cathay, Ganges: Hyde (2009), 71, 88; Phillips (2000), 37–39; Bacon adopted this in opus magnum, I, pp. 387–388.
77. Von den Brincken (1992), 98, 105, 119–120; Phillips (1988), 79; Hyde (2009).
78. Rubr. XVIII,5 S. 211 with Schmieder (1994) on the Caspian Sea.
79. Phillips (2009), 5; Rubiés (2009), 45–50; Hyde (2009), 172–173. Rubruck's letters were hardly read. Jackson (2009), 284. The Mongols were identified with Gog and Magog.
80. Autopsy, eyewitness, experiments: Schmieder (2013), 240–241.
81. Edson (2007), 94–95.
82. Greenblatt (1998), 52–53; Schmieder (1994), 319.
83. Christian (2000), 6; Hyde (2009), 88; Steinicke (2005), 115. Idealized image of India and the counter-world (with minimal real knowledge): Le Goff (2009), 161–162; Sarnowsky (2015), 11 on Mandeville's sources.
84. 214–215; cited in Greenblatt (1998), 52; Scafi (2006), 241; Giovanni Marignolli (mid-fourteenth century) transferred it forty Italian miles beyond the Sri Lankan coast; Hyde (2009), 99–100; Flint (2009), 336. The only travel report to mention Paradise is Mandeville's novel.
85. Krüger (2012), 92; von den Brincken (1992), 125, 201; 136–167. John Mandeville II, 331, 333.
86. Mayerson (1993); Schneider (2004).
87. Gervase of Tilbury (1150–1235). Robert Grosseteste speaks of theologians who suppose Paradise to lie below the equator; Wright (1965), 262.
88. Macr. Sat. 2,5,22–36; Mart. Cap. 6,602–608; 7,874; Moretti (1994), 269–270; Scafi (2006), 170, 176 on Michael Scot. 193. Criticism in John Scotus; Scafi (2006), 194–195. The convergence of the Antipodes with Paradise was perhaps facilitated by ancient authors (Servius) seeing the land of the Antipodes as the abode of the reincarnated, just as the earthly paradise was the abode of souls.

89. Wright (1965), 163–164; Scafi (2006), 176–178, 218–220. Aristot. cael. 2,2,285b15–28.
90. Knefelkamp (1986), 74–77; Edson (2007), 98. Even in antiquity, motifs could migrate from India to Africa and vice versa: the Isles of the Blessed were placed in the Antipodes; Wright (1965), 28.
91. Krüger (2000), 15–16; Krüger (2012), 86; Wright (1965), 162–163; Metzler (2009), 382–383 on Arab models, Marco Polo, and Albertus Magnus, who postulated the inhabitability of the torrid zone in 1260. Ptolemy had already said the same (geogr. 4,8). A work ascribed to Bede (seventh century) was the first to assert the impassability of the torrid zone.
92. Plin. nat. 2,75,183–185; Ambr. Hex. 4,5,23.
93. Pierre d'Ailly, L'imago 6–12, ed. Burton 1, 194–196; Epilogus 2, 520–522; von den Brincken (1992), 143.
94. Scafi (2006), 240; Prest (1981), 27–37; Hamilton (2009), 139–140; Le Goff (2009), 162.
95. Fernández-Armesto (1987), 76, 90, 185–190.
96. Fernández-Armesto (1987), 189–190.
97. Schmitt/Verlinden (1986), 40–47; Le Goff (1998), 193.
98. Schmitt/Verlinden (1986), 100.
99. Sanchez (1994), 199–202.
100. Fernández-Armesto (1991), 23–44.
101. Strab. 1,4,6 (p. 65). The fact that a cartouche in a map attributed to his brother features Strabo alongside Ptolemy, Pliny, and Isidore makes it likely that Columbus had read Strabo; Fernández-Armesto (1991), 29.
102. Christobal Colón, ed. Varela (1982), 327. Quoted in Pagden (1993), 22; Moretti (1994), 277–278.
103. Moretti (1994), 271–275; Padgen (1993), 19.
104. Fernández-Armesto (1991), 29.
105. Pietri Martyris Anglerii Opus Epistolarum, ep. 131, p. 360; Moretti (1994), 275–276.
106. Fernández-Armesto (1991), 29.
107. Padgen (1993), 10; Scafi (2006), 242; Moretti (1994), 281. Garden of Eden at the Gulf of Paria: Rubiés (2009), XXXIII. Many fourteenth- and fifteenth-century Italian authors saw the Canaries as an important stepping stone on the path to Elysium.
108. Phillips (2009), 11; Grimm (1977), 106.
109. Sanchez (1994), 197–198; Ophir in India: Wright (1965), 275.
110. Fernández-Armesto (1991), 32; Flint (2009), 344.
111. Fernández-Armesto (1991), 35–36; Stückelberger (1987), 333–335.
112. Fernández-Armesto (1991), 37.
113. Fernández-Armesto (1991), 30–36; Stückelberger (1987), 335.
114. Flint (2009), 338.
115. Grafton (1992), 77.

116. Cf. Knefelkamp (1986), 110–111.
117. Fernández-Armesto (1991), 35–36.
118. Grafton (1992), 54; Falchetta (2008); Wright (1965), 87. The first mediaeval map with an open Indian Ocean was that of Albertinus de Virga (1415), accepted by Martellus Germanus (1489) and Martin Behaim.
119. Schmitt (1984), 92.
120. Damiao de Gois, in Schmitt (1984), 53.
121. Padgen (1993), 34, 38–39; Flint (2009), 339–342.
122. Columbus, Letter from the New World (Jane 1989), 198, 200 (monsters); Ptol. geogr. 7,2,27–31.
123. Journal (Jane 1989), 143.
124. Columbus, Journal (Jane 1989), 102; Letter from the New World (Jane 1989), 200; Decot (1993), 117; Flint (1992); Flint (2009), 336; Sanchez (1994), 203–205.
125. Journal (Jane 1989), 52.
126. Journal (Jane 1989), 23–36, 43–51 for communications with the 'Indians'. He often describes this as 'telling by signs' (e.g. 54, 56, 92–93). Characteristically, Columbus always seems to understand his native interlocutors especially well when they refer to gold.
127. Amerigo Vespucci, Mundus novus, 4; Grafton (1992), 83; Peter Martyr: Grafton (1992), 55.
128. Padgen (1993), 10, 30, Amazons and Ophir: Grafton 1992, 243–244. Ophir = Peru: Sanchez (1994), 198.
129. Grafton (1992), 36.
130. Grafton (1992), 138–140; Pritchett (1993), 289.
131. Grafton (1992), 164–166.
132. Quoted in Padgen (1993), 58.

EPILOGUE

1. For authenticity: Delekat (1969) with admittedly far-reaching speculations on Phoenician goals.
2. Broodbank (2013), 60–61 on 'mediterranoid regions' of the world.
3. Yates (1997); Lewis (2006), 136–187.
4. Arr. anab. 7,1,4.
5. Plat. Phaedrus 274c/d. On the link between enlightenment and exploration see 4 Mos. 13,17–20, 2 Sam. 24,1:1; 1 Chron. 21:1.
6. Herod. 4,10,2–3. When poets (Prop. 3,4,1–4; 3,1,15–16; Hor.carm. 1,12,53–57) have the emperor Planning a war against India or declaring India part of the Empire, they are recalling the example of Alexander. In fact, no emperor seriously contemplated conquering the subcontinent.
7. Bang (2008), 66–77, 142–145, 174. In the mid-first century, Seleucia supposedly had a population of 600,000; Plin. nat. 6,122.
8. Di Cosmo (2000), 405.

9. Bang (2008), 299.
10. Liu (1990), 8; Ferguson (1978), 590.
11. Leslie/Gardiner (1996), 162, 218; Gopal (1961).
12. Plin. nat. 34,41; PME 39; Ferguson (1978), 589.
13. Philostr. Ap. 3–5; Plin. nat. 12,29; 18,10,55; Dion. Per. 1126; Silvae 4,9,12; Bang (2008), 138–139 and 194.
14. Bang (2008), 152; Rathbone (2003), 219; Ray (1994), 43.
15. On the south: Hall (2010), 59. No ideology of extending rule 'usque ad fines': Yü (1967), 67.
16. Hom. Od. 1,3.
17. Hom. Od. 9,174.
18. This is nicely illustrated in the case of the centurions whom Nero—according to Sen. nat. 6,8,3—dispatched 'ad investigandum Nili caput', supposedly because Nero had a pronounced love of knowledge (*veritatis in primis amantissimus*). What was really at stake is made clear in Plin. nat. 6,181: preparations for a campaign against Ethiopia (Sudan/Meroë): ... *inter reliqua bella et Aethiopicum cogitanti* (s. Neroni).
19. Lewis (2006), 252–260.
20. See Stuurman (2008), 22: 'but the entire ethnography cannot be reduced to an admire-your-enemies'-enemies logic'.
21. Aristot. Cael. 2,14; Strab. 1,4,6 (64–65). Cf. Sen. Nat. pr.13.
22. Ptol. geogr. 1,14,1; 13,5–9; 7,1,12,16; 8,1,15; 2,3; 3,3.

ACKNOWLEDGEMENTS

1. The translator wishes to thank the author for his helpfulness in responding to queries and Oscar Wilson for his sage advice.

Bibliography

PRIMARY SOURCES: EDITIONS, TRANSLATIONS, AND COMMENTARIES USED

The Acts of Thomas. Intr., Text and comm. A. J. F. Klijn. Leiden, 2003; Brill.

Agatharchides of Cnidos. *On the Erythraean Sea*. Transl. and ed. M. Burstein. London, 1989: Hakluyt Society.

Aischylus. *Persians and Other Plays*. Transl. C. Collard. Oxford, 2008: Oxford University Press.

The Amarna Letters. Ed. and transl. W. Moran. Baltimore, 1987: Johns Hopkins University Press.

Ancient Egyptian Literature: A Book of Readings. Vol. 2: *The New Kingdom*. Transl. M. Lichtheim. Berkeley/Los Angeles/London, 1976: University of California Press.

The Apocryphical New Testament: A Collection of Apocryphai Christian Literature in English Translation. Transl. J. K. Elliott. Oxford, 2005: Oxford University Press.

Asheri, A. B., and A. Corcella. 2007. *A Commentary on Herodotus Books I–IV*. Oxford: Oxford University Press.

Averroes' Questions in Physics. Transl. H. T. Goldstein. Boston, 1991: Kluwer Academics.

Avienus. *Ora maritima*. Ed. A. Bertholet. Paris, 1934: Libraire ancienne H. Champion.

Avienus. *Ora maritima or Description of the Seacoast*. Ed. and transl. J. P. Murphy. Chicago, 1977: Ares.

Berggren, J. L., and A. Jones. 2000. *Ptolemy's Geography: An Annotated Translation of the Theoretical Chapters*. New York: Princeton University Press.

Ctesias. 'Introduction'. In *On India*. Transl. and comm. A. Nichols. London, 2011: Bloomsbury.

Ctésias de Cnide. *La Perse, L'Inde. Autres Fragments*. Transl. and comm. B. D. Lenfant. Paris, 2004: Les Belles Lettres.

Der lateinische Text der Apokalypse des Esdra. Ed. A. F. J. Klijn. Texte und Untersuchungen zur Geschichte der altchristlichen Literatur 131. Berlin, 1983: Akademie-Verlag.

Dicks, D. R. 1960. *The Geographical Fragments of Hipparchus*. London: University of London/Athlone Press.

The Edicts of Asoka. Ed. and transl. N. A. Nikam and R. M. McKeon. Chicago/London, 1959: University of Chicago Press.

The El-Amarna Correspondence: A New Edition of the Cuneiform Letters from the Site of El-Amarna Based on Collations of All Extant Tablets. Ed. A. F. Rainey and W. M. Schniedewind. Boston, 2014: Brill.

Ephraim the Syrian. *Hymns on Paradise*. Transl. S. Brock. Crestwood/New York, 1990: St. Vladimir's Seminary Press.

Erman, A. *Reise um die Erde durch Nord-Asien und die beiden Ozeane in den Jahren 1828, 1829 und 1830*. Erste Abteilung: Historischer Bericht 1. Berlin, 1833: Reimer.

Eustathius. *Ancienne version latine des neuf Homélies sur l'Hexaéméron de Basile de Césarée*. Ed. E. Amand de Mendieta and S.Y. Rudberg. Berlin, 1958: Akademie-Verlag.

The Fragments of the Persika of Ktesias. Ed. J. Gilmore. London/New York, 1888: .

Geminos. *Introduction to the phenomena*. Ed. and transl. J. Evans. Princeton, 2006: Princeton university Press.

Hanno the Carthaginian, Periplus. Ed. and transl. V. A. N. Oikonomodes and M. C. Miller. 2nd ed. Chicago, 1995: Ares.

Herodotus. *The Histories*. Transl. Waterfield and edited with an introduction and notes C. Dewald. Oxford World's Classics. Oxford, 2008: Oxford University Press.

Hill, J. E. *Through the Jade Gate to Rome: A Study of the Silk Routes during the Later Han Dynasty, 1st to 2nd Centuries CE. An annotated Translation of the Chronicle on the 'Western Regions' in the Hou Hanshu*. Charleston, SC, 2009: BookSurge.

Hippocrates. *Ancient Medicine. Airs, Waters, Places. Epidemics 1 and 3. Precepts. Nutriment. L CL 147*. Ed. and transl. P. Potter. Cambridge, MA/London, 2022: Harvard University Press.

Hirschberger, M. 2004. *Gynaikôn Katalogos und Megalai Ehoiai. Ein Kommentar zu den Fragmenten zweier hesiodeischer Epen*. BzA 198. Munich/Leipzig: K. G. Saur.

How, W. W., and J. Wells. 1928. *A Commentary on Herodotus: With Introduction and Appendixes*. Vols. 1–2. Oxford: Oxford University Press.

Horner, I. B. 1963–1964. *Milinda's Questions*. London: Luzac.

The Hymn of Pearls: The Syriac and Greek Texts with Introduction. Transl. and Notes J. Ferreira. Sydney, 2002: St. Pauls Publications.

The Journal of Christopher Columbus. Transl. C. Jane, with an appendix by R. A. Skelton. New York, 1989: Bonanza Books.

Kaplan, P. 'Skylax of Karyanda'. In *Brill's New Jacoby*. Leiden. http://referenceworks.brillonline.com/entries/brill-s-new-jacoby/skylax- of-karyanda-709-a709. Accessed 17 September 2009: Brill.

Leslie, D., D. Kenneth, and H. J. Gardiner, eds. *The Roman Empire in Chinese Sources*. Studi Orientali 15. Rome, 1996: Bardi.

López-Ruiz. L., ed. *Gods, Heroes, and Monsters. A Sourcebook of Greek, Roman, and Near Eastern Myths in Translation*. Oxford, 2014: Oxford University Press.

Mahâvamsa: The Great Chronicle of Sri Lanka. A New Annotated Translation with Prolegomena. A.W.P. Guruge. Colombo, 1989: Associated Newspapers of Ceylon.

The Mahâvamsa or the Great Chronicle of Ceylon. Ed. W. Geiger and M. H. Bode. Repr. Of the original edition 1912. Colombo, 1950: Government Information Department.

Marcian of Heraclea. *Periplus of the Outer Sea: East and West, and of the Great Islands Therein*. Transl. and comm. W. H. Schoff. Philadelphia, 1927: Commercial Museum of Philadelphia.

Mette, H. J. *Pytheas von Massilia*. Berlin, 1952: De Gruyter.

Milinda's Questions. Vol. 1. Transl. I. B. Horner. London, 1963: Luzac & Company.

Müller, K., ed. *Geographi Graeci Minores*. Paris, 1855 (1–3). Repr. Hildesheim, 1965: Olms.

Mundus Novus. Letter to Lorenzo Pietro Di Medici. Transl. G. T. Northup. Princeton, NJ, 1916: Princeton University Press.

Murphy, J. P., ed. 1977. *Avienus: Ora maritima or Description of the Seacoast*. Chicago: Ares.

Mynářová, J. 'Discovery, Research, and Excavation of the Amarna Tablets: The Formative Stage'. In *The El-Amarna Correspondence: A New Edition of the Cuneiform Letters from the Site of El-Amarna Based on Collations of All Extant Tablets*, edited by Anson F. Rainey, 37–46. Leiden, 2015: Brill.

New Testament Apocrypha II: Writings Relating to the Apostles; Apocalypses and Related Subjects. Ed. W. Schneemelcher, transl. R. L. Wilson. Rev. ed. Louisville, 1992: Westminster John Knox Press.

Olivelle, P., ed. *King, Governance, and Law in Ancient India: Kautilya's Arthasastra*. Oxford, 2013: Oxford University Press.

The Periplus Maris Erythraei. Transl. and comm. L Casson. Princeton, NJ, 1989: Princeton University Press.

The Periplus of Hanno: A Voyage of Discovery down the West African Coast, by a Carthaginian Admiral of the Fifth Century B.C. Transl. W. H. Schoff. Philadelphia, 1912: Commercial Museum Philadelphia.

'The Periplous of Skylax of Karyanda'. Transl. and comm. M. L. Allain. PhD dissertation, Ohio State University, 1977: Ohio State University Press.

The Periplus of the Erythraean Sea by an unknown Author. With some extracts from Agatharchid's 'On the Erythraean Sea'. Ed. and transl. G. W. B. Huntingford. London, 1980: Hakluyt Society.

Platon. *Phaidon*. Transl. and comm. T. Ebert. Göttingen, 2004: Vandenhoel & Ruprecht.

Plutarch. *On the Face Which Appears in the Orb of the Moon*. Ed., transl., and comm. to the Critical Edition L. L. Gárriga. Brill's Plutarch Studies. Brill's Plutarch Text Editions 7. Leiden/Boston, 2021: Brill.

Pomponius Mela's Description of the World. Transl. F. E. Romer. Ann Arbor, MI, 1998: University of Michigan Press.

Poseidonios. *Part 1: The Fragments, Part 2: Commentary*. Ed. L. Edelstein and I. G. Kidd. Sec. Ed. Cambridge, 1989/1982: Cambridge University Press.

Pownall, F. *Hekataios of Miletos*. In *Brill's New Jacoby*. http://dx.doi.org/10.1163/1873-5363_bnj_a1.: Leiden, 2013: Brill

Pseudo-Skylax's Periplous: The Circumnavigation of the Inhabited World. Ed. G. Shipley. Bristol, 2011: Phoenix Press.

The Questions of King Milinda. 2. vols. Transl. T. W. Rhys Davids. Oxford, 1890–1894: Clarendon Press.

The Report of Wenamun. Transl. H. Goedicke. Baltimore, MD, 1975: Johns Hopkins University Press.

'The Report of Wenamon'. Transl. J. H. Breasted. In *The American Journal of Semitic Languages and Literatures* 21 (1905): 100–209: University of Chicago Press.

Roseman, C. H. *Pytheas of Massilia: A Critical Examination of the Texts.* Seattle, WA, 1983: University of Washington Press.

Schmitt, E. (ed.). 1984. *Die großen Entdeckungen.* Dokumente zur Geschichte der europäischen Expansion 2. Munich: Harrassowitz.

Schmitt, E., and Ch. Verlinden, eds. 1986. *Die mittelalterlichen Ursprünge der europäischen Expansion.* Dokumente zur Geschichte der europäischen Expansion 1. Munich: Harrassowitz.

Schneider, U., ed. *Die großen Felsen-Edikte Aśokas.* Kritische Ausgabe, Übersetzung und Analyse der Texte. Wiesbaden, 1978: Harrassowitz.

Scott, L. *Pytheas of Massalia: Texts, Translation, and Commentary.* Routledge Classical Translations. Abingdon/New York, 2022: Routledge.

Sima Qian. *Records of the Grand Historian of China: Han Dynasty.* 2 vols. Ed. and transl. B. Watson. New York, 1993: Columbia University Press.

Sophokles. *Antigone.* Ed. and transl. R. Gibbons and C. Segal. Oxford, 2007: Oxford University Press.

Sprague, R. K. (ed.). *The Older Sophists: A Complete Translation by Several Hands of the Fragments in die Fragmente der Vorsokratiker.* Ed. Diels-Kranz. Columbia, 1972: University of South California Press.

Stoneman, R. *Megasthenes' 'Indica': A New Translation of the Fragments with Commentary.* Routledge Classical Translation. Abingdon/New York, 2021: Routledge.

Texts of Greek and Latin Authors on the Far East from the 4th C. B.C.E. to the 14th C. C.E. Transl. J. Sheldon. Turnhout, 2010: Brepols.

Theiler, W., ed. *Poseidonios. Die Fragmente.* 2 vols. Berlin/New York, 1982: De Gruyter.

Vamsatthappakâsinî Commentary on the Mahâvamsa. Ed. G. P. Malalasakera. London, 1935: Humphrey Mitford.

The Voyage of Pedro Álvares Cabral to Brazil and India. From Contemporary Documents and Sources. Transl. W. B. Greenlee. London, 1938, sec. impr. 2020: Gyan.

Whitby, M. '*Nearchos*'. In *Brill's New Jacoby.* http://dx.doi.org/10.1163/1873-5363_bnj_a133. Accessed 7 December 2020: Brill.

'Ymago Mundi' de Pierre d'Ailly. Texte latin et traduction française des quatre traits cosmographiques d'Ailly E. Burton. Paris, 1930: Maison neuve frères.

SECONDARY SOURCES

Aalders, G. J. 1978. 'Die Meropes des Theopomp'. *Historia* 27: 317–327.

Abel, K. 1974. 'Zone'. *E Suppl.* 14: 989–1188.

Abeydeera, A. 2009. 'A Raki's Mission to Romanukharattha: New Evidence in Favour of Pliny's Account of Taprobane, N.H. 6.84–91'. *Habis* 40: 145–165.

Abulafia, D., ed. 2003. *The Mediterranean in History.* London.

Abulafia, D. 2019. *The Boundless Sea: A Human History of the Oceans*. London: J.Paul Getty Museum.

Ahl, F.M. 1982. 'Amber, Avallon, and Apollo's Singing Swan'. *AJPh* 103: 373–411.

Allchin, R., et al. eds. 1997. *Gandharan Art in Context. East West Exchanges at the Crossroades of Asia*. New Delhi.

Almagor, E., and J. Skinner, eds. 2013. *Ancient Ethnography: New Approaches*. London: Bloomsbury.

Alram, M. 2002. 'Die Geschichte der Seidenstraße im Spiegel der Münzen'. *HONG* 42: 34–45.

Alster, B. 1983. 'Dilmun, Bahrain, and the Alleged Paradise in Sumerian Myth and Literature'. In *Dilmun: New Studies in the Archaeology and Early History of Bahrain*, edited by D.T. Potts, 39–74. Berlin: Reimer.

Alston, R. 1995. *Soldier and Society in Roman Egypt*. London: Routledge.

Amigiues, S. 2005. 'Anaxikrates' Expedition to Western Arabia'. In *A Gateway From the Eastern Mediterranean to India*, edited by J. M. F. Boussac and J. F. Salles, 189–195. New Delhi: Manohar.

Anawati, G. C., L Hödl, and H. Greive. 1980. 'Averroes'. *Lexikon des Mittelalters* 1: 1291–1295: Artemis.

Andrade, N. 2015/2016. 'The Voyage of Maes Titianus and the Dynamics of Social Connectivity between the Roman Levant and Central Asia/West China'. *Mediterraneo antico* 16 (2): 41–74.

Arnaud, P. 2005. *Les routes de la navigation antique: itineraries en Méditerranée*. Paris: Errance.

Arnaud, P. 2011a. 'Ancient Sailing-Routes and Trade Patterns. The Impact of Human Factors'. In *Maritime Archaeology and Ancient Trade in the Mediterranean*, edited by D. Robinsohn and A. Wilson, 61–80. Oxford: Oxbow Books.

Arnaud, P. 2011b. 'Sailing 90 Degrees from the Wind: Norm or Exception.' In *Maritime Technology in the Ancient Economy: Ship-Design and Navigation*, edited by W.V. Harris and K. Iara, 147–160. Portsmouth/Rhode Island: Journal of Roman Archaeology.

Artzy, M. 1997. 'Nomads of the Sea'. In *Res Maritimae. Cyprus and the Mediterranean from Prehistory to Late Antiquity*, edited by R. L. Hohlfelder, S. Swiny, and H. W. Swiny, 1–16. CAARI 1. Atlanta: Scholar's Press.

Artzy, M. 1998. 'Routes, Trade, Boats and "Nomads at the Sea"'. In *Mediterranean Peoples in Transition: Thirteenth to Early Tenth Centuries* BCE, edited by S. Gitin, A. Mazar, and E. Stern, 439–448. Jerusalem: Israel Exploration Society.

Aubet, M. E. 2001. *The Phoenicians and the West. Politics, Colonies, and Trade*. Sec. Ed. Cambridge: Cambridge University Press.

Austen, R. A. 2010. *Trans Saharan Africa in World History*. Oxford: Oxford University Press.

Bacon, H. 1961. *Barbarians in Greek Tragedy*. New Haven, CT: Yale University Press.

Ballabriga, A. 1998. *Les Fictions d'Homère. L'invention mythologique et cosmographique dans l'Odyssée*. Paris: Presses universitaires de France.

Bang, P. F. 2008. *The Roman Bazaar. A Comparative Study of Trade and Markets in a Tributary Empire*. Cambridge: Cambridge University Press.

Bang, P. F. 2009. 'Commanding and Consuming the World. Empire, Tribute, and Trade in Roman and Chinese History'. In *Rome and China: Comparative Perspectives on Ancient World Empires*, edited by W. Scheidel, 100–120. Oxford: Oxford University Press.

Barako, T. J. A. 2003. 'Rebuttal: Philistines Upon the Seas'. *Biblical Archaeology Review* 29: 22–23.

Bartlett, R. 2009. 'Gerald's Ethnographic Achievement'. In *Medieval Ethnographies: European Perceptions of the World Beyond*, edited by J. P. Rubiés, 231–272. The Expansion of Latin Europe 9. Farnham: Routledge.

Beaujeu, J. 1955. 'L'Antiquité'. In *Histoire Universelle des explorations. De la Préhistoire à la fin du Moyen Âge*, edited by L.-H. Parias, 113–251. Paris: Nouvelle Librairie des France.

Beckwith, C. 2009. *Empires of the Silk Road: A History of Central Eurasia From the Bronze Age to the Present*. Princeton, NJ/Oxford: Princeton University Press.

Beeston, A. F. L. 2005. 'The Arabian Aromatics Trade in Antiquity'. In *A. F. L. Beeston at the Arabian Seminar and Other Papers*, edited by M. C. A. MacDonald and C. S. Philipps, 53–64. Oxford: Archaeopress.

Bell, B. M. 1995. 'The Contribution of Julius Caesar to the Vocabulary of Ethnography'. *Latomus* 54: 753–767.

Bennet, J. 2013 . 'The Aegean Bronze Age.' In W. Scheidel et al. (eds.). *The Cambridge Economic History of the Greco-Roman World*. Cambridge (Pb): 175–210: Cambridge University Press.

Beresford, J. 2013. *The Ancient Sailing Season*. Mnemosyne Suppl. 351. Leiden/Boston: Brill.

Berger, E. H. 1903. *Geschichte der wissenschaftlichen Erdkunde der Griechen*. Leipzig: Veit.

Bernard, L. 2000. 'Massilia und sein Hinterland als Ausgangspunkt von Fernkontakten mit der Celtica'. In *Fernkontakte in der Eisenzeit*, edited by A. Lang and V. Salac, 147–159. Prag.

Bichler, R. 2011. 'Die Fahrt zu den Grenzen der Erde. Von Herodot bis zur Alexander-Historiographie'. *Gymnasium* 118: 314–344.

Bichler, R. 2007. 'Ktesias "korrigiert" Herodot. Zur literarischen Einschätzung der Persika'. In R. Bichler, *Historiographie – Ethnographie – Utopie. Gesammelte Schriften*, edited by R. Rollinger, 229–245. Part 1: Studien zu Herodots Kunst der Historie (Philippika 18,1). Wiesbaden: Harrassowitz.

Bikai, P. 1987. 'Trade Networks in the Early Iron Age: The Phoenicians at Palaepaphos'. In *Western Cyprus: Connections*, edited by B. W. Rupp, 125–128. Göteburg: Astrom.

Bikai, P. 1992. 'The Phoenicians'. In *The Crisis Years: The 12th Century*, edited by W. A. Ward and M. Joukowsky, 132–141. Dubuque, IA: Kendall Hunt.

Blomquist, J. 1984 'Reflections of Carthaginian Commercial Activity in Hanno's Periplus'. *Orientalia Suecana* 33–34: 53–62.

Blue, L., J. Whitewright, and R. Thomas. 2011. 'Ships and Ships' Fittings'. In *Myos Hormos – Quseir al-Qadim. Roman and Islamic Ports on the Red Sea*, part 2: *Finds from the Excavations 1999–2003*, edited by L. Blue and D. Peacock, 179–209. BAR International Series 2286. Oxford: Archaeopress.

Boardman, J. 2006. 'Early Euboean Settlements in the Carthage Area'. *Oxford Journal of Archaeology* 25: 195–200.

Bockius, R. 2007. 'Spuren griechisch-etruskischen Knowhows im keltischen Schiffbau'. In *Forschungen zur Vorgeschichte und Römerzeit im Rheinland. FS H.-E. Joachim*, edited by H. Kelzenberg, P. Kußling, and St. Weber, 253–267. BJ Beiheft 57. Bonn: Phipp von Zabern.

Bolchert, P. 1908. *Aristoteles' Erdkunde von Asien und Libyen*. Berlin: Weidmamm.

Bolton, J. D. P. 1962. *Aristeas of Proconnesus*. Oxford: Oxford Reprints.

Bosch-Gimpera, P. 1944. 'The Phokaians in the Far West. An Historical Reconstruction'. *CQ* 38: 53–59.

Bosworth, A. B. 1996. 'The Historical Setting of Megasthenes' Indica'. *CPh* 91: 113–127.

Bosworth, A. B. 1998a. *Alexander and the East: The Tragedy of Triumph*. Oxford: Clarendon Press.

Bosworth, A. B. 1998b. 'Calanus and the Brahman Opposition'. In *Alexander der Große. Eine Welteroberung und ihr Hintergrund*, edited by W. Will, 173–203. Bonn: Habelt.

Bouffier, S. 2013. 'Evacuer l'eau hors des fortifications en occident grec'. In *L'occident grec de Marseille à Mégara Hyblaea. FS H. Tréziny*, edited by S. Bouffier, A. Hermary, 121–136. BAMA 13. Aix-en- Provence/Paris: publications du Centre Camille Jullian Etidions Errance.

Boulnois, L. 2004. *Silk Road, Monks, Warriors and Merchants on the Silk Road*. Geneva: Odyssey.

Boussac, J. M. F., and J. F. Salles, eds. 2005. *A Gateway from the Eastern Mediterranean to India*. New Delhi: Manohar.

Bowen, R. L. 1960. 'Egypt's Earliest Sailing Ships'. *Antiquity* 34: 117–131.

Bowra, C. M. 1964. *Heldendichtung. Eine vergleichende Phänomenologie der heroischen Poesie aller Völker und Zeiten*. Stuttgart: Metzlerische Verlagsbuchhandlung.

Braun, T. 2004. "'Hecataios' Knowledge of the Western Mediterranean."'. In K. Lomas (ed.). *Greek Identity in the Western Mediterranean. FS B. Shefton*, edited by K. Lomas, 287–347. Leiden/Boston: Brill.

Braun, T. F. R. G. 1982. 'The Greeks in the Near East'. In *The Cambridge Ancient History*, part 3: *The Expansion of the Greek World. Eighth to sixth Century B.C.*, edited by J. Boardman and N. G. L. Hammond, 1–31. 2nd ed. Cambridge: Cambridge University Press.

Breton, J.–P. 1999. *Arabia Felix from the Time of the Queen of Sheba: Eighth Century B.C. to First Century A.D.* Notre Dame: University of Notre Dame Press.

Bretzl, H. 1903. *Botanische Forschungen des Alexanderzuges*. Leipzig: Teubner.

Briant, P. 2002. *From Cyrus to Alexander: A History of the Persian Empire.* Winona Lake, IN: Penn State University Press.

Bridgman, T. P. 2005. *Hyperboreans: Myth and History in Celtic Hellenic Contacts.* London: Routledge.

Brodersen, K. 1995. *Terra Cognita. Studien zur Römischen Raumerfassung.* Hildesheim: Olms.

Brodersen, K., and Elsner, J. eds. 2009. *Images and Texts on the 'Artemidorus Papyrus'.* Stuttgart: Steiner.

Brody, J. A. 1998. *Each Man Cried Out to His God: The Specialized Religion of Canaanite and Phoenician Seafarers.* Harvard Semitic Museum Publications 58. Atlanta: Scholar Press.

Brok, R. 2000. 'Sickness in the Body Politic. Medical Imagery in the Greek Polis'. In *Death and Disease in the Ancient City*, edited by V. M. Hope and E. Marshall, 24–34. London/New York: Routledge.

Brommer, F. 1986. *Heracles: The Twelve Labors of the Hero in Ancient Art and Literature.* New York. (= Brommer, F. 1986. *Die zwölf Taten des Helden in antiker Kunst und Literatur.* 5th ed. Darmstadt: Wissenschaftliche Buchgesellschaft.)

Broodbank, C. 2013. *The Making of the Middle Sea: A History of the Mediterranean from the Beginning to the Emergence of the Classical World.* Oxford: Thames & Hudson.

Brown, C. G. 1992. 'The Hyperboreans and Nemesis in Pindar's "Tenth Pythian"'. *Phoenix* 46: 95–107.

Brown, T. S. 1962. 'Herodotus' Portrait of Cambyses'. *Historia* 31: 387–403.

Brown, T. S. 1978. 'Suggestions for a Vita of Ctesias of Cnidos'. *Historia* 27: 1–19.

Bryce, T. 1998. *The Kingdom of the Hittites.* Oxford: Oxford University Press.

Buchner, G. 1982. 'Die Beziehungen zwischen der euböischen Kolonie Pithekussai auf der Insel Ischia und dem nordwestsemitischen Mittelmeerraum in der zweiten Hälfte des 8. Jhs. v. Chr.'. In *Phönizier im Westen*, edited by H. G. Niemeyer, 277–306. Madrider Beiträge 8. Mainz: Philipp von Zabern.

Bulliet, R. W. 1975. *The Camel and the Wheel.* Cambridge, MA: Harvard University Press.

Burgess, G. S., and C. J. Strijbosch. 2006. *The Brendan Legend. Texts and Versions.* Leiden: Brill.

Burkert, W. 1972. *Lore and Science in Ancient Pythagoreanosm.* Cambridge, MA: Harvard University Press.

Burkert, W. 1979. *Structure and History in Greek Mythology and Ritual.* Sather Classical Lectures 47. Berkeley: University of California Press.

Burkert, W. 1987. *Greek Religion: Archaic and Classic.* Oxford: Blackwell.

Burkert, W. 1992. *The Orientalizing Revolution. Near Eastern Influence on Greek Culture in the Early Archaic Age.* Cambridge, MA/London: Harvard University Press.

Burns, B. E. 2010a. *Mycenaean Greece, Mediterranean Commerce, and the Formation of Identity.* Cambridge: Cambridge University Press.

Burns, B. E. 2010b. 'Trade'. In *The Oxford Handbook of the Bronze Age Aegean (ca. 3000–*1000 BC), edited by E. H. Cline, 291–304. Oxford: Oxford University Press.

Burr, V. 1947. 'Das geographische Weltbild Alexanders des Großen'. *WJ* 1: 91–99.

Burstein, S. M. 1976. 'Alexander, Callisthenes, and the Sources of the Nile'. *GRBS* 17: 135–146.

Burstein, S. M. 1993. 'The Hellenistic Fringe. The Case of Meroe'. In *Hellenistic History and Culture*, edited by P. Green, 38–66. Berkeley: University of California Press.

Burstein, S. M. 1996. 'Ivory and Ptolemaic Exploration of the Red Sea: The Missing Factor'. *Topoi* 6: 799–807.

Bury, J. B. 1906. 'The Homeric and the Historic Kimmerians'. *Klio* 6: 79–88.

Büttner, M. 1979. 'Die geographisch-cosmographischen Schriften des Aristoteles und ihre Bedeutung für die Entwicklung der Geographie in Deutschland. Ursachen und Folgen'. In *Wandlungen im geographischen Denken von Aristoteles bis Kant. Dargestellt an ausgewählten Beispielen*, edited by M. Büttner, 14–34. Paderborn: Schöningh.

Carpenter, R. 1966. *Beyond the Pillars of Hercules*. London: Methuen.

Carswell, J. 1991. 'The Port of Mantai, Sri Lanka'. In *Rome and India: The Ancient Sea Trade*, edited by V. Begley and R. D. De Puma, 197–203. Madison: University of Wisconsin Press.

Cartledge, P. 2002. *The Greeks. A Portait of Self and Other*. 2nd ed. Oxord: Oxford University Press.

Cary, G., and E. H. Warmington. 1949. *The Geographic Background of Greek and Roman History*. Oxford: Clarendon Press.

Cary, G., and E. H. Warmington. 1963. *The Ancient Explorers, revised edition Penguin*. London: Penguin Books.

Cary, M. 1956. 'Maes, Qui et Titianos'. *CQ* 6: 130–134.

Casson, L. 1991. 'Ancient Naval Technology and the Route to India'. In *Rome and India. The Ancient Sea Trade*, edited by V. Begley, R. D. De Puma, 8–11. Madison: University of Wisconsin Press.

Casson, L. 1994. *Travel in the Ancient World*. London: Johns Hopkins University Press.

Caubet, A. 2000. 'Ras Shamra–Ugarit Before the Sea People'. In *The Sea Peoples and Their World: A Reassessment*, edited by E. D. Oren, 35–51. Philadelphia: University of Pennsylvania Press.

Chakravarti, R. 2002. *Traders and Trade in Early Indian Society*. Delhi: Manohar.

Chami, F. 1999. 'Graeco-Roman Trade Link and the Bantu Migration Theory'. *Anthropos* 94: 205–215.

Chami, F., and P. J. Msemwa. 1997. 'A New Look at Culture and Trade on the Azanian Coast'. *Current Anthropology* 38: 673–677.

Chami, F. A. 1999. *The Early Iron Age on Mafia Island and Its Relationship with the Mainland. Azania* 34: 1–10.

Chandra, M. 1977. *Trade and Trade Routes in Ancient India*. New Delhi: Abhina Publications.

Chang, H. 2005. 'The Cities of the Hippocratic Doctors'. In *Hippocrates in Context*, edited by P. Van der Eiyk, 156–170. Boston/Leiden.

Christian, D. 2000. 'Silk Roads or Steppe Roads? The Silk Roads in World History'. *Journal of World History* 11: 1–26.

Clarke, G. W. 1967. 'Ancient Knowledge of the Gulf Stream'. *CPh* 62: 25–31.

Clarke, K. 1999. *Between Geography and History. Hellenistic Constructions of the Roman World*. Oxford: Clarendon Press.

Cline, E. H. 2014. *1177 B.C. The Year Civilization Collapsed*. Princeton/Oxford: Princeton University Press.

Cline, E. H., and D. O'Connor. 2007. 'The Mystery of the "Sea Peoples"'. In *Mysterious Lands*, edited by D. O'Connor and S. Quirke, 107–138. London: UCL Press.

Cobb, M. A. 2018. *Rome and the Indian Ocean Trade from Augustus to the Early Third Century* CE. Mnemosyne Suppl. 418. Leiden/Boston: Brill.

Coldstream, J. N. 1982. 'Greeks and Phoenicians in the Aegean'. In *Phönizier im Westen*, edited by H. G. Niemeyer, 261–275. Madrider Beiträge 8. Mainz: Philipp von Zabern.

Comfort, H. 1991. 'Terra Sigillata from Arikamedu'. In *Rome and India: The Ancient Sea Trade*, edited by V. Begley, R. D. De Puma, 134–150. Madison: University of Wisconsin Press.

Cook, E. 1992. 'Ferrymen of Elysium and the Homeric Phaeacians'. *JIES* 20: 239–269.

Coones, P. 1983. 'The Geographical Significance of Plutarch's Dialogue *Concerning the Face Which Appears in the Orb of the Moon*'. *Transactions of the Institute of British Geographers* 8: 361–372.

Cooper, J. P. 2011. 'The Nile versus the Red Sea in Ancient and Medieval N-S Navigation'. In *Maritime Technology in the Ancient Economy: Ship-Design and Navigation*, edited by W. V. Harris and K. Iara, 189–210. Journal of Roman Archaeological Suppl. Series 84. Portsmouth/Rhode Island. RI.

Corral, M. A. 2002. *Ezekiel's Oracles against Tyre. Historical Reality and Motivations*. Biblia and Orientalia 46. Rome: Biblica and Orientalia.

Couprie, D. L. 2011. *Heaven and Earth in Ancient Greek Cosmology: From Thales to Heraclides Ponticus*. Astrophysics and Space Science Library 374. New York: Springer.

Crone, P. 1987. *Meccan Trade and the Rise of Islam*. Princeton, NJ: Gorgias Press.

Culican, W. 1986. *Opera selecta: From Tyre to Tartessos*. Philadelphia: Coronet Books.

Cunliffe, B. 1997. *The Ancient Celts*. Oxford/New York: Oxford University Press.

Cunliffe, B. 1999. 'Atlantic Sea-Ways'. *Revista de Guimaraes* 1: 93–105.

Cunliffe, B. 2001. *Facing the Ocean: The Atlantic and its Peoples, 8000 BC–AD 1500*. Oxford: Oxford University Press.

Cunliffe, B. 2002. *The Extraordinary Voyage of Pytheas the Great*. New York: Penguin.

Cunliffe, B., 2011. *Europe between the Oceans 9000 BC–AD 1000. Themes and Variations: 9000 BC–AD 1000*. New Haven, CT: Yale University Press.

Daebritz, R. 1914. 'Hyperboreer'. *RE* 9 (1): 258–279.

Dan, A. 2013. 'Achaemenid World Representations in Herodotos' Histories. Some Geographic Examples of Cultural Translation'. In *Herodots Wege des Erzählens. Logos und Topos in den Historien*, edited by K. Geus, E. Irwin, and T. Poiss, 83–121. Frankfurt am Main: Peter Lang.

Dayton, J. 1984. 'Herodotus, Phoenicia, the Persian Gulf and India in the First Millenium'. In *Arabié orientale: Mésopotamie et Iran méridionale de l'âge du fer au début de la période islamique*, edited by R. Boucharlat and J. F. Salles, 363–375. Paris: Editions Recherche sur les Civilisations.

De Angelis, F. 2003. *Megara Hyblaia and Selinous. : The Development of Two Greek City-States in Archaic Sicila*. Oxford.

De Give, B. 2005. *Les rapports de l'Inde et de l'Occident des origines au règne d'Aśoka*. Paris: Les Indes savants.

De Jong, J. W. 1973 'The Discovery of India by the Greeks'. *Asiatische Studien* 27: 115–142.

De Maigret, A. 1991. 'The Frankincense Trade'. In *Ancient Rome and India: Commercial and Cultural Contacts between the Roman World and India*, edited by R. M. Cimino, 60–61. New Delhi: Munashier Manohar.

De Romanis, F. 1996. *Cassia, cinnamomo, ossidiana*. Rome: L'Erma di Bretschneider.

De Romanis, F. 1997. *Crossings: Early Mediterranean Contacts with India*. New Dehli: Manhohar.

De Romanis, F. 2005. 'Greek Graffiti Found in the Wadi Menih El-Her: A Vestorius Between Coptos and Berenike'. In *A Gateway from the Eastern Mediterranean to India*, edited by J. M. F. Boussac and J. F. Salles, 43–57. New Delhi: Manohar.

De Romanis, F., ed. 2020. *The Indo-Roman Pepper Trade and the Muziris Papyrus*. Oxford Studies on the Roman Economy. Oxford: Oxford University Press.

Decot, R. 1993. 'Weltbild und Erdform in der theologischen Betrachtung von 1450–1550'. In *Entdeckungen und frühe Kolonisation*, edited by Chr. Dipper and M. Vogt, 107–134. Darmstadt: Verlag TH Darmstadt.

Delekat, L. 1969. *Phönizier in Amerika. Die Echtheit der 1873 bekanntgewordenen kanaanäischen (altsidonischen) Inschrift aus Paraiba in Brasilien nachgewiesen*. Bonner biblische Beiträge 32. Bonn: Hanstein.

Demand, N. H. 2013. *A History of Ancient Greece in Its Mediterranean Context*. 3rd ed. Cornwall-on-Hudson: Sloan.Deme, A., and S. K. McIntosh, S.K. 2006. 'Excavations at Walaldé. : New Light on the Settlement of the Middle Senegal Valley by Iron-using Using Peoples.' *Journal of African Archaeology* 4: 317–347.

Dench, E. 2007. 'Ethnography and History'. In *A Companion to Greek and Roman Historiography*, edited by J. Marincola, 493–503. Oxford: Blackwell.

Desanges, J. 1978. *Recherchers sur l'activité des méditerranéens aux confins de l 'Afrique*. Rome: École française de Rome.

Di Cosmo, N. 2000. 'Ancient City-States of the Tarim Basin'. In M.H. Hansen (ed.). *A Comparative Study of Thirty City-State Cultures*, edited by M. H. Hansen, 393–407. Kopenhagen: 393–407.

Di Cosmo, N. 2002. *Ancient China and Its Enemies: The Rise of Nomadic Power in East Asian History*. Cambridge: Cambridge University Press.

Dickie, M. 1995. 'The Geography of Homer's World'. In *Homer's World: Fiction, Tradition, Reality*, edited by O. Andersen and M. Dickie, 29–56. Bergen: Aström.

Dickinson, O. 2010. 'The Collapse at the End of the Bronze Age'. In *The Oxford Handbook of the Bronze Age Aegean (ca. 3000–1000 BC)*, edited by E. H. Cline, 483–490. Oxford: Oxford University Press.

Dicks, D. R. 1970. *Early Greek Astronomy to Aristotle*. Bristol: Thames and Hudson.

Dihle, A. 1978. 'Die entdeckungsgeschichtlichen Voraussetzungen des Indienhandels der römischen Kaiserzeit'. *ANRW*: 546–580.

Dihle, A. 1984a. 'Der Seeweg nach Indien'. In A. Dihle, *Antike und Orient. Gesammelte Aufsätze*, edited by V. Pöschl and H. Petersmann, 109–117. Heidelberg: Carl Winter Universitätsverlag.

Dihle, A. 1984b. 'Die Sendung des Inders Theophilos'. In A. Dihle, *Antike und Orient. Gesammelte Aufsätze*, edited by V. Pöschl and H. Petersmann, 102–108. Heidelberg: Carl Winter Universitätsverlag.

Dihle, A. 1984c. 'Serer und Chinesen'. In A. Dihle, *Antike und Orient. Gesammelte Aufsätze*, edited by V. Pöschl and H. Petersmann, 201–215. Heidelberg: Carl Winter Universitätsverlag.

Dihle, A. 1984d. 'Indische Philosophen bei Clemens Alexandrinus'. In A. Dihle, *Antike und Orient. Gesammelte Aufsätze*, edited by V. Pöschl and H. Petersmann, 78–88. Heidelberg: Carl Winter Universitätsverlag.

Dihle, A. 1984e. 'Buddha und Hieronymus'. In A. Dihle, *Antike und Orient. Gesammelte Aufsätze*, edited by V. Pöschl and H. Petersmann, 98–101. Heidelberg: Carl Winter Universitätsverlag.

Dihle, A. 1984f. 'Plinius und die Geographische Wissenschaft in der Römischen Kaiserzeit'. In A. Dihle, *Antike und Orient. Gesammelte Aufsätze*, edited by V. Pöschl and H. Petersmann, 174–190. Heidelberg: Carl Winter Universitätsverlag.

Dihle, A. 1994. *Die Griechen und die Fremden*. Munich: C. H. Beck.

Dihle, A. 2000. 'Die Philosophie der Barbaren'. In *Gegenwelten zu den Kulturen Griechenlands und Roms in der Antike*, edited by T. Hölscher, 183–203. Munich/Leipzig: De Gruyter.

Dodds, E. R. 1951. *The Greeks and the Irrational*. Berkeley: University of California Press.

Domínguez, A. J. 2000. 'Phocaeans and Other Ionians in Western Mediterranean'. In *Die Ägäis und das westliche Mittelmeer. Beziehungen und Wechselwirkungen 8. bis 5. Jh. v. Chr.*, edited by F. Krenzinger, 507–513. Archäologische Forschungen 4. Vienna: Verlag der Österreichischen Akademie der Wissenschaften.

Domínguez, A. J. 2006. 'Greeks in the Iberian Peninsula'. In *Greek Colonisation: An Account of Greek Colonies and Other Settlements Overseas*, Vol. 1, edited by G. R. Tsetskhladzem, 429–505. Boston/Leiden: Brill.

Donlan, W. 1980. *The Aristocratical Ideal in Ancient Greece*. Colorado: Coronado Press.

Dorati, M. 1995. 'Ctesia falsario?'. *Quaderni di Storia* 21: 33–52.

Dornseiff, F. 1937. 'Odysseus' letzte Fahrt'. *Hermes* 72: 353–355.

Dossin, G. 1970. 'La route de l'etain en Mesopotamie au temps de Zimri-Lim'. *Revue d'Assyriologie* 64: 97–106.

Dothan, T. u. M. 1992. *People of the Sea: The Search for the Philistines*. New York: Scribner.

Dougherty, C. 1993. *The Poetics of Colonization. From City to Text in Archaic Greece*. New York/Oxford: Oxford University Press.

Dougherty, C. 2001. *The Raft of Odysseus. The Ethnographic Imagination of Homer's Odyssey*. Oxford: Oxford University Press.

Dousa, T. M. 2011. 'Common Motifs in the "Orphic" B Tablets and Egyptian Finery Texts. Continuity or Convergence?' In *The 'Orphic' Gold Tablets and Greek Religion: Further Along the Path*, edited by R. G. Edmonds III, 120–164. Cambridge: Cambridge University Press.

Dowden, K. 1980. 'Deux Notes sur les Scythes et les Arimaspes'. *Revue des Études Grecques* 93: 486–492.

Drews, R. 1993. *The End of the Bronze Age: Changes in Warfare and the Catastrophe ca. 1200 B.C.* Princeton, NJ: Princeton University Press.

Driessen, J., and C. MacDonald. 1984. 'Some Military Aspects of the Aegean in the Late 15th and 14th Centuries B.C.'. *BSA* 79: 49–74.

Dueck, D., and K. Brodersen. 2012. *Geography in Classical Antiquity*. Key Themes in Ancient History. Cambridge: Cambridge University Press.

Dunbabin, T. J. 1968. *The Western Greeks: The History of Sicily and South Italy from the Foundation of the Greek Colonies to 480 BC*. Oxford: Oxford University Press.

Duncan-Jones, R. 1994. *Money and Government in the Roman Empire*. Cambridge: Cambridge University Press.

Ebner, E. 1906. *Geographische Hinweise und Anklänge in Plutarchs Schrift De facie in orbe lunae*. Munich: Theodor Ackermann.

Edson, E., ed. 2007. *The World Map 1300–1492: The Resistance of Tradition and Transformation*. Baltimore, MD: Johns Hopkins University Press.

Ehrlich, C. S. 1996. *The Philistines in Transition: A History from ca. 1000–730 B.C.E.* Studies in the History and Culture of the Ancient Near East 10. Leiden/New York/Cologne: Brill.

Eliade, M. 1992. *Schamanen, Götter und Mysterien. Die Welt der alten Griechen*. Freiburg et al.: Herder.

Elliot, H. 1970. *The Old World and the New*. Cambridge: Cambridge University Press.

Ellmers, D. 2010. 'Der Krater von Vix und der Reisebericht des Pytheas von Masssilia'. *AKB* 40: 363–381.

Emanuel, J. 2013. 'Cretan Lie and Historical Truth. Examining Odysseus' Raid on Egypt in its Late Bronze Age Context'. In *Donum natalicium digitaliter confectum Gregorio Nagy septuagenario a discipulis collegis familiaribus oblatum*, edited by D. Elmer, D. Frame, L. Muellner, and V. Bers, 1–41. Cambridge, MA: Harvard University Press.

Emanuel, J. P. 2021. *Naval Warfare and Maritime Conflict in the Late Bronze and Early Iron Age Mediterranean*, Vol. 2, *Ancient Warfare.* Culture and History of the Ancient Neasr East 117. Leiden/Boston: Brill.

Erdrich, M. 2014 'Römische Importe im Barbaricum—ein Reflex des Bernsteinhandels'. In *Die Bernsteinstraße, Archäologie in Deutschland Sonderheft 4*, edited by D. Quast, M. Erdrich, 72–81. Darmstadt: Wissenschaftliche Buchgesellschaft/Theiss.

Fabre, D. 2004. *Seafaring in Ancient Egypt.* London: Periplus Publishing.

Fabre, P. 1992. 'Les grecs à la découverte de l'Atlantique'. *REA* 94: 11–21.

Fage, J. D. 2002. *A History of Africa.* 4th ed. London/New York: Routledge.

Falchetta, P. 2006. *Fra Mauro's World Map: With a Commentary and Translation of the Inscriptions.* Terrarum orbis 5. Turnhout: Brepols.

Falchetta, P. 2008. 'The Use of Portolan Charts in European Navigation During the Middle Ages'. In *Europa im Weltbild des Mittelalters. Kartographische Konzepte* 10, edited by I. Baumgärtner and H. Kugler, 269–276. Berlin: de Gruyter.

Faure, P. 1993. *Magie der Düfte. Eine Kulturgeschichte der Wohlgerüche.* Munich: Dtv.

Fentress, E. 2011. 'Slavers on Chariots'. In *Money, Trade and Trade Routes in Pre-Islamic North Africa*, edited by A. Dowler and E. R. Galwin, 65–71. British Museum Research Publication 176. London: British Museum Press.

Ferguson, J. 1969. 'Classical Contacts with West Africa'. In *Africa in Classical Antiquity: Nine Studies*, edited by L. A. Thompson and J. Fertuson, 1–25. Ibadan: Ibadan University Press.

Ferguson, J. 1978. 'China and Rome'. *ANRW* II 9, 2: 581–603.

Fernández-Armesto, F. 1987. *Before Columbus: Exploration and Colonization from the Mediterranean to the Atlantic: 1229–1492.* London: Red Globe Press.

Fernández-Armesto, F. 1991. *Columbus.* New York: Oxford University Press.

Fernández-Armesto, F. 2001. 'Maritime History and World History'. In *Maritime History as World History: New Perspectives on Maritime History*, edited by D. Finamore, 7–34. Gainesville: University Press of Florida.

Fernández-Armesto, F. 2006. *Pathfinders: A Global History of Exploration.* New York/London: W.W. Norton.

Filliozat, J. 1964. *The Classical Doctrine of Indian Medicine. Its Origins and Its Greek Parallels.* Delhi: Munshiram Manoharlal Oriental Booksellers and Publishers.

Finkelstein, I., and N. A. Silberman. 2006. *David and Solomon: In Search of the Bible's Sacred Kings and the Roots of the Western Tradition.* New York: Free Press.

Flint, V. I. J. 1984. 'Monsters and Antipodes in the Early Middle Ages and Enlightment'. *Viator* 15: 65–80.

Flint, V. I. J. 1992. *The Imaginative Landscape of Christopher Columbus.* Princeton, NJ: Princeton University Press.

Flint, V. I. J. 2009. 'Travel Fact and Fiction in the Voyages of Columbus'. In *Medieval Ethnographies: European Perceptions of the World Beyond*, edited by J. P. Rubiés, 329–345. The Expansion of Latin Europe 1000–1500. Farnham/Burlington: Routledge.

Follis, E. R. 1978. 'Israel and the Sea: A Test Case in Hellenosemitic Studies'. *Society of Biblical Literature: Seminar Papers* 13: 407–415.

Foxhall, L. 2005. 'Cultures, Landscapes, and Identities in the Mediterranean World'. In *Mediterranean Paradigms and Classical Antiquity*, edited by I. Malkin, 75–92. London/New York: Routlidge.

Fraser, P. M. 1994. 'The World of Theophrastus'. In *Greek Historiography*, edited by S. Hornblower, 167–191. Oxford: Clarendon Press.

Fynes, R. C. C. 1993. 'Isis and Pattinī: The Transmission of a Religious Idea from Roman Egypt to India'. *Journal of the Royal Asiatic Society of Great Britain and Ireland* 3: 377–391.

Gabrielsen, V. 2013. 'Rhodes and the Ptolemaic Kingdoms: The Commercial Infrastructure'. In *The Ptolemies, the Sea, and the Nile: Studies in Waterborne Power*, edited by K. Buraselis, M. Stefanou, and D. J. Thompson, 66–81. Cambridge: Cambridge University Press.

Gail, A. 2009. 'A New Discovery: Aśoka's Minor Rock Edict I'. *Pandanus* 3: 127–129.

Garrard, T. F. 1982. 'Myth and Metrology. The Early Trans-Saharan Gold Trade'. *JAH 32,4*: 443–461.

Gawlikowski, M. 1994. 'Palmyra as a Trading Centre'. *Iraq* 56: 27–33.

Gehrig, U. 1990. 'Die Phönizier in Griechenland.' In *Die Phönizier im Zeitalter Homers*, edited by U. Gehrig and H. G. Niemeyer, 23–32. Mainz: Philipp von Zabern.

Georganas, I. 2010. 'Weapons and Warfare'. In *The Oxford Handbook of the Bronze Age Aegean (ca. 3000– 1000 BC)*, edited by E. H. Cline, 305–314. Oxford: Oxford University Press.

Georges, P. 1994. *Barbarian Asia and the Greek Experience: From the Archaic Period to the Age of Xenophon*. Baltimore/London: John Hopkins University Press.

Geus, K. 2000. 'Utopie und Geographie. Zum Weltbild der Griechen in frühhellenistischer Zeit'. *Orbis Terrarum* 6: 54–91.

Geus, K. 2002. *Eratosthenes von Kyrene. Studien zur hellenistischen Kultur- und Wissenschaftsgeschichte*. Municher Beiträge zur Papyrusforschung und antiken Rechtsgeschichte 92. Munich: C. H. Beck.

Geus, K. 2003. 'Space and Geography'. In *A Companion to the Hellenistic Culture*, edited by A. Erskine, 232–245. Malden/Oxford: Blackwell.

Geus, K. 2013. 'Claudius Ptolemy on Egypt and East Africa'. In *The Ptolemies, the Sea, and the Nile. Studies in Waterborne Power*, edited by K. Buraselis, M. Stefanou, and D. J. Thompson et al., 218–231. Cambridge: Cambridge University Press.

Gisinger, F. 1924. 'Geographie'. *RE Suppl.* 4: 521–685.

Gisinger, F. 1963. 'Pytheas (1)'. *RE* 24: 314–366.

Gómez-Espelósin, F. J. 2000. *El Descubrimiento del mundo. Geografía y viajeros en la Antigua Grecia*. Madrid: Ediciones AKAL.

Gopal, L. 1961. 'Textiles in Ancient India'. *JESHO* 4: 42–64.

Graf, D. F. 1996. 'The Roman East from the Chinese Perspective'. *AAAS* 42: 199–216.

Grafton A., 1992. *New Worlds, Ancient Texts: The Power of Tradition and the Shock of Discovery*. Cambridge, MA/London: Harvard University Press.

Grainger, J. D. 1990. *Seleukos Nikator: Constructing a Hellenistic Kingdom*. London/New York: Routledge.

Green, P. 1991. *Alexander of Macedon, 356–323 B.C.: A Historical Biograph*. Revised and enlarged ed. Berkeley/Los Angeles/London: University of California Press.

Greenblatt, S. 1998. *Wunderbare Besitztümer. Die Erfindung des Fremden. Reisende und Entdecker*. Berlin: Wagenbach.

Grimm, R. R. 1977. *Paradisus Coelestis. Paradisus Terrestris. Zur Auslegungsgeschichte des Paradieses im Abendland bis um 1200*. Medium Aevum 33. Munich: Fink.

Groom, N. 1981. *Frankincense and Myrrh*. New York: Longman.

Gruen, E. S. 2012. *Rethinking the Other in Antiquity*. Princeton, NJ/Oxford: Princeton University Press.

Gunawardana, R. A. L. H. 1990. 'Seaways to Sielediba. Changing Patterns of Navigation in the Indian Ocean and their Impact on Precolonial Sri Lanka'. In *Sri Lanka and the Silk Road of the Sea*, edited by S. Bandaranayake, 25–44. Colombo: Sri Lanka National Commion for Unesco and the Central Cultural Fund.

Gupta, S. 2005. 'Monsoon Environments and the Indian Ocean Interaction Sphere in Antiquity. 3000 B.C.–A.D. 300'. In *Monsoon and Civilization*, edited by Y. Yasuda, 133–160. New Delhi: Roli Books.

Habicht, C. 2013. 'Eudoxos of Cyzicus and Ptolemaic Exploration of the Sea Route to India'. In *The Ptolemies, the Sea and the Nile. Studies in Waterborne Power*, edited by K. Buraselis et al., 197–206. Cambridge: Cambridge University Press.

Hänger, C. 2001. *Die Welt im Kopf. Raumbilder und Stretegie im römischen Kaiserreich*. Göttingen: Vandenhoek & Ruprecht.

Halkias, G. T. 2014. 'When the Greeks Converted the Buddha. Asymmetrical Transfers of Knowledge in Indo-Greek Cultures'. In *Religion and Trade: Religious Formation, Transformation and Cross-Cultural Exchange between East and West*, edited by P. Wick and V. Rabens, 65–115. Leiden/Boston: Brill.

Hall, E. 1989. *Inventing the Barbarian: Greek Self-Definition through Tragedy*. Oxford: Clarendon Press.

Hall, K. R. 2010. *A History of Early Southeast Asia: Maritime Trade and Social Developments 100–1500*. Lanham: Rawan & Littlefield.

Hamel, G. 1995. 'Taking the Argo to Ninive: Jonah and Jason in a Mediterranean Context'. *Judaism* 44: 341–359.

Hamilton, B. 2009. 'Continental Drift: Prester John's Progress Through the Indies'. In *Medieval Ethnographies: European Perceptions of the World Beyond*, edited by J. P. Rubiés, 121–153. The Expansion of Latin Europe 9. Farnham/Burlington: Routledge.

Hands, A. R. 1969. 'The Consolidation of Carthaginian Power in the Fifth Century B.C.'. In *Africa in Classical Antiquity. Nine Studies*, edited by L. A. Thompson and J. Ferguson, 81–98. Ibadan: Ibadan University Press.

Hänger, C. 2001. *Die Welt im Kopf. Raumbilder und Strategie im Römischen Kaiserreich.* Göttingen: Vandenhoeck & Ruprecht.

Harding, A. 1984. *The Myceneans and Europe.* Bath 1984: Emerald.

Harding, A. 1990. 'The Wessex Connection. Developments and Perspectives' In *Orientalisch-Ägäische Einflüsse in der Europäischen Bronzezeit*, edited by P. Schauer, 139–154. Römisch-Germanisches Zentralmuseum Monographien 15. Bonn: Habelt

Harris, W.V., and K. Iara, eds. 2011. *Maritime Technology in the Ancient Economy. Ship-Design and Navigation.* Portsmouth, RI: Journal of Roman Archaeology.

Harris, W.V. (ed.) 2005. *Rethinking the Mediterranean.* Oxford: Oxford University Press.

Harrison, J. E. 1904. 'Mystica Vannus Iacchi'. *JHS* 24: 241–254.

Harrison, T. 2012. *The Horse Road.* New York: Bloomsbury.

Hartog, F. 2001. *Memories of Odysseus: Frontier Tales from Ancient Greece.* Edinburgh: University of Chicago Press.

Hauben, H. 1985. 'Ceux qui naviguent sur la mer extérieure (SB III 7169)'. *ZPE* 59: 135–136.

Hawkes, C. F. 1975. *Pytheas: Europe and the Greek Explorers: A Lecture Delivered at New College, Oxford on 20th May.* Oxford: Blackwell.

Healy, J.F. 1999. *Pliny the Elder on Science and Technology.* Oxford.

Healy, J. F. 1996. "'Palmyra and the Arabian Gulf Trade."'. *ARAM* 8: 33–37.

Healy, J. F. 1999. *Pliny the Elder on Science and Technology.* Oxford.

Heckel, W. 1992. *The Marshals of Alexander's Empire.* London: Routledge.

Heil, M., and R. Schulz. 2015. 'Who Was Maes Titianus?' *Journal of Ancient Civilizations* 30: 72–84.

Heilen, S. 2000. 'Eudoxos von Knidos und Pytheas von Massilia'. In *Geographie und verwandte Wissenschaften*, edited by W. Hübner, 55–74. Stuttgart: Steiner.

Heimberg, U. 1981. *Gewürze, Weihrauch, Seide. Welthandel in der Antike.* Schriften Limesmuseum Aalen 27. Stuttgart: Regierungspräsidium Stuttgart.

Heinen, H. 2001. 'Greeks, Iranians and Romans on the Northern Shore of the Black Sea'. In *North Pontic Archaeology: Recent Discoveries and Studies*, edited by G. R. Tsetskhladze, 1–23. Leiden: Brill.

Heinimann, F. 1965. *Nomos und Physis. Herkunft und Bedeutung einer Antithese im griechischen Denken des 5. Jahrhunderts.* Schweizerische Beiträge zur Altertumswissenschat 1. Basel: Friedrich Reinhardt.

Helck, W. 1995. *Die Beziehungen Ägyptens und Vorderasiens zur Ägäis bis ins 7. Jahrhundert v. Chr.* 2nd ed. Darmstadt: Wissenschaftliche Buchgesellschaft.

Hennig, R. 1926. 'Neue Erkenntnisse zur Geographie Homer'. *RhM* 75: 266–286.

Hennig, R. 1934. *Die Geographie des homerischen Epos. Eine Studie über die erdkundlichen Elemente der Odyssee.* Leipzig/Berlin: Teubner.

Hennig, R. 1935. 'Herodots Handelsweg zu den sibirischen Issedonen'. *Klio* 28: 242–254.

Hennig, R. 1944. *Terrae Incognitae. Eine Zusammenstellung und kritische Berertung der wichtigen vorcolumbischen Entdeckungsreisen an Hand der darüber vorliegenden Originalberichte.* Leiden: Brill.

Hermary, A. 2004. 'The Greeks in Marseilles and the Western Mediterranean'. In *The Greeks Beyond the Aegean. From Marseilles to Bactria*, edited by V. Karageorghis, 59–77. Nicosia: Brill.

Herrmann, A. 1926. 'Die Irrfahrten des Odysseus'. *Meereskunde* 15 (3): 1–32.

Herzfeld, E. 1968. *The Persian Empire.* Wiesbaden: Steiner.

Hiller, S. 1991. 'The Mycenaeans and the Black Sea'. In *Thalassa. L'Egée préhistorique et la mer*, edited by R. Laffineur and L. Basch, 207–216. Aegaeum 7. Liège: Universitè de Liège.

Hess, R. 1992. 'Caphtor'. In *Anchor Bible Dictionary*, Vol. 1, edited by D. N. Freedman, 869–870. New York: Yale University Press.

Hiltebeitel, A. 2011. *Dharma: Its Early History in Law, Religion, and Narrative.* Oxford: Oxford University Press.

Hinkkanen, M.-L., and D. Kirby. 2000. *The Baltic and the North Seas.* New York: Routledge.

Hirsch, S. W. 1985. *The Friendship of the Barbarians: Xenophon and the Persian Empire.* Hannover/London: University Press of New England.

Hitchener, R. B. 2005. 'The Advantages of Wealth and Luxury. The Case for Economic Growth in the Roman Empire'. In *The Ancient Economy: Evidence and Models*, edited by G. Manning and I. Morris, 207–222. Stanford: Stanford University Press.

Hodge, A. T. 1998. *Ancient Greek France.* Bristol: Bristol Classical Press.

Hoekstra, A. 1981. *Epic Verse before Homer: Three Studies.* Amsterdam: Royal Netherlands Academy.

Hoessly, F. 2001. *Katharsis. Reinigung als Heilverfahren. Studien zum Ritual der archaischen und klassischen Zeit sowie zum Corpus JHippocraticum.* Göttingen: Vandenhoeck & Ruprecht.

Hoffner, H. A. 1968. 'A Hittite Analogue to the David and Goliath Contrest of Champions?' *Catholic Biblical Quarterly* 30: 220–225.

Hoftijzer, J., and W. H. Van Soldt. 1998. 'Texts from Ugarit Pertaining to Seafraing'. In *Seagoing Ships and Seamanship in the Bronze Age Levant,* edited by S. Wachsmann, 333–344. College Station: Texas A&M University Press.

Hölbl, G. 1994. *Geschichte des Ptolemäerreiches. Politik, Ideologie und religiöse Kultur von Alexander dem Großen bis zur römischen Eroberung.* Darmstadt: Wissenschaftliche Buchgesellschaft.

Hölscher, G. 1949. *Drei Erdkarten. Ein Beitrag zur Erderkenntnis des hebräischen Altertums.* SAH 1944/8, 3. Abhandlung. Heidelberg: Carl Winter Universitätsverlag.

Hölscher, U. 1990. *Die Odyssee. Epos zwischen Märchen und Roman.* 2nd ed. Munich: C. H. Beck.

Holt, F. L. 1988. *Alexander the Great and Bactria.* Leiden: Brill.

Holzberg, N. 1996. 'Utopias and fantastic travel: Euhemerus, Iambulus'. In *The Novel in the Ancient World*, edited by G. Schmeling, 621–628. Leiden: Brill.

Horden, P. 2005. 'Travel Sickness. Medicine and Mobility in the Mediterranean'. In *Rethinking the Mediterranean*, edited by W.V. Harris, 179–199. Oxford: Oxford University Press.

Horden, P., and N. Purcell. 2000. *The Corrupting Sea: A Study of Mediterranean History*. Malden: Wiley Blackwell.

Horowitz, W. 1998. *Mesopotamian Cosmic Geography*. Mesopotamian Civilizations 8. Winona Lake, IN: Eisenbrauns/Pennsylvania University Press.

Hosten, H. 1912. 'The Mouthless Indians'. *JPASB* 8: 291–301.

Hubbell, M. 1935. 'Ptolemy's Zoo'. *CJ* 31: 68–77.

Hudson, G. F. 1924. 'The Land of the Budini: A Problem in Ancient Geography'. *CR* 38: 158–162.

Hughues-Brock, H. 2005. 'Amber and Some Other Travellers in the Bronze Age Aegean and Europe'. In *Autochthon: Papers Presented to O. T. P. K. Dickinson*, edited by A. Dakouri-Hild, 301–316. Oxford: Archaeopress.

Hundt, H.-J. 1969. 'Über vorgeschichtliche Seidenfunde'. *JRGZ* 16: 59–71.

Hurwit, J. M. 1987. *The Art and Culture of Early Greece: 1100–480 B.C.* Ithaca, NY/London: Cornell university Press.

Huss, W. 1989. 'Die antike Mittelmeerwelt und Innerafrika bis zum Ende der Herrschaft der Karthager und Ptolemäer'. In *Afrika. Entdeckung und Erforschung eines Kontinents*, edited by H. Duchhardt et al., 1–29. Cologne/Vienna: Böhlau.

Huss, W. 1985. *Geschichte der Karthager*. Munich: C. H. Beck.

Huss, W. 2001. *Ägypten in hellenistischer Zeit 332–30 v. Chr.* Munich: C. H. Beck.

Hyde, J. K. 2009. 'Ethnographers in Search of an Audience'. In *Medieval Ethnographies: European Perceptions of the Worlds Beyond*, edited by J. P. Rubiés, 65–119. The Expansion of Latin Europe 1000–1500. Farnham/Burlington: Routledge.

Immerwahr, H. R. 1966. *Form and Thought in Herodotus*. Cleveland, OH: American Philological Association.

Isaac, B. H. 2004. *The Invention of Racism in Classical Antiquity*. Princeton, NJ/Oxford: Princeton University Press.

Ivantchik, A. I. 2005. *Am Vorabend der Kolonisation. Das nördliche Schwarzmeergebiet und die Steppennomaden des 8. – 7. Jhs. v. Chr. in der klassischen Literaturtradition. Mündliche Überlieferung, Literatur und Geschichte*. Pontus Septentrionalis 3. Berlin/Moscow: Paleograph Press.

Jackson, P. 2009. 'William of Rubruck in the Mongol Empire. Perception and Prejudices'. In *Medieval Ethnographies: European Perceptions of the Worlds Beyon*, edited by J. P. Rubiés, 273–290. The Expansion of Latin Europe 1000–1500. Farnham/Burlington: Routledge.

Jacoby, F. 1912. 'Hekataios (3)'. *RE* 7, 2: 2667–2750.

Jansari, S., and R. Ricot. 2016. 'Megasthenes and the Astomoi: A Case Study'. In *Megasthenes und seine Zeit/Megasthenes and His Time*, edited by J. Wiedehöfer, H. Brinkhaus, R. Bichler, 191–201. Wiesbaden: Harrassowitz.

Jha, D. N. 2004. *Early India. A Concise History*. Dehli: Manohar.

Jones, B. E., and L. Vagnetti. 1991. 'Traders and Craftsmen in the Central Mediterranean. Archaeological Evidence and Archaeometric Research'. In *Bronze Age Trade in the Mediterranean*, edited by N. H. Gale, 127–147. Studies in Mediterranean Archaeology 90. Gothenburg: Aströms.

Jongman, W. M. 2007. 'The Early Roman Empire: Consumption'. In *The Cambridge Economic History of the Greco-Roman World*, edited by W. Scheidel et al., 592–618. Cambridge, MA: Cambridge University Press.

Journès, H., Y. Georgelin. 2000. *Pythéas, Explorateur et Astronome*. Ollioules: Éditions de la Nerthe.

Jung, R. 2009. 'Sie vernichteten sie, als ob sie niemals existiert hätten. Was blieb von der Zerstörung der Seevölker?' In *Schlachtfeldarchäologie*, edited by H. Meller, 31–48. Halle: Landesamt für Denkmalpflege und Archäologioe Sachsen Anhalt.

Jung, R., and M. Mehofer. 2005–2006. 'A Sword of Naue II Type from Ugarit and the Historical Significance of Italian-Type Weaponry in the Eastern Mediterranean' *AEA* 8: 111–135.

Jung, R., and M. Mehofer. 2013. 'Mycenaean Greece and Bronze Age Italy. Cooperation, Trade or War?' *AkorrBl* 43 (2): 175–193.

Káadáar, Z. 1972. "'Some Problems Concerning the Scientific Authenticity of Classical Authors on Libyan Fauna."'. *ACD* 8: 11–16.

Kahn, C. H. 1985. *Anaximander and the Origins of Greek Cosmology.* 2nd ed. New York/London: Philadelphia Centium.

Kahn, H. A. 1994. *The Birth of the European Identity: The Europe-Asia Contrast in Greek Thought 490–322 B.C.* Nottingham: University of Nottingham.

Kalogerakos, I. G. 1996. *Seele und Unsterblichkeit. Untersuchungen zur Vorsokratik bis Empedokles*. Stuttgart/Leipzig: Teubner.

Käppel, L. 2001. 'Bilder des Nordens im frühen antiken Griechenland'. In *Ultima Thule. Bilder des Nordens von der Antike bis zur Gegenwart*, edited by A. Engel-Braunschmidt et al., 11–27. Imaginatio Borealis 1. Frankfurt am Main: Peter Lang.

Karttunen, K. 1986. 'On the Contacts of South India with the Western World in Ancient Times and the Mission of the Apostle Thomas'. In *South Asian Religion and Society: Studies on Asian Topics*, edited by A. Parpola and B. Smidt Hansen, 189–204. Kopenhagen/London: Riverdale.

Karttunen, K. 1987. 'The Country of Fabulous Beasts and Naked Philosophers. India in Classical and Medieval Literature'. *Arctos* 21: 43–52.

Karttunen, K. 1989. *India in Early Greek Literature*. Studia Orientalia 65. Helsinki: Finnish Oriental Society.

Karttunen, K. 1991. 'The India of Ctesias and Its Criticism'. In *Graeco-Indica: India's Cultural Contects with the Greek World*, edited by U. P. Arora, 74–85. New Delhi: Ramanand Vidya Bhawan.

Karttunen, K. 2002. 'The Ethnograpy of the Frings'. In *Brill's Companion to Herodotos*, edited by E. J. Bakker, I. F. de Jong, and H. van Wees, 457–474. Leiden: Brill.

Kehoe, D. 2012. 'Contract Labor'. In *The Cambridge Companion to the Roman Economy*, edited by W. Scheidel, 114–130. Cambridge: Cambridge University Press.

Kenoyer, J. M. 2006. 'New Perspectives on the Mauryan and Kushan Periods'. In *Between the Empires: Society in India 300 BCE to 400 CE*, edited by P. Olivelle, 33–49. Oxford: Oxford University Press.

Killick, D. 2004. 'Review Essay: What Do We Know About African Iron Working'. *Journal of African Archaeology* 2: 97–112.

Kim, H. J. 2009. *Ethnicity and Foreigners in Ancient Greece and China*. London: Duckworth.

Kim, H. J. 2013. 'The Invention of the "Barbarian" in Late Sixth Century BC Ionia.' In *Ancient Ethnography: New Approaches*, edited by E. Almagor and J. Skinner, 25–48. London: Bloomsbury Academics.

Kingsley, P. 1994. 'Greeks, Shamans and Magi'. *Studia Iranica* 23: 187–198.

Kingsley, P. 1995. *Ancient Philosophy, Mystery, and Magic. Empedocles and Pythagorean Tradition*. Oxford: Oxford University Press.

Kleineberg, A., et al., eds. 2011. *Germania und die Insel Thule. Die Entschlüsselung von Ptolemaios' Atlas der Oikumene*. Darmstadt: Wissenschaftliche Buchgesellschaft.

Knapp, A. B. 1991. 'Spice, Drugs, Grain and Grog. Organic Goods in the Bronze Age East Mediterranean Trade'. In *Bronze Age Trade in the Mediterranean*, edited by N. H. Gale, 21–68. Jonsered. Aströms.

Knapp, A. B. 1993. 'Thalassocracies in Bronze Age Eastern Mediterranean Trade. Making and Breaking the Myth'. *World Archaeology* 24: 332–347.

Knefelkamp, U. 1986. *Die Suche nach dem Reich des Priesterkönigs Johannes*. Gelsenkirchen: Andreas Müller.

Koch, I. 2017. 'Early Philistia Revisited and Revised'. In *Rethinking Israel: Studies in the History and Archaeology of Ancient Israel in Honour of Israel Finkelstein*, edited by O. Lipschits et al., 189–205. Winona Lake, IN: Eisenbrauns. Pennsylvania State University Press.

Kominko, M. 2008. 'New Perspectives on Paradise. The Levels of Reality, Byzantine and Latin Medieval Maps'. In *Cartography in Antiquity and the Middle Ages: Fresh Perspectives, New Methods*, edited by R. J. A. Talbert and R. W. Unger, 139–153. Leiden: Brill.

Kordosis, M. 1992. *China and the Greek World. An Introduction to the Greek-Chinese Studies with Special Reference to the Chinese Sources: Hellenistic-Roman-Early Byzantine period (2nd c. B.C.–6th c. A.D.)*. Thessaloniki: M. Kordosis.

Kordosis, M. 1999. 'The Limits of the Known Lands (Ecumene) in the East according to Cosmas Indicopleustes: *Tzinista (China) and the Ocean*'. *Byzantium* 69: 99–106.

Kortenbeutel, H. 1931. *Der ägyptische Süd- und Osthandel in der Politik der Ptolemäer und römischen Kaiser*. Berlin: Haffmann.

Kosak, J. C. 2000. 'Polis Nosousa: Greek Ideas about the City and Disease in the Fifth Century BC.' In *Death and Disease in the Ancient City*, edited by V. M. Hope and E. Marshall, 35–54. London/New York: Routledge.

Kosmin, P. J. 2014. *The Land of the Elephant Kings: Space, Territory, and Ideology in the Seleucid Empire*. Cambridge, MA/London: Harvard University Press.

Koster, A. 2014. 'Römische Bernsteinkunst aus der Provinz Germania inferior'. In *Die Bernsteinstraße, Archäologie in Deutschland Sonderheft 4*, edited by D. Quast and M. Erdrich, 65–71. Darmstadt: Wissenschaftliche Buchgesellschaft/Theiss.

Kranz, W. 1915. 'Die Irrfahrten des Odysseus'. *Hermes* 50: 93–112.

Krebs, C. B. 2006. '"Imaginary Geography" in Caesar's Bellum Gallicum'. *AJPh* 127: 111–136.

Krings, V., ed. 1995. *La civilization phénicienne et punique. Manuel de recherché*. Leiden: Brill.

Kristensen, A. K. G. 1988. *Who Were the Cimmerians, and Where Did They Come From? Sargon II, the Cimmerians, and Rusa I*. Historisk-filosofiske Meddelelser 57. Kopenhagen: The Royal Dutch Academy of Science and Letters.

Krüger, R. 2000. *Das Überleben des Erdkugelmodells in der Spätantike (ca. 60 v. u. Z–ca. 550)*. Eine Welt ohne Amerika 2. Berlin: Weidler.

Krüger, R. 2012. *Moles globosa, globus terrae und arenosus globus in Spätantike und Mittelalter. Eine Kritik des Mythos von der Erdscheibe*. Berlin: Weidler.

Kuckenberg, M. 2010. *Das Zeitalter der Keltenfürsten. Eine europäische Hochkultur*. Stuttgart: Klett-Cotta.

Kulke, H., and D. Rothermund. 2016. *A History of India*. 6th ed. London/New York: Routledge.

Kuhrt, A. 2000. *The Ancient Near East c. 3000–330 BC*, Vol. 1. 1st ed. Abingdon, 1995; repr. London/New York: Routledge.

Kumar Thaplyal, K. 2009. *A New Aśokan Inscription from Ratanpurwa*. Jnana-Pravaha Monograph 1. Benares: Irtāna Ravāha. Center for Cultural Studies.

Lane Fox, R. 2004. *Alexander the Great*. London: Penguin.

Lane Fox, R. 2008. *Travelling Heroes: Greeks and their Myths in the Epic Age of Homer*. London: Penguin.

Lanfranchi, G. 2000. 'The Ideological and Political Impact of the Neo-Assyrian Imperial Expansion on the Greek World in the 8th and 7th Century'. In *The Heirs of Assyria*, edited by R. Whiting, S. Aro, 7–34. Helsinki: Pennsylvania State University Press.

Lange, D. 2010. 'The Emergence of Social Complexity in the Southern Chad Basin toward 500 BC: Archaeological and Other Evidence'. *Borno Museum Society Newsletter*, 68–71.

Lange, D. 2011. *The Founding of Kanem by Assyrian Refugees ca. 600 BCE: Documentary, Linguistic, and Archaeological Evidence*, 23–27. Boston: University Working Papers African Studies.

Lascarides-Zannas, E. 1981. 'Greece and South India. From Ptolemy Philadelphus (283–246 B.C.) to Cosmas Indicopleustes (c. 545 A.D.)'. In *Proceedings of the Fifth International Conference-Seminar of Tamil Studies*, edited by M. Arun. ācalam, 1–11. Madras: International Association of Tamil Research.

. "'A Millenary of Greek Chroniclers in India.'". In U. P. Arora (ed.). *Graeco-India. India's Cultural Contacts with the Greek World*, edited by U. P. Arora, 63–73. New u-Delhi: 63–73.

Law, R. 1980. *The Horse in African History*. Oxford: Oxford University Press.

Law, R. C. C. 1967. 'The Garamantes and Trans-Saharan Enterprise in Classical Times'. *JAH* 8: 181–200.

Lawler, A. 2012. 'Diving Into the Indian Ocean's Past'. *Science Magazine* 337: 288–289.

Le Goff, J. 1998. *Das Hochmittelalter, Weltbildr Weltgeschichte*. Frankfurt am Main: Fischer.

Le Goff, J. 2009. 'The Medieval West and the Indian Ocean. An Oneiric Horizon'. In *Medieval Ethnographies: European Perceptions of the Worlds Beyond*, edited by J. P. Rubiés, 155–173. The Expansion of Latin Europe 1000–1500. Farnham/ Burlington: Routledge.

Lerner, J. 2015. 'Regional Study: Baktria—the Crossroads of Ancient Eurasia.' In *The Cambridge World History*, Vol. IV 4, *A World with States, Empires, and Networks: 1200 BCE–900 CE*, edited by C. Benjamin, 300–324. Cambridge: Cambridge University Press.

Lesky, A. 1948. 'Aia'. *WS* 63: 22–68.

Lewis, D. M. 1984. 'Persians in Herodotus'. In *The Greek Historians: Literature and History: FS A. E. Raubitschek*, edited by M. H. Jameson, 101–117. Stanford: ANMA Libri.

Lewis, M. E. 2006. *The Construction of Space in Early China*. New York: State University of New York Press.

Lewis, M. E. 2007. *The Early Chinese Empires. Qin and Han*. Cambridge, MA/ London: Belknap Press of Harvard University Press.

Lhote, H. 1982. *Les chars rupestres sahariens. Des Syrtes au Niger, par le pays des Garamantes et des Atlantes*. Toulouse: Editions de Hespérides.

Linder, E. 1981. 'Ugarit: A Canaanite Thalassocracy'. In *Ugarit in Retrospect: Fifty years of Ugarit and Ugaritic*, edited by G. D. Young, 31–42. Winona Lake, IN: Eisenbrauns/ Penn State University Press.

Lindgren, U. 1997. 'Geographie in der Zeit der Karolinger'. In *Karl der Große und sein Nachwirken. Wissen und Weltbild*, part 1, edited by P. Butzer et al., 507–519. Brepols: Turhaut.

Lipinski, E. 2004. *Itineraria Phoenicia*. Orientalia Lovaniensia Analecta 127. Leuven/ Paris: Peeters.

Liu, X. 1990. *Ancient India and Ancient China: Trade and Religious Exchanges AD 1–600, Sec. Impr.* Oxford: Oxford University Press.

Liu, X., and L. N. Shaffer. 2007. *Connections across Eurasia: Transportation, Communication, and Cultural Exchange on the Silk Roads*. New York: McGraw Hill.

Liverani, M. 1987. 'The Collapse of the Near Eastern Regional System at the End of the Bronze Age: The Case in Syria'. In *Centre and Periphery in the Ancient World*, edited by M. Rowlands, M. Larsen, K. Kristiansen, 66–73. Cambridge: Cambridge University Press.

Liverani, M. 1999–2000. 'The Sargon Geography and the Late Assyrian Mensuration of the Earth'. *State Archives of Assyria Bulletin* 13: 57–85.

Liverani, M. 2000. 'The Libyan Caravan Road in Herodotus IV.181–189'. *JESHA* 43: 496–500,

Liverani, M. 2005. *Israel's History and the History of Israel.* Translated by C. Perei and P. R. Davies. London/Oakville: Equinox.

Llothe, H. 1982. *Les chars rupestres sahariens. Des Syrtes au Niger, par le pays des Garamantes et des Atlantes.* Toulouse: Éditions des Hespérides.

Lloyd, G. E. R., and N. Sivin. 2002. *The Way and the Word: Science and Medicine in Early Greece and China.* New Haven, CT/London: Yale University Press.

Lo Cascio, E. 2007. 'The Early Roman Empire: The State and the Economy'. In *The Cambridge Economic History of the Greco-Roman World*, edited by W. Scheidel et al., 619–647. Cambridge: Cambridge University Press.

Loewe, M. 1986. 'The Former Han Dynasty'. In *The Cambridge History of China*, Vol. 1, *The Ch'in and Han Empires 221 B.C.–A.D. 220*, edited by D. Twitchett, M. Loewe, 103–222. Cambridge: Cambridge University Press.

Londey, P. 1990. 'Greek Colonists and Delphi'. In *Greek Colonists and Native Populations*, edited by J.-P. Descoudres, 117–127. Oxford: Oxford University Press.

Lonis, R. 1978. 'Les conditions de la navigation sur la côte atlantique de l'Afrique dans l'antiquité. Le problème du retour'. In *Afrique noire et monde méditerranéen dans L'antiquité*, edited by R. Lonis, 147–162. Dakar: Les Nouvelles éditions africaines.

Lordkipanidze, O./Léveque, and P. Léveque, (eds.). 1990. *Sur les traces des Argonautes. Actes du 6e Symposion de Vani.* Colchide.

Lorton, D. 1971. 'The Supposed Expedition of Ptolemy II to Persia'. *JEA* 57: 160–164.

Lozovsky, N. 2000. *'The Earth Is Our Book'. Geographical Knowledge in the Latin West ca. 400–1000.* Ann Arbor: University of Michigan Press.

Maaß, O. 1915. *Die Irrfahrten des Odysseus im Pontos. Wissenschaftliche Beilage des Jahresberichtes des Evangelischen Gymnasiums in Gütersloh.* Gütersloh: Bertelsmann.

MacDonald, K. C. 1998. 'Before the Empire of Ghana. Pastoralism and the Origins of Cultural Complexity in the Sahel'. In *Transformations in Africa: Essays on Africa's Later Past*, edited by G. Connah, 71–103. London: Leicester University Press.

MacDonald, K. C. 2011. 'A View from the South: Sub-Saharan Evidence for Contacts Between North Africa, Mauretania and the Niger 1000 BC–AD 700'. In *Money, Trade and Trade Routes in Pre-Islamic North Africa*, edited by A. Dowler and E. R. Galwin, 72–82. British Museum Research Publication 176. London: The British Museum.

Machinist, P. 2000. 'Biblical Traditions: The Philistines and Israelite History'. In *The Sea Peoples and Their World: A Reassessment*, edited by E. D. Oren, 53–83. Philadelphia: University of Pennsylvania Press.

Madreiter, I. 2012. *Stereotypisierung—Idealisierung—Indifferenz. Formen der Auseinandersetzung mit dem Achaimeniden-Reich in der griechischen Persika-Literatur.* Classica et Orientalia 4. Wiesbaden: Harrassowitz.

Maeir, A. M., and L. A. Hitchcock. 2017. 'Rethinking the Philistines'. In *Rethinking Israel: Studies in the History and Archaeology of Ancient Israel in Honour of Israel Finkelstein*, edited by O. Lipschits et al., 247–266. Winnona Lake, IN: Eisenbrauns.

Magnavita, C. et al. 2006. 'Zilum: A Mid-first Millennium BC Fortified Settlement Near Lake Chad'. *Journal of African Archaeology* 4 (1): 153–169.

Mair, H. 1995. 'Mummies of the Tarim Bassin'. *Archaeology* 48 (2): 28–35.

Mairs, R. 2014. *The Hellenistic Far East: Archaeology, Language, and Identity in Greek Central Asia.* Cambridge: Oakland University of California Press.

Malinowski, G. 2014. 'Alexander and the Beginning of the Greek Exploration in Nilotic Africa'. In *Alexander the Great and Egypt: History, Art, Tradition*, edited by V. Grieb et al., 273–286. Philippika 60. Wiesbaden: Harrassowitz.

Malkin, I. 1987. *Religion and Colonization in Ancient Greece.* Leiden: Brill.

Malkin, I. 2011. *A Small Greek World: Networks in the Ancient Mediterranean.* Oxford: Oxford University Press.

Mallory, J. P., and V. H. Mair. 2000. *The Tarim Mummies: Ancient China and the Mystery of the Earliest Peoples from the West.* London: Thames and Hudson.

Mango, M. M. 1996. 'Byzantine Maritime Trade with the East (4th–7th Century)'. *Aram* 8: 139–163.

Manning, J. G. 2005. 'The Relationship of Evidence to Models in the Ptolemaic Economy (322 BC–30 BC)'. In *The Ancient Economy*, edited by J. G. Manning and I. Morris, 163–186. Stanford: Stanford University Press.

Manthe, U. 2014. 'Soldaten der Crassus-Armee in China?' *Gymnasium* 121: 477–492.

Margalith, O. 1994. *The Sea People in the Bible.* Wiesbaden.

Marinatos, N. 1995. 'Circe and Liminality: Ritual Backgrounds and Narrative Structure'. In *Homer's World: Fiction, Tradition, Reality*, edited by O. Andersen and M. Dickie, 133–140. Bergen: Aström.

Marks, J. H. 1985. *Visions of One World: Legacy of Alexander.* Guilford: Tour Quarter.

Marshall, E. 2000. 'Death and Disease in Cyrene: A Case Study'. In *Death and Disease in the Ancient City*, edited by V. M. Hope and E. Marshall, 8–23. London/New York: Routledge.

Marzano, A. 2011. 'Snails, Wine and Winter Navigation'. In *Maritime Technology in the Ancient Economy: Ship-Design and Navigation*, edited by W. V. Harris and K. Iara, 179–188. Journal of Roman Archaeology Supplementary Series 84. Portsmouth: .

Mattingly, R. 2011. 'The Garamantes of Fazzan. An Early Libyan State with Trans-Saharan Connections'. In *Money, Trade and Trade Routes in Pre-Islamic North Africa*, edited by A. Dowler and E. R. Galwin, 49–60. British Museum Research Publication 176. London: the British Museum.

Mattingly, R. 2015. 'Transsaharahandel'. In *Frühgeschichte der Mittelmeerkulturen. Historisch-archäologisches Handbuch*, edited by A.-M. Wittke, 779–783. Der Neue Pauly Suppl. 10. Stuttgart/Weimar: Metzler.

Mauny, R. 1947. 'Une route préhistorique á travers le Sahara occidentale'. *BIFAN* 9: 341–357.

Mauny, R. 1970. *Les siècles obscures de l'Afrique noire. Histoire et Archéologie*. Nancy: Fayard.

Mauny, R. 1978. 'Trans-Saharan Contacts and the Iron Age in West Africa'. In *The Cambridge History of Africa*, Vol. 2, *From c. 500 BC to AD 1050*, edited by J. D. Page, 272–341. Cambridge: Cambridge University Press.

Mauny, R. 1993. 'A Confusion of Indias: Asian India and African India in the Byzantine Sources'. *Journal of the American Oriental Society* 113: 169–174.

Mayerson, P. 1995. 'Aelius Gallus at Cleopatris (Suez) and on the Red Sea'. *GRBS* 36: 17–24.

Mayor, A. 2014. *The Amazons: Lives and Legends of Warrior Women Across the Ancient World*. Princeton, NJ/Oxford: Princeton University Press.

Mayor, A., and M. Heaney. 1993. 'Griffins and Arimaspeans'. *Folklore* 104: 40–66.

McClish, M. R. 2009. 'Political Brahmanism and the State: A Compositional History of the Arthaśāstra'. PhD dissertation, University of Texas. https://repositories.lib.utexas.edu/ handle/2152/10568.

McGrail, S. 2001. *Boats of the World: From the Stone Age to Medieval Times*. Oxford: Oxford University Press.

McLaughlin, R. 2010. *Rome and the Distant East: Trade Routes to the Ancient Lands of Arabia, India and China*. London/New York: Bloomsbury.

McLaughlin, R. 2014. *The Roman Empire and the Indian Ocean: The Ancient World Economy and the Kingdoms of Africa, Arabia, and India*. Barnsley: Pen & Sword.

McPherson, K. 1990. *Traditional Indian Ocean Shipping Technologies: Sri Lanka and the Silk Road of the Sea, ed. Bandaranayake, S., Dewaraja, L., Silva R., Wimalaratne K.D.A.* The Central Cultural Fund. Colombo: Sri Lanka National Commission for Unesco anmd the Central Cultural Fund.

Medas, S. 2004. *De rebus nauticis: L'arte della navigazione nel mondo antico*. Rome: L'Erma di Bretschneider.

Mee, C. 'Mycenaean Greece, the Aegean and Beyond'. In *The Cambridge Companion to the Aegean Bronze Age*, edited by C. W. Shelmerdine, 362–386. Cambridge: Cambridge University Press.

Mehofer, M. 2005–2006. "'A Sword of Naue II Type from Ugarit and the Historical Significance of Italian-Type Weaponry in the Eastern Mediterranean."'. *AEA* 8: 111–135.

Meier, C. 1990. *The Greek Discovery of Politics*. Cambridge, MA: Harvard University Press.

Meijer, F. 1986. *A History of Seafaring in the Classical World*. London/Sydney: Routledge.

Meister, K. 1990. *Die griechische Geschichtsschreibung. Von den Anfängen bis zum Ende des Hellenismus*. Stuttgart: Kohlhammer.

Meister, K. 2010. *'Aller Dinge Maß ist der Mensch'. Die Lehren der Sophisten*. Munich: Fink.

Metzler, I. 2009. 'Perceptions of Hot Climate in Medieval Cosmography and Travel Literature'. In *Medieval Ethnographies: European Perceptions of the World Beyond*, edited by J. P. Rubiés Mirabet, 379–415. The Expansion of Latin Europe 9. Aldershot: Routledge.

Meuli, K. 1921. *Odyssee und Argonautika. Untersuchungen zur griechischen Sagengeschichte und zum Epos*. Basel: Buchdruck Mehr.

Meuli, K. I. 1935. 'Scythica'. *Hermes* 70: 121–176.

Meyer, D. 1998. 'Hellenistische Geographie zwischen Wissenschaft und Literatur. Timosthenes von Rhodos und der griechische Periplus'. In *Gattungen wissenschaftlicher Literatur in der Antike*, edited by W. Kullmann et al., 193–215. ScriptOralia 95. Tübingen: Gunter Narr.

Michaux, G. 2003. 'Gilgamesh and Homer: A Comparative Study of Motif Sets, Distinctions and Similarities'. *Mathesis* 12: 9–25.

Miller, J. I. 1969. *The Spice Trade of the Roman Empire: 29 B.C. to A.D. 641*. Oxford: Clarendon Press.

Miller, M. C. 1997. *Athens and Persia in the Fifth Century BC: A Study in Cultural Receptivity*. Cambridge: Cambridge University Press.

Mitchell, L. G. 2007. *Panhellenism and the Barbarian in Archaic and Classical Greece*. Swansea: Classical Press of Wales.

Möller, A. 2000. *Naukratis: Trade in Archaic Greece*. Oxford: Oxford University Press.

Mondi, R. 1983. 'The Homeric Cyclopes. Folktale, Tradition, and Theme'. *Transactions of the American Philological Association* 113: 17–38.

Montiglio, S. 2005. *Wandering in the Ancient Greek Culture*. Chicago/London: University of Chicago Press.

Morgan, R. J. 'Lucian's True Histories and the Wonders Beyond Thule of Antonius Diogenes'. *Classical Quarterly (n.s.)* 35 (2009): 475–490.

Moore, K., Lewis, D. 1999. *Birth of the Multinational. : 2000 Years of Ancient Business History. : From Ashur to Augustus*. Copenhagen Aarhus: Copenhagen Business School Press.

Moorey, R. P. S. 2001. 'The Mobility of Artisans and Opportunities for Technology Transfer Between Western Asia and Egypt in the Late Bronze Age'. In *The Social Context of Technological Change. Egypt and the Near East 1650–1550 BC*, edited by A. J. Shortland, 1–14. Oxford: Oxbow Books.

Morel, J.-P. 2006. 'Phocaean Colonisation'. In *Greek Colonisation: An Account of Greek Colonies and Other Settlements Overseas*, Vol. 1, edited by G. R. Tsetskhladze, 359–428. Boston/ Leiden: Brill.

Moretti, G. 1994. 'The Other World and the "Antipodes". The Myth of the Unknown Countries Between Antiquity and the Renaissance'. In *The Classical Tradition and the Americas*, Vol. 1, *European Images of the Americas and the Classical Tradition*, edited by W. Haase, M. Reinhold, 241–284. Berlin/New York: De Gruyter.

Morgan, I. 1988. *The Miniature Wall Paintings of Thera: A Study in Aegean Culture and Iconography*. Cambridge: Cambridge University Press.

Morgan, J. R. 1993. 'Make-believe and Make Believe: The Fictionality of the Greek Novels'. In *Lies and Fiction in the Ancient World*, edited by C. Gill and T. P. Wiseman, 175–229. Austin: University of Texas.

Morley, N. 2007. 'The Early Roman Empire: Distribution'. In *The Cambridge Economic History of the Greco-Roman World*, edited by W. Scheidel et al., 570–591. Cambridge: Cambridge University Press.

Morris, S. P. 1989. 'A Tale of Two Cities: The Miniature Frescoes from Thera and the Origins of Greek Poetry'. *AJA* 93: 511–535.

Morrison, J. 1956. 'Pythagoras of Samos'. *CQ* 6: 135–156.

Morrison, J. S., and R. T. Williams. 1968. *Greek Oared Ships 900–322 B.C.* Cambridge: Cambridge University Press.

Morton, J. 2001. *The Role of the Physical Environment in Ancient Greek Seafaring*. Leiden: Brill.

Mourre, C. 1964. 'Euthyménès de Marseille'. *Revue d'Études ligures* 1: 133–139.

Moynihan, R. 1985. 'Geographical Mythologie and Imperial Ideology'. In *The Age of Augustus*, edited by R. Winkes, 149–162. Louvrain/Rhode Island: Brown University.

Müller, K. E. 1997. *Geschichte der antiken Ethnologie*. Reinbeck/Hamburg: Rowohlt.

Munson, R. V. 2001. *Telling Wonders: Ethnographic and Political Discourse in the Work of Herodotus*. Ann Arbor: University of Michigan Press.

Murphy, E. M./Mallory, and J. P. Mallory. 2000. "'Herodotus and the Cannibals.'". *Antiquity* 74: 388–394.

Murphy, T. 2004. *Pliny the Elder's Natural History: The Empire in the Encyclopedia*. Oxford: Oxford University Press.

Murray, O. 2001. 'Herodotus and Oral History'. In *The Historian's Craft in the Age of Herodotus*, edited by N. Luraghi, 16–44. Oxford: Oxford University Press.

Naas, V. 2011. 'Imperialism, Mirabilia and Knowledge: Some Paradoxes in the Naturalis Historia'. In *Pliny the Elder: Themes and Contexts*, edited by R. K. Gibson and R. Morello, 57–70. Leiden/Boston: Brill.

Nachtigall, G. 1881. 'Sahara und Sudan'. *II. Berlin 1881. ND* 2016 *Vol. II: Kawar, Bornu, Kanem, Borku, Ennedi*. Translated from the original German with an introduction and notes by A. G. B. Fisher and H. J. Fisher. London: C. Hurst & Co. Publishers.

Nappo, D. 2007. 'The Impact of the Third Century Crisis on the International Trade with the East'. In *Crises and the Roman Empire*, edited by O. Hekster et al., 233–244. Impact of Empire 7. Leiden/Boston: Brill.

Narain, A. K. 1957. *The Indo-Greeks*. Oxford: Oxford University Press.

Nebes, D. 2009. 'Die Nabatäer in Südarabien. Eine datierte nabatäisch-sabäische Inschrift (Bilingue) aus Sirwah/Jemen'. *AW* 40: 52–53.

Neiman, D. 1980. 'Ethiopia and Kush. Biblical and Ancient Greek Geography'. *The Ancient World* 3: 35–42.

Neville, A. 2007. *Mountains of Silver and Rivers of Gold: The Phoenicians in Iberia*. Oxford: Oxbow Books.

Nicolet, C. 1991. *Space, Geography, and Politics in the Early Roman Empire.* Ann Arbor: The University of Michigan Press.

Nielsen, H. 1987. *Medicaments Used in the Treatment of Eye Diseases in Egypt, the Countries of the Near East, India, and China in Antiquity*. Odense: University Press of Southern Denmark.

Niemeyer, W.-D. 1998. 'The Mycenaeans in Western Anatolia and the Problem of the Origins of the Sea Peoples'. In *Mediterranean Peoples in Transition: Thirteenth to Early Tenth Century* BCE, edited by S. Gitin, A. Mazar, and E. Stern, 17–65. Jerusalem: Israel Exploration Society.

Nippel, W. 1990. *Griechen, Barbaren und 'Wilde'. Alte Geschichte und Sozialanthropologie.* Frankfurt am Main: Fischer.

Noort, E. 1994. *Die Seevölker in Palästina.* Kampen: Peeters.

Norman, K. R. 2007. 'Asokan Envoys and Buddhist Missionaries'. In *Collected Papers VIII*, edited by K. R. Norman, 183–198. Lancester: The Pali Text Society.

Norman, K. R. 2012. 'The Language of the Composition and Transmission of the Asokan Inscriptions'. In *Reimagining Aśoka: Memory and History*, edited by P. Olivelle et al., 38–82. Delhi: Oxford University Press.

O'Connor, D., and S. Quirke, eds. 2003. *Mysterious Lands.* London: UCL Press.

O'Doherty, M. 2013. *The Indies and the Medieval West: Thought, Report, Imagination.* Turnhout: Brepols Publishers.

O'Grady, P. A. 2002. *Thales of Miletus: The Beginnings of Western Science and Philosophy.* London/New York: Routledge.

O'Sullivan, J. N. 1990. 'Nature and Culture in Odyssey?' *SO* 65: 7–17.

Okhotnikov, S. B. 2001. 'Settlements in the Lower Reaches of the Dniester (6th–3rd Century BC)'. In *North Pontic Archaeology: Recent Discoveries and Studies*, edited by G. R. Tsetskhladze, 91–115. Leiden: Brill Academic.

Olivelle, P., ed. 2013. *King, Governance, and Law in Ancient India. Kautilya's Arthasastra.* Oxford: Oxford University Press.

Osborne, R. 2007. 'Archaic Greece'. In W. Scheidel et al. (eds.). *The Cambridge Economic History of the Greco-Roman World*, edited by W. Scheidel et al., 277–301. Cambridge: 277–301.

Padgen, A. 1993. *European Encounters with the New World.* New Haven, CT: Yale University Press.

Page, D. L. 1973. *Folktales in Homer's Odyssey.* Cambridge: Harvard University Press.

Panchenko, D. 1998. 'Scylax's Circumnavigation of India and Its Interpretation in Early Greek Geography: Ethnography and Cosmography. Part 1'. *Hyperboreus* 4: 211–241.

Panchenko, D. 1998. 'Scylax's Circumnavigation of India and Its Interpretation in Early Greek Geography: Ethnography and Cosmography. Part 2'. *Hyperboreus* 9: 274–295.

Pape, J. 2000. 'Die attische Keramik der Heuneburg und der keramische Südimport in der Zone nördlich der Alpen während der Hallstattzeit'. In *Importe und mediterrane Einflüsse auf der Heuneburg*, edited by W. Kimmig, 71–176. Mainz: Philipp von Zabern.

Pappa, E. 2013. *Early Iron Exchanges in the West: Phoenicians in the Mediterranean and the Atlantic*. Ancient Near Eastern Studies. Suppl. 43. Leuven/Paris/Walpole, MA: Peeters uitgeverij.

Paranavitana, S. 1971. *The Greeks and the Mauryas*. Colombo: Lake House Investments.

Pare, C. 1991. 'Fürstensitze. Celts and the Mediterranean World: Developments in the West Hallstatt Culture in the 6th and 5th Centuries BC'. *Proceedings of the Prehistoric Society* 57: 183–202.

Park, D. P. 2011. *Climate Change, Human Response, and the Origins of Urbanism at Timbuktu: Archaeological Investigations into the Prehistoric Urbanism of the Timbuktu Region of the Niger Bend, Mali, West Africa*. Ann Arbor, MI: Yale University ProQuest Dissertations Publishing.

Parke, H. W. 1985. *The Oracles of Apollo in Asia Minor*. London: Croom Helm.

Parke, H. W., and D. E. Wormell. 1956. *The Delphic Oracle*. 2 vols. Oxford: Blackwell.

Parker, G. R. 2008. *The Making of Roman India*. Cambridge/New York: Cambridge University Press.

Parker, R. 1995. 'Early Orphism'. In *The Greek World*, edited by A. Powell, 483–510. London/New York: Routledge.

Parzinger, H. 2004. *Die Skythen*. Munich: C. H. Beck.

Paul, B. 2005. 'De l'Euphrate à la Chine avec la caravane de Maes Titianos'. *CRAI* 3: 929–969.

Peatfield, A. 2008. 'Minoan and Mycenean Warfare'. In *The Ancient World at War*, edited by P. De Souza, 87–99. London: Thames & Hudson.

Peddie, J. 1998. *Conquest: The Roman Invasion of Britain*. Sutton: Bramley Books.

Pédech, P. 1980. 'L'Expédition d'Alexandre et la science grecque'. In *Megas Alexandros*, edited by M. Vapheiadou Vogiatzake, 135–156. Thessalonike: Hetaireia Makedonikon Spoudon.

Pedersén, O. 2005. 'Foreign Professionels in Babylon: Evidence from the Archive in the Palace of Nebuchadnezzar II'. In *Ethnicity in Ancient Mesopotamia*, edited by W. H. Van Soldt, 267–272. CRRAI 48. Leiden: Peeters Publishers.

Perera, B. J. 1951. 'The Foreign Trade and Commerce of Ancient Ceylon'. *The Ceylon Historical Journal* 1: 109–119.

Petersmann, H. 1981. 'Homer und das Märchen'. *WS* 15: 43–68.

Petropoulos, E. K. 2005. *Hellenic Colonization in Euxeinos Pontos: Penetration, Early Establishment, and the Problem of the "Emporion" Revisited*. BAR International Series 1394. Oxford: British Archaeological Reports Oxford.

Philipp, H. 1911. *Die historisch-geographischen Quellen in den Etymologiae des Isidorus von Sevilla*. Berlin: Weidemann.

Phillips, E. D. 1955. 'The Legend of Aristeas. Fact and Fancy in early Greek Notions of East Russia, Siberia, and Inner Asia'. *Artibus Asiae* 18: 161–177.

Phillips, J. R. S. 1988. *The Medieval Expansion of Europe*. Oxford: Oxford University Press.

Phillips, S. 2000. 'The Outer World in the European Middle Ages'. In *Medieval Ethnographies: European Perceptions of the Worlds Beyond (The Expansion of Latin Europe 1000–1500)*, edited by J. P. Rubiés, 1–41. Farnham: Ashgate.

Picard. C. 1982. 'Les navigations de Carthage vers l'ouest. mit einer Textabbildung'. In *Phönizier im Westen*, edited by H. G. Niemeyer, 167–173. Madrider Beiträge 8. Mainz: Philipp von Zabern.

Picard, G. Ch. 1992. 'Der Periplus des Hanno'. In *Karthago (WdF 654)*, edited by W. Huss, 182–192. Darmstadt: Harrassowitz.

Plischke, S. 2014. *Seleukiden und Iran. Die seleukidische Herrschaftspolitik in den östlichen Satrapien*. Classica et orientalia 9. Wiesbaden.

Pomey, P. 2011. 'Les consequences de l'évolution des techniques de construction navale sur l'économie maritime antique: quelques exemples.' In *Maritime Technology in the Ancient Economy: Ship-Design and Navigation*, edited by W. V. Harris and K. Iara, 39–55. Portsmouth/Rhode Island: Journal of Roman Archaeology.

Potts, D.T. 1990. *The Arabian Golf in Antiquity*. 2 vols. Oxford: Oxford University Press.

Potts, D. T. 1995. 'Distant Shores: Ancient Near Eastern Trade with South Asia and Northeast Africa'. In *Civilizations of the Ancient Near East III*, edited by J. M. Sasson, 1451–1463. New York: Simon & Schuster.

Potts, D.T. 2011. 'Old Arabia in Historic Sources'. In *Roads of Africa: The Archaeological Treasures of Saudi Arabia*, edited by U. Franke and J. Gierlichs, 86–101. Tübingen: Ernst Wasmuth.

Pralon, D. 1992. 'La légende de la fondation de Marseille'. In *Marseille grecque et la Gaule*, edited by M. Bats et al., 51–56. Ètudes Massaliètes 3. Aix-en-Provence: Adam Pub.

Prasad, P. C. 1977. *Foreign Trade and Commerce in Ancient India*. New Delhi: Abhinav Publications.

Préaux, C. 1957. 'Les grecs à la découverte de l'Afrique per l'Egypte'. CE 32: 284–312.

Prest, J. M. 1981. *The Garden of Eden: The Botanic Garden and the Re-creation of Paradise*. New Haven, CT: Yale University Press.

Prickett-Fernando, M. 1990. 'Durable Goods: The Archaeological Evidence of Sri Lanka's Role in the Indian Ocean Trade'. In *Sri Lanka and the Silk Road of the Sea*, edited by S. Bandaranayake et al., 61–84. Colombo: Sri Lanka Institute of International Relations.

Pritchard, J. B. 1968. *New Evidence on the Role of the Sea Peoples in Canaan at the Beginning of the Iron Age*. In *The Role of the Phoenicians in the Interaction of Mediterranean* Civilizations, edited by W. A. Ward, 99–112. Beirut: American University of Beirut.

Pritchett, W. K. 1993. *The Liar School of Herodotos*. Amsterdam: Brill Academic.

Prontera, F. 2013. 'Timosthenes and Eratosthenes. Sea Routes and Hellenistic Geography'. In *The Ptolemies, the Sea, and the Nile. Studies in Waterborne Power*, edited by K. Buraselis et al., 207–217. Cambridge: Cambridge University Press.

Pulak, C. 1997. 'The Uluburun Shipwreck'. In *Res Maritimae: Cyprus and the Mediterranean from Prehistory to Late Antiquity*, edited by S. Swiny, R. L. Hohlfelder, and H. Wylde Swiny, 232–262. ASOR Archaeological Reports 4. Atlanta.

Pulleyblank, E. G. 1999. 'The Roman Empire as Known to Han China'. *Journal of the American Oriental Society* 119: 71–79.

Raaflaub, K. A., and R. J. A. Talbert, eds. 2010. *Geography and Ethnography: Perceptions of the World in Pre-Modern Societies*. The Ancient World: Comparative Histories. Malden/Oxford: Wiley-Blackwell.

Radermacher, L. 1903. *Das Jenseits im Mythos der Hellenen. Untersuchungen über antiken Jenseitsglauben*. Bonn: A. Marcus & E. Weber's Verlag.

Radermacher, L. 1916. 'Die Gründung von Marseille. Ein Versuch zur Geschichte von Sage und Sitte'. *RhM* 71: 1–16.

Raman, K. V. 1991. 'Further Evidence of Roman Trade from Coastal Sites in Tamil Nadu'. In *Rome and India: The Ancient Sea Trade*, edited by V. Begley, R. D. De Puma, 125–133. Madison: University of Wisconsin Press.

Randles, W. G. L. 1994. 'Classical Models of World Geography and Their Transformation Following the Discovery of America'. In *The Classical Tradition and the Americas*, Vol. 1, Part 1, edited by W. Haase and M. Reinhold, 5–76. Berlin/New York: De Gruyter.

Raschke, M. G. 1978. 'New Studies in Roman Commerce with the East'. *ANRW* II.9.2 : 604–1378.

Rathbone, D. 2003. 'The Financing of Maritime Commerce in the Roman Empire I–II AD'. In *Credito et moneta nel mondo romano*, edited by E. Lo Cascio, 197–230. Bari: Edipuglia.

Ray, H. P. 2003. *The Archaeology of Seafaring in Ancient South Asia*. Cambridge World Archaeology. Cambridge: Cambridge University Press.

Ray, H. P. 1994. *The Winds of Change: Buddhism and the Maritime Links of Early South Asia*. Delhi/Oxford: Oxford University Press.

Rebuffat R. 1995. 'Les penteconteres d'Hannon'. *Karthago* 23: 20–30.

Reger, G. 2009. 'On the Road to India with Apollonios of Tyana and Thomas the Apostle'. In *Greek and Roman Networks in the Mediterranean*, edited by J. Malkin et al., 249–263. London: Taylor & Francis.

Reichert, F. E. 1992. *Begegnungen mit China. Die Entdeckung Ostasiens im Mittelalter*. Sigmaringen: Jan Thorbecke.

Reinhardt, K. 1921. *Poseidonios*. Munich: C. H. Beck.

Rice, M. 1985. *Search for the Paradise Land: An Introduction to the Archaeology of Bahrein and the Arabian Gulf: From the Earliest Time to the Death of Alexander*. London: Prentice Hall Press.

Rice, M. 1994. *The Archaeology of the Arabian Gulf c. 5000–323 BC*. London/New York: Routledge.

Ridgway, D. 1992. *The First Western Greeks*. Cambridge: Cambridge University Press.

Rihll, T. 1996. 'The Origin and Establishment of Ancient Greek Slavery'. In *Serfdom and Slavery: Studies in Legal Bondage*, edited by M. L. Bush et al., 89–111. London/New York: Routledge.

Robert, J.-N. 1993. *De Rome à la Chine. Sur les routes de la soie au temps des Césars.* Paris: Les belles lettres histoire antiquité.

Roberts, O. T. P. 1987. 'Wind-power and the Boats from the Cyclades'. *International Journal of Nautical Archaeology* 16: 309–311.

Robinson, D., and A. Wilson, eds. 2011. *Maritime Archaeology and Ancient Trade in the Mediterranean.* Oxford: Oxford University School of Archaeology.

Rochberg, F. 2012. 'The Expression of Terrestrial and Celestial Order in Ancient Mesopotamia'. In *Ancient Perspectives: Maps and Their Place in Mesopotamia, Egypt, Greece and Rome*, edited by A. Talbert, 9–46. Chicago/London: University of Chicago Press.

Röd, W. 1988. *Die Philosophie der Antike. Teil 1: Von Thales bis Demokrit.* 2nd ed. Munich: C. H. Beck.

Roller, D. W. 2003. *The World of Juba II and Kleopatra Selene: Royal Scholarship on Rome's African Frontier.* London/New York: Taylor & Francis.

Roller, D. W. 2006. *Through the Pillars of Herakles.* New York: Taylor & Francis.

Roller, D. W. 2010. *Eratosthenes' Geography.* Princeton, NJ: Princeton University Press.

Roller, D. W. 2015. *Ancient Geography: The Discovery of the World in Classical Greece and Rome.* London: I. B. Tauris.

Roller, D. W. 2018. *A Historical and Topographical Guide to the Geography of Strabo.* Cambridge: Cambridge University Press.

Roller, D. W., ed. 2019. *New Directions in the Study of Ancient Geography.* Publications of the Association of Ancient Historians 12. University Park: Pennsylvania State University Press.

Röllig, W. 1982. 'Die Phönizier des Mutterlandes zur Zeit der Kolonisierung'. In *Phönizier im Westen*, edited by H. G. Niemeyer, 15–30. Madrider Beiträge 8. Mainz: Philipp von Zabern.

Rollinger, R. 2013. 'The View from East to West: World View and Perception of Space in the Neo-Assyrian Empire'. In *Aneignung und Abgrenzung. Wechselnde Perspektiven auf die Antithese von 'Ost' und 'West' in der griechischen Antike*, edited by N. Zenzen et al., 93–161. Oikumene. Studien zur antiken Weltgeschichte 10. Heidelberg: Verlag Antike.

Romm, J. 2010. 'Continents, Climates, and Cultures. Theories of Global Structure'. In *Geography and Ethnography: Greek Perceptions of the World in Pre-modern Societies*, edited by K. A. Raaflaub and R. J. A. Talbert, 215–235. Malden/Oxford: Wiley-Blackwell.

Romm, J. 1987. 'Dragons and Gold at the Edges of the Earth: A Folktale Motiv Developed by Herodotus'. *Wonders and Tales* 1: 45–55.

Romm, J. 1989. 'Aristoteles' Elephant and the Myth of Alexander's Scientific Patronage'. *AJPh* 110: 566–575.

Romm, J. 1992. *The Edges of the Earth in Ancient Thought: Geography, Exploration, and Fiction*. Princeton, NJ: Princeton University Press.

Rood, T. 2006. 'Herodotus and Foreign Lands'. In *The Cambridge Companion to Herodotus*, edited by C. Dewald and J. Marincola, 290–305. Cambridge: Cambridge University Press.

Rougé, J. 1981. *Ships and Fleets of the Ancient Mediterranean*. Transl. S. Frazer. Middleton: Wesleyan University Press.

Routledge, B., and K. McGeough. 2009. 'Just What Collapsed? A Network Perspective on "Palatial" and "Private" Trade at Ugarit'. In *Forces of Transformation: The End of the Bronze Age in the Mediterranean*, edited by Ch. Bachhuber and R. G. Roberts, 22–29. Themes from the Ancient Near East BANEA Publication Series 1. Oxford: Oxbow Books.

Rubiés, J. P. 2009. 'The Emergence of a Naturalistic and Ethnographic Paradigm in Late Medieval Travel Writing'. In *Medieval Ethnographies: European Perceptions of the Worlds Beyond (The Expansion of Latin Europe 1000–1500)*, edited by J. P. Rubiés, 43–64. Farnham/Burlington: Taylor & Francis.

Ruffing, K. 2014 'Cultural Encounters between Rome and the East'. In *Case Studies in Transmission*, edited by L. Lindstedt et al., 143–157. JHMNE 1. Münster: Ugarit-Verlag.

Salles, J.-F. 1987. 'The Arab-Persian Gulf under the Seleucids'. In *Hellenism in the East: The Interaction of Greek and non-Greek Civilizations from Syria to Central Asia after Alexander*, edited by A. Kuhrt and S. Sherwin-White, 75–109. London: Duckworth.

Salles, J.-F. 1988. 'La circumnavigation de l'Arabie dans l'antiquité Classique'. In *L'Arabie et ses mers bordières. Teil 1: Itinéraires et voisinages*, edited by F.-J. Salles, 75–102. Lyon/Paris: Maison de l'Orient et de la Méditerranée Jean Poullioux.

Salles, J.-F. 1995. 'The Periplus of the Erythraean Sea and the Arab-Persian Gulf'. In *Athens, Aden, Arikamedu: Essays on the Interrelations between India, Arabia, and the Eastern Mediterranean*, edited by J. M. F. Boussac and J.-F. Salles, 115–146. New Delhi: Manohar.

Salmon, J. B. 1984. *Wealthy Corinth. A History of the City to 338 B.C.* Oxford: Oxford University Press.

Sanchez, J.-P. 1994. 'Myths and Legends in the Old World and European Expansionism on the American Continent'. In *The Classical Tradition and the Americas*, Vol. 1, Part 1, edited by W. Haase and M. Reinhold, 189–240. Berlin/New York: De Gruyter.

Sarao, K. T. S. 2007. *Urban Centres and Urbanisation as Reflected in the Pāli Vinaya and Sutta Pitakas*. 2nd ed. Dehli: University of Delhi.

Sarnowsky, J. 2015. *Die Erkundung der Welt. Die großen Entdeckungen von Marco Polo bis Humboldt*. Munich: C. H. Beck.

Sasson, J. M. 1966. 'Canaanite Maritime Involvement in the Second Millennium B.C.'. *Journal of the American Oriental Society* 86 (2): 126–138.

Sauter, H. 2000. *Studien zum Kimmerierproblem*. Bonn: Habelt.

Scafi, A. 2006. *Mapping Paradise: A History of Heaven on Earth.* Chicago: University of Chicago Press.

Scheidel, W. 2011. 'A Comparative Perspective on the Determinants of the Scale and Productivity of Maritime Trade in the Roman Mediterranean'. In *Maritime Technology in the Ancient Economy. Ship-Design and Navigation*, edited by W. v. Harris and K. Iara, 21–37. Journal of Roman Archaeology Supplementary Series 84. Portsmouth.

Schipper, B. U. 2005. *Die Erzählung des Wenamun. Ein Literaturwerk im Spannungsfeld von Politik, Geschichte und Religion.* Göttingen: Vandenhoeck & Ruprecht.

Schleicher, F. 2014. *Cosmographia Christiana. Kosmologie und Geographie im frühen Christentum.* Paderborn: Ferdinand Schöningh.

Schmid, P. 1985. 'Der Handel der römischen Kaiserzeit im niedersächsischen Nordseeküstengebiet aufgrund archäologischer Zeugnisse'. In *Untersuchungen zu Handel und Verkehr der vor- und frühgeschichtlichen Zeit in Mittel- und Nordeuropa, Teil 1: Methodische Grundlagen und Darstellungen zum Handel in vorgeschichtlicher Zeit und in der Antike*, edited by K. Düwel et al., 451–459. Göttingen: Vandenhoeck & Ruprecht.

Schmidt, G. 2002. *Rabe und Krähe in der Antike. Studien zur archäologischen und literarischen Überlieferung.* Wiesbaden: Reichert.

Schmieder, F. 1994. *Europa und die Fremden. Die Mongolen im Urteil des Abendlandes vom 13. bis in das 15. Jahrhundert.* Sigmaringen: Jan Thorbecke.

Schmieder, F. 2013. 'Nachdenken auf der Karte. Mappae Mundi als Spiegel spätmittelalterlichen Weltwissens'. In *Weltwissen vor Kolumbus*, edited by J. Cobet, 236–257. Periplus 23. Berlin: Lit Verlag.

Schmitt, P. 1968. 'Connaissance des îles Canaries dans l'antiquité'. *Latomus* 27: 362–391.

Schneider, C. 1970. *Geistesgeschichte der christlichen Antike.* Munich: C. H. Beck.

Schneider, P. 2004. *L'Éthopie et L'Inde. Interférences et confusions aux extrémités du monde antique.* Collection de l'École Francaise de Rome 335. Rome: École francaise de Rome.

Schniedewind, W. M. 2005. *How the Bible Became a Book: The Textualization of Ancient Israel.* Cambridge: Cambridge University Press.

Schoff, W. H. 1912. *The Periplus of the Erythraean Sea: Travel and Trade in the Indian Ocean.* New York: Longmans, Green, and Co.

Schottenhammer, A. 2006. 'Schifffahrt und Überseebeziehungen bis ins 3. Jahrhundert: Ein Überblick'. In *Han-Zeit. Festschrift für Hans Stumpfeldts*, edited by M. Friedrich, R. Emmerich, and H. v. Ess, 600–621. Wiesbaden: Harrassowitz.

Schulz, R. 2005. *Die Antike und das Meer.* Darmstadt: Wissenschaftliche Buchgesellschaft.

Schulz, R. 2020. *Als Odysseus staunte: Die Griechische Sicht des Fremden und das ethnographische Vergleichen.* Göttingen: Vandenhoeck & Ruprecht.

Schulz, R. 2021. 'Travelers'. In *A Cultural History of the Sea in Antiqity.* Vol. 1, edited by M.-C. Beaulieu, 129–151. London: Bloomsbury.

/1966. 'Griechenland und Indien im Spiegel der antiken Literatur'. *Jahresbericht des Bundesgymnasiums und Bundesrealgymnasiums Fürstenfeld für das Schuljahr* 36: 62–86.

Schwarz, F. F. 1969. 'Deimachos von Plataiai. Zum geistesgeschichtlichen Hintergrund seiner Schriften'. In *Beiträge zur Alten Geschichte und deren Nachleben*, edited by R. Stiehl and H. E. Stier, 293–304. FS F. Altheim I. Berlin.

Schwarz, F. F. 1974. 'Ein singhalesischer Prinz in Rom'. *RhM* 117: 166–176.

Schwarz, F. F. 1982. 'The Itinerary of Iambulus—Utopianism and History'. In *Indology and Law: Studies in Honour of J. D. M. Derrett*, edited by G. Sontheimer, 18–55. Wiesbaden: Steiner.

Scodel, E. 2005. 'Odysseus' Ethnographic Digressions'. In *Approaches to Homer: Ancient and Modern*, edited by R. J. Rabel, 147–165. Swansea: The Classical Press of Wales.

Scodel, R. 2004. 'The Story-Teller and His Audience'. In *The Cambridge Companion to Homer*, edited by R. Fowler, 45–55. Cambridge: Cambridge University Press.

Scott, D. A. 1985. 'Ashokan Missionary Expansion of Buddhism Among the Greeks in North West India, Bactria and the Levant'. *Religion* 15: 131–141.

Scott, M. 2014. *Delphi: A History of the Center of the Ancient World*. Princeton, NJ/ Oxford: Princeton University Press.

Sedlar, J. W. 1980. *India and the Greek World: A Study in the Transmission of Culture*. Totowa, NJ: Rowman & Littlefield.

Segal, C. P. 1968. 'Circean Temptations in Homer, Vergil, Ovid'. *TAPA* 99: 419–442.

Segert, S. 1969. 'Phoenician Background of Hanno's Periplus'. *Mélanges de l'Université Saint Joseph* 45: 501–518.

Seland, E. H. 2007. *The Indian Ocean in the Ancient Period*. Oxford: BAR Publishing.

Seland, E. H. 2008. 'The Indian Ocean and the Globalisation of the Ancient World'. *Ancient West & East* 7: 65–77.

Seland, E. H. 2009a. 'Shipwreck, Maroons and Monsters: The Hazards of Ancient Red Sea Navigation'. In *Connected Hinterlands: Proceedings of the Red Sea Project 4*, edited by L. Blue et al., 179–185. Oxford: Archeopress.

Seland, E. H. 2009b. 'The Periplus' Report of a Roman Attack on Aden: An Unintended Result of Successful Propaganda?' *SO* 80: 60–67.

Seland, E. H. 2011. 'The Persian Gulf or the Red Sea? Two Axes in Ancient Indian Ocean Trade: Where to Go and Why'. *World Archaeology* 43: 398–409.

Seland, E. H. 2012. 'Trade and Christianity in the Indian Ocean During Late Antiquity'. *Journal of Late Antiquity* 5: 72–86.

Seland, E. H. 2013. 'Networks and Social Cohesion in Ancient Indian Ocean Trade'. *Geography, Ethnicity, Religion, Journal of Global History* 8: 373–390.

Seland, E. H. 2014. 'Archaeology of Trade in the Western Indian Ocean. 300 BC–AD 700'. *Journal of Archaeological Research* 22: 367–402.

Selvakumar, V., K. P. Shajan, and R. Tomber. 2009. 'Archaeological Investigations at Pattanam, Kerala. New Evidence for the Location of Ancient Muziris'. In *Migration, Trade and Peoples, Teil 1: Indian Ocean Commerce and the Archaeology of*

Western India, edited by R. Tomber, L. Blue, and S. Abraham, 29–41. London: The British Association for South Asian Studies.

Severin, T. 1985. *The Jason Voyage: The Quest for the Golden Fleece*. London: Hutchinson.

Shankman, S., and S. Durrant. 2000. *The Siren and the Sage: Knowledge and Wisdom in Ancient Greece and China*. London/New York: Bloomsbury.

Sharma, R. S. 2005. *India's Ancient Past*. Oxford: Oxford University Press.

Sharples, R. W. 1990. 'The School of Alexander?' In *Aristotle Transformed: The Ancient Commentators and Their Influence*, edited by R. Sorabji, 83–111. Ithaca/New York: Cornell University Press.

Shaw, J. W. 2004. 'Kommos: The Sea-Gate to Southern Crete'. In *Crete beyond the Palaces*, edited by L. P. Day et al., 43–51. Philadelphia: INSTAP Academic Press.

Shefton, B. B. 1982. 'Greeks and Greek Imports in the South of the Iberian Peninsula: The Archaeological Evidence'. In *Phönizier im Westen*, edited by H. G. Niemeyer, 337–370. Madrider Beiträge 8. Mainz.

Shefton, B. B. 1994. 'Massilia and Colonization in the North-eastern Mediterranean'. In *The Archaeology of Greek Colonization: FS Sir J. Boardman*, edited by G. R. Tsetskhladze and D. De Angelis, 61–86. Oxford.

Shefton, B. B. 2000. 'On the Material in Its Northern Settings'. In W. Kimmig (ed.). *Importe und mediterrane Einflüsse auf der Heuneburg*, edited by W. Kimmig, 27–41. (Heuneburgstudien 11). Mainz: 27–41.

Sherratt, A., and S Sherratt. 1991. 'From Luxuries to Commodities: The Nature of Mediterranean Bronze Age Trading Systems'. In *Bronze Age Trade in the Mediterranean*, edited by N. H. Gale, 351–382. Studies in Mediterranean Archaeology 90. Jonsered: Aströms.

Shipley, G. 2000. *The Greek World after Alexander 323–30 B.C.* London: Routledge.

Sidebotham, S. E. 2011. *Berenike and the Ancient Maritime Spice Route*. New York: University of California Press.

Sidebotham, S. E. 1986. *Roman Economic Policy in the Erythra Thalassa 30 B.C.–A.D. 217*. Leiden: Brill.

Sidky, H. 2000. *The Greek Kingdom of Bactria: From Alexander to Eucradides the Great*. Philadelphia: Rowman and Littlefield.

Silk, M. 2004. 'The Odyssee and its Explorations'. In *The Cambridge Companion to Homer*, edited by R. Fowler, 31–44. Cambridge: Cambridge University Press.

Simek, R. 1996. *Heaven and Earth in the Middle Ages: The Physical World before Columbus*. Suffolk: Boydell & Brewer.

Singer, I. 2000. 'New Evidence on the End of the Hittite Empire'. In *The Sea Peoples and their World: A Reassessment*, edited by E. D. Oren, 21–33. Philadelphia: University of Pennsylvania Press.

Singh, U. 2008. *A History of Ancient and Early Medieval India: From the Stone Age to the 12th Century*. Delhi: Pearson Education India.

Siriweera, W. I. 1990. 'Pre-colonial Sri Lanka's Maritime Commerce with Special Reference to Its Port'. In *Sri Lanka and the Silk Road of the Sea*, edited by S.

Bandaranayake et al., 125–133. Colombo: Sri Lanka Institute of International Relations.

Skinner, J. E. 2012. *The Invention of Greek Ethnography: From Homer to Herodotus*. Oxford: Oxford University Press.

Smith, I. G. 2022. 'Demetrius of Tarsus` Exploration of the Island in the West: An Unusual Excursion of the Roman Navy in Britain'. *Historia* 71 (2): 225–258.

Snodgrass, A. M. 1991. 'Bronze Age Exchange: A Minimalist Position'. In *Bronze Age Trade in the Mediterranean*, edited by N. H. Gale, 15–20. Studies in Mediterranean Archaeology 90. Jonsered: Paul Aströms Förlag.

Snowden, F. M. 1970. *Blacks in Antiquity: Ethiopians in the Greco-Roman Experience*. Cambridge, MA: The Belknap Press.

Solomou, S. 1992. 'Greek Knowledge of India before the Fourth Century B.C.'. MA- thesis, University of. British Columbia. http://circle.ubc. ca/bitstream/handle/2429/1735/ubc_1993_ spring_solomou_stavros.pdf?sequence=3 (2. 11. 2015).

Sommer, M. 2001. 'Der Untergang des Hethitischen Reiches. Anatolien und der Östliche Mittelmeerraum um 1200 v.Chr.'. *Saeculum* 52: 157–176.

Sommer, M. 2011. 'Trans-Saharan Long-Distance Trade and the Helleno-Punic Mediterranean'. In *Money, Trade and Trade Routes in Pre-Islamic North Africa*, edited by A. Dowler and E. R. Galwin, 61–64. British Museum Research Publication 176. London: British Museum Press.

De Souza, P., and P. Arnaud, eds. 2017. 'The Sea in History: The Ancient World'. *La Mer dans l'Histoire*. New York: The Boydell Press.

Speidel, M. A. 2007. 'Außerhalb des Reiches? Zu neuen lateinischen Inschriften aus Saudi-Arabien und zur Ausdehnung der römischen Herrschaft am Roten Meer'. *ZPE* 163: 296–306.

Speidel, M. A. 2016. 'Fernhandel und Freundschaft. Zu Roms Amici an den Handelsrouten nach Südarabien und Indien'. *Orb Terr* 14: 155–193.

Stahl, W. H. 1962. *Roman Science, Origins, Development, and Influence to the Later Middle Ages*. Madison, WI: Praeger Publishers.

Stanford, W. B. 1963. *The Ulysses Theme: A Study in the Adaptability of a Traditional Hero*. 2nd ed. Oxford: Blackwell.

Starr, C. G. 1956. 'The Roman Emperor and the King of Ceylon'. *CPh* 51: 27–30.

Stauffer, A. 2007. 'Textilien aus Xinjiang. Textilherstellung und Kulturtransfer entlang der Handelsrouten an der Taklamakan'. In *Ursprünge der Seidenstraße. Sensationelle Neufunde aus Xinjiang*, edited by A. Wieczorek and C. Lind, 73–86. Stuttgart: Wissenschaftliche Buchgesellschaft.

Steinicke, M. 2005. 'Apokalyptische Heerscharen und Gottesknechte. Wundervölker des Ostens in abendländischer Tradition vom Untergang der Antike bis zur Entdeckung Amerikas'. PhD dissertation, FU Berlin. http://www.diss.fu-berlin.de/2005/290/.

Stern, M. 1991. 'Early Roman Export Glass in India'. In *Rome and India: The Ancient Sea Trade*, edited by V. Begley and R. D. De Puma, 113–124. Madison: University of Wisconsin Press.

Stewart, A. 1990. *Greek Skulpture*. Vol. 1. New Haven, CT: Yale University Press.

Stoneman, R. 1994. 'Romantic Ethnography: Central Asia and India in the Alexander Romance'. *AncW* 25: 93–107.

Stoneman, R. 2019. *The Greek Experience of India: From Alexander to the Indo-Greeks*. Princeton: Princeton University Press.

Stos-Gale, Z. 2001. 'Minoan Foreign Relations and Copper Metallurgy in MMIII–LMIII Crete.' In *The Social Context of Technological Change: Egypt and the Near East 1650–1550 BC*, edited by A. J. Shortland, 195–210. Oxford: Oxbow Books.

Strijbosch, C. 2000. *The Seafaring Saint: Sources and Analogues of the Twelfth-Century Voyage of Saint Brendan*. Dublin: Four Courts Press.

Stückelberger, A. 1987. 'Kolumbus und die antiken Wissenschaften'. *AKG* 69: 331–340.

Stuurman, S. 2008. 'Herodotus and Sima Qian: History and the Anthropological Turn in Ancient Greece and Han China'. *Journal of World History* 19: 1–40.

Swanson, J. T. 1975. 'The Myth of Transsaharan Trade during the Roman Era'. *International Journal of African Historical Studies* 8: 582–600.

Szabó, A. 1992. *Das geozentrische Weltbild. Astronomie, Geographie und Mathematik der Griechen*. Munich: dtv.

Tadmor, H. 1975. 'Assyria and the West: The Ninth Century and Its Aftermath'. In *Unity and Diversity*, edited by H. Goedicke and J. J. M. Roberts, 36–48. Baltimore: Johns Hopkins University.

Tarn, W. 1929. 'Ptolemy II and Arabia'. *Journal of Egyptian Archeology* 15: 9–25.

Tartaron, T. R. 2013. *Maritime Networks in the Mycenaean World*. Cambridge: Cambridge University Press.

Taylor, T. 2001. 'Thracians, Scythians, and Dacians, 800 BC–AD 300'. In *The Oxford History of Prehistoric Europe*, edited by B. Cunliffe, 373–410. Oxford: Oxford University Press.

Tchernia, A. 2009. 'L'exportation du vin. Interprétations actuelles de l'exception gauloise'. In *Agricoltura e scambi nell' Italia zardo-reüubblicana*, edited by J. Carlsen and E. Lo Cascio, 91–113. Bari: Edipuglia.

Tchernia, A. 1997. 'The Dromedary of the Peticii and Trade with the East'. In *Crossings: Early Mediterranean Contacts with India*, edited by F. De Romanis and A. Tchernia, 238–249. New Dehli/Manohar: Manohar Publishers & Distributors.

Tchernia, A. 1998. 'Arikamedu et le graffito naval d'Alagankulam'. *Topoi* 8: 447–463.

Temin, P. 2006. 'Mediterranean Trade in Biblical Times'. In E. Heckscher, *International Trade and Economic History*, edited by R. Findlay, R. G. H. Henriksson, H. Lindgren, and M. Lundahl, 141–156. Cambridge, MA: MIT Press.

Thapar, R. 1987. *The Mauryas Revisited*. Kalkutta: K. P. Bagchi.

Thapar, R. 2002. *The Penguin History of Early India. From the Origins to AD 1300*. . London: Penguin.

Thapar, R. 1997. *Aśoka and the Decline of the Mauryas: With a New Afterword, Bibliography, and Index*. Delhi: Oxford University Press.

Thapar, R. 1998. *Recent Perspectives on Early Indian History*. Bombay: South Asia Books.

Thiel, J. H. 1967. *Eudoxus of Cyzicus: A Chapter in the History of the Sea-Route to India and the Route Round the Cape in Ancient Times*. Groningen: J. B. Wolters.

Thierry, F., and C. Morrisson. 1994. 'Sur les monnaies byzantines trouvées en Chine'. *RN* 36: 109–145.

Thomas, R. 2000. *Herodotus in Context: Ethnography, Science and the Art of Persuasion*. Cambridge: Cambridge University Press.

Thomson, J. O. 1948. *History of Ancient Geography*. New York: Cambridge University Press.

Thorley, J. 1969. 'The Development of Trade between the Roman Empire and the East under Augustus'. *G&R* 16: 209–222.

Thorley, J. 1971. 'The Silk Trade between China and the Roman Empire at Its Height'. *G&R* 18: 71–80.

Thornton, A. 1970. *People and Themes in Homer's Odyssey*. London: Routledge.

Thrane, H. 1990. 'The Mycenaean Fascination: A Northerner's View'. In *Orientalisch-Ägäische Einflüsse in der Europäischen Bronzezeit*, edited by P. Schauer, 165–179. Römisch-Germanisches Zentralmuseum Monographien 15. Bonn: Habelt.

Tierney, J. J. 1960. 'The Celtic Ethnography of Posidonius'. *PRIA C* 60: 189–275.

Timpe, D. 1989. 'Entdeckungsgeschichte'. *RGA* 7: 307–389.

Timpe, D. 1995. *Romano-Germanica*. Stuttgart.

Todd, M. 1992. 'The Early Germans'. Oxford: Blackwell.

Tomber, R. 2008. *Indo-Roman Trade: From Pots to Pepper*. London: Bristol Classical Press.

Tov, E. E. 1986. 'The David and Goliath Saga: How a Biblical Editor Combined Two Versions'. *BibRev* 11: 34–41.

Tsetskhladze, G. R. 1994. 'Greek Penetration of the Black Sea'. In *The Archaeology of Greek Colonization*, edited by G. R. Tsetskhladze and F. De Angelis, 111–136. FS Sir J. Boardman. Oxford: Oxford University School of Archaeology.

Tsetskhladze, G. R. 2002. 'Ionians Abroad'. In *Greek Settlements in the Eastern Mediterranean and the Black Sea*, edited by A. M. Snodgrass and G. R. Tsetskhladze, 81–96. Oxford: British Archaeological Reports Oxford.

Tsitsiridis, S. 2011. "Greek Mime in the Roman Empire." (P.Oxy. 413: Charition and Moicheutria). *Logeion* 1: 184–232.

Tsetskhladze, G. R. 2004. 'On the Earliest Greek Colonial Architecture in the Pontos'. In *Pontus and the Outside World: Studies in Black Sea History: Historiography and Archaeology*, edited by C. J. Tuplin, 226–278. Colloquia Pontica 9. Leiden/Boston: Brill Academic.

Tuplin, A. 2004. 'Doctoring the Persians: Ctesias of Cnidus: Physician and Historian'. *Klio* 86: 305–347.

Tuplin, C. J. 1999. 'Greek Racism? Observations on the Character and Limits of Greek Ethnic Prejudice'. In *Ancient Greeks West and East*, edited by G. R. Tsetskhladze, 47–75. Mnemosyne Suppl. 196. Leiden: Brill Academic.

Turcan, R. 1996. *The Cults of the Roman Empire*. Oxford: Blackwell.

Van der Waerden, B. L. 1988. *Die Astronomie der Griechen*. Darmstadt: Wissenschaftliche Buchgesellschaft.

Van den Boom, H., and J. Pape. 2000. 'Die massaliotischen Amphoren'. In *Importe und mediterrane Einflüsse auf der Heuneburg*, edited by W. Kimmig, 43–70. Mainz: Philipp von Zabern.

Van den Broek, R. 1972. *The Myth of the Phoenix according to Classical and Early Christian Traditions*. Leiden: Brill.

Vanschoonwinkel, J. 2006. 'Mycenaean Expansion'. In *Greek Colonisation: An Account of Greek Colonies and Other Settlements Overseas*, Vol. 1, edited by G. R. Tsetskhladze, 41–113. Boston/ Leiden: Brill Academic.

Vassilaides, D. 2004. 'Greeks and Buddhism: Historical Contacts in the Development of a Universal Religion'. *The Eastern Buddhist* 36: 134–183.

Veenhof, K. R. 2001. *Geschichte des Alten Orients bis zur Zeit Alexander des Großen*. Göttingen: Vandenhoeck & Ruprecht.

Verger, S. 2006. 'Des hyperboréens aux Celtes. L'extreme-nord occidental des grecs à l'épreuve des contacts avec les cultures de l'Europe tempérée'. In *Celtes et Gaulois. L'archéologie face à l'histoire. La préhistoire des celtes*, edited by D. Vitali, 48–53. Bibracte/Glux-en-Glenne: Centre archéologique européen.

Vian, F. 1982. 'Les navigations des Argonautes. Élaborations d'une légend'. *BAGB* 1: 273–285.

Vichos, S. 1999. 'The Point Iara Wreck. The Nautical Dimension'. In *The Point Iara Wreck. Interconnections in the Mediterranean ca. 1200 B.C.*, edited by W. Phelps, 77–98. Athens: Hellenistic Institute of Marine Archaeology.

Villeneuve, F. 2005–2006. 'Farasân Inscriptions and Bukharin's Ideas: No Pontifex Herculis and Other Comments'. *Arabia* 3: 289–296.

Vivenza, G. 1980. 'Altre Considerazioni sul periplu di Annone'. *Economia e storia* 1: 101–110.

Vlassopoulos, K. 2013. 'The Stories of the Others: Storytelling and Intercultural Communication in the Herodotean Mediterranean'. In *Ancient Ethnography: New Approaches*, edited by E. Almagor and J. Skinner, 47–75. London: Bloomsbury.

Vogel, K. A. 2001. 'Sphaera terrae. Das mittelalterliche Bild der Erde und die kosmographische Revolution'. PhD dissertation, Göttingen. http://webdoc.sub.gwdg.de/diss/2000/vogel/.

Vogelsang, K. 2013. *Geschichte Chinas*. 4th ed. Stuttgart: Reclam.

Von den Brincken, A.-D. 1992. *Fines Terrae. Die Enden der Welt und der Vierte Kontinent auf mittelalterlichen Weltkarten*. Hannover: Hahnsche Buchhandlung.

Von Hinüber, O. 2000. *A Handbook of Pali Literature*. Indian Philology and South Asian Studies 2. Berlin/New York: De Gruyter.

Von Hinüber, O. 2010. "'Did Hellenistic Kings Send Letters to Asoka?"' *JAOS* 130: 261–266.

Von Soden, W. 1959. 'Die Eremboi der Odyssee und die Irrfahrt des Menelaos'. *WS* 72: 26–29.

Voutsaki, S., ed. 2001. *Economy and Politics in the Mycenaean Palace States*. Cambridge: Cambridge Philological Society.

Wachsmann, S. 1998. *Seagoing Ships and Seamenship in the Bronze Age Levant*. London: Chatham Publishing.

Wachsmann, S. 2000. 'To the Sea of the Philistines'. In *The Sea Peoples and Their World: A Reassessment*, edited by E. D. Oren, 103–143. Philadelphia: University of Pennsylvania.

Waldbaum, J. C. 1994. 'Early Greek Contacts with the Southern Levant ca. 1000–600 B.C.: The Eastern Perspective'. *BASOR* 293: 53–66.

Wallinga, H. T. 1993. *Ships and Sea-Power before the Great Persian War: The Ancestry of the Ancient Trireme*. Leiden: Brill Academic.

Warnecke, H. 2006. 'Schiffahrtswege'. In *Mensch und Landschaft in der Antike. Lexikon der Historischen Geographie*, edited by H. Sonnabend, 442–446. Stuttgart/Weimar: J. B. Metzler.

Warnecke, H. 2002.' Zur Phänomenologie und zum Verlauf antiker Überseewege'. In *Zu Wasser und zu Land– Verkehrswege in der antiken Welt*, edited by E. Olshausen, 93–107. Stuttgart: Steiner.

Waters, M. 2014. *Ancient Persia: A Concise History of the Achaemenid Empire 550–330 BCE*. Cambridge: Cambridge University Press.

Watson, G. 1966. *Theriac and Mithridatium: A Study in Therapeutics*. London: Wellcome Historical Medical Library.

Webster, G. 1999. *The Roman Invasion of Britain*. London/New York: Routledge.

Wedde, M. 2005. "'The Mycenaean Galley in Context. : From Fact to Idée Fixe."'. In R. Laffineur, E. Greco (eds.). *Emporia. : Aegeans in the Central Mediterranean*, edited by R. Laffineur and, E. Greco, 29–38. (Aegaeum 25). Liège: 29–38.

Weerakkody, D. P. M. 1997. *Taprobane: Ancient Sri Lanka as Known to Greeks and Romans: Indicopleustoi: Archaeology of the Indian Ocean*. Turnhout: Brepols.

Wells, J. 1923. 'The Persian Friends of Herodotus'. In *Studies on Herodotus*, edited by J. Wells, 95–111. Oxford: Blackwell.

Wells, P. S. 1980. *Culture Contact and Culture Change: Early Iron Age Central Europe and the Mediterranean World*. Cambridge: Cambridge University Press.

Werake, M. 1978. 'A New Date for the Beginning of Sino-Sri Lankan Relations'. *The Sri Lanka Journal of the Humanities* 4: 64–73.

Werake, M. 1990. 'Sino-Sri Lankan Relations During the Pre-colonial Times'. In *Sri Lanka and the Silk Road of the Sea*, edited by S. Bandaranayake et al., 221–223. Colombo: Central Cultural Fund.

West, M. L. 1986. *The Hesiodic Catalogue of Women: Its Nature, Structure, and Origins*. Oxford: Oxford University Press.

West, M. L. 1988. 'The Rise of the Greek Epic'. *JHS* 58: 151–172.

West, M. L. 2002. 'Eumelos: A Corinthian Epic Cycle?' *JHS* 122: 109–133.

West, S. 2003. '"The Most Marvellous of All Seas": The Greek Encounter with the Euxine'. *G&R* 50: 151–167.

White, D. 1991. *Myths of the Dog Man*. Chicago: University of Chicago Press.

Whitelaw, T. 2001. 'Reading between the Tablets: Assessing Mycenean Palatial Involvement in Ceramic Production and Consumption'. In *Economy and Politics in the Mycenean Palace States*, edited by S. Voutsaki and J. T. Killen, 51–79. Cambridge: Cambridge Philological Society.

Whitewright, J. 2007. 'How Fast Is Fast? Technology, Trade and Speed under Sail in the Roman Red Sea'. In *Natural Resources and Cultural Connections in the Red Sea*, edited by J. Starkey et al., 77–87. Oxford: Archaeopress.

Whitewright, J. 2011a. 'The Potential Performance of Ancient Mediterranean Sailing Rigs'. *The International Journal of Nautical Archaeology* 40 (1): 2–17.

Whitewright, J. 2011b. 'Efficiency or Economies? Sail Developments in the Ancient Mediterranean'. In *Maritime Technology in the Ancient Economy: Ship-Design and Navigation*, edited by W. V. Harris and K. Iara, 89–102. Journal of Roman Archaeology Supplementary Series 84. Portsmouth.

Whittaker, C. R. 2004a. *Rome and Its Frontiers: The Dynamics of Empire*. London/New York: Routledge.

Whittaker, C. R. 2004b. 'Indian Trade Within the Roman Imperial Network'. In *Rome and Its Frontiers: The Dynamics of Empire*, edited by C. R. Whittaker, 163–180. London/New York: Routledge.

Whittaker, C. R. 2004c. '"To Reach Out to India and Pursue the Dawn": The Roman View of India'. In *Rome and Its Frontiers: The Dynamics of Empire*, edited by C. R. Whittaker, 144–162. London/New York: Routledge.

Wielowiejski, J. 1984. 'Bernsteinstrasse und Bernsteinweg während der römischen Kaiserzeit im Lichte der neueren Forschung'. *MBAH* 3: 69–87.

Wilcken, U. 1925. 'Punt-Fahrten in der Ptolemäerzeit'. *Zeitschrift für Ägyptische Sprache und Altertumskunde* 60: 86–102.

Wilcken, U. 1967. *Alexander the Great*. New York: W. W. Norton & Co.

Will, E. 1991. 'The Mediterranean Shipping Amphoras from Arikamedu'. In *Rome and India: The Ancient Sea Trade*, edited by V. Begley and R. D. De Puma, 151–156. Madison: University of Wisconsin Press.

Willeitner, J. 2013. *Die Weihrauchstraße*. Darmstadt: Philipp von Zabern.

Wilson, A. 2006. 'The Spread of Foggara-Based Irrigation in the Ancient Sahara'. In *The Libyan Desert: Natural Resources and Cultural Heritage*, edited by D. Mattingly et al., 205–216. London: Society for Lybian Studies.

Wilson, A. I. 2011. 'The Economic Influence of Developments in Maritime Technology in Antiquity'. In *Maritime Technology in the Ancient Economy: Ship-Design and Navigation*, edited by W. V. Harris and K. Lara, 211–233. Portsmouth, RI: Journal of Roman Archaeology.

Wilson, J. P. 2013. 'Literacy'. In *A Companion to Archaic Greece*, edited by K. A. Raaflaub and H. van Wees, 542–563. Malden/Oxford: Wiley-Blackwell.

Winiarczyk, M. 2011. *Die hellenistischen Utopien.* Berlin: De Gruyter.

Winston, D. 1976. 'Iambulos' Island of the Sun and Hellenistic Literary Utopias'. *Science-Fiction Studies* 3: 219–227.

Wittkower, R. 1977. 'Die Wunder des Ostens. Ein Beitrag zur Geschichte der Ungeheuer'. In *Allegorie und der Wandel der Symbole in Antike und Renaissance*, edited by R. Wittkower, 87–150. Cologne: DuMont.

Wolters, R. 1999. *Nummi signati. Untersuchungen zur römischen Münzprägung und Geldwirtschaft.* Munich: C. H. Beck.

Woolf, G. 2011. *Tales of the Barbarians: Ethnography and Empire in the Roman West.* London: Wiley-Blackwell.

Wright, J. K. 1965. *The Geographical Lore of the Time of the Crusades: A Study in the History of Medieval Science and Tradition in Western Europe: With a New Introduction by C. J. Glacken.* New York: Dover Publications.

Xushan, Z. 2004. 绪山: 《关于"公元100年罗马商团到达中国"问题的–点思考》.《世界历史》. 2004 年第2期. 111–114页。= 'Some Consideration on Roman Merchants Arrived China in AD 100年100罗马商团到达中国'100问题的–100点思考100》.《100世界100历史100》. 2004 100年第2期100. 111–114 *World History* 2: 111–114.

Xu-Shan, Z. 2004. 'The Name of China and Its Geography in Cosmas Indicopleustes'. *Byzantium* 74: 452–462.

Yasur-Landau, A. 2010. *The Philistines and Aegean Migration at the End of the Late Bronze Age.* Cambridge: Cambridge University Press.

Yasur-Landau, A. 2012. 'The "Feathered Helmets" of the Sea Peoples: Joining the Iconographic and Archaeological Evidence.' *Talanta* 44: 27–40.

Yates, R. D. S. 1997. 'The City-State in Ancient China'. In *The Archaeology of City-States: Cross-Cultural Approaches*, edited by S. L. Nichols and T. H. Charlton, 71–90. Washington, DC: Smithsonian Institution Press.

Ying, L. 2004. 'Rulers of the Treasure Country: The Image of the Roman Empire in Chinese Society from the First to the Fourth Century AD'. *Latomus* 63: 327–339.

Yon, M. 1992. 'The End of the Kingdom of Ugarit'. In *The Crisis Years: The 12th Century B.C. from beyond the Danube to the Tigris*, edited by W. A. Ward and M. S. Joukowski, 111–122. Dubuque: Kendall Hunt.

Young, G. K. 1997. 'The Customs Officer at the Nabatean Port of Leuke Kome'. *ZPE* 119: 266–268.

Young, G. K. 2001. *Rome's Eastern Trade: International Commerce and Imperial Policy 31 BC–AD 305.* London/New York: Taylor & Francis.

Yü, Y.-S. 1967. *Trade and Expansion in Han China: A Study in the Structure of Sino-Barbarian Economic Relations.* Berkeley: University of California Press.

Yü, Y.-S. 1986. 'Han Foreign Relations'. In *The Cambridge History of China*, Vol. 1, *The Ch'in and Han Empires, 221 B.C.–A.D. 220*, edited by D. Twitchett and M. Loewe, 377–462. Cambridge: Cambridge University Press.

Yü, Y.S. 1990. 'The Hsiung-nu'. In *The Cambridge History of Early Inner Asia*, edited by D. Sinor, 118–150. Cambridge: Cambridge University Press.

Zaccagnini, C. 1983. 'Patterns of Mobility among Ancient Near Eastern Craftsmen'. *Journal of Near Eastern Studies* 42: 245–264.

Zaikov, A. V. 2004. 'Alcman and the Image of Scythian Steed'. In *Pontus and the Outside World: Studies in Black Sea History: Historiography and Archaeology*, edited by C. J. Tuplin, 69–84. Colloquia Pontica 9. Leiden/Boston: Brill.

Zambrini, A. 1982. 'Gli Indica di Megastene'. *ASNP* 12,1: 71–149.

Zhmud, L. 1997. *Wissenschaft, Philosophie und Religion im frühen Pythagoreismus*. Berlin: De Gruyter.

Zysk, K. 2000. *Ascetitism and Healing in Ancient India: Medicine in the Buddhist Monastery.* Corrected ed. Dehli 1998. repr. Dehli: Mortilal Banaesidass.

Index

For the benefit of digital users, indexed terms that span two pages (e.g., 52–53) may, on occasion, appear on only one of those pages.

Figures are indicated by *f* following the page number